BizTalk 2013 Recipes

A Problem-Solution Approach

Mark Beckner

Kishore Dharanikota

BizTalk 2013 Recipes: A Problem-Solution Approach

ISBN-13 (pbk): 978-1-4302-6373-9

ISBN-13 (electronic): 978-1-4302-6374-6

President and Publisher: Paul Manning
Lead Editor: Jonathan Gennick
Technical Reviewer: Triston Arisawa and Rebecca Arisawa
Editorial Board: Steve Anglin, Mark Beckner, Ewan Buckingham, Gary Cornell, Louise Corrigan, Morgan Ertel, Jonathan Gennick, Jonathan Hassell, Robert Hutchinson, Michelle Lowman, James Markham, Matthew Moodie, Jeff Olson, Jeffrey Pepper, Douglas Pundick, Ben Renow-Clarke, Dominic Shakeshaft, Gwenan Spearing, Matt Wade, Tom Welsh
Coordinating Editor: Christine Ricketts
Copy Editor: Michele Bowman and Michael G. Laraque
Compositor: SPi Global
Indexer: SPi Global
Artist: SPi Global
Cover Designer: Anna Ishchenko

Distributed to the book trade worldwide by Springer Science+Business Media New York, 233 Spring Street, 6th Floor, New York, NY 10013. Phone 1-800-SPRINGER, fax (201) 348-4505, e-mail orders-ny@springer-sbm.com or visit www.springeronline.com. Apress Media, LLC is a California LLC and the sole member (owner) is Springer Science+Business Media Finance Inc (SSBM Finance Inc). SSBM Finance Inc is a Delaware corporation.

For information on translations, please e-mail rights@apress.com or visit www.apress.com.

Apress and friends of ED books may be purchased in bulk for academic, corporate, or promotional use. eBook versions and licenses are also available for most titles. For more information, reference our Special Bulk Sales–eBook Licensing web page at www.apress.com/bulk-sales.

Any source code or other supplementary materials referenced by the author in this text is available to readers at www.apress.com. For detailed information about how to locate your book's source code, go to www.apress.com/source-code/.

Contents at a Glance

Contents

About the Authors

Mark Beckner is a technical consultant specializing in business strategy and enterprise application integration. He runs his own consulting firm, Inotek Consulting Group, LLC, delivering innovative solutions to large corporations and small businesses. His projects have included engagements with numerous clients throughout the U.S. and range in nature from mobile application development to complete integration solutions. He has authored a number of titles including *BizTalk 2013 EDI for Health Care, BizTalk 2013 EDI for Supply Chain Management, Microsoft Dynamics CRM API Development, Pro EDI in BizTalk Server 2006 R2*, and *Pro RFID in BizTalk Server 2009*. He has spoken at a number of venues, including Microsoft TechEd. He works with BizTalk, Dynamics CRM, SharePoint, SQL Server, and custom .NET development. Mark, his wife Sara, and his boys Ciro and Iyer Blue live in the rugged deserts and/or mountains of the American West. His web site is www.inotekgroup.com, and he can be contacted directly at mbeckner@inotekgroup.com.

Kishore Dharanikota has years of experience developing and integrating enterprise-scale business applications in a wide range of industries. He specializes in integration of on-premise and line-of-business (LOB) systems and software as a service (Saas)–based solutions. He is the founder of Plural Hub LLC, a boutique consulting firm for integration and custom development services. He believes highly in constant learning and mentoring. He is a certified SOA architect and holds the MCAD.NET, MCSD.NET, and MCTS BizTalk certifications. He has a master's degree in computer science and an M.B.A. in marketing. He lives with his family in a small town in the foothills of the Saddleback Mountains in Southern California. He can be reached at kishore@pluralhub.com.

About the Technical Reviewers

Triston Arisawa brings a broad range of talents to any engagement, ranging from computer sciences to the culinary arts. He has extensive experience in the health care industry, working primarily with Microsoft BizTalk for HIPPA-compliant EDI solutions, utilizing many of the common EDI formats found in health care technology today. Specifically, he has managed several EDI projects involving small teams for EDI 834, 835, and 837 transactions. He has also developed a number of Dynamics CRM solutions. Whether it is BizTalk integrations, HL7 solutions, CRM plugins, or custom JavaScript—no project is too big or too small. Triston translates his desire for quality BizTalk and CRM implementations directly into success for his clients. He also makes one mean dragon roll (he has worked as a sushi chef in a variety of ritzy locations, including Aspen, Colorado). Triston holds several degrees, including a B.S. in computer information systems, a B.A.S. in business management, an A.A.S. in computer aided design, and an A.A.S. in culinary arts. He can be reached at tarisawa@inotekgroup.com.

Rebecca Arisawa is a business applications developer working in a variety of fields, including publishing, manufacturing, and health care. Rebecca's strength lies in her attention to detail, and she has leveraged this to create many successful and scalable BizTalk solutions. She enjoys spending her free time with her two boys, encouraging their creativity and enthusiasm for technology and the arts.

CHAPTER 1

∎∎∎

Recent Developments

The two latest releases of BizTalk (2010 and 2013) provide a number of new features that will aid developers and increase the ability of the platform to support solutions built on it.

New Functionalty in BizTalk 2013

BizTalk 2013 introduces a number of new adapters, but the main focus of this release is on cloud-based technologies and functionality. Recipes 1-1 through 1-16 outline several aspects to this functionality, while Chapter 6 has coverage for many of the new adapters and Chapter 12 focuses entirely on cloud-based concepts. The following bullets list some of the key areas of functionality:

- Updates for HL7, SWIFT, X12, and EDIFACT. These schemas and processes are updated to support the latest requirements for the various standards. Chapter 8 demonstrates how to work with X12 EDI.

- View artifact dependencies (see Recipe 1-12).

- New adapters (SFTP, SharePoint, REST support, LOB, etc.). There is coverage of numerous adapters in Chapter 6.

- Simplified setup of ESB (see Recipe 1-11).

- Host handler association of dynamic send ports. See Chapter 10 for a recipe associated with administration.

- XslCompiledTransform maps (see Recipe 1-14).

- Building hybrid on-premise and cloud-based applications, connecting to Azure Service Bus and Azure Storage, Access Control Service, paying for use and other cloud-based solutions are covered in Chapter 12.

- Hosting BizTalk rapidly in the cloud (see Recipe 1-15).

New Functionalty in BizTalk 2010

The primary updates in BizTalk 2010, which are all still available in BizTalk 2013, centered around the BizTalk mapper user interface and EDI trading partner configuration and management. Additional updates included improvements to administrative functionality and the consolidation of tools within the BizTalk Admin Console. Recipes 1-1 through 1-10 are meant to introduce this new functionality, while Chapter 8 focuses entirely on the EDI components.

The most obvious piece of new functionality for all BizTalk developers was the mapper interface. A new toolbar offers a number of features allowing for better navigation, smarter linking, and an overall better user experience. Figure 1-1 shows this new toolbar.

Figure 1-1. *The BizTalk 2010 mapper toolbar*

The most innovative piece of new functionality released was the EDI Trading Partner management interface. The entire engine was revamped, and what was impossible before became possible. Exchanging documents among multiple business divisions and multiple partners with different envelope and document configurations and tracking settings became a snap. Developers of EDI solutions found this functionality refreshing and much needed.

Almost as important as asking "What's new?" is considering "What's gone?" Several core pieces of functionality were removed in BizTalk 2010. The most notable was the Health and Activity Tracking (HAT) application and the ability to do administration of ports and orchestrations directly from Visual Studio using BizTalk Explorer. These were both central to a developer's everyday use of BizTalk, and in many respects, it is unfortunate that these tools are gone. Everything is now centralized in the BizTalk Administration Console, and most of the functionality of HAT and BizTalk Explorer became available in that console.

1-1. Using the Relevance Tree View

Problem

You have complex schemas in your map, and you are having difficulty seeing what nodes are being used.

Solution

By using the relevance tree view, only the nodes that are actually being used in mapping the active tab will be shown. Use the following steps to work with this functionality:

1. Open an existing map in Visual Studio. By default, the full tree view will be shown. Dotted lines show that some child node is being mapped, but the schema would have to be manually expanded to see what specific node it is. An example of this is shown in Figure 1-2.

```
□ 📂 <Schema>
   □ 📄 X12_00401_837_P
      □ 📄 ST
         ⑤ ST01
         📄 ST02----------------------------------------------------
         ⑤ ST03
      ⊞ 📄 BHT_BeginningOfHierarchicalTransaction_TS837Q1
      ⊞ 📄 REF_TransmissionTypeIdentification_TS837Q1
      ⊞ 📄 TS837Q1_1000A_Loop
      ⊞ 📄 TS837Q1_1000B_Loop
      □ 📄 TS837Q1_2000A_Loop
         ⊞ 📄 HL_BillingPaytoProviderHierarchicalLevel_TS837Q1
         ⊞ 📄 PRV_BillingPaytoProviderSpecialtyInfomation_TS83
         ⊞ 📄 CUR_ForeignCurrencyInfomation_TS837Q1_2000A
         ⊞ 📄 TS837Q1_2010A_SubLoop
         □ 📄 TS837Q1_2000B_Loop
            □ 📄 HL_SubscriberHierarchicalLevel_TS837Q1_200
               📄 HL01__HierarchicalIDNumber-------------
               ⑤ HL02__HierarchicalParentIDNumber
               ⑤ HL03__HierarchicalLevelCode
               ⑤ HL04__HierarchicalChildCode
         ⊞ 📄 SBR_SubscriberInformation_TS837Q1_2000B
```

Figure 1-2. *Default full tree view*

2. Click the first button on the mapping toolbar to show the relevant links for the source schema, or click the last button to show them for the target schema. Clicking this button causes only the mapped nodes to be displayed, as shown in Figure 1-3.

3

Figure 1-3. *Showing only the nodes that are being mapped*

3. Click the button again to return to the full tree view.

How It Works

Showing only the nodes that are actually being mapped can save a lot of time on schemas that have more than a few nodes. Developers of EDI maps will find these particularly helpful, since there can be hundreds or thousands of nodes and elements in a schema. Having to manually sort through all of the nodes can be confusing and time consuming.

There also exists the ability to show only links that are relevant. The mapping surface can become crowded with all of the links, and it can help to turn off any that are not pertinent to the current mapping taking place. The relevant links can be turned on and off by clicking the second button that appears on the mapping toolbar. An example of a map with all of the links turned on is shown in Figure 1-4, while the same map with only the relevant links showing appears in Figure 1-5.

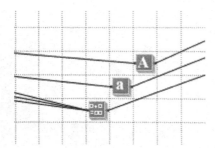

Figure 1-4. *Showing all links*

Figure 1-5. *Showing only relevant links*

1-2. Navigating the Mapping Surface

Problem

You want to be able to access elements of the mapping surface as rapidly as possible and need to understand how to use the new functionality.

Solution

There are a number of new tools that can be used to move and view the mapping surface. These include

- Panning
- Zooming
- Searching
- Grid preview

This solution walks through the use of each of them.

1. Open an existing map in Visual Studio.

2. To pan a map from top to bottom or left to right, click the hand button on the mapping toolbar, which is shown in Figure 1-6. You can now drag the mapping surface in any direction needed.

Figure 1-6. *The pan button*

3. To zoom in and out on the map, use the zoom functionality on the mapper toolbar. Zooming out can give you perspective on where your functoids are and allow you to easily locate and modify mappings. If you zoom in and the functoids loose focus, you will notice flashing blue arrows to guide you to where the components are (see Figure 1-7).

Figure 1-7. *Arrow indicating where functoids are after zooming in*

4. To find a specific value or word in a schema or a functoid, you can use the search functionality (see Figure 1-8). You can search on name, label, comments, inputs, and scripts in functoids. Searching on a value will highlight all of the results; you can use the up and down arrows to navigate through the results (see Figure 1-9).

Figure 1-8. *Searching for a value in a functoid*

Figure 1-9. *Search results are highlighted*

5. To use the grid preview functionality, right-click the mapping surface, and select Grid Preview. This will pop up a window that shows a box and all of the functoids (see Figure 1-10). You can drag and drop the box over the area of the map you want to scroll to, and the map will automatically move.

Figure 1-10. *Using the grid preview functionality*

How It Works

There are a variety of ways to move around a map now. Prior to BizTalk 2010, the mapping interface was pretty rudimentary and didn't provide a lot of options. Based on feedback from developers, the mapper user interface has been greatly improved.

■ **Note** Make sure to comment your functoids so that you can use the search functionality to more easily find them. If you've got more than a handful of advanced scripting functoids, for example, you will find that by adding comments you will save a lot of time trying to figure out which ones contain the methods you are looking for.

1-3. Correcting Errors in Functoids
Problem

You have some complex mappings using various functoids, and you want to make sure you don't have any obvious errors.

Solution

The new mapper brings intelligence to the functoids, showing errors prior to the testing of a map. This allows you to rapidly assess where incomplete mappings exist and eases development by indicating possible fixes to the errors. To see how this is done, follow these steps:

1. Open an existing map in Visual Studio.

2. Drop a functoid onto the mapping surface.

3. An exclamation mark will be on top of the functoid, indicating that an error exists. Roll your mouse cursor over the top of the functoid to see the details of the error (as shown in Figure 1-11).

Figure 1-11. *Functoid error information*

How It Works

There are a number of upgrades to the coding of maps in addition to the quick overview of the error as shown in the solution to this recipe. Another valuable update is that the functoid interface actually forces the selection of required inputs (see Figure 1-12). For example, if there are two inputs required, they will appear in the functoid configuration window, and the functoid will continue to show an error until these are configured. You can scroll over the warning icons for each input to see the exception message.

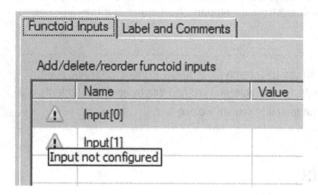

Figure 1-12. *Configuring the required inputs to the functoid*

1-4. Indicating Matches in Maps
Problem
You want some help mapping the source schema nodes to the target schema nodes.

Solution
There is now some intelligence built into the mapper that aids in mapping source nodes to target nodes. A developer can request that all nodes in the target schema that appear to be matches be highlighted. This can be done using the following steps:

1. Open an existing map in Visual Studio.

2. Right-click a node in the source schema and select Indicate Matches.

3. One or more links should appear with suggested matches (see Figure 1-13). Clicking a link will cause the link to be made permanent in the map.

Figure 1-13. *A suggested match*

■ **Note** Not all recommendations by the mapper are accurate! There is no requirement to use this feature.

How It Works
The mapper tries to find a match based largely on name, though it also looks at the structure of nodes in the source and target schemas. A related piece of new functionality allows for the auto-linking based on name or structure of the source nodes. This functionality appears when you drag a source schema record (not an element or attribute, but the record itself) and drop it on a target schema record. When the link is dropped, a context menu appears (as shown in Figure 1-14).

Figure 1-14. *Linking by structure or name*

1-5. Configuring Core Server Settings

Problem

You want to set throttles, thresholds, tracking, polling intervals, and other systemwide settings that will be used to optimize and control processes running within BizTalk.

Solution

Prior to BizTalk 2010, configuring core settings was done through a variety of methods, including manually setting registry keys. Now, the BizTalk Settings Dashboard has been introduced. To access this dashboard, take the following steps:

1. Open the BizTalk Administration Console.

2. Right-click the BizTalk Server Group, and select Settings. In the BizTalk Settings Dashboard that opens, you will notice a variety of properties that can be set (see Figure 1-15).

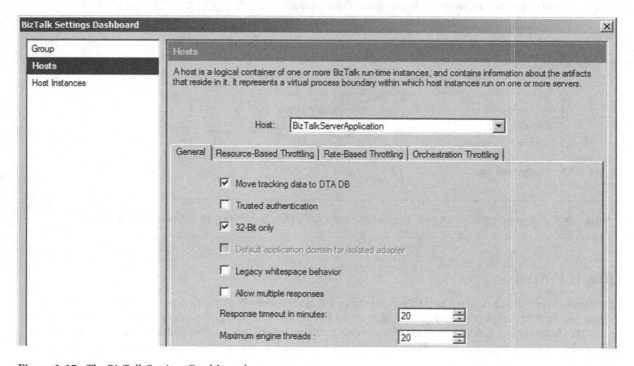

Figure 1-15. *The BizTalk Settings Dashboard*

How It Works

A great deal of performance tuning is available through the use of the BizTalk Settings Dashboard. It centralizes all of the throttles, timeouts, thread handling, and other functionality that used to be manually configured. Take a look at the different properties available prior to deployment and become familiar with the settings in order to better support your BizTalk environment.

1-6. Transfering Files Using SFTP

Problem

You need to use the BizTalk FTP adapter to transfer files using SFTP.

Solution

In previous versions of BizTalk Server, the FTP adapter did not support SFTP transactions. Now, support for SFTP is built into the standard adapter and can be easily configured using these steps:

1. Open the BizTalk Administration Console, and right-click the Send Ports folder under a BizTalk application.

2. Select New Static One-way Receive Port.

3. On the General tab, select FTP for the Type property. Once selected, click the Configure button.

4. There is a new section in the FTP Transport Properties configuration window called SSL (see Figure 1-16), which allows for the specification of the client certificate hash (among other things). Set the properties for the Firewall, FTP, and SSL Sections as needed, and save the settings.

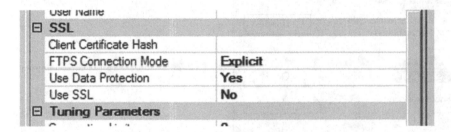

Figure 1-16. Configuring the SSL settings for SFTP

How It Works

In addition to supporting SFTP, the FTP Adapter has some additional feature updates. These include support for the following:

- *Downloading files from read-only FTP sites*: In previous versions, when BizTalk retrieved a file from an FTP site, it would automatically delete the file. This prevented the FTP adapter from being used successfully with read-only FTP sites.

- *Atomic ASCII-based file transfers*: Previous versions only supported binary atomic transactions.

1-7. Accessing the EDI Version 5010 HIPAA Schemas

Problem

You are building an EDI (Electronic Document Interchange) solution that requires the use of 5010 HIPAA-compliant schemas.

Solution

BizTalk ships with thousands of precreated schemas that support the various EDI documents. Shipping with BizTalk 2010 are a number of HIPAA 5010-compliant schemas. These schemas can be accessed using the following steps:

1. Using Windows Explorer, browse to `$\Program Files\Microsoft BizTalk Server 2010\ XSD_Schema\EDI`.

2. Double-click the `MicrosoftEdiXSDTemplates.exe` file to extract all of the schemas (see Figure 1-17).

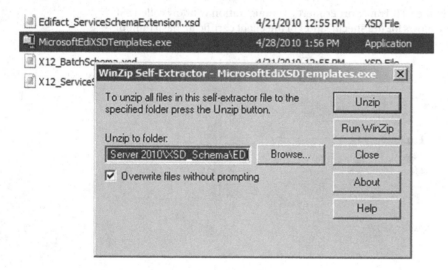

Figure 1-17. *Extracting the EDI schemas*

■ **Note** It can take a substantial amount of time to extract all of the schemas.

---

3. The 5010 documents will be available in the `HIPAA\00501` subfolder (see Figure 1-18).

Figure 1-18. *The extracted 5010 schemas*

How It Works

EDI schemas are identical to other BizTalk schemas and can be added to any Visual Studio solution. Generally speaking, they are more complex in structure and contain many more nodes and elements than other BizTalk schemas. An example of a 5010 HIPAA Schema in Visual Studio is shown in Figure 1-19. There are continual updates to EDI schemas. The HIPAA 5010 schemas are primarily related to health care, so given the volatility of health care laws today, it is very likely that there will continue to be other versions of these (and other) schemas.

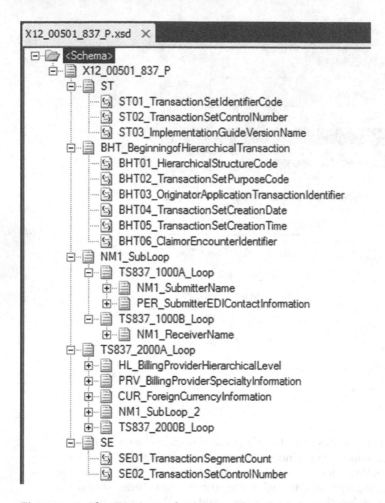

Figure 1-19. *The HIPAA compliant 837P 5010 schema in Visual Studio*

1-8. Configuring EDI Trading Partners

Problem

You are developing an EDI solution, and you need to configure a new trading partner.

Solution

Trading partner management is the most significant new functionality presented in BizTalk Server 2010. The new mapper has some nice features, but it doesn't bring new functionality to the product. The trading partner configuration, on the other hand, allows for the development of EDI solutions that could not be done before. This solution outlines how to create a trading partner in BizTalk Server.

> ■ **Note** An entire chapter in this book (Chapter 8) is dedicated to EDI solutions and the configuration of trading partners. This recipe introduces the most basic aspect of this new functionality.

1. Open the BizTalk Administration Console, and click Parties (see Figure 1-20).

Figure 1-20. *The Parties folder in BizTalk*

2. Right-click any area in the Parties and Business Profiles area and select New ➤ Party.

3. In the Party Properties dialogue box, give the party an appropriate name. This should be the name of the trading partner you will be exchanging documents with.

4. Enable the option for the Local BizTalk processing (see Figure 1-21). This setting is used to indicate that BizTalk Server will be used to process messages to or from the party (rather than being the default party itself).

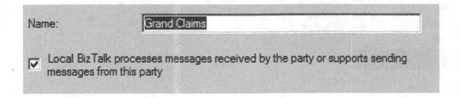

Figure 1-21. *Configuring the base party object*

5. Click the "Send ports" tab. This is where ports are associated with a party, and it is used in instances where all outbound EDI documents on this port should have envelope information configured as specified in the EDI properties of the party being configured. Add any relevant send ports, and click OK.

Now that the party object has been created, a new business profile must be created. A business profile contains all of the EDI configurations for a given business of a trading partner. For example, a trading partner may be a single company with multiple departments or divisions. Each department has its own integrations with internal and external vendors, and each uses its own X12 or EDIFACT settings. One business profile for each department must be created in order to ensure that the envelopes on the EDI documents being exchanged are set properly, and that all other EDI specific configurations are accurate for that department.

6. Right-click the party that was created, and select New ➤ Business Profile (see Figure 1-22).

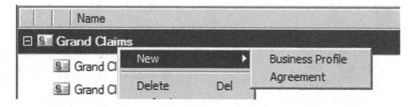

Figure 1-22. *Creating a business profile on a party*

7. Give the business profile a name representative of the business unit or department being set up. In many cases, a party will only have a single business profile.

8. On the identities screen, set the trading partner ID(s) and qualifier(s) (see Figure 1-23). These values are given to you directly by the trading partner, and are the way trading partners are uniquely identified.

Figure 1-23. *Setting the Business Profile's identities*

9. Once the business profile is fully configured, click OK.

With the business profile and core party configured, an agreement can be made. However, to create an agreement, you must have two parties configured. One party represents the recipient, and one is the sender. In many cases, BizTalk is going to be one of the parties. However, in the cases where BizTalk is acting as a value added network (VAN)—essentially, as a router of documents between parties—there may be many parties sending and receiving documents to many other parties. All of the configurations representing document communication between parties are known as agreements.

10. To create an agreement, right-click the business profile, and select New ➤ Agreement.

11. Initially, there will be only a single tab to configure. You must specify the party being interacted with and the protocol being used. To do so, set the Protocol property to (for example) X12, and the Party and Business properties to an available party. Once these have been set, two new tabs will appear (see Figure 1-24). These tabs are where all of the EDI specific information is configured for the given agreement.

Figure 1-24. Setting the general properties of the Agreement

17

12. Click each of the tabs to set the EDI-specific values based on the trading partner configuration specifications. An example of the Identifiers screen is shown in Figure 1-25. Once you are finished, click OK to save the trading partner configuration.

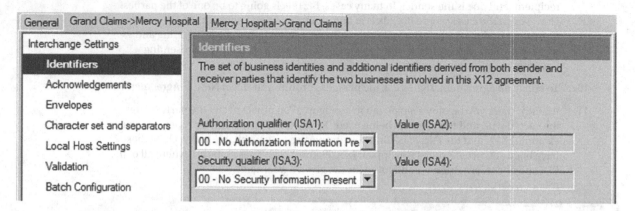

Figure 1-25. *Setting values within the agreement*

How It Works

This recipe outlined how to configure the different components that make up a trading partner, but without the full story, understanding all of the settings is difficult. Chapter 8 of this book covers a number of aspects of configuring EDI solutions, and much of it deals with trading partner configurations. Make sure to read through the appropriate sections to understand how parties, business profiles, agreements, and other components all tie together.

1-9. Zooming Out on an Orchestration
Problem

You need to be able to zoom out on an orchestration to see more of the design surface.

Solution

Right-click the design surface of an orchestration and select the Zoom option. Different levels of zooming are available, as shown in Figure 1-26.

Figure 1-26. *Zooming options on an orchestration*

How It Works

It is very simple to zoom in and out on an orchestration, but the value and benefits are great. For large orchestrations, it is invaluable to be able to get a bird's eye view of the full flow. In previous versions of BizTalk Server, no zooming was available, which was a hinderance to development and code reviews.

■ **Note**   You can get more granular levels of zooming by holding the Ctrl key and using the wheel on your mouse to zoom in and out on the orchestation.

1-10. Installing BizTalk Server RFID 2010
Problem

You want to insall BizTalk Server RFID (Radio-Frequency Identification) on the same server as BizTalk Server 2010.

Solution

BizTalk Server RFID 2010 must be installed with BizTalk Server 2010; it is not compatible with previous versions of BizTalk. Take the following steps to install it:

1. BizTalk RFID can be installed from the standard setup screen of BizTalk Server 2010. Click the Install Microsoft BizTalk RFID option shown in Figure 1-27.

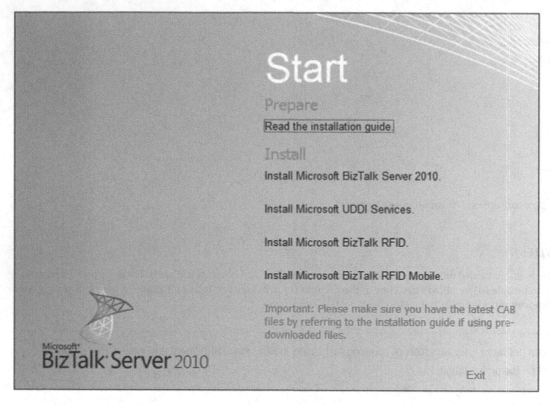

Figure 1-27. *Install link for BizTalk RFID*

2. Click through the initial setup screens, indicating the database to connect to and other basic information.

■ **Note** During the System Configuration Check, you may get a message warning that MSMQ is not installed. This can be remedied by enabling MSMQ on your operating system. Figure 1-28 shows this for Windows Server 2008 R2.

Figure 1-28. *Enabling message queuing for BizTalk RFID Install*

How It Works

Many developers assume that BizTalk RFID is built into the standard BizTalk Server application, but it is not. BizTalk Server RFID is a completely separate application from BizTalk Server 2010. It is a part of the BizTalk family, which includes applications like Host Integration Server (HIS), the Enterprise Service Bus (ESB) Framework, and the Adapter Pack. BizTalk RFID allows for the administration of RFID devices. The way in which it collects data allows for easy integration with BizTalk Server 2010, but in no way is it tied to the core product. The most common way to integrateBizTalk RFID with BizTalk Server is to use the SQL tables representing the RFID data. This integration does not differ in any way from that of any other external system.

■ **Note** *Pro RFID in BizTalk Server 2009* (Apress, 2009) is solely focused on BizTalk RFID. While it is based on the previous version of BizTalk RFID, virtually all of the concepts and process apply to the 2010 version.

1-11. Installing and Configuring the Enterprise Service Bus with BizTalk Server 2013

Problem

You want to install Enterprise Service Bus Tool kit with BizTalk Server 2013.

Solution

Enterprise Service Bus (ESB) is an add-on to base BizTalk Server 2013 installation. To install and configure ESB take the following steps:

1. The option to install ESB is added to the standard installation screen of BizTalk. Click on Install Microsoft BizTalk ESB Tool kit link to start the installation, as shown in Figure 1-29.

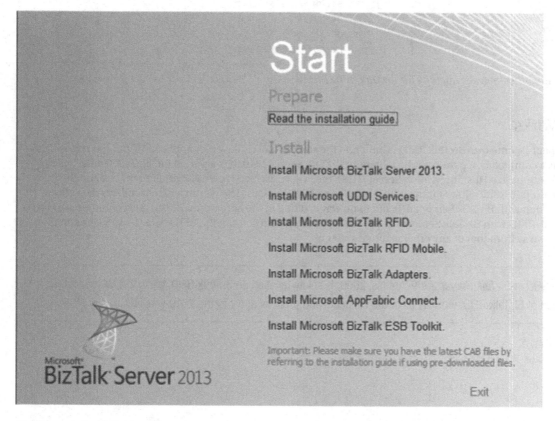

Figure 1-29. *Install Link for BizTalk ESB Toolkit*

2. Agree to the License agreement and select the components to install. In the current case all the components are selected, as shown in Figure 1-30.

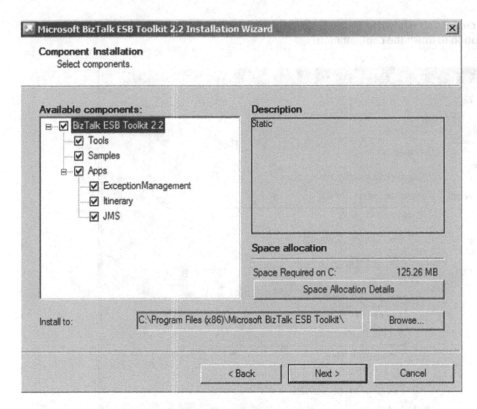

Figure 1-30. *BizTalk ESB Toolkit Component Installation*

3.   Select the ESB Configuration tool to configure ESB Tool kit (see Figure 1-31).

Figure 1-31. *ESB Configuration tool selection*

4. Input the proper credentials (shown in Figure 1-32), proper BizTalk User Groups, and Database information to finish the configuration.

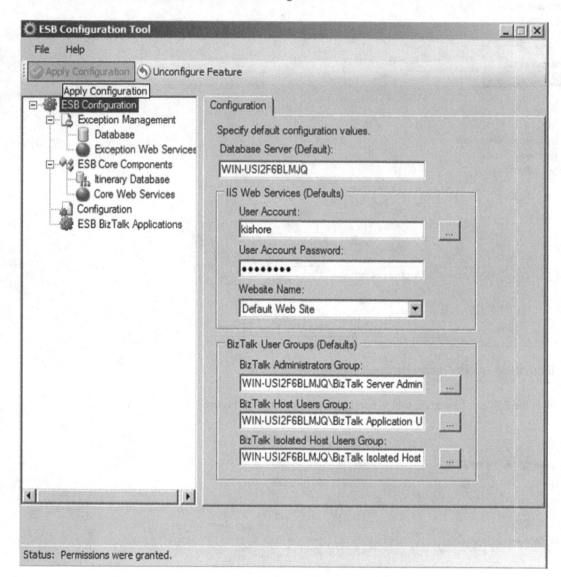

Figure 1-32. *ESB Configuration tool set up*

How It Works

Enterprise Service Bus (ESB) Framework provides an infrastructure for developing a loosely coupled Service Oriented architecture based solutions. BizTalk's publish-subscribe mechanism provides a scalable platform for Service-Oriented Architecture (SOA)-based applications. BizTalk has been supporting ESB framework since BizTalk 2006 R2. Over the years new capabilities are added to the ESB framework. Some of the feedback received from the clients included a request to simplify the installation process. In previous versions of BizTalk Servers a number of steps needed to be taken to successfully install ESB. The process was not integrated into the core installation. In the current version, it only requires selecting ESB on the root installation menu to finish it.

■ **Note**   The core installation includes BizTalk ESB Toolkit Core and ESB Exception Management Framework. Even though the configuration is significantly simplified, a few more steps are needed to configure the ESB portal. The source code for portal needs to be downloaded to the machine on which the portal is being configured and the install scripts need to be executed. Multi-node ESB Tool Kit Configuration requires a lot of attention to service accounts, database servers, and Active Directory groups for BizTalk. The current Recipe highlights the simplification of the installation and configuration. Refer to the product documentation for detailed instructions on ESB configuration.

1-12. Viewing BizTalk Artifact Dependencies
Problem

You need to identify the dependencies between BizTalk artifacts in case some of the artifacts need to be stopped or redeployed.

Solution

Dependency between the artifacts can be viewed in a deployed application by following the below steps in BizTalk Administration Console:

1. Open the BizTalk Administration Console and select the BizTalk application.

2. Right click any BizTalk artifact and select the View Dependencies option from the menu (see Figure 1-33). In this case, the dependencies for an orchestration are viewed.

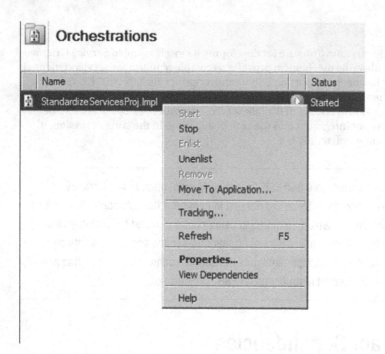

Figure 1-33. Menu Option to View Dependencies

3. Look at current orchestration's dependency on the Receive port as shown in Figure 1-34

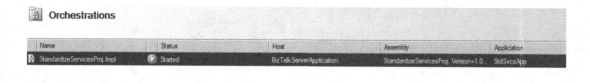

Figure 1-34. Dependency Statistics for an Orchestration

4. Look at the Receive Location's Dependency on pipelines, as shown in Figure 1-35.

Receive Ports

WcfService_StandardizeSer... > Receive Ports

Name	Two Way	Application
WcfReceivePort_StandardizeServices/StandardizeServicesProj_l...	Yes	StdSvcsApp

Dependency Statistics: WcfService_StandardizeServices/StandardizeServicesPr...

Used by:		Using:	
Receive Ports	1	Pipelines	2

Last Updated:	8/31/2013 5:38:18 PM

Figure 1-35. *Dependency Statistics for a Receive Location*

How It Works

Dependency tracking is a long awaited feature in BizTalk Administration. It will significantly simplify upgrading the BizTalk artifacts when there is a deep dependency hierarchy. The typical BizTalk artifacts are Orchestrations, Send Ports, receive ports, pipelines, maps and schemas. There are two types of dependencies for every artifact. A "Used By" type of dependency shows the dependency of another artifact on this artifact. And a "Using" type of dependency shows the dependency of this artifact on another artifact.

In the current scenario, the orchestration has a dependency on a receive port. In other words, orchestration has a using dependency on a receive port. The receive location is used by receive port, and receive location uses two pipelines (XMLReceive pipeline for receiving request and PassThrough send Pipeline for sending response).

1-13. Configuring Dynamic Send Ports

Problem

You need to configure a dynamic send port and assign a send handler for it.

Solution

Perform the following steps in BizTalk Administration Console:

1. Open the BizTalk Administration Console and select the BizTalk application.

2. To create a Send port, right click the Send Port and click on New ➤ Dynamic One-way Send Port.

3. Double click the send port and click on the Configure button to set the Send Handler Information (see Figure 1-36).

Figure 1-36. *Handler Configuration for a Dynamic Send Port*

How It Works

BizTalk 2013 now offers the ability to select the appropriate host for the dynamic send port. Till the current version, BizTalk framework did not offer this capability. It is a limitation if the dynamic send port is participating in a high volume scenario. The Administration console always selected the Default Host (BizTalkServerApplication) for all dynamic send ports. With this new feature, the hosts can be separated based on the scenario.

1-14. Verifying Performance Improvments in BizTalk Maps
Problem

You are trying to understand the performance improvements of the Maps in BizTalk 2013 that come about from the compiler's use of the XslCompliedTransform class

Solution

The XslCompiledTransform class in BizTalk 2013 is used by the compiler, instead of XslTransform class. The developer will still perform the same activities on the map's design surface as before, and saves the map file in a BizTalk project. At run time, when the map is invoked by either a port or an orchestration, BizTalk framework loads the map into the context. And when invoked, this compiled map will be executed.

The best way to observe this performance improvement is by executing a complex Map from EDI document to a canonical XML schema. Then compare the time taken in execting the map in the BizTalk 2013 environment with the exection time of the same map in BizTalk 2010.

> ■ **Note** Refer to Recipe 8-2 for creating a complex EDI map. Build and deploy a BizTalk Project to the BizTalk Administration Console by following the steps in Recipe 9-4.

How It Works

BizTalk supports very mature mapping capabilities. Mapping simplifications are being worked on in various versions of BizTalk. Now in BizTalk 2013, the mapping framework uses XslCompiledTransform class instead of XmlTransform class as in previous versions. XslCompiledTransform class provides huge performance improvements (about four fold improvement), and it will be glaringly obvious in a complicated map with lot of mappings between input schemas to the output schema. The first improvement is in the multithreading support. Once the loading of the map is completed, the transform method can be called simultaneously from various threads. The second improvement is in caching the map. The new XSLT processor compiles the XSLT style sheet to a common intermediate format. Once the style sheet is compiled, it can be cached and reused.

1-15. Hosting BizTalk Server 2013 in the Cloud
Problem

You are tasked to quickly set up infrastructure for a BizTalk 2013 Development environment for an upcoming execution of a project.

Solution

Create your environment quickly and easily via Microsoft's Azure service. Microsoft provides a series of prebuilt images for virtual machines in their Azure data centers. Once a Microsoft Azure subscription for the enterprise is set up, it is just the matter of subscribing to the correct virtal machine by following certain payment model.

> ■ **Note** The details of Azure Subscriptions, payment models, and Azure portal and Service Bus are discussed in detail in Chapter 12.

Here is the process to follow, to create a BizTalk 2013 environment in the cloud:

1. Open the Microsoft Azure Management Portal for creating a BizTalk environment on demand. To create BizTalk environment from the pre-built gallery of virtual machines, click on '+ NEW' at the bottom left corner of the portal Management Default page ➤ COMPUTE ➤ VIRTUAL MACHINE ➤ FROM GALLARY. See Figure 1-37.

Figure 1-37. *Azure Portal's Create a Virtual machine from a Gallery option*

2. Select the most appropriate BizTalk virtual machine image suitable for your current need – an example of this is shown in Figure 1-38.

Figure 1-38. *Virtal Machine image selection option*

3. Fill the configuration details for the virtual machine:

- A descriptive name

- A new user

- Select the subscription

- Region of the data center

- Availalability set

4. The above steps will provision a virtual machine. The details can be viewed in Azure portal, as shown in Figure 1-39 and 1-40.

Figure 1-39. *Provisioned Virtual machine*

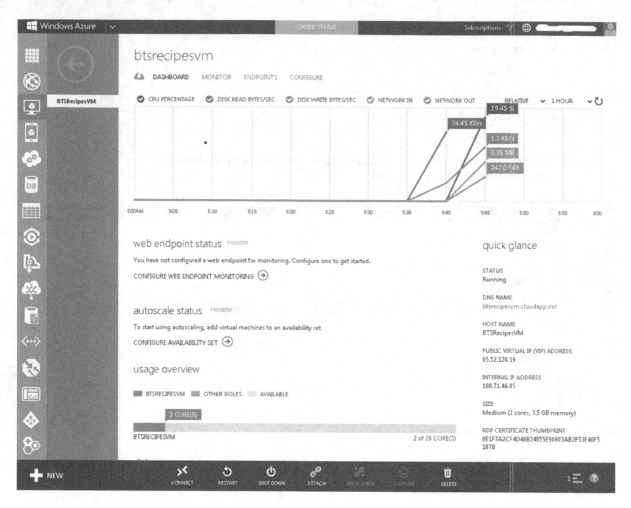

Figure 1-40. *Provisioned Virtual machine - Details*

How It Works

In a typical enterprise, installing and configuring a BizTalk environment takes several days. It requires budget approval from the management, acquiring licenses for the software, allocating physical or virtual machines for the environment, and finally installing and configuring the software. This process is repeated every time a new BizTalk environment is set up or an existing environment is upgraded. Going to a cloud-based solution sidesteps much of that work, and can be done more quickly.

Before getting approval for BizTalk environment changes, IT professionals need to figure out usage patterns and link them to business scenarios. Is the new environment for a short term project initiative? Is it to resolve the burst in traffic in a specific time of the year (For example, holiday shopping seasons will have a burst of orders that need to be fulfilled)? Or, is the new environment for a scaling-up scenario in which more application servers and database servers are being added to the existing configuration?

Microsoft considered all these complexities and came up with the Windows Azure BizTalk Infrastructure-as-a-service (IaaS) model.

The BizTalk environment in cloud can help out in various ways. For example:

- Lower budget overhead – The pay-as-you-go model requires only enuogh budget to resolve the current, short-term business need. This avoids huge, upfront software licensing and acquisition costs

- Decreased set up time – The set up and configuration steps are decreased, because the pre-built images simplify what needs to be done to ramp up in a new environment. A BizTalk environment can be set up in then cloud in a few minutes instead of taking days.

- Scaled by demand – The scaling up or scaling out of the BizTalk environment can be achieved on an on-demand basis to resolve burst scenarios.

- Migration of existing licenses- Using Software license mobility, existing licenses can be migrated to the Windows Azure BizTalk environment.

- Decreased effort in Environment Management – Much less effort is now required in managing, upgrading and patching the BizTalk nodes in Windows Azure. This is because much of the work is now handled by Microsoft professionals in their Data Centers.

- Distribution of Data Centres - Geographic distribution of the BizTalk environment will make transactions run faster in a global enterprise which is spanning multiple countries.

- Customised prebuilt BizTalk images – With the help of customized Scripting and APIs, a BizTalk environment can be tailored to your needs.

- Centralized Management - Unified access to Azure Portal in managing the BizTalk environment will significantly simplify monitoring and reporting tasks.

1-16. Configure Windows Azure BizTalk Services
Problem
You are tasked to configure Windows Azure BizTalk services for an upcoming hybrid integration with on-premise ERP system.

Solution

Windows Azure BizTalk Services is one of the most exciting features released as part of BizTalk 2013. It significantly decreases the complexity in building, deploying and managing a hybrid integration. It requires three components to facilitate the communication from Windows Azure BizTalk Services to an on-premise ERP system. The development and deployment of the integration is done in Visual Studio with an add-on template which is installed as part of BizTalk Services SDK. Windows Azure BizTalk services need to be set up for your subscription in Windows Azure portal. BizTalk Adapter Services need to be installed to connect to the on-premise ERP system. The current recipe highlights the set up of Windows Azure BizTalk Services for an existing Azure subscription.

▧ **Note**   Refer to BizTalk product documentation for installation instructions on BizTalk Services SDK and BizTalk Adapter Services . Since, it is mostly a double click installation; these instructions are not covered in the recipe.

Here are the steps in the solution:

1. Before BizTalk Services are configured under your Windows Azure subscription, few required prerequisites need to be configured.

    a. Configure Windows Azure Access Control Service namespace, to authenticate BizTalk Services.

    b. Configure Windows Azure SQL Data base, for storing tables, views and stored procedures that are required for BizTalk Services.

    c. Configure Windows Azure Storage Account, to access tables, blobs and queues. It stores logging and tracking information.

    d. Configure SSL Certificate, for communicating with BizTalk Services URL over HTTPS.

2. Log into Azure Management Portal using Windows Live account.

3. To configure BizTalk Service, click on '+ NEW' at the bottom left corner of the portal Management Default page ➤ APP SERVICES ➤ BIZTALK SERVICE➤ CUSTOM CREATE, as shown in Figure 1-41.

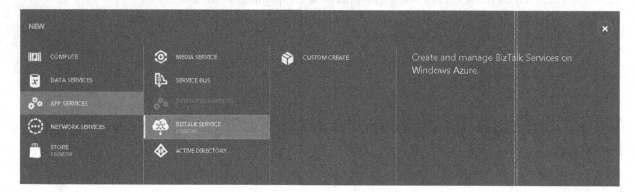

Figure 1-41. *Azure Portal's Custom Create BizTalk Service option*

1. Configure the BizTalk Service specific properties as listed in Table 1-1.

Table 1-1. *BizTalk Service Configuration Properties*

Grouping - Configuration Property	Description
BizTalk Service Settings - BizTalk Service Name	Name of the BizTalk Service.
BizTalk Service Settings - Domain URL	By default the Domain URL is constructed from the BizTalk Service Name. It can be changed to something other than BizTalk Service name.
BizTalk Service Settings - BizTalk Service Settings - Edition	Possible editions are – Developer, Standard, Basic and Premium. Based on the business scenario a version of these editions is selected.
BizTalk Service Settings - Region	Select the region of the data center closest to your needs.
BizTalk Service Settings - Tracking Data base	The SQL Database which stores the tracking data.
BizTalk Service Settings - Subscription	Optional. Select the subscription that is most appropriate for your BizTalk Service.
Database Settings - Subscriptions	Optional. This option is available only when there are multiple applicable Azure subscriptions.
Database Settings – Data base	Name of the SQL Data base instance, which is created as one of the prerequisites.
Database Settings – Login Name	Login user name for the SQL Data base instance
Database Settings – Login Password	Password for the SQL Data base
Data base Settings - Region	Geographic Region to host the SQL Data base.
Access Control Settings – Access Control Namespace	Name of the ACS namespace
Access Control Settings – Access Control Management Service Username	Username for the ACS Namespace
Access Control Settings – Access Control Management Service Password	Password for the ACS Namespace
Access Control Settings – Monitoring/Arching Storage Account	Select the existing Storage account from the list
BizTalk Service Certificate - Certificate	Browse and select the private SSL Certificate file (.pfx) which includes BizTalk Service name.
BizTalk Service Certificate - Password	Enter the password for the certificate.

How It Works

BizTalk Services on Windows Azure provides a simple, yet powerful integration platform to extend on-premise applications to the cloud. These managed services significantly simplify the integration by providing a no code drag and drop feature to hybrid integrations. BizTalk Services are helpful in cloud based EAI and EDI transmissions.

Microsoft provides these EAI and B2B integration capabilities through something called a bridge. A bridge is a combination of a pipeline, a source and a destination. In a EAI scenario, when a source sends a message to the bridge, it is picked up by the pipeline which performs validation or enrichment, and the resulting message is routed to the specified destination. In a B2B scenario, when a trading partner submits a X12 message to the bridge it is validated, transformed and routed to the destination. A service bus destination can relay the message to the on premise end point through BizTalk Adapter services framework.

The development, deployment and management are simplified with new set of features. An integration portal provides a unified view of all the Windows Azure deployments. Visual Studio is extended include templates for developing and deploying the custom integrations to Windows Azure. B2B services provide trading partner management (Partners, Agreements, and Profiles). The pipelines provide one-way and two-way message transmission, formatting and routing capabilities. The core framework provides monitoring; configuration and tracking stores save and view.

■ **Note**   As of third Quarter of 2013, BizTalk Services are in Preview mode. Until these services are released to the general audience, Microsoft doesn't commit to full Service Level Agreements, but can selectively work with individual clients in taking the integrations to production. In the coming releases, robust business process orchestration capabilities will be added to the current feature set.

CHAPTER 2

∎∎∎

Document Schemas

The BizTalk tool set enables exchanging information among computer systems. Each area of BizTalk's rich set of capabilities addresses the common development tasks of building an integration solution. For example, BizTalk has tools for the common task of translating information from a structure understood by a source computer system into a structure understood by a destination computer system. Other BizTalk tools focus on defining integration processes or patterns of information flows.

This chapter focuses on the capabilities of the BizTalk Editor tool. The BizTalk product team designed the Editor tool specifically for defining the structure of the information that flows through BizTalk. BizTalk calls these definitions *schemas*, and the BizTalk Editor creates them.

For example, suppose a customer message flows through BizTalk. This message may contain customer demographic information such as occupation and gender, logistical information such as address, and information about the particular products of interest to the customer. BizTalk needs to collect and organize this information in a structured format to fully utilize it.

Sometimes, BizTalk needs to examine messages to handle them correctly. For example, suppose additional verification steps are needed if a customer's purchase is very expensive and outside normal buying patterns. A BizTalk schema can promote the purchase amount and make it available throughout BizTalk. BizTalk can examine the purchase amount and take an additional step to send a notification message to the customer's representative. This property promotion process creates a property schema defining information about the message. The BizTalk runtime engine uses property schemas extensively, capturing information such as the location where BizTalk accepts a message or the message's intended destination.

XML standards form the core of BizTalk. At no time is this more evident than when defining messages with the BizTalk Editor development tool. Use the Editor to define the structure of information. For example, you can create a hierarchy in which a customer message contains a demographic section, an address section, and a section for customer preferences. Each of these sections can contain details relevant only to that section.

The XML Schema Definition (XSD) language natively defines message structure to BizTalk. Since the Editor defines messages in XSD by default, any XSD-compliant XML editor can define BizTalk messages. However, the BizTalk Editor supports many of the rich capabilities of XSD, such as importing common schemas to facilitate reuse and consistency across message formats.

In addition to message structure, the BizTalk Editor can also define the data types of specific fields, thus completing the message definition. These data type definitions can be interoperable XSD primitive types, such as xs:string or xs:decimal, or complex data types. For example, complex types may require values adhering to regular expressions or a list of enumerated values enforced with the schema.

Finally, while XML standards are the core for BizTalk messages and the Editor, a message structure can extend beyond XML to apply to other formats such as a comma-delimited flat file representation. BizTalk can efficiently parse a diverse population of message formats into XML for processing within the core BizTalk runtime engine. XML must still define the message structure and fields, but a schema can specify additional information defining how the XML message translates to and from the file format.

2-1. Creating Simple Document Schemas

Problem

As part of your business process or messaging solution, you need to create an XML schema from scratch. You can't generate a schema based off of an existing XML document, as this schema represents data that has not been modeled before.

Solution

The following steps outline how to create a simple schema and add it to your BizTalk project.

1. Open an existing project or create a new project in Visual Studio.

2. As shown in Figure 2-1, right-click the project name in the Solution Explorer and select Add ➤ Add New Item.

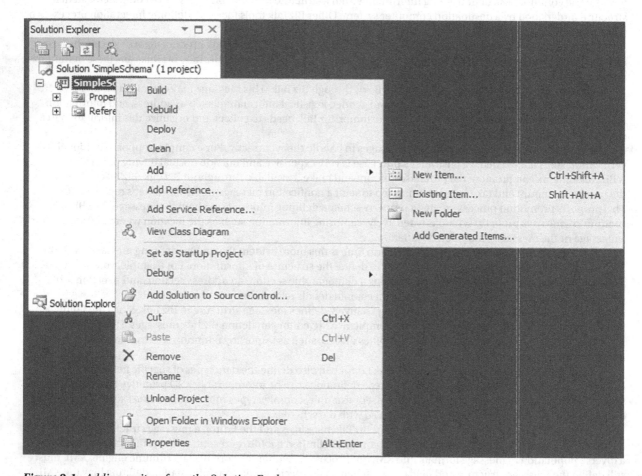

Figure 2-1. *Adding an item from the Solution Explorer*

3. The Add New Item dialog box will appear, as shown in Figure 2-2. Select Schema as the type of item, type in a name for the item, and click OK.

Figure 2-2. *Add New Item dialog box*

4. To change the name of the root node, right-click the node, and select Rename.

5. To add nodes, right-click a node, and select Insert Schema Nodes. Then select from the following options, as shown in Figure 2-3:

    - Child Record, to add a new record indented one level from the selected node

    - Child Field Attribute, to add a new attribute node indented one level from the selected node

    - Child Field Element, to add a new element node indented one level from the selected node

    - Sibling Record, to add a new record node at the same level of the selected node

    - Sibling Field Attribute, to add a new attribute node at the same level of the selected node

    - Sibling Field Element, to add a new element node at the same level of the selected node

Figure 2-3. *Adding schema nodes*

6. Select a node to view and modify its properties.

How It Works

XML schemas are the foundation of all scenarios and document exchanges with BizTalk Server. Once you have created your schema, you can create your scenario. Whether it is a pure messaging solution or involves business process automation scenarios implemented as orchestrations, the schema is available to all other projects and solutions simply by referencing it. Additionally, once you have created your schema, you can generate instances of the document that will adhere to the schema definition. This feature makes it very easy to create test data.

To generate a test instance, follow these steps:

1. Open the schema Properties, shown in Figure 2-4, by right-clicking the schema in the Solution Explorer and selecting Properties.

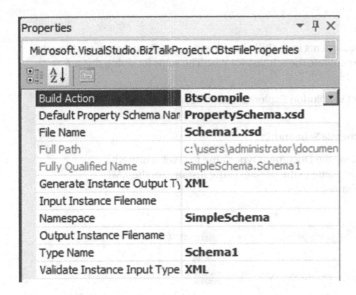

Figure 2-4. *Schema Properties*

2. Type a path and file name next to Output Instance Filename, or select the ellipsis to use the common file dialog box to browse to a file location and name the file. Then click OK.

3. Right-click the schema, and select Generate Instance. A test instance of the document will be created and named based on the Output Instance Filename property specified.

Similarly, BizTalk Server provides the ability to validate that an instance of a document adheres to a schema definition. To validate an instance, follow these steps:

1. Open the schema Properties by right-clicking the schema name in the Solution Explorer and selecting Properties.

2. Type a path and file name next to Input Instance Filename, or select the ellipsis to use the common file dialog box to browse to a file location and select a file. Then click OK.

3. Right-click the schema, and select Validate Instance. The document specified in the Input Instance Filename property will be validated against the schema.

2-2. Creating a Schema Based on an Existing XML Document
Problem

You have an existing XML document that you want to create a BizTalk schema for.

Solution

In many situations, you will need to consume XML documents in BizTalk that already exist. Rather than creating the schema by hand, you can have BizTalk automatically generate the schema for you. The steps for doing this are as follows:

1. In a BizTalk project, right-click the project in Solution Explorer, and select Add ➤ Add Generated Items.

2. In the dialogue box that opens, select Generate Schemas.

3. The Generate Schemas window appears. Set the Document type value to "Well-Formed XML (Not Loaded)" and set the "Input file" value to the pre-=existing instance of the XML that you are basing the schema on. See Figure 2-5.

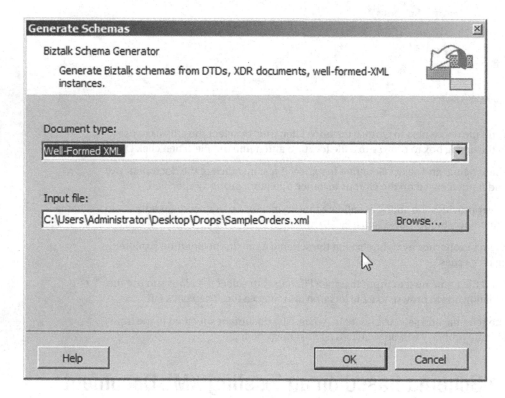

Figure 2-5. *Specifying a well-formed XML instance*

■ **Note** You may get an error similar to that shown in Figure 2-6. If so, simply run the `InstallWFX.vbs` script in the file path specified in the error message and run the schema generator tool again.

Figure 2-6. The error message that occurs the first time the schema generator is run

4. Click OK. The schema will be automatically created and added to your BizTalk project.

How It Works

There are several other options for generated items, but this is the most helpful of the group. You would be amazed at the number of developers who try to hand code their own schemas based on XML documents that already exist.

2-3. Creating Schema Namespaces
Problem

You need to create two schemas that have the same name for the root node.

Solution

BizTalk Server uses a combination of namespaces and root nodes to resolve schema references. Therefore, it is possible to have two schemas with the same root node as long as their namespace designation is different. By default, the BizTalk Editor will set the namespace of a schema to http://[solution].[schema], where solution refers to the name of the solution file and schema refers to the name of the schema file. This default namespace designation may be modified as follows:

1. Open the project that contains the schema.

2. Double-click the schema to open it.

3. Select the <Schema> node.

4. Right-click and select Properties.

5. Modify the Target Namespace property as desired.

When you modify the Target Namespace property, BizTalk Server will automatically modify the Default Namespace (element name xmlns) of the schema to match the Target Namespace. Once the two schemas with the same root node have different namespace designations, they may be used without any conflicts.

How It Works

Namespaces are used to allow elements and attributes from different schemas to share names. For example, two schemas may have an element named FirstName. If the schemas did not have different namespaces, BizTalk Server would not know which FirstName you were referencing. In addition to adopting naming standards and conventions for all BizTalk artifacts, you should adopt a standard for namespaces in schemas. An example of a standard is as follows:

```
http://[Company Name].[Project].BizTalk.Schemas.[Schema].[Version]
```

where Company Name is your company name, Project is the name of the project, Schema is the name of the schema, and Version is the version number of the schema.

■ **Note**   "EDI" should not be used in the namespace of any project that uses the BizTalk EDI engine. During runtime, you may run into conflicts with this that will not allow your components to function as expected.

2-4. Promoting Properties

Problem

You have a scenario where you want to subscribe to a message differently based on the contents or context of the message, and you need to understand how BizTalk Server exposes this metadata.

Solution

In order to promote instance-specific data fields (data that resides in the actual message instances, such as a customer name or the ID of an order), you must create a property schema. You then promote the specific schema elements, attributes, or records you need to subscribe to into the property schema. This task is accomplished in Visual Studio, and can be done in one of two ways: quick promotion and regular promotion. For more information on both of these methods, see Recipe 2-5, which describes how to create a property schema.

In addition to instance-specific data fields, a number of system- or exchange-specific properties are automatically promoted by BizTalk Server. A description of these exchange-specific properties, and the fundamental difference between them and instance-specific properties, is provided in the following "How It Works" section.

All properties that have been promoted, regardless of whether they are associated with a specific instance or the message exchange in general, are available for subscription by other BizTalk Server objects, including send ports, send port groups, and orchestrations. Promoted properties are also available for tracking purposes, which allow them to be used in troubleshooting and reporting.

How It Works

The importance of promoted properties in BizTalk Server's publish/subscribe architecture cannot be overstated. Understanding how they work is absolutely critical when designing and building an integration solution.

From a simplistic perspective, a publish/subscribe integration architecture involves source systems publishing or outputting messages to a centralized hub. After the hub receives these messages, it delivers them to the destination, or subscribing, systems. Within BizTalk Server, promoted properties are the key data that determine which messages are delivered to subscribing systems or processes. Without promoted properties, messages would be received by BizTalk Server, but they would not be sent out, resulting in a sort of black hole of messages. This would obviously not be a good situation, and BizTalk Server will actually throw an error if a message is received without having a system or process that subscribes to it. This keeps with the theory that it is not a good idea for a publish/subscribe integration hub to accept messages for which it does not have a subscriber.

A term that is commonly used to describe a message's promoted properties is *message context*. The message context includes all the instance-specific and exchange-specific data fields and essentially is the metadata that the messaging engine of BizTalk Server uses to process messages. As previously noted, instance-specific properties are those that pertain to a specific message instance, and they must be promoted explicitly during development. A common example of this type of property is an XML element containing a unique ID, which may capture an important data field such as an order number. From a message schema, XML elements, attributes, and records may be promoted.

■ **Note**   In order for an XML record to be promoted, its `ContentType` property must be set to `SimpleContent`. All promoted properties, regardless of whether they are populated by XML elements, attributes, or records, have a maximum length of 255 characters.

Along with being the key data elements allowing message subscription, promoted properties are also commonly used in orchestrations to determine business process. Orchestrations can handle messages dynamically by interrogating promoted properties that hold key metadata elements of a message. For example, sales orders being delivered domestically may need to be handled differently than those being sent overseas. By capturing the destination country of an order in the document schema and flagging the element as a promoted property, this data element can easily be used as a decision point in the orchestration. Domestic orders could be handled on one branch of decision logic, and international orders handled on another. It is important to note here that as an alternative to using promoted properties, the actual XML message could be interrogated within the orchestration to determine the destination of a sales order. While this method could be used, leveraging promoted properties simplifies programming and has performance benefits, as promoted properties can be accessed directly without incurring the cost of opening the entire XML message.

For additional performance gains, *distinguished fields* can be used as opposed to promoted properties within orchestrations. Distinguished fields provide functionality similar to promoted properties (allowing access to instance- or exchange-specific metadata items on a message), with a few key differences:

- Distinguished fields are available only within a single orchestration instance, and they are not available to other BizTalk Server objects, such as receive locations, send ports, send port groups, and tracking utilities.

- Distinguished fields can be of any length; promoted properties have a maximum length of 255 characters.

- Distinguished fields have less of a performance impact than promoted properties, as they are not persisted to the MessageBox database. Instead, they are essentially XPath aliases, which simply point to the appropriate XML data field. Additionally, adding the `DistinguishedField` attribute to a field on a .NET class allows it to be exposed as a distinguished field.

- Distinguished fields are accessed through a reference to the name of the message, the name of the record structure containing the distinguished field (which could include multiple levels of child records), and the name of the distinguished field, with each named item separated by periods: `MessageName.RecordName.ChildRecordName.DistinguishedFieldName`. Promoted properties, on the other hand, are accessed through a reference to the name of the message, the name of the property schema, and a name of the promoted property, via the following format:

  `MessageName(PropertySchameName.PromotedPropertyName)`.

Certain scenarios will call for sensitive information, such as a bank account number, to be used as a promoted property. To allow for enhanced troubleshooting and detailed reporting, promoted properties can be viewed in tools such as the Group Hub reports in the BizTalk Admin Console and Business Activity Monitor (BAM). Based on privacy regulations, these data fields may need to be hidden from these tools, which can be accomplished by setting the promoted property's `Sensitive Information` property to `True` (this configuration is applied on the property schema).

System- or exchange-specific properties are those that are automatically promoted by BizTalk Server and allow the successful processing of those documents by the messaging engine. The fundamental difference between the two types of properties is that exchange-specific properties can all be determined without looking into the actual contents, or payload, of the message. Instance-specific properties, on the other hand, are all populated with actual values within a message instance.

Exchange-specific properties come in various types. Table 2-1 lists the default exchange-specific property types that come with a complete installation of BizTalk Server. Additional properties may be added as other BizTalk related items are installed, such as the MQ Series adapter.

Table 2-1. *Default Exchange-Specific Property Types*

Type	Description
BizTalk Framework (BTF2)	Properties that support the BizTalk Framework. These are very rarely used in the routing of documents.
BizTalk Server (BTS)	Properties that support core BizTalk Server messaging. These are extremely common in routing and include things like `ReceivePortName` and other standard properties that are useful to route on.
EDI (EDI)	These are the base EDI properties are available when the BizTalk EDI components have been installed. They include envelope information, party information, and other data related to EDI message processing.
AS2 (EdiIntAS)	These properties are related to AS2 (also known as EDI over the Internet) messages and are available on messages processed using the AS2 protocol.
EDI Override (EDIOverride)	These properties are used primarily to override the values of EDI messages at runtime. They include envelope segments and several other related properties.
Error Reporting (ErrorReport)	Properties that support error reporting and handling. These are used when subscribing to documents that have failed on ports that have been enabled for routing of failed documents.
Legacy (LEGACY)	Properties that support BizTalk Server 2002 properties.
Message Tracking (MessageTracking)	Properties that support message tracking.
Orchestration (Microsoft.BizTalk. XLANGs.BTXEngine)	Properties that support the BizTalk Server orchestration engine.
MIME (MIME)	Properties that support the processing of MIME-encoded messages.
Various BizTalk Adapters (FILE, FTP, HTTP, MQSeries, MSMQ, MSMQT, POP3, SMTP, SOAP, SQL, WCF, WSS, etc.)	Properties that support the different adapters, both standard (such as File and FTP) and third-party adapters. These properties are available for documents that have been processed using the specific adapter (for example, if a message was received on a File adapter, the file promoted properties will be populated).
XML Document (XMLNorm)	Properties that support the processing of XML documents.

BizTalk Server processes promoted properties as messages are received into or sent out of the MessageBox. Specifically, pipelines handle this task. System- or exchange-specific properties are promoted by default, through pipelines such as XML or PassThru (both the receive and send variety). For instance-specific properties to be promoted, a pipeline other than the PassThru must be used, as this pipeline does not attempt to match messages to their associated schemas (and therefore property schemas).

As properties are promoted, their XSD data types are converted to Common Language Runtime (CLR) data types. Table 2-2 shows XSD data types and their associated CLR data types.

Table 2-2. *XSD Data Types and Associated CLR Data Types*

XSD	CLR	XSD	CLR
anyURI	String	Name	String
Boolean	Boolean	NCName	String
byte	sbyte	negativeInteger	Decimal
date	DateTime	NMTOKEN	String
dateTime	DateTime	nonNegativeInteger	Decimal
decimal	Decimal	nonPositiveInteger	Decimal
double	Double	normalizedString	String
ENTITY	String	NOTATION	String
float	Single	positiveInteger	Decimal
gDay	DateTime	QName	String
gMonth	DateTime	short	Int16
gMonthDay	DateTime	string	String
ID	String	time	DateTime
IDREF	String	token	String
int	Int32	unsignedByte	Byte
integer	Decimal	unsignedInt	Uint32
language	String	unsignedShort	Uint16

In addition to pipelines, orchestrations may also be used to explicitly set promoted properties. This is important if your business process requires the copying or creation of messages. Since messages are immutable (meaning once a message has been created, it cannot be modified) in BizTalk Server, a new message must be created prior to any of its promoted properties being set. When a message is constructed in an orchestration as a copy of another message, the message context (its promoted properties), by default, are all copied to the new message. Once this new message is created, its properties may be explicitly set to something different than in the original message. This must be done in the same Message Assignment shape in the orchestration as the duplicate message.

■ **Note**　When a copy of a message is created in an orchestration, it is important to consider how the properties on the original message are configured. If any of its properties are configured to use `MessageContextPropertyBase` for the `Property Schema Base` (a property of the promoted field found in the property schema), they will not be copied to the new message in the orchestration. By contrast, all those properties that are configured to use the `MessageDataPropertyBase` (the default value) for the `Property Schema Base` will be copied to the new message. For more information about the `Property Schema Base` property, see Recipe 2-5.

2-5. Creating Property Schemas
Problem

You want to subscribe to a message based on the contents of the message.

Solution

Property schemas allow you to promote properties so that they can be used when setting up filter expressions. As long as the PassThruReceive pipeline is not used, these promoted properties are added to the message context during pipeline processing. Once added to the message context, they can be used as filter expressions on send ports. These properties are also available to be evaluated or modified in orchestrations. To create a property schema and promote a property, follow these steps:

1.　Open the project that contains the schema.

2.　Double-click to open the schema.

3.　Select the node that you wish to promote.

4.　Right-click and select Promote ➤ Quick Promotion, as shown in Figure 2-7.

Figure 2-7. *Completing a quick promotion of a property*

5. You will be asked if you wish to add the property schema to the project. Click OK. The property schema is created with a reference to the promoted property, as well as a default property of Property1. This may be removed from the property schema.

■ **Note** You may also add a property schema by highlighting the project in the Solution Explorer and selecting Add ➤ New Item ➤ Property Schema. Once the property schema is added to the project, you must associate it with a schema. To do this, select the schema in the Solution Explorer, right-click a node in the schema, and select Promote ➤ Show Promotions. In the dialog box, select the Property Fields tab, and click the Folder icon to launch the BizTalk Type Picker dialog box. Browse to the property schema, select it, and click OK.

---

6. To view all promoted properties, select any node in the schema and select Promote ➤ Show Promotions to open the Promote Properties dialog box.

7. Select the Property Fields tab to view all of the promoted properties, as shown in Figure 2-8.

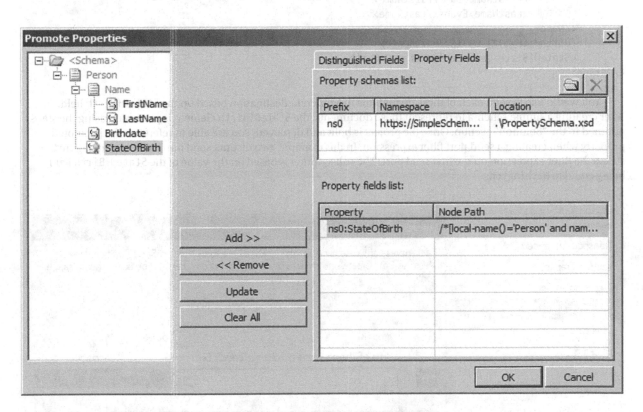

Figure 2-8. Viewing the promoted properties in the Promote Properties dialog box

8. You may promote additional fields directly from this dialog box, or repeat steps 3 and 4 to promote other fields.

How It Works

Once you have deployed the solution with the promoted properties, they may be used to perform content-based routing on the documents. Following is a simple example of content-based routing. Assume you have the following two documents:

```
<Person>
        <Name>
                <FirstName>John</FirstName>
                <LastName>Doe</LastName>
        </Name>
        <Birthdate>1979-05-31</BirthDate>
        <StateOfBirth>Washington</StateOfBirth>
</Person>

<Person>
        <Name>
                <FirstName>Sam</FirstName>
                <LastName>Evans</LastName>
        </Name>
        <Birthdate>1973-03-15</BirthDate>
        <StateOfBirth>California</StateOfBirth>
</Person>
```

You would like to send each of these documents to a different destination based on the StateOfBirth field. After creating a simple schema to represent these documents, the StateOfBirth element is promoted using the steps outlined in the "Solution" section. Once the project is built and deployed, you are able to reference the promoted property when creating a send port filter expression. In this example, two distinct send ports are created. Figure 2-9 shows the filter expression on the first send port. The subscription is based on the value of the StateOfBirth field being equal to Washington.

Figure 2-9. *Subscription for Washington*

On the second send port, the subscription is based on the value of the `StateOfBirth` field being equal to `California`, as shown in Figure 2-10.

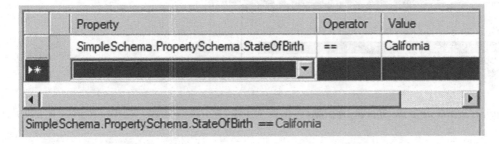

Figure 2-10. *Subscription for California*

Although this example is simple, it is easy to see how you can leverage this feature to create content-based routing scenarios through the use of promoted properties.

It is also possible to create message context properties that do not exist in the message itself, but only in the message context. This may be valuable when you are not allowed to modify the schema but would like to associate additional information with the document. This may be accomplished by adding a node to a property schema and setting its `Property Schema Base` property to `MessageContextPropertyBase`. This property is then available and can be set in an orchestration, and ultimately, the document may be routed based on its value. For example, perhaps you would like to calculate the age for each person processed in the preceding example, but you cannot add an Age element to the schema. As opposed to adding a node to the schema, a node is added to the property schema, as shown in Figure 2-11.

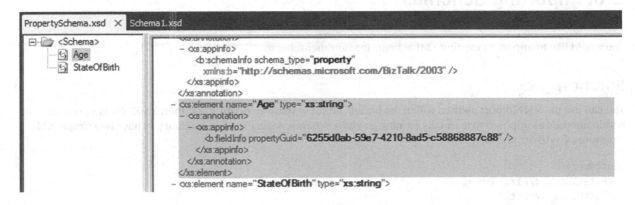

Figure 2-11. *Adding a property to message context*

After building and redeploying the solution, a second property, Age, is now available (see Figure 2-12) for generating filter expressions.

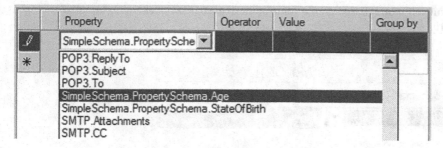

Figure 2-12. *The new value is available in the filter expressions*

To complete the scenario, you would do the following:

- Create an orchestration that subscribes to all of the documents with no value for Age.

- In this orchestration, calculate the Age value based on the birth date, and set the property accordingly.

- Send the document back into the MessageBox database.

- Add a second filter expression to the existing send ports to subscribe based on the StateOfBirth and if the Age value is present.

In summary, content-based routing is a typical scenario, and property schemas are used to extend the message context properties that come with BizTalk Server.

2-6. Importing Schemas
Problem

You would like to import an existing XML schema into another schema.

Solution

You can use the XSD Import method within the BizTalk Editor to reuse an existing common XML object structure within another, as opposed to manually creating an entire schema. As an example, assume you have two simple XML structures, Customer and Address:

```
<Customer>
  <FirstName> </FirstName>
  <LastName> </LastName>
  <MiddleInit> </MiddleInit>
  <Age></Age>
</Customer>

<Address>
  <AddrLine1> </AddrLine1>
  <AddrLine2> </AddrLine2>
  <AddrLine3> </AddrLine3>
  <Zip> </Zip>
  <State> </State>
  <Country> </Country>
</Address>
```

To use the XSD Import method to allow this scenario within BizTalk, follow these steps:

1. Open the project that contains the existing schema (in this case, the Customer schema).

2. Double-click the Customer schema to open it.

3. Right-click the root node of the Customer schema, and select Properties.

4. In the Properties window, click the ellipsis next to Imports to open the Imports dialog box, which is shown in Figure 2-13.

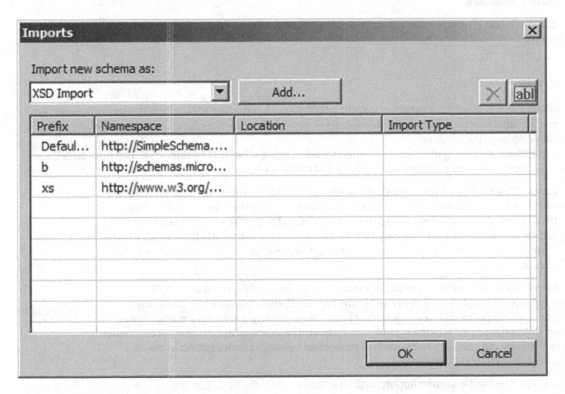

Figure 2-13. *Imports dialog box*

5. Select XSD Import as the import type, and click the Add button.

6. In the BizTalk Type Picker dialog box, select the Schemas tree node, and select the Address schema.

■ **Note** In this example, the Address schema is within the current BizTalk project. If the schema existed outside the BizTalk project, the schema could be imported by selecting the Reference tree node.

The preceding procedure imports the Address schema into the Customer schema. To use the Address schema, follow these steps:

1. Click the Customer node in the Customer schema.

2. Right-click and select Insert Child Record.

3. Click the newly created child record.

4. In the Properties window, click the Data Structure Type drop-down list, and select the Address reference.

The Customer schema is now referencing and using the Address schema via the Imports schema method within the BizTalk tool set.

How It Works

Within the BizTalk tool set, there are a variety of ways in which you can construct XML schemas. The choices revolve around common architecture principles such as reuse, development best practices for schema organization, and fundamental development preferences.

This example illustrated using the Imports method for referencing schema. The Imports dialog box offers three choices for achieving the schema reference activity (step 5 of the recipe):

> *Include*: This method physically includes a schema definition within another. The common usage would be to create a static reference of a schema during the schema build process. This choice could be used to leverage previously defined XSD schema (for example, publicly available schema). The include schema must be the same target namespace of the schema you are including. Alternatively, the target namespace of the include schema can be blank.

> *Import*: The most commonly used import method within BizTalk, the Import option includes XSD Imports statements within the source schema definition. By using this option, namespaces and XSD object structures within the target schema are available for use within the source schema in read-only fashion. The practical application for this choice revolves around common reuse, such as reuse of an existing schema artifact or use of a publicly available XML schema.

> *Redefine*: The least-common import method within BizTalk, the Redefine option, like the Import option, allows namespaces and XSD object references to be used within the source definition. However, the Redefine option allows objects and data structures to be overridden within the source definition. Common uses could be to create an inheritance model or to reuse and customize an existing XSD structure.

This example demonstrated referencing other schemas within the BizTalk tool set. However, while BizTalk provides and implements standard XSD instructions to achieve this functionality, common architecture usage and choices should not be ignored to ensure the correct schema reference method is selected.

2-7. Referencing Schemas
Problem

You would like to reference an XML schema in your BizTalk project, because you want to reuse an existing BizTalk artifact or prebuilt schema component.

Solution

As an example, assume you have a simple Customer XML schema (CustomerSchema.dll) stored in an existing BizTalk project:

```
<Customer>
  <FirstName> </FirstName>
  <LastName> </LastName>
  <MiddleInit> </MiddleInit>
  <Age></Age>
</Customer>
```

To reference an existing schema, follow these steps:

1. Open your source project.

2. Within the Solution Explorer, right-click the References tree node, and select Add Reference.

3. Select the Projects tab in the Add References dialog box if the schema you are after is in the same project, or click the Browse tab, navigate to CustomerSchema.dll, and then click the OK button.

You now have referenced CustomerSchema.dll and can use the inherent BizTalk artifacts in your current project. For example, suppose that you want to use the DLL in a new map within your current project. Follow these steps:

1. Right-click the project, and select Add ➤ New Item.

2. In the Add New Item dialog box, double-click Map. This opens a blank map with left and right panes where you can enter the source and destination schema, respectively.

3. Click Open Source Schema in the left pane.

4. In the BizTalk Type Picker dialog box, select the References tree node, and select the Client Schema reference.

5. Select the Schemas node.

6. Select the Customer schema.

How It Works

Referencing schemas gives you the ability to reuse and reference existing BizTalk artifacts, as you would normally reference other .NET artifacts. While this can be powerful, you should always keep in mind partitioning and change scenarios. For example, if you were to reference an existing deployed artifact, to make changes to the referenced artifact, you would need to remove the referenced artifact in the dependent project.

■ **Note**   One of the most important things you can do is plan how to organize your BizTalk artifacts into separate projects (and, in turn, assemblies). Intelligent namespacing is the first step, separating schemas into appropriate projects is the next. Since schemas are referenced by maps and by orchestrations, the map and orchestration artifacts often should be kept in their own, separate projects. Using small assemblies that have just a few artifacts is the ideal approach, as these are far more easy to update and redeploy than other methods of organization.

This example explored how to reference a schema artifact in another project. BizTalk also gives you the ability to reference schemas in Schema Import tasks. For information on how to import schema references, refer to Recipe 2-6.

2-8. Creating Envelopes to Split Inbound Data

Problem

You are receiving a message that contains multiple records in a batch fashion. In order to import this information into the appropriate systems, each record must be handled individually, as opposed to processing them all in a single batch.

Solution

Envelopes allow you to define a container schema that wraps a number of child schemas or subschemas. By defining which child records it contains, the envelope allows BizTalk Server to access the subrecords individually (a process commonly known as *debatching*) and process them as distinct messages. For this solution, it is assumed that the schema defining the child record has already been created (see Recipe 2-1 for how to create a schema). In this case, our child record schema is Order – the incoming document contains one or more "Orders," and we want to split these into individual orders using an envelope.

To create an envelope schema, follow these steps:

1. Open the project that contains the child record schema. In this case, "Order" would be the child record.

2. Right-click the project, and select Add ➤ New Item to open the Add New Item dialog box.

3. Select Schema Files from the BizTalk Project Items category and Schema from the list of templates. Enter a descriptive name for your new schema and then click Add. In this case, OrderEnvelope will be used.

4. Right-click the Root node of the new schema, and change it to the root name of the incoming schema containing the batch of records (OrderEnvelope in this example).

5. Click the Schema node (directly above the newly renamed root node), and change the Envelope property of the schema to Yes (in the Properties window), as shown in Figure 2-14.

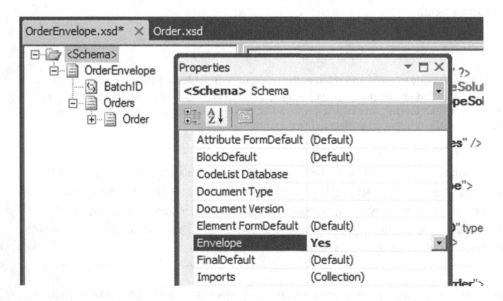

Figure 2-14. *Configuring the schema to be an envelope*

6. Right-click the newly renamed root node, and select Insert Schema Node ➤ Child Record, Child Field Attribute, or Child Field Element, to add the appropriate envelope elements. In this example, a child field element named BatchID and a child record named Orders, which will contain the child records, are added.

7. Right-click the record that will contain the child records (Orders in this example) and select Insert Schema Node ➤ Child Record to add a container for the child records. In this example, a child record named Order is added.

8. Right-click the container child record (Order in this example), and select Insert Schema Node ➤ Any Element to add a placeholder for the child elements. The resulting envelope schema has the structure shown in Figure 2-15.

Figure 2-15. *Envelope schema structure*

9. Click the root node (OrderEnvelope in this example), and click the Body XPath property of the schema (in the Properties window), which will open the Body XPath dialog box.

10. Navigate through the schema structure displayed in the tree view, and select the container record for the child records you wish to process individually (the Orders record in this example), as shown in Figure 2-16. Then click OK.

Figure 2-16. Specifying a child record

11. Build and deploy the solution.

12. The next step is to create the receive port, receive location, and send port. The basics are as follows:

    a. Create a Receive Port and an associated File Receive Location. Set the Receive pipeline property as XMLReceive. See Figure 2-17.

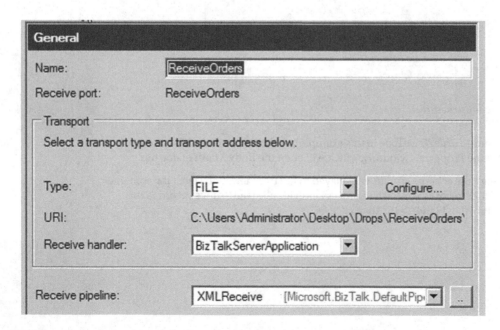

Figure 2-17. Configuring the Receive Port for Splitting

b. Create a File Send Port. Set the filter to subscribe to the Receive Port (BTS.ReceivePortName) and the Send Pipeline property to XMLTransmit. See Figure 2-18.

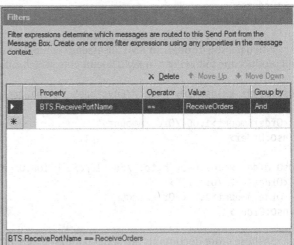

Figure 2-18. *Configuring the Send Port for Splitting*

c. Enlist the Send Port and enable the Receive Location.

13. Drop an instance of the Orders XML document on the File Receive Location. The split of the inbound Orders document will occur automatically in the pipelines.

■ **Note** You can create a sample instance to work from by right-clicking the OrderEnvelope schema and selecting Generate Instance. Paste this into Notepad or some other text editor. Next, right-click the Order schema, and select Generate Instance. Paste this into the correct node in the Orders document in the text editor. Save this manually created document and use it as a test input document.

How It Works

Envelopes provide the means to group multiple messages into one XML document. In the preceding example, the envelope was used to disassemble individual order documents from a single enveloped document containing a batch of orders. Once the envelope and document schemas (OrderEnvelope and Order in the example) have been deployed, BizTalk Server has the ability to leverage the two in message processing. The following XML represents one possible instance of the envelope schema:

```
<ns0:OrderEnvelope xmlns:ns0="http://EnvelopeSolution.OrderEnvelope">
  <BatchID>BatchID_0</BatchID>
  <Orders>
    <ns0:Order xmlns:ns0="http://EnvelopeSolution.Order">
      <OrderID>1</OrderID>
      <OrderAmount>1.00</OrderAmount>
    </ns0:Order>
```

```
      <ns0:Order xmlns:ns0="http://EnvelopeSolution.Order">
        <OrderID>2</OrderID>
        <OrderAmount>2.00</OrderAmount>
      </ns0:Order>
    </Orders>
</ns0:OrderEnvelope>
```

When passed through an XML disassembler pipeline component in BizTalk Server, the preceding XML message will produce the following two XML documents, which can be processed individually:

```
<ns0:Order xmlns:ns0="http://EnvelopeSolution.Order">
  <OrderID>1</OrderID>
  <OrderAmount>1.00</OrderAmount>
</ns0:Order>
```

```
<ns0:Order xmlns:ns0="http://EnvelopeSolution.Order">
  <OrderID>2</OrderID>
  <OrderAmount>2.00</OrderAmount>
</ns0:Order>
```

As these order documents are split up into separate messages within BizTalk Server, they can undergo different forms of business logic or be delivered to a different destination, depending on their properties (see Recipe 2-4 for more information about property-based subscriptions).

The key data element that allows envelope processing in BizTalk server is the Body XPath property. This data element acts as a pointer to the container record that encapsulates or surrounds the child records. On the OrderEnvelope root node, the Body XPath property was set to the Orders record, which contains the individual Order records. In envelope schemas containing a single root node, the Body XPath property must be set to that root node.

For envelope schemas with multiple root nodes, the following apply:

- If the Root Reference property is not set on the envelope schema, the Body XPath property must be set for all root nodes.

- If the Root Reference property is set on the envelope schema, the Body XPath property must be set for the root node configured in the Root Reference property. The Body XPath property can be set for the other root nodes, but it is not required.

- It is not required to set the Root Reference property, but the Body XPath property must always be set on at least one root node.

In addition to encapsulating multiple messages, envelopes can also supply header information that applies to all the records it contains. In the example, the BatchID element is defined once at the envelope level, but applies to all the individual order documents. This functionality of supplementing the individual message data with header data or metadata can be seen in the common example of SOAP envelopes (see Recipe 2-13 for more information about SOAP envelopes).

Within BizTalk Server, envelope processing for received messages occurs in the disassemble stage of a receive pipeline. The out-of-the-box XML receive pipeline handles the removing and parsing of any envelope data contained within the inbound document. The subschemas are dynamically determined at runtime by the envelope's properties (specifically, the Body XPath), and used to validate the child documents' structure and split each out into an individual message.

A custom receive pipeline can also be used to more precisely process inbound enveloped documents. By leveraging the XML disassembler pipeline component, the envelope and document (child document) schemas can be set explicitly in the properties of the component. All envelope and document schemas explicitly set should have unique target namespaces.

■ **Note**   If envelope or document schemas are explicitly set on an XML disassembler component, only documents matching those schemas will be processed within the pipeline. The order of envelope schemas is enforced based on the configuration within the Envelope property on the XML disassembler component. In contrast, the order of the document schemas is not enforced.

After the inbound enveloped document has been debatched into individual messages, the disassembler promotes any properties of the envelope to each individual message. In the example, if the BatchID had been configured as a promoted property, it would have been attached to each individual message during disassembly.

Implementing envelopes for outbound messages is also possible within BizTalk Server. This process is handled in the assembling stage of a send pipeline. By leveraging the XML assembler pipeline component in a custom send pipeline, the envelope schemas can explicitly be set in the properties of the component. As it passes through the custom pipeline, the message will be wrapped in the specified envelope(s) and have the appropriate message properties demoted to the envelope(s). If a batch of outbound messages is sent through the custom send pipeline, the batch of messages will all be combined into a single document and wrapped in the specified envelope.

In addition to having a single envelope, a group of messages can be wrapped in a series of nested envelopes. Using nested envelopes provides a flexible way for transferring message batches that have a complex structure or relationship.

While the preceding solution used BizTalk Server's pipeline capabilities to handle inbound envelope processing, there are other implementation options to consider when designing a solution. A loop can be used within an orchestration to iterate over child records within an enveloped document, splitting out each submessage individually using XPath queries or a node list object. An orchestration can also be used to call out to an external assembly to handle message debatching. When determining which method to use, it is important to consider the following:

- Does the entire batch need to be handled transactionally (for example, if one of the messages fails to process correctly, should the entire batch be canceled)?

- Do the individual records within the batch need to be processed in a specific order (for example, in the same order in which they appear in the original document)?

- Does there need to be any event or notification after all messages in the batch are successfully processed?

- Is business logic (orchestration) implemented on each individual message after it has been debatched?

If your business scenario would lead you to answer yes to any of these questions, using an orchestration to handle the parsing of an enveloped document may be required. The main benefit of using an orchestration is enhanced control over the processing of the individual messages. The order of the messages can be maintained; scopes can be used to implement transactionality across the entire message batch; compensating and error handling are more robust; and it is simple to implement logic required when all messages within a batch have completed processing. The major downsides to using orchestrations for debatching are performance and ease of modification to the solution (as changing the orchestration requires you to redeploy the BizTalk Server solution).

If the requirements of your business scenario allow for envelope processing to be handled via pipelines, you will realize performance gains. Additionally, the solution will be simplified by minimizing the number of implemented artifacts.

2-9. Creating Complex Types

Problem

You want to create an address data type that can be reused, rather than creating the same set of data for every address type.

Solution

You can use XSD complex types within the BizTalk Editor. As an example, assume that you need to create your own complex data type for storing shipping addresses for an Order schema:

```
<Order>
  <CompanyName> </CompanyName>
  <OrderID> </ OrderID>
  <OrderDate> </OrderDate>
  <OrderAmount></ OrderAmount >
  <ShipTo>
          <CompanyID> </CompanyID>
          <AddressLine1> </AddressLine1>
          <AddressLine2> </AddressLine2>
          <AddressLine3> </AddressLine4>
          <Zip> </Zip>
  </ShipTo>
  <ShipFrom>
          <CompanyID> </CompanyID>
          <AddressLine1> </AddressLine1>
          <AddressLine2> </AddressLine2>
          <AddressLine3> </AddressLine4>
          <Zip> </Zip>
  </ShipFrom>
</Order>
```

For this example, the Order schema has been built with Order Header nodes and the <ShipTo> record. The following steps outline how to create a complex type to be the data type for the <ShipTo> and <ShipFrom> addresses. You will model the data type of the existing <ShipTo> record.

1. Open the project that contains the schema.

2. Double-click the schema (the Order schema in this example) to open it, as shown in Figure 2-19.

```
<?xml version="1.0" encoding="utf-16" ?>
- <xs:schema xmlns="http://CreatingComplexTypes.Schema1" xmlns:b="http://schemas.microsoft.com/BizTalk/2003"
    targetNamespace="http://CreatingComplexTypes.Schema1" xmlns:xs="http://www.w3.org/2001/XMLSchema">
  - <xs:element name="Order">
    - <xs:complexType>
      - <xs:sequence>
          <xs:element name="CompanyName" type="xs:string" />
          <xs:element name="OrderID" type="xs:string" />
          <xs:element name="OrderDate" type="xs:string" />
          <xs:element name="OrderAmount" type="xs:string" />
        - <xs:element name="ShipTo">
          - <xs:complexType>
            - <xs:sequence>
                <xs:element name="AddressLine1" type="xs:string" />
                <xs:element name="AddressLine2" type="xs:string" />
                <xs:element name="AddressLine3" type="xs:string" />
                <xs:element name="Zip" type="xs:string" />
              </xs:sequence>
            </xs:complexType>
          </xs:element>
        </xs:sequence>
      </xs:complexType>
    </xs:element>
  </xs:schema>
```

Figure 2-19. *Order schema*

3. Click the existing record on which you want to base the complex type (the <ShipTo> record in the Order schema in this example).

4. In the Properties window, click Data Structure Type, and type **Address** in the box. This step will now automatically recognize the record as a complex data type.

Now you can reuse the complex type. For example, here are the steps to create a record that uses the sample complex type:

1. Click the Order schema node.

2. Right-click and select Insert Schema Node ➤ Child Record. Type the record name **ShipFrom**.

3. In the Properties window of the newly created ShipForm child record, click Data Structure Type, and select the complex type that is now available, Address.

This procedure creates the Address complex type element structure under the ShipFrom record. A sequence instruction is created under both the ShipFrom and ShipTo records to implement the complex type. Figure 2-20 shows the finished schema.

Figure 2-20. *Order schema with the Address complex type*

How It Works

The example demonstrated creating a complex type data type based on an existing schema record within the schema. By XSD definition, a *complex type* is an element (record) that has child elements or attributes. Complex types can be used to implement custom schema rules and XSD data structure considerations for records, elements, and attributes. For example, you might use complex data types for validation rules via XSD regular expressions, schema cardinality, and order. In addition, you can make data type references to your complex types, allowing you to reuse record structures and XSD implementations.

A complex type is derived from the base data type anyType; that is, in the purest form, a complex type is in essence a stand-alone base type, in which you can define your own XSD structure representation and schema rules.

■ **Note** A *simple type* is an element that in itself is defined and does not have children. For example, you might have a simple type named Order ID, which has a length limit of six and must start with an *A* character. In this instance, an XSD length restriction could be defined, along with a regular expression to check that the order starts with the letter *A*: <OrderID> Axxxxx </ OrderID>.

2-10. Defining Regular Expressions
Problem

You have field elements or attributes in your schema for which you want to restrict the valid content beyond data type, enumerations, length, and minimum and maximum values.

Solution

You can use the Pattern property of a field element or attribute to place a collection of regular expressions. Regular expressions are used to do pattern matching against the inbound data for the node. If the inbound data adheres to the pattern(s) defined for a node, then the input instance document will pass XML validation. If the inbound data for the node does not match the pattern(s), then the input instance document will fail XML validation. From within the BizTalk Editor, follow these steps to add a regular expression to a field element or an attribute:

1. Select the field element or attribute node to which you wish to add restriction patterns.

2. Right-click and select Properties.

3. Set the Derived By property to Restriction. This will enable the Restriction properties within the Properties window.

4. Select the ellipsis next to the Pattern property to launch the Pattern Editor dialog box, as shown in Figure 2-21.

Figure 2-21. *Pattern Editor dialog box*

5. Add one to many valid regular expressions, and then click OK. The BizTalk Editor will add these restriction patterns to the schema definition.

■ **Note**   Although XSD regular expressions are similar to those in other programming languages that allow for pattern matching, there are some differences. Refer to the W3C specification for the specifics of the regular expression syntax for XSD.

How It Works

More restrictive validation of the input data may be of value for numerous types of data, such as phone numbers, IP addresses, and Social Security numbers. In these cases, you can use regular expressions to restrict the type of data that will be considered valid.

Once you have created a schema that has nodes with pattern value restrictions, you can use the Generate Instance and Validate Instance capabilities of the BizTalk Editor to test your patterns. See Recipe 2-1 for more information about these two features.

> ■ **Note** If you have pattern restrictions for a node(s) in your schema, the Generate Instance option will not create an instance document with valid data for those nodes. You will need to edit the instance document created. However, the Validate Instance option will validate the schema, including restriction patterns.

At runtime, neither the PassThruReceive nor the XMLReceive pipeline will complete a strict validation of the inbound document against the schema including the pattern matching. To complete a thorough validation of an inbound document, you must create a validation pipeline and add the document schema to the Document Schema property of the XML validator. If the document fails schema validation in the pipeline, the instance will terminate.

In practice, it may be more beneficial to handle the strict validation of data more gracefully than terminating the instance when the validation fails. This is especially true if the document is coming from an outside source or from a system that is outside your control. However, restriction patterns can be used to safeguard downstream systems and processes from bad data.

2-11. Creating Flat File Schemas
Problem

You are consuming an inbound message in a flat file structure and must represent the data in an XML schema. The inbound flat file contains records that are both positional and delimited.

> ■ **Note** *Delimited files* contain characters (such as commas) that separate the data. Files that are positional in nature contain data items that are a predefined length within the file. The physical position of the data defines what the data represents.

Solution

The solution outlined in this recipe consumes an inbound flat file schema message that may have a structure similar to the flat file shown in Listing 2-1. Additionally, this recipe outlines the steps required to manually create a schema for a flat file. BizTalk 2010 also includes a Flat File Wizard for creating flat file schemas (see Recipe 2-12)

> ■ **Note** The number bar at the top of Listing 2-1 is included for reference only and is not part of the file content. The number bar is for counting the position of the characters.

Listing 2-1. CustomerSalesOrder.txt

```
12345678901234567890123456789012345678901234567891234567890123456789
ORDER2004-10-24
SoldTo Shauna Marie     1223 Buttercup Lane Seattle      WA 98155
ShipTo Jen Schwinn      3030 Moby Road      Kent         WA 98110
ITEMS,ITEM111-AA|Grape|1|2.00|Bottle of Pop,ITEM111-AB|Cola|
1|2.00|Bottle of Pop
```

Additionally, the outbound BizTalk schema may have a structure similar to the XML file shown in Listing 2-2.

Listing 2-2. *CustomerSalesOrder.xml*

```
<ns0:order xmlns:ns0="http://Schema_Chapter_Project.CustomerSalesOrder">
  <date>10/24/2004</date>
  <customerHeader>
    <customerType>SoldTo</customerType>
    <fullName>Shauna Marie</fullName>
    <street>1223 Buttercup Lane</street>
    <city>Seattle</city>
    <state>WA</state>
    <postal>98155</postal>
  </customerHeader>
  <customerHeader>
    <customerType>ShipTo</customerType>
    <fullName>Jen Schwinn</fullName>
    <street>3030 Moby Road</street>
    <city>Kent</city>
    <state>WA</state>
    <postal>98110</postal>
  </customerHeader>
  <items>
    <item>
      <productId>ITEM111-AA</productId>
      <productName>Grape</productName>
      <quantity>1</quantity>
      <unityPrice>2.00</unityPrice>
      <description>Bottle of Pop</description>
    </item>
    <item>
      <productId>ITEM111-AB</productId>
      <productName>Cola</productName>
      <quantity>1</quantity>
      <unityPrice>2.00</unityPrice>
      <description>Bottle of Pop</description>
    </item>
  </items>
</ns0:order>
```

Follow these steps to create the flat file schema:

1. Create a new BizTalk schema, and select the Flat File Schema template.

2. Determine the structure and layout of your message schema. The structure and layout of the message schema will largely determine how the inbound document is parsed. In the XML sample in Listing 2-2, all data fields were defined as string elements. The customerHeader, items, and item nodes are defined as records.

3. Select the root node (the orders node in this example), and specify the child delimiter to be a carriage return and a line feed (CRLF). The most straightforward way to set the delimiter to a CRLF is by setting the child delimiter type to be Hexadecimal.

4. Specify the `child delimiter` property to be 0x0D 0x0A.

5. Set `child order` to be `Infix`.

6. Set `tag identifier` to read `ORDER`. The `tag identifier` property tells the schema where the data begins for the message. The children data for the root node of `order` are delimited by commas that appear in the middle of the data.

7. Based on the fact that there are two instances of `customerHeader` information, the `max cardinality` property for `customerHeader` record must be set to 2.

8. Set the structure for `customerHeader` to `positional`, since all of the child elements that represent customer information are related in a positional format within the flat file. Each child node that exists under `customerHeader` must have the position defined for the length of the data and the offset for where that value begins in the file. The way the value is represented starts from the left of the data element. For the length and offset of each element, see Table 2-3.

Table 2-3. *Customer Header Child Elements*

Element	Positional Length	Offset
customerType	7	0
fullName	16	0
street	20	0
city	14	0
state	3	0
postal	5	0

9. Set the `next node` tag value to `ITEMS` since `Items` is the next heading in the flat file.

10. Identify the `delimiter` as a comma, and set the `child-order` to `prefix`, since each item will be prefixed with a comma to indicate the beginning of that item.

11. Make sure that `child delimiter type` is set to `character`. Select `item`, and make sure the `child delimiter` is set to the pipe character (|), since the attributes for the items are delimited by the pipe character in the flat file.

12. Set the pipe character to `infix`, since each line has pipe characters set in between the delimited characteristics.

To test the flat file output of the schema, follow these steps:

1. Verify that `Generate Instance Output Type` on your schema reads `Native`. The `Native` property allows the schema to generate the native file format, which is a flat file, for that schema.

2. Right-click the schema, and select Generate Instance. You should see the default generated flat file.

To test the flat file schema to see the XML generated based on the provided flat file, follow these steps:

1. Verify that `Generate Instance Output Type` on your schema reads XML. The XML property allows the schema to process the inbound flat file and translate that flat file to an XML representation.

2. Right-click the schema, and select Validate Instance. You should see the XML version of the processed flat file.

How It Works

BizTalk is capable of processing both positional and delimited data, either in individual files or in a single file. The *child delimiter* is the key concept to keep in mind when creating a flat file schema. Any parent-level record that contains child elements or attributes must define whether the data in the flat file for those child records is delimited or positional and how the data is delimited.

Based on the layout of the destination message schema, you should consider the following when dealing with records versus dealing with child elements and attributes:

Records: If you use records to group child elements or attributes, consider how the child records will be demarcated. Will the child data be delimited, or is the child data positional? In the example in Listing 2-1, each line of data is delimited by a CRLF. Knowing that each line of data is delimited by a CRLF aids in determining whether the output schema must support that specific delimiter. The basic line delimiter information points to the need of specifying a delimiter of a CRLF for the parent record of the output schema.

Tag identifiers: Records may contain tag identifiers to distinguish one type of record from another record. A tag value also allows you to identify where data begins in the file.

Positional elements/attributes: In the XML example in Listing 2-2, the `customerHeader` data is stored in positional format. For each child node, you must provide the offset (where to start reading the data) and the length for that data item. Additionally, the parent record must specify that the child data structure is `Positional`.

Delimited elements/attributes: The flat file example in Listing 2-1 shows multiple items occurring on the same line delimited by the pipe (|) character. The attributes related to a single item are then further delimited by the comma character. The item's parent record must specify that the child data structure is `Delimited`. Additionally, the child delimiter for the item's parent record must specify that each item is delimited by a pipe character.

Cardinality for records: By default, BizTalk sets the cardinality field for records and elements/attributes to a default value of 1. The value of 1 means that you expect to receive a maximum and minimum of one instance of that record and associated child values. If you expect an inbound flat file to contain more than a single record instance, you must change the `max occurs` value to a number equal to *unbounded* or the number of instances you expect to receive.

Wrap characters: If the incoming data contains characters that have been identified as delimiting characters (for example, commas), those characters can be ignored through the use of wrap characters. For example, if the record contained the name Shauna, Marie and you wanted to have the comma included as part of the name, you could define a wrap character of " (double quote) and enclose the name within the wrap character: "Shauna, Marie". BizTalk will treat any special characters defined within a set of wrap characters as field-level data.

Escape characters: The purpose of escape characters is very similar to that of wrap characters. Escape characters specify the character to be used to escape reserved characters, and then the reserved characters will be treated as literal characters in a message.

If the records are delimited, you must determine how the records are delimited. For managing CRLF type transactions, child delimiter type is set to hexadecimal, and the delimiter is set to 0x0D 0x0A. If the delimiter is a character value like a comma, set child delimiter type to character. The other key consideration for using delimiters is defining the child-order of the delimiter:

- If the delimiter appears after the set of data, the child-order of the delimiter is postfix.

- If the delimiter appears before the set of data, the delimiter is prefix.

- If the delimiter appears in the middle of the set of data, the delimiter is infix.

The default child-order for a record is conditional default. The conditional default value means that if a tag value has been set for that record, then the child-order will be prefix. Otherwise, the child-order will be infix.

If the records are positional, you must determine the spacing of the delimited data. In the example, it was assumed that there were no spaces between the data (offsets set to 0) and the beginning of the data fields started at the left of each data value.

Another key consideration to keep in mind is the cardinality of the data groupings. When a BizTalk schema is created, by default, the cardinality is set to 1 (even if no cardinality value is explicitly set for a field). In the example, keeping the cardinality of the items set to the default would have caused some data to be lost when parsing both the customerHeader values and the item values. In the example, the cardinality of max value was changed to 2 to account for both the shipTo and soldTo values.

2-12. Creating Flat File Schemas via the Wizard
Problem

You are receiving an order file in flat file format from one of your customers. You would like to use the Flat File Schema Wizard to expedite the creation of an XML schema.

Solution

To demonstrate how to use the Flat File Schema Wizard, we will use the flat file sample shown in Listing 2-1 (used in Recipe 2-11). To create the flat file schema using the Flat File Schema Wizard, follow these steps:

1. Open a new BizTalk Server project.

2. Right-click the project, and select Add ➤ New Item.

3. In the Add New Item dialog box, select the Flat File Schema Wizard template. Click Add. Figure 2-22 demonstrates this step.

Figure 2-22. Creating a new flat file schema

4. On the Welcome screen of the BizTalk Server Flat File Wizard page, click Next.

5. On the Flat File Schema Information page (shown in Figure 2-23), specify the information that will be used as input to generate the specifics of the desired flat file schema:

BizTalk Flat File Schema Wizard

Flat File Schema Information

Specify the flat file document instance and schema information.

Instance file:

`C:\Users\Administrator\Documents\Visual Studio 2010\Projects\FlatF`   Browse...

Record name:

`CustomerSalesOrder`

Target namespace:

`http://FlatFileSchemaWizard.CustomerSalesOrder`

Code page: `UTF-8 (65001)`

☐ Count positions in bytes

Help   < Back   Next >   Cancel

Figure 2-23. Flat File Schema Information page

- *Instance File*: Use this to specify where your source instance file is located.

- *Record Name*: Specify the Root node of the schema you want to create. For this example, enter **CustomerSalesOrder**.

- *Target Namespace*: Specify the namespace of the schema you'd like to create.

- *Code Page*: This identifies the encoding format of a file. In this instance, use the default, which is UTF-8 (65001).

- *Count Positions in Bytes*: This specifies whether positions are calculated by bytes. If this box is not checked, positions will calculated by characters.

6. Click Next.

7. On the Select Document Data page, specify the data contents that will be used to generate the schema. The data contents are based on the instance file specified on the Flat File Schema Information page. Highlight the contents of the file that will be used to define the document data, as shown in Figure 2-24.

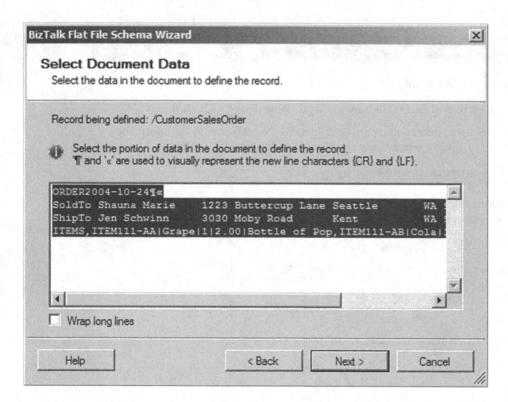

Figure 2-24. Source Document Data page

8. Click Next.

9. Now define the record format. In this example, the record is delimited by a carriage return and a line feed, as shown by the record identifier ORDER2004-10-24. Select the By Delimiter Symbol radio button, as shown in Figure 2-25.

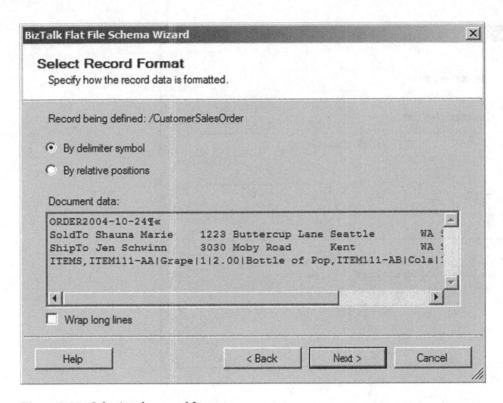

Figure 2-25. *Selecting the record format*

10. Click Next.

11. Now, specify the properties of the record (as shown in Figure 2-26). This step will define the makeup of the record to represent CustomerSalesOrder:

    a. Specify the child delimiter. Given that the record is defined by delimiter, select the child delimiter {CR}{LF}.

    b. Select the Record Has a Tag Identifier box. In this example, the tag identifier will be ORDER.

Figure 2-26. *Specifying the properties of the delimited record*

■ **Note** ORDER is the identifier based on it being the text identifier that is specified in the source record. This text will be searched for to identify the continuation or creation of a new record. Not all text files will have a record tag identifier; in these cases, leave this box unchecked.

---

12. Click Next.

13. Now, specify the properties of the child elements for the record (as shown in Figure 2-27). This step will identify the makeup of the elements for CustomerSalesOrder. Using the grid on the Child Elements page, define the record's child elements. In this example, set the values shown in Table 2-4.

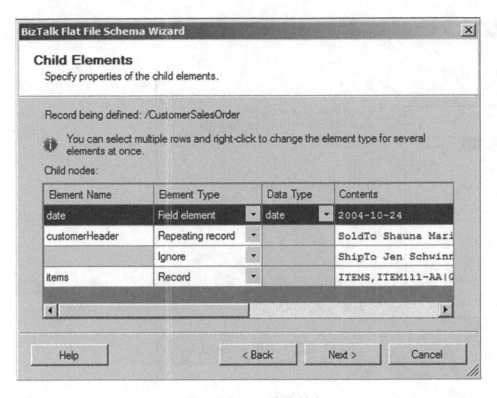

Figure 2-27. *Specifying the properties of the record's child elements*

Table 2-4. *Child Element Properties*

Element Name	Element Type	Data Type
date	Field Element	Date
customerHeader	Repeating Record	
	Ignore	
items	Record	

■ **Note** Observe that the customer ShipTo information is ignored because the record is the same structure as the customer SoldTo. Instead, the customer Header can be modeled using the Repeating Record element type.

---

14. Click Next.

15. On the Schema View page, the fundamental structure of the CustomerSalesOrder schema appears. Now, you'll define the individual characteristics of the child records of the schema. Figure 2-28 shows the page showing the schema structure.

Figure 2-28. *Schema view of the CustomerSalesOrder schema*

16.   Select the customerHeader element. Click Next to continue.

17.   On the Select Document Data page, select the data that will be used to define the customerHeader record by ensuring the first line is selected, as shown in Figure 2-29.

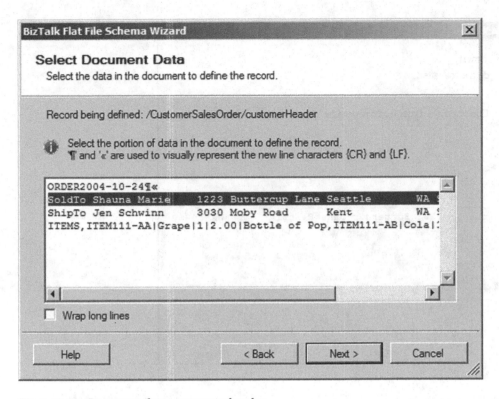

Figure 2-29. Document data—customer header

18. Click Next.

19. Now, you will select the record format for the customer header. In this example, select the By Relative Positions radio button, as shown in Figure 2-30.

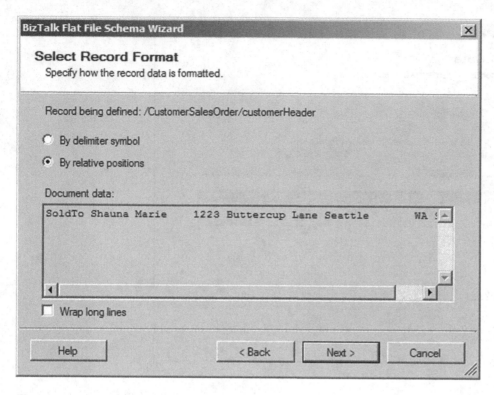

Figure 2-30. *Record format—customer header*

20. Click Next.

21. The wizard will give a visual representation of the record's element positions. Use this tool by selecting the starting position of each record element. You can do this by clicking the mouse at each element's starting point, as shown in Figure 2-31.

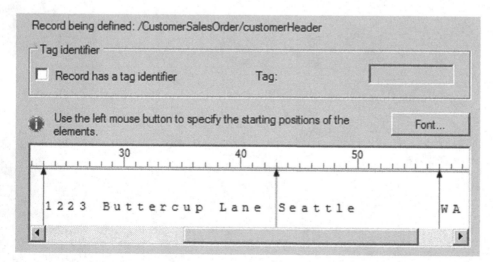

Figure 2-31. *Specifying the positional record*

22. Click Next.

23. Next, you will specify the properties of the child elements for the customer header record. This step will identify the makeup of the elements for `CustomerSalesOrder/customerHeader`. These XML elements are derived from the positional representation of the record elements on the previous page. So, using the grid on the Child Elements page, define the record's child elements. In this example, set the values shown in Table 2-5.

Table 2-5. *Child Element Properties*

Element Name	Element Type	Data Type
customerType	Field Element	string
fullName	Field Element	string
street	Field Element	string
city	Field Element	string
state	Field Element	string
postal	Field Element	string

24. Click Next.

25. On the Schema View page, the `CustomerSalesOrder` schema appears with an updated `customerHeader` structure, as shown in Figure 2-32. Next, you'll define the characteristics of the `items` record, so click Next.

Figure 2-32. *Schema view of CustomerSalesOrder*

26. On the Select Document Data page, select the data that will be used to define the `items` record. Ensure the items data line is selected, as shown in Figure 2-33.

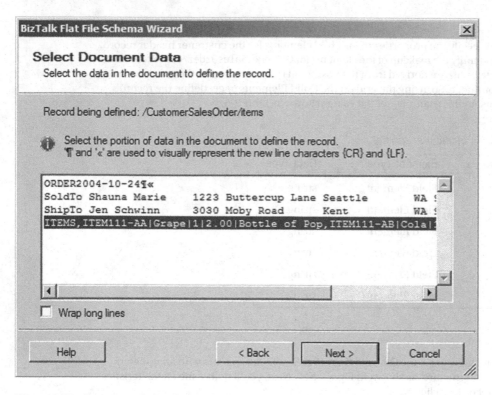

Figure 2-33. Document data—items

27. Click Next.

28. Now you will select the record format for the items data. In this example, select the By Delimiter Symbol radio button.

29. Click Next.

30. Next, you will specify the properties of the items record (as shown in Figure 2-34). This step will define the makeup of the record to represent CustomerSalesOrder/items:

   a. Specify the child delimiter. Given that the record is defined by a comma delimiter, select the comma (,) child delimiter.

   b. Check the Record Has a Tag Identifier box. In this example, the tag identifier will be ITEMS.

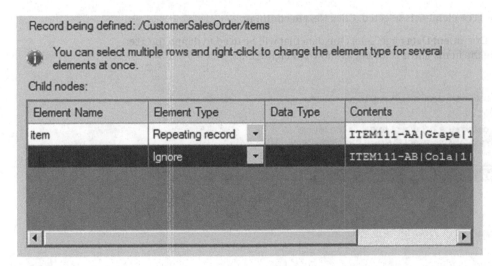

Record being defined: /CustomerSalesOrder/items

Child delimiter: `·` ▼   Escape character:

┌─ Tag identifier ──────────────────────────────────────┐
│ ☑ Record has a tag identifier   Tag: `ITEMS`   │
└───┘

Document data:

```
ITEMS,ITEM111-AA|Grape|1|2.00|Bottle of Pop,ITEM111-AB|Cola|:
```

☐ Wrap long lines

Figure 2-34. *Properties of the delimited record—items*

31. Click Next.

32. You will now specify the properties of the child elements for the items record (as shown in Figure 2-35). This step will identify the makeup of the elements for the CustomerSalesOrder/items that are derived from the delimiter specified on the previous page. Using the grid in the Child Elements page, define the items record's child elements. In this example, set the values shown in Table 2-6.

Record being defined: /CustomerSalesOrder/items

ℹ You can select multiple rows and right-click to change the element type for several elements at once.

Child nodes:

Element Name	Element Type	Data Type	Contents
item	Repeating record ▼		ITEM111-AA|Grape|1
	Ignore ▼		ITEM111-AB|Cola|1|

Figure 2-35. *Specifying properties of the items record's child elements*

Table 2-6. *Child Element Properties—Items*

Element Name	Element Type	Data Type
item	Repeating Record	
	Ignore	

81

33. Click Next.

34. On the Schema View page, the structure of the CustomerSalesOrder schema is updated. Now, you can define the individual characteristics of the items record's child elements. Figure 2-36 shows the page with the schema structure.

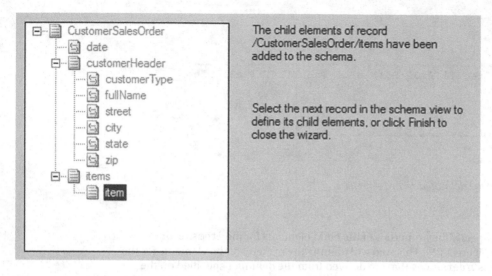

Figure 2-36. *Schema view of the CustomerSalesOrder schema*

35. Make sure the item element is selected. Click Next to continue.

36. On the Select Document Data page, select the data that will be used to define the item record. Ensure the items line is selected, as shown in Figure 2-37.

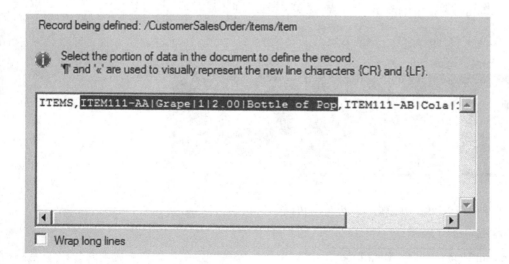

Figure 2-37. *Document data—items data*

37. Click Next.

38. Now, select the record format for the items data. This example will use delimited, so select the By Delimiter Symbol radio button, and click Next.

39. Next, you will specify the properties of the items data elements. This step will define the makeup of the data elements to represent CustomerSalesOrder/items. You'll now specify the child delimiter: given that the record is defined by the pipe delimiter (|), select the child delimiter |, as shown in Figure 2-38.

Figure 2-38. Properties of the delimited record—items data

40. Click Next.

41. Next, you will specify the properties of the child elements for the items record (as shown in Figure 2-39). This step will identify the makeup of the elements for the CustomerSalesOrder/items/item and are derived from the delimited specification. Using the grid on the Child Elements page, define the record's child elements. In this example, set the values as shown in Table 2-7.

Figure 2-39. Specifying the properties of the record item's child elements

Table 2-7. *Child Element Properties*

Element Name	Element Type	Data Type
productId	Field element	string
productName	Field element	string
quantity	Field element	int
unitPrice	Field element	float
description	Field element	string

42. Click Next.

43. This completes the creation of the schema, so click Finish to complete the schema. Figure 2-40 shows the finished product.

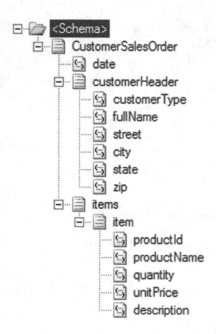

Figure 2-40. *The finished schema*

44. To test the schema, check that the Input Instance File in the properties is set to a valid flat file instance. Right-click the CustomerSalesOrder.xsd file in Solution Explorer, and select Validate. This will generate an XML version of the flat file, which is shown in Figure 2-41.

```
- <CustomerSalesOrder xmlns="http://FlatFileSchemaWizard.CustomerSalesOrder">
    <date xmlns="">2004-10-24</date>
  - <customerHeader xmlns="">
      <customerType>SoldTo</customerType>
      <fullName>Shauna Marie</fullName>
      <street>1223 Buttercup Lane</street>
      <city>Seattle</city>
      <state>WA</state>
      <zip>98155</zip>
    </customerHeader>
  - <customerHeader xmlns="">
      <customerType>ShipTo</customerType>
      <fullName>Jen Schwinn</fullName>
      <street>3030 Moby Road</street>
      <city>Kent</city>
      <state>WA</state>
      <zip>98110</zip>
    </customerHeader>
  - <items xmlns="">
    - <item>
        <productId>ITEM111-AA</productId>
        <productName>Grape</productName>
        <quantity>1</quantity>
        <unitPrice>2.00</unitPrice>
        <description>Bottle of Pop</description>
      </item>
    - <item>
        <productId>ITEM111-AB</productId>
        <productName>Cola</productName>
        <quantity>1</quantity>
        <unitPrice>2.00</unitPrice>
        <description>Bottle of Pop</description>
      </item>
    </items>
  </CustomerSalesOrder>
```

Figure 2-41. *XML version of the flat file, created by validating the schema*

How It Works

In this recipe, we demonstrated how to use the Flat File Schema Wizard. To recap the scenario, you used the wizard to create a fairly complex illustration of a flat file to XML schema creation using different positional and delimited flat file references at the record, line, and field levels. The tool allows a developer to reverse engineer a schema based on a sample flat file instance.

Not demonstrated in this example but a common consideration when working with flat files is the usage of escape characters. You can accommodate escape characters when defining the properties at the record, line, or field level.

The Flat File Schema Wizard makes the process of defining schemas simpler, because the user sees the schema being modeled through the process and, in addition, is not exposed to the complexity of the schema syntax.

As helpful as the tool might be, it is still important to understand what the requirements are for the schema and how specifically the file will be implemented. Given this, you should spend some design time trying to understand exactly what the schema will do and how this relates to other processes (such as other interfaces and other trading partners).

2-13. Creating SOAP Header Schemas
Problem

You are using the publish/subscribe method in your orchestration architecture with many different schemas, and there are a number of common fields that need to be passed with all documents delivered to the BizTalk MessageBox (using direct binding on all ports). You want to be able to pass these fields without adding them to all of the individual schemas.

Solution

Assume that you have three XML instances schemas as follows (XML instances are shown for clarification):

```
<Person>
  <ID>ID_0</ID>
  <TraceFlag>true</TraceFlag>
  <Name>Name_1</Name>
</Person>

<Company>
  <ID>ID_0</ID>
  <TraceFlag>true</TraceFlag>
  <CompanyName>CompanyName_2</CompanyName>
</Company>

<Address>
  <ID>ID_0</ID>
  <TraceFlag>true</TraceFlag>
  <AddressLine>AddressLine_1</AddressLine>
</Address>
```

Two of the elements are common in all three of the schemas and represent values that are common: ID represents a common tracking ID, and TraceFlag represents whether logging should occur in an orchestration. The elements are not truly part of the description of a Person, Company, or Address, but their values need to be available. Your goal is to move these common fields out of the schemas so that they look as follows:

```
<Person>
  <Name>Name_1</Name>
</Person>

<Company>
  <CompanyName>CompanyName_2</CompanyName>
</Company>

<Address>
  <AddressLine>AddressLine_1</AddressLine>
</Address>
```

All messages in BizTalk are passed through the MessageBox wrapped in a SOAP envelope. A SOAP envelope consists of two sections: the Header and the Body, wrapped in an envelope, as shown in Listing 2-3. The Header can be common across all schemas, while the Body contains the actual XML instance of any given schema. Adding and accessing fields within orchestrations at the SOAP Header level is made available in a simple and straightforward way. This is a powerful and useful tool that has multiple applications depending on the solution architecture.

Listing 2-3. Sample SOAP Envelope Structure

```
<soap:Envelope xmlns:xsi="http://www.w3.org/2001/XMLSchema-instance"
 xmlns:xsd="http://www.w3.org/2001/XMLSchema"
 xmlns:soap="http://schemas.xmlsoap.org/soap/envelope/"
  <soap:Header>
        <MessageId>uuid:bbbb-cccc-dddd-eeee</MessageId>
        <TraceFlag>true</TraceFlag>
  </soap:Header>
  <soap:Body>
        <Person><Name>Name_1</Name></Person>
  </soap:Body>
</soap:Envelope>
```

In Listing 2-3, the Header contains two fields and the Body consists of an XML document that is an instance of the Person schema. This is an actual representation of what a document looks like when placed in the MessageBox by an orchestration when using the SOAPHeader property schema and Person schema described in this recipe.

By default, BizTalk will strip the XML document out of the envelope's Body and deliver it to the appropriate subscribers. These subscribers see the XML document that was originally contained in the Body and do not have context to the Header. However, if a SOAPHeader property schema has been defined, the subscriber will also have access to the envelope's Header information.

The SOAPHeader property schema shows which fields will be promoted and available at the Header level on all schemas within a given project. The SOAPHeader property schema must reference the namespace http://schemas.microsoft.com/BizTalk/2003/SOAPHeader and have each of the elements on it with their Property Schema Base set to MessageContextPropertyBase. The steps for creating a SOAPHeader property schema are as follows:

1. Add a new schema to a BizTalk project.

2. In the Properties window of the schema, set the Target Namespace to the BizTalk SOAPHeader namespace and the Schema Type to Property, as shown in Figure 2-42.

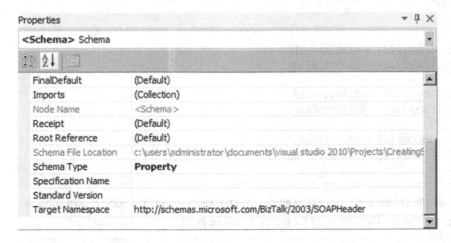

Figure 2-42. *SOAP Header property values*

3. Add the desired elements to the schema. There is no root node on a SOAPHeader property schema; it has only elements. In this example, there would be two elements added to the schema: MessageId and TraceFlag. See Figure 2-43.

Figure 2-43. *Defining the elements*

4. On each element created, set the Property Schema Base in the Properties window to MessageContextPropertyBase, as shown in Figure 2-44.

Namespace	http://schemas.microsoft.com/BizTalk/2003/SOAPHeader
Nillable	False
Node Name	MessageId
Notes	
Property Schema Base	**MessageContextPropertyBase**
RootNode TypeName	**MessageId**
Sensitive Information	(Default)

Figure 2-44. *Element property values*

5. Build and deploy the solution.

Once compiled, the elements in the SOAPHeader property schema will be available on all messages within an orchestration and can be accessed and set in Expression shapes and Message Assignment shapes. Listing 2-4 shows how to set these elements.

Listing 2-4. Setting Properties in a Message Assignment Shape

```
// populate the SOAP Header information
strMessageId = "111-222-333-444";
blnTraceFlag = true;

msgAddress(CreatingSOAPHeaders.MessageId) = strMessageId;
msgAddress(CreatingSOAPHeaders.TraceFlag) = blnTraceFlag;

msgPerson(CreatingSOAPHeaders.MessageId) = strMessageId;
msgPerson(CreatingSOAPHeaders.TraceFlag) = blnTraceFlag;

msgCompany(CreatingSOAPHeaders.MessageId) = strMessageId;
msgCompany(CreatingSOAPHeaders.TraceFlag) = blnTraceFlag;
```

■ **Note**   The value available in the properties of the messages will be equal to the namespace given the SOAP Header schema. In this project, it was set to CreatingSOAPHeaders; therefore, all of the properties will be listed, as shown in Figure 2-45.

```
// populate the SOAP Header information
msgSecondary(CreatingSOAPHeaders.MessageId) = System.Convert.ToString(System.Guid.NewGuid());
msgSecondary(
```

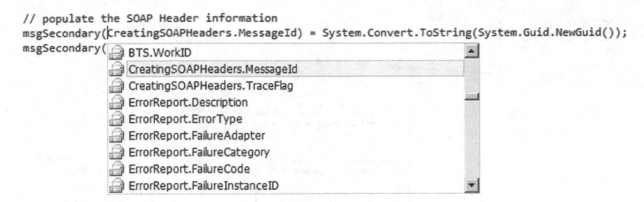

Figure 2-45. *The properties are based on the namespace given to the SOAP Header schema*

How It Works

The project accompanying this recipe (CreatingSOAPHeaders) demonstrates the practical application of the SOAP Header. The basic architecture of the solution is this:

- Primary orchestration receives an incoming document from a file receive location.

- Orchestration sets the promoted SOAP Header properties in a Message Assignment shape.

- Orchestration delivers the message to the BizTalk MessageBox via direct binding on a port.

- A secondary orchestration subscribes to the MessageBox and is instantiated when a document matching the schema it is subscribing to arrives.

- The secondary orchestration reads the values of the SOAP Header and writes them to the Windows event viewer.

Figure 2-46 illustrates the flow of the primary orchestration and the use of a Message Assignment shape to set the SOAP Header properties before delivering to the MessageBox (port_2 is direct binding).

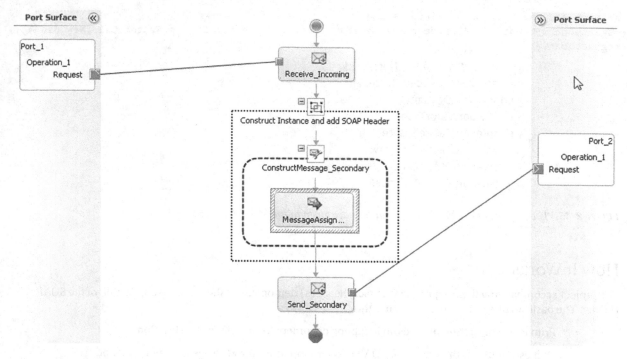

Figure 2-46. *Sample solution primary orchestration*

The secondary orchestration subscribes to the MessageBox and writes the values of the SOAP Header properties to the Windows Event Log. Figure 2-47 shows the secondary orchestration.

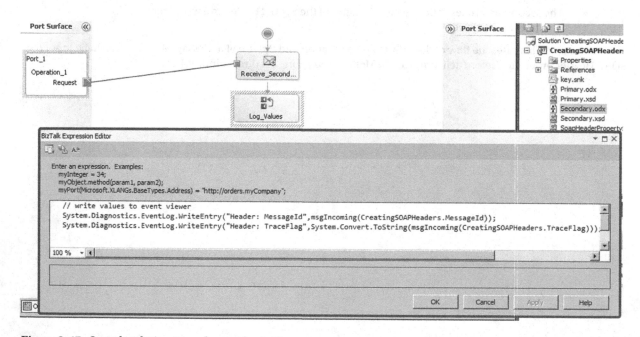

Figure 2-47. *Sample solution secondary orchestration*

How do you access incoming documents wrapped in SOAP envelopes? Incoming documents can be wrapped in a SOAP envelope (by an external client to BizTalk), but by default, only those that are delivered via a SOAP transport receive location will be automatically promoted and made available within an orchestration.

For example, with orchestrations exposed as web services, additional properties can be set at the SOAP Header level using the BizTalk Web Services Publishing Wizard. These properties are then available to any client who calls the web service, accessible in the same way as all of the standard web methods and properties. However, if the delivery of a message wrapped in a SOAP envelope via a different transport is required (such as MSMQ or file drop), you need to use a custom pipeline component.

Listing 2-5 demonstrates a process to promote incoming values to the SOAPHeader property schema. This example is a complete custom pipeline intended to be placed on the decode stage of a BizTalk custom pipeline, followed by a standard XML disassembler. It demonstrates how to do the following:

- Load the incoming message stream into an XML document, which can be accessed via the Document Object Model (DOM).

- Load the MessageId value located at the Header level of the incoming SOAP envelope. The incoming message matches the structure of the document shown in Listing 2-3.

- Promote the field to the SOAP Header, and make it available once the document is delivered to the MessageBox.

- Return the document within the Body of the SOAP envelope as a stream.

Listing 2-5. Pipeline Property Promotion

```
public IBaseMessage Execute(IPipelineContext pc, IBaseMessage inmsg)
{
        try
        {
                string strMessageId = "";

                // declare XML Document
                System.Xml.XmlDocument xmlDoc = new System.Xml.XmlDocument();

                // prepare the fields to be promoted
                xmlDoc.Load(inmsg.BodyPart.Data);

                // if values are not present, default to empty string
                try
                {
                        strMessageId = xmlDoc.SelectSingleNode
("//*[local-name()='Header'/*[local-name()='MessageID']").
InnerText;
                }
                catch {}

                // strip off the envelope and return just what is within the Body
                System.IO.MemoryStream ms = new
System.IO.MemoryStream(System.Text.Encoding.UTF8.GetBytes
(xmlDoc.SelectSingleNode("//*[local-name()='Body']").InnerXml));

                inmsg.BodyPart.Data = ms;
```

```
                // promote the SOAP Header fields
                inmsg.Context.Promote("MessageId",
"http://schemas.microsoft.com/BizTalk/2003/SOAPHeader"
.ToString(),strMessageId);

            }
            catch (Exception ex)
            {
            throw new Exception("Pipeline component exception - " + ex.Message);
            }
        return inmsg;
}
```

CHAPTER 3

■ ■ ■

Document Mapping

At the core of integration projects is the need to exchange data. When systems are required to pass data, the data must either be in a common format or the systems must have a way in which to map the data from one system to another. Historically, mapping was spread across multiple components and entities, such as the database layer, the data access layer, and even the publishing and consuming systems themselves. When additional systems were added to the integration, or requirements around the mapping logic changed, many systems and components involved in the integration would need to be customized. Integration applications, such as BizTalk Server, offer a centralized and organized platform for handling mapping and provide tools to aid in the development of these mappings.

■ **Note**   There is a book focused solely on mapping, *Pro Mapping in BizTalk Server 2009* (Apress, 2009). Make sure to refer to it for more advanced mapping examples (including EDI).

Exchanging data requires that all systems have a common way in which data is interpreted or a common way in which data can be mapped from one system to another. BizTalk provides for this through several approaches, the most prominent of which is the BizTalk Mapper (additional approaches include XSLT style sheets, custom .NET assemblies, message assignment within orchestrations, and other code-driven solutions). The BizTalk Mapper is a graphical interface with which to develop transformations of data between any number of schemas of disparate systems or entities. These maps consist of the business logic necessary to transform the data into the format that the target systems require.

Rather than storing the business logic for transformations across many different components and systems, the rules should be contained in only the integration layer. All that is required of the systems being integrated should be the ability to make available their data (either through the system publishing its data to the integration platform or by the integration hub initiating the request for the data). There is absolutely no need to customize any system based on the way that another system may need to receive the data. If the system data is available, the integration layer will be able to consume and manipulate the data into the needed format. By keeping the business logic needed for transforming data in the integration hub (in this case, BizTalk orchestrations and maps), there is a single, common location for all mapping, and no need to modify individual systems when the mapping requirements change.

When mapping rules change or additional systems are added to an integration solution, one of the greatest objectives is to modify as few components as possible. With a well organized mapping solution, the only components that will need to be modified, compiled, and redeployed are the map components themselves (mapping assemblies, XSLT, or any other component). None of the individual systems will be affected, none of the business workflows (orchestrations) will be influenced, and none of the schemas will need to be changed. Additional systems should be able to be added to an integration without modifying any of the existing maps for other systems. An intelligently organized mapping solution can eliminate the need for complex modifications across an integration solution.

This chapter will describe how to use BizTalk for data transformation and mapping. As with the rest of the BizTalk platform, there are numerous ways to solve the same problem, and mapping components can range from any variety and combination of traditional BizTalk graphical maps, XSLT, and .NET assemblies. The business requirements should drive the technical solution, and there is no single approach that will suit all situations. The recipes in this chapter introduce the fundamental mapping techniques that will aid in the development of a solid mapping design and architecture, and ultimately in a scalable and configurable integration solution.

3-1. Creating Simple Maps
Problem

You would like to map one XML format to another using the BizTalk tool set. This may be for a variety of reasons, such as application mapping with an internal application, format specifics (such as flat file to database object), or an external business scenario where a business partner requires the core data for a business process in a different format (such as an industry standard) than your schema provides.

Solution

The BizTalk Mapper enables you to perform XML message transformation. The tool is shipped with the core BizTalk product and provides numerous capabilities to support message transformation and translation via straight mapping and functoids, as well as unit test support.

■ **Note** The term *functoids* refers to predefined functions within the BizTalk Mapper tool set. Functoids support a number of useful translations and transformations. As a point of interest, *functoid* is a term coined by Microsoft and is commonly described as "functions on steroids."

As an example, suppose that you have the following simple customer schema (`Customer`):

```
<Customer>
  <FirstName> </FirstName>
  <LastName> </LastName>
  <MiddleInit> </MiddleInit>
  <Age></Age>
  <Address>
  <AddrLine1> </AddrLine1>
  <AddrLine2> </AddrLine2>
  <AddrLine3> </AddrLine3>
  <Zip> </Zip>
  <State> </State>
  <Country></Country>
  </Address>
</Customer>
```

And you want to map to another customer schema (CustomerRecord) that is slightly different in structure and format:

```
<CustomerRecord >
  <Name> </Name>
  <MiddleInit> </MiddleInit>
  <Address> </Address>
  <Zip> </Zip>
  <State> </State>
  <Country> </Country>
  <DateTime> </DateTime>
</CustomerRecord>
```

The example involves mapping values from a source to a destination schema that subsequently demonstrates different structure and invariably, message transformation. To create the BizTalk map for the example, follow these steps:

1. Open the project that contains the schemas.

2. Right-click the project, and select Add ➤ New Item.

3. In the Add New Item dialog box, shown in Figure 3-1, click Map and give the file name a valid name. Once completed, click the Add button.

Figure 3-1. *Adding a map*

4. A blank map will now be opened, with left and right panes for the source and destination schema, respectively, as shown in Figure 3-2. Click the Open Source Schema link in the left pane.

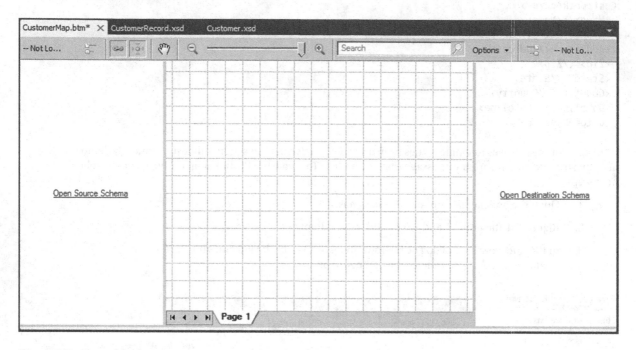

Figure 3-2. *A new blank map*

5. In the BizTalk Type Picker dialog box, select the Schemas tree node, and then select the Customer schema (see Figure 3-3). Click OK.

Figure 3-3. *The BizTalk Type Picker*

6. Click the Open Destination Schema link in the right pane.

7. In the BizTalk Type Picker dialog box, select the Schemas tree node, select the CustomerRecord schema, and click OK. The source and destination schemas will now be displayed.

8. Perform the straight-through mapping. Click the MiddleInit element in the source schema, and drag it across to the MiddleInit element in the destination schema. Repeat this for the Zip, State, and Country elements.

9. Perform the concatenation mapping.

■ **Note**   The term *concatenation mapping* within the BizTalk Mapper refers to the joining of two or more values to form one output value.

Here are the steps to follow in order to perform the concatenation.

1. In the left pane, click the Toolbox, and click the String Functoids tab.

2. Click and drag two String Concatenate functoids onto the map surface, as shown in Figure 3-4.

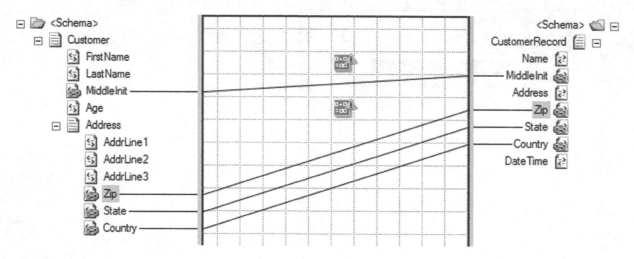

Figure 3-4. *String Concatenate functoids on the design surface*

3. Click the FirstName element in the source schema and drag it across to the left point on the first String Concatenate functoid. Click the right side of the String Concatenate functoid, and drag it across to the Name element in the destination schema.

4. Double-click the first String Concatenate functoid. Click the Plus button (this will add a new input), and create a constant that has a space in it (see Figure 3-5).

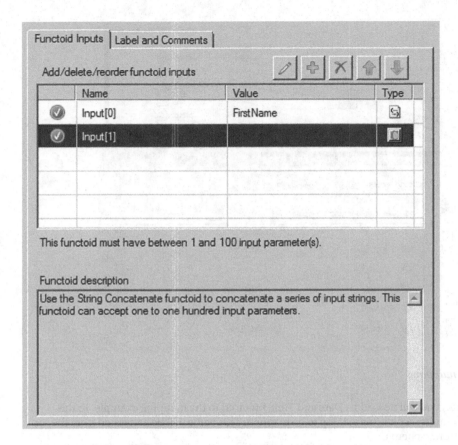

Figure 3-5. *String concatenate functoids on the design surface*

5. Click the LastName element in the source schema, and drag it across to the left point on the first String Concatenate functoid. This will complete the mapping of Name.

6. Click the AddrLine1 element in the source schema, and drag it across to the left point on the second String Concatenate functoid. Click the right side of the String Concatenate functoid, and drag it across to the Address element in the destination schema.

7. Repeat step 6 for AddrLine2 and AddrLine3, adding a comma between each address field. Figure 3-6 shows the completed concatenation mapping.

Figure 3-6. *String concatenation mappings*

To demonstrate functoid usage, you will now add a Date and Time functoid to the mapping example. In this instance, the destination schema requires a date/time stamp to be mapped. This value will be generated from the Date and Time functoid, not the source schema.

1. In the left pane, click the Toolbox, and then click the Date/Time Functoids tab (See Figure 3-7).

Figure 3-7. *Date/Time functoids in the Toolbox*

2. Click and drag a Date and Time functoid onto the map surface.

3. Click the right side of the Date and Time functoid, and drag it across to the `DateTime` element in the destination schema.

The map is now complete, as shown in Figure 3-8.

Figure 3-8. *Completed customer map*

How It Works

The BizTalk Mapper is used to map XML messages (instances of XML schema at runtime) to an alternate format based on transformation and/or translation. It is built on XSLT and shields the user from complex XSLT transformation logic, by providing a GUI environment to facilitate the transformation. The tool comes with numerous functoids and mapping capabilities to support straight-through and deterministic transformation. In addition, the tool gives the built-in ability to perform unit testing.

The maps created within the BizTalk Mapper environment can be used within other BizTalk runtime environments. For example, they can be used with receive/send ports, for transforming a message to and from application end points. Port mapping might be advantageous when the mapping involves minimal process considerations or the need to apply multiple maps to a given message. Changes to maps on ports can be completed without recompilation of currently deployed BizTalk assemblies. Maps can also be used with transformation shapes, for message transformation within a BizTalk orchestration. Mapping within an orchestration might be preferred when the mapping process involves broad process considerations or process support via robust exception and error handling.

The choices for where and when to map vary depending on a number of factors. A number of these have to do with common development principals (such as consistency and readability) and standards enforced by the environment in which you are operating. However, a few common rules of thumb should be noted:

> *Keep it simple*: Keep maps logically organized. Across maps, ensure that the same look and feel are applied for consistency.

■ **Note** Just because you can create a map using the mapper and functoids doesn't always mean you should. Make sure that whatever maps you create are simple and maintainable. Highly complex maps with many interlocking functoids can become unwieldy and next to impossible to support. Alternatives to mapping (most notably XSLT) are often very intelligent alternatives.

> *Keep business rules in mind*: Based on the deterministic ability of mapping, be careful or keep in mind the usage of business rules within maps. If you find you are using rules within maps (for example, If OrderTotal > $1000), keep in mind maintenance and where in your organization a decision may be made to change this rule. In addition, always consider the right place to maintain rules and context domain knowledge from an operation and support perspective.

> *Consider performance*: While mapping is powerful, complex and/or large maps can affect performance. As with all common development activities, always ensure that the logic performed is the most efficient and tested for scale in your practical operating conditions and requirements. If you experience performance issues, employ techniques such as revisiting design by exploring the solution breakdown. Consider simplifying the development task at hand.

Like all good development processes, maps should be designed and tested for desired application operation conditions.

The example in this recipe showed a baseline solution of what can be performed with the BizTalk Mapper. Throughout this chapter, other mapping capabilities will be demonstrated, illustrating the use of functoids and mapping techniques for structure and transformation control.

3-2. Organizing Maps
Problem

Maps can become very complex and hence difficult to read and maintain.

Solution

BizTalk Sever provides a number of features to aid in the readability and maintainability of maps. One of these features is *grid pages*. BizTalk Server allows you to create, name/rename, and order grid pages. When you create links between source and destination elements, the links will appear on only the selected grid page. Therefore, you can segment groups of links onto different grid pages. By default, a map file is created with one grid page named Page 1. Once you have selected source and destination schemas, you can access the grid page menu by right-clicking the tab at the bottom of the grid page, as shown in Figure 3-9.

Figure 3-9. *Click the tab at the bottom of the grid page to access the grid page menu*

From this menu, you can perform the following functions:

- Select Add Page to add a new grid page to the map.

- Select Delete Page to delete the selected grid page. (If you delete a grid page, all of the links associated with that grid page will also be removed.)

- Select Rename Page to rename the selected grid page.

- Select Reorder Pages to launch the Reorder Pages dialog box, as shown in Figure 3-10. From this dialog box, you can change the order in which the grid pages appear when viewing the map file.

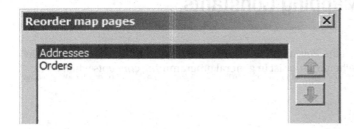

Figure 3-10. *Reorder Pages dialog box*

Another feature provided by BizTalk Server for facilitating the readability and maintainability of maps is the ability to label links. While the labels do not appear on the grid pages, they will be used to designate the input parameters for functoids. By default, a functoid will show the XPath designation if it is linked directly to a source field, or it will show the name of the previous functoid if it is linked from another functoid. However, if the input links to a functoid are labeled, and the Label property of the link will be shown. To label a link, follow these steps:

1. Open the project that contains the map.

2. Open the map file.

3. Select the grid page that contains the link to be labeled.

4. Select the link to be labeled, right-click, and select Properties.

5. Fill in the Label property.

The ability to label and add comments to individual functoids is helpful in organization, especially when there are a large number of functoids on the page. To comment a functoid, simply double click the functoid, and click on the Label and Comments tab (as shown in Figure 3-11).

Figure 3-11. *Commenting a functoid*

How It Works

There are many ways to segment a map into multiple grid pages. For example, you can create a grid page for each major node in a source schema that requires complex mapping. Regardless of how you divide the map, the goal of using multiple grid pages should be to improve the readability and maintainability of the map.

3-3. Adding and Configuring Mapping Constants
Problem

You would like to use constant values within a BizTalk map. This might be because of preset output map values within a destination schema (that do not exist in the source schema) to assist in general programming concepts when using functoids, or for other reasons.

Solution

To demonstrate how to add map constants using the BizTalk Mapper, suppose that you want to use a constant in conjunction with a String Extraction functoid. In this example, you would like to extract a specified number of characters (five) from the left of the source element value. In the source schema, Customer, you have Zip elements like this:

```
<Zip>98103-00001</Zip>
```

In the destination schema, CustomerRecord, you have Zip elements like this:

```
<Zip>98103</Zip>
```

To map constants, follow these steps:

1. Set up the BizTalk map with the appropriate source and destination schema, as shown in Figure 3-12.

Figure 3-12. *The source and destination schema for the constant mapping example*

2. In the left pane, click the Toolbox, and then click the String Functoids tab.

3. Click and drag a String Left functoid onto the map surface.

4. Click the Zip element in the source schema and drag it across to the left point of the String Left functoid.

5. Click the String Left functoid on your map surface, and select Input Parameters in the Properties window. The Configure Functoid Inputs dialog box is now displayed, as shown in Figure 3-13. Notice the first input parameter is the source schema's Zip element. This is automatically configured as a result of dragging the source Zip element onto the map surface.

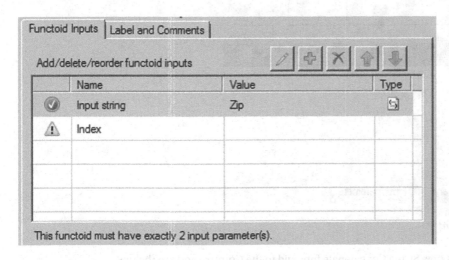

Figure 3-13. *Configure Functoid Inputs dialog box*

6. In the Configure Functoid Inputs dialog box, click the Index row (BizTalk will automatically add required input variables).

7. Type in the value 4. As noted, you are extracting five characters for the zip code. Because the functoid is zero-based, the start position will be 0 and the end position will be 4, resulting in five characters.

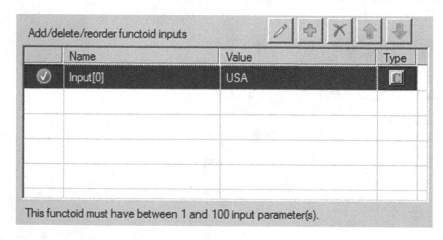

Figure 3-14. *With the constant configured*

8. Click OK to complete the functoid configuration.

9. Click on the right side of the String Left functoid and drag it across to the Zip element in the destination schema.

10. Now, drag a String Concatenate functoid onto the mapping surface. Double-click the functoid. A default input will be available; ignore this, and click the Plus button. Type the value **USA**. Delete the unused input (you may have to reorder using the up/down arrows). The final values should look like that shown in Figure 3-15. Click OK.

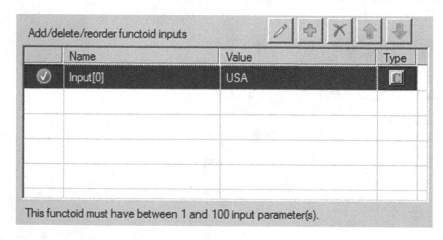

Figure 3-15. *Adding a new constant*

11. Drag the output of this new String Concatenate functoid to the Country node in the map.

How It Works

You might use constant mapping for the following:

- To support functoid configuration, as in the example in this recipe, which used the String Left functoid.

- For values declared and assigned within a Scripting functoid. In essence, these values can be mapped as output into destination values. Furthermore, they can be declared once and accessed as global variables within other Scripting functoids in the context of the working BizTalk map.

- With the String Concatenate functoid. Use the input parameter of this functoid as the constant value required. This functoid does not require any input values from the source schema. In this usage, a String Concatenate functoid would simply be mapped through to the desired destination value.

The best use of constant mapping depends on the situation and requirements you are developing against. Examine the likelihood of change within the scenario where you are looking to apply the functoid constant. If there is a high likelihood that values and their application will change, consistency should be the major factor to facilitate maintenance.

If constants are set via deterministic logic or complex or embedded business rules, it might be worth thinking about whether the constant should be applied in the map or applied within a scripting component or upstream/downstream BizTalk artifacts. The key is understanding where rules and deterministic values are set to support the specific situation. Apply the appropriate design principles to ensure the correct constant assignment technique is applied.

You might decide it would be best to map values outside the mapping environment. This could be a result of deterministic logic or business rules being the major requirement in the constants implementation. Furthermore, rules that derive constants may exist outside the BizTalk map. Constants may need to change dynamically, and it may be too cumbersome to perform a recompile/deployment for such changes within a BizTalk map.

3-4. Mapping Any Element Nodes

Problem

You need to create a mapping between two schemas containing elements and attributes that are unknown when building the map, and you must include the unknown schema structures in your mapping.

Solution

You can include unknown schema structures in a map by using the <Any> element.

1. Build a source message schema containing an <Any> element. This can be done by right-clicking the record in the schema and selecting Insert Schema Node ➤ Any Element, as shown in Figure 3-16.

Figure 3-16. *Creating a source message with an Any element*

2. Build a destination schema containing an <Any> element, as shown in Figure 3-17.

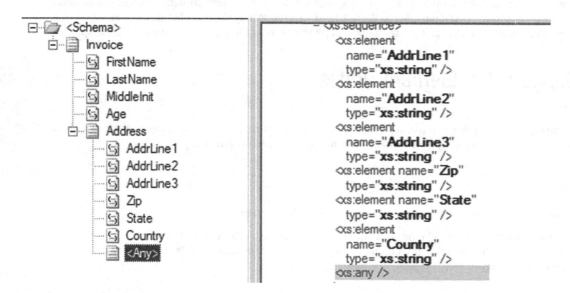

Figure 3-17. *Creating a destination message*

3. Add a new map to the solution. Set the source and target schemas appropriately.

4. Click the Toolbox, and then click the Advanced Functoids tab. Drag a Mass Copy functoid onto the map surface. Connect the Address element from the source message to the Mass Copy functoid, and connect the Mass Copy functoid to the Address field of the destination message.

5. Create other desired mapping links normally, as shown in Figure 3-18.

Figure 3-18. *Configuring the Mass Copy functoid*

How It Works

An <Any> element in a schema designates a specific location in the schema where new elements or attributes can be added. When BizTalk uses the schema to process a message containing unknown elements or attributes in the designated location, the schema will still consider the message valid. If this source message is mapped into a different schema that also has a location designated for extensibility with an <Any> element, then the information must be copied to that location with the Mass Copy functoid.

■ **Note** By default, BizTalk will examine only the namespace and root node name of a message to identify the schema, and will not detect extra elements in the message body. To perform a deep validation of a message format, create a receive pipeline with the XML disassembler, specify the schema to validate messages against, and set Validate Document Structure to true. See Chapter 3 for more information about how to configure receive pipelines.

The contents of an <Any> element cannot be mapped with most of the default BizTalk functoids. Other functoids require establishing an explicit link from a source field, and that is not possible if the source field is not known at design time. The Mass Copy functoid can be linked only directly to an ancestor of the <Any> element, which may not give the granularity of control desired. Consider using an XSLT script with the Scripting functoid to achieve finer control. For example, if you know some element will be present at runtime but cannot predict the element name of its parent, an XSLT script can still perform the mapping.

Note that you can override the mapping of the mass copy on a line by line basis. For instance, if the Zip field needs to be mapped differently, simply add the appropriate functoid(s) and map it; this will override whatever the Mass Copy functoid has created (see Figure 3-19).

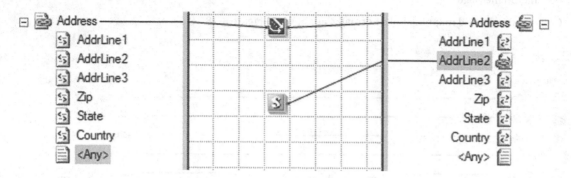

Figure 3-19. *Overriding AddrLine2 within a Mass Copy functoid*

Sometimes, the BizTalk development environment has difficulty validating schemas containing <Any> elements. It can incorrectly determine that elements and attributes appearing in the location designated by the schema should not be there, causing validation for the schema to fail. This complicates schema development because the developer must deploy the schema with a pipeline capable of validating the document structure to check if the schema is correct according to a sample source message. To avoid this deployment effort while developing the schema, wait to add <Any> elements until the rest of the schema is developed and verify that those other elements are defined correctly. Then, when adding the <Any> elements to the schema, there will be a baseline of what is working correctly.

The Mass Copy functoid allows source records and containing elements and attributes to be copied and mapped across to the destination schema. This in turn, allows large structures to be mapped quickly in design time, without the need of performing 1:1 detailed mapping on all subsequent schema nodes. The Mass Copy functoid performs the recursive copying by applying a wildcard (/*) XSLT template match on source to destination XML elements. This is of particular benefit when the destination is defined as an <xs:any> type.

When mapping from source to destination, only the structure under the destination parent XML record will be copied. This often results in having to re-create the parent record element to allow all subsequent children nodes to be mapped to the destination schema. For example, consider the following two schemas, Customer and Customers:

```
<Customer>
  <Name> </Name>
  <AccountID> </AccountId>
  <DOB> </DOB>
</Customer>

<Customers>
  <Customer>
  <Name> </Name>
  <AccountID> </AccountId>
  <DOB> </DOB>
  </Customer>
</Customers>
```

In this instance, the <Customers> record cannot be mapped to the <Customer> record on the destination schema. A containing element <Customer> will need to be defined on the destination schema to enable the correct operation of the Mass Copy functoid mapping.

When mapping source to destination elements, always be cautious of underlying XSD schema rules, such as cardinality, order, and data types. For example, the Mass Copy functoid will "blindly" copy all child elements specified to the destination schema. It will not copy elements out of order or check for required values in the destination schema.

Changes to the source and destination schema may result in the need to update your impacted maps leveraging the Mass Copy functoid. This, in turn, will mandate a recompile and deployment of your BizTalk solution.

Using the Mass Copy functoid within the BizTalk Mapper is one of a variety of ways to recursively copy elements. The following are three key approaches to recursively copy XML structures:

Mass Copy functoid: Creates a wildcard XSLT template match to recursively copy elements. This approach may provide a performance benefit, as each source and destination element does not require a 1:1: XSLT template match. This, in turn, requires fewer XSLT code instructions to be interpreted and executed at runtime.

Recursive mapping: This is achieved by holding down the Shift key and mapping from a source to destination record element. This is a usability design feature that enables a developer to perform recursive mapping via one keystroke. This approach implements 1:1 XSLT template matches on all source and destination elements.

Straight-through mapping: This approach is to manually link all source and associated destination elements within the BizTalk Mapper tool. This method does 1:1 template matches on all source and destination elements.

3-5. Using the Value Mapping Functoids
Problem

You need to understand how and when to use the Value Mapping and the Value Mapping (Flattening) functoids.

Solution

BizTalk provides two Value Mapping functoids: Value Mapping and Value Mapping (Flattening). Both will cause a new record to be created in the destination for every record in the source. The Value Mapping (Flattening) functoid is used when the destination document has a flat structure.

Both functoids require two input parameters: a Boolean value and the node that is to be mapped. If the Boolean value is true, the value will be mapped; otherwise, it will not be mapped.

The following steps demonstrate the use of the Value Mapping functoid in a map, using the source document shown in Listing 3-1.

Listing 3-1. Source Document for the Value Mapping Functoid Example

```
<nsO:NewHireList xmlns:nsO="http://UsingValueMappingFunctoids.NewHireList">
  <DateTime>DateTime_O</DateTime>
  <Person>
    <ID>1</ID>
    <Name>Jonesy</Name>
    <Role>.NET Developer</Role>
    <Age>47</Age>
  </Person>
```

```
<Person>
  <ID>2</ID>
  <Name>Scott</Name>
  <Role>Database Developer</Role>
  <Age>40</Age>
</Person>
<Person>
  <ID>3</ID>
  <Name>Austin</Name>
  <Role>QA</Role>
  <Age>33</Age>
</Person>
</ns0:NewHireList>
```

These steps refer to the Value Mapping functoid but are identical for the Value Mapping (Flattening) functoid.

1. Click the Toolbox, and click the Advanced Functoids tab. Drop the Value Mapping functoid on the map surface between the source and destination schemas.

2. The first parameter for the Value Mapping functoid needs to be a Boolean value. For this example, a Not Equal functoid will be used to generate the Boolean value. In the Toolbox, click the Logical Functoids tab, and drop a Not Equal functoid to the left of the Value Mapping functoid. The first input parameter for the Not Equal functoid should be the value from the Role element. The second input parameter should be a constant value. Set this value to QA. This will ensure that only those records that are not in this role will be mapped across. See Figure 3-20.

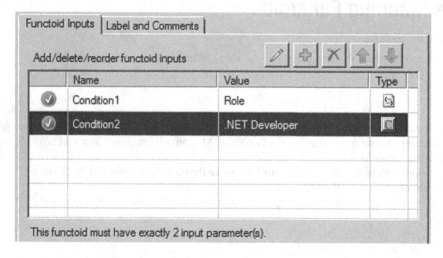

Figure 3-20. *Configuring the Not Equal functoid*

3. The second parameter for the Value Mapping functoid in this example is the Name element from the source document. Ensure that a line exists between this node and the functoid.

4. Drop the output line from the Value Mapping functoid on the target node in the destination document, as shown in Figure 3-21.

Figure 3-21. *Using the Value Mapping functoid*

At this point, the map can be tested. Using the source document shown in Listing 3-1, output of the map is the document shown in Listing 3-2.

Listing 3-2. Output Document Using the Value Mapping Functoid

```
<ns0:Company xmlns:ns0="http://UsingValueMappingFunctoids.Company">
 <Employees>
  <Employee>
   <Name>Jonesy</Name>
  </Employee>
  <Employee>
   <Name>Scott</Name>
  </Employee>
  <Employee>
  </Employee>
 </Employees>
</ns0:Company>
```

■ **Note**   If the Value Mapping (Flattening) functoid does not map a value across, the node is not created on the destination schema, whereas if the Value Mapping functoid does not map a value, an empty destination node will be created. To change this behavior, you will need to use additional functoids or scripting.

If the Value Mapping functoid is replaced with the Value Mapping (Flattening) functoid (as shown in Figure 3-22), the document in Listing 3-3 will be output.

Figure 3-22. *Map with Value Mapping (Flattening) functoid*

Listing 3-3. Output Document Using the Value Mapping (Flattening) Functoid

```
<nsO:Company xmlns:nsO="http://UsingValueMappingFunctoids.Company">
 <Employees>
  <Employee>
   <Name>Jonesy</Name>
   <Name>Scott</Name>
  </Employee>
 </Employees>
</nsO:Company>
```

How It Works

This example showed the default behavior of the Value Mapping functoid. However, the default output of the Value Mapping functoids can be altered through the use of additional functoids and scripting. For example, notice that the output in Listing 3-3 is flat instead of nested (two Person nodes within the Employee node). By adding a Looping functoid to the Name element in the source document and attaching it to the Employee root node in the destination document (see Figure 3-23), you can obtain nested output, as in Listing 3-4. The output is identical to using the Value Mapping functoid as shown in Listing 3-2.

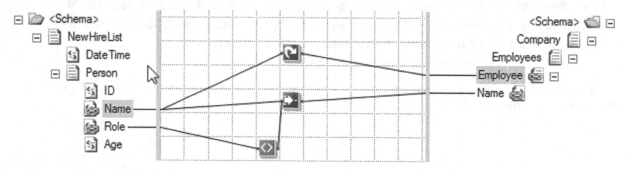

Figure 3-23. *Using the Value Mapping (Flattening) and Looping functoids*

Listing 3-4. Output Using Value (Mapping) Flattening and Looping Functoids

```
<nsO:Company xmlns:nsO="http://UsingValueMappingFunctoids.Company">
 <Employees>
  <Employee>
   <Name>Jonesy</Name>
  </Employee>
  <Employee>
   <Name>Scott</Name>
  </Employee>
  <Employee>
  </Employee>
 </Employees>
</nsO:Company>
```

One of the most common situations in XML document mapping is working with nonexistent elements. By default, if an element does not exist in an incoming document but is mapped to the destination document in a BizTalk map, the node on the destination document will be created with a null value (<Node/>). The use of a Value Mapping (Flattening) functoid causes the node to be created in the destination document only if the source node exists in the source document.

3-6. Using the Table Looping Functoid

Problem

You need to create a repeating structure in an output document with no equivalent repeating structure in an input document.

Solution

BizTalk Sever provides two functoids, the Table Looping functoid and the Table Extractor functoid, for creating a repeating node structure from a flattened input structure, from constant values, and from the output of other functoids. The Table Looping functoid is used to create a table of information based on inputs. The functoid will generate output for each row from this table. The Table Extractor functoid is used to direct data from each column in the table to a node in the destination document. Following are the basic steps for configuring these functoids.

1. Click the Toolbox, and then click the Advanced Functoids tab. Drag the functoid onto the map surface, and create links to the functoid.

   a. Set the first input parameter, which is a link from a node structure in the input document that defines the scope of the table. If this node repeats in the input document, the number of occurrences of this element in the input document will be used to control the number of times the set of Table Extractor functoids will be invoked at runtime.

   b. Set the second input parameter, which is a constant that defines the number of columns for each row in the table.

   c. Set the next input parameters, which define the inputs that will be placed in the table. These inputs can come from the input document, the output from other functoids, constant values, and so on.

2. Configure the table based on inputs for the Table Looping functoid.

   a. Select the ellipsis next to the `TableFunctoidGrid` property in the Properties window to launch the Table Looping Configuration dialog box.

   b. For each cell, select a value from the drop-down list. The drop-down list will contain a reference to all of the inputs you defined in step 1c.

   c. Check or uncheck the Gated check box. If checked, column 1 will be used to determine whether a row in the table should be processed as follows: When the value in column 1 of the row is the output from a logical functoid, if the value is `True`, the row is processed, and if the value is `False`, the row is not processed. Similarly, if the value in column 1 of the row is from a field, the presence of data equates to `True`, and the row is processed, and the absence of data equates to `False`, and the row is not processed and subsequently missing from the output structure.

   d. Select OK to close the dialog box.

3. Configure the outputs for the Table Looping functoid.

   a. Link the Table Looping functoid to the repeating node structure in the output document.

   b. Link the Table Looping functoid to a Table Extractor functoid for each column in the table. The Table Extractor functoid can be found in the Toolbox on the Advanced Functoids tab.

4. Configure the input parameters for each Table Extractor functoid.

   a. Set the first input parameter, which is the output link from the Table Looping functoid.

   b. Set the second input parameter, which is the column number of the data to be extracted from the table.

5. Configure the outputs for each Table Extractor functoid. Link the functoid to a node in the destination schema that is part of a repeating structure.

■ **Note** It is very helpful to label all of the links so that meaningful names are displayed when configuring these functoids.

How It Works

The Table Looping and Table Extractor functoids are used together. As an example, suppose that you have the sample input document shown in Listing 3-5.

Listing 3-5. Flattened Input Structure

```
<AliasesFlat>
    <Names>
        <Alias1FirstName>John</Alias1FirstName>
        <Alias1LastName>Doe</Alias1LastName>
        <Alias2FirstName>Sam</Alias2FirstName>
```

```
        <Alias2LastName>Smith</Alias2LastName>
        <Alias3FirstName>James</Alias3FirstName>
        <Alias3LastName>Jones</Alias3LastName>
    </Names>
</AliasesFlat>
```

The goal is to use these two functoids to create an output document of the format shown in Listing 3-6.

Listing 3-6. Repeating Nested Structure

```
<AliasesRepeating>
    <AliasNames>
        <FirstName>John</FirstName>
        <LastName>Doe</LastName>
    </AliasNames>
    <AliasNames>
        <FirstName>Sam</FirstName>
        <LastName>Smith</LastName>
    </AliasNames>
    <AliasNames>
        <FirstName>James</FirstName>
        <LastName>Jones</LastName>
    </AliasNames>
</AliasesRepeating>
```

Figure 3-24 shows the configuration for the input parameters for the Table Looping functoid. The first parameter is a reference to the node structure Names in the input schema. The second parameter is a constant value of 2 indicating there will be two columns in the table. The remaining parameters are the first and last name of each alias from the input document.

	Name	Value	Type
✓	Input[0]	Names	
✓	Input[1]	2	
✓	Input[2]	Alias1FirstName	
✓	Input[3]	Alias1LastName	
✓	Input[4]	Alias2FirstName	
✓	Input[5]	Alias2LastName	
✓	Input[6]	Alias3FirstName	
✓	Input[7]	Alias3LastName	

Add/delete/reorder functoid inputs

Figure 3-24. *Table Looping input parameters*

Figure 3-25 shows the completed Table Looping Configuration dialog box for the Table Looping functoid. It has been configured so that each row contains an alias first name in column 1 and an alias last name in column 2. There will be three rows in the table to process, one for each alias provided as input.

Figure 3-25. *Table Looping Configuration dialog box*

The output links from the Table Looping functoid are configured as follows:

- An output link to the AliasNames repeating node structure in the destination schema

- An output link to a Table Extractor functoid for processing first names (column 1) from the table

- An output link to a Table Extractor functoid for processing last names (column 2) from the table

Figure 3-26 shows the configuration for the Table Extractor functoid that will process column 1 from the table. The first parameter is a link from the Table Looping functoid, and the second parameter is a constant value of 1, which indicates it will process the first column from each row as it is processed.

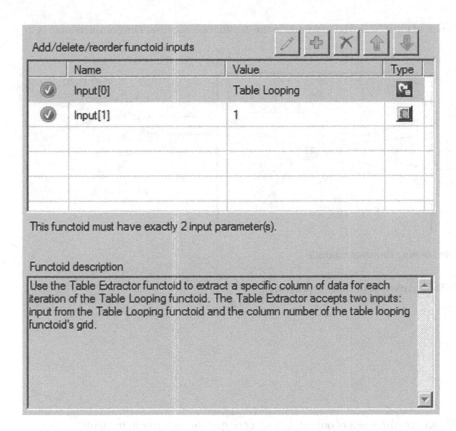

Figure 3-26. *Table Extractor functoid configuration for column 1*

Figure 3-27 shows the configuration for the Table Extractor functoid that will process column 2 from the table. The first parameter is a link from the Table Looping functoid, and the second parameter is a constant value of 2, which indicates it will process the second column from each row as it is processed.

Figure 3-27. *Table Extractor functoid configuration for column 2*

Finally, each Table Extractor functoid must be linked to a node in the destination schema. The complete map is shown in Figure 3-28.

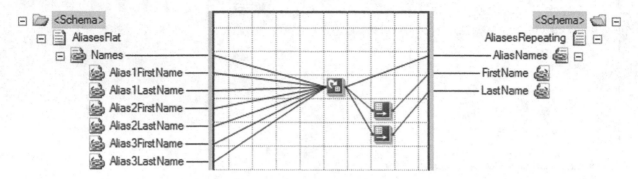

Figure 3-28. *Final map for the Table Looping functoid example*

Here is what the data table will look like when the map is processed:

Column 1	Column 2
John	Doe
Sam	Smith
James	Jones

Once the table is loaded, it will generate three sets of output: one set of output for each row in the table. This, in turn, will create three repetitions of the AliasNames node structure in the destination document: one for each row in the table. A repeating node structure has been created, even though one did not exist in the input document.

3-7. Using the Database Lookup Functoid
Problem

You need to map an incoming node to a database table column to reference a specific set of data via a BizTalk Server map. Specifically, for an inbound author ID, you need to retrieve the person attributes that are stored in a SQL based table. Additionally, the data that is stored in the database table is dynamic, and coding the values within the BizTalk map is not possible.

■ **Note**   The Database Lookup functoid can communicate with any ODBC-compliant data source. For this recipe, SQL Server is the assumed data source.

Solution

BizTalk provides the Database Lookup functoid, which can retrieve a recordset. For example, suppose that the inbound message specifies an author's Social Security number but no personal information. The map must retrieve the author's information and map the information to the outbound message. The Database Lookup functoid can retrieve the information from a specific SQL table using the author's Social Security number as the value for which to search. The inbound XML message may have a format similar to the following and a table with data as show in Figure 3-29.

```
<ns0:PersonSearch xmlns:ns0="http://DatabaseLookupFunctoid.PersonSearch">
  <ID>172321176</ID>
</ns0:PersonSearch>
```

ID	FirstName	LastName
172321176	Juno	Dos
544651234	Trays	Quatro
781232222	Sing-Ko	Says

Figure 3-29. *Record data*

You can use the Database Lookup functoid by taking the following steps:

1. Click the Toolbox, and then click the Database Functoids tab. On the map surface, in between the source and destination schemas, drag and drop a Database Lookup functoid.

2. Connect the left side of the Database Lookup functoid to the inbound document node that will specify the value used in the search.

3. Configure the input parameters of the Database Lookup functoid, as shown in Figure 3-30. This functoid requires four parameters to be specified either through mapping the inbound source data to the functoid or through setting constants in the functoid.

	Name	Value	Type
✓	Input[0]	ID	
✓	Input[1]	Provider=SQLOLEDB;Server=WIN-LUNNMMJU...	
✓	Input[2]	People	
✓	Input[3]	ID	

Add/delete/reorder functoid inputs

This functoid must have exactly 4 input parameter(s).

Figure 3-30. *Database Lookup Functoid input parameters dialog box*

    a.   For the first input parameter, verify that the inbound node, connected in step 2, is the first value in the list of properties. This is a value to be used in the search criteria. It's basically the same as the value used in a SQL WHERE clause.

    b.   Set the second parameter, which is the connection string for the database. The connection string must be a full connection string with a provider, machine name, database, and either account/password or a flag indicating the use of Trusted Security mode in SQL. The connection string must include a data provider attribute. A lack of data provider attribute will generate a connection error when the map tries to connect to the database.

■ **Note**   The easiest connection string to start with is integrated security, which has the format of `Provider=SQLOLEDB;Server=[servername];Database=[dbname];Integrated Security=SSPI;`.

---

    c.   Set the third parameter, which is the name of the table used in search.

    d.   Set the fourth parameter, which is the name of the column in the table to be used in search.

4.   Again, click the Toolbox, and click the Database Functoids tab. On the map surface, after the Database Lookup functoid, drag and drop the Error Return functoid.

5.   Connect the right side of the Database Lookup functoid to the left side of the Error Return functoid. Connect the right side of the Error Return functoid to the outbound schema node that is a placeholder for error messages.

6.   Again, click the Toolbox, and click the Database Functoids tab. On the map surface, above the Error Return functoid, drag and drop the Value Extractor functoid for each extracted value from the return recordset. For example, if you are returning five values in the recordset, you would need five Value Extractor functoids.

7.   For each Value Extractor functoid, connect the left side of the functoid to the right side of the Database Lookup functoid.

8.   Configure the properties of each Value Extractor functoid to retrieve the appropriate value by specifying the column name of the extracted value. For example, if the value returned resides in a column named FirstName, you would create a constant in the Value Extractor functoid named FirstName. The Value Extractor functoid's Configure Functoid Inputs dialog box should look similar to Figure 3-31.

	Name	Value	Type
✓	Input[0]	Database Lookup	▣→
✓	Input[1]	First Name	▣

Add/delete/reorder functoid inputs

This functoid must have exactly 2 input parameter(s).

Figure 3-31. *Value Extractor functoid input parameters dialog box*

9. For each Value Extractor functoid, connect the right side of the functoid to the appropriate target schema outbound node. The completed map should look similar to the sample map in Figure 3-32.

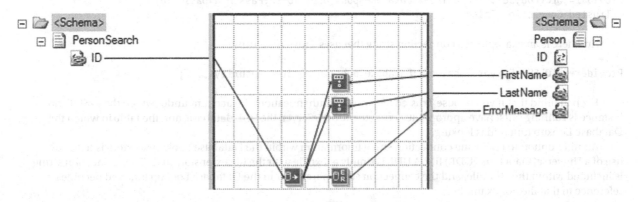

Figure 3-32. *The final mapping*

How It Works

The Database Lookup functoid requires four parameters as inputs, and it outputs an ActiveX Data Objects (ADO) recordset. Keep in mind that the recordset returns only the first row of data that matches the specific criteria provided to the Database Lookup functoid.

In addition to the input parameters, the Database Lookup functoid requires two helper functoids for optimal use:

- The Error Return functoid, which returns SQL-related errors or exceptions. The Error Return functoid requires the Database Lookup functoid as the input and a link to an output node in the target schema. To avoid runtime errors, verify that the only inbound connection to the Error Return functoid is that of the Database Lookup functoid and not any other database functoids. A generated error looks like that shown in Figure 3-33.

```
<ns0:Person xmlns:ns0="http://DatabaseLookupFunctoid.Person">
  <ID>ID_0</ID>
  <FirstName />
  <LastName />
  <ErrorMessage>[DBNETLIB][ConnectionOpen (Connect()).]SQL Server
    does not exist or access denied.</ErrorMessage>
</ns0:Person>
```

Figure 3-33. *An error has been generated*

- The Value Extractor functoid, which retrieves a specific column from the returned recordset. The Value Extractor will retrieve the value based on the specific column specified in the input parameters.

Security Considerations

Whenever you use SQL authentication (SQL username and password), there is potential for a security risk. Consider using trusted security for access to the database rather than specifying the username and password in the connection string used by the Database Lookup functoid. For example, here is a connection string that uses SQL security:

```
Provider=SQLOLEDB;Server=localhost;Database=pubs;User ID=sa;Password=password;
  Trusted_Connection=False
```

And here is an example of a connection string that uses Trusted Security:

```
Provider=SQLOLEDB;Server=localhost;Database=pubs;Integrated Security=SSPI;
```

Keep in mind that if you choose Trusted Security for authentication, the account under which the BizTalk host instance is running must have appropriate access to the SQL Server, the SQL database, and the table in which the Database Lookup functoid is looking.

Another option to enclosing connection string information within the Database Lookup functoid is to make use of a Universal Data Link (UDL) file. A UDL is simply a text file with the file extension .udl. The connection string is included within the UDL file, and the connection string parameter in the Database Lookup functoid becomes a reference to that file, for example:

```
File Name=c:\BizTalkConfig\ConnectionString.UDL
```

Once the UDL file is created, it can be made available on a secure file share.

■ **Note** UDL files are external to the BizTalk map and therefore must be parsed every time a connection to the database is open. The parsing activity will cause some performance degradation.

Additionally consider the use of a SQL view, versus direct table access, and having the Database Lookup functoid point to the database view. A SQL view offers the ability to manage table security permissions or the abstraction of the physical table structure.

Architecture Considerations

The Database Lookup functoid is convenient to implement in mappings. For straightforward data retrieval, this functoid performs adequately. However, the following items should be taken into consideration when evaluating when to use the Database Lookup functoid:

> *Database availability*: If you cannot guarantee that the data source being queried will be available when BizTalk is available, using the Database Lookup functoid may not make sense.

> *Error management*: Mapping will occur and not trap the SQL errors in the .NET exception style. Errors should be trapped and managed when mapping. When implementing the Database Lookup functoid, consider using the Error Return functoid. Additionally, after the mapping, it would be wise to query the Error Return node for an error message and implement error handling if one exists.

> *Performance*: Evaluate your performance requirements and determine if accessing a SQL database will negatively affect your overall mapping performance. Implementing the Database Lookup functoid may not impact performance greatly, but consider the effect if you must run the Database Lookup functoid multiple times in a single map. Database Lookup functoids that are part of a looping structure will cause a level of performance degradation. Make sure that the latest BizTalk service packs are applied when using the Database Lookup functoid, as they include performance-enhancing features such as caching.

> *Database support*: Evaluate if the database that you must access will support the necessary security requirements and also allow table (or at least view level) access.

Advanced Database Lookup Functoid Usage

The BizTalk map translates the Database Lookup functoid information into a dynamic SQL SELECT statement. If you run a SQL Profiler trace during testing of the BizTalk map, you will see the SELECT call with the dynamic SQL. Knowing that dynamic SQL is created by the Database Lookup functoid allows you to use it to perform some relatively powerful database lookups. The Database Lookup functoid allows only a single value and single column name to be referenced in the query. However, with a bit of extra mapping, you can use this functoid to query against multiple columns. The map in Figure 3-32 generates the following SQL query code:

```
exec sp_executesql N'SELECT * FROM people WHERE ID= @P1', N'@P1 nvarchar(9)',
N'172321176'
```

This query performs a SELECT to retrieve all rows from the People table where the author ID is equal to the value in the inbound XML document (for example, 172321176).

Keep in mind that the Database Lookup functoid returns only the first row that it encounters in the recordset. If multiple authors had the same ID, you would potentially retrieve the incorrect author. For example, if the author ID is the last name of the author, you may retrieve multiple authors that share the same last name. One way to ensure uniqueness, aside from querying on a unique column, is to specify additional columns in the query. The Database Lookup functoid accepts only four parameters, so additional concatenation must occur before submitting the parameters to the Database Lookup functoid.

After configuring the inbound concatenated value, the next step is to specify multiple column names as the input parameter in the Database Lookup functoid. Figure 3-34 demonstrates a sample Database Lookup functoid configuration with multiple columns specified. The output from the Database Lookup functoid to the Value Extractor functoid does not change.

	Name	Value	Type
✓	Input[0]	String Concatenate	
✓	Input[1]	Provider=SQLOLEDB;Server...	
✓	Input[2]	People	
✓	Input[3]	FirstName+LastName	

This functoid must have exactly 4 input parameter(s).

Figure 3-34. Database Lookup functoid with multiple columns

■ **Note**   A plus symbol (+) is used between the column names in the Database Lookup functoid, whereas in the Concatenation functoid, no + is required. If a + is specified in the Concatenation functoid, you will receive incorrect results, as the dynamic SQL statement created will be incorrect.

In this example, the inbound message specifies an author's first name and last name instead of a unique author ID. The map must still retrieve the author's information and map the information to the outbound message. The inbound XML message may have a format to the following message:

```
<ns0:PersonSearch xmlns:ns0="http://DatabaseLookupFunctoid.PersonSearch">
  <FirstName>Juan</FirstName>
  <LastName>Dos</LastName>
</ns0:PersonSearch>
```

The following is the dynamic SQL created in the map that accepts multiple columns:

```
exec sp_executesql N'SELECT * FROM authors WHERE FirstName+LastName= @P1', N'@P1
nvarchar(12)', N'JuanDos'
```

The dynamic SQL created shows the inbound author's first name and last name parameters as a concatenated parameter. The SQL statement also shows a combination WHERE clause with FirstName + LastName.

There are some limitations to specifying multiple columns through the concatenation approach. Specifically, string data types are the only data types that work reliably due to the concatenation operation that occurs in SQL. Integer data types may also be used, but in the case of integer (or other numeric data types), SQL will perform an additive operation versus a concatenation operation. Adding two numbers together, as what would happen when specifying numeric data types, and comparing the result to another set of numbers being added together may yield multiple matches and may not achieve the desired results. The mix of varchar and numeric fields will not work with this approach, as you will receive a data casting exception from your data provider.

3-8. Seeding Cross-Reference Tables with ID Cross-References

Problem

You wish to dynamically cross-reference unique identifiers between two or more systems. The reference data already exists, so you wish to load the data into the BizTalk cross-reference tables before you use the cross-reference functoids or application programming interface (API).

Solution

Within an XML configuration file you name List_Of_App_Type.xml, insert the XML shown in Listing 3-7, and insert an appType node for each system that will have cross-references.

Listing 3-7. List_Of_App_Type.xml

```xml
<?xml version="1.0" encoding="UTF-8"?>
<listOfAppType>
    <appType>
        <name>Oracle</name>
        <description/>
    </appType>
    <appType>
        <name>Siebel</name>
        <description/>
    </appType>
</listOfAppType>
```

■ **Note**   These node values in Listings 3-7 through 3-10 have been placed in the XML as an example. You should remove them and insert your own.

Within an XML configuration file you name List_Of_App_Instance.xml, insert the XML shown in Listing 3-8.

Listing 3-8. List_Of_App_Instance.xml

```xml
<?xml version="1.0" encoding="UTF-8"?>
<listOfAppInstance>
        <appInstance>
            <instance>Oracle_01</instance>
            <type>Oracle</type>
            <description/>
        </appInstance>
        <appInstance>
            <instance>Siebel_01</instance>
            <type>Siebel</type>
            <description/>
        </appInstance>
```

```
        <appInstance>
            <instance>Siebel_12</instance>
            <type>Siebel</type>
            <description/>
        </appInstance>
</listOfAppInstance>
```

Since unique identifiers are often different for each unique instance of a system, you must create different cross-references for each system. Therefore, you must insert an appInstance node for each instance of an application you will cross-reference, inserting a common type value across instances that are of the same type of system, and which correspond to the appType you created in the List_Of_App_Type.xml configuration file. For instance, you may be running two instances of Siebel, so you would insert two appInstance nodes with a type of Siebel, but give each a unique value in the instance node (for example, Siebel_01 and Siebel_12).

Within an XML configuration file you name List_Of_IdXRef.xml, insert the XML shown in Listing 3-9.

Listing 3-9. List_Of_IdXRef.xml

```
<?xml version="1.0" encoding="UTF-8"?>
<listOfIDXRef>
    <idXRef>
        <name>Customer.ID</name>
        <description/>
    </idXRef>
    <idXRef>
        <name>Order.PONumber</name>
        <description/>
    </idXRef>
</listOfIDXRef>
```

For each ID field you plan to cross-reference, insert an idXRef node with a unique name child node. This value will be used to identify the ID field that you are cross-referencing. For instance, if you plan to cross-reference a customer that is in different systems, you would insert an idXRef with a name like Customer.ID.

Within an XML configuration file you name List_Of_IdXRef_Data.xml, insert the XML shown in Listing 3-10.

Listing 3-10. List_Of_IdXRef_Data.xml

```
<?xml version="1.0" encoding="UTF-8"?>
<listOfIDXRefData>
    <idXRef name="Customer.ID">
        <appInstance name="Oracle_01">
            <appID commonID="100"> CARA345</appID>
        </appInstance>

        <appInstance name="Siebel_01">
            <appID commonID="100">99-4D976</appID>
        </appInstance>
        <appInstance name="Siebel_12">
            <appID commonID="100">440L</appID>
        </appInstance>
    </idXRef>
</listOfIDXRefData>
```

For each field you create in the List_Of_IdXRef.xml file, insert an idXRef node. For each system you create in the List_Of_App_Instance.xml file, insert an appInstance node. Insert one or more appID nodes for each unique identifier. Insert a commonID attribute to store a common identifier, and set the application-specific value within the node. The common ID will be repeated for each appID that is cross-referenced.

Within an XML configuration file you name Setup-Config.xml, insert the XML shown in Listing 3-11.

Listing 3-11. Setup-Config.xml

```
<?xml version="1.0" encoding="UTF-8"?>
<Setup-Files>
    <App_Type_file>C:\List_Of_App_Type.xml</App_Type_file>
    <App_Instance_file>C:\List_Of_App_Instance.xml</App_Instance_file>
    <IDXRef_file>C:\List_Of_IDXRef.xml</IDXRef_file>
    <IDXRef_Data_file>C:\List_Of_IDXRef_Data.xml</IDXRef_Data_file>
</Setup-Files>
```

Each node should point to the physical location where you have created the corresponding XML configuration files.

Seed the BizTalk cross-reference tables by opening a command-line window and running the BizTalk cross-reference import tool, BTSXRefImport.exe (found in the BizTalk installation directory), passing in the path to the cross-reference XML file created in Listing 3-11:

```
BTSXRefImport.exe -file=C:\Setup-Config.xml
```

How It Works

During installation of BizTalk, several cross-reference tables are created in the BizTalkMgmtDb database. All the cross-reference tables begin with the prefix xref_, and the BTSXRefImport tool imports the data from the XML files provided into the table structure for access at runtime. It is not necessary to use the BTSXRefImport.exe tool to insert data into the cross-reference tables. You may insert data directly into the following tables:

- xref_AppInstance
- xref_IdXRef
- xref_IdXRefData

After running the BTSXRefImport tool, and if the data were in a denormalized form, the data would look like this:

AppType	AppInstance	IdXRef	CommonID	Application ID
Oracle	Oracle_01	Customer.ID	100	CARA345
Siebel	Siebel_01	Customer.ID	100	99-4D976
Siebel	Siebel_12	Customer.ID	100	44OL

There are subtle differences between ID and value cross-referencing. Value cross-references, as the name implies, deal with static values, while ID cross-references deal with cross-referencing unique identifiers. Since most value cross-references are not updated at runtime, a functoid and API method are not provided to update the references at runtime. ID cross-references, though, may be updated using the Set Common ID functoid or API method.

■ **Note**   The Set Common ID functoid is poorly named, as it actually sets the `application` ID and the `CommonID`. If `CommonID` is not provided, the method will return a new `CommonID` Instance.

3-9. Seeding Cross-Reference Tables with Value Cross-References

Problem

You wish to statically cross-reference state values between two or more systems. The reference data already exists, but you must load the data into the BizTalk cross-reference tables before you may use the cross-reference functoids or API.

Solution

Within an XML configuration file you name `List_Of_App_Type.xml`, insert the XML shown in Listing 3-12, and insert an appType node for each system that will have static cross-references.

Listing 3-12. List_Of_App_Type.xml

```
<?xml version="1.0" encoding="UTF-8"?>
<listOfAppType>
    <appType>
        <name>Oracle</name>
        <description/>
    </appType>
    <appType>
        <name>Siebel</name>
        <description/>
    </appType>
</listOfAppType>
```

■ **Note**   The node values in Listings 3-12 through 3-14 have been placed in the XML as an example. You should remove them and insert your own.

Within an XML configuration file you name `List_Of_ValueXRef.xml`, insert the XML shown in Listing 3-13.

Listing 3-13. List_Of_ValueXRef.xml

```
<?xml version="1.0" encoding="UTF-8"?>
<listOfValueXRef>
    <valueXRef>
        <name>Order.Status</name>
        <description/>
    </valueXRef>
</listOfValueXRef>
```

For each field you plan to statically cross-reference, insert a valueXRef node with a unique child node name. This value will be used to identify the static field. For instance, if you plan to map between order status codes, you might create a common value of Order.Status.

Within an XML configuration file you name List_Of_ValueXRef_Data.xml, insert the XML shown in Listing 3-14.

Listing 3-14. List_Of_ValueXRef_Data.xml

```xml
<?xml version="1.0" encoding="UTF-8"?>
<listOfValueXRefData>
<valueXRef name="Order.Status">
    <appType name="Oracle">
        <appValue commonValue="Open">OP</appValue>
        <appValue commonValue="Pending">PD</appValue>
        <appValue commonValue="Closed">CD</appValue>
    </appType>
    <appType name="Siebel">
        <appValue commonValue="Open">1:Open</appValue>
        <appValue commonValue="Pending">2:Pending</appValue>
        <appValue commonValue="Closed">3:Closed</appValue>
    </appType>
</valueXRef>
</listOfValueXRefData>
```

For each static field you create in the List_Of_ValueXRef.xml file, insert a valueXRef node. For each system you create in the List_Of_App_Type.xml file, insert an appType node. Insert one or more appValue nodes for each value that is permissible for this valueXRef field. Insert a commonValue attribute to store the common name for the value, and set the application-specific value within the node. The common value will be repeated for each appType that is cross-referenced.

Within an XML configuration file you name Setup-Config.xml, insert the XML shown in Listing 3-15.

Listing 3-15. Setup-Config.xml

```xml
<?xml version="1.0" encoding="UTF-8"?>
<Setup-Files>
<App_Type_file>c:\List_OF_App_Type.xml</App_Type_file>
<ValueXRef_file>c:\List_Of_ValueXRef.xml</ValueXRef_file>
<ValueXRef_Data_file>c:\List_Of_ValueXRef_Data.xml</ValueXRef_Data_file>
</Setup-Files>
```

Each node should point to the physical location where you have created the corresponding XML configuration files.

Seed the BizTalk cross-reference tables by opening a command-line window and running the BizTalk cross-reference import tool, BTSXRefImport.exe (found in the BizTalk installation directory), passing in the path to the Setup-Config.xml cross-reference file:

```
BTSXRefImport.exe -file=C:\Setup-Config.xml
```

How It Works

During installation of BizTalk, several static cross-reference tables are created in the `BizTalkMgmtDb` database. All the cross-reference tables begin with the prefix `xref_`, and the `BTSXRefImport` tool imports the data from the XML files provided to the table structure for access at runtime. It is not necessary to use the `BTSXRefImport.exe` tool to insert data into the cross-reference tables. You may insert data directly into the following tables:

- `xref_AppType`
- `xref_ValueXRef`
- `xref_ValueXRefData`

In a denormalized form, the table would look like this after running the `BTSXRefImport` tool:

AppType	ValueXRef	CommonValue	AppValue	AppType
Oracle	Order.Status	Open	OP	Oracle
Siebel	Order.Status	Open	1:Open	Siebel
Oracle	Order.Status	Pending	PD	Oracle
Siebel	Order.Status	Pending	2:Pending	Siebel
Oracle	Order.Status	Closed	CD	Oracle
Siebel	Order.Status	Closed	3:Closed	Siebel

3-10. Using the ID Cross-Reference Functoids

Problem

Within a map, you wish to dynamically cross-reference unique identifiers between two or more systems, and the identifier cross-references have already been loaded into the cross-reference tables. For example, a source system publishes an `Account` with a unique identifier of `1234`, and you want to cross-reference and dynamically translate that identifier to the unique identifier in a destination system of `AA3CARA`.

■ **Note**   If you have not already loaded the identifier cross-reference data, see Recipe 3-8 for more information.

Solution

To cross-reference the identifiers within a map, take the following steps:

1. Click the Database Functoids tab in the Toolbox.

2. Drag the Get Common ID functoid onto to the map surface.

3. Open the Input Parameters dialog box for the Get Common ID functoid.

4. Add a constant parameter and set the value to the ID type you wish to cross-reference. For instance, you may set the value to something like `Customer.ID`.

5. Add a second constant parameter to the Get Common ID functoid, and set the value to the source system application instance. For instance, you may set the value to something like Siebel_01.

6. Click OK.

7. Connect the unique source identifier node you wish to cross-reference from the source schema to the Get Common ID functoid.

8. Drag the Get Application ID functoid from the Database Functoids tab onto the map surface, and place it to the right of the Get Common ID functoid.

9. Open the Input Parameters dialog box for the Get Application ID functoid.

10. Add a constant parameter and set the value to the ID type you wish to receive. For instance, you may set the value to something like Customer.ID.

11. Add a second constant parameter to the Get Common ID functoid and set the value to the destination system application instance. For instance, you may set the value to something like Oracle_01.

12. Click OK.

13. Connect the Get Common ID functoid to the Get Application ID functoid.

14. Connect the functoid to the unique destination identifier node.

15. Save and test the map.

How It Works

Identifier cross-referencing allows entities to be shared across systems. Although cross-referencing functionality is often not required in small integration projects, as usually there is a single system for a given entity type, in larger organizations, it is common to find several systems with the same entities (for example, Account, Order, and Invoice). These entities are often assigned a unique identifier that is internally generated and controlled by the system. In other words, from a business perspective, the entities are the same, but from a systems perspective, they are discrete. Therefore, in order to move an entity from one system to another, you must have a way to create and store the relationship between the unique identifiers, and to discover the relationships at runtime.

BizTalk Server provides this functionality through cached cross-referencing tables, API, an import tool, and functoids. Using the import tool, you can load information about systems, instances of those systems, the entities within those systems you wish to cross-reference, and the actual cross-reference data into a set of cross-reference tables that are installed with BizTalk in the BizTalkMgmtDb database. Then, using the functoids or API at runtime, you access the tables to convert an identifier from one recognized value to another. The basic steps for converting from one system to another are as follows:

1. Using the source identifier, source instance, and source entity type, retrieve the common identifier by calling the Get Common ID functoid.

■ **Note** The common identifier is commonly not stored in any system. It is an identifier used to associate one or more identifiers.

---

2. Using the common identifier, destination system instance, and destination entity type, retrieve the destination identifier by calling the Get Application ID functoid.

This recipe has focused on accessing identifier cross-referencing functionality through BizTalk functoids, but an API is also available. The cross-referencing class may be found in the `Microsoft.Biztalk.CrossRreferencing.dll`, within the namespace `Microsoft.BizTalk.CrossReferencing`. This class has several members that facilitate storing and retrieving identifier cross referencing relationships, as listed in Table 3-1.

Table 3-1. *ID Cross-Referencing API*

Member	Description
GetCommonID	With an application instance, entity/ID type, and application identifier value, retrieves a common identifier. If a cross-reference does not exist, a blank will be returned. If the application instance or entity/ID type does not exist, an exception will be thrown.
GetAppID	With a common identifier, application instance, and entity/ID type, retrieves the application identifier value. If a cross-reference does not exist, a blank will be returned. If the application instance or entity/ID type does not exist, an exception will be thrown.
SetCommonID*	With an application instance, entity/ID type, application identifier value, and optionally a common identifier, create a relationship in the cross-referencing tables. If a common identifier is not passed to the method, one will be created and returned. If the application instance or entity/ID type does not exist, an exception will be thrown.

* The `SetCommonID` method does set the common identifier and will create one if not passed to the method, but more importantly, it creates the relationship between the application-specific identifier and the common identifier. Perhaps a better name would have been `SetIDCrossReference`.

3-11. Using the Value Cross-Reference Functoids
Problem

Within a map, you wish to statically cross-reference state values between two or more systems, and the value cross-references have already been loaded into the cross-reference tables. For example, a source system publishes an Order with a status of 1:Open, and you want to cross reference and translate the static state value to the static value in a destination system of OP.

■ **Note**   If you have not already loaded the value cross-reference data, see Recipe 3-9 for more information.

Solution

To cross-reference the static values within a map, take the following steps:

1. Click the Database Functoids tab in the Toolbox.

2. Drag the Get Common Value functoid to the map surface.

3. Open the Input Parameters dialog box for the Get Common Value functoid.

4. Add a constant parameter, and set the value to the static value type you wish to cross-reference. For instance, you may set the value to something like Order.Status.

5. Add a second constant parameter to the Get Common Value functoid, and set the value to the source system application type. For instance, you may set the value to something like Siebel.

6. Click OK.

7. Connect the state value source node you wish to cross-reference from the source schema to the Get Common Value functoid.

8. Drag the Get Application Value functoid from the Database Functoids tab to the map surface, and place it to the right of the Get Common Value functoid.

9. Open the Input Parameters dialog box for the Get Application Value functoid.

10. Add a constant parameter, and set the value to the static value type you wish to cross-reference. For instance, you may set the value to something like Order.Status.

11. Add a second constant parameter to the Get Common Value functoid, and set the value to the destination system application type. For instance, you may set the value to something like Oracle.

12. Click OK.

13. Connect the Get Common Value functoid to the Get Application Value functoid.

14. Connect the functoid to the unique destination state value node.

15. Save and test the map.

How It Works

Identifier and value cross-referencing are similar in concept, with the following differences:

- Value cross-referencing is commonly between enumeration fields. Identifier cross-referencing is commonly between entity unique identifiers.

- Value cross-referencing occurs between system types. Identifier cross-referencing occurs between instances of system types.

- Identifier cross-references may be set at runtime. Value cross-references are static and may be loaded only through the import tool or direct table manipulation.

The basic steps for converting from one system to another are as follows:

1. Using the source application type, source application static value, and source entity value type, retrieve the common value by calling the Get Common Value functoid.

■ **Note** The common value is generally not stored in any system. It is a value used to associate multiple values.

---

2. Using the common static value, destination system type, and destination entity value type, retrieve the destination static value by calling the Get Application Value functoid.

This recipe has focused on accessing value cross-referencing functionality through BizTalk functoids, but an API is also available. The cross-referencing class may be found in the `Microsoft.Biztalk.CrossRreferencing.dll`, within the namespace `Microsoft.BizTalk.CrossReferencing`. This class has several members that facilitate storing and retrieving value cross-referencing relationships, as listed in Table 3-2.

Table 3-2. *Value Cross-Referencing API*

Member	Description
GetCommonValue	With an application type, entity/node value type, and application value, this member retrieves a common value. If a cross-reference does not exist, a blank will be returned. If the application type or entity/node value type does not exist, an exception will be thrown.
GetAppValue	With a common value, application type, and entity/node type, this retrieves the application value. If a cross-reference does not exist, a blank will be returned. If the application type or entity/node value type does not exist, an exception will be thrown

3-12. Using the Looping Functoid
Problem

The structure of a message from a source system you are integrating with contains multiple repeating record types. You must map each of these record types into one record type in the destination system. In order for the message to be imported into the destination system, a transformation must be applied to the source document to consolidate, or standardize, the message structure.

Solution

Create a map that utilizes the BizTalk Server Looping functoid, by taking the following steps:

1. Click the Toolbox, and then click the Advanced Functoids tab. On the map surface, between the source and destination schemas, drag and drop a Looping functoid. This functoid accepts 1 to 100 repeating source records (or data elements) as its input parameters. The return value is a reference to a single repeating record or data element in the destination schema.

2. Connect the left side of the Looping functoid to the multiple repeating source data elements that need to be consolidated.

3. Connect the right side of the Looping functoid to the repeating destination data element that contains the standardized data structure.

How It Works

An example of a map that uses the Looping functoid is shown in Figure 3-35.

Figure 3-35. *Using the Looping functoid*

In this example, multiple types of plane flight reservations are consolidated into a single list of records capturing passengers and their associated seats. The XML snippet in Listing 3-16 represents one possible instance of the source schema.

Listing 3-16. *Source Schema Instance for the Looping Functoid Example*

```
<ns0:PassengerReservations xmlns:ns0="http://LoopingFunctoid.PassengerReservations">
  <FlightNumber>666</FlightNumber>
  <OnlineReservation>
    <Name>Lucifer Smith</Name>
    <Seat>13A</Seat>
    <Website>www.greatdeals.com</Website>
    <Confirmed>True</Confirmed>
  </OnlineReservation>
  <OnlineReservation>
    <Name>Beelzebub Walker, Jr.</Name>
    <Seat>13B</Seat>
    <Website>www.hellofadeal.com</Website>
    <Confirmed>False</Confirmed>
  </OnlineReservation>
  <TravelAgentReservation>
    <PassengerName>Jim Diablo</PassengerName>
    <Seat>13C</Seat>
    <AgentName>Sunny Rodriguez</AgentName>
  </TravelAgentReservation>
  <AirlineReservation>
    <Name>Imin Trouble</Name>
    <Seat>13D</Seat>
    <BookingDesk>Chicago</BookingDesk>
  </AirlineReservation>
</ns0:PassengerReservations>
```

Based on this source XML, the looping map displayed in Figure 3-35 will produce the XML document shown in Listing 3-17, containing a single passenger seat assignment list.

Listing 3-17. Destination Schema Instance for the Looping Functoid Example

```
<ns0:Manifest FlightNumber="666" xmlns:ns0="http://LoopingFunctoid.Manifest">
  <Passenger Name="Lucifer Smith" SeatNumber="13A" />
  <Passenger Name="Beelzebub Walker, Jr." SeatNumber="13B" />
  <Passenger Name="Jim Diablo" SeatNumber="13C" />
  <Passenger Name="Imin Trouble" SeatNumber="13D" />
</ns0:Manifest>
```

This example displays a simplistic but useful scenario in which the Looping functoid can be used. Essentially, this functoid iterates over the specified repeating source records (all those with a link to the left side of the functoid), similar to the For...Each structure in coding languages, and maps the desired elements to a single repeating record type in the destination schema.

■ **Note**   The four source records in the XML instance (the two OnlineReservations records, the one TravelAgentReservation record, and the one AirlineReservation record) produced four records in the output XML. If the source instance had contained five records, the resulting output XML document would also contain five records.

Based on this simple principle, you can develop much more complex mappings via the Looping functoid. One example of a more advanced use of the Looping functoid is conditional looping. This technique involves filtering which source records actually create destination records in the resulting XML document. The filtering is done by adding a logical functoid to the map, which produces a true or false Boolean value based on the logic. Common examples of filtering are based on elements that indicate a certain type of source record, or numeric elements that posses a certain minimum or maximum value.

The previous flight reservation example can be extended to implement conditional looping, in order to map only those online reservations that have been confirmed. This can be accomplished via the following steps:

1. Click the Toolbox, and click the Logical Functoids tab. On the map surface, in between the source and destination schemas, drag and drop a logical Equal functoid. This functoid accepts two input parameters, which are checked for equality. The return value is a Boolean true or false.

2. Specify the second input parameter for the logical Equal functoid as a constant with a value of True.

3. Connect the left side of the logical Equal functoid to the data element whose value is the key input for the required decision (Confirmed in the OnlineReservation node, in this case) logic.

4. Connect the right side of the logical Equal functoid to the element in the destination schema containing the repeating destination data element that contains the standardized data structure.

An example of the enhanced map is shown in Figure 3-36.

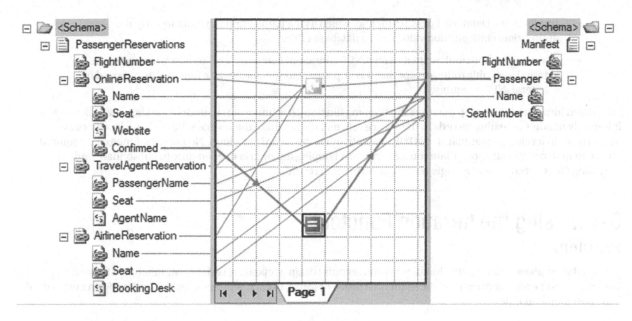

Figure 3-36. *Conditional looping*

Based on the same source XML outlined earlier in Listing 3-16, the looping map displayed in Figure 3-36 will produce the following XML document, containing a single passenger seat assignment list with only three passengers (Lauren Jones's reservation, which was not confirmed, is filtered out by the conditional looping logic):

```
<ns0:Manifest FlightNumber="666" xmlns:ns0="http://LoopingFunctoid.Manifest">
  <Passenger Name="Lucifer Smith" SeatNumber="13A" />
  <Passenger Name="Jim Diablo" SeatNumber="13C" />
  <Passenger Name="Imin Trouble" SeatNumber="13D" />
</ns0:Manifest>
```

■ **Note** Due to the fact that the `Confirmation` element is not being mapped over to the destination schema, the output of the logical Equal functoid is tied to the `Passenger` record. If the logical Equal functoid were being applied to an element that is being mapped to the destination schema, such as the `Seat` element, the output of the Equal functoid could be tied directly to the `SeatNumber` element in the destination schema.

In this example of conditional looping, the second input parameter of the logical Equal functoid is a hard-coded constant set to `True`. In real-world scenarios, it may not be ideal for this value to be hard-coded. You may prefer to have it driven off a configurable value. Several alternatives exist:

- Implement a Scripting functoid to the map, which passes the name of a configuration value to an external assembly. This external assembly would then handle the lookup of the actual configuration value.

- Implement a Database Lookup functoid, which as the name implies, would look up the appropriate configuration value from a database table.

- Use a custom functoid, written in any .NET-compliant language. This option is similar to the external assembly route, except that it is implemented specifically as a functoid as opposed to a general .NET assembly.

When implementing a map that uses the Looping functoid, it is important to understand how BizTalk Server inherently handles repeating records in the source schema. If a record in the source schema has a Max Occurs property set to a value greater than 1, BizTalk Server handles the record via a loop. No Looping functoid is required for the map to process all appropriate source records. A Looping functoid is needed only to consolidate multiple repeating source records into a single repeating destination record.

3-13. Using the Iteration Functoid
Problem

You need to implement a map that handles certain records within a repeating series in an intelligent fashion. The map must be able to determine the sequential order, or index, of each repeating record, and perform customized logic based on that index.

Solution

Develop a BizTalk Server map, and leverage the Iteration functoid by taking the following steps.

1. Click the Toolbox, and click the Advanced Functoids tab. On the map surface, between the source and destination schemas, drag and drop an Iteration functoid. This functoid accepts a repeating source record (or data element) as its one input parameter. The return value is the currently processed index of a specific instance document (for a source record which repeated five times, it would return 1, 2, 3, 4, and 5 in succession as it looped through the repeating records).

2. Connect the left side of the Iteration functoid to the repeating source record (or data element) whose index is the key input for the required decision logic.

3. Connect the right side of the Iteration functoid to the additional functoids used to implement the required business logic.

How It Works

An example of a map that uses the Iteration functoid is shown in Figure 3-37.

Figure 3-37. *Using the Iteration functoid*

In this example, all the peak hourly energy values from the source XML are mapped over to the destination XML. The Iteration functoid is used to determine the index of each `HourlyUsage` record, with those having an index value of 3 or higher being flagged as peak hours. Additionally, the output from the Iteration functoid is also used to create the Hour element in the destination XML, defining to which hour the energy reading pertains. The XML snippet in Listing 3-18 represents one possible document instance of the source schema.

Listing 3-18. *Sample Source Instance for the Iteration Functoid Example*

```
<ns0:HourlyUsage xmlns:ns0="http://IterationFunctoid.HourlyUsage">
  <Date>09/06/2010</Date>
  <Usage>
    <Hour>01</Hour>
    <EnergyUsage>2.4</EnergyUsage>
    <Adjustments>0</Adjustments>
  </Usage>
  <Usage>
    <Hour>02</Hour>
    <EnergyUsage>1.7</EnergyUsage>
    <Adjustments>1</Adjustments>
  </Usage>
  <Usage>
    <Hour>03</Hour>
    <EnergyUsage>3.9</EnergyUsage>
    <Adjustments>0</Adjustments>
  </Usage>
  <Usage>
    <Hour>04</Hour>
    <EnergyUsage>12.4</EnergyUsage>
    <Adjustments>3</Adjustments>
  </Usage>
  <Usage>
    <Hour>05</Hour>
    <EnergyUsage>15</EnergyUsage>
    <Adjustments>0</Adjustments>
  </Usage>
```

```
<Usage>
  <Hour>06</Hour>
  <EnergyUsage>3.2</EnergyUsage>
  <Adjustments>1</Adjustments>
</Usage>
</ns0:HourlyUsage>
```

When passed through the map displayed in Figure 3-37, this XML will produce the XML document shown in Listing 3-19, containing all the peak hourly energy usage values with their associated Hour value.

Listing 3-19. Sample Destination Instance for the Iteration Functoid Example

```
<ns0:PeakHourUsage xmlns:ns0="http://IterationFunctoid.PeakHourUsage">
  <Date>09/06/2010</Date>
  <Usage>
    <Hour>4</Hour>
    <Amount>12.4</Amount>
  </Usage>
  <Usage>
    <Hour>5</Hour>
    <Amount>15</Amount>
  </Usage>
  <Usage>
    <Hour>6</Hour>
    <Amount>3.2</Amount>
  </Usage>
</ns0:PeakHourUsage>
```

The Iteration functoid can be a crucial tool for those business scenarios that require the current index number of a looping structure within a map to be known. In the energy usage example, it allows a generic list of chronological usage values to be mapped to a document containing only those values that occur in the afternoon, along with adding an element describing to which hour that usage pertains. As the map processes the repeating HourlyUsage records in the source XML in a sequential fashion, the index from the Iteration functoid is passed to the logical Greater Than functoid, which compares the index with a hard-coded value of 3. If the index value is 4 or greater, the element is created in the destination XML, and its hour ending value is set.

This example works well for the purposes of our simple scenario, but those who have dealt with hourly values of any kind know that days on which daylight saving time (DST) falls need to be handled carefully. Since the time change associated with DST actually occurs early in the morning, there are 13 morning (before afternoon) hourly values in the fall occurrence of DST, and 11 morning hourly values in the spring occurrence.

The map in Figure 3-37 can easily be enhanced to account for this by adding logic based on the record count of hourly values in the source XML document. You can accomplish this via the following steps:

1. Click the Toolbox, and click the Advanced Functoids tab. On the map surface, between the source and destination schemas, drag and drop a Record Count functoid. This functoid accepts a repeating source record (or data element) as its one input parameter. The return value is the count of repeating source records contained in a specific instance document.

2. Connect the left side of the Record Count functoid to the repeating source record (or data element) whose index is the key input for the required decision logic.

3. Drag and drop a Subtraction functoid from the Mathematical Functoids tab onto the map surface, positioning it to the right of the Record Count functoid. This functoid accepts a minimum of 2 and a maximum of 99 input parameters. The first is a numeric value, from which all other numeric input values (the second input parameter to the last) are subtracted. The return value is a numeric value equaling the first input having all other inputs subtracted from it.

4. Connect the right side of the Record Count functoid to the left side of the Subtraction functoid.

5. Specify the second input parameter for the Subtraction functoid as a constant, with a value of 12.

6. Connect the right side of the Subtraction functoid to the left side of the Greater Than functoid. Ensure that this input to the Greater Than functoid is the second input parameter.

In this modified example, the repeating source record's count has 12 subtracted from it to adjust for the two DST days of the year (this works since we are interested in only the afternoon energy usage values, which are always the final 12 readings for a day). This adjusted value is then passed through the same logical Greater Than functoid as in the previous example, and the DST issue is effectively handled.

The use of the Iteration functoid is common in a number of other scenarios. One such scenario is when dealing with a document formatted with comma-separated values (CSV). Often, the first row in a CSV document contains column header information, as opposed to actual record values. The following flat file snippet shows one possible representation of energy usage values in CSV format:

```
EnergyUsage,Adjustments
2.4,0
2.5,0
2.8,0
```

In cases like these, it is likely that you do not want to map the column headers to the destination XML document. You can use an Iteration functoid to skip the first record of a CSV document. The index from the Iteration functoid is passed to a logical Not Equal functoid, which compares the index with a hard-coded value of 1. If the index is anything other than 1 (the record at index 1 contains the column header information), the values are mapped to the destination XML.

■ **Note** You can also strip out column headers by using envelope schemas.

Another common use of the Iteration functoid is to allow the interrogation of records preceding or following the currently processed record. This can be helpful when mapping elements in a repeating record in the source schema that require knowledge of the next or previous record.

3-14. Creating a Custom Functoid

Problem

You have a mapping need that requires the repeated use of complex functionality.

Solution

Rather than writing the same inline code (C#, XSLT, and so on) and pasting it in multiple shapes, or using a combination of multiple existing functoids, you can develop your own custom functoid.

As an example, we'll describe the process to develop, deploy, and use a custom functoid that replaces the ampersand (&), greater than (>), and less than (<) symbols with their HTML/XML equivalents. The functoid will have one input parameter and one output parameter, representing the string on which to run the replacement. This functoid would be used primarily with XML that may be returned from an external source, such as a .NET assembly, where the XML may not have been validated and contains characters that must be escaped.

Use the following steps to create, deploy, and use a custom functoid. Refer to the sample solution SampleCustomFunctoid.sln included with this book.

1. Create a new Class Library .NET project. Functoids can be coded in any .NET language. This example is implemented in C#.

2. Add a reference to the `Microsoft.BizTalk.BaseFunctoids.dll` assembly located in the `%\Program Files\Microsoft BizTalk Server 2010\Developer Tools` directory.

3. Create a resource file (`resx`) to store the functoid configuration parameters. The name of the file and the parameters should match what is shown in Listing 3-20.

■ **Note** Adding a bitmap (or any file) to a resource file may require using a third-party application. You can download such applications freely from the Internet.

---

4. Code the functoid. The functoid code should match that shown in Listing 3-20. This is a complete C# class library and will compile into a deployable functoid.

    Listing 3-20. Custom Functoid Class Library

    ```
    using System;
    using Microsoft.BizTalk.BaseFunctoids;
    using System.Reflection;

    namespace SampleCustomFunctoid
    {
        /// <summary>
        /// See sample solution (SampleCustomFunctoid.sln)
        /// which accompanies this recipe
        /// </summary>
    ```

```
[Serializable]
public class EncodeFunctoid : BaseFunctoid
{
    public EncodeFunctoid() : base()
    {
        //Custom functoids should begin with 6000 or higher
        this.ID = 6667;

        // resource assembly reference
        SetupResourceAssembly
            ("SampleCustomFunctoid.SampleCustomFunctoidResource",
            Assembly.GetExecutingAssembly());

        //Set the properties for this functoid
        SetName("SAMPLECUSTOMFUNCTOID_NAME");
        SetTooltip("SAMPLECUSTOMFUNCTOID_TOOLTIP");
        SetDescription("SAMPLECUSTOMFUNCTOID_DESCRIPTION");
        SetBitmap("SAMPLECUSTOMFUNCTOID_BITMAP");

        // one parameter in, one parameter out
        this.SetMinParams(1);
        this.SetMaxParams(1);

        //Function code below
        SetExternalFunctionName(GetType().Assembly.FullName,
          "SampleCustomFunctoid.EncodeFunctoid", "EncodeChars");

        //Category in Toolbox where this functoid will appear
        this.Category = FunctoidCategory.String;

          //output of functoid can go to all nodes indicated
        this.OutputConnectionType = ConnectionType.All;

        // add one of the following lines of code for every input
        // parameter. All lines would be identical.
        AddInputConnectionType(ConnectionType.All);
    }

    // Actual function which does the replacement of symbols
    public string EncodeChars(String strInputValue)
    {
        strInputValue = strInputValue.Replace("&","&amp;");
        strInputValue = strInputValue.Replace("<","&lt;");
        strInputValue = strInputValue.Replace(">","&gt;");

        return strInputValue;
    }
}
```

5. Add a strong name key, and build the project.

6. Place a copy of the assembly in the following directory: `%\Program Files\Microsoft BizTalk Server 2010\Developer Tools\Mapper Extensions`.

7. To add the functoid to the toolbox, on the window toolbar, click Tools ➤ Choose Toolbox Items. In the Choose Toolbox dialog box, click the Mapper Functoids tab. Click the Browse button, and select the functoid DLL from step 5, as shown in Figure 3-38. Then click OK.

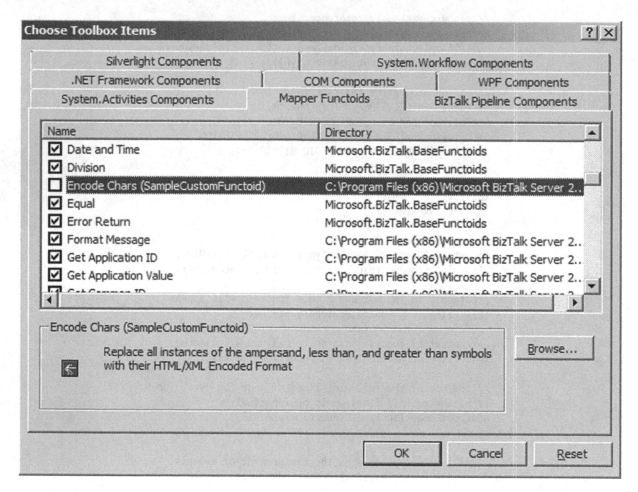

Figure 3-38. Adding a custom functoid to the Toolbox

8. Add the functoid to the Global Assembly Cache (GAC).

■ **Note** Functoids can be tested in maps without deploying to the GAC.

This completes the steps for creating a custom functoid. You can now add the functoid to a BizTalk map and test it. When a map is ready for deployment, the functoid will need to be copied to the `Mapper Extensions` folder (see step 6) and the GAC on the production server. Figure 3-39 shows the new functoid with custom bitmap in the toolbox in Visual Studio.

Figure 3-39. *The new functoid in the toolbox*

How It Works

One of the biggest benefits to using custom functoids is that you have full access to the .NET libraries. Inline code within maps gives only limited access to libraries, and coding is often primitive. Custom functoids are created as .NET class libraries, and they have all of the related coding benefits.

The example shown in this recipe is very simple. Custom functoids do not have to be limited to the two functions shown in the code. For example, assume that you need a functoid that does some sort of interaction with a database. You may need to include an `Init()` function and a deconstructor to terminate a connection, all of which can be included in the class library.

Additionally, you may need multiple input parameters for your functoid. Additional parameters can be added very easily. See Listing 3-21 for an example of a functoid with three input parameters.

Listing 3-21. Multiple Input Parameters for a Custom Functoid

```
SEE CODE FROM Listing 3-20.

// three parameters in, one parameter out
this.SetMinParams(3);
this.SetMaxParams(3);

...

// add one of the following lines of code for every input
// parameter. All lines would be identical.
AddInputConnectionType(ConnectionType.All); // input parameter 1
```

```
AddInputConnectionType(ConnectionType.All); // input parameter 2
AddInputConnectionType(ConnectionType.All); // input parameter 3

}

// Actual function which does the replacement of symbols
public string EncodeChars(String strInputValue, strReplace1, strReplace2)
{
strInputValue = strInputValue.Replace("&",strReplace1);
strInputValue = strInputValue.Replace("<",strReplace2);

return strInputValue;
}
```

3-15. Using the Date and Time Functoids
Problem

You are mapping a message in BizTalk Server and need to manipulate date and time fields. Specifically, you must use the current date in order to determine a required date and time in the future, which is added to the outbound message during mapping. Additionally, you must apply the processing time for each document during mapping.

Solution

Within a map, use the Date and Time functoids provided with BizTalk Server. To apply the current processing time to the outbound document within the map, take the following steps:

1. Click the toolbox, and then click the Date and Time Functoids tab. On the map surface, in between the source and destination schemas, drag and drop a Date and Time functoid. Since this functoid simply outputs the current date and time, it requires no input values.

2. Connect the right side of the Date and Time functoid to the element in the destination schema containing the date and time the message is processed.

To determine a future date based on the current date, take the following steps:

1. Drag and drop a Date functoid from the Date and Time Functoids tab of the toolbox onto the map surface. This functoid is similar to the Date and Time functoid but returns only the current date, as opposed to the current date and time. It also requires no input values.

2. Drag and drop an Add Days functoid from the Date and Time Functoids tab onto the map surface, positioning it to the right of the Date functoid. This functoid accepts two input parameters: a date or datetime value, and a numeric value indicating the number of days to add to the date supplied in the first input parameter. The return value is the date with the specified amount of days added.

3. Connect the right side of the Date functoid to the Add Days functoid.

4. Specify the second input parameter for the Add Days functoid as a constant with a value of 1.

5. Connect the right side of the Add Days functoid to the element in the destination schema containing the future date.

How It Works

An example of a map that uses the Date and Time functoids is shown in Figure 3-40.

Figure 3-40. *Using the Date and Time Functoids*

This example captures the current date and time in the `TransactionProcessingDateTime` element, which is supplied by the Date and Time functoid. The format of the date and time produced by the Date and Time functoid is YYYY-MM-DDThh:mm:ss, which is ISO 8601-compliant. The time values are notated in 24-hour format.

The future date that the deposited funds will be available is captured in the `FundsAvailableDateTime` element. This value is based off the current date, supplied by the Date functoid, with a single day added to it to provide tomorrow's date, which is supplied by the Add Days functoid. The format of the Date functoid's output is YYYY-MM-DD, while the Add Days functoid accepts dates formatted as YYYY-MM-DD or YYYY-MM-DDThh:mm:ss. The format of the Add Days functoid's output is YYYY-MM-DD. All date formats used by these two functoids are ISO 8601–compliant. The time values are notated in 24-hour format.

The XML in Listing 3-22 represents one possible instance of the source schema.

Listing 3-22. Sample Source Instance for the Date/Time Functoid Example

```
<ns0:ATMDeposit xmlns:ns0="http:// DateTimeFunctoids.ATMDeposit">
  <ATMNumber>00111</ATMNumber>
  <AccountNumber>123456</AccountNumber>
  <Amount>100.00</Amount>
  <Currency>USD</Currency>
</ns0:ATMDeposit>
```

When passed to the map in Figure 3-40, this XML message will produce the outbound XML document shown in Listing 3-23.

Listing 3-23. Sample Output Instance for the Date/Time Functoid Example

```
<ns0:BankDeposit xmlns:ns0="http://Mapping.BankDeposit">
  <TransactionSourceNumber>00111</TransactionSourceNumber>
  <Account>123456</Account>
  <Amount>100.00</Amount>
  <Currency>USD</Currency>
  <TransactionProcessingDateTime>2010-09-06T16:32:05</TransactionProcessingDateTime>
  <FundsAvailableDateTime>2010-09-07</FundsAvailableDateTime>
</ns0:BankDeposit>
```

The Date and Time functoids provide a baseline set of functionality when needing to interrogate and manipulate date and time values. In the bank account example, the Date and Time functoid provides the current date and time, allowing a timestamp to be applied to the outbound document, indicating the time that the message was processed. Often, messages include an element or elements detailing the time that the message pertains to, or the time at which a message was created. The Date and Time functoid is useful when the actual processing time (in this example, the time a deposit is processed within a bank's integration system) is required, which will likely be different from any time value embedded in the source document. The difference between date and time values within a source instance message and the actual processing time of the message can be particularly important when dealing with batched or time-delayed processes.

This example also shows how you can use the Date and Add Days functoids in conjunction to calculate a future date based on the day a message is processed. The current date is provided by the Date functoid, which is used by the Add Days functoid to come up with a date that is a specified number of days in the future. In the bank account scenario, this functionality is used to determine the day on which deposited funds are available. Business rules like this can be common among financial institutions, as validation procedures are often required when dealing with monetary transactions.

■ **Note** You can also use a negative numeric value with the Add Days functoid, resulting in a date that is the specified number of days in the past. For this example, the Date and Time functoid (substituting for the Date functoid) could have been used as the first input parameter for the Add Days function, and the map would be functionally equivalent. This is due to the fact that the Add Days functoid can accept either date or datetime values, and in either case, produces only a value indicating a date (excluding a time element).

This bank account example can be extended to illustrate how the Time functoid can be used to add a time component to the data capturing the date at which deposited funds are available. Currently, the example simply calculates a date for this value, but it is likely that a financial institution would additionally need to know the time at which deposited funds should be made available for use. Since the Add Days functoid produces only date values (without a time component), you must use a Time functoid, in addition to a String Concatenate functoid. To implement this enhancement, take the following steps:

1. On the mapping grid, in between the source and destination schemas, drag and drop a Time functoid. Since this functoid simply outputs the current time, it requires no input values.

2. Drag and drop a String Concatenate functoid onto the mapping grid. This functoid allows multiple string values to be concatenated, or added, together.

3. Delete the current connection between the Add Days functoid and the element in the destination schema containing the future date that the deposited funds will be available in the bank account.

4. Connect the right side of the Add Days functoid to the String Concatenate functoid.

5. Specify the second input parameter for the String Concatenate functoid as a constant, with a value of T. This value is required in between the date and time portions of a datetime value for ISO 8601–compliant values.

6. Connect the right side of the Time functoid to the String Concatenate functoid. The String Concatenate functoid should look like Figure 3-41.

	Name	Value	Type
✓	Input[0]	Add Days	
✓	Input[1]	T	
✓	Input[2]	Time	

This functoid must have between 1 and 100 input parameter(s).

Figure 3-41. *The String Concatenate functoid with time values*

7. Connect the right side of the String Concatenate functoid to the element in the destination schema containing the future date that the deposited funds will be available in the bank account.

Figure 3-42 shows an example of a map implementing these changes.

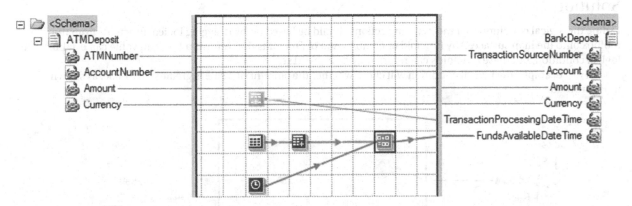

Figure 3-42. *Using the Time functoid*

Based on the same source XML used in the preceding example, the map in Figure 3-42 will produce the XML document shown in Listing 3-24, with a time component included in the FundsAvailableDateTime element.

Listing 3-24. Sample Output Instance for the Time Functoid Example

```
<ns0:BankDeposit xmlns:ns0="http://Mapping.BankDeposit">
  <TransactionSourceNumber>00111</TransactionSourceNumber>
  <Account>123456</Account>
  <Amount>100.00</Amount>
  <Currency>USD</Currency>
  <TransactionProcessingDateTime>2010-09-06T16:32:04</TransactionProcessingDateTime>
  <FundsAvailableDateTime>2010-09-07T16:32:05</FundsAvailableDateTime>
</ns0:BankDeposit>
```

One common challenge when dealing with datetime values is standardizing on a common format. This issue can be seen with dates adhering to the MM-DD-YYYY (common in the United States) or DD-MM-YYYY (common in Europe and other areas) format. Unfortunately, BizTalk Server does not have any Date and Time functoids that do complex datetime formatting. There are a number of ways to handle this issue. The simplest way is to use string functoids provided with BizTalk Server to manipulate and standardize the order of year, month, and day values. Specifically, you can use String Extract functoids to pull out values within a date (in this scenario, you would pull out the DD, MM, and YYYY values in three separate String Extract functoids), and then a String Concatenate functoid to combine the individual values in the correct format (in this scenario, you would append the three values in an order of YYYY-MM-DD).

There are also more robust ways of implementing complex date/time formatting. One option is to use the Scripting functoid, which provides access to the libraries of C#, VB .NET, and JScript .NET (either via inline code embedded in the map, or by referencing external assemblies written in one of the .NET-compliant languages). Additionally, you could use a custom functoid (which would leverage the datetime functionality of a .NET language).

3-16. Creating Functoid If-Then-Else Logic

Problem

You need to map values from the source to the destination message depending on whether a logical condition evaluates to true or false.

Solution

Define the logical condition that the mapping actions should be based on by dragging logical functoids from the toolbox onto the map surface. Any functoid or combination of functoids that returns a Boolean value can establish the logical condition, but these functoids can return only true or false.

In this example, the logical condition will check whether the amount of a sale is greater that 1,000, as shown in Figure 3-43.

Figure 3-43. *Creating the logical operator*

Only large sales should appear under the <BigSales> element in the destination message, so the logical condition will check if the Amount in the source message is greater than 1,000. The following steps define the logical operation that determines mapping actions, as shown in Figure 3-44.

	Name	Value	Type
✓	Condition1	Amount	
✓	Condition2	1000	

Add/delete/reorder functoid inputs

This functoid must have exactly 2 input parameter(s).

Figure 3-44. Defining the comparison value

1. Drag a Greater Than functoid from the Logical Functoids tab of the toolbox onto the map surface.

2. Select the Amount field of the input message. Drag the cursor over the Greater Than functoid while pressing the mouse button to establish the first comparison value.

3. Right-click the functoid on the map surface, and select Properties.

4. In the Properties window, click the Input Parameters field, and select the ellipsis that appears.

5. Define the constant value in the Configure Functoid Inputs dialog box.

Next, define the mapping actions that depend on the evaluation of the logical condition. In this example, the contents of the <Sales> elements should map to different parts of the destination message, so the map must use the Boolean outcome of the logical comparison as input to a Value Mapping functoid.

1. Drag a Value Mapping functoid from the Advanced Functoids tab of the toolbox to the right and below the Greater Than functoid.

2. Create a link from the Greater Than functoid to the Value Mapping functoid.

3. Create a link from the Amount field of the input message to the Value Mapping functoid to determine the value mapped when the logical condition is true.

4. Create a link from the Value Mapping functoid to the SaleAmount field appearing under the BigSales record to define where the large value will occur in the destination message.

The Value Mapping functoid defines the action the map should take when the logical condition evaluates to true. Both the amount of the big sale and the name of the sales representative must appear in the destination message in this example, so the map must use two Value Mapping functoids, as shown in Figure 3-45.

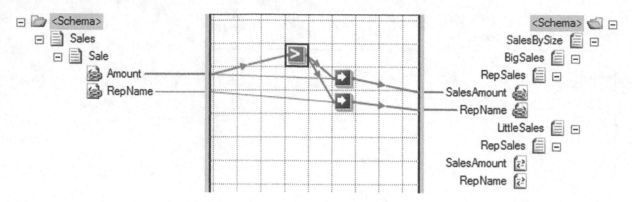

Figure 3-45. *Defining conditional mapping actions*

BizTalk must also know that it should create only the <RepSales> element in the destination message when the amount is greater that 1,000. Establishing a link from the logical operator to the RepSales element will ensure that BizTalk creates this parent to the actual values mapped.

When the logical condition evaluates to false, BizTalk should map the sale to the <SmallSales> part of the destination message. The map can check this directly by placing a Not Equal functoid on the mapping surface and comparing to the result of the logical comparison established earlier with a constant value equal to true, as shown in Figure 3-46.

	Name	Value	Type
✓	Condition1	Greater Than	>
✓	Condition2	true	⬛

Add/delete/reorder functoid inputs

This functoid must have exactly 2 input parameter(s).

Figure 3-46. *Defining the else condition*

Finally, define the mapping actions that BizTalk should take when the logical comparison is not true. In this example, the Value Mapping functoids simply need to map under the <SmallSales> element in the destination message.

1. Drag a Value Mapping functoid onto the map surface.

2. Create a link from the Not Equal functoid that represents the else case to the Value Mapping functoid.

3. Create a link from the Amount field of the source message to the Value Mapping functoid.

4. Create a link from the Value Mapping functoid to the SaleAmount field appearing under the SmallSales record to define where the small value will occur in the destination message, as shown in Figure 3-47.

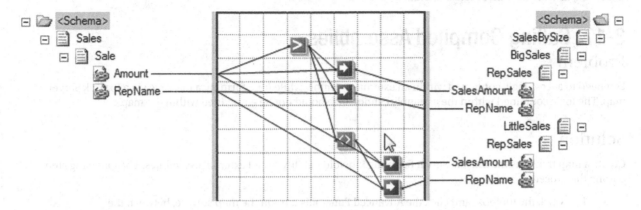

Figure 3-47. *Completed If-Then-Else map*

How It Works

Working with the BizTalk Mapper can be an unfamiliar process, even to experienced programmers. Business rules defined in source code can be procedural and explicit, but the graphical depiction of a BizTalk map can abstract the runtime behavior.

The link to the logical condition defines the information on which the map will perform the logical operation. BizTalk will evaluate the logical condition for each occurrence of the information in the source message, and remember the context of the logical condition when performing the output actions dependent on it. This means that the Value Mapping functoid will automatically know the right Amount and RepName values to map when the map executes.

The order of the Value Mapping functoid inputs is critical. The first input parameter must be either true or false. The second input parameter specifies the value that the functoid will return when the first parameter is true. While the order is established based on the order in which the inputs are connected to the Value Mapping functoid, sometimes the order can get mixed up when modifying the functoid links. There is no indication of the input parameter order on the mapping surface, but fortunately, it is easy to check. Open the Configure Functoid Inputs window, and the Boolean value should appear first in the list. Modify the order here by selecting one of the input parameters and clicking the up and down arrows.

■ **Note** In many cases, If-Then-Else logic using functoids like this can becoming complex and frustrating to implement (and maintain!). The best approach frequently is to use an Advanced Scripting functoid with either XSLT or C# to implement the logic.

This example establishes a logical condition and defines mutually exclusive mapping actions that are directly determined from the evaluation of the logical conditions. Alternatively, a map can define separate logical conditions independently. With this alternative approach, the developer must carefully define the logical conditions to ensure that every input message will map to some outcome, and never both. This becomes an increasingly important consideration as the logical comparison becomes more and more complex.

When there are more than two mutually exclusive outcomes, the Not Equal functoid in this example can be combined with additional logical comparisons by linking its result to the Logical AND functoid. The result of the Logical AND functoid also evaluates to true or false, and the developer can define actions to take based on this result, as with any other logical operator.

3-17. Calling Compiled Assemblies

Problem

You need to access logic contained within an external assembly while transforming a message via a BizTalk Server map. The logic contained within the assembly cannot and should not be embedded within the map.

Solution

Create a map that uses the BizTalk Server Scripting functoid's ability to call external assemblies. The following steps outline the procedure:

1. Click the toolbox, and click the Advanced Functoids tab. On the map surface, between the source and destination schemas, drag and drop a Scripting functoid. This functoid's input and output values are dependent on the logic contained within the Scripting functoid.

2. Connect the left side of the Scripting functoid to the appropriate source data elements or records. In this solution, no source data elements are used.

3. Configure the Scripting functoid.

   a. While the Scripting functoid is highlighted on the mapping grid, right-click the functoid, and select Configure Functoid Inputs.

   b. In the Configure Scripting Functoid dialog box, on the Script Functoid Configuration tab, select External Assembly for Script Type and the appropriate assembly, class, and method for Script Assembly, Script Class, and Script Method, as shown in Figure 3-48. Then click OK.

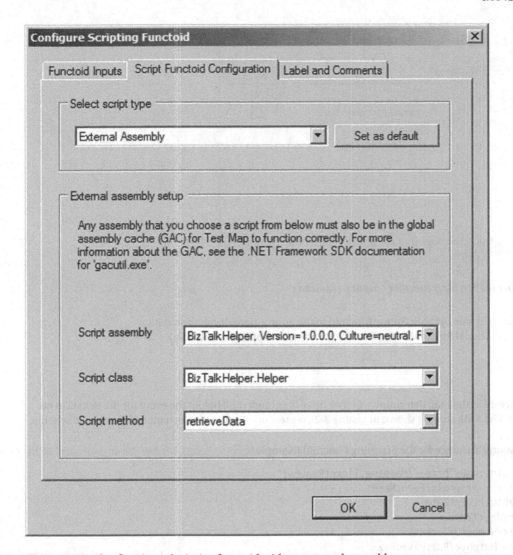

Figure 3-48. Configuring a Scripting functoid with an external assembly

■ **Note**   You must add a reference to the external assembly to the Visual Studio project containing the map for it to be available in the Configure Functoid Script dialog box. The external assembly must also be placed in the GAC.

    c.   To pass in a parameter, click the ellipsis to the right of Input Parameters in the Properties window.

    d.   In the Configure Functoid Inputs dialog box, on the Functoid Inputs tab, create or order the appropriate input parameters for the method specified in step 2, as shown in Figure 3-49, and then click OK.

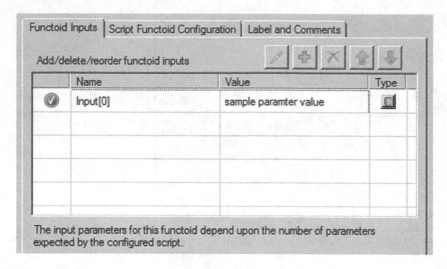

Figure 3-49. *Configuring the Scripting functoid's input parameters*

4. Connect the right side of the Scripting functoid to the appropriate destination data element or additional functoid (if further logic needs to be applied to the data).

How It Works

In this example, the functoid in the map determine whether there is enough time before the event for the tickets to be mailed to the purchaser. The XML snippet shown in Listing 3-25 represents one possible instance of the source schema.

Listing 3-25. *Sample Source Instance for the Scripting Functoid Example*

```
<nsO:TicketRequest xmlns:nsO="http://Mapping.TicketRequest">
  <EventName>Chelsea vs. Arsenal</EventName>
  <EventDate>08/06/2010</EventDate>
  <Venue>Stamford Bridge</Venue>
  <NumberOfTickets>2</NumberOfTickets>
  <PurchasedBy>George Murphy</PurchasedBy>
  <MailTicketFlag>True</MailTicketFlag>
</nsO:TicketRequest>
```

Based on this source XML, the map will produce the XML document (assuming that the current date is prior to August 4, 2010) shown in Listing 3-26, with the MailedTicketFlag appropriately set.

Listing 3-26. *Sample Output Instance for the Scripting Functoid Example*

```
<nsO:TicketOrder xmlns:nsO="http://Mapping.TicketOrder">
  <Title>Chelsea vs. Arsenal</Title>
  <Date>08/06/2010</Date>
  <Venue>Stamford Bridge</Venue>
  <NumOfTickets>2</NumOfTickets>
  <TicketHolder>George Murphy</TicketHolder>
  <MailedTicketFlag>True</MailedTicketFlag>
</nsO:TicketOrder>
```

This example demonstrates one of the many reasons why external assemblies may need to be called from a BizTalk Server map. Here, the external assembly provides access to a configuration value. This value is held in a configuration file (but alternatively could be held in a database or other data store), which is updated over time by system administrators and business analysts. For the purposes of this example, the following configuration value was used.

```
<add key="MinimumDaysAdvanceForMailedTickets" value="-2" />
```

The value of -2, which represents the minimum number of days required to mail tickets to a purchaser, is added to the EventDate element (by the Add Days functoid), resulting in a date value two days prior to the event (08/04/2006 in this example). The current date (supplied by the Date functoid) is then compared to the calculated date value (by the Less Than logical functoid) to determine if there is enough time to mail the purchased tickets. Finally, if there is ample time to mail the tickets, and the source document indicates the purchaser requested tickets to be mailed, the MailedTicketFlag element in the destination message is set to true.

The benefit of having the MinimumDaysAdvanceForMailedTickets value stored in a file external to BizTalk, as opposed to being hard-coded within the actual map, is that a change to the value does not require a redeployment of BizTalk Server artifacts for the modification to be applied. Additionally, by encapsulating the custom logic in an external assembly, any changes to that logic will require only that the external assembly is rebuilt and redeployed to the GAC. No changes to the BizTalk Server environment (aside from a BizTalk service restart to immediately apply the changes in the redeployed custom assembly) are required. Implementing this logic in an external assembly has the additional benefits of allowing reuse of the logic, minimizing code maintenance, and providing access to the debugging utilities within Visual Studio.

■ **Note**   You can step into the external assembly in debug mode by running the external assembly solution in Visual Studio in debug mode, attaching to the process of the Visual Studio solution containing the BizTalk Server map, and testing the map.

In addition to using a generic external assembly, a custom functoid could also have been used to implement the configuration value retrieval logic. It is important to consider the differences between the two options prior to selecting your design. The main benefit of using a custom functoid is that the assembly is hosted within the BizTalk Server environment. The actual assembly file is located within the BizTalk Server program file directory, and the functoid can be added to the Functoid Toolbox within the development environment. Using generic external assemblies is sometimes a requirement, however, such as when the existing logic contained within them needs to be accessed directly (without modification to the source code or assembly location). This may be the case when using third-party or proprietary assemblies, where you do not have access to the source code.

Other common examples of logic contained in external assemblies are complex database-retrieval mechanisms, calculations above and beyond what is possible with the out-of-the-box mathematical functoids, and complex date and string formatting.

■ **Caution**   Care should be taken with regard to data types for values passed into and out of external assemblies. For example, if a source document element having a data type of xs:int is used as an input parameter for a method contained in an external assembly, it will be passed as an integer. Likewise, if the output from an external assembly is used to populate a destination document element having a data type of xs:int, it should be returned as an integer.

3-18. Using Inline C#

Problem

You are mapping a message in BizTalk Server and must implement custom logic via an inline C# code snippet. The custom logic should be embedded within the map.

Solution

Create a map that uses the BizTalk Server Scripting functoid's ability to call inline C#. The following steps outline the procedure:

1. Click the toolbox, and click the Advanced Functoids tab. On the map surface, between the source and destination schemas, drag and drop a Scripting functoid. This functoid's input and output values are dependent on the logic contained within the Scripting functoid.

2. Connect the left side of the Scripting functoid to the appropriate source data elements or records. This specifies the order and location of the Scripting functoid's input parameters.

3. Configure the Scripting functoid.

   a. While the Scripting functoid is highlighted on the mapping grid, click the ellipsis to the right of the `FunctoidScript` item in the Properties window.

   b. In the Configure Scripting Functoid dialog box, on the Script Functoid Configuration tab, select Inline C# for Script Type and enter your custom C# logic in the Inline Script Buffer text box, as shown in Figure 3-50 (the code for this is shown in Listing 3-27. Then click OK.

Figure 3-50. *Configuring a Script functoid to call inline C#*

■ **Note** You can import tested C# code from a file by clicking the Import from file button.

Listing 3-27. Inline C# Code

```
string EUDateTimeFormat = "dd/MM/yyyy HH:mm:ss";
string EUDateFormat = "dd/MM/yyyy";

public string UStoEUDateFormatter(string USDate)
{
 return Convert.ToDateTime(USDate).ToString(EUDateFormat);
}
```

c. Drag the appropriate source field and drop it on the left-hand side of the Scripting functoid (as the input parameter).

d. In the Configure Functoid Inputs dialog box, create or order the appropriate input parameters for the method specified in step 2, and then click OK.

e. Connect the right side of the Scripting functoid to the appropriate destination data element or additional functoid (if further logic needs to be applied to the data).

How It Works

An example of a map that uses the BizTalk Server Scripting functoid's ability to call inline C# is shown in Figure 3-51.

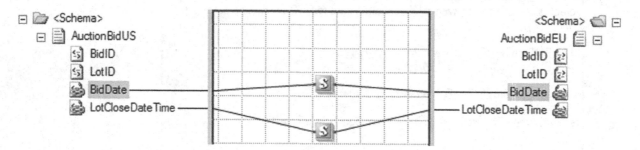

Figure 3-51. *Using the Scripting functoid to call inline C#*

In this example, auction bids from the United States are transformed into European Union (EU) bids. The Scripting functoids used in the map format the date and datetime values common in the United States to those that are common in the EU. The XML snippet in Listing 3-28 represents one possible instance of the source schema.

Listing 3-28. Sample Source Instance for the Inline C# Example

```
<ns0:AuctionBidUS xmlns:ns0="http://Mapping.AuctionBidUS">
  <BidID>12345</BidID>
  <LotID>123-456</LotID>
  <BidDate>09/25/2010</BidDate>
  <LotCloseDateTime>09/18/2010 23:59:59</LotCloseDateTime>
</ns0:AuctionBidUS>
```

Based on this XML snippet, the map displayed will produce the XML document shown in Listing 3-29. Notice that the format of the BidDate and LotClosedDateTime values have been changed from MM/DD/YYYY and MM/DD/YYYY hh:mm:ss format to DD/MM/YYYY and DD/MM/YYYY hh:mm:ss format, respectively.

Listing 3-29. Sample Output Instance for the Inline C# Example

```
<ns0:AuctionBidEU xmlns:ns0="http://Mapping.AuctionBidEU">
  <BidID>12345</BidID>
  <LotID>123-456</LotID>
  <BidDate>25/09/2010</BidDate>
  <LotCloseDateTime>18/09/2010 23:59:59</LotCloseDateTime>
</ns0:AuctionBidEU>
```

Date formatting like this is one of countless examples where custom logic could be needed within a BizTalk Server map. In the auction bid example, date and datetime values were formatted with inline C# to account for regional differences. Additionally, in the first Scripting functoid, two variables were defined that specify the date and datetime format for the EU. This illustrates another helpful use of Scripting functoids: the ability to create global variables that can be used by any other functoid within the map. In the example, the `UStoEUDateFormatter` method in the second Scripting functoid referenced the `EUDateTimeFormat` variable that was defined in the first Scripting functoid.

■ **Note**   All methods defined in inline Scripting functoids should have unique names. This is important to avoid naming conflicts, as all inline script is embedded within the map inside CDATA tags.

You can format dates in a number of different ways within a BizTalk Server map. In our example, we used inline C#, but we could have used either of the other available script languages (VB .NET or JScript .NET), an external assembly, or a custom functoid.

■ **Note**   You can reuse methods within other Scripting functoids by calling them just like you would as if they were being called in standard .NET. There is no need to copy and paste the methods with the exact same code and a different name. You can simply declare them as public and then call them from other Scripting functoids.

Inline scripting is a good option when a simple implementation of custom logic is needed, and the logic is unlikely to be leveraged outside the map. It is important to recognize a key limitation of inline scripting: debugging utilities. Because the inline script is embedded into the map's XSLT, stepping into the code at runtime is not possible. One possible way to allow easier debugging of an inline script is to first create and test it in a separate executable or harness. This will allow you to use the robust debugging utilities of Visual Studio. Once the code has been fully tested, it can be placed into a Scripting functoid.

The fact that the inline script is saved in the XSLT of the map has another important consequence: only those libraries available to XSLT style sheet scripts may be leveraged. The following are available namespaces:

- `System`: The system class

- `System.Collection`: The collection classes

- `System.Text`: The text classes

- `System.Text.RegularExpressions`: The regular expression classes

- `System.Xml`: The XML classes

- `System.Xml.Xsl`: The XSLT classes

- `System.Xml.Xpath`: The XPath classes

- `Microsoft.VisualBasic`: The Visual Basic script classes

3-19. Passing Orchestration Variables into Maps

Problem

You need to include information from variables in an orchestration in the destination message of a BizTalk mapping.

Solution

Begin by creating a new message schema with fields for capturing the information from the orchestration, as shown in Figure 3-52. The information from the orchestration variables must be set in a separate message from the input message, referred to here as a *context message*. In this recipe, the mapping will transform a customer purchase message for the customer support department, and the orchestration will define the support information with the business process. BizTalk will use the new message schema to capture the support information.

Figure 3-52. *Defining the context message schema*

Follow these steps to set up the orchestration.

1. To access the fields of this message easily from within the orchestration, define them as distinguished fields. Right-click the context message schema tree, and select Promote ➤ Show Promotions. In the Promote Properties dialog box, select each field in the left window, and click the Add button, as shown in Figure 3-53. Then click OK.

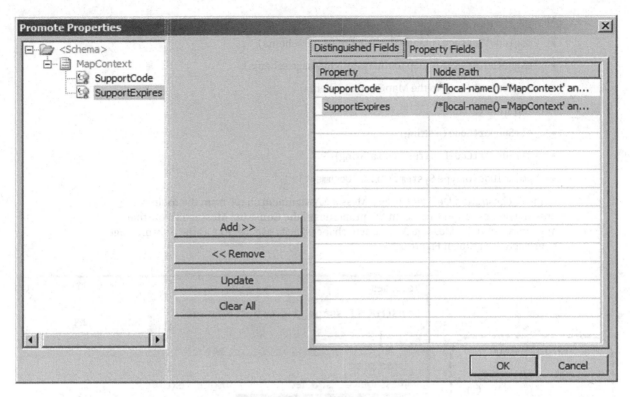

Figure 3-53. *Designating the distinguished fields*

2. Define the following orchestration properties on the Orchestration View tab (see Figure 3-54):

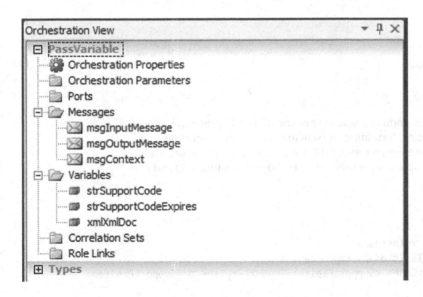

Figure 3-54. *The orchestration messages and variables*

- Messages

  - msgInputMessage (map to the Input message schema)

  - msgOutputMessage (map to the Output message schema)

  - msgContext (map to the MapContext schema)

- Orchestration variables

  - strSupportCode (a string)

  - strSupportCodeExpires (also a string)

  - xmlXmlDoc (of type System.Xml.XmlDocument)

3. In the Orchestration Designer, drag a Message Assignment shape from the toolbox onto the orchestration surface. In the properties of the Construct Message shape that appears around the Message Assignment shape, specify msgContext as the only message constructed, as shown Figure 3-55.

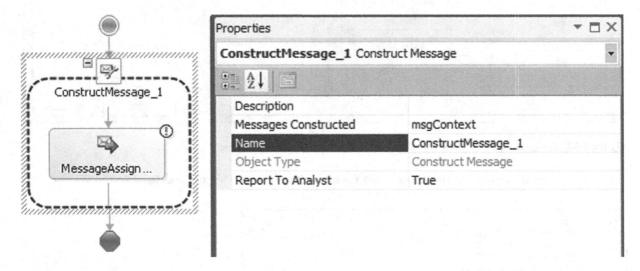

Figure 3-55. *The Construct Message*

4. Double-click the Message Assignment shape to open the BizTalk Expression Editor window. Load an XML string conforming to the schema of the context message into the xmlXmlDoc variable. Then create the msgContext message by assigning the loaded XmlDocument variable to it. This example uses the code shown in Listing 3-30 and in Figure 3-56.

Listing 3-30. Build the Context Message

```
xmlXmlDoc.LoadXml("<ns0:MapContext xmlns:ns0=
'http://PassingOrchestrationVariablesIntoMaps.MapContext'>
<SupportCode>SupportCode_0</SupportCode> <SupportExpires>SupportExpires_0</SupportExpires>
</ns0:MapContext>");

msgContext = xmlXmlDoc;
```

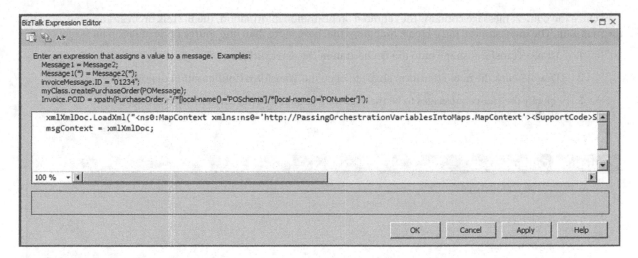

Figure 3-56. *The Message Assignment*

■ **Note**   Obtain a sample XML string by right-clicking the schema in the Solution Explorer and selecting Generate Instance. Copy and paste this into the LoadXml method.

Once instantiated, the values in MapContextMsg can be set anywhere in the orchestration. For simplicity in this example, they are created and set in the same Message Assignment shape, and the expiration is the same day that the context message is created, as shown in Listing 3-31 and Figure 3-57.

Listing 3-31. Set the Values in the Orchestration

```
msgContext.SupportCode = "R-2";
msgContext.SupportExpires = System.DateTime.Now.ToString("yyyy-MM-dd");
```

```
xmlXmlDoc.LoadXml("<ns0:MapContext xmlns:ns0='http://PassingOrchestrat
msgContext = xmlXmlDoc;

msgContext.
                    ♦ SupportCode        distinguished-field System.String SupportCode
00 %    ▾ ◀        ♦ SupportExpires
```

Figure 3-57. *Setting the values of the context message*

Once the context message contains the required orchestration information, the BizTalk orchestration must create the mapping. The orchestration must create mappings that have more than one source or destination message.

1. Drag a Transform shape onto the Orchestration Designer surface.

2. Double-click the new Transform shape to open the Transform Configuration dialog box.

3. Specify the source messages to be the msgInputMessage and MapContextMsg messages, as shown in Figure 3-58.

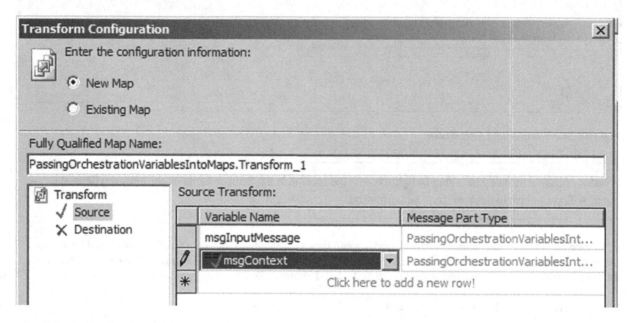

Figure 3-58. *Configuring map source messages*

4. Specify msgOutputMessage for the destination message, and then click OK.

BizTalk will generate a new transformation with two input messages and one output message. One of the input messages will be the MapContextMsg message containing the values from the orchestration. The developer can choose to either drive mapping logic from these values or map them directly to the destination message as in this example, as shown in Figure 3-59.

Figure 3-59. *Defining mapping logic from the source messages*

■ **Caution** BizTalk may not be able to recognize the second schema if the project name begins with a number.

How It Works

BizTalk developers often think about translation among message types when defining integration processes in an orchestration. They can place a Transform shape directly within an orchestration to transform a message into different formats, so it seems that the transformation and orchestration are integral to each other. However, the BizTalk mapper cannot directly access the contextual information of the business process and the logic existing in the orchestration.

The BizTalk Mapper can natively access many resources outside the map with the default functoids. For example, the Database Lookup functoid can access records in a database, and the Scripting functoid can invoke an external assembly. However, the most direct way to access information about the context of the business process is by creating a message specifically for capturing the state of the business process. Add the information required in the mapping to this additional message, and then add the context message as an additional input message to the map.

The possible reasons for passing information from an orchestration into a mapping with a second message are as varied as the capabilities of BizTalk orchestrations. However, in all cases, the mapping destination message must contain information that cannot or should not be added to the schema of the input message. Here are some examples:

- A standards body such as RosettaNet sets the source message schema, and it should not change.

- The mapping must access message context properties. A map cannot access these values. For example, if the SMTP adapter is used, an orchestration can access the sender with the SMTP.From property but not directly from the BizTalk Mapper. The destination message may need this information.

- The mapping must include information about the business process that is not known until runtime and is required in the orchestration. Rather than duplicating the logical definitions, define each definition once within the orchestration and pass the information to the mapping.

- BizTalk must be capable of modifying the mapped values without redeploying the BizTalk artifacts. For example, the BizTalk rules engine can be easily invoked from within an orchestration and facilitates additional capabilities like rule versioning and seamless deployment.

3-20. Using Inline XSLT

Problem

You need to map an incoming document with a node containing a document that matches exactly the destination schema. All of the nodes in the source document need to be mapped in their entirety to the destination document. Both the source and the destination schemas have target namespaces, and the namespaces must be preserved.

Solution

By using inline XSLT within a Scripting functoid, you can create the target document with the appropriate nodes and the correct namespace. Listing 3-32 shows a sample input document.

Listing 3-32. Sample Input Document for the Inline XSLT Example

```
<nsO:SampleSource xmlns:nsO="http://Sample.Source">
  <ID>ID_0</ID>
  <Payload>
    <SampleDestination>
      <Name>Name_0</Name>
      <Address>Address_0</Address>
      <Company>Company_0</Company>
    </SampleDestination>
  </Payload>
</nsO:SampleSource>
```

The inline XSLT is written to parse the incoming document as a whole; there is no need to have an input to the Scripting functoid. The output of the Scripting functoid occurs under the node that the output is tied to—in this case, the XSLT output will be directly below the SampleDestination element. When XML documents contain namespaces, use the local-name() qualifier to reference a specific node by name. Because of the requirement that the namespaces be preserved, it is necessary to copy each of the nodes in the source document's Payload node (which consists of an Any element that can contain any XML structure) separately to the destination document.

Figure 3-60 shows the configuration for the Scripting functoid with the inline XSLT for the <Name> element. Additional nodes (such as Address and Company) can be added using the same code pattern. See Listing 3-33 for the XSLT code.

Listing 3-33. XSLT Code

```
<xsl:if test="//*[local-name()='SampleDestination'])/*[local-name()='Name']">
 <xsl:element name="Name">
 <xsl:value-of select="//*[local-name()='SampleDestination']/*[local-name()='Name']"/>
</xsl:element>
</xsl:if>
```

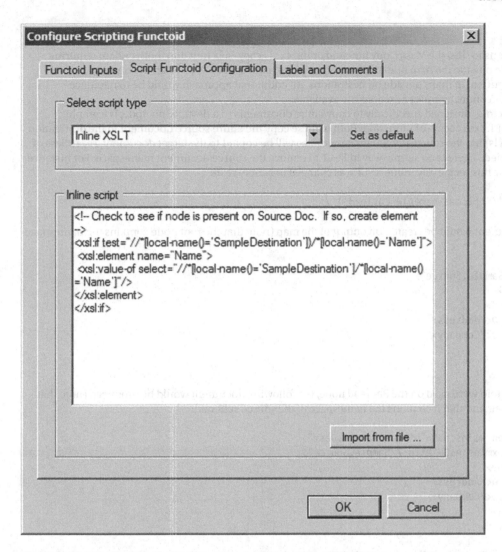

Figure 3-60. *Configuring the Scripting functoid to use inline XSLT*

This XSLT script will produce the desired XML document on output, as shown in Listing 3-34.

Listing 3-34. Sample Output Document for the Inline XSLT Example

```
<ns0:SampleDestination xmlns:ns0="http://Sample.Dest">
  <Name>Name_0</Name>
  <Address>Address_0</Address>
  <Company>Company_0</Company>
</ns0:SampleDestination>
```

How It Works

The two expected solutions to this, the Mass Copy functoid or the `<xsl:copy-of>` function, both end up requiring additional logic and code outside the map due to the presence of the namespaces. These can be solved in orchestration mapping but not in maps outside orchestrations. An additional approach would be to reference an external XSLT file where more complex functions are available.

The Mass Copy functoid, designed specifically to copy entire documents to a destination node, is a graphic representation of the XSLT `<xsl:copy-of>` function. Both of these copy the entire source document to the destination document. The problem is that the source document namespace will be copied to the target document, regardless of the node level being copied. There is no simple way in XSLT to remove the source document namespace. For instance, if in the given solution for this recipe, the inline XSLT was changed to simply read:

```
<xsl:copy-of select="//*[local-name()='Payload']"/>
```

The following document would be created on output of the map (note that the root node contains the namespace of the source schema):

```
<Payload xmlns:ns0="Sample.Source">
  <SampleDestination>
    <Name>Name_0</Name>
    <Address>Address_0</Address>
    <Company>Company_0</Company>
  </SampleDestination>
</Payload>
```

If a Mass Copy functoid were used on the `Payload` node, the following document would be produced (note that the root node repeats itself and that it contains the namespace of the source schema):

```
<ns0:SampleDestination xmlns:ns0="http://Sample.Dest">
  <SampleDestination xmlns:ns0="http://Sample.Source">
    <Name>Name_0</Name>
    <Address>Address_0</Address>
    <Company>Company_0</Company>
  </SampleDestination>
</ns0:SampleDestination>
```

The output document for both of these approaches is not the desired outcome. However, if the mapping is being done in an orchestration, the output document will be in a message that can now be accessed and corrected in a Message Assignment shape, using the code in Listing 3-35.

Listing 3-35. Message Assignment

```
// xmlDoc is a variable of type System.Xml.XmlDocument()
// msgSampleDestination contains the output of the map

// xpath will access the contents of the SampleDestination node
xmlDoc = xpath(msgSampleDestination, "/*/*");

// populate the message
msgSampleDestination = xmlDoc;
```

Another option would be to move the entire solution to an external XSLT document, where more complex functions such as templates are available, and reference it in the map directly rather than using the mapping functions. This can be done by selecting properties on the map being developed and indicating the path to the XSLT file in the Custom XSLT Path property.

■ **Note**   One of the greatest skills in BizTalk mapping is becoming proficient with XSLT. Functoids are great, but knowing how to code is even better! Do yourself a favor and learn how to apply Inline XSLT scripting to your maps. You will be astounded at how much easier it is to write a map that is intelligent and maintainable.

In summary, a number of approaches can be taken to map an incoming document with a node containing a document that matches exactly the destination schema. The cleanest and most viable approach is described in this recipe's solution. Quicker and more convoluted solutions involve using the Mass Copy functoid and <xsl:copy-of> function. An additional approach is to move the mapping completely out of the map into a separate XSLT document. The appropriate solution must be decided by the developer.

3-21. Using XSLT Call Templates
Problem

You want to use the inline XSLT call template functionality within the Scripting functoid and understand the difference between inline XSLT and an inline XSLT call template.

Solution

Use the following steps to add an Inline XSLT Call Template functoid call to a map. The steps assume the schemas shown in the map in Figure 3-61 are being used.

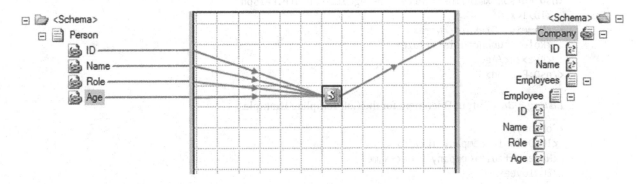

Figure 3-61. *Scripting/XSLT call template in a map*

1. Click the toolbox, and then click the Advanced Functoids tab. Drop a Scripting functoid onto the map surface.

2. While the Scripting functoid is highlighted on the mapping grid, click the ellipsis to the right of the FunctoidScript item in the Properties window. In the Configure Scripting Functoid dialog box, on the Script Functoid Configuration tab, select Inline XSLT Call Template for Script Type, place the code shown in Listing 3-36 into the Inline Script Buffer text box, and then click OK.

Listing 3-36. Template Code

```xsl
<xsl:template name="CreateCompanySchema">
<xsl:param name="ID" />
<xsl:param name="Name" />
<xsl:param name="Role" />
<xsl:param name="Age" />
<xsl:element name="Company">
 <xsl:element name="ID">Default Company ID</xsl:element>
 <xsl:element name="Name">Default Company Name</xsl:element>
 <xsl:element name="Employees">
  <xsl:element name="Employee">
   <xsl:element name="ID"><xsl:value-of select="$ID" /></xsl:element>
   <xsl:element name="Name"><xsl:value-of select="$Name" /></xsl:element>
   <xsl:element name="Role"><xsl:value-of select="$Role" /></xsl:element>
   <xsl:element name="Age"><xsl:value-of select="$Age" /></xsl:element>
  </xsl:element>
 </xsl:element>
</xsl:element>
</xsl:template>
```

3. Create four input parameters by dropping each of the four nodes (ID, Name, Role, and Age) in the source document onto the Scripting functoid.

4. Drop the output of the functoid onto the root node (Company) of the destination schema.

5. Test the map. Assuming that the input document that is shown in Listing 3-37 is used as input, the document shown in Listing 3-38 will be output.

Listing 3-37. Input Document for the Call Template Example

```xml
<ns0:Person xmlns:ns0="http://UsingCallTemplate.Person">
 <ID>1</ID>
 <Name>S. Brekalo</Name>
 <Role>Acupuncturist</Role>
 <Age>33</Age>
</ns0:Person>
```

Listing 3-38. Output Document for the Call Template Example

```xml
<Company>
 <ID>Default Company ID</ID>
 <Name>Default Company Name</Name>
 <Employees>
  <Employee>
   <ID>1</ID>
   <Name>S. Brekalo</Name>
   <Role>Acupuncturist</Role>
   <Age>33</Age>
  </Employee>
 </Employees>
</Company>
```

How It Works

Calling an XSLT template is very similar to using inline XSLT. The main difference is the way in which values within the source document are passed and accessed. With inline XSLT, node values in the source document are accessed through XSL methods, whereas with called XSLT templates, the values are passed in as parameters.

In the case where code may need to be reused for multiple nodes, it may be more advantageous to create a template that can be reused without modifying the code. Templates will also allow for more traditional programming techniques, such as setting and updating variables dynamically within the template (for example, the ability to update a variable to store the number of loops that have occurred within a for-each loop).

Listing 3-39 demonstrates the use of inline XSLT rather than a called XSLT template. The output of Listing 3-39 will produce the same output as that of the XSLT template code shown earlier in Listing 3-36.

Listing 3-39. Inline XSLT for Comparison

```
<xsl:element name="Company">
 <xsl:element name="ID">Default Company ID</xsl:element>
 <xsl:element name="Name">Default Company Name</xsl:element>
 <xsl:element name="Employees">
  <xsl:element name="Employee">
   <xsl:element name="ID">
    <xsl:value-of select="//*[local-name()='ID']" />
   </xsl:element>
   <xsl:element name="Name">
    <xsl:value-of select="//*[local-name()='Name']" />
   </xsl:element>
   <xsl:element name="Role">
    <xsl:value-of select="//*[local-name()='Role']" />
   </xsl:element>
   <xsl:element name="Age">
    <xsl:value-of select="//*[local-name()='Age']" /></xsl:element>
   </xsl:element>
  </xsl:element>
 </xsl:element>
</xsl:element>
```

3-22. Using XSLT Group-By

Problem

You need to define mapping from an input message with a flat structure to an output message grouping elements by the values of fields in the input message.

Solution

The input message must have records containing a field on which the grouping should be performed, as well as the information that needs to be grouped together. The output message needs to define records for each group and a field containing the aggregated information. The input message may have a structure similar to the XML in Listing 3-40.

Listing 3-40. Sample Source Message for the XSLT Group-By Example

```
<ns0:Sales xmlns:ns0="http://tempURI.org">
  <Sale>
    <Amount>100.01</Amount>
    <RepName>Megan</RepName>
  </Sale>
  <Sale>
    <Amount>200.01</Amount>
    <RepName>Megan</RepName>
  </Sale>
  <Sale>
    <Amount>10.10</Amount>
    <RepName>Leah</RepName>
  </Sale>
  <Sale>
    <Amount>2000</Amount>
    <RepName>Misti</RepName>
  </Sale>
  <Sale>
    <Amount>50.10</Amount>
    <RepName>Leah</RepName>
  </Sale>
</ns0:Sales>
```

To create the mapping, follow these steps:

1. Click the toolbox, and click the Advanced Functoids tab. Place a Scripting functoid on the map surface and connect it to the record that will contain each group in the destination message.

2. While the Scripting functoid is highlighted on the map surface, click the ellipsis to the right of the `FunctoidScript` item in the Properties window. In the Configure Scripting Functoid dialog box, on the Script Functoid Configuration tab, select Inline XSLT for Script Type.

3. Create an `xsl:for-each` element in the inline XSLT script, and define the groups to create in the output message by selecting the unique values of the grouping field. This statement will loop through each unique value appearing in the input message.

4. Inside the `xsl:for-each` element, create the record that should contain the group and the field containing the value that must be aggregated for the group. The `current()` function obtains the current iteration value of the `xsl:for-each` element's select statement. Listing 3-41 shows the inline XSLT.

Listing 3-41. Inline XSLT Group-By Script

```
<xsl:for-each select="//Sale[not(RepName=preceding-sibling::Sale/RepName)]/RepName">
  <RepSales>
    <RepTotalAmount>
        <xsl:value-of select="sum(//Sale[RepName=current()]/Amount)"/>
    </RepTotalAmount>
    <RepName>
        <xsl:value-of select="current()"/>
    </RepName>
  </RepSales>
</xsl:for-each>
```

This XSLT script will produce the XML message shown in Listing 3-42, containing one `RepSales` element for each sales representative with the total sales and name of the representative.

Listing 3-42. Sample Destination Message for the XSLT Group-By Example

```
<ns0:SalesByRep xmlns:ns0="http://tempURI.org">
  <RepSales>
    <RepTotalAmount>300.02</RepTotalAmount>
    <RepName>Megan</RepName>
  </RepSales>
  <RepSales>
    <RepTotalAmount>60.2</RepTotalAmount>
    <RepName>Leah</RepName>
  </RepSales>
  <RepSales>
    <RepTotalAmount>2000</RepTotalAmount>
    <RepName>Misti</RepName>
  </RepSales>
</ns0:SalesByRep>
```

How It Works

The key feature of this inline XSLT example is the `select` statement appearing in the `xsl:for-each` element. This statement will create a list of values to create a group for, containing the distinct values of `RepName` in our example. Each `RepName` is located at `//Sale/RepName` in the input message. However, the `select` statement should obtain only the first occurrence of each distinct group value. This inline example achieves this by adding the filter `[not(RepName=preceding-sibling::Sale/RepName)]` to the `select` statement. The `xsl:for-each` element will loop through the first occurrence of each unique grouping value, and the value can be obtained within the `xsl:for-each` element with the `current()` function.

When the filter expression evaluates a `Sale` element, the condition `RepName=preceding-sibling::Sale/RepName` is true whenever there is an element appearing before it with the same `RepName` value. Placing the condition inside the `not()` function makes it true only when there are no preceding elements with the same `RepName` value, so it is only true for the first occurrence of each distinct `RepName` value.

The inline XSLT script in Listing 3-41 calculates the total sales of each representative and creates one record in the output message containing the total sales and the sales representative's name.

In addition to grouping fields in the output message, the map may need to perform aggregations for the groups of input message values. Perhaps BizTalk cannot determine the specific groupings that the map needs to perform until runtime, or static links may not be practical because of a large number of possible groups.

When inline XSLT performs the grouping, BizTalk applies the filter expression to the `//Sale` statement, which means BizTalk applies the filter expression to every `Sale` element in the input message. For each input message, the expression checks the value of every `preceding-sibling` and returns `true` when none of the `preceding-sibling` elements has the same `RepName` value. This algorithm is not efficient for large messages.

There is a generally more efficient alternative XSLT approach to the group by problem. This alternative approach is the Muenchian method. The Muenchian method is generally more efficient than the inline solution presented here, but the default BizTalk functoids cannot implement it. The Muenchian method declares an `xsl:key` element at the top level of the XSLT style sheet. The map directly obtains a node set for each distinct `RepName` with an `xsl:key`, eliminating the computational cost of checking every preceding sibling incurred with inline XSLT. However, since the top level of the `xsl:stylesheet` element must declare the `xsl:key` element, inline XSLT cannot implement it. Only a separate style sheet file can implement the Muenchian method. Place the XSLT style sheet in Listing 3-43 in a separate file for this example.

Listing 3-43. Sample Group-By Style Sheet

```
<?xml version="1.0"?>
<xsl:stylesheet xmlns:xsl="http://www.w3.org/1999/XSL/Transform" version="1.0">
    <xsl:key name="SalesByRepKey" match="Sale" use="RepName"/>
    <xsl:template match="/">
        <ns0:SalesByRep xmlns:ns0='http://tempURI.org'>
<xsl:apply-templates select="//Sale[generate-id()=
generate-id(key('SalesByRepKey', RepName)[1])]"/>
        </ns0:SalesByRep>
    </xsl:template>
    <xsl:template match="Sale">
        <RepSales>
            <RepTotalAmount>
<xsl:value-of select="sum(key('SalesByRepKey', RepName)/Amount)" />
            </RepTotalAmount>
            <RepName>
<xsl:value-of select="RepName" />
            </RepName>
        </RepSales>
    </xsl:template>
</xsl:stylesheet>
```

Specify the external XSLT file used by a BizTalk map (see the next recipe for steps on doing this).

3-23. Using an External XSLT File for a Map
Problem

You are fed up with the mapper and can't stand using functoids. You have a complex map that you feel like getting done programmatically, and you want to shell out to real XSLT.

Solution

It is quite simple to shell out to an XSLT document. Take these steps:

1. Right-click the map surface, and select Properties.

2. Click the ellipsis next to the Custom XSLT Path property, and open the file containing the custom XSLT.

3. Compile the map. The XSLT file is included in the BizTalk assembly and does not need to be deployed separately.

How It Works

Sometimes, it is best to use XSLT directly, instead of using the BizTalk mapping functionality. This can be for a variety of reasons but generally is useful when there is a lot of complex mapping that uses If-Then-Else to populate fields. Because this type of logic can get complex with the use of Value Mapping functoids, pure XSLT can be much easier to use. See Figure 3-62.

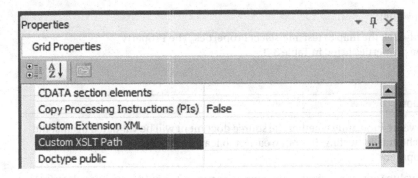

Figure 3-62. *Shelling out to an external XSLT style sheet*

■ **Note** You cannot use both an external XSLT style sheet and functoids within a single map.

3-24. Testing Maps

Problem

You have developed a map and are ready to test and view its output.

Solution

For the purposes of testing, there are two basic types of maps:

- Simple maps, which consist of a single source schema and single destination schema

- Complex maps, which consist of two or more source schemas and/or two or more destination schemas

This solution will work through both types, illustrating several techniques for creating the necessary input documents and obtaining the test results. Figure 3-63 shows a simple map, with a Company schema being mapped from a combination of a Person schema and hard-coded values in two String Concatenate functoids.

Figure 3-63. *A simple map*

Use the following steps to test a simple map:

1. In the Solution Explorer, right-click the map to test and select Properties. The Property Pages dialog box contains the properties listed in Table 3-3.

Table 3-3. *Map Properties*

Property	Description
Validate TestMap Input	Boolean value indicating whether the source document will be validated against the source schema. For testing, it is often easiest to leave this to False in the early stages of development.
Validate TestMap Output	Boolean value indicating whether the output document should be validated against the destination schema. For testing, it is often easiest to leave this to False in the early stages of development.
TestMap Input Instance	Path to the file that contains an instance of the source schema. Used when the TestMap Input property is not set to Generate Instance.
TestMap Input	Indicates the origin of the source document. If set to Generate Instance, BizTalk will generate an instance in memory that contains values for all attributes and elements in the source schema. If set to XML or Native, BizTalk will look for an instance of the document in the location specified in the TestMap Input Instance property. Native indicates a non-XML file, such as a flat file.
TestMap Output	Indicates the format of the output document. The document will be output to a file stored in a temporary directory on Windows and accessible through Visual Studio.

■ **Note** All test map output files are stored in the following directory: $\Documents and Settings\[current user] \Local Settings\Temp_MapData.

2. If you're testing with the TestMap Input property set to Generate Instance, right-click the map, and select Test Map (see Figure 3-64). This will cause BizTalk to write to the Output window in Visual Studio and display any errors that may exist. If no errors exist in the map, a link to the test's output XML file will be made available.

Figure 3-64. *The context menu of a map*

3. If you're testing with the TestMap Input property set to XML or Native, and no instance currently exists, follow these steps:

    a. Right-click the source schema in the Solution Explorer, and select Properties. Set the path where an instance of the output document should be written. Click OK when the properties have been set appropriately.

    b. Right-click the source schema, and select Generate Instance.

    c. Open the document created in the previous step. BizTalk will give default values to all of the elements and attributes in the schema. Edit these with appropriate values for your testing needs. When you're generating instances from schemas, all Any elements and Any attributes will be created. These will fail validation when a map is tested. Either delete these from the generated instance or replace them with a value that would be expected.

    d. Right-click the map in the Solution Explorer, and select Properties.

    e. Set the TestMap Input Instance property to the path of the instance created in step 3c. Set the Test Map Input property to the appropriate type. Click OK.

    f. Right-click the map, and select Test Map. This will produce an output document that can be validated for accuracy. Check the Output window in Visual Studio for details in case of failure.

Testing complex maps requires several more steps to create a valid input instance. The main difference in testing the two types of maps lies in how the input instances are generated.

When a map has multiple source schemas, they are wrapped in a hierarchy created by BizTalk. This hierarchy must be matched if using anything other than Generate Instance for the TestMap Input. In cases where nodes such as Any elements or Any attributes exist in the source documents, generated instances will fail during testing. It then becomes a requirement to create by hand an instance of the multipart input document.

A map can have two or more source documents specified through the use of a Transform shape in a BizTalk orchestration (as shown in Figure 3-65).

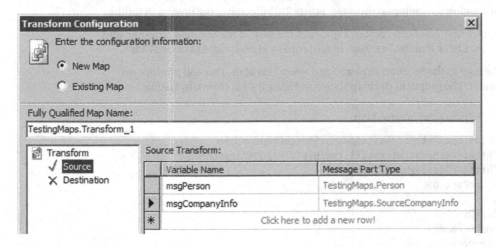

Figure 3-65. *Specifying two source schemas on a map in a Transform shape*

Figure 3-66 shows a complex map with a Company schema being mapped from a combination of two source schemas, Person and SourceCompanyInfo.

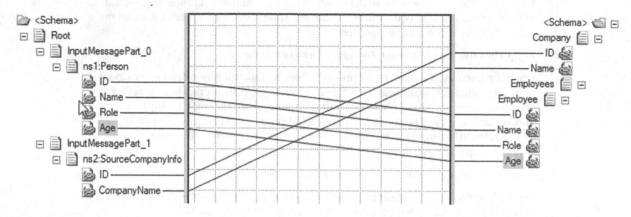

Figure 3-66. *A complex map*

There is never a time in which multiple native instances can be set as source, since the only place that a map with multiple source schemas can be created is in a Transform shape within an orchestration. Therefore, the following steps are specific to creating XML instances that match the multipart input instance needed and can be taken to aid in producing a valid source instance:

4. To generate an instance of the source schema, create a temporary map that is the inverse of what you are trying to produce. In the case of the example shown in Figure 3-67, the map would consist of the Company schema being the single source schema, with the Person and SourceCompanyInfo being the two destination schemas. The intention is to have BizTalk generate an output message that closely resembles the needed input instance. When namespaces are involved, this is all the more important, as prefixes will be added by BizTalk when creating the multipart message. Figure 3-67 illustrates the inverse mapping.

5. Once a temporary map has been created, right-click the map in the Solution Explorer, and select Properties. Check that the TestMap Input property is set to Generate Instance.

6. Right-click the map in the Solution Explorer, and select Test Map. This will produce an output document. The output of the map shown in Figure 3-69 is shown in Listing 3-44.

Listing 3-44. Output of the Inverse Map

```
<ns0:Root xmlns:ns2="http://TestingMaps.SourceCompanyInfo"
xmlns:ns0="http://schemas.microsoft.com/BizTalk/2003/aggschema"
xmlns:ns1="http://TestingMaps.Person">
 <OutputMessagePart_0>
  <ns1:Person>
   <ID>ID_0</ID>
   <Name>Name_0</Name>
   <Role>Role_0</Role>
   <Age>Age_0</Age>
  </ns1:Person>
 </OutputMessagePart_0>
 <OutputMessagePart_1>
```

```
        <ns2:SourceCompanyInfo>
         <ID>ID_0</ID>
         <CompanyName>Name_0</CompanyName>
        </ns2:SourceCompanyInfo>
       </OutputMessagePart_1>
      </ns0:Root>
```

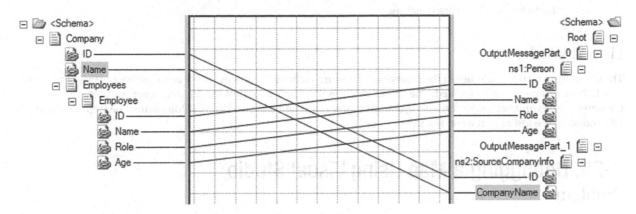

Figure 3-67. *Inverse complex map used to generate an input instance*

7. Copy the output document into a text editor, and manually change the names of the OutputMessage nodes to InputMessage nodes so that the outcome is a valid instance of the input document for the true map. In this case, you want a document that can be used as the input for the map shown in Figure 3-66, as shown in Listing 3-45. The bold elements in the example are the only elements that need to be modified.

Listing 3-45. Input Instance Produced by Modifying Output from Listing 3-44

```
<ns0:Root xmlns:ns2=http://TestingMaps.SourceCompanyInfo
xmlns:ns0="http://schemas.microsoft.com/BizTalk/2003/aggschema"
xmlns:ns1="http://TestingMaps.Person">
<InputMessagePart_0>
<ns1:Person>
<ID>ID_0</ID>
<Name>Name_0</Name>
<Role>Role_0</Role>
<Age>Age_0</Age>
</ns1:Person>
</InputMessagePart_0>
<InputMessagePart_1>
<ns2:SourceCompanyInfo>
<ID>ID_0</ID>
<CompanyName>Name_0</CompanyName>
</ns2:SourceCompanyInfo>
</InputMessagePart_1>
</ns0:Root>
```

8. Once the modifications have been made to the document, save it to a file. This document can now be used as a valid input instance for the valid map (you can delete the temporary map at this time). Right-click the valid map in the Solution Explorer, and select Properties. Set the TestMap Input property to XML and TestMap Input Instance to the file that you just created.

9. Right-click the map in the Solution Explorer, and select Test Map. This will produce an output document that can be validated for accuracy. Check the Output window in Visual Studio for details in case of failure.

How It Works

The difficulty in testing maps lies in the creation of the source schema instances. There are a number of ways in which these instances can be created. The objective of this solution was to provide the steps necessary for creating documents that would allow for the testing of both simple maps and complex maps. Additionally, the steps necessary for producing the test output were described.

3-25. Debugging a Map Using Visual Studio
Problem

You need to step through your map code just like you would with other .NET code in order to debug.

Solution

Debugging a map can be done using the following steps:

1. Specify an input document to test the map with (right-click the map, and set it in the properties).

2. In the Solution Explorer, right-click the map to debug, and select Debug Map (see Figure 3-68).

Figure 3-68. *Selecting Debug Map*

3. Immediately, the map will open in a classic debugger. You can set breakpoints in the XSL that is shown (see Figure 3-69).

```
SalesMap.xsl* ✕  SalesMap.btm      SalesBySize.xsd      Sales.xsd
      <?xml version="1.0" encoding="UTF-16"?>
    ⊟<xsl:stylesheet xmlns:xsl="http://www.w3.org/1999/XSL/Transform" xmlns:msxsl="urn:schema
        <xsl:output omit-xml-declaration="yes" method="xml" version="1.0" />
  ⊙ ⊟ <xsl:template match="/">
          <xsl:apply-templates select="/s0:Sales" />
        </xsl:template>
  ● ⊟ <xsl:template match="/s0:Sales">
    ⊟   <ns0:SalesBySize>
    ⊟     <BigSales>
    ⊟       <xsl:for-each select="Sale">
                <xsl:variable name="var:v1" select="userCSharp:LogicalGt(string(Amount/text())
                <xsl:variable name="var:v3" select="string(Amount/text())" />
                <xsl:variable name="var:v4" select="userCSharp:LogicalGt($var:v3 , &quot;10008
    ⊟         <RepSales>
```

Figure 3-69. *Actively Debugging*

How It Works

Debugging a map is very straightforward, and can be useful in many situations. With some maps, such as Inline XSLT Call Templates, the debugger is not of much use, but for the majority of cases, it can be very helpful. Prior to BizTalk 2010, there were some techniques to debug the map, but they were not as readily available and easy to implement. Standard debug shortcuts apply, including

- F10 to step over the code
- F11 to step into the code (includes stepping into inline scripts, such as C#, and functoids)
- F9 to toggle a breakpoint
- F5 to continue

CHAPTER 4

■ ■ ■

Messaging and Pipelines

Messaging is the core functionality provided within BizTalk Server. On a very basic level, it is the plumbing that moves messages from one location to another. A number of different parts or objects make up this plumbing, taking actions at each step of a message's path through BizTalk Server. Generally speaking, messaging objects can be split into two categories: receive and send. Figure 4-1 outlines the stages a message goes through as it is processed.

Figure 4-1. BizTalk messaging architecture

The receive objects enable the publishing side of BizTalk Server's publish/subscribe architecture. They publish messages into the MessageBox database, the central repository for all messages handled by BizTalk Server. The following objects are involved with receiving messages:

- *Receive location*: Handles the actual retrieval of messages from a specified location. The following are the main objects included within receive locations:

- The *receive adapter* defines the location and method (file, MSMQ, SQL, and so on) to retrieve messages.

- The *receive pipeline* allows decoding, decryption, disassembling, and validating messages against a schema. Receive pipelines also enable party resolution. A custom pipeline component can implement custom logic.

- *Receive port*: Groups one to many receive locations and defines any transformation (or mapping) that occurs on messages being received by the receive port.

The send objects enable the subscribing side of BizTalk Server's publish/subscribe architecture. They subscribe to messages in the MessageBox database and deliver the messages onward to destination locations. The following objects are involved with sending messages:

- *Send port*: Handles the actual delivery of messages to a specified location. The following are the main objects included within send ports:

- A *filter* defines the subscriptions for the send port. *Promoted properties* define these subscriptions and determine which messages the send port will handle. (See Recipe 1-3 for details on promoted properties.)

- A *map* defines any transformation occurring on messages sent through the send port. (See Chapter 2 for details on document mapping.)

- The *send pipeline* allows assembling, validating against a schema, encoding, and encrypting messages. A customer pipeline component can also implement custom logic.

- *Send port group*: Groups one to many send ports and defines the filter(s) used to determine the messages handled by the send ports.

As the MessageBox database receives a message, BizTalk Server checks to see what active subscriptions (send port filters, for example) there are for that message and routes the message to each of the appropriate subscribers. This publish/subscribe architecture facilitates adding new consumers of information, making it easy to deliver messages to additional systems if needed. Once the MessageBox database receives a message, BizTalk can deliver it to any number of subscribing destination systems.

While the MessageBox database holds all messages that are processed by BizTalk Server, messaging objects (receive ports, receive locations, send ports, and send port groups) are stored in the Management database. In BizTalk Server 2010, messaging objects can be associated with an *application*, which is a logical grouping of all objects related to a specific application or solution (including messaging objects, orchestrations, schemas, and so on). The application concept facilitates the management of a wide variety of BizTalk objects that are essentially part of one unit of work.

Messaging objects are created and managed through the BizTalk Administration Console. A number of other tools are also available for managing messaging objects. This chapter focuses on using the tools provided with BizTalk Server to "lay the pipes" for your integration solutions.

■ **Note**   In previous editions of BizTalk Server, some administration could be done through BizTalk Explorer in Visual Studio. This option is no longer available in BizTalk 2010.

4-1. Configuring Receive Ports and Locations
Problem

You have messages from an external application or system that you want to receive into BizTalk Server.

Solution

In BizTalk, receive ports and receive locations are configured to receive data from other applications, systems, or processes. As an example, the following solution describes the procedure for configuring a one-way receive port and a location to receive data from another application via a file input.

1. Open the BizTalk Administration Console.

2. Under the appropriate BizTalk application, right-click the `Receive Ports` folder, and add a new one-way receive port.

3. In the Name text box, name the receive port (`PubSubReceive` in our example).

4. Click the Receive Locations tab, and create a new receive location.

5. In the Name text box, enter a name for this location (`PubSubFileReceive` in this example).

6. Set the properties as follows (see Figure 4-2), and then click OK.

Figure 4-2. *Receive location properties*

- Type: FILE
- URI (address): Click the ellipsis, and navigate to or enter the path to a location where the sample instance will be dropped (in this example, `C:\Users\Administrator\Desktop\Drops\ReceivePubSub`)
- Receive pipeline: `Microsoft.BizTalk.DefaultPipelines.XMLReceive` pipeline

How It Works

Receive ports and receive locations are used in tandem to receive data into the BizTalk environment. Data could be from an internal application or an external entity across the Internet, for instance. Receive locations are tied to a receive port; however, there can be many receive locations per port. There are two types of receive ports:

- *Static one-way*: A port defined to receive data into BizTalk.

- *Request response port*: A port that is used to receive data, but then submit a response back to the sending entity. An example of this could be a web service or HTTP request (request/response–based transport).

Within the receive port configuration, an XML message can be transformed via inbound maps.

Associated with a receive port are one to many receive locations. Receive locations are the physical entry point into the BizTalk MessageBox. The following receive location options can be configured:

- *General*: Configure the transport type and location. The transport type includes all BizTalk out-of-the-box adapters (FILE, MSMQ, SQL, HTTP, and so on). The location includes the physical location, input masking, authentication, and batching options based on the transport type.

- *Receive handler*: The physical BizTalk host the receive location is to run under.

- *Receive pipeline*: Receive pipelines are BizTalk components that support various types of message construction. In addition, pipelines can be extended via .NET code through the BizTalk interface iComponent. Common uses of pipelines are to enable message transformation for non-XML messages, such as a flat file format or a recordset from a database. In addition, receive pipelines can also be specified for well-formed XML messages.

- *Service window*: Service window properties enable constraints on when a receive location is active by date and time filters. This might be useful when dealing with cost-prohibitive communication entities or nondedicated transport.

4-2. Configuring Send Ports

Problem

You have a document that you would like to send to a downstream application, partner, or process.

Solution

You use a send port to send documents from the BizTalk Server platform to other applications, partners, or processes. Send ports are configured using the BizTalk Administration Console and can be used in a pure messaging scenario (no orchestration) or from an orchestration.

■ **Note**   The ability to configure BizTalk artifacts via the BizTalk Explorer in Visual Studio is no longer available in BizTalk Server 2010.

The steps for creating and configuring a send port are as follows:

1. From the BizTalk Administration Console, right-click Send Ports, and select New ➤ Static One-way Send Port. The details behind the types of send ports are as follows:

   - *Static one-way port*: *Static* indicates that the properties are fixed and set at design time. *One-way* indicates that there will be no response back to BizTalk after the message is sent.

   - *Static solicit-response port*: *Static* indicates that the properties are fixed and set at design time. *Solicit-response* indicates that there will be a response back to BizTalk after the message is sent.

   - *Dynamic one-way port*: *Dynamic* indicates that properties will be set at runtime to define the ultimate destination of the message. *One-way* indicates that there will be no response back to BizTalk after the message is sent.

   - *Dynamic solicit-response port*: *Dynamic* indicates that properties will be set at runtime to define the ultimate destination of the message. *Solicit-response* indicates that there will be a response back to BizTalk after the message is sent.

2. The Send Port Properties dialog box will appear. Send port configurations are divided into these categories: General, Transport, Maps, Filters, Certificates, and Tracking properties. Set the properties as required (see the "How It Works" section). Then, click OK to save the configurations and create the send port.

How It Works

Send ports are one of the fundamental BizTalk artifacts and are used to send any types of messages or data from the BizTalk platform to physical locations, systems, or processes. Determining the type of send port to create is important when constructing a solution. You may use send ports in pure messaging or orchestration-based solutions.

You can configure various properties for send ports. Transport properties are available only for static port types (one-way or solicit-response). Both a primary and a secondary transport can be defined. The secondary transport will take effect if an error is encountered sending to the primary transport and all retries as defined by the primary transport Retry Count setting were also attempted. Table 4-1 describes the Transport properties.

Table 4-1. *Send Port Transport Properties*

Property	Description
Transport Type	The type of adapter. If you chose a solicit-response port type, only those adapters that support solicit-response, such as HTTP and SOAP, will be available in the drop-down list.
Address (URI)	Click the Configure button to launch a window for configuring the properties specific to the adapter chosen as the transport type.
Retry Count	Represents the number of times BizTalk Server will retry sending the message if there is a problem during transmission.
Retry Interval	Represents the number of minutes between retry intervals.
Ordered Delivery	When set to True, BizTalk will guarantee the ordered delivery of messages.
Enable Routing for Failed Messages	With this checked, failed messages will have certain context properties promoted so that they can be routed to orchestrations or send ports.

(*continued*)

Table 4-1. (*continued*)

Property	Description
Enable the Service Window	When set to False, BizTalk will send messages at any time of day. When set to True, BizTalk will send messages only within the Start Time and Stop Time settings.
Start Time	Indicates when BizTalk will start sending messages if Enable the Service Window is set to True. Time is represented as HH:MM AM/PM.
Stop Time	Indicates when BizTalk will stop sending messages if Enable the Service Window is set to True. Time is represented as HH:MM AM/PM.

Send properties are the general properties that apply to all send ports. Table 4-2 describes the send properties.

Table 4-2. *Send Port Send Properties*

Property	Description
Tracking	Sets how messages will be tracked. There are a number of options around tracking message bodies and message properties. These can be invaluable in troubleshooting or accessing failed documents.
Certificate Name	A drop-down list of all certificates installed and available for use on the send port.
Thumbprint	The certificate's thumbprint, which will fill in automatically if a certificate name is selected.
Send Pipeline	A drop-down list of the send pipelines available. You can select a pipeline for processing messages sent over this send port.
Receive Pipeline	A drop-down list of the receive pipelines available. For solicit-response send ports, you can select a pipeline for processing the responses received over this port.

Filters are used to create subscriptions when orchestrations are not part of the scenario. From the Filters dialog box, you can create one or more filter expressions, which are used to filter messages to the send port. There is a set of BizTalk properties for use in filtering, and promoted message properties can be used for filtering as well. If you bind a send port directly to an orchestration port, the filters do not apply. Maps are used to transform the document being sent. You may edit one or more maps to the collection, but there may only be one map with a given source schema. Only maps deployed in assemblies are available for selection.

Send ports have few requirements for basic operation. For example, you must specify the transport mechanism, the transport location (such as the HTTP URL), and the BizTalk pipeline that will process the message outbound from BizTalk.

4-3. Configuring Port Maps
Problem

Before receiving an XML message, you would like to transform a message into a predetermined XML format.

Solution

Within BizTalk, you can map source messages into a destination format. You can map with a receive port, an orchestration, or send port. Here, we will outline the steps for mapping in a receive port.

1. Open a receive port that you wish to configure a map on.

■ **Note**   Remember that when setting a map on a receive port, it will apply to all receive location associated with that port.

---

2. Click the Inbound Maps tab.

3. In the grid that opens, select a deployed map. It will automatically fill in the source and target schemas, based on the map. A receive port can have multiple maps associated with it. See Figure 4-3.

Figure 4-3. *Selecting maps for port mapping*

How It Works

This recipe's solution described how to configure a receive port to perform inbound mapping transformation. Remember that when you're using a receive port, the inbound message must be in an XML format. If inbound mapping is configured, the message must also conform to the schema of that specified in the inbound format of the map in question. If the message does not match, the message will fail in the map, and the message interchange will be marked for exception processing.

Another key concept to keep in mind when configuring receive port maps is that more than one map can be specified on a receive port. Multiple XML schemas can be accepted by the receive port; it is not tied to one specific schema. For example, if you have three purchase order document formats arriving from external entities, you could transform each format to a common (canonical) format via port maps on the receive port. This process is commonly referred to as *document normalization*. In this instance, you could have three maps to support each format and a single receive port to satisfy the solution. This scenario is demonstrated in Figure 4-4.

Figure 4-4. Document normalization

A key consideration when applying receive port maps is how you plan to handle exceptions, such as an XML message that does not conform to a map, invalid XML received, and data enrichment required during or before transformation. All of these exceptions could be handled within a port map or receive location, or with downstream BizTalk orchestration functionality.

4-4. Using Send Port Groups

Problem

You want BizTalk Server to send the same message to multiple downstream systems for further processing.

Solution

To demonstrate how to send a message to multiple systems, we will use the example of sending data to an enterprise resource planning (ERP) system. Suppose that you have an orchestration that sends sales order information to your company's ERP system. The business requires sales order information to be available to other departments in your company that do not have access to the ERP system. The business would like to see the data available via the internal data warehouse. Additionally, the business requires minimal downtime for the existing deployed solution due to the need to process orders 24 hours a day, 7 days a week.

The solution is to create a send port to the data warehouse and create a send port group that will manage sending messages from the orchestration to the existing ERP send port as well as the new data warehouse send port. This recipe assumes that the orchestration already exists.

1. To create the new send port group, in the BizTalk Administration Console, right-click Send Port Groups, and select New ➤ Send Port Group.

2. In the Send Port Group Properties dialog box, add one or more existing send ports, as shown in Figure 4-5.

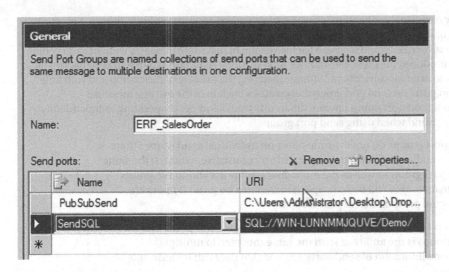

Figure 4-5. Adding send ports to a send port group

3. Update the send port binding of the deployed orchestration, and choose the send port group, as shown in Figure 4-6.

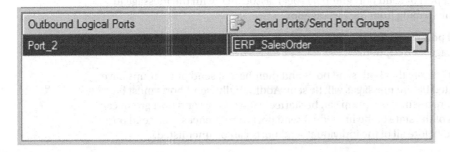

Figure 4-6. Updating your orchestration binding

4. Verify the send port group and referenced send ports are enlisted and started before testing the updated orchestration binding.

How It Works

Send port groups are collections of send ports through which BizTalk Server can publish the same message to multiple destinations using a single configuration. Send port groups are similar to send ports in their ability to be bound to orchestrations, as well as be implemented in pure messaging scenarios (via filter subscriptions).

Send ports that are included in a send port group process messages in two ways:

- As a participant in a send port group
- As a direct recipient of messages routed from BizTalk

Send port groups are incredibly useful in the situations where multiple parties are subscribing to the same message using different messaging protocols or different message formats. For example, one subscriber could receive an XML version of a message, and a separate subscriber could receive a flat file version of that same message, without extra coding or changes to the orchestration that produced the message. Another good use for a send port group is to keep backup files of the transactions sent from BizTalk to external subscribers. Without changing the existing orchestration and with little effort, you can implement a new send port and send port group that creates a backup of the existing message.

Send ports that are included in a send port group operate differently from send ports operating independently. Keep the following considerations in mind when using send port groups:

Filters: Filters on send port groups do not override filters on individual send ports. Filters used on both send ports and a send port group operate in a cumulative nature. If the same filter is used on a send port group as well as the individual send ports within the group, it is likely that duplicate messages will be sent. Special care must be given if filters are implemented on both send ports and send port groups.

One-way static ports: Send port groups can use only static one-way send ports. The strength of send port groups is the ability to send the same message to multiple subscribers. However, one limitation of send port groups is that they can include only static one-way send ports.

Operating states: The operating state between send ports and send port groups is independent. The states between send ports and send port groups are identical:

- *Bound*: The send port or send port group has been physically linked to an orchestration.

- *Enlisted*: The send port or send port group has been associated with the message to which it will be subscribing from the MessageBox.

- *Started*: The send port or send port group is ready to process messages matching the appropriate message subscription.

Enlisted ports: You must verify that both send ports and their parent send port groups have been enlisted and started before messages will be sent. Additionally, send ports must be enlisted or started before a send port group can be started. However, a send port group can be enlisted, regardless of the state of the individual send ports it references. The send port group must be stopped before all of the individual send ports can be unenlisted.

Table 4-3 shows how state affects the behavior of message processing.

Table 4-3. *Send Port and Send Port Group States*

Message Published	Send Port Group State	Send Port State	Description
Send port	Any state	Started	Message processed
Send port	Any state	Stopped	Message suspended
Send port group	Started	Started	Message processed
Send port group	Any state	Stopped	Message suspended
Send port group	Stopped	Any state	Message suspended

Send port groups are powerful tools for allowing multiple subscribers to subscribe to the same message. Individual mappings for each subscriber can be maintained and implemented without affecting other subscribers. Additionally, send port groups allow the ability to resubmit suspended messages, if there is a communication problem, to a single system without having to resubmit to other systems in the send port group.

4-5. Creating Validation Pipelines

Problem

You have an inbound or outbound document that requires validation beyond checking for well-formed XML.

Solution

You can use a send or receive pipeline to perform a strict validation of an instance of an XML document by providing validation against an XSD schema. BizTalk Server provides an XML Validator pipeline component for validating XML (schema) documents. If the inbound or outbound document is not XML, it must be converted to XML prior to validation. The following steps define how to create a receive pipeline that can be used to validate an XML document. The steps are similar to those for configuring a send pipeline.

1. Open the project that will contain the pipeline.

2. Right-click the project, and select Add ➤ New Item.

3. In the Add New Item dialog box, select Receive Pipeline, and provide a name. Then click Add.

4. Drag the XML Validator component from the BizTalk Pipeline Components section of the toolbox to the Drop Here location under the Validate label, as shown in Figure 4-7.

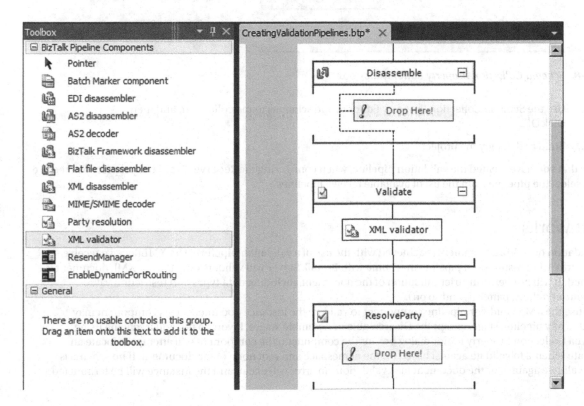

Figure 4-7. *Creating an XML validator pipeline*

5. Select the ellipsis next to the Document Schemas property for the XML Validator component (in the Properties window) to launch the Schema Collection Property Editor dialog box, shown in Figure 4-8.

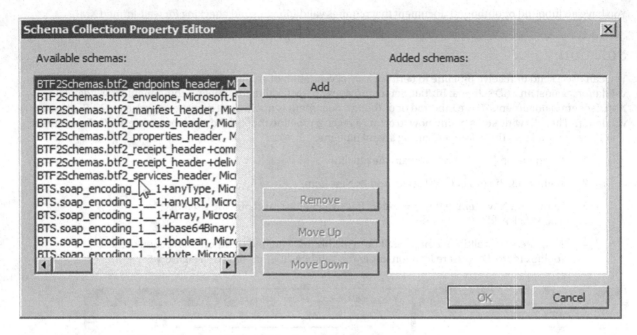

Figure 4-8. *Schema Collection Property Editor dialog box*

6. Use the Schema Collection Property Editor to add schemas to the collection, and then click OK.

7. Build and deploy the project.

Now that you have created the validation pipeline, when configuring the Receive Pipeline property of a receive location, select the pipeline from the list of available receive pipelines.

How It Works

Strict validation of an XML document is achieved with the use of a validation pipeline. The XMLReceive receive pipeline and XMLTransmit send pipeline that come with BizTalk Server will validate only that an XML document is well formed. It will not perform strict validation of the document, including data types and restriction values (length, enumerations, patterns, and so on).

You use the XML Validator pipeline component to validate the instance document. This component may be placed in any pipeline stage, except the Disassemble or Assemble stages. If you do not add a schema using the Schema Collection Property Editor dialog box for the component, the component will attempt to locate an appropriate schema to validate against based on the namespace and root node of the document. If no schema is found to validate against, or the document fails validation, an error will occur, and the instance will be terminated.

4-6. Creating Encryption Pipelines

Problem

You need to guarantee that only the intended recipient of a message can understand it by encrypting the message. The recipient needs to verify the message sender by checking a digital signature included with the message.

Solution

You can implement an encryption mechanism for outgoing messages, as well as a decryption mechanism for the inbound messages. As an example, suppose that you need BizTalk to send this message shown in Listing 4-1 across the Internet to move the requested amount of money between the specified accounts. This message contains sensitive information, including bank account numbers and a Social Security number.

Listing 4-1. Sensitive Information

```
<ns0:MoneyTransfer xmlns:ns0="http://Creating_EncryptionPipelines.Confidential">
    <TransferAmount>108.37</TransferAmount>
    <TransferInitDate>2005-09-30</TransferInitDate>
    <FromAccount>0987-654-321</FromAccount>
    <ToAccount>1234-567-890</ToAccount>
    <RequestedBySSN>123-45-6789</RequestedBySSN>
    <RequestedByName>StacyR</RequestedByName>
</ns0:MoneyTransfer>
```

BizTalk sends the message with the encryption pipeline constructed in this recipe. The message becomes encrypted, as shown in Listing 4-2. No one but the intended recipient can understand the message.

Listing 4-2. Encrypted Message

```
Content-ID: {51572541-E6CE-4DD6-913C-B7C7558D2269}
Content-Description: body
Bcc:
MIME-Version: 1.0
Content-type: application/x-pkcs7-mime; smime-type=enveloped-data; name="smime.p7m"
Content-Transfer-Encoding: base64
```

```
MIAGCSqGSIb3DQEHA6CAMIACAQAxgbwwgbkCAQAwIjAUMRIwEAYDVQQDEwlkZXZvbmx5Y2ECCmEI
BAMAAAAAAAIwDQYJKoZIhvcNAQEBBQAEgYAH+kU66z4r4lZYzq1eOKNfoYt1HVMBaYL61W5wrTPt
...
qQ+ubHBbgHMXyJl/SPylOtSN9XeQGZgBGKb2j+MeBONEjHlRE22aDnazailnmgu2x588820wnQAA
AAAAAAAAAA=
```

The message recipient decrypts the message with the decryption pipeline constructed in this recipe, obtaining the same message as before encryption (see Listing 4-1).

The following sections show how to enable message encryption and decryption.

Send an Encrypted Message

To implement an encryption mechanism for outgoing message, follow these steps on the BizTalk Server responsible for encrypting the message and sending it:

1. Obtain the public key certificate from the party that will securely receive the message, and install it in the Local Computer\Other People folder, as shown in Figure 4-9.

Figure 4-9. *Installing the public key of the receiver*

■ **Note**   BizTalk provides native support for MIME encryption decryption using X.509 version 3 certificates. Microsoft Certificate Services can generate the certificates used by BizTalk.

■ **Note**   The certificate store can be opened by typing **mmc** at a command prompt. Click File ➤ Add/Remove Snap-in.

---

2. Create an empty BizTalk solution, and add a new send pipeline to the solution (right-click the project, select Add ➤ New Item, and select Send Pipeline from the Add New Item dialog box). Give the send pipeline an appropriate name.

3. Drag the MIME/SMIME Encoder component from the BizTalk Pipeline Components section of the toolbox to the Encode stage of the send pipeline, as shown in Figure 4-10.

Figure 4-10. *Adding the MIME/SMIME encoder*

4. Right-click the encoder in the pipeline, and select Properties. Change the value of the Enable encryption property to True, as shown in Figure 4-11.

Figure 4-11. *Enabling pipeline encryption*

5. Build and deploy the BizTalk project containing the send pipeline.

6. Create a send port to deliver the message to the recipient, using any transport adapter desired.

7. In the Send section of the Send Port Properties dialog box, select the send pipeline with the MIME/SMIME encoder component. Then select the public-key certificate of the message receiver for the Certificate Name property.

Receive an Encrypted Message

To configure a decryption mechanism for an incoming message, follow these steps on the BizTalk Server responsible for decrypting the message upon receipt:

1. Obtain a certificate from a certification authority (CA) containing a private key.

2. Log in to the BizTalk Server with the BizTalk service account credentials. Open the certificate file containing the private key, and install it into the Current User\Personal\ Certificates folder of the BizTalk service account.

3. Create an empty BizTalk solution, and add a new receive pipeline to the solution (right-click the project, select Add ➤ New Item, and select Receive Pipeline from the Add New Item dialog box).

4. Drag the MIME/SMIME Decoder component from the BizTalk Pipeline Components section of the toolbox to the Decode stage of the receive pipeline, as shown in Figure 4-12.

Figure 4-12. *Adding the MIME/SMIME decoder*

5. Build and deploy the BizTalk project containing the receive pipeline.

6. Create a receive port and a receive location to accept the encrypted message from the sender, using any desired transport adapter.

7. In the Receive Location Properties dialog box, specify the receive pipeline with the MIME/SMIME decoder, as shown in Figure 4-13.

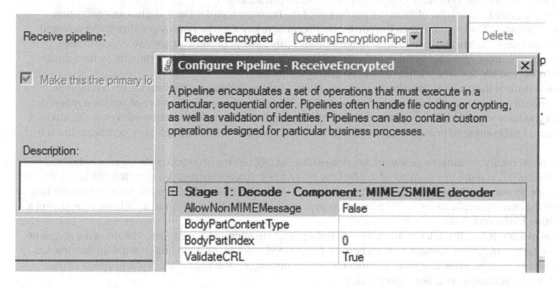

Figure 4-13. *Configuring the decryption pipeline*

8. Using the BizTalk Administration Console, open Platform Settings and select Host Instances. Right click the BizTalk host that will receive the encrypted message and select Properties.

9. Specify the decryption certificate BizTalk will use to receive messages. Secure messages by pasting the thumbprint of the certificate containing the private key into the Thumbprint field in the Certificates section of the Host Properties dialog box.

How It Works

Organizations often deal with confidential information that only the message sender and recipient should understand. For example, financial information may contain sensitive information such as Social Security or bank account numbers. Medical information may contain private information protected by law. Use the encryption capabilities of BizTalk to protect the confidentiality of sensitive information, while still allowing two parties to share it easily.

BizTalk can transmit encrypted information across a network securely. This is particularly important when transmitting messages over a public network, such as the Internet. If the two parties must keep the message confidential, encryption can ensure only the intended recipient can understand it.

One option for ensuring the confidentiality of messages is to use a secure transport like HTTPS. Securing the message transport can be effective, but the transport generally secures only communication directly between two machines on a network. When a message has several network hops before it arrives at the final destination, each hop must be secured individually, providing multiple chances for a configuration error to expose the sensitive information. For example, HTTPS may securely transmit a message to a trading partner, but then be transmitted without encryption over an insecure transport within the trading partner's internal network. To ensure a higher level of confidentiality, you should encrypt the contents of the message, rather than depend on the communication protocol. Message content encryption provides confidentiality over any transport, including transports or BizTalk adapters that cannot support encryption, such as the FTP and SMTP adapters.

BizTalk's encryption capabilities use certificates containing cryptographic key pairs of a public key and a private key. The owner of a certificate can share the public key freely with anyone who wants to send the owner confidential information. However, only the certificate's owner should know its private key.

To encrypt a message, the sender obtains the public key of the message recipient and applies an encryption algorithm to the message. The recipient uses the corresponding private key and the same algorithm to decrypt and understand the message. Certificate owners must fiercely protect private keys because anyone who possesses a private key can decrypt messages encrypted with the corresponding public key. However, certificate owners must distribute public keys to anyone who wishes to send an encrypted message.

BizTalk can securely transmit information to many recipients, using a different certificate for each recipient. BizTalk will detect all certificates placed in the Local Computer\Other People certificate store of the local machine. For example, if you have several trading partners that you must securely exchange information with over the Internet, you can configure a different send port for each trading partner and specify a different public key certificate in each send port.

The decryption certificate must be in the private store of the BizTalk service account receiving encrypted messages. While BizTalk can use any number of public keys to send encrypted information, each BizTalk host can have only one decryption certificate. Each certificate contains a unique identifier called a *thumbprint*, which BizTalk uses to identify the correct certificate from this store to decrypt messages. The thumbprint is calculated by applying a hashing algorithm to the certificate.

In addition to encryption, BizTalk can also add a digital signature to encrypted messages. The message recipient can verify the signature using the sender's public key to be guaranteed that the message originated with the original sender and was not modified while in transit. To enable message signing, set the Signature type property of the MIME/SMIME encoder component, as shown in Figure 4-14.

Figure 4-14. *Enabling message signing*

While each BizTalk host can have a unique decryption certificate, an entire BizTalk group can have only one signing certificate. Specify the signing certificate by entering the thumbprint of the certificate in the Group Properties dialog box for the BizTalk group, as shown in Figure 4-15. This can be accessed by right-clicking the BizTalk Group in BizTalk Administration Console and selecting Properties.

Figure 4-15. Specifying the signing certificate

4-7. Creating Flat File Send and Receive Pipelines

Problem

You are integrating two systems that can communicate only via flat file messages and must provide the mechanisms for receiving and sending the messages within BizTalk Server.

Solution

Create a flat file receive and send pipeline, as follows (these steps assume that a flat file schema has already been created):

1. Open a project that contains a flat file schema.

2. Right-click the project, and select Add ➤ New Item.

3. In the Add New Item dialog box, select Receive Pipeline from the list of templates. Give a descriptive name to your new pipeline, as shown in Figure 4-16, and then click Add.

Figure 4-16. *Adding a new receive pipeline to a project*

4. From the BizTalk Pipeline Components section of the toolbox, drag and drop a Flat File Disassembler component into the Disassemble stage of the receive pipeline.

5. With the Flat File Disassembler component highlighted, set the Document schema property in the Properties window to the flat file schema (CustomerSalesOrder in the example), as shown in Figure 4-17.

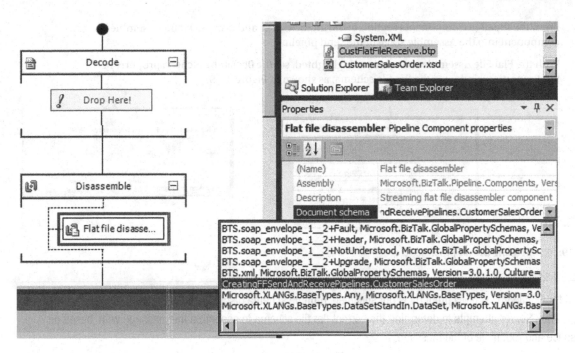

Figure 4-17. *Configuring a receive pipeline for a flat file schema*

■ **Note** Setting the Document schema property is required when using the Flat File Disassembler component. All other properties are optional.

---

6. Save the receive pipeline.

7. Now create the Send Pipeline. Right-click the project, and select Add ➤ New Item.

8. In the Add New Item dialog box, choose Send Pipeline from the list of templates. Give a descriptive name to your new pipeline, as shown in Figure 4-18, and then click Add.

Figure 4-18. *Adding a new send pipeline to a project*

9. From the Pipeline Components section of the toolbox, drag and drop a Flat file assembler component into the Assemble stage of the send pipeline.

10. With the Flat File Assembler component highlighted, set the Document schema property in the Properties window to the flat file schema, as shown in Figure 4-19.

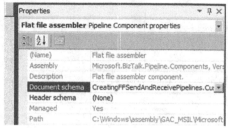

Figure 4-19. *Configuring a send pipeline*

■ **Note** If the Document schema property is not specified, runtime schema discovery will be attempted. During schema discovery, BizTalk Server attempts to determine the correct flat file schema to assemble the message with, based on the namespace and root node of the message.

---

11. Save the send pipeline.

12. Build and deploy the solution.

Once the flat file schema and pipelines (CustomerSalesOrder, CustFlatFileReceive, and CustFlatFileSend in this example) have been deployed, BizTalk Server can use them in message processing.

How It Works

Many systems in use today were designed and engineered prior to the advent of XML. To communicate with these systems, it is often necessary to use flat file formats such as positional, delimited, or a combination of the two. In our example, a simple positional flat file message is parsed into XML as BizTalk Server receives the document. BizTalk Server then assembles the XML back into its correct flat file format when sending the message to the appropriate subscribers.

More specifically, the custom receive pipeline created in the example (CustFlatFileReceive) is used in a receive location that retrieves inbound flat file messages. This receive pipeline disassembles the flat file message into an XML document by leveraging the out-of-the-box Flat File Disassembler pipeline component. By setting the Document schema property on the Flat File Disassembler component, BizTalk Server is instructed to apply the correct schema to inbound documents, thereby producing the appropriate XML representation of the original flat file.

Figure 4-20 represents one possible instance of the inbound flat file document.

URL: C:\Users\Administrator\Documents\Visual Studio 2010\Projects\CreatingFFSendAndReceivePipelines\CreatingFFSendAndReceiveF

```
ORDER2004-10-24
SoldTo Shauna Marie       1223 Buttercup Lane Seattle        WA 98155
ShipTo Jen Schwinn        3030 Moby Road      Kent           WA 98110
ITEMS,ITEM111-AA|Grape|1|2.00|Bottle of Pop,ITEM111-AB|Cola|1|2.00|Bottle of Pop
```

Figure 4-20. *Example instance of the flat file*

When passed through the FlatFileReceive pipeline created in the solution (which can be implemented via a receive location), BizTalk Server disassembles the flat file into the following XML message, based on the details defined within the CustomerSalesOrder.xsd schema (see Figure 4-21).

```xml
- <CustomerSalesOrder xmlns="http://FlatFileSchemaWizard.CustomerSalesOrder">
    <date xmlns="">2004-10-24</date>
  - <customerHeader xmlns="">
      <customerType>SoldTo</customerType>
      <fullName>Shauna Marie</fullName>
      <street>1223 Buttercup Lane</street>
      <city>Seattle</city>
      <state>WA</state>
      <zip>98155</zip>
    </customerHeader>
  - <customerHeader xmlns="">
      <customerType>ShipTo</customerType>
      <fullName>Jen Schwinn</fullName>
      <street>3030 Moby Road</street>
      <city>Kent</city>
      <state>WA</state>
      <zip>98110</zip>
    </customerHeader>
  - <items xmlns="">
    - <item>
        <productId>ITEM111-AA</productId>
        <productName>Grape</productName>
        <quantity>1</quantity>
        <unitPrice>2.00</unitPrice>
        <description>Bottle of Pop</description>
      </item>
    - <item>
        <productId>ITEM111-AB</productId>
        <productName>Cola</productName>
        <quantity>1</quantity>
        <unitPrice>2.00</unitPrice>
        <description>Bottle of Pop</description>
      </item>
    </items>
  </CustomerSalesOrder>
```

Figure 4-21. *Example instance of the XML*

Since the CustFlatFileSend pipeline (which can be implemented via a send port) is configured to assemble instances of the CustomerSalesOrder.xsd message type back into flat file format, the original flat file document would be output again (as shown previously in Figure 4-20).

As well as the required Document schema property, you can configure other optional properties for the Flat File Disassembler component, as shown in Table 4-4.

Table 4-4. *Flat File Disassembler Optional Properties*

Property	Description
Header schema	Defines the schema to apply to any header included in the flat file message.
Preserve header	Specifies if the flat file header should be stored in the message context (properties). The message context contains metadata about the message and is attached to the message throughout its lifetime in BizTalk Server.
Recoverable interchange processing	Specifies if the flat file disassembler should attempt to recover from errors occurring during message processing.
Trailer schema	Defines the schema to apply to any trailer included in the flat file message.
Validate Document Structure	Specifies if the configured schemas (document, header, and trailer schemas) should be used to validate their respective message parts (document, header, and trailer, respectively).

The custom send pipeline created is then used in a send port to deliver flat file messages to subscribers. This send pipeline assembles the XML messages back into flat file format by using the Flat File Assembler pipeline component provided with BizTalk Server. By setting the Document schema property on the Flat File Assembler component, BizTalk Server is instructed to apply the correct schema to outbound documents, thereby producing the appropriate flat file representations of the original XML document.

Along with the required Document schema property, you can set the optional properties listed in Table 4-5 for the Flat File Assembler component.

Table 4-5. *Flat File Assembler Optional Properties*

Property	Description
Header schema	Defines the schema to apply to the header portion of the flat file message. If a header schema is defined on an instance message via the XMLNORM. HeaderSpecName context property, it will override this property setting.
Preserve byte order mark	Specifies if a byte order mark (BOM) should be added to messages passing through the pipeline.
Target charset	Specifies the target character set, which is used as the outbound message is encoded.
Trailer schema	Defines the schema to apply to the trailer portion of the flat file message.

You can configure encoding of outbound messages in a number of different locations, and you should understand the logic BizTalk Server uses to determine which to use if there are discrepancies. Table 4-6 lists the methods that can be used to specify message encoding, ordered to reflect their precedence. If none of the methods listed in Table 4-6 is used to configure message encoding, UTF-8 is used.

Table 4-6. *Methods for Encoding Outbound Messages*

Method	Description
Message- XMLNORM.TargetCharset	This message context property takes precedence over all other encoding configurations and will be used if its value is set.
Component- Target Charset	This Flat File Assembler pipeline component property will be used if its value is set and none of the higher precedence (XMLNORM.TargetCharset) values are set.
Schema- CodePage	This schema property will be used if its value is set and none of the higher precedence values (Target Charset or XMLNORM.TargetCharset) are set.
Message- XMLNORM.SourceCharset	This message context property will be used if its value is set and none of the higher precedence values (CodePage, Target Charset, or XMLNORM.TargetCharset) are set.

You can also configure flat files through their message headers. In addition to configuring the header schema via the Flat File Disassembler or Flat File Assembler pipeline components, you can use the XMLNORM.HeaderSpecName message context property.

One common challenge encountered when receiving flat file messages from source systems is determining which schema to apply to different messages. This is particularly important when multiple message types (for example, customer and order message types) are received from the same location. Since flat file messages are not inherently self-describing, as XML messages are, it can be difficult to determine which flat file message schema to apply to the inbound messages. In these scenarios, you can use a solution similar to the Schema Resolver Component SDK example that comes with BizTalk Server. This example shows how to implement a custom Flat File Disassembler pipeline component to dynamically associate message types to inbound instances based on an identifier contained in each instance message.

Finally, to assist in testing the assembling and disassembling of flat file messages, the FFAsm.exe and FFDasm.exe tools are provided with BizTalk Server. These tools allow you to run the flat file assembler and disassembler directly against instance messages. These tools can be particularly useful and time-saving when working with large or complex flat file schemas.

4-8. Creating Custom Pipeline Components
Problem

You need to create a context property to assist in the routing of the inbound message.

Solution

The BizTalk custom pipeline component can promote a context property of an inbound message. The component does not alter the content of the original message, but rather creates a property and promotes the property to the message context.

As an example of implementing a custom pipeline, we will use the code shown in Listing 4-3, which is a complete C# class library that will compile into a complete custom pipeline assembly.

Listing 4-3 Sample Pipeline Assembly Class Library

```csharp
//---------------------------------------------------------------------
// File: PropertyPromotionPipelineExample.cs
//
// Summary: A sample of how to write a pipeline component that
//          creates a context property.
//---------------------------------------------------------------------

using System;
using System.IO;
using System.Collections;
using System.ComponentModel;
using System.Resources;
using System.Reflection;
// BizTalk classes
using Microsoft.BizTalk.Message.Interop;
using Microsoft.BizTalk.Component.Interop;

namespace PropertyPromotionPipelineExample
{
    /// <summary>
    /// BizTalk Server custom pipeline component that creates
    /// a custom context property for the inbound message.

    /// </summary>
    ///
    // Attribute declarations to identify this class is a pipeline component
    // and that the assembly can be used in any pipeline stage
    [ComponentCategory(CategoryTypes.CATID_PipelineComponent)]
    [ComponentCategory(CategoryTypes.CATID_Any)]
    [System.Runtime.InteropServices.Guid("63ed4b26-63cd-4d29-9661-f584c94cf858")]
    public class PropertyPromotionPipelineExample :
        Microsoft.BizTalk.Component.Interop.IBaseComponent
        , Microsoft.BizTalk.Component.Interop.IComponent
        , Microsoft.BizTalk.Component.Interop.IComponentUI
        , Microsoft.BizTalk.Component.Interop.IPersistPropertyBag
    {
        //Key for storage on property bag:
        private string m_propbagkey_customproprop
                = "SAMPLECUSTOMPROPROP";
        private string m_propbagkey_custompropropnamespace
                = "SAMPLECUSTOMPROPROPNAMESPACE";

        //Var to store design time value
        private string m_propname = "";
        private string m_propnamespace = "";

        static ResourceManager resManager = new ResourceManager("SampleCustom
PipelineComponent.SampleCustomPipelineComponent", Assembly.GetExecutingAssembly());
```

```csharp
public PropertyPromotionPipelineExample ()
{
    // Default constructor logic
}

#region Public Properties
// Display the following public properties for design time
public string CustomContextPropertyName
{
    get {    return m_propname;}
    set {    m_propname = value;}
}

// Display the following public properties for design time
public string CustomContextPropertyNamespace
{
    get {    return m_propnamespace;}
    set {    m_propnamespace = value;}
}
#endregion

#region IBaseComponent members defines Description, Name, and Version
public string Description
{
    get
    {
        return "Sample Custom Pipeline Component";
    }
}

public string Name
{
    get
    {
        return "Sample Custom Pipeline Component";
    }
}

public string Version
{
    get
    {
        return "1.0";
    }
}
#endregion

#region IComponent members contains the main implementation
public IBaseMessage Execute(IPipelineContext pContext
                    , IBaseMessage pInMsg)
```

```
        {
            // Create custom context property on message
            pInMsg.Context.Promote(m_propname, m_propnamespace, string.Empty);
            return pInMsg;
        }
        #endregion

        #region IComponentUI members contains design time information
        // Include a validate method used by BizTalk
        public IEnumerator Validate(object obj)
        {
            IEnumerator enumerator = null;
            // Return a null
                return enumerator;
        }
        // We do not have an icon for this custom component
        [Browsable(false)]
        public System.IntPtr Icon
        {
            get
            {
                // No icon associated with this pipeline component
                return  IntPtr.Zero;
            }
        }
        #endregion

        #region IPersistPropertyBag members contains placeholders
        public void GetClassID(out Guid classid)
        {
            // Return class ID of this component for usage from unmanaged code.
            classid = new System.Guid("63ed4b26-63cd-4d29-9661-f584c94cf858");
        }

        public void InitNew()
        {
            // Initialization not implemented
        }

        public void Load(IPropertyBag propertyBag, Int32 errorlog)
        {
            // Load configuration property for component.
            string val = (string)ReadPropertyBag(propertyBag,
                    m_propbagkey_customproprop);

            if (val != null)
                m_propname = val;

            val = (string)ReadPropertyBag(propertyBag,
                    m_propbagkey_custompropropnamespace);
            if (val != null)
                m_propnamespace = val;
        }
```

```csharp
        public void Save(IPropertyBag propertyBag
                , Boolean clearDirty, Boolean saveAllProperties)
        {
            // Saves the current component configuration into the property bag.
            object val = (object)m_propname;
            WritePropertyBag(propertyBag,
                m_propbagkey_customproprop, val);

            val = (object)m_propnamespace;
            WritePropertyBag(propertyBag,
                m_propbagkey_custompropropnamespace, val);
        }

        private static object ReadPropertyBag(IPropertyBag propertyBag
                , string propertyName)
        {
            // Reads property value from property bag.
            object val = null;
            try
            {
                propertyBag.Read(propertyName, out val, 0);
            }
            catch(ArgumentException)
            {
                return val;
            }
            catch(Exception ex)
            {
                throw new ApplicationException(ex.Message);
            }
            return val;
        }

        private static void WritePropertyBag(IPropertyBag propertyBag
                , string propertyName, object val)
        {
            // Writes property values into a property bag.
            try
            {
                propertyBag.Write(propertyName, ref val);
            }
            catch(Exception ex)
            {
                throw new ApplicationException(ex.Message);
            }
        }
        #endregion
    }
}
```

Use the following steps to create, install, and implement a custom pipeline component.

1. Create a new Class Library .NET project as shown in Figure 4-22. Custom pipeline components can be coded in any .NET language. This example is implemented in C#.

Figure 4-22. *Creating a C# Library for the custom pipeline component*

2. Add a reference to the `Microsoft.BizTalk.Pipeline.dll` assembly located in the `%\Program Files\Microsoft BizTalk Server 2010` directory.

3. Develop the custom component code, which should match that shown in Listing 4-3.

4. Build the component, and place a copy of the assembly in the pipeline components folder located where BizTalk is installed (for example, `C:\Program Files\Microsoft BizTalk Server 2010\Pipeline Components`).

5. To add the pipeline component to the Visual Studio toolbox, select ToolsChoose Toolbox Items. In the dialog box, select the BizTalk Pipeline Components tab, and then select the pipeline assembly created in step 4. The component should appear in your toolbox, as shown in Figure 4-23.

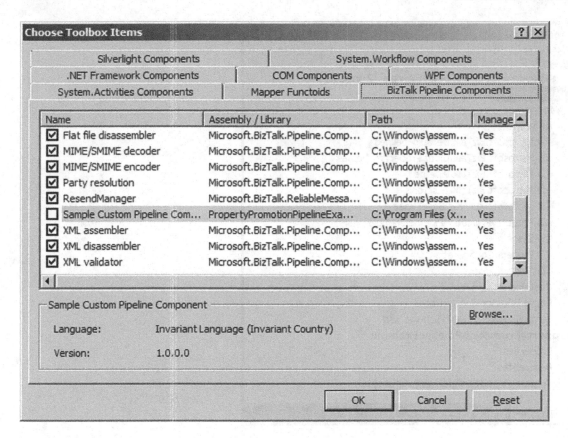

Figure 4-23. Adding a custom pipeline component to the toolbox

---

■ **Note** Loading the Choose Toolbox Items dialog box may take some time.

---

6. To add and configure the custom component as a receive pipeline, create a new BizTalk solution with the following items (see Figure 4-24 for the full solution layout):

- Schema containing the message to be received.

- Property schema containing the context property implemented in the solution. For this example, create a property schema that contains a string element named Routing.

- A receive pipeline that implements the custom pipeline component.

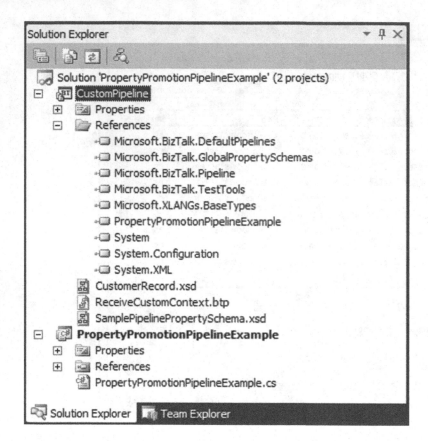

Figure 4-24. *Pipeline solution layout*

How It Works

BizTalk includes out-of-the-box functionality for processing messages within receive and send pipelines. However, situations may arise where custom processing of messages is required. For example, you may need custom message validation, processing of flat files, or formatting of messages to HTML that BizTalk does not natively support. Custom pipeline components offer incredible flexibility for preprocessing or postprocessing messages via send and receive pipelines. Additionally, custom pipeline components can coexist with native BizTalk pipeline components in the same pipeline.

In BizTalk solutions where message content or context determines routing, you may need to route messages based on the lack of existence of a property. BizTalk does not have the ability to route on the lack of property existence. However, you can use a custom pipeline component to create a property that is always part of a message. Rather than check for the existence of the property, you can check whether the property contains an empty string value. The solution that accompanies this recipe creates a custom pipeline component that creates a context property for every message that is processed by the component.

Creating custom pipeline components may seem like an extensive task due to the code required for hosting the component in a BizTalk pipeline, as well as setting the design-time properties. In actuality, there is a single method that contains the processing logic, and the remainder of the code supports the component design-time properties.

Your first task in creating a custom pipeline component is to create a project reference to the `Microsoft.BizTalk.Pipeline.dll` file contained in the main BizTalk installation folder. After you have added the appropriate project reference, you must consider the implementation of the custom pipeline component. There are three logical areas to a custom pipeline component to consider:

- Attributes and class declaration

- Design-time properties

- Implementation of the four pipeline interfaces: IBaseComponent, IComponentUI, IPersistPropertyBag, and IComponent

The following sections describe each of these areas in more detail.

Attributes and Class Declaration

Consider how you plan on using the custom component, such as in a send or receive pipeline. Additionally, consider the pipeline stage in which you plan on implementing the custom component. The attributes and class declaration indicate to Visual Studio that the assembly is a custom pipeline component. If you do not properly identify that you are creating a BizTalk custom pipeline component, you will not be able to add the component to the Visual Studio toolbox or be able to add the component to a pipeline stage. Here is the header section from the sample code shown previously in Listing 4-3:

```
[ComponentCategory(CategoryTypes.CATID_PipelineComponent)]
    [ComponentCategory(CategoryTypes.CATID_Any)]
    [System.Runtime.InteropServices.Guid("63ed4b26-63cd-4d29-9661-f584c94cf858")]
    public class PropertyPromotionPipelineExample :
        Microsoft.BizTalk.Component.Interop.IBaseComponent
        , Microsoft.BizTalk.Component.Interop.IComponent
        , Microsoft.BizTalk.Component.Interop.IComponentUI
        , Microsoft.BizTalk.Component.Interop.IPersistPropertyBag
```

The sample custom component is identified, via the `ComponentCategory` attributes, as a pipeline component for use in any pipeline stage. Additionally, the class declaration specifies that four interfaces (IBaseComponent, IComponent, IComponentUI, and IPersistPropertyBag) will be implemented within the class. The GUID is required for use in COM interop with unmanaged code.

Design-Time Properties

Custom component design-time properties are exposed via public declarations and appropriate get/set methods. The following is the section of Listing 4-3 that demonstrates how two design-time properties are exposed.

```
#region Public Properties
        // Display the following public properties for design time
        public string CustomContextPropertyName
        {
            get {    return m_propname;}
            set {    m_propname = value;}
        }
```

```
        // Display the following public properties for design time
        public string CustomContextPropertyNamespace
        {
            get {    return m_propnamespace;}
            set {    m_propnamespace = value;}
        }
#endregion
```

Implementation of the Four Pipeline Interfaces

The final logical area required in the creation of a custom pipeline component is the implementation of four interfaces, as summarized in Table 4-7. The four interfaces provide the design-time and runtime implementations for the custom component and serve as a guide. Not all of the interfaces must contain code, and the IComponent interface contains the function that performs the message processing.

Table 4-7. *Interface Implementation*

Interface	Description	Implementation Notes
IBaseComponent	Properties related to the basic information about the custom component.	Contains three properties that enable the engine to retrieve the component name, version, and description.
IComponentUI	Defines the properties for displaying the custom component in the design-time user interface as well as the validation rules for design-time properties.	Contains two methods: one that allows the validation of the component's configuration and another that provides a pointer reference to the icon that will be displayed in the development tool set for the custom component. If null is set for the pointer, the default icon will be used.
IPersistPropertyBag	Custom pipeline properties that are displayed at runtime when using the custom assembly in a pipeline.	Enables a component to store and receive its configuration information.
IComponent	Defines the method used by all pipeline components. Assembler/disassembler custom components implement their own interface.	Contains the main function that performs the heavy lifting and processing of the inbound/outbound message. This method takes as parameters the pipeline context and incoming message.

■ **Note**   If the custom component is to reside in either the Assemble or Disassemble pipeline stages, the component must also implement the appropriate assemble/disassemble interface.

IBaseComponent

IBaseComponent contains three read-only properties that return the description, version, and name of the component to the design-time environment and other tools interested in basic component information. Implementing the IBaseComponent is straightforward and requires implementing only the three read-only properties. Here is the section of the code in Listing 4-3 that demonstrates the implementation of the three properties.

```
#region IBaseComponent members defines Description, Name, and Version
    public string Description
    {
        get
        {
            return "Sample Custom Pipeline Component";
        }
    }

    public string Name
    {
        get
        {
            return "Sample Custom Pipeline Component";
        }
    }

    public string Version
    {
        get
        {
            return "1.0";
        }
    }
#endregion
```

IComponentUI

IComponentUI serves to present the component icon in the design-time tool set. The two methods implemented in the IComponentUI are Icon and Validate. The Icon method provides a pointer to the graphic icon displayed in the design-time user interface. If no icon is specified, Visual Studio will display the default icon in the BizTalk Pipeline Components section of the Toolbox. The Validate method allows processing of any design-time properties. For example, if you have a custom design-time property that requires information, you can include validation rules within the Validate method to verify the design-time information entered.

The following portion of Listing 4-3 shows both the Validate and Icon methods. In the solution example included with this recipe, the default Visual Studio icon will be used, and no special validation rules are required for the specified user data.

```
#region IComponentUI members contains design time information
    // Include a validate method used by BizTalk
    public IEnumerator Validate(object obj)
```

```
    {
        IEnumerator enumerator = null;
        // Return a null
            return enumerator;
    }
    // We do not have an icon for this custom component
    [Browsable(false)]
    public System.IntPtr Icon
    {
        get
        {
            // No icon associated with this pipeline component
            return  IntPtr.Zero;
        }
    }
}
#endregion
```

IPersistPropertyBag

The purpose of the IPersistPropertyBag interface is to provide access to your object to unmanaged code. If you are familiar with .NET, then you may have used property bags in other projects. IPersistPropertyBag also allows access to design-time configuration values. There are four public methods that exist in the IPersistPropertyBag interface: GetClassID, initNew, Load, and Save. The GetClassID function must return a unique ID that represents the component. The initNew function can be used to establish structures (data, caching, and memory) used by the other IPersistPropertyBag methods. The final functions facilitate the loading and saving of property values. In the solution example accompanying this recipe, two additional methods were created to wrap the actual read/write functions of the property bag; however, the read and write functions could also be called directly from the Load and Save functions.

The following portion of the code from Listing 4-3 demonstrates the implementation of the four IPersistPropertyBag functions as well as the two helper functions.

```
#region IPersistPropertyBag members contains placeholders
    public void GetClassID(out Guid classid)
    {
        // Return class ID of this component for usage from unmanaged code.
        classid = new System.Guid("63ed4b26-63cd-4d29-9661-f584c94cf858");
    }

    public void InitNew()
    {
        // Initialization not implemented
    }

    public void Load(IPropertyBag propertyBag, Int32 errorlog)
    {
        // Load configuration property for component.
        string val = (string)ReadPropertyBag(propertyBag,
                m_propbagkey_customproprop);
```

```csharp
        if (val != null)
            m_propname = val;

        val = (string)ReadPropertyBag(propertyBag,
                m_propbagkey_custompropropnamespace);
        if (val != null)
            m_propnamespace = val;
    }

    public void Save(IPropertyBag propertyBag
            , Boolean clearDirty, Boolean saveAllProperties)
    {
        // Saves the current component configuration into the property bag.
        object val = (object)m_propname;
        WritePropertyBag(propertyBag,
            m_propbagkey_custompropprop, val);

        val = (object)m_propnamespace;
        WritePropertyBag(propertyBag,
            m_propbagkey_custompropropnamespace, val);
    }

    private static object ReadPropertyBag(IPropertyBag propertyBag
            , string propertyName)
    {
        // Reads property value from property bag.
        object val = null;

        try
        {
            propertyBag.Read(propertyName, out val, 0);
        }
        catch(ArgumentException)
        {
            return val;
        }
        catch(Exception ex)
        {
            throw new ApplicationException(ex.Message);
        }
        return val;
    }

    private static void WritePropertyBag(IPropertyBag propertyBag
            , string propertyName, object val)
    {
        // Writes property values into a property bag.
        try
        {
            propertyBag.Write(propertyName, ref val);
        }
```

```
        catch(Exception ex)
        {
            throw new ApplicationException(ex.Message);
        }
    }
#endregion
```

IComponent

IComponent is the most important interface in the component, as it contains the processing logic for messages. This interface contains a single method, Execute, which takes two parameters. BizTalk calls the Execute method to process the message, and then passes the message and the context of the message as the two parameters. The following outlines the Execute method declaration and the two required parameters in Listing 4-3.

```
#region IComponent members contains the main implementation
        public IBaseMessage Execute(IPipelineContext pContext
                                    , IBaseMessage pInMsg)
        {
            // Create custom context property on message
            pInMsg.Context.Promote(m_propname, m_propnamespace, string.Empty);
            return pInMsg;
        }
#endregion
```

The IPipelineContext parameter refers to the environment in which the component is running. For example, the IPipelineContext object contains pipeline property information, including the pipeline stage in which the component is running. The IPipelineContext object also contains a resource tracker, which cleans up objects. The IBaseMessage object contains the inbound message. The main purpose of the custom component is to perform some level of processing on the inbound message object.

The Execute method returns the IBaseMessage object, which represents all parts of the processed message (such as the message content and context). You may perform any type of message or context processing if you return the IBaseMessage object at the end of the function. When BizTalk processes messages through pipelines, it streams the messages, rather than passing the whole messages. Additionally, the message passed through the pipeline is a read-only data object. The solution example accompanying this recipe demonstrates only adding a context property and does not demonstrate updating the content of the message. You must perform the following steps if you plan to alter the message content:

1. Create a memory stream object to hold the contents on the updated message or a copy of the inbound message. Remember that an inbound message is read-only, and you need a new container to perform updates to the inbound message. The new memory stream object is a container for the updated message.

2. Process the inbound message stream. The easiest way of processing the inbound message is to copy the stream to a string and load the message into an XMLDocument. However, using an XMLDocument object does not perform well and is not recommended for a production-type solution. A better method involves using a stream reader to manipulate the inbound stream. Consider the following approaches for manipulating the inbound memory stream:

   - Use Stream.Read() as the primary mechanism for dealing with message content.

   - Use XMLReader.Read() as the secondary mechanism for dealing with message content.

   - Use the XML message in the DOM as a last resort option due to the performance hit. Specifically, if you're dealing with large messages, do not load the entire message into the DOM for processing.

3. Set the message body part. After processing the message, you must return the updated message. If you used a memory stream object, you can set the return IBaseMessage.Data object to the memory stream object. Remember to rewind the updated memory stream object so you are passing the whole message and not the end of the memory stream. The pipeline processor will not attempt to rewind the stream, and you will receive a pipeline if the stream is not rewound.

4. Add the memory stream to the resource tracker. If you used a new memory stream object, make sure to add the memory stream object to the IPipelineContext.Resource tracker for cleanup.

Pipelines are the first line of processing before a message is received by the BizTalk MessageBox or before the message is received by a target system. Out-of-the-box functionality supports the ability to perform straightforward processing of messages. There may be situations that require more complex processing, data validation, or interaction with .NET objects. In those situations, implementing a custom pipeline component offers the flexibility of adding processing logic within the BizTalk framework.

The main function required for implementing a custom pipeline component is the Execute function in the IComponent interface. The other interfaces serve for design-time and component interactions with the runtime engine.

Manipulation of the inbound message requires making a copy of the inbound message stream, as the inbound message stream is read-only. Before a memory stream can be returned to the IBaseMessage.Data object, it must be rewound, as the BizTalk pipeline engine does not perform this function. You should also clean up memory stream objects by adding the object to the pipeline resource tracker.

■ **Note**   There are several pipeline component creation tools available on the Internet that may be used to reduce overall coding effort.

4-9. Handling Pipeline Errors
Problem

You need to implement custom logic within a pipeline for an integration solution you are building. Based on the solution's requirements, message delivery must be guaranteed, with no messages being lost once they are received by BizTalk Server. Any errors within the custom pipeline must result in a notification e-mail being sent to the appropriate system administrators.

Solution

BizTalk Server 2010 has some very convenient, easy-to-use error-handling functionality called *error reporting*, which enables simplified handling of pipeline (and other) errors. Error reporting is specified on receive and send ports within the BizTalk Administration Console, as shown in Figure 4-25.

Figure 4-25. *Configuring error reporting on a send port*

By enabling this feature on a port, you instruct BizTalk Server to take a number of steps in the event an error is encountered during message processing (which includes adapter, pipeline, mapping, and routing processing). Specifically, a clone of the errored message is created, with all the original promoted properties demoted. The message does, however, have the appropriate error reporting properties promoted, such as the failure code and receive port/send port name. This message is then delivered to the MessageBox, and can be subscribed to by an SMTP send port via the error reporting promoted properties. This SMTP send port can be configured to deliver notification messages to a system administrator.

■ **Note**   If error reporting is enabled, and an error occurs when BizTalk Server attempts to deliver the cloned message to the MessageBox, the original message is placed in the suspended queue.

How It Works

Error reporting allows a variety of receive/send port errors to be trapped and managed. The details of the error are promoted as properties on a copy of the original message, which is sent to the MessageBox database. This allows you to handle error messages just like any other message: via subscriptions. You can define error-handling mechanisms specific to a single integration point, an application, or an entire BizTalk environment. Your error-handling mechanisms can be a simple notification e-mail (as shown in this solution), or a complex set of processes implemented as orchestrations.

The Error Reporting properties are available on Filters in send ports and orchestrations (See Figure 4-26). This allows messages to be routed to the appropriate destinations.

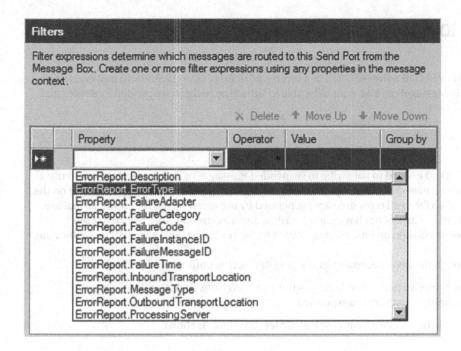

Figure 4-26. *The Error Report properties available in filters*

Table 4-8 shows the error-reporting properties promoted on errored messages.

Table 4-8. *Error-Reporting Properties Promoted on Errored Messages*

Property	Description
FailureCode	The code identifying the error.
FailureCategory	The category of the failure.
MessageType	The BizTalk message type of the failed message. This property may be empty if BizTalk Server could not determine the type of message.
ReceivePortName	The name of the receive port where the failure occurred. This property is populated and promoted only if the failure occurred on a receive port.
InboundTransportLocation	The URI of the receive location where the failure occurred. This property is populated and promoted only if the failure occurred on a receive port.
SendPortName	The name of the send port where the failure occurred. This property is populated and promoted only if the failure occurred on a send port.
OutboundTransportLocation	The URI of the send port where the failure occurred. This property is populated and promoted only if the failure occurred on a send port.
ErrorType	The type of message that the error report contains.
RoutingFailureReportID	The ID of the related routing failure report message in the MessageBox. The routing failure report message contains the properties (context) of the original message and can be queried to provide additional information about the errored message.

4-10. Subscribing to Suspended Messages

Problem

A message fails at some point in your BizTalk solution (such as a receive port, map, or orchestration) and ends up as a suspended message on the BizTalk MessageBox. You want to be able to subscribe to these suspended messages and route them to a file drop.

Solution

This solution will introduce the method needed to subscribe to suspended messages by demonstrating how to use a receive port/filtered send port combination. The receive port will listen for messages of a certain type to arrive on the MessageBox. The send port will subscribe to all error messages generated by the receive port. All messages that are picked up by the receive port will fail because of not having a subscriber, and an error message will be written to the MessageBox. These messages will then be immediately routed to the send port, and a file will be written out to a specified file location.

The following steps walk through the steps necessary for creating the receive port:

1. Creating a new one-way receive port in the BizTalk Administration Console. Enter the name of this port as **SampleSubscribeToSuspended**.

2. On the General Tab, click the Enable Routing for Failed Messages box, as shown in Figure 4-27.

Figure 4-27. Enabling routing

3. On the Receive Locations tab, add a receive location to the port. Give a valid file path for the address of this location (such as `C:\drop`).

4. Click OK. The receive port has been successfully configured and created.

5. Right-click the receive location, and enable it.

The following steps walk through the steps necessary for the send port. You can set up additional subscribers—for instance, an orchestration—to allow for more complex processing. In this solution, the send port will simply write the suspended message out to a file drop. For any properties not listed in the following steps, keep the default values.

1. Create a new one-way send port in the BizTalk Administration Console. Enter the name of this port as **SampleSuspendedToFile**.

2. On the General tab, set Transport Type to File, and enter a valid file path to which to write outgoing files. Set `Send Pipeline` to `PassThruTransmit`.

3. On the Filters tab, click the Property drop-down list, and select `ErrorReport.ReceivePortName`. Set the value equal to the name of the receive port created in the earlier steps (`SampleSubscribeToSuspended`). Do not use quotes.

4. Click OK. You have successfully configured and created the send port.

5. Do not enlist or start the send port at this time. At this point, the solution is complete—aside from the enlistment of the send port. Dropping a file on the receive location will cause the receive port to throw an exception and log to the Event Viewer—there is no subscriber. The error message has been routed to the MessageBox, but there is no subscriber for it either.

6. Now, enlist and start the send port. The receive location will fail to find a subscriber. This time, however, the error will be routed to the send port, and the message will be written out to the send port file location.

How It Works

A number of properties are available on the `ErrorReport` object. This solution worked with one of these, `ReceivePortName`. Building a more complex solution using an orchestration will allow access to all the remaining properties. For example, assume that instead of a send port subscribing to the `ErrorReport` as shown in this solution, you have an orchestration with a receive port. The orchestration will receive the message, and you can then access the `ErrorReport` properties in the send port filter, receive filter of an orchestration, or within an Expression shape, as shown in Figure 4-28.

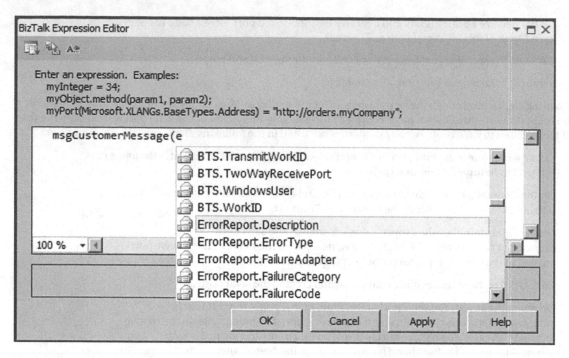

Figure 4-28. *Accessing the* ErrorReport *properties*

■ ■ ■

CHAPTER 5

Orchestrations

If publish/subscribe messaging capabilities are at the heart of BizTalk, then process orchestration capabilities are BizTalk's brain. A BizTalk orchestration can define a complex integration process, coordinating the flow of information when simple data synchronization will not suffice. BizTalk provides a graphical design tool for defining these integration processes. These orchestration capabilities build upon the foundational publish/subscribe architecture of the BizTalk messaging runtime.

In the simplest cases, integration is strictly about receiving information from one system and delivering it to another. Accordingly, a BizTalk orchestration receives and sends messages through orchestration ports. However, many real-world situations require more than simple message delivery. With an orchestration, the BizTalk developer can graphically define additional processing steps in Visual Studio. For example, these processing steps may involve examining a message or invoking a .NET assembly and deciding on the appropriate actions to take. An orchestration can define an integration process with sequential processing steps or perform independent activities simultaneously. Define higher-level integration services in an orchestration by composing the messaging capabilities of BizTalk with additional integration processing logic. Future integration requirements can reuse the higher-level integration services to reduce implementation effort and enable greater agility.

BizTalk orchestrations support many of the capabilities needed to compose integration activities together, as follows:

- Atomic and long-running transactions help ensure that all systems involved in an integration process come to a consistent result.

- Transformations convert from a format understood by a source system to a format understood by a destination system.

- Orchestrations can invoke an external .NET assembly or use expressions defined with custom code.

- Exceptions can be handled by defining the scope of integration activities.

- Orchestrations support transaction compensation and rollbacks.

BizTalk orchestrations also provide terrific support for interacting with services defined by interoperable contracts. With BizTalk 2010, an orchestration can directly consume Windows Communication Framework (WCF) services and ASMX .NET web services (WSDL), exposing the service operations within the graphical orchestration design environment. The BizTalk developer can also expose an orchestration as a service, which any service consumer can invoke without having to know that BizTalk technology implements the service.

5-1. Receiving Messages
Problem

You are building a solution that requires the implementation of a business process. You must configure an orchestration to receive messages, which begins the business process.

Solution

BizTalk Server orchestrations receive messages either through a Receive shape or directly from another orchestration as an orchestration input parameter. A Receive shape allows messages to be routed from the MessageBox to the orchestration, as demonstrated in this solution.

To create an orchestration that receives messages via a Receive shape, follow these steps:

1. Open a project that contains a schema that represents the message that will be received.

2. Right-click the project in Solution Explorer, and select Add ➤ New Item.

3. In the Add New Item dialog box, select Orchestration Files from the Installed Templates list, choose the BizTalk Orchestration template, and give a descriptive name to your new orchestration, as shown in Figure 5-1. In our example, the orchestration is named `ReceiveShapeOrchestration`. Then, click Add.

Figure 5-1. Adding a new orchestration to a project

4. In the Orchestration View window, expand the top node of the tree view (this node will have the same name as the orchestration), so that the `Messages` folder is visible. (If the Orchestration View window is not visible, select View ➤ Other Windows ➤ Orchestration View.)

5. Right-click the `Messages` folder, and select New Message, which creates a message called Message_1 by default.

6. Click the new message, and give it a descriptive name in the Properties window. In our example, the message is named `msgCustomerMessage`.

7. Click the Message Type property in the Properties window, and select the appropriate type to associate with the message, as shown in Figure 5-2. In our example, we select the CustomerSchema message type.

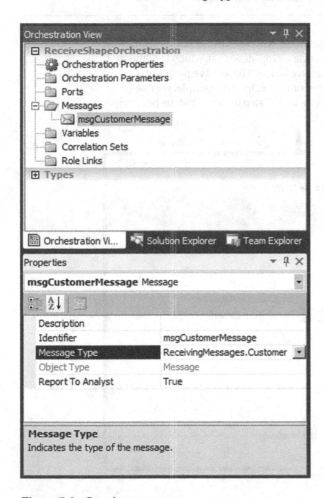

Figure 5-2. *Creating a message*

■ **Note** Notice all of the types available for setting the message. A very common option is to set a message to System.Xml.XmlDocument, which allows an XML document of any format to be received (rather than strongly typed against a specific XSD). Of course, subscribing to the generic XMLDocument will cause *all* documents on the MessageBox to be picked up, so make sure your filtering is set up!

---

8. From the toolbox, drag a Receive shape onto the orchestration directly beneath the green circle at the top of the design surface.

■ **Note** In addition to dragging and dropping shapes from the toolbox, you can also add shapes to an orchestration by right-clicking a section of the vertical process flow arrow and selecting Insert Shape.

9. With the Receive shape selected, specify the shape's Name, Message, and Activate properties, as shown in Figure 5-3. The Message property is set via a drop-down list, which is populated with all the messages that are in scope for the Receive shape. The Active property is also set via a drop-down list, with the choices True or False. In our example, we use ReceiveCustomerMessage, msgCustomerMessage (created in step 6), and True, respectively.

Figure 5-3. *Adding a Receive shape*

10. To configure a port and port type for the orchestration to use to receive a message, right-click the Port Surface area, and select New Configured Port. This will start the Port Configuration Wizard.

11. Step through the Port Configuration Wizard, specifying the following items (accept all other defaulted values):

- *Port name*: oprtReceiveCustomerMessagePort.

- *New port type name*: oprtTypeCustomerMessagePortType.

- *Port binding*: Select Specify Now, and configure the appropriate receive adapter to consume inbound messages, as shown in Figure 5-4. In this example, we configure the port to use the FILE adapter, which receives XML messages from the C:\Users\Administrator\Desktop\Drops\ReceiveShapeOrchestration folder.

Port direction of communication:

I'll always be receiving messages on this port. ▼

Port binding:

Specify now ▼

URI: Transport:

\Drops\ReceiveShapeOrchestration*.xml   FILE ▼

(example: c:\PurchaseOrders*.xml)

Receive pipeline: Send pipeline:

Microsoft.BizTalk.DefaultPipelines.XML ▼   Microsoft.BizTalk.DefaultPipelines.XML ▼

Figure 5-4. *Configuring an orchestration port for receiving messages*

■ **Caution**   Using Specify Now as your method of port binding can make your development and deployment process easier, but be careful when using this feature. It is not the recommended method for production code, because you should not embed port bindings inside an orchestration. A better approach is to use a binding file.

---

12.   Connect the orchestration port's request operation to the Receive shape, as shown in Figure 5-5.

Figure 5-5. *Connecting an orchestration port to a Receive shape*

13.   The project can now be deployed. During the deployment process, the port will automatically be created, along with all bindings to the orchestration (this does not happen when a port is set up using the Specify Later option). Figure 5-6 shows the port created for this solution.

Figure 5-6. *The receive port created automatically during deployment*

How It Works

Understanding how messages are received into orchestrations is critical when designing and implementing orchestrations in BizTalk Server. Receive shapes are the most common method used to deliver messages to orchestrations. In this recipe's solution, we showed how to add a Receive shape to an orchestration, configure the Receive shape's Message Type and Activate properties, and connect it to a receive port.

If the Receive shape is the first shape in the orchestration, it must have its Activate property set to True. If an orchestration does not have an activating Receive shape, it must be called or started (instantiated) from another orchestration.

The data a Receive shape accepts is defined by its Message property, which relates to a message that has been defined within the orchestration. All messages in BizTalk are bound to a specific type, which can be an XSD schema or a .NET class. This allows orchestrations to receive instances of XSD schemas or .NET classes as inputs. While our example used a single Receive shape, orchestrations can use many Receive shapes to accept different types of messages at different points in the business logic.

Each Receive shape must be bound to an operation, or orchestration port. An orchestration port is the interface through which messages pass on their way into or out of orchestration instances. Orchestration ports define the direction messages flow (receiving into an orchestration, sending from an orchestration, or both), and are bound to a physical port, another orchestration, or directly to the MessageBox database. The topic of binding orchestrations is covered in more detail in Recipe 5-4, but it is important to understand the methods by which orchestration ports can be bound and how they affect the way messages are received into an orchestration:

- *Physical receive port*: All messages that are consumed by the specified receive port are routed to the orchestration. This setting creates subscriptions in the MessageBox database, which deliver messages passing through the physical receive port to the orchestration port.

- *Another orchestration*: Only those messages explicitly being passed from the calling orchestration are routed to the orchestration.

- *Directly to the MessageBox*: All messages in the MessageBox database that validate against the Receive shape's message type are routed to the orchestration.

Each Receive shape has a number of properties associated with it, as listed in Table 5-1.

Table 5-1. *Receive Shape Properties*

Property	Description
Activate	Flag indicating whether the Receive shape activates the orchestration instance.
Description	Summary of the Receive shape.
Filter Expression	A filter that is applied to all messages being received via the Receive shape.
Initializing Correlation Sets	A list of correlation sets that are initialized as messages pass through the Receive shape.
Following Correlation Sets	A list of correlation sets that are followed as messages pass through the Receive shape. This property is not available on the first Receive shape of an orchestration.
Message	The message that will be created when a document is passed through the Receive shape. A message with a message type of XmlDocument can be used to receive a generic XML message, without limiting documents to a specific XSD schema.
Name	Name of the Receive shape.
Object Type	Name of the object type (read-only, automatically set to Receive).
Operation	Specifies through which orchestration port operation the Receive shape receives its message.
Report To Analyst	Flag indicating whether the message part should be exposed via the Visual Business Analyst Tool.

The Filter Expression property allows you to be a bit more specific about which messages make it into your orchestration. Clicking the ellipsis in the input box for the Filter Expression property launches the Filter Expression dialog box. This dialog box allows you to create specific filters, which include one to many logical expressions that must be met in order for a message to be received into the orchestration. These logical expressions are based on a property, an operator, and a value and can be grouped by using the And and Or keywords.

A filter expression can be set on only a Receive shape that has its Activate property set to True. When the value portion of the filter expression is a string, you must put double quotes around the actual value for the expression to work properly.

The Initializing Correlation Sets and Following Correlation Sets properties specify which correlation is followed when messages are received on the Receive shape. Generally speaking, correlation sets allow you to send and receive messages in and out of orchestrations that directly relate to one another.

5-2. Sending Messages

Problem

You want to send messages from within a BizTalk orchestration for processing by other orchestrations.

Solution

Within a BizTalk orchestration, messages are sent using the Send shape. To use the Send shape, follow these steps:

1. Open the BizTalk project that contains the orchestration with the messages you want to send. For this exercise, it is assumed that the orchestration is already configured to receive a message.

2. Drag a Send shape from the toolbox. Place the shape underneath the orchestration Receive shape.

3. In the Orchestration View window, expand the top node of the tree view so that the Messages folder is visible.

4. Right-click the Messages folder, and select New Message, which creates a message.

5. Click the new message, and give it a descriptive name in the Properties window (msgCustomer in our example).

6. Click the Message Type property in the Properties window, select the Schema node, and select the appropriate schema. In this example, it uses the Customer.xsd schema.

7. Select the Send shape, and in the Properties window, assign the message to msgCustomer.

■ **Note** The type of port you are creating is not a physical BizTalk port. This is an orchestration port that will be bound later to the physical port.

---

8. To configure a port and port type for the orchestration to use to send a message, right-click Port Surface, and click New Port, as shown in Figure 5-7.

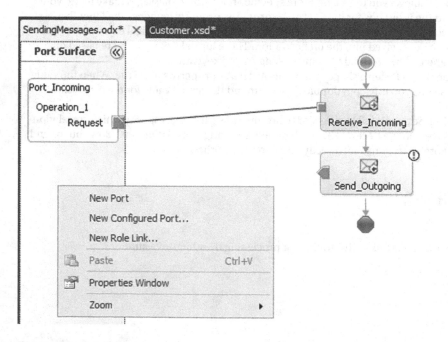

Figure 5-7. *Creating a new port*

9. Click the exclamation mark (tool tip), and select "No port type has been specified." This starts the Port Configuration Wizard.

10. On the Select a Port Type page, name the port oprtSendCustomer, and click Next.

11. On the Configure Port page, enter the following details, as shown in Figure 5-8, and then click Next:

    • Select the "Create a new Port Type" radio button.

    • Name the port type oprtTypeSendCustomer.

    • Select the One-Way radio button under Communication Pattern.

    • Select the "Internal - limited to this project" radio button under Access Restrictions.

Select the port type to be used for this port:

(•) Create a new Port Type

( ) Use an existing Port Type

Port Type Name:

| oprtTypeSendCustomer |

Communication Pattern:

(•) One-Way

( ) Request-Response

Access Restrictions:

( ) Private - limited to the containing module

(•) Internal - limited to this project

( ) Public - no limit

Figure 5-8. Configuring an orchestration port for sending messages

12. On the Port Binding page, select "I'll always be sending messages on this port" for the port direction of communication. For port binding, select Direct, and select the first radio button. Routing between ports will be defined by filter expressions on incoming messages in the MessageBox database. Click Finish after making your selections.

■ **Note** In this example, we are implementing a standard publish/subscribe model; that is, the message implementation does not need to be physically specified. The BizTalk MessageBox database will be responsible for initializing one or more downstream messaging subscriptions.

---

13. From the port on the Port Surface area, click the green square, and drag it to the Send shape on the orchestration design surface, as shown in Figure 5-9.

Figure 5-9. *Send message configuration*

How It Works

In this recipe's solution, we demonstrated how to send messages out of an orchestration to BizTalk messaging and downstream BizTalk endpoints. To review, the following are the key steps to perform to send a message:

1. Identify a message to send. This can be a .NET class, multipart message, web reference message, or schema.

2. Create an orchestration port. Specify the port type and access restrictions.

3. Se et the port direction and binding (dynamic or direct) to BizTalk messaging artifacts.

When sending messages out of an orchestration, it is also important to consider the type of request you would like to implement. Should the message not be returned (one-way), or should the orchestration wait for a response (request/response)? In essence, the port choice should support the type of communication being implemented.

Another important consideration is the message context. Within the orchestration, is the message its own instance, or should it be aware of correlation implications? Within the Send shape, you have the ability to address correlation message context by setting the `Following Correlation Sets` or `Initializing Correlation Sets` property.

5-3. Creating Multipart Messages
Problem

You are building an integration solution and receive multiple documents that together form a single logical message in your back-end system. You must group these documents into one message by using a multipart message in BizTalk Server.

Solution

Multipart messages are created in BizTalk Server orchestrations, as opposed to being created as schemas. Multipart messages are a collection of message parts, with each part having a specific type. Message part types can be defined by an XSD schema or a .NET class. This solution describes how to use XSD schemas to define each of the message parts.

To create an orchestration and a multipart message, follow these steps:

1. Open the project that contains the schemas. In this sample, we will use an order header schema and an order line item schema to demonstrate the use of multipart messages, as shown in Figure 5-10.

Figure 5-10. *The schemas being used*

2. Right-click the project, and select Add ➤ New Item.

3. In the Add New Item dialog box, select Orchestration Files from the Categories list and BizTalk Orchestration as the template, and give a descriptive name to your new orchestration. In our example, the orchestration is named `MultiPartMessageOrchestration`. Then, click Add.

4. In the Orchestration View window, expand the Types node of the tree view so that the `Multi-part Message Types` folder is visible, as shown in Figure 5-11. (If the Orchestration View window is not visible, select View ➤ Other Windows ➤ Orchestration View.)

Figure 5-11. *Viewing multipart message types*

5. Right-click the Multi-part Message Types folder, and select New Multi-part Message Type, which creates a new multipart message type. A default message part is automatically added to all newly created multipart message types.

6. Click the new multipart message type, and give it a descriptive name in the Properties window. In our example, the multipart message is named Order.

7. Expand the new multipart message type, click the default message part, and give it a descriptive name in the Properties window. In our example, the message part is named Header. Note that the Message Body Part property is set to True.

8. Click the Type property in the Properties window, and select the appropriate schema to associate with the message part, as shown in Figure 5-12. In our example, the schema is named OrderHeader.

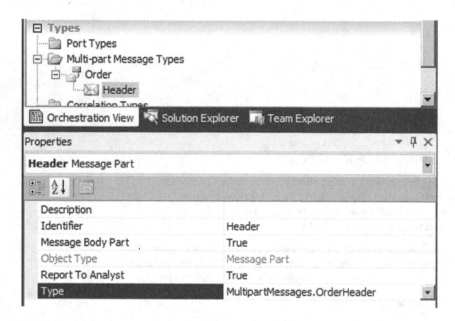

Figure 5-12. *Setting the default message part's type*

9. Right-click the Order multipart message type, and select New Message Part, which creates a new message part.

10. Click the new message part, and give it a descriptive name in the Properties window. In our example, the message part is named LineItems. Note that the Message Body Part property is set to False.

11. Click the Type property in the Properties window, and select the appropriate schema to associate with the message part, as shown in Figure 5-13. In our example, the schema is named OrderLineItems.

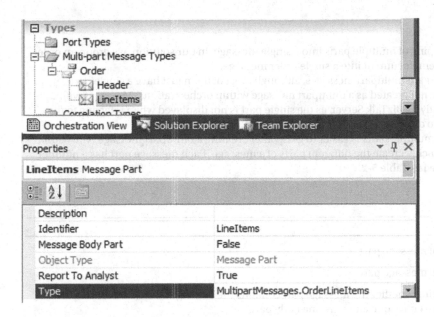

Figure 5-13. *Setting an additional message part's type*

12. In the Orchestration View window, expand the top node of the tree view so that the Messages folder is visible.

13. Right-click the Messages folder, and select New Message, which creates a message.

14. Click the new message, and give it a descriptive name in the Properties window. In our example, the message is named MultiPartOrderMessage.

15. Click the Message Type property in the Properties window, and select the appropriate type to associate with the message, as shown in Figure 5-14. In our example, we select the Order multipart message type.

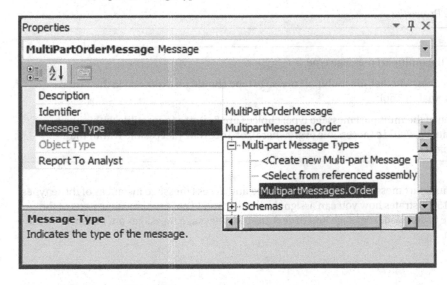

Figure 5-14. *Creating a multipart message*

How It Works

Multipart messages allow for the grouping of multiple parts into a single message. In our solution, we group an order header document and an order line item document into a single order message.

All messages within BizTalk Server are multipart messages, although most of them just have a single part (the message body) and, therefore, are not created as a multipart message within orchestrations. Messages with a single part are treated slightly differently by BizTalk Server, as the single part is not displayed when referring to the message and the message is referred to directly.

The concept of messages having multiple parts is easier to grasp after creating a multipart message type within an orchestration, where you must explicitly create the different parts of a message. Each message part has a number of properties associated with it, as listed in Table 5-2.

Table 5-2. *Message Part Properties*

Property	Part
Description	Summary of message part
Identifier	Name of the message part
Message Body Part	Flag indicating whether the message part contains the message body (every multipart message must have one and only one body part)
Report To Analyst	Flag indicating whether the message part should be exposed via the Visual Business Analyst Tool
Type	The type defining the message part's content

The type of message part can be either a .NET class or an XSD schema. If a .NET class is specified, the class must be XML-serializable or support custom serialization. If an XSD schema is used, the schema must be included in the same BizTalk Server project as the multipart message type or in a referenced assembly. By specifying the XmlDocument type, a message part can contain any valid XML document. The multipart message type has the properties listed in Table 5-3 associated with it.

Table 5-3. *Multipart Message Type Properties*

Property	Part
Identifier	Name of the multipart message type
Report To Analyst	Flag indicating whether the multipart message type should be exposed via the Visual Business Analyst Tool
Type Modifier	The scope of the multipart message type; choices are Private (accessible within the orchestration), Public (accessible everywhere), or Internal (accessible within the same project)

Once you have defined your multipart message types, you can create and access message instances of those types within the orchestration. Figure 5-15 illustrates how you can assign the Header and LineItems message parts of the Order message. In this example, the OrderHeaderMessage and OrderLineItemsMessage messages are instances of the Header and LineItems schemas.

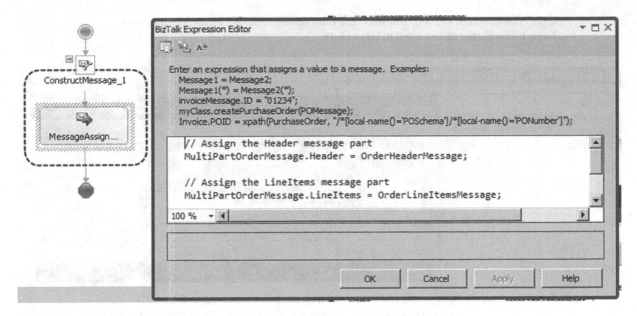

Figure 5-15. *Assigning message parts*

Some common uses of multipart messages in BizTalk Server are when you are consuming a service or processing e-mail messages within orchestrations. When you add a web service reference to an orchestration, a multipart message type is generated automatically, with one part created for each message part defined in the web service's WSDL file. For those scenarios where e-mail messages are being processed, it is common to use multipart message types to handle MIME multipart messages; the body message part would contain the body of the e-mail, and subsequent parts could contain e-mail document attachments.

5-4. Binding Orchestrations
Problem

You need to bind an orchestration to a physical port, to associate a process with a BizTalk messaging port, and consequently, a downstream BizTalk process.

Solution

Binding orchestrations to physical ports is the activity that enables defined processes (orchestration) to be associated with physical connectivity and communication, such as file, HTTPS, or web/WCF service. BizTalk enables two methods of binding orchestrations. You can choose to specify the binding immediately within the BizTalk Orchestration Designer (by choosing the Specify Now option during the port binding process) or later using the BizTalk Administration Console (by choosing Specify Later). When you choose Specify Later, this indicates that binding information will not be determined at design time. This recipe demonstrates using the Specify Later option.

1. Deploy an orchestration, and choose the Specify Later method during the port binding process.

2. Open the BizTalk Administration Console and under the Orchestrations tree, locate your orchestration.

3. Right-click the orchestration, and select the Bind option. The Port Bindings Properties dialog box will appear, as shown in Figure 5-16.

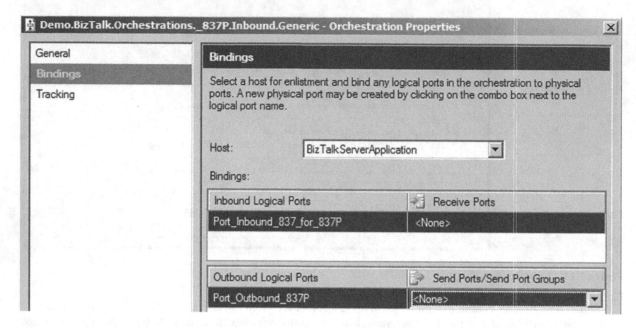

Figure 5-16. *Port Bindings Properties dialog box*

4. For each orchestration port, select the desired BizTalk messaging port. The port choices available for selection will be filtered based on the port type (send or receive).

How It Works

Binding orchestrations enables processes to be associated with BizTalk messaging ports and consequently, downstream BizTalk processes and artifacts.

Binding can be completed within the BizTalk Orchestration Designer (when you choose Specify Now) or within the BizTalk Administration Console (when you choose Specify Later). The two binding choices allow for separation between process and configuration activities for both task and environment orientation.

Consider the separation of roles between a developer and administrator. The developer would be responsible for development activities within BizTalk, whereas the administrator would be responsible for deployment activities. These activities can be abstracted to allow for environment-specific configuration, without development involvement or consideration. To illustrate this point, consider testing and production BizTalk environments, and how the specification of port values (such as URLs, file locations, and so on) and physical receive locations can be achieved via this abstraction.

5-5. Configuring a Send Port at Runtime
Problem

You need to send a message from BizTalk Server but will not have all of the required information to do so until the orchestration is executing.

Solution

To be able to configure a send port at runtime, you create a dynamic send port within the orchestration. This recipe demonstrates how to configure the outbound dynamic send port in the Message Construct shape. The first step is to copy the contents of the inbound message to the outbound message. Listing 5-1 shows an example of a dynamic XML message.

Listing 5-1. Sample Dynamic XML Message

```
<ns0:DynamicMessage xmlns:ns0="http://DynamicSendPortProject.xsdDynamicMessage">
  <Header>
    <FTPServer>myFTPServer.com</FTPServer>
    <FTPUserName>FTPUserName</FTPUserName>
    <FTPPassword>FTPPassword</FTPPassword>
    <Retry>3</Retry>
    <RetryInterval>5</RetryInterval>
    <FileName>FileName.xml</FileName>
  </Header>
  <Body>
    <Content>This is a test message.</Content>
  </Body>
</ns0:DynamicMessage>
```

Next, configure the address that BizTalk will use to communicate the message. The address uses the same format as a standard URL. In this example, we specify ftp:// to transmit the file via FTP. The FTP transport protocol requires additional properties to be specified (such as the username and password). Listing 5-2 shows an example of a construct message configuration.

The following steps outline the procedure:

1. Open the project containing the orchestration that will be processing the inbound message and sending that message via a dynamic send port.

2. Create a new orchestration send port with a port binding that is dynamic (named oprtSendDynamic in this example).

■ **Note** You will be required to choose a send pipeline when configuring the send port. You can choose from any deployed send pipeline, any send pipeline referenced by your project, or any send pipeline that is part of your existing solution.

---

3. Verify that you have a message that contains all of the properties required for configuring the send port and that the properties are promoted or distinguished. Your message may look similar to the message shown earlier in Listing 5-1.

4. Select the Message Assignment shape from the BizTalk Orchestrations section of the toolbox, and drag it to the appropriate location within the orchestration.

5. Select the Message Assignment shape, and update the properties.

    - Change the default name if desired.

    - Add a description if desired.

    - Identify the output message(s) constructed.

    - Set the Report To Analyst property. Leave the property as True if you would like the shape to be visible to the Visual Business Analyst Tool.

6. Update the Message Assignment shape to contain the information that constructs the outbound message as well as configures the properties on the outbound dynamic send port. Your construct message may look similar to the one shown earlier in Listing 5-2.

    Listing 5-2. Sample Message Assignment Code

    ```
    // Construct Message
    msgDynamicOut = msgDynamicIn;

    // Set the FTP properties based on message content.
    // Reference the send port to set properties.
    oprtSendDynamic(Microsoft.XLANGs.BaseTypes.Address) =
        "ftp://" + msgDynamicIn.Header.FTPServer + "/"
        + msgDynamicIn.Header.FileName;

    // Set message context properties for ftp.
    msgDynamicOut(FTP.UserName) = msgDynamicIn.Header.FTPUserName;
    msgDynamicOut(FTP.Password) = msgDynamicIn.Header.FTPPassword;
    msgDynamicOut(BTS.RetryCount) =
                    System.Convert.ToInt32(msgDynamicIn.Header.Retry);
    msgDynamicOut(BTS.RetryInterval) =
                    System.Convert.ToInt32(msgDynamicIn.Header.RetryInterval);
    ```

7. Complete the orchestration (as shown in Figure 5-17).

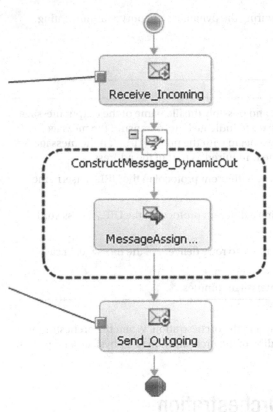

Figure 5-17. *Completed dynamic send port orchestration*

How It Works

Dynamic ports allow the physical location of a physical send port (one-way or solicit-response) to be determined at runtime. The only requirement for a dynamic port is setting a pipeline at design time. The ability to specify the transport protocol and address at runtime allows for the flexibility of routing messages based solely on message content or on the output of message processing in an orchestration.

For example, implementing the SMTP send adapter to send an e-mail from BizTalk requires configuration information (SMTP server, e-mail recipient, and subject). Rather than specifying the configuration information at design time, you can use a dynamic port, which allows you to configure the information programmatically and modify it based on the message content or processing. Additionally, dynamic send ports can be set via content returned from the Business Rule Engine.

This recipe's solution demonstrated setting up a dynamic send port to send a message via FTP. The inbound message contains the message content as well as the configuration information for transmitting the message to the FTP recipient. The properties of the message are distinguished fields and are therefore easily referenced. Depending on the transport protocol being specified for the dynamic port, different properties will be required and optional.

■ **Caution**   If you attempt to set the `Microsoft.XLANGs.BaseTypes.Address` field with an orchestration port that is not a dynamic port in BizTalk, you will receive a compile-time error.

Table 5-4 shows the required and optional properties for configuring the dynamic send port communicating via FTP.

Table 5-4. *Dynamic Send Port Properties*

Name	Description
Address	A required property that contains the location and possibly the file name of the output message to create. The Address property uses URL prefixes to indicate how to transmit the message. To transmit a message via FTP, the address must begin with the prefix ftp://. If the message is being sent via FTP or FILE, a file name attribute is required as part of the address.
UserName	Specifies the FTP username. If you are specifying a different protocol in the URL, a username may not be required.
Password	Specifies the FTP password. If you are specifying a different protocol in the URL, a password may not be required.
RetryCount	An optional property that specifies how many times to retry delivery of the message, in case there is a problem transmitting the message.
RetryInterval	An optional property that specifies the retry interval in minutes.

This recipe's solution demonstrated creating a dynamic send port in the orchestration. When the orchestration is deployed, the physical send port will be created, and specific binding of the orchestration to a physical send port is already done.

5-6. Creating Branching Logic in an Orchestration
Problem

From within an orchestration, you would like to execute different processing based on the evaluation of available information.

Solution

A Decide shape is the equivalent of an If...Then...Else statement in standard programming. It allows you to direct different processing at runtime based on the evaluation of information. The following steps outline how to add a Decide shape to an orchestration and configure it.

1. Open the project containing the orchestration.

2. Open the orchestration.

3. Select the Decide shape from the toolbox, and drag it to the appropriate location within the orchestration.

4. Select the Decide shape, and update its properties.

   - Change the default name if desired.

   - Add a description if desired.

   - Set the Report To Analyst property. Leave the property as True if you would like the shape to be visible to the Visual Business Analyst tool.

5. Select the rule branch named Rule_1, and update its properties (click it, and set its properties in the Properties window).

   - Change the default name if desired.

   - Add a description if desired.

   - Set the Report To Analyst property. Leave the property as True if you would like the shape to be visible to the Visual Business Analyst Tool.

   - Right-click the ellipsis next to the Expression property, and enter a valid Boolean expression for the rule.

6. To add an additional rule, right-click the Decide shape, and select New Rule Branch.

■ **Note** To delete a branch, right-click the branch, and select Delete. To delete the Decide shape, right-click the shape, and select Delete.

How It Works

Decide shapes can be used to complete different processing based on information available at runtime. The following is a simple example of using and configuring the Decide shape from within an orchestration. Assume you have a document as follows:

```
<Employee>
    <FirstName>John</FirstName>
    <LastName>Doe</LastName>
    <SSN>111-22-3333</SSN>
    <State>Washington</State>
    <HireDate>1999-05-31</HireDate>
</Employee>
```

From within an orchestration, you would like to complete different processing under the following scenarios:

   - The State is "Washington", and an SSN is provided.

   - The State is "Washington", and no SSN is provided.

   - The State is not "Washington".

To set up this different processing based on these three scenarios, you add a Decide shape to the orchestration and configure two rule branches and the else branch. For the first rule branch, define the expression to ensure the state is Washington and that a Social Security number was provided, as shown in Figure 5-18.

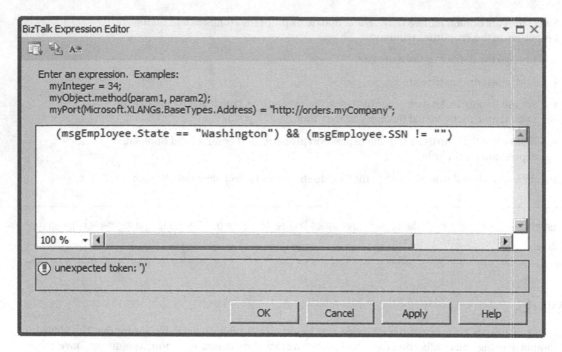

Figure 5-18. First rule branch

> ■ **Note** To access schema nodes from within an orchestration, you must set the nodes as distinguished fields from within the schema editor. In cases where the schema can't be altered – or fields can't be promoted – xpath can be used within the orchestration to access values in the data.

For the second rule branch, configure the expression to ensure the state is Washington and that no Social Security number was provided, as shown in Figure 5-19.

```
Enter an expression. Examples:
    myInteger = 34;
    myObject.method(param1, param2);
    myPort(Microsoft.XLANGs.BaseTypes.Address) = "http://orders.myCompany";

    (msgEmployee.State == "Washington") && (msgEmployee.SSN == "")
```

Figure 5-19. Second rule branch

> ■ **Note** Refer to the BizTalk help file for a complete list of valid operators in orchestration expressions. It uses what many refer to as ".NET Lite," which means only a subset of libraries are available for use.

The else branch will accommodate all other inbound documents where the state is not Washington. Figure 5-20 shows a completed orchestration with a Decide shape configured as described in this example. In this example, a document will be sent to different locations depending on whether the State is "Washington" and whether or not the document contains an SSN. If the State is not "Washington", no document will be sent. It is not required that the branch of a Decide shape contain any actions.

Figure 5-20. *Decide shape orchestration example*

5-7. Receiving Multiple Message Formats in a Single Orchestration

Problem

You need to execute the same orchestration logic for two or more different schemas.

Solution

Instead of creating separate orchestrations with identical logic, you can have one orchestration that uses the Listen shape and multiple Receive shapes. The Listen shape enables an orchestration to listen for any messages matching the schemas of any Receive shapes within the Listen shape. A Listen shape can contain multiple Receive shapes, all listening for different messages. In this solution, we will look at how to create an orchestration that listens for either of two messages to arrive.

The first step in the process is to define two different schemas to represent the different documents for which the orchestration will be listening. A typical example of this would be two versions of the same schema, where the elements defined differ enough to warrant a completely different schema. For instance, several required nodes on version 1 may not exist on version 2. Another example would be two different schemas representing similar data (such as customer, order, and so on) from two different legacy systems. In both cases, you would need to have both of the documents instantiate the same orchestration and be subject to the same rules and workflow.

For this solution, we will assume the following two documents are being used, representing different versions of the Person schema:

```
<ns0:Person xmlns:ns0="http://SampleListenShape.Person.V2">
  <ID/>
  <Name/>
  <Role/>
  <Age/>
</ns0:Person>

<ns0:Person xmlns:ns0="http://SampleSolution.Person">
  <ID/>
  <FirstName/>
  <MiddleName/>
  <LastName/>
  <Role/>
  <Age/>
</ns0:Person>
```

1. In an empty orchestration, drop a Listen shape onto the design surface.

2. Add two Receive shapes within the Listen shape.

    a. Set the Activate property on both Receive shapes to True.

    b. Rename the Receive shapes to Receive_Ver_1 and Receive_Ver_2. This is for reference purposes only.

    c. Create two message variables in the orchestration (click the Orchestration tab, right-click Messages, and select New Message), named msgVer1 and msgVer2, pointing them to the appropriate schema.

    d. Set the message type of Receive_Ver_1 to msgVer1 and Receive_Ver_2 to msgVer2.

3. Add a new port to the Port Surface with the following properties (using the Port Configuration Wizard).

    a. Name the new port Port_Receive_Incoming.

    b. Create a new port type of PortType_ReceiveIncoming.

    c. Select "I'll always receive messages on this port."

    d. Set the port binding to Specify Later, or give a file path and set it to Specify Now.

4. Create two operations on the port (there will be one created automatically). Right-click the port, name the operation Operation_VI, and set the Message Type to msgVer1. Repeat this to add Operation_V2 with the Message Type set to msgVer2.

5. Add a map to transform the version 1 documents into version 2. This will allow the orchestration to work with one message type throughout.

    a. Add a construct message with a Transform shape under the Receive_Ver_1 shape.

    b. Create a new map.

    c. Set the source schema to msgVer1 and the destination schema to msgVer2. The orchestration will resemble Figure 5-21.

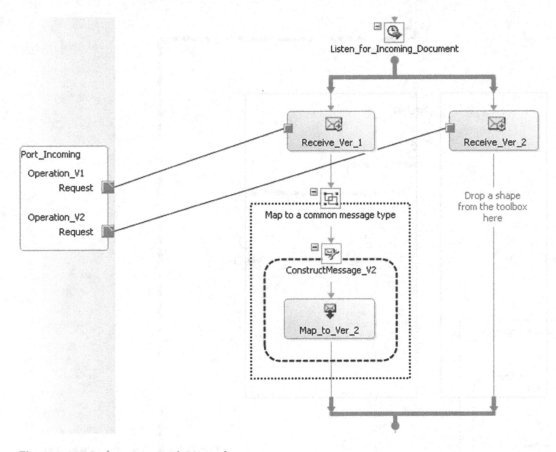

Figure 5-21. *Orchestration with Listen shape*

At this point, the orchestration can be deployed, bound to a receive port, and started. If either version of the Person schema is dropped on the MessageBox (via a port or directly bound), the orchestration will instantiate.

How It Works

This recipe demonstrated how to uses the Listen shape with multiple Receive shapes. There are alternative ways to use the Listen shape. One of the most common is a combination of a Receive shape and a Delay shape. This can be used for polling behavior in a long-running orchestration. For example, an orchestration could be set up to listen for a document to be dropped on a file directory. If a file is not dropped within a certain amount of time (as specified in the Delay shape), a series of steps could take place (such as notifying an administrator). By adding a Loop shape, the orchestration could return to listening for the document to arrive. An example of this is shown in Figure 5-22.

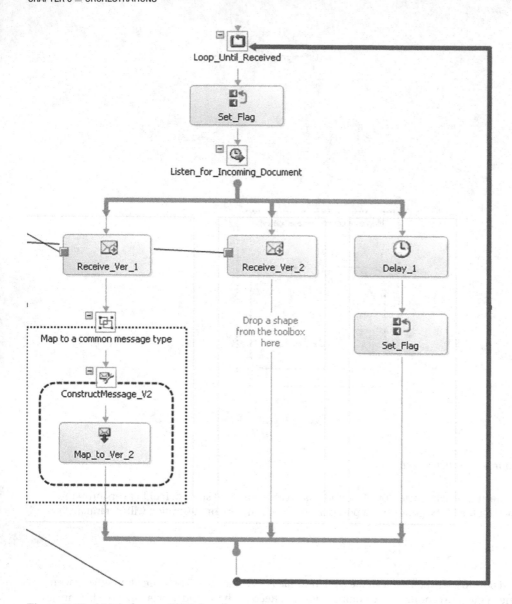

Figure 5-22. *Listen shape with Delay shape*

5-8. Calling External Assemblies
Problem

You need to call a method contained in a .NET class library assembly. You want to understand how to reference this assembly within your BizTalk project and how to call it from an Expression shape.

Solution

This solution will walk you through referencing an external assembly and calling the assembly from code within an Expression shape. Assume that the assembly is called SampleClass.dll, which contains a class called Helper. The Helper class has a function to set a string of characters to uppercase, as shown in Listing 5-3.

Listing 5-3. Sample C# Assembly

```
using System;
using System.Collections.Generic;
using System.Linq;
using System.Text;

namespace SampleClass
{
 [Serializable]
 public class SampleClass
 {
  public string strToUpperCase(string input)
  {
   input = input.ToUpper();
   return input;
  }
 }
}
```

Once the C# assembly has been built and the DLL is available, use the following steps to reference the assembly.

1.   Open a BizTalk project in Visual Studio.

2.   In the Solution Explorer, right-click References under the project header, and select Add Reference.

3.   In the Add Reference dialog box, click the Browse tab, find the SampleClass.dll assembly, and then click OK.

4.   Now that the assembly is available in the BizTalk project, create a new orchestration variable. With an orchestration open, click the Orchestration View window. Right-click the Variables folder, and select New Variable from the drop-down menu.

5.   In the Properties window of the variable, set the following properties (see Figure 5-23):

   •   Name the variable objSample.

   •   Add a description, such as Demonstration Object.

   •   Specify the variable's .NET type by clicking the drop-down box for the Type property and selecting <.NET Class>. In the Select Artifact Type dialog box, select the SampleClass class, as shown in Figure 5-24.

Figure 5-23. *Variable Properties window*

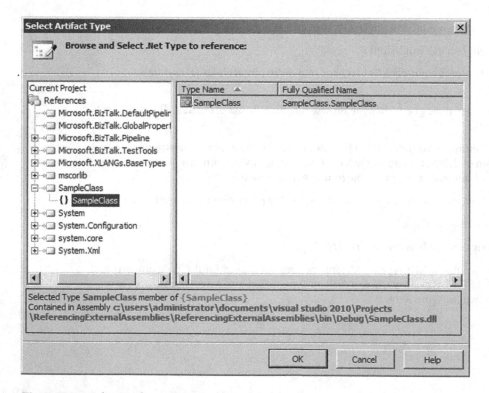

Figure 5-24. *Selecting the artifact type*

6. Drop an Expression shape in the orchestration, and enter the following code to invoke the external assembly, as shown in Figure 5-25.

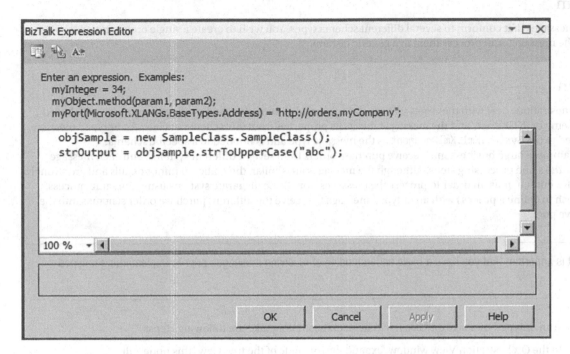

Figure 5-25. *Adding code to the Expression shape*

How It Works

When creating a .NET class variable in BizTalk, an option exists to Use Default Constructor. This property causes an instance of the object to be constructed when the orchestration instantiates. If this property is set to False, the variable will need to be instantiated in an Expression shape through the *new* keyword (as in step 6 of the solution).

Another property that should be noted is on the referenced assembly itself: Copy Local. This property indicates whether the assembly referenced should be copied into the local bin directory when a project is built. Several factors will help decide whether the assembly should be copied locally; if a reference is to a dynamic assembly (such as another BizTalk project that is built at the same time as the project in which it is referenced), you probably will not want to copy the assembly locally.

It is important to note that when calling a .NET assembly that is not marked as serializable, it must be called from an atomic scope. When creating an assembly that will be used primarily by BizTalk, it is appropriate to mark all classes as serializable. The following example demonstrates doing this in C#.

```
[Serializable]
public class Example { }
```

5-9. Receiving Untyped Messages

Problem

You have messages that conform to several different schema types. You wish to create a single orchestration to consume the messages and process them in a generic fashion.

Solution

BizTalk orchestrations deal with messages that are strongly typed. A strongly typed message conforms to a selected BizTalk schema or .NET class, and the message inherits its properties from this schema or class. An untyped message is configured to use System.Xml.XmlDocument as the message type and is not tied to a specific schema.

For example, a large business may receive purchase orders from several different systems, and each message must follow the same processing steps. Although the messages are similar, they differ in minor details and are strongly typed to different schemas. In order to process the messages from these disparate systems using the same process, you may wish to define a process with an untyped message to receive the different purchase order schemas into the same receive port.

■ **Note**   It is important that you have a basic understanding of receiving messages prior to implementing untyped messages.

To create an untyped message and use it within an orchestration, take the following steps:

1. In the Orchestration View window, expand the top node of the tree view (this node will have the same type name as the orchestration) so that the Messages folder is visible.

2. Right-click the Messages folder, and select New Message, which creates a message.

3. Click the new message, and give it a descriptive name in the Properties window. In this example, the message is named incomingOrder.

4. Click the Message Type property in the Properties window, and select the .NET type System.Xml.XmlDocument.

5. From the toolbox, drag a Receive shape onto the orchestration directly beneath the green circle at the top of the design surface.

6. With the Receive shape selected, specify the shape's Name, Message, and Activate properties. In our example, we use ReceiveOrder, incomingOrder (created in step 3), and True, respectively.

■ **Note**   All message types will be received by an untyped port. Therefore, if you directly bind your port to the MessageBox, you will receive every message received into the MessageBox. This could create unintended behavior down the road.

---

7. Right-click one of the Port Surface areas, and select New Configured Port. This will open the Port Configuration Wizard.

8. Step through the Port Configuration Wizard, specifying the following items (accept all other default values):

- *Port name*: ReceiveOrderPort

- *New port type name*: ReceiveOrderPortType

- *Port binding*: Specify Later

- *Configure the Request*: Connect the orchestration port's Request operation to the Receive shape.

How It Works

Untyped messages are a deceptively complex and powerful BizTalk feature. Untyped messages are powerful, because they allow for abstracted processes. For instance, rather than create three processes for three different purchase orders that your company receives from trading partners, you could create a single process that handles the different messages in the same process. Although the single process may increase in complexity, it reduces the amount of maintainable code.

When implementing untyped messages, pay attention to the following areas:

Direct binding: Creating an untyped message that is directly bound to the MessageBox is not recommended. All schema-based messages within BizTalk have a base type of System.Xml.XmlDocument. The implication of this fact is that using a message variable that is typed as System.Xml.XmlDocument will set up a receive subscription for all messages that are received into the MessageBox through the directly bound port. Since, in almost every case, this is not the desired functionality, take caution when implementing this type of scenario.

Casting: Creating an untyped message will negate many of the common operations available for that schema type. For instance, accessing common promoted properties (MessageDataBaseProperties) and using Transform shapes are not supported with untyped messages. It is possible, though, to cast between an untyped message and a typed message. To cast a message, create an instance of the typed message in a Construct/Assignment shape, and assign the untyped message to the typed message. You now have the ability to use the typed message with all associated orchestration functionality.

Promoted properties: Although it is not possible to access common promoted properties (MessageDataBaseProperties) for an untyped message, it is possible to create and access a type of promoted property known as a MessageContextPropertyBase property for an untyped message. Refer to the BizTalk help file for more information about how to create this type of context property within your property schema. Setting the MessageContextPropertyBase property is done in the same manner as setting other promoted properties.

■ **Note** MessageContextPropertyBase properties of untyped messages may be set within the orchestration, but the context property cannot be filtered on within other services unless a correlation set containing the MessageContextPropertyBase property is first initialized. In addition, it is not possible to map on a send port, because the MessageType property, which is required to match a message to a map, is not promoted for untyped messages.

By considering direct binding, casting, and promoted properties, you can safeguard your solution from complex bugs that are difficult to identify and triage.

5-10. Using the Parallel Action Shape

Problem

From within an orchestration, you would like to complete numerous activities at the same time and independently of one another.

Solution

A Parallel Action shape may be added to an orchestration to implement the concurrent processing of all parallel branches when the orchestration executes. Processing beyond the parallel branches will not occur until all branches of the Parallel Action shape have completed. The following steps outline how to add a Parallel Action shape to your orchestration.

1. Open the project containing the orchestration.

2. Open the orchestration.

3. Select the Parallel Action shape from the toolbox, and drag it to the appropriate location within the orchestration.

4. Select the Parallel Action shape and update its properties.

    a. Change the default name if desired.

    b. Add a description if desired.

5. To add an additional branch, right-click the Parallel Action shape, and select New Parallel Branch.

■ **Note**   To delete a branch, right-click the branch, and select Delete. To delete the Parallel Action shape, right-click the shape, and select Delete.

How It Works

You can use the Parallel Action shape within an orchestration to create concurrent processing. Care should be taken when accessing data from within parallel actions to avoid contention or deadlock situations. This can also be avoided by using synchronized scopes in conjunction with parallel actions. Additionally, if an orchestration is terminated from within a branch of a Parallel Action shape, the process will terminate regardless of the status of the processing within the other parallel branches.

5-11. Using the Loop Shape

Problem

You need to repeat a series of steps in an orchestration until a certain condition is met.

Solution

You can use the Loop shape in a BizTalk orchestration, in a manner similar to using a loop in any programming language, such as this looping logic:

```
int a = 0;
while(a < 3)
{
  System.Console.WriteLine(a);
  a = a + 1;
}
```

As an example, the following steps show how to implement a loop that terminates after a counter variable has been incremented to a certain value. The orchestration will loop three times, logging its progress to the Windows Event Viewer.

■ **Note**   The example demonstrates a complete orchestration that could be called from another orchestration using the Call or Start Orchestration shape. To make this a stand-alone orchestration, simply add a Receive shape as the first step and bind it to a port.

---

1. In an empty orchestration, create a new variable called intCount. Make it of type Int32. This will represent the loop counter.

2. Drop an Expression shape on the design surface. Rename this shape to Set_Count. Then double-click the shape, and type in the following code:

   ```
   //initialize counter
   intCount = 0;
   ```

3. Drop a Loop shape below the Set_Count shape. Double-click the Loop shape, and enter the following code (note there is no semicolon):

   ```
   //loop while count is less than 3
   intCount < 3
   ```

4. Drop another Expression shape inside the Loop shape, and rename it Increase_Count. Enter the following code:

   ```
   //increase counter
               intCount = intCount + 1;
               //log to the event viewer
               System.Diagnostics.EventLog.WriteEntry("Count",
   System.Convert.ToString(intCount));
   ```

The orchestration is shown in Figure 5-26.

Figure 5-26. *Loop shape with counter*

How It Works

The Loop shape has many applications, from looping through XML documents to supplementing the Listen shape, exception handling routines, and so on. Orchestrations can mimic the behavior of long-running Windows services with the proper placement of a Loop shape. For example, if you need to poll for data on a timed interval, you could set up an orchestration to do this. An initial Receive shape would instantiate the orchestration and immediately enter a loop. Once in the loop, it would never exit, looping every [x] number of minutes to reexecute a series of steps. The orchestration would be long-running and would never end until terminated manually. An example of this type of orchestration is shown in Figure 5-27.

Figure 5-27. *Long-running polling orchestration*

5-12. Using the Transform Shape

Problem

You would like to transform an XML message, or multiple XML messages, into the format of another specified XML schema.

Solution

Using the Transform shape within the BizTalk Orchestration Designer allows you to transform XML messages into the format of another specified XML schema. As an example, assume an orchestration message (Customer schema) requires transformation (mapping) in preparation for a publication to another line-of-business application.

```
<Customer>
  <FirstName> </FirstName>
  <LastName> </LastName>
  <MiddleInit> </MiddleInit>
  <Age></Age>
  <Address>
  <AddrLine1> </AddrLine1>
  <AddrLine1> </AddrLine1>
  <AddrLine1> </AddrLine1>
  <Zip> </Zip>
  <State> </State>
  <Country></Country>
  </Address>
</Customer>
```

In this example, the outbound specification (CustomerRecord) has a different structure and form than that required by the line-of-business application.

```
<CustomerRecord >
  <Name> </Name>
  <MiddleInit> </MiddleInit>
  <Address> </Address>
  <Zip> </Zip>
  <State> </State>
  <Country> </Country>
  <DateTime> </DateTime>
</CustomerRecord>
```

To use the Transform shape within the Orchestration Designer, follow these steps:

1. Open the BizTalk project that contains the orchestration.

2. Ensure that two orchestration messages have been created. The msgCustomers message should reference the Customer schema, and the msgCustomerRecords message should reference the CustomerRecord schema.

3. Drag a Transform shape from the BizTalk Orchestrations section of the toolbox. Place the shape under the Receive shape on the design surface. This automatically creates a Construct Message container and a Transform shape.

4. Click the exclamation mark (tool tip) on the Transform message shape within the Construct Message boundary.

5. Click the missing or invalid mapping configuration value in the drop-down list. The Transform Configuration dialog box will appear.

6. In the Enter Configuration Information Input section of the Transform Configuration dialog box, select the Existing Map radio button. (The New Map option allows you to configure the Construct shape by creating a new map.)

7. For the Fully Qualified Map Name Input option, select the map desired for the transformation. In this example, the Transform_Sample.mapCustomer map was selected.

8. Under the Transform node, select Source. Then, click the Source_Transform input, and select the msgCustomers orchestration message. This is the orchestration message assigned to the orchestration and is the same schema as that of the inbound map: Transform_Sample.mapCustomer.

9. Under the Transform node, select Destination. Then, click the Destination_Transform input, and select the msgCustomerRecords orchestration message. This is the orchestration message assigned to the orchestration and is the same schema as that of the outbound map, Transform_Sample.mapCustomer. Figure 5-28 shows the completed configuration.

Figure 5-28. *Transform Configuration dialog box*

10. Click OK to complete the configuration of the Transform shape. Notice that the Construct Message shape is automatically configured with the Messages Constructed property of CustomerRecords. This indicates that the message constructed in the message transform is that of the destination schema specified in the transform map.

How It Works

The Transform shape allows you to map messages from one format to another within the BizTalk Orchestration Designer. This functionality assists in addressing common enterprise integration challenges, where destination processes and systems require a different format to that specified by the source process or system.

The Transform shape allows the assignment of an existing map or the creation of a new map within the Transform Configuration dialog box. Also, you can transform one or multiple source messages into one or multiple destination formats. To enable this, create a new map within the Transform shape configuration, by specifying multiple input messages and/or multiple destination messages. This will automatically create a map with the specified source and destination messages. This capability is useful when you need to partition message calls for the destination process or system. Figure 5-29 shows creating a destination with three schemas (two are identical in this example), and Figure 5-30 illustrates a BizTalk map with multiple messages.

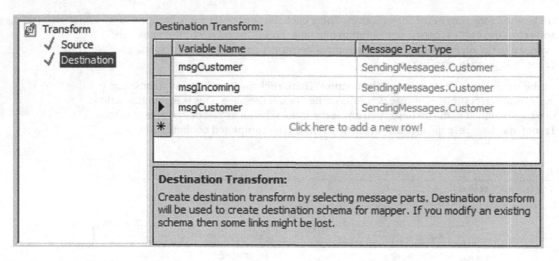

	Variable Name	Message Part Type
	msgCustomer	SendingMessages.Customer
	msgIncoming	SendingMessages.Customer
▶	msgCustomer	SendingMessages.Customer
*	Click here to add a new row!	

Destination Transform:

Create destination transform by selecting message parts. Destination transform will be used to create destination schema for mapper. If you modify an existing schema then some links might be lost.

Figure 5-29. *Creating multiple messages in the destination mapping*

Figure 5-30. *The map with the multi-message target*

■ **Note** Native multiple message mapping can be done only inside an orchestration.

Message transformation may be required to perform deterministic data enrichment, required by the destination system. For example, this scenario is very common within the enterprise resource planning (ERP) application paradigm, where target integration processes (for example purchase orders, advance shipment notices, and invoices) require additional information to persist and update ERP process information based on the process and source context of a message.

A further consideration of using the Transform shape is that of implementing exception handling. By using the Transform shape in conjunction with a Scope shape, you can handle exceptions. Based on message transformation failure, orchestration logic can be implemented to take a course of action to handle the exception. This approach is different from that of implementing mapping within send or receive ports. Here, exceptions must be handled by the failure context of the port object.

Message transformation and message mapping are fundamental requirements for any enterprise integration platform, and BizTalk enables this capability via its mapping and orchestration tool set.

5-13. Using the Call Orchestration and Start Orchestration Shapes

Problem

Within a BizTalk orchestration, you would like to reuse common process logic across BizTalk processes.

Solution

Within a BizTalk orchestration, you can call or start other orchestrations without sending a message outside an orchestration's context. BizTalk orchestrations can function as traditional functions, calling one another synchronously or asynchronously. Using the Call Orchestration shape allows a parent orchestration to call a child orchestration with a set of parameters and receive output back (synchronous). Using the Start Orchestration shape allows a parent orchestration to call a child orchestration with any set of parameters and move on, independent of receiving a result back (asynchronous).

As an example, assume that you would like to synchronously call an orchestration to perform a validation routine on a message.

1. Open the BizTalk project that contains the orchestration that you would like to perform the Call Orchestration functionality.

2. Drag a Call Orchestration shape from the toolbox onto your design surface.

3. Click the exclamation mark (tool tip) on the shape. Select No Called Orchestration - Click to Configure. The Call Orchestration Configuration dialog box appears.

4. In the Call Orchestration Configuration dialog box, select the orchestration you wish to call, as shown in Figure 5-31. In this dialog box, you can also select parameters that can be passed by an orchestration. Parameters are passed in the form of .NET variables. Only orchestration types that have Activation set to False—that is, only orchestrations that are invoked from another process—will be available for selection. In this instance, this is the calling orchestration rather than message instantiation.

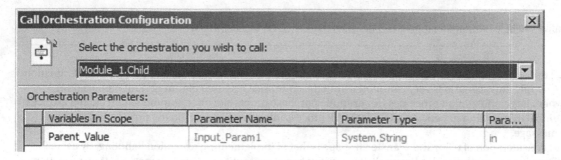

Figure 5-31. Call Orchestration Configuration dialog box

5. Click OK to complete the Call Orchestration shape configuration.

How It Works

Orchestration shapes in the BizTalk Orchestration Designer allow for the calling of other orchestrations synchronously or asynchronously. The choice of shape depends on the scenario and design requirements specified for the operating solution.

Calling an orchestration synchronously gives you the ability to nest functionality, similar to calling a method synchronously in any programming language. Calling an orchestration asynchronously allows an orchestration's functionality to be abstracted and performed independently without creating dependencies on the calling and invoking orchestration process.

In addition to calling an orchestration, you can optionally pass parameters to the calling orchestration. Parameters can be used to complement or aid in message processing without the need for custom code development to construct process-centric message context logic. To achieve this within a BizTalk orchestration, parameters are defined in the form of .NET BizTalk type variables. For example, messages, variables, and correlation sets are all BizTalk type variables eligible to be passed with the calling orchestration. Figure 5-32 shows the configuration of a callable orchestration (note that there is no Receive shape required) with a single input parameter.

Figure 5-32. *Configuring a callable orchestration*

5-14. Configuring Basic Correlations

Problem

You need to send a message out of an orchestration and receive a response back into the same orchestration instance.

Solution

You can use a correlation set to tell an orchestration to accept only messages that have the same information as a message sent by the orchestration. As an example, suppose you have a customer support website where customers can place support requests and expect a response to appear on the website within two days. When a customer places a request, the website sends a support request message containing a unique SupportID to BizTalk, which BizTalk forwards to a customer relationship management (CRM) system. Once support personnel monitoring the CRM system respond to the customer request, the response containing the same SupportID goes through BizTalk and posts to the customer support website for the customer to view.

Occasionally, the support personnel cannot respond within two days, either because the request is not clear or because it is an extraordinarily tough request. When support personnel cannot solve the customer's request in time, the business policy is to elevate the request to a special support team that will work one-on-one with the customer to help with the problem. Unfortunately, the CRM system does not have the functionality to escalate the support request after the standard time period. However, fortunately for your customers, BizTalk can implement the business process and coordinate these two messages easily using correlation sets.

The same orchestration instance that forwards the request to the CRM system must receive the correlating response. In this example, BizTalk will know to receive the response with the same SupportID as the message forwarded to the other system.

1. Create an orchestration that defines the basic flow of messages. Figure 5-33 illustrates a basic message flow where the orchestration receives a message, forwards the message on to another system, and waits for a response. If the orchestration does not receive a response within a specified amount of time, the orchestration sends the original message to another location for higher priority processing.

Figure 5-33. *Defining the message flow*

2. A correlation type defines the information that BizTalk uses to decide which orchestration instance gets the response. To create the correlation type, in the Orchestration View window, right-click Correlation Types, and select New Correlation Type, as shown in Figure 5-34. The Correlation Properties dialog box appears.

Figure 5-34. *Creating the correlation type*

3. In the Correlation Properties dialog box, select the promoted property that defines the correlation information, and click the Add button. In this example, select the `ServiceID` promoted property of the `ServiceRequest` schema, as shown in Figure 5-35. Select OK to complete the creation of the new correlation type, and rename it to `ServiceIDType`.

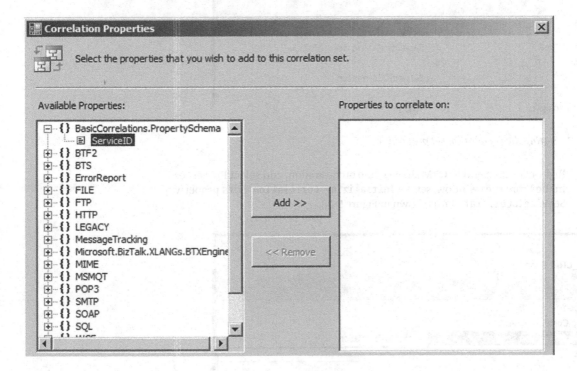

Figure 5-35. *Defining the members of the correlation type*

■ **Note** While a correlation set type can contain any promoted property, it cannot contain distinguished fields.

---

4. To create the correlation set, right-click `Correlation Sets` in the Orchestration View window, and select New Correlation Set, as shown in Figure 5-36.

Figure 5-36. Creating the correlation set

5. In the Properties window, change the name of the new correlation set to `ServiceIDCorrelation`, and set the correlation type to the `ServiceIDType` created in steps 2 and 3, as shown in Figure 5-37.

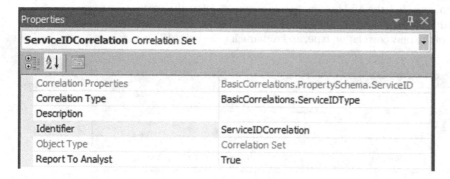

Figure 5-37. Setting the correlation set properties

6. Right-click the Send to CRM shape in the orchestration, and select Properties. In the Properties window, set the `Initializing Correlation Sets` property to `ServiceIDCorrelation`, as shown in Figure 5-38.

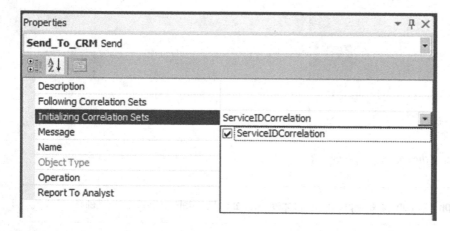

Figure 5-38. Initializing the correlation set

7. Right-click the Get CRM Response shape, and select Properties. In the Properties window, set the Following Correlation Sets property to ServiceIDCorrelation, as shown in Figure 5-39. This ensures that the orchestration will accept only messages with the same information at runtime, which is the specific support identifier in this example. While sending the outbound message, BizTalk creates an instance subscription with the properties of the correlation set to receive the correlated inbound message.

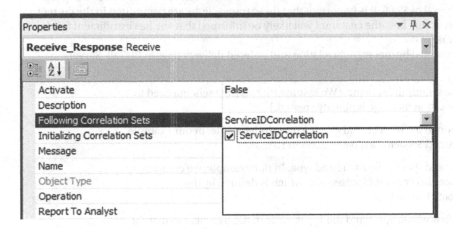

Figure 5-39. *Following the initialized correlation set*

How It Works

The orchestration in Figure 5-33 defines the basic flow of messages that BizTalk needs to coordinate. However, the time between when BizTalk sends the support message to the CRM system and receives a response could be as long as two days. You would expect that there could be any number of outstanding customer support requests during two days. Moreover, because many support requests are sent to the CRM system, many BizTalk orchestrations would be waiting concurrently for a response. Further, suppose one request has already taken over a day of research, when a new one arrives that will take only a few minutes to handle. BizTalk creates a new orchestration instance to forward each message to the CRM system, but how will BizTalk know which orchestration instance should receive the response message?

By using a correlation set, you can tell an orchestration to accept only messages that have the same information as a message sent by the orchestration. A *correlation set* is a container for holding information of a particular correlation type. A *correlation type* defines the correlation set, telling BizTalk the fields in a message that will create the correlation set. In this example, we have only one SupportID to keep track of, so we create only one correlation set. When BizTalk initially sends the support request to the CRM system, the orchestration instance initializes the correlation set containing the SupportID to keep track of the specific SupportID in the messages. The action receiving the response from the CRM system follows the same correlation set, meaning that the orchestration instance will accept only messages with the same SupportID as the message sent to the CRM system.

5-15. Maintaining Message Order
Problem

You are implementing an integration point where message order must be maintained. Messages must be delivered from your source system to your destination system in first-in/first-out (FIFO) sequence.

Solution

In scenarios where FIFO-ordered delivery is required, *sequential convoys* handle the *race condition* that occurs as BizTalk attempts to process subscriptions for messages received at the same time. Ordered message delivery is a common requirement that necessitates the use of sequential convoys. For example, FIFO processing of messages is usually required for financial transactions. It is easy to see why ordered delivery is required when looking at a simple example of a deposit and withdrawal from a bank account. If a customer has $0.00 in her account, makes a deposit of $10.00, and then makes a withdrawal of $5.00, it is important that these transactions are committed in the correct order. If the withdrawal transaction occurs first, the customer will likely be informed that she has insufficient funds, even though she has just made her deposit.

Sequential convoys are implemented by message correlation and ordered delivery flags in BizTalk Server, as outlined in the following steps.

1. Open the project that contains the schema. (We assume that an XSD schema used to define a financial transaction message is already created.)

2. Add a new orchestration to the project, and give it a descriptive name. In our example, the orchestration is named SequentialConvoyOrchestration.

3. Create a new message, and specify the name and type. In our example, we create a message named FinancialTransactionMessage, which is defined by the FinancialTransactionSchema schema.

4. In the Orchestration View window, expand the Types node of the tree view so that the Correlation Types folder is visible.

5. Right-click the Correlation Types folder, and select New Correlation Type, which creates a correlation type and launches the Correlation Properties dialog box.

6. In the Correlation Properties dialog box, select the properties that the convoy's correlation set will be based on. In our example, we select the BTS.ReceivePortName property, which indicates which receive port the message was received through.

7. Click the new correlation type, and give it a descriptive name in the Properties window. In our example, the correlation type is named ReceivePortNameCorrelationType.

8. In the Orchestration View window, right-click the Correlation Set folder, select New Correlation Set, and specify a name and correlation type. In our example, we create a correlation set named ReceivePortNameCorrelationSet and select ReceivePortNameCorrelationType.

9. From the toolbox, drag the following onto the design surface in top-down order. The final orchestration is shown in Figure 5-40.

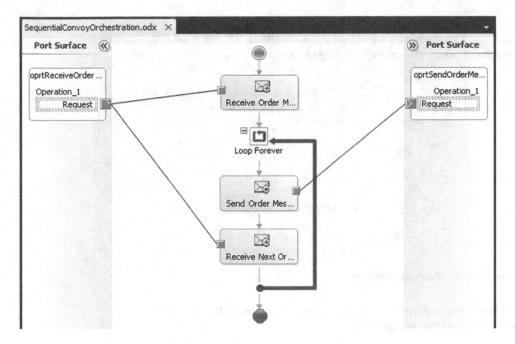

Figure 5-40. *Configuring a sequential convoy*

- *Receive shape to receive the initial order message*: Configure this shape to use the FinancialTransactionMessage, activate the orchestration, initialize ReceivePortNameCorrelationSet, and to use an orchestration receive port.

- *Loop shape to allow the orchestration to receive multiple messages*: Configure this shape with the expression Loop == true (allowing the orchestration to run in perpetuity).

- *Send shape within the Loop shape*: This delivers the financial transaction message the destination system. Configure this shape to use an orchestration send port.

- *Receive shape within the Loop shape*: This receives the next message (based on the order messages were received) in the convoy. Configure this shape to use the FinancialTransactionMessage, to follow the ReceivePortNameCorrelationSet and to use the same orchestration receive port as the first Receive shape.

10. Build and deploy the BizTalk project.

11. Create a receive port and receive location to receive messages from the source system.

12. Create a send port to deliver messages to the destination system. In our solution, we send messages to an MSMQ queue named TransactionOut. In the Transport Advanced Options section of the Send Port Properties dialog box, select the Ordered Delivery option, as shown in Figure 5-41.

Figure 5-41. *Configuring an ordered delivery send port*

13. Bind the orchestration to the receive and send ports, configure the host for the orchestration, and start the orchestration.

How It Works

In this solution, we show how a convoy can be used to sequentially handle messages within an orchestration. The sequential convoy consists of the ReceivePortNameCorrelationSet and the ordered delivery flags specified on the receive location and send port. The first Receive shape initializes the correlation set, which is based on the receive port name by which the order was consumed. Initializing a correlation set instructs BizTalk Server to associate the correlation type data with the orchestration instance. This allows BizTalk to route all messages that have identical correlation type criteria (in our case, all messages consumed by the receive port bound to the orchestration) to the same instance. The Ordered Processing flag further instructs BizTalk Server to maintain order when determining which message should be delivered next to the orchestration.

■ **Note** The adapter used to receive messages into sequential convoy orchestrations must implement ordered delivery. If an adapter supports ordered delivery, the check box will appear on the Transport Advanced Options tab.

The Send shape in the orchestration delivers the financial transaction message to a destination system for further processing. The second Receive shape follows the correlation set, which allows the next message consumed by the receive port to be routed to the already running orchestration instance. Both the Send and second Receive shapes are contained within a loop, which runs in perpetuity. This results in a single orchestration instance that processes all messages for a given correlation set, in sequential order. This type of orchestration is sometimes referred to as a *singleton* orchestration.

Working with Sequential Convoys

The term *convoy set* is used to describe the correlation sets used to enforce convoy message handling. While our example used only a single correlation set, you can use multiple correlation sets to implement a sequential convoy. Regardless of how many correlation sets are used, sequential convoy sets must be initialized by the same Receive shape and then followed by a subsequent Receive shape.

Sequential convoys can also accept untyped messages (messages defined as being of type XmlDocument). You can see how this is important by extending the financial transaction scenario, and assuming that a deposit and withdrawal are actually different message types (defined by different schemas). In this case, a message type of XmlDocument would be used on the convoy Receive shapes.

Fine-Tuning Sequential Convoys

While our example does implement a sequential convoy, you can fine-tune the solution to handle sequential processing in a more efficient and graceful manner. As it stands now, the SequentialConvoyOrchestration handles each message received from the source MSMQ queue in order. This essentially single-threads the integration point, significantly decreasing throughput. Single-threading does achieve FIFO processing, but it is a bit heavy-handed. In our example, *all* transactions do not have to be delivered in order—just those for a particular customer. By modifying the convoy set to be based on a customer ID field in the financial transaction schema (instead of the receive port name), you can allow transactions for different customers to be handled simultaneously. This change would take advantage of BizTalk Server's ability to process multiple messages simultaneously, increasing the performance of your solution.

■ **Note**   In this scenario, you must use a pipeline that promotes the customer ID property (such as the XmlReceive pipeline) on the receive location bound to the sequential convoy orchestration. The PassThru receive pipeline cannot be used in this scenario.

Changing the convoy set to include a customer ID field would also impact the number of orchestrations running in perpetuity. Each new customer ID would end up creating a new orchestration, which could result in hundreds, if not thousands, of constantly running instances. This situation is not particularly desirable from either a performance or management perspective. To address this issue, you can implement a timeout feature allowing the orchestration to terminate if subsequent messages are not received within a specified period of time. Take the following steps to implement this enhancement. The updated orchestration is shown in Figure 5-42.

Figure 5-42. *Configuring a terminating sequential convoy*

1. Add a Listen shape in between the Send shape and second Receive shape.

2. Move the second Receive shape to the left-hand branch of the Listen shape.

3. Add a Delay shape to the right-hand branch of the Listen shape. Configure this shape to delay for the appropriate timeout duration. In our example, we set the timeout to be 10 seconds by using the following value for the Delay property:

```
new System.TimeSpan(0,0,0,10)
```

4. Add an Expression shape directly below the Delay shape. Configure this shape to exit the convoy by using the following expression:

```
Loop = false;
```

Finally, you can enhance the solution to ensure that messages are successfully delivered to the destination system before processing subsequent messages. In the current solution, messages are sent out of the orchestration to the MessageBox database via the orchestration port. Once this happens, the orchestration continues; there is no indication that the message was actually delivered to its end destination. For example, if the destination MSMQ queue was momentarily offline, a message may be suspended while subsequent messages may be delivered successfully. Take the following steps to implement this enhancement. The updated orchestration portion is shown in Figure 5-43.

Figure 5-43. *Capturing delivery failure exceptions*

1. Change the orchestration send port's Delivery Notification property to Transmitted.

2. Add a Scope shape directly above the Send shape.

3. Move the Send shape inside the Scope shape.

4. Add an exception handler by right-clicking the Scope shape. Configure this shape to have an Exception Object Type property of Microsoft.XLANGs.BaseTypes.DeliveryFailureException. Enter a descriptive name for the Exception Object Name property.

5. Add an Expression shape inside the exception handler block added in the previous step. Configure this shape to appropriately handle delivery failure exceptions. In our solution, we simply write the event to the trace log via the following code:

```
System.Diagnostics.Trace.Write("Delivery Failure Exception Occurred - " +
deliveryFailureExc.Message);
```

5-16. Configuring Parallel Convoys

Problem

You are implementing a data aggregation integration point, which requires data to be retrieved from multiple systems. Each source system publishes messages, and a message from each system must be received before further processing can take place.

Solution

A *parallel convoy* is a business process (orchestration) that receives multiple messages in parallel (at the same time) that relate to each other. Parallel convoys handle the *race condition* that occurs as BizTalk attempts to process subscriptions for messages received at the same time.

A common scenario requiring parallel convoys is where multiple messages for a specific event must be received before a business process can start. As an example, suppose your company's policy allows an order to be shipped only once payment has been approved and stock level has been verified. Payment approval comes from a financial system, and stock-level information comes from an inventory system. Once both systems publish their respective messages for a specific order, that order can be delivered to the customer.

Parallel convoys are implemented by message correlation and Parallel Action shapes in BizTalk Server, as shown in the following steps.

1. Open the project that contains the schemas. (We assume that XSD schemas used to define payment approval and stock-level verification messages are already created.)

2. Add a new orchestration to the project, and give it a descriptive name. In our example, the orchestration is named `ParallelConvoyOrchestration`.

3. Create two new messages, and specify the name and type of each. In our example, we create messages named `PaymentApprovalMessage` and `StockLevelConfirmationMessage`, which are defined by the `PaymentApprovalSchema` and `StockLevelConfirmationSchema` schemas, respectively.

4. In the Orchestration View window, expand the `Types` node of the tree view so that the `Correlation Types` folder is visible.

5. Right-click the `Correlation Types` folder, and select New Correlation Type, which creates a correlation type and launches the Correlation Properties dialog box.

6. In the Correlation Properties dialog box, select the properties that the correlation will be based on. In our scenario, we select the `OrderID` property, which has been promoted from the `PaymentApprovalSchema` and `StockLevelConfirmationSchema` schemas.

7. Click the new correlation type, and give it a descriptive name in the Properties window. In our example, the correlation type is named `OrderIDCorrelationType`.

8. In the Orchestration View window, right-click the `Correlation Set` folder, select New Correlation Set, and specify a name and correlation type. In our example, we create a correlation set named `OrderIDCorrelationSet` and select `OrderIDCorrelationType`.

9. From the toolbox, drag the following onto the design surface in top-down order; the parallel convoy configuration is shown in Figure 5-44:

- Parallel Actions shape to receive the response from the financial and inventory systems.

- Receive shape to receive messages from the financial system. Place this shape on the left-hand branch of the Parallel Actions shape. Configure this shape to use the PaymentApprovalMessage, to initialize the OrderIDCorrelationSet, to activate the orchestration, and to use an orchestration receive port.

- Receive shape to receive messages from the inventory system. Place this shape on the right-hand branch of the Parallel Actions shape. Configure this shape to use the StockLevelConfirmationMessage, to initialize the OrderIDCorrelationSet, to activate the orchestration, and to use an orchestration receive port.

- Expression shape to deliver the ship the order. Configure this shape to send the order to the appropriate recipient. In our solution, we simply write a message to the trace log via the following code:

```
System.Diagnostics.Trace.Write("Shipping Order with ID = " +
                        PaymentApprovalMessage
    (ParallelConvoyOrchestration.PropertySchema.OrderID));
```

Figure 5-44. *Configuring a parallel convoy*

How It Works

In this solution, we show how a convoy can be used to concurrently handle messages within an orchestration. The parallel convoy, also referred to as a *concurrent convoy*, consists of the OrderIDCorrelationSet and the Parallel Actions shape. Each Receive shape in the Parallel Actions shape initializes the correlation set, which is based on the order ID. Initializing a correlation set instructs BizTalk Server to associate the correlation type data with the orchestration instance. This allows BizTalk to route all messages that have identical correlation type criteria (in our case, all messages with a specific order ID) to the same instance.

Each of the Receive shapes has its Activate property set to True and its Initializing Correlation configured to the same correlation set. The Receive shape that receives the first message will handle the activation of the orchestration instance and the initializing of the correlation set. The second Receive shape will not activate a new orchestration instance (even though its Activate property is set to True) and will actually follow the correlation set that the other Receive shape initialized.

Based on this example, messages for two order IDs would be handled in the following manner:

1. A payment approval message for order ID 1 is received, which instantiates orchestration instance 1.

2. A stock-level confirmation message for order ID 2 is received, which instantiates orchestration instance 2.

3. A payment approval message for order ID 2 is received, which is correlated and delivered to orchestration 2. The orchestration continues processing, ships order ID 2, and terminates successfully.

4. A stock-level confirmation message for order ID 1 is received, which is correlated and delivered to orchestration 1. The orchestration continues processing, ships order ID 1, and terminates successfully.

While our example used only a single correlation set, multiple correlation sets can be used to implement a parallel convoy. Parallel convoys are defined as having a convoy set that is initialized on multiple branches of a Parallel Actions shape within an orchestration. Regardless of how many correlation sets are used, if multiple Receive shapes initialize a convoy set in a Parallel Actions shape, the same correlation sets must be initialized on all of the Receive shapes.

5-17. Using XPath Queries on Messages

Problem

You need to get and/or set values in a message within an orchestration. There are a number of nodes that cannot be promoted because they are not unique, and you need to be able to access these values.

Solution

To access values in a message, you can use XPath. XPath queries are used to navigate the tree of a given XML document and are typically used within orchestration Message Assignment and Expression shapes. BizTalk XPath queries require two parameters: the first parameter references the XML message, and the second is the query path.

As an example, assume that an orchestration message called msgDemo contains the XML shown in Listing 5-4.

Listing 5-4. Sample XML Instance for XPath Query Example

```
<ns0:NewHireList xmlns:ns0="http://SampleSolution.NewHireList">
  <DateTime>1999-04-05T18:00:00</DateTime>
  <ns1:Person xmlns:ns1="http://SampleSolution.Person">
    <ID>1</ID>
    <Name>S. Jonesy</Name>
    <Role>Embedded Programmer</Role>
    <Age>40</Age>
  </ns1:Person>
  <ns1:Person xmlns:ns1="http://SampleSolution.Person">
    <ID>2</ID>
    <Name>D. Hurley</Name>
    <Role>Artist</Role>
    <Age>45</Age>
  </ns1:Person>
</ns0:NewHireList>
```

The following steps demonstrate getting values, getting a node count, getting an entire XML node, and setting values.

1. To get the value of the <DateTime> element, use the following XPath query. The output of this query is 1999-04-05T18:00:00.

```
xpath(msgDemo,"string(//*[local-name()='DateTime'])")
```

2. To get the value of the <Name> element that is in the same <Person> node as the <ID> which is equal to 2, use the following XPath query. The output of this query will be D. Hurley.

```
xpath(msgDemo,"string(//*[local-name()='Name' and ../*

[local-name()='ID'] = '2'])")
```

3. To get the count of <Person> nodes within the document, use the following XPath query. The output of this query is 2.

```
xpath(msgDemo,"count(//*[local-name()='Person'])")
```

4. To get the entire XML node representation of the second <Person> node, use the following XPath query. Note that this requires formatting the query using the System.String.Format function. The result of this query will be a full XML node.

```
strXPathQuery = System.String.Format("//*[local-name()='Person'][{0}]",2);
            xmlDoc = xpath(msgIncoming,strXPathQuery);

                <ns1:Person xmlns:ns1="http://SampleSolution.Person">
                 <ID>2</ID>
                 <Name>D. Hurley</Name>
                 <Role>Artist</Role>
                 <Age>45</Age>
</ns1:Person>
```

5. To set the value of the <DateTime> element, use the following XPath query. Note that this must be done in a Message Assignment shape, since the value of the message is changing. The message used must first be constructed.

```
xpath(msgDemo, "//*[local-name()='DateTime']") = strDateTime;
```

How It Works

This recipe's solution demonstrated several of the many uses of XPath. One question that often arises is when to use XPath instead of using promoted properties. The ability to promote properties is limited. Elements that repeat within a schema cannot be promoted. Only unique values can be promoted. When you need to set the value of repeating nodes, XPath is the quickest and most versatile approach.

5-18. Using Nontransactional Orchestration Scopes
Problem

You need to define how your orchestration behaves under possible exception conditions.

Solution

Any orchestration can have Scope shapes in it. Place other orchestration shapes within the Scope shape to define the expected behavior of the orchestration. If BizTalk encounters an exception performing the steps inside a Scope shape, it will jump to separate actions defined in an exception handler. The solution demonstrates how to add exception handling to an orchestration.

■ **Note** A scope functions exactly like a traditional try/catch block.

---

1. Create a new orchestration. Drag a Scope shape from the toolbox onto the orchestration design surface.

2. Right-click the name of the Scope shape, and select Properties from the context menu.

3. Set the Transaction Type property to None and the Name property to Controlled Exceptions Scope.

4. Right-click the name of the new Scope shape, and select New Exception Handler from the context menu, as shown in Figure 5-45.

Figure 5-45. *Creating an exception handler*

5. Right-click the name of the exception handler created in the previous step, and select Properties Window from the context menu.

6. Set the Exception Object Type property to General Exception and the Name property to Log Exception, as shown in Figure 5-46.

Figure 5-46. *Setting the Exception object type and name*

7. From the toolbox, drag an Expression shape into the exception handler.

8. Double-click the Expression shape to open the Expression Editor, and add the following code to record the exception.

```
System.Diagnostics.EventLog.WriteEntry("A Simple BizTalk Source",
        "An exception was encountered in my sample orchestration.  ");
```

9. Build the orchestration logic inside the Scope shape. If BizTalk encounters an exception processing the orchestration logic, it will invoke the Expression shape.

How It Works

The BizTalk Orchestration Designer is a development tool. Just as when building a component with any other development tool, exception conditions can occur long after the component is constructed. The developer may misunderstand how the component should behave, or changes to the other systems BizTalk interacts with may cause exception conditions. Regardless of the cause, the developer always needs to plan for the unexpected.

■ **Note** In addition to defining how an orchestration reacts to possible exception conditions, orchestration scopes can also define atomic or long-running transactions.

This recipe demonstrates how to respond to exception conditions by invoking an Expression shape that writes an error message to the Windows application log. However, an exception handler can define more rigorous error-resolution procedures. The compensation block can simply log the exception, can invoke an exception-handling framework, or can invoke another BizTalk orchestration defining a series of resolution actions. In addition, if an orchestration defines the procedures for resolving exceptions, then the BizTalk Business Activity Monitor (BAM) can generate reports on exception-resolution processes.

Error Information

This solution's example uses the default General Exception object type, as shown earlier in Figure 5-46. This is useful when you want to log where and when errors occur but do not need specific information about the actual errors encountered.

An exception handler can identify more specific error information when the exception handler's Object Type property is set to any class inheriting from System.Exception. When the Object Type is a .NET Exception, as shown in Figure 5-47, the exception object can retrieve additional information such as an error message.

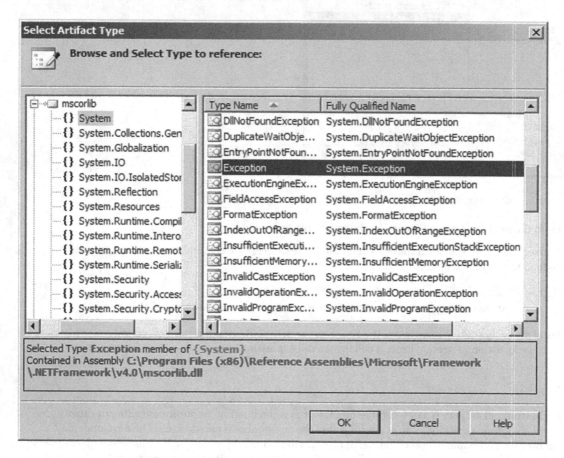

Figure 5-47. *Setting the exception handler type*

Modify the Expression shape as follows to include the error message in the application log entry.

```
System.Diagnostics.EventLog.WriteEntry("A Simple BizTalk Source",
        "An exception was encountered: " + ex.Message);
```

Multiple Exception Handlers

A single Scope shape can also specify multiple exception handlers to define different reactions to different exceptions encountered by the orchestration. When the Scope shape encounters an exception, it will check each exception handler from top to bottom. The Scope shape invokes the first exception handler matching the type of exception encountered and stops looking for a match. Therefore, more specific exception handlers must appear above more general exception handlers, or the general exception handler will handle all errors and the Scope shape will never invoke the specific exception handlers. Define an additional exception handler with the following steps.

1. Define the first exception handler as presented in this recipe's solution.

2. Right-click the name of the Scope shape, and select New Exception Handler.

3. Move the handler for the General Exception defined in the solution by selecting the name and dragging the mouse over the lower line defining the new exception handler. The General Exception handler should appear below the new one.

4. Right-click the name of the new exception handler, and select Properties Window.

5. Change the `Name` property to `Handle Arithmetic Exception`.

6. For the `Exception Object Type` property, select `<.NET Exception...>`. In the Select Artifact Type dialog box that appears, select the Arithmetic Exception, as shown in Figure 5-48, and then click OK.

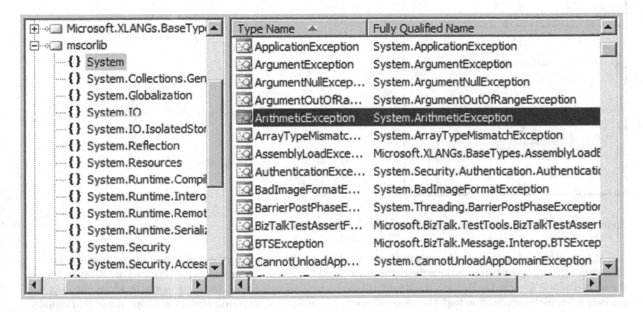

Figure 5-48. *Selecting the ArithmeticException*

7. Change the `Exception Object Name` property to `ex`.

8. Add shapes to the new exception handler to handle arithmetic exceptions specifically, as shown in Figure 5-49.

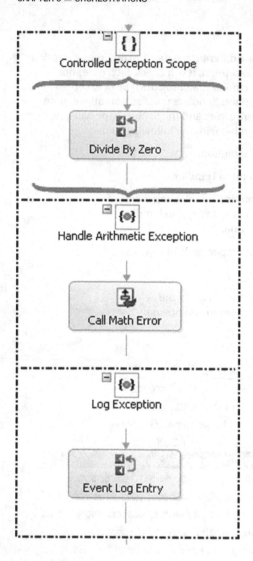

Figure 5-49. *Defining arithmetic exception-specific shapes*

While a Scope shape will invoke only the first exception handler matching the type of exception encountered, sometimes there are consistent actions the orchestration should take for different kinds of errors. For example, what if the orchestration depicted in Figure 5-49 should call the orchestration for resolving math errors in addition to logging the exception to the application log? The Throw shape can propagate an exception from the Scope shape that initially catches it to an outer Scope shape defining the consistent error actions. Figure 5-50 depicts an example of a Scope shape contained within another Scope shape.

■ **Note**   You can drag and drop the catch blocks from one exception block to another.

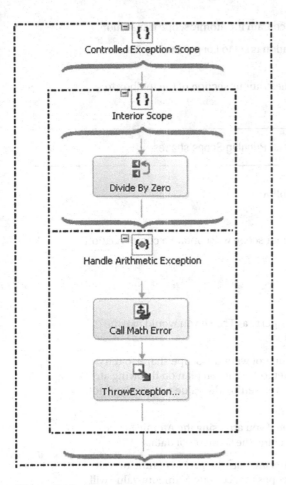

Figure 5-50. *Nested scopes*

5-19. Creating Atomic Scopes

Problem

You are building an orchestration process that contains actions that must complete together as a group or fail as a group.

Solution

BizTalk supports the notion of completing small units of work following the Atomicity, Consistency, Isolation, and Durability (ACID) transaction model. The Atomic Scope shape implements the ACID transaction model. Atomic scopes are the most flexible and restrictive of the transaction models in BizTalk. The use of an atomic scope within BizTalk ensures that a group of steps either succeeds or fails together. The following instructions outline the steps required to create and configure an atomic scope.

1. Open the project containing the orchestration that will contain the atomic scope transaction.

2. Verify the `Transaction Type` property of the orchestration is set to `Long Running`. This is required for orchestrations containing atomic scopes.

3. Select and drag the Scope shape from the BizTalk Orchestrations section of the toolbox to the appropriate location within the orchestration.

■ **Note** Atomic scopes may not contain nested Atomic Scope or Long Running Scope shapes.

---

4. Select the Scope shape, and update the properties as follows.

   • Change `Transaction Type` to `Atomic`.

   • Change `Compensation` from `Default` to `Custom` if your scope will contain a compensation handler.

   • Change `Isolation Level` to the correct value.

   • Change `Name` if desired.

   • Set the `Report To Analyst` property. Leave the property as `True` if you would like the shape to be visible to the Visual Business Analyst tool.

   • Change the `Retry` value from `True` to `False` if you do not want the Scope shape to retry in the event of a failure. The `Retry` value must be set to `True` if you plan on throwing an exception to cause the atomic scope to retry. However, setting the value to `true` does not mean the atomic scope will retry by default.

   • Change the `Synchronized` value from `False` to `True` if you are using the Atomic Scope shape within a Parallel Actions shape and manipulating the same set of data.

   • Change the `Timeout` value if desired. Scope timeouts indicate the period of time to wait (in seconds) before the transaction fails. Atomic scopes that contain a timeout value will stop the transaction and be suspended if the timeout value is reached.

   • Change the `Transaction Identifier` if desired.

5. Add the appropriate orchestration actions to the Atomic Scope shape.

How It Works

BizTalk supports the ACID model by providing the following features:

   • *Atomicity*: Atomic Scope shapes guarantee all actions within the Scope shape are either performed completely or not performed at all.

   • *Consistency*: System properties (messages and variables) are preserved through the transaction. In the situation where an atomic scope cannot be committed and the system properties are updated, the system properties are rolled back to their previous state.

■ **Note** All variables, regardless of whether they are local to the scope or global to the orchestration, will be rolled back to their previous state when an atomic scope fails.

- *Isolation*: Each atomic scope allows controlled visibility to other scopes' and transactions' data.

- *Durability*: Once an atomic scope has been committed, the only way the action can be undone is through the use of a BizTalk compensation handler.

Atomic Scope Considerations

Atomic scopes are extremely useful, but there is an associated cost with the use of any transactional model inside an orchestration. Consider the following when deciding whether to use an atomic scope:

- Atomic scopes cannot contain a send and a receive port that are referencing the same two-way request/response orchestration port. For example, if you are referencing an HTTP/SOAP port in your orchestration, you cannot have the Send and Receive shapes in a single Atomic Scope shape. Additionally, you cannot have Send and Receive shapes that implement the same correlation set within the same Atomic Scope shape. The rationale for this is that as soon as context has left the orchestration (a message is sent via a Send shape), the atomic scope action is complete, and a response cannot be matched to the request.

- If an Atomic Scope shape contains a Send, Receive, or Start Orchestration shape, BizTalk will wait to perform those actions until the scope has been committed. BizTalk considers the boundary of the transaction to be the point that a message has been committed to the BizTalk MessageBox.

- A single atomic scope is not that expensive in the context to processing of an entire orchestration. However, the use of multiple atomic scopes can be expensive because BizTalk sets a checkpoint before and after an atomic scope is executed. Consider ways to combine multiple atomic scopes into fewer atomic scopes. The checkpoint takes place so that the orchestration can be resumed if it is suspended due to an exception in the atomic scope.

■ **Note** Think of a checkpoint as BizTalk serializing its current processing state to persist and prepare for a rollback in the case of an exception in the atomic scope. The serialization and persistence of the current processing state reduces performance incrementally. The more atomic scopes in an orchestration, the more points of persistence that will be created and the greater the overall degradation in the performance of the orchestration.

- An object that is not serializable (does not implement the ISerializable interface or is not marked with a serializable attribute) must be in an atomic scope. For example, if you are using the XmlNodeList object, the variable must be declared local to the scope and referenced within the Atomic Scope shape. The XmlDocument data type is an exception to this rule.

- Using an Atomic Scope shape to perform multiple send operations does not guarantee that the send operations will be rolled back in the case one send fails. For example, if you have two Send shapes each sending a message to a SQL database, if there is a failure in one or both SQL databases, the Atomic Scope shape does not guarantee that the data will be backed out from either database call. BizTalk considers the boundary of a transaction to be the point that a message is committed to the MessageBox. True rollbacks are guaranteed only in true Microsoft Distributed Transaction Coordinator (MSDTC) transactions.

Atomic Scope Benefits

Even though atomic scopes are the more restrictive of the two transaction models, they offer significant benefits over the use of long-running scopes. Atomic scopes allow the specification of an `Isolation Level` property, as follows:

- Specifying `Serializable` means that concurrent transactions will not be able to make data modifications until the transaction is committed.

- Specifying `Read Committed` means that the existing transaction is prevented from accessing data modifications until the transaction is committed.

- Specifying `Repeated Read` means that read locks are required until the existing transaction is committed.

Atomic scopes also implement a retry capability that is enabled through the use of the `Retry` flag. An atomic scope will retry if the Scope shape's `Retry` property is set to `True` and at least one of the following exceptions occurs:

- `Microsoft.XLANG.BaseTypes.RetryTransactionException` is thrown or in the event that BizTalk cannot commit the transaction. Additionally, all variables will be reset to their state prior to entry of the scope.

- `Microsoft.XLANG.BaseTypes.PersistenceException` occurs due to BizTalk's inability to persist state.

Exception Handling

One challenge to using atomic scopes is the fact that you cannot have an exception handler on the Atomic Scope shape itself. Atomic scopes are defined to either succeed or fail, hence there is no direct need to have an exception handler. In the situation where an exception should be caught in an error handler, the items that cause an exception can be enclosed in a nontransactional scope (with an error handler) inside the atomic scope.

Consider the following scenario: you must pass a nonserializable object to a custom assembly that, in turn, makes a database call. You want to catch any communication exceptions and force the atomic scope to retry. One option for this scenario would be to implement an atomic scope to manipulate the nonserializable object and within that Atomic Scope shape, include a nontransactional Scope shape with an error handler that will throw a `Microsoft.XLANG.BaseTypes.RetryTransactionException`. This scenario would allow you use a nonserializable object and force a retry in the case of a communication problem.

■ **Note** When throwing a `RetryTransactionException` to perform a retry, validate that conditions have changed so that you do not continually throw a `RetryTransactionException` and create an infinite retry loop.

Compensation Handling

Atomic Scope shapes (as well as other Scope shapes) support the notion of compensation to facilitate undoing a logical piece of work regardless of the successful commit. Suppose that the atomic scope executes and commits successfully, but there is a business-error problem with the message data. The atomic scope, from a technical aspect, executed and committed correctly. However, due to the business validation failing, the transaction must be undone. Compensations allow definition of a process that details how the previously committed atomic transaction is to be rolled back.

The structure of a compensation handler is similar to that of an exception handler but functionally different. BizTalk will use the default compensation handler if no custom compensation handler is defined. The default BizTalk compensation handler calls the compensation blocks of any nested transactions, in reverse order of completion. Compensation handlers must be called explicitly, unlike error handlers, through the use of the Compensation shape. A common use for a compensation handler is to create a message that indicates business data needs to be backed out of a specific system or process.

MSDTC Transactions

An Atomic Scope shape behaves like an MSDTC transaction but is not an explicit DTC transaction by default. To clarify, if you send a message to SQL Server via the SQL adapter, the actions performed in the SQL call will not roll back, and a compensation handler is required to back out any committed changes. The reason a compensation handler is required is due to the SQL adapter not enrolling in an explicit DTC transaction.

Atomic scopes do support the use of a DTC transaction as long as the objects referenced in the scope are serviced components (COM+ objects) derived from the System.EnterpriseServices.ServicedComponents class. Additionally, the isolation levels must agree and be compatible between transaction components and what is specified in the atomic scope. The atomic scope does not require a configuration value to be set on the shape itself, as it will automatically enroll in an MSDTC transaction if possible.

Listing 5-5 serves as an outline for what to include in your assembly for creating a serviced component. Your assembly must reference System.EnterpriseServices and System.Runtime.InteropServices (for the Guid attribute reference). Verify that your component is registered in the Global Assembly Cache (GAC) (for example, using gacutil) and that you also register the component in COM+ (for example, using regsvcs).

Listing 5-5. Serviced Component

```
using System;
using System.EnterpriseServices;
using System.Runtime.InteropServices;

namespace MSDTCTestLibrary
{
    /// <summary>
    /// Summary description for Class1.
    /// </summary>
    ///
    [Guid("9943FB26-F4F5-4e80-B746-160AB9A6359E")]
    [Transaction(TransactionOption.Required)]
    public class ClassMSDTCTest : ServicedComponent
    {
        public ClassMSDTCTest(){}
        public String Test()
        {
            try
            {
                // Commit the transaction
                ContextUtil.SetComplete();
                return "Test";
            }
```

```
        catch (Exception ex)
        {
            // Abort the transaction
            ContextUtil.SetAbort();
            return ex.ToString();
        }

    }

  }
}
```

5-20. Using Long-Running Transactions

Problem

You have separate tasks to accomplish in an orchestration that must all succeed or fail together. These tasks may take a long time to complete.

Solution

Long-running transactions can help ensure a single consistent outcome across multiple BizTalk tasks. As an example, suppose you have a web site where customers can make purchases using credit. Creating a new customer involves two steps. First, the customer needs a login to access your web site. Second, the customer also needs credit established to make purchases. Sometimes, your web site cannot create a login because the customer has chosen a login already assigned to another customer. Other times, BizTalk cannot establish credit for the customer. If one of these tasks succeeds and the other fails, the user may experience undesirable behavior on your web site.

By defining actions to reverse each of the two tasks required in this example, BizTalk can automatically reverse the effects of one task in the event that the other fails. If BizTalk creates a login but cannot establish credit, it will detect the failure and invoke the compensation logic to disable the login. If credit is established but BizTalk cannot create the login, it will invoke the compensation logic to suspend credit.

The following steps demonstrate how to set up a long-running transaction for this example.

1. Create a new BizTalk project, and add an orchestration.

2. Right-click the orchestration design surface, and select Properties Window.

3. Set the Transaction Type property to Long Running.

4. Place a Receive shape on the design surface with the Activate property set to True. Configure BizTalk to receive a NewCustomerMsg message.

5. Place a Parallel Actions shape under the Receive shape.

6. Place a Scope shape under the left branch of the Parallel Actions shape.

7. Select the icon in the upper-right corner of the Create Login shape, and select Long Running from the menu, as shown in Figure 5-51.

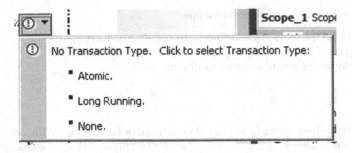

Figure 5-51. *Setting the scope transaction type*

8. Place a Send shape inside the Scope shape.

9. Set the Send shape's `Message` property to `NewCustomerMsg`.

10. Create a one-way send port named `CustomerActivation`.

11. Set the `CustomerActivation` send port's `Delivery Notification` property to `Transmitted`.

■ **Note**   Use delivery notification to determine if a delivery failure occurs. BizTalk will not complete the long- running transaction until the messages with delivery notification are successfully delivered and will report an error if any of the messages are suspended.

---

12. Right-click the top portion of the Scope shape, and select New Compensation Block from the context menu, as shown in Figure 5-52.

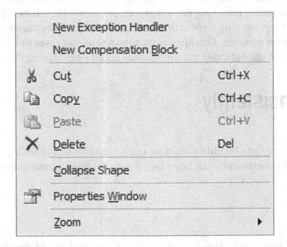

Figure 5-52. *Creating the compensation block*

13. Place a Send shape inside the compensation block, and attach it to a new port. This defines the actions to reverse the transaction if another transaction fails.

14. Repeat steps 6 to 13 to define the Create Credit Account scope.

15. Deploy the orchestration and bind the ports to file locations. To simulate delivery failure to the `CustomerActivation` and `CreditApplication` ports, deny the BizTalk Application Users group access to the file locations bound to the orchestration ports.

How It Works

The goal of a *transaction* is to ensure that many separate tasks will all either succeed or fail together. With long-running transactions, BizTalk performs each task independently. If one task fails, then BizTalk must roll back the changes of the successful tasks. Rolling back successful tasks because of another's failure is called *compensation*. A BizTalk orchestration can determine when successful transactions need to compensate for a failed transaction, but the BizTalk developer must define the specific compensation logic.

The solution's example consists of two tasks, each with custom compensation logic defined. If BizTalk cannot establish credit for the customer, the Create Login transaction must compensate by taking actions to disable the login. Similarly, BizTalk compensates the Create Credit Account transaction by taking action to rescind credit. BizTalk will detect the error in the Create Credit Account transaction and call the compensation logic of all the long-running transactions in the same scope that have completed successfully. If the Create Login transaction also fails, then both transactions arrived at the same result, and BizTalk has nothing to compensate for. BizTalk will compensate only long-running transactions that complete successfully.

Long-running transactions are a great way to ensure a consistent outcome under circumstances such as the following:

- Tasks take longer than a split-second to complete.

- Results can be inconsistent for a short while before the compensating logic completes.

- BizTalk needs to send or receive messages with a transport that cannot participate in an atomic transaction, like an ASMX web service.

In addition to long-running transactions, BizTalk scopes can also support atomic transactions. An atomic transaction differs by locking all the resources involved until the transaction knows they can all succeed. If they cannot all succeed, the transaction reverses all changes before releasing the resources. Because of this locking behavior, atomic transactions should be very quick. A long-running transaction executes each task separately and follows up with compensating logic if one task encounters an error. This approach allows separate tasks to have different results for a short time while the compensating logic executes but also allows greater processing flexibility.

5-21. Catching Exceptions Consistently
Problem

You want to be able to catch all exceptions in the same way and be able to handle retries automatically with a configurable delay. You also want to be able to resubmit documents that have failed without losing context to what step in the orchestration flow was last executed.

Solution

The `ExceptionHandlerPatternDemo` project shows the use of the pattern, with a single Business Flow orchestration calling two different paths in a single Task Processing orchestration. Neither the Business Flow orchestration (`SAMPLEMainBusinessFlow.odx`) nor the Task Processing orchestration (`SAMPLEExternalComponentCall.odx`) are required in a true implementation. They are provided for demonstration purposes only. All of the files in the `Common Schemas` project and all of the files in the `Exception Handler Buffer` project are required, and *need no modifications (aside from possible namespace modifications) to be used in any other solution.*

The SAMPLEMainBusinessFlow orchestration demonstrates calling the other orchestrations with multiple input parameters (as demonstrated in the first Task Request grouping) and with an XML document that needs to be mapped (as demonstrated in the second Task Request grouping). Use the following steps to deploy and test the solution.

1. Open the ExceptionHandlerPatternDemo project.

2. Deploy the project using Visual Studio. All of the files necessary for a complete deployment are included in the solution (including the strong name key). For ease of deployment, place the base folder, ExceptionHandlerPatternDemo, on the C:\ drive root. If the C: drive is not available, several of the ports will need to be modified, as they reference physical paths for file send and receive locations.

3. Once the orchestrations and schemas are deployed, bound, and started, drop the SampleKickOff.xml file in the Input folder. This will kick off the flow. Monitor the progress in the Windows Event Viewer (all steps are logged to the Event Viewer).

How It Works

Based on a publish/subscribe architecture, the Exception Handler pattern can be used to buffer calls to components that may throw exceptions from the actual business flow of a process. The Exception Handler buffer allows for a common mechanism to catch, process, and retry exceptions (including notification to an administrator) that can be reused across multiple solutions. Figure 5-53 shows the high-level architecture of a request, and Figure 5-54 shows the high-level architecture of a response.

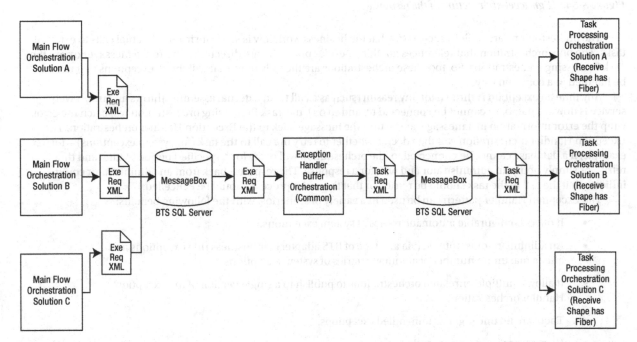

Figure 5-53. *High-level architecture of the request*

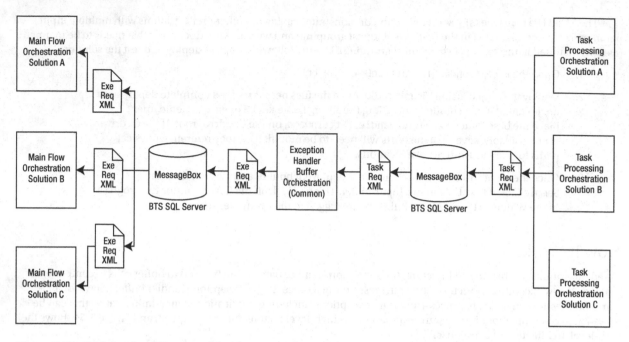

Figure 5-54. *High-level architecture of the response*

The orchestrations are built in such a way that the business workflow is separate from the actual calls to external tasks. The only orchestration that references anything besides ports that are directly bound to the MessageBox are the Task Processing orchestrations. So, too, these orchestrations are the only ones that will throw exceptions that need to be handled in a common way.

Any time an exception is thrown for any reason (such as a call to an external assembly throws an error, a web service is down, a database cannot be connected to, and so on), the Task Processing orchestration will catch the error, wrap the error information in a message, and return the message back to the Exception Handler orchestration. The Exception Handler orchestration will then decide whether to retry the call to the task (for system exceptions)—for example, if a database cannot be connected to, the orchestration will delay for a specified period of time and then retry—or simply notify an administrator and wait for a response. The response back from an administrator could indicate that the call to the task should be retried or that the entire process should be cancelled.

The Exception Handler pattern can be used in a variety of scenarios, with the following benefits:

- It offers configurable automatic retries of system exceptions.

- An administrator is notified (via any type of BTS adapter) for business rule exceptions and after a maximum number of automatic retries of system exceptions.

- It allows multiple unrelated orchestrations to publish to a single version of the Exception Handler orchestration.

- There are no uncaught or unhandled exceptions.

- No messages end up suspended.

- It offers complete visibility into the life cycle of an orchestration.

The orchestrations communicate with one another through the publish/subscribe model, meaning that the publishing orchestration drops a message on the BizTalk MessageBox to which the subscribing orchestration is subscribing. The following sections describe these schemas and how they are used.

Exception Handler Buffer Call Request Schema

This schema is published by the Business Flow orchestration(s) and subscribed to by the Exception Handler Buffer orchestration. It contains all of the data needed to call a task and all of the configurable information needed by the exception handler to process and retry exceptions (such as maximum number of retries, delay between retries, and so on). Table 5-5 shows the schema definition.

Table 5-5. *Exception Handler Buffer Call Request Schema*

Element	Description
CorrelationID	A unique identifier that is assigned in the Main Flow orchestration and travels with each message through the entire request and full response.
OrchestrationFilter	The unique identifier specifying which Task Processing orchestration should instantiate based on the call. All Task Processing orchestration instances will subscribe to messages that are based on the TaskProcessingLogicCall schema. To ensure that the correct Task Processing orchestration is kicked off, the Receive shape in the Task Processing orchestration must be filtered on this field. Note that if only one instance of the Task Processing orchestration is being used, there is no need to implement this filter.
TaskName	The name of the task that is to be executed in the Task Processing orchestration. The Task Processing orchestration can have multiple branches in a Decide shape. The branch that is executed is based on the value in this parameter.
MaxRetryCount	Maximum number of retries for a task that has thrown an exception. For example, if a call is being made to a database, and the connection to the database is unavailable, the Task Processing orchestration will return an exception. The Exception Handler orchestration will then retry (after a delay) the call to the task. Use this parameter to specify the maximum number of retries before notifying an administrator.
RetryDelay	Amount of time between retries. This parameter is in seconds.
InputParameter	If the call to the task is a call with one single simple type parameter (such as a string, integer, and so on), this parameter can be used. It is a distinguished field and can be easily accessed.
InputParameter (Node)	This is a repeating node allowing for multiple input parameters. Use this structure when multiple input parameters are needed. Values can be accessed using XPath queries in the Task Processing orchestration (see the demonstration for examples). Name: Name of the parameter. Type: The parameter type (integer, string, and so on). This parameter is not required. Value: The value of the parameter. The XPath query can find the Value based on the Name.
XMLParameter	This <Any> element can be populated with any type of XML document that may need to be passed to the Task Processing orchestration. There can be multiple XMLParameter values passed. See the demonstration for examples of how this parameter can be populated and read.

Exception Handler Buffer Call Response Schema

This schema is published by the Exception Handler orchestration and subscribed to by the Main Business Flow orchestration(s). It contains the output information needed by the Main Business Flow to determine what (if any) the result of the Task Processing orchestration call may have been. Table 5-6 shows the schema definition.

Table 5-6. *Exception Handler Call Buffer Response Schema*

Element	Description
CorrelationID	A unique identifier that is assigned in the Main Flow orchestration and travels with each message through the entire request and full response.
SuccessFlag	Boolean value indicating success or failure of call. If an administrator canceled the process, this value would be returned as false. If the call was made, regardless of the outcome, this value will be returned as true.
OutputParameter	If the response from the task is a single simple type parameter (such as a string, integer, and so on), this parameter can be used. It is a distinguished field and can be easily accessed.
OutputParameter (Node)	This is a repeating node allowing for multiple output parameters. Use this structure when multiple output parameters are needed. Values can be set and accessed using XPath queries in the Task Processing orchestration (see the demonstration for examples).
	Name: Name of the parameter.
	Type: The parameter type (integer, string, and so on). This parameter is not required.
	Value: The value of the parameter. The XPath query can find the Value based on the Name.
XMLParameter	This <Any> element can be populated with any type of XML document that may need to be passed back from the Task Processing orchestration. There can be multiple XMLParameter values passed. See the demonstration for examples of how this parameter can be populated and read.

Task Processing Logic Call Schema

This schema is published by the Exception Handler orchestration and is subscribed to by the Task Processing orchestration(s). All Task Processing orchestration instances subscribe to this schema type. Use a filter expression on the individual Task Processing orchestration's initial Receive shape to indicate which instance to kick off (based on the OrchestrationFilter parameter). Table 5-7 shows the schema definition.

Table 5-7. *Task Processing Logic Call Schema*

Element	Description
CorrelationID	A unique identifier that is assigned in the Main Flow orchestration and travels with each message through the entire request and full response.
OrchestrationFilter	The unique identifier specifying which Task Processing orchestration should instantiate based on the call. All Task Processing orchestration instances will subscribe to messages that are based on the TaskProcessingLogicCall schema. To ensure that the correct Task Processing orchestration is kicked off, the Receive shape in the Task Processing orchestration must be filtered on this field. Note that if only one instance of the Task Processing orchestration is being used, there is no need to implement this filter.
TaskName	The name of the Task that is to be executed in the Task Processing orchestration. The Task Processing orchestration can have multiple branches in a Decide shape. The branch that is executed is based on the value in this parameter.
InputParameter	If the call to the Task is a call with one simple type parameter (such as a string, integer, and so on), this parameter can be used. It is a distinguished field and can be easily accessed.

(continued)

Table 5-7. (*continued*)

Element	Description
InputParameter (Node)	This is a repeating node allowing for multiple input parameters. Use this structure when multiple input parameters are needed. Values can be accessed using XPath queries in the Task Processing orchestration (see the demonstration for examples).
	Name: Name of the parameter.
	Type: The parameter type (integer, string, and so on). This parameter is not required.
	Value: The value of the parameter. The XPath query can find the Value based on the Name.
XMLParameter	This <Any> element can be populated with any type of XML document that may need to be passed to the Task Processing orchestration. There can be multiple XMLParameter values passed. See the demonstration for examples of how this parameter can be populated and read.

Task Processing Logic Response Schema

This schema is published by the Task Processing Logic orchestration(s) and subscribed to by the Exception Handler Buffer orchestration. It contains the output information needed by the Main Business Flow to determine what (if any) the result of the Task Processing orchestration call may have been and by the Exception Handler Buffer orchestration to determine what exceptions may be present and if the call needs to be retried (based on the presence of exceptions). Table 5-8 shows the schema definition.

Table 5-8. *Task Processing Logic Response Schema*

Element	Description
CorrelationID	A unique identifier that is assigned in the Main Flow orchestration and travels with each message through the entire request and full response.
SuccessFlag	Boolean value indicating success or failure of call. This is not a success/failure indicating the result of the call, but an actual indicator of whether or not the call was made. If an exception was thrown, or an administrator canceled the process, this value would be returned as false. If the call was made, regardless of the outcome, this value will be returned as true.
ErrorMessage	The text of the exception message (if an exception was thrown).
BaseException	The base exception type (if an exception was thrown).
StackTrace	The full stack trace thrown (if an exception was thrown).
OutputParameter	If the response from the task is a single simple type parameter (such as a string, integer, and so on), this parameter can be used. It is a distinguished field and can be easily accessed.
OutputParameter (Node)	This is a repeating node allowing for multiple output parameters. Use this structure when multiple output parameters are needed. Values can be set and accessed using XPath queries in the Task Processing orchestration (see the demonstration for examples).
	Name: Name of the parameter.
	Type: The parameter type (integer, string, and so on). This parameter is not required.
	Value: The value of the parameter. The XPath query can find the Value based on the Name.
XMLParameter	This <Any> element can be populated with any type of XML document that may need to be passed back from the Task Processing orchestration. There can be multiple XMLParameter values passed. See the demonstration for examples of how this parameter can be populated and read.

Error To Administrator Schema

This schema is published by the Exception Handler orchestration and is published to an administrator. This may be as simple as writing to a file, or it could be set up to write to a database or any other protocol desired. The Error To Administrator schema contains all of the information that an administrator would need to understand what error was thrown. Once the administrator is ready to resubmit the document to the process, the same schema type is resubmitted. Table 5-9 shows the schema definition.

Table 5-9. *Error To Administrator Schema*

Element	Description
CorrelationID	A unique identifier that is assigned in the Main Flow orchestration and travels with each message through the entire request and full response.
CancelFlag	Boolean value indicating that the administrator wants to cancel the entire process. There may be times when the exception being thrown may require some amount of rewrite. For whatever reason, an administrator may cancel the process by simply dropping the XML file back into the process with this flag set to true.
OriginalMessage	This node will contain the XML of the original message passed into the Exception Handler orchestration.
ErrorMessage	The text of the exception message (if an exception was thrown).
BaseException	The base exception type (if an exception was thrown).
StackTrace	The full stack trace thrown (if an exception was thrown).

5-22. Creating Role Links

Problem

You need to send a specific type of request based on a certain element within a document.

Solution

You can send specific request types based on certain document elements by using role links. Role links offer the flexibility of defining functions or roles for the inbound and outbound ports of your orchestration. Additionally, role links also offer the flexibility of abstracting the interactions between orchestration and external parties.

The following instructions outline the steps required to create and configure role links within a BizTalk orchestration. Before implementing role links, you must create an orchestration and role links within the orchestration. Next, you must deploy the orchestration and create the parties that participate in the processes.

This solution uses two sample XML files to demonstrate how role links route messages based on message content. The first XML instance requires a manager party's approval, and the second XML instance requires a human resources (HR) department party's approval.

We've divided the solution for this recipe into several tasks, as described in the following sections.

Create the BizTalk Solution

First, you must create a BizTalk orchestration for this example.

1. Create a new BizTalk solution that will process new hire requests that require approvals. The message structure should match the sample outline in Listing 5-6.

    Listing 5-6. *Sample New Hire XML Instance*

    ```
    <ns0:ApplicantApproval
        xmlns:ns0="http://Sample_Role_Link_Recipe.SampleNewHireRequest">
      <ApplicantID>1000</ApplicantID>
      <Approver>Manager</Approver>
      <Detail>

        <SSN>508-03-4433</SSN>
        <Name>Wally McFally</Name>
        <Position>Technician</Position>
        </Detail>
    </ns0:ApplicantApproval>
    ```

2. Create an orchestration to process the new hire requests. The orchestration requires the artifacts listed in Table 5-10.

Table 5-10. *Role Links Recipe Artifacts*

Name	Type	Description
ReceiveNewHireRequest	Receive port	The Receive port.
ReceiveRequest	Receive shape	The Receive shape to receive messages.
InitializeRoleLinks	Expression shape	The Expression shape to initialize role links for outbound message routing.
SendRequest	Send shape	Send shape for the outbound message.
msgNewHire	Message matching schema defined in step 1.	The name of the message is crucial, because it must match the name referenced in the expression code that is entered to initialize role links. Make sure that the Approver element in the message is a distinguished property, because the value in this field is used for routing.

Create the Orchestration Role Links

Next, you need to create and initialize the role links send port for message approval. The Role Link shape will contain a single Approval consumer role.

1. Select the Role Link shape form the BizTalk Orchestrations section of the toolbox, and drag the shape to the orchestration.

2. The Role Link Wizard will launch (see Figure 5-55). Follow the Role Link Wizard, and specify the following:

    - For the role link name, specify NewHireApproval.

    - For the role link type, specify NewHireApprovalRoleLinkType.

    - For the role link usage, specify that you are creating a Consumer role, as this orchestration will be providing messages.

Figure 5-55. *Role Link Wizard*

3. Click the Finish button to complete the wizard.

4. Once the wizard has completed, remove the Provider role from the newly created role link, as the Provider role will not be used in this example.

___

■ **Note** When following the Role Link Wizard, select either the Provider role or Consumer role for your application. The Role Link Wizard will create both roles, but you are free to remove the role that does not apply to your given situation.

___

Create the Role Link Send Port Type

After creating the role link, the next task is to create a send port type implemented by the role link. A send port type is required because it defines the type of message a send port will send.

1. Right-click the Provider section of the Role Link shape, and choose Add Port Type.

2. In the Port Type Wizard, select Create a New Port Type, and enter SendPortType for the name. Click the Finish button to complete the wizard.

3. Connect the orchestration send port to the newly created send port type in the role link Consumer role. The orchestration should resemble Figure 5-56.

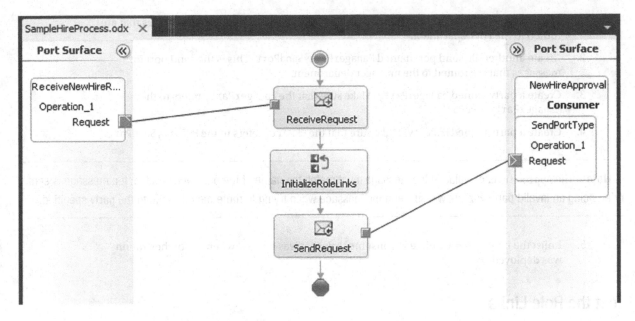

Figure 5-56. *New Hire orchestration with role links*

4. BizTalk uses the destination party for routing of the message. Add the following code to the Expression shape in your orchestration.

```
//set the approver name
            NewHireApproval(Microsoft.XLANGs.BaseTypes.DestinationParty) = new
Microsoft.XLANGs.BaseTypes.Party(msgNewHire.Approver, "OrganizationName");
```

5. Build and deploy the solution after completing the orchestration. When you deploy the solution, a new Consumer role is created in the Role Links folder located in the BizTalk Administration Console.

■ **Note** The Expression shape code performs the party resolution. The line of code uses the Approver distinguished field to determine to which party to route the message. When you create a party, a party alias is also created to use for party resolution. In the Expression shape, we use the default alias, OrganizationName, which is created with each party. However, multiple aliases can be created for a party and then referenced in an Expression shape. For example, an alias of PhoneNumber could be created during the party creation and then referenced in the Expression shape.

Create Parties and Physical Send Ports

The final steps involve creating the BizTalk parties and physical send ports for the solution. Within the BizTalk Administration Console, create the physical send ports and parties that will receive the approval messages.

1. Create a file send port named HRPartySendPort. This is the send port for messages that are routed to the HR department.

2. Create another file send port named ManagerPartySendPort. This is the send port for messages that are routed to the manager department.

3. Create a party named ManagerParty. Make sure that the ManagerParty refers to the ManagerPartySendPort.

4. Create a party named HRParty. Make sure that the HRParty refers to the HRPartySendPort.

■ **Note**   The Approver name value in the message must match the name of the party you created. If a message is sent referencing an invalid party, BizTalk will suspend the message when trying to route the message to the party specified.

---

5. Enlist the two parties within the Consumer role that was created when the orchestration was deployed.

Test the Role Links

After completing the preceding tasks, you will be able to enlist and start your solution to test the implemented role links. When you submit a message with Manager as the value for the Approver element, the message will be routed to the send port associated with the Manager party. When you submit a message with HR as the value for the Approver element, the message will be routed to the send port associated with the HR party.

How It Works

Role links are extremely useful for loosely coupling your physical solution from the trading partner or disparate system. Processes that implement role links benefit from the abstraction by being able to stand independent of the implementation of the trading partner or subscribing system.

Imagine having a business process that is the same for multiple trading partners or systems. Some of the consumers of the process need the information in a flat file format or must receive the information using a proprietary communication protocol. You could implement this scenario through the use of dynamic ports or a send port group, but the maintenance of subscribers becomes a challenge. Updating a dynamic send port requires updating the process that provides the configuration information. Implementing role links allows the subscribers to be independent and updated without impacting other subscribers.

Implementing role links is straightforward and requires few steps in configuration. The first set of configuration steps is performed in the solution design-time environment. The final set of steps is performed after the process has been deployed. You must identify whether you are consuming or providing a service, identify the parties that will be interacting with the service, and specify the role under which the parties will operate. The Role Link Wizard in Visual Studio will create two default roles automatically. You are not required to use the two roles, and you can create additional roles after the wizard has executed.

The following are the required components when implementing role links:

- *Parties*: The specific entities interacting with your organization's orchestration either providing or consuming information from that orchestration. Typically, each party represents a single organization that interacts with your organization.

- *Roles*: Logical entities that define a specific business process. Roles either consume or provide services.

- *Role links*: Describe the relationship or connection (link) between two roles. The Role Link shape within Visual Studio will launch the Role Link Wizard to assist in creating roles within your orchestration.

- *Role link types*: Describe how your orchestration participates in the service. Role link types are similar to port types in that you specify whether you are consuming a message or publishing a message.

In the sample solution accompanying this recipe, a New Hire process has been created that contains a single Approver role. We required only a single role and removed one role from the role link after the wizard was complete. For the role created in our role link, we specified a send port type. Each role must implement a port type for communication to outside entities. The final step was to programmatically determine party resolution. For illustration purposes, an Expression shape implemented party resolution via code. BizTalk must always know which party will be receiving the message, and the party resolution can either be performed in the orchestration or within a pipeline.

5-23. Calling Web Services

Problem

You want to call a web service from within your business process, using the standard SOAP adapter.

Solution

When calling a web service, the first item that is needed is the Web Services Description Language (WSDL). The WSDL contains the interfaces indicating how a web service can be called. BizTalk imports this WSDL and turns it into a schema that can be read in the same way as a standard XSD, with each web method defining its own schema. This solution will walk through the steps required to reference a WSDL, create a message to post to a web service (via a web method), and get the web service result message.

1. Open a BizTalk project in Visual Studio.

2. In the Solution Explorer, right-click the References node under the project header, and select Add Service Reference.

3. In the Add Service Reference dialog box, you can manually enter the URL of the WSDL into the URL box at the top of the window. This can be a standard web URL (http://) or a file path to a WSDL or SVC file (useful for developing in a disconnected environment). Alternatively, use any of the other Browse methods to locate the service.

4. After entering a valid URL path, all available web services will be displayed (see Figure 5-57). Select the desired web service from this list. Make sure that the namespace shown in the text box is appropriate (usually, you will want to rename this to something more descriptive than the default; the name entered here will be how the web service is referred to in the rest of the project)

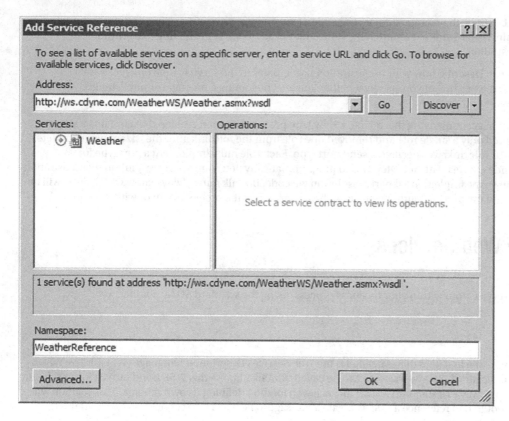

Figure 5-57. Referencing a web service

5. Click the OK button. The newly referenced web service should now appear under the Service References folder in the Solution Explorer (see Figure 5-58).

Figure 5-58. The referenced service in the Solution Explorer

6. In an orchestration, right-click Port Surface, and select New Configured Port. This will start the Port Configuration Wizard. Use the following settings to configure the new port.

   - Name the port appropriately.

   - For Port Type, select Existing Port Type. In the window that appears, highlight the web port that is a post (as opposed to a response back), and then click Next.

   - The final screen should be automatically configured indicating that BizTalk will always be set to sending a request and receiving a response, with the port binding set to Specify Now. There is no need to make any changes. Click Next, and then click Finish.

■ **Note** Web service calls can be request/response (two-way) or simply request (one-way). Some of the parameters in the configuration will be slightly different in the case of a one-way web service.

---

7. In the orchestration, add a new Send shape. This shape will require a message to be associated with it. You will want to create a message that has the same type as the outgoing port you configured in step 6, as follows:

   a. In the Orchestration View window, right-click the Messages folder, and select New Message.

   b. Give this message an appropriate name, such as msgRequest.

   c. In the Properties window of the message, click the Message Type drop-down list, expand Web Message Types, and select the message type that corresponds to the port type you indicated in step 6.

   d. Set the Send shape Message Type property to this message.

8. Connect the Send shape to the outgoing method on the port created in step 6.

9. Drop a Receive shape on the orchestration, immediately after the Send shape created in step 7. You will need to create a message that has the type as the response back from the web service call, as follows:

   a. In the Orchestration View window, right-click the Messages folder, and select New Message.

   b. Give this message an appropriate name, such as msgResponse.

   c. In the Properties window of the message, click the Message Type drop-down list, expand Web Message Types, and select the message type that corresponds to the response of the web service web method indicated in step 6.

   d. Set the Receive shape Message Type property to this message.

10. Create an instance of the message that you are sending to the web service (msgRequest). This can be done through a map or a Message Assignment shape. The following steps will show how to do this through a map.

   a. Drop a Transform shape in the orchestration immediately before the Send shape created in step 6. This will automatically create a Construct Message shape.

   b. In the Properties window of the Construct Message shape, click the Messages Constructed property, and select the message created in step 6 (msgRequest).

    c.   Double-click the Transform shape. In the Transform Configuration dialog box, the target document should be `msgRequest`, and the source document can be any document (you will need to create a message, not included in these steps, of any given schema type and set it to the source).

    d.   After setting the source and target schemas, click OK. The map should open, and you can map fields as needed.

How It Works

The complexity around calling and mapping to web services is greatly reduced by using a BizTalk orchestration, the standard SOAP adapter, and the steps described in this solution. However, there may be times when these steps do not provide the result needed. In cases where the called web service is too complex a structure to consume, the web service could be called from an external .NET component, removing the complexity of calling it from BizTalk altogether.

Calling a web service from an external assembly lets developers use the full functionality of .NET to make the call. While complex web services with arrays or strongly typed data sets can be called from an orchestration, moving the call to an external component may be easier.

There are important benefits to calling a web service with the BizTalk SOAP adapter and following the steps described in this solution. The ability to turn the WSDL into a schema, the ability to have retries automatically occur, and the simplicity of creating the message through the BizTalk Mapper are all excellent reasons to invoke the web service from within an orchestration.

5-24. Exposing an Orchestration as a Service
Problem

You would like to expose an orchestration process as a service to be called from an outside application.

Solution

Using BizTalk, an orchestration can be exposed as a service via the BizTalk WCF Service Publishing Wizard. Using this tool, the effort to expose an orchestration as a service is considerably simplified. To expose an orchestration as a service, take the following steps:

1.   Open the BizTalk WCF Services Publishing Wizard by selecting Start ➤ Programs ➤ BizTalk 2010 ➤ BizTalk WCF Services Publishing Wizard.

2.   On the Welcome page, click the Next button.

3.   On the WCF Service Type page, click the Service Endpoint radio button.

4.   Set the Adapter name to WCF-BasicHttp (see Figure 5-59).

Figure 5-59. *Setting the port as public*

5. On the next page, you will have the option of publishing a schema or an orchestration as a WCF service. Select the orchestration option.

6. On the BizTalk Assembly page, browse to the DLL that contains the orchestration you are publishing.

7. On the Orchestration and Ports screen, ensure that the ports you want to expose are selected.

8. On the WCF Service Properties page, set the namespace to a descriptive value.

9. On the WCF Service Location, browse to the web directory where this will be published (see Figure 5-60).

Figure 5-60. *Setting the Web Directory*

How It Works

Exposing orchestrations as services allows you to reuse orchestration processes by creating BizTalk configurations to support the passing of a service call to a BizTalk orchestration. This way, you can take advantage of core BizTalk capabilities such as error handling, document tracking, and integration into downstream BizTalk via the publish/subscribe architecture. In addition, you can extend outside your BizTalk environment, to enable a service-oriented approach, composite application paradigms, and so on.

The WCF Services Publishing Wizard interrogates the BizTalk orchestration and receive ports and creates a service application to support the calling of the target BizTalk orchestration. This is achieved by creating a service

(SVC) that calls a C# .NET code behind that implements the mechanism of publishing the message instance to the BizTalk MessageBox.

Just as BizTalk orchestrations can be exposed as services, so too can XSD schemas. XSD schema services are also generated using the WCF Services Publishing Wizard, where one or more XSD schemas are selected and corresponding services are generated. The service handles sending the message directly to the BizTalk MessageBox, offering a way to implement publish/subscribe without the need to create a BizTalk orchestration.

5-25. Calling Pipelines from Within an Orchestration
Problem

You are developing an orchestration and need to use pipeline-processing stages within the workflow. Specifically, you need to validate a document and batch multiple messages into a single interchange. You want the orchestration to be efficient, minimizing the interactions between the orchestration and the MessageBox database.

Solution

BizTalk Server exposes a programmatic interface into pipelines, allowing you to call both receive and send pipelines directly from orchestrations. Assume your orchestration has the following steps:

1. Receive an order message in an industry-standard format.

2. Transform the message to a canonical version of the order schema.

3. Send the canonical order message to an external application for processing.

4. Receive a status message from the external application indicating the success or failure of the message processing.

In addition to the orchestration, you have also created a receive pipeline to validate the canonical order schema, an envelope, and a send pipeline to batch the canonical order and order response documents into a single interchange.

Open your orchestration in Visual Studio, and perform the following steps to implement the pipeline calls:

1. From the toolbox, drag the following shapes onto the orchestration design surface:

   a. Drag a Scope shape named Execute Receive Pipeline directly below the Construct Canonical Order Message shape, and set the Transaction Type property to Atomic.

■ **Note** The orchestration's Transaction Type property must be set to Long Running in order for it to hold an Atomic Scope shape.

---

   b. Drag an Expression shape named Execute Receive Pipeline inside the Scope shape added in the previous step.

   c. Drag a Construct Message shape named Construct Validated Message directly below the Execute Receive Pipeline Expression shape (also inside the Execute Receive Pipeline Scope shape), and set the Messages Constructed property to a message defined by your validating schema—in this solution, a message named CanonicalOrderValidatedMessage defined by the canonical order schema.

   d. Drag a Message Assignment shape named Assign Validated Message inside the construct message shape added in the previous step.

e. Drag a Construct Message shape named `Construct Batched Message` directly below the `Receive Order Status` receive shape, and set the `Messages Constructed` property to an XML message—in this solution, a message named `BatchedOrderMessage` of type `System.Xml.XmlDocument`.

f. Drag a Message Assignment shape named `Assign Batched Message` inside the construct message shape added in the previous step.

2. Add a reference in your BizTalk project to the `Microsoft.XLANGs.Pipeline.dll` (found in the root BizTalk installation folder), which holds the classes required for calling pipelines from orchestrations.

3. Create a new variable named `ValidatePipelineOutput` of type `Microsoft.XLANGs.Pipeline.ReceivePipelineOutputMessages` in the `Execute Receive Pipeline` Scope shape. This variable will hold the validated output of the call to the receive pipeline, containing the validated canonical order message.

4. Add the following code to the `Execute Receive Pipeline` Expression shape in order to call the appropriate receive pipeline:

```
ValidatePipelineOutput = Microsoft.XLANGs
                .Pipeline.XLANGPipelineManager.ExecuteReceivePipeline
                (typeof(OrderProcessing.ValidateCanonical
                OrderSchemaReceivePipeline),
        CanonicalOrderMessage);
```

5. Add the following code to the Assign Validated Message shape in order to extract the validated canonical order message:

```
CanonicalOrderValidatedMessage = null;
        ValidatePipelineOutput.MoveNext();
ValidatePipelineOutput.GetCurrent(CanonicalOrderValidatedMessage);
```

■ **Note** To handle multiple output messages from a receive pipeline (when using an envelope for message debatching, for example), you may need to use a loop in order to iterate through the message collection and handle each appropriately.

---

6. Create a new variable named `BatchingPipelineInput` of type `Microsoft.XLANGs.Pipeline.SendPipelineInputMessages`. This variable will hold the output of the call to the send pipeline, containing the batched order messages.

7. Add the following code to the Assign Flat File Message shape to call the appropriate send pipeline (`BatchedOrderMessages` is a BizTalk message of type `System.XML.XmlDocument` and is used to hold the output of the `ExecuteSendPipeline` method call):

```
BatchedOrderMessages = null;
        BatchingPipelineInput.Add(CanonicalOrderValidatedMessage);
        BatchingPipelineInput.Add(CanonicalOrderStatusMessage);
        Microsoft.XLANGs.Pipeline.XLANGPipelineManager.ExecuteSendPipeline
        (typeof(OrderProcessing.BatchOrderAndStatusMessagesSendPipeline),
    BatchingPipelineInput, BatchedOrderMessages);
```

5. Build and deploy the solution.

How It Works

This solution shows how to leverage pipeline processing directly from orchestrations. First, we discuss the mainline process involved in the solution. Then, we discuss exception handling.

Mainline Process

The `Microsoft.XLANGs.Pipeline.XLANGPipelineManager` class exposes an API for calling pipelines programmatically.

■ **Note**   To use this class, you must add a reference in your BizTalk project to the `Microsoft.XLANGs.Pipeline` assembly.

In this scenario, you needed to use both a receive pipeline and a send pipeline. The receive pipeline allows you to validate a message that you create in the orchestration. You call the receive pipeline via the `ExecuteReceivePipeline` method, which has the following signature:

- Type: The fully qualified type of the receive pipeline you need to call. You format this parameter as `typeof(FullyQualifiedNameOfReceivePipeline)`. You can easily find the fully qualified type name of your receive pipeline by clicking the pipeline file in the Solution Explorer and viewing the `Fully Qualified Name` property.

- `XLANGMessage`: The XLANG message object you need to pass into the receive pipeline.

This method returns an instance of the `Microsoft.XLANGs.Pipeline.ReceivePipelineOutputMessages` class, which contains an enumeration of output messages from the receive pipeline. In this solution, the pipeline produces a single message, and you are able to easily extract the message by using the `MoveNext` and `GetCurrent` methods of the class. If multiple messages could be returned by the receive pipeline, you would need to loop through the `ReceivePipelineOutputMessages` object to extract each message. You can accomplish this by using a Loop shape configured with `ValidatePipelineOutput.MoveNext()` as the expression and an Assign Message shape configured with `ValidatePipelineOutput.GetCurrent(CanonicalOrderValidatedMessage);` as the expression.

■ **Note**   You must place the code (usually contained within an Expression shape) that calls the receive pipeline in an Atomic Scope shape, because the `ReceivePipelineOutputMessages` class is not serializeable and cannot be persisted to the MessageBox.

The send pipeline batches multiple messages within the orchestration into a single interchange. You call the send pipeline via the `ExecuteSendPipeline` method, which has the following signature:

- Type: The fully qualified type of the send pipeline you need to call. You format this parameter as `typeof(FullyQualifiedNameOfSendPipeline)`.

- `SendPipelineInputMessage`: The collection of messages you need to pass into the send pipeline.

- `XLANGMessage`: The XLANG message object you will receive as output from the send pipeline.

■ **Note**   You must place the code that calls the send pipeline in a Message Assignment shape, because the ExecuteSendPipeline method constructs the XLANGMessage it passes as an output parameter.

Although calling pipelines from an orchestration generally results in the same functionality and processing as when they are executed via BizTalk messaging objects, you need to be aware of some differences. One of the most important discrepancies is the input and output XLANG message objects that are passed to ExecuteReceivePipeline and ExecuteSendPipeline, respectively. Although XLANG message objects allow you define them as being of any type (XmlDocument, String, DateTime, and so on), the XLANG message instances you pass to the pipeline execute methods must be XML documents. This means that the XLANG message objects should be defined by either the System.Xml.XmlDocument type or an XML schema to ensure consistent behavior. This limitation is because the pipeline execution methods treat their XLANG message parameters as XmlDocument objects. Although it is possible to use a different type to define your XLANG message objects (such as System.String), it is advised you do so with caution and careful consideration and validate that any data written to the message is in XML format.

■ **Note**   One shortcoming of this limitation is that it is not straightforward to call a send pipeline that assembles an XML document into flat file format, because the flat file string is returned as an XmlDocument object but likely does not conform to XML.

Another difference to be aware of is how tracking and monitoring data is handled. When calling pipelines from an orchestration, pipeline components leveraging the BAM Interceptor API are not supported, and the assembler/disassembler stages do not process tracking information. Additionally, transactional pipeline components are not supported when called from orchestrations.

Exception Handling

Any errors occurring in pipelines called from orchestrations cause an XLANGPipelineManagerException exception object to be thrown. Messages are not suspended, as they would be if the pipeline were executed by a messaging object (receive location or send port). This exception object can be handled via a catch exception block, which is configured on a Scope shape within an orchestration. Once the exception is caught, the exception's properties can be interrogated and the event handled appropriately.

Using an invalid document (using a character in the Identifier element, which expects an integer value) in this solution produces the following error:

```
There was a failure executing pipeline "OrderProcessing.ValidateCanonicalOrderSchema
    ReceivePipeline".
Error details:
    "The 'Identifier' element has an invalid value according to its data type.".
Exception type: XLANGPipelineManagerException
Source: Microsoft.XLANGs.Pipeline
Target Site: Microsoft.XLANGs.Pipeline.ReceivePipelineOutputMessages ExecutePipeline
    (Microsoft.BizTalk.PipelineOM.ReceivePipeline, Microsoft.
    XLANGs.BaseTypes.XLANGMessage)
```

As you can see, the exception thrown has a type of XLANGPipelineManagerException, and the description indicates the specific validation failure.

5-26. Consume a WCF Service in an Orchestration

Problem

You want to create an orchestration that consumes a WCF web service.

Solution

The following steps will guide you through the implementation:

1. Open the BizTalk project where you want to create a WCF service reference.

2. Right click on the BizTalk Project. It opens a Pop-up Menu. Select Add ➤ Add Generated Items from the menu. See Figure 5-61.

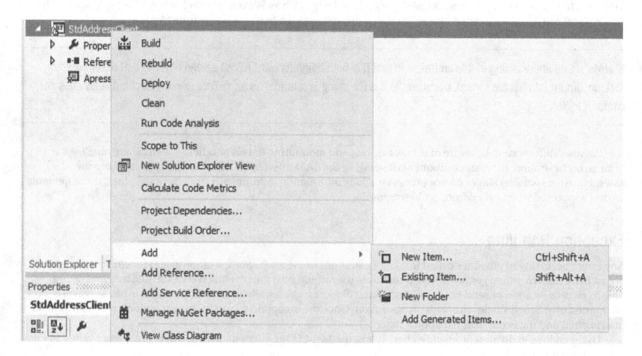

Figure 5-61. *Add Generated Items option in Visual Studio*

3. This opens Add Generated Items Wizard. In the Wizard select Generated Schema Files in the Pane, select Consume WCF Service, and click the Add button to start the generation of WCF service related artifacts. See Figure 5-62.

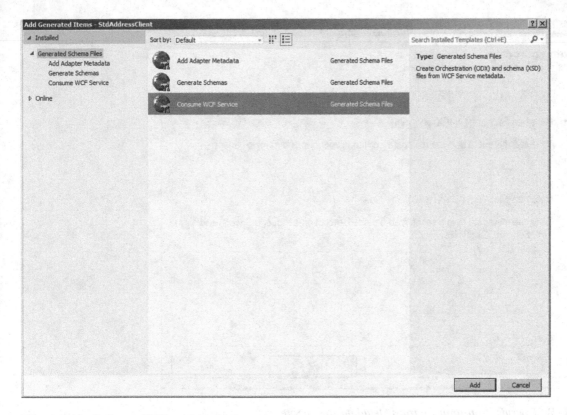

Figure 5-62. Consume WCF service selection screen

4. Click on the Next button on the Welcome screen of WCF Consuming Wizard.

5. On the Metadata Source screen, you have an option to consume the Metadata either from a running web service or from existing WSDL file as shown in Figure 5-63. This former option reads the WSDL from the URL and generates the artifacts. In the case of an existing WSDL file or XSD schemas, select the latter option. In the current case, select the first option.

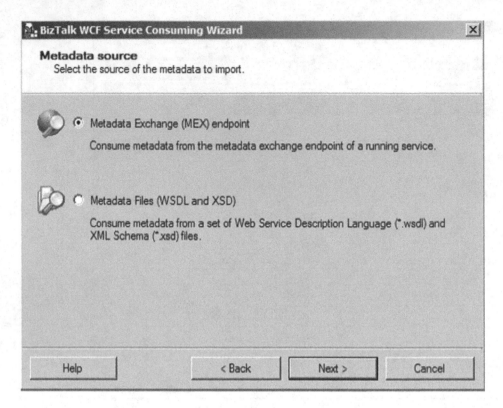

Figure 5-63. *WCF Service Consuming Wizard Metadata Source Screen*

6. On the Metadata Endpoint screen (shown in Figure 5-64), type the URL to the WSDL in the Metadata URL text box, click on the Get button to verify the connection, and retrieve the WSDL. Then click on the Next button.

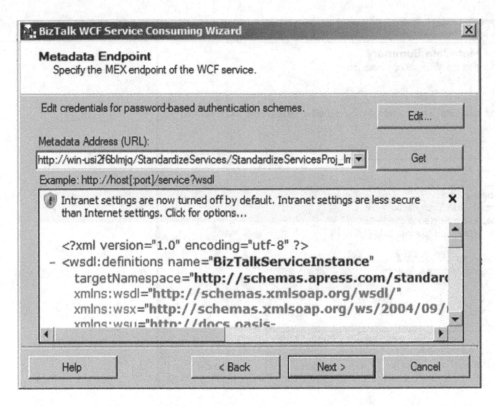

Figure 5-64. *WCF Service Consuming Wizard Metadata Endpoint Screen*

7.   In the Import WCF Service Metadata Summary page, enter the Namespace, and click on
     the Import button (shown in Figure 5-65).

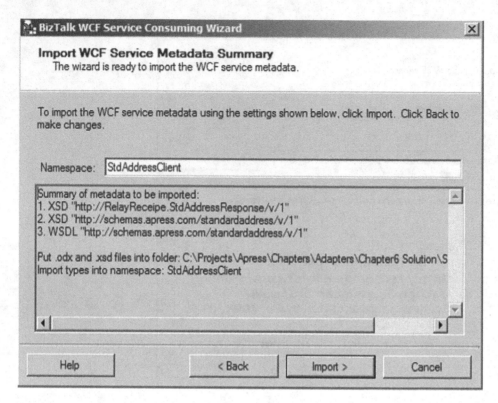

Figure 5-65. *WCF Service Consuming Wizard Import WCF Service Metadata Summary Screen*

8. Next, click on the Finish button on the Wizard's summary screen. This activity will generate the needed Schemas, binding files, and a starter orchestration with port types in the Visual Studio Project, as shown in Figure 5-66.

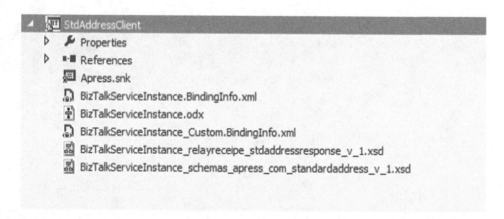

Figure 5-66. *Generated Items in BizTalk Project*

The starter orchestration with the SOAP port types and Multi-part Message Types will give a starting point in case a new orchestration needs to be created. In some cases, if you have an existing orchestration, you will need to bind the WCF endpoint. In this case, you can refer to the port types that are created in the starter orchestration, as shown in Figure 5-67.

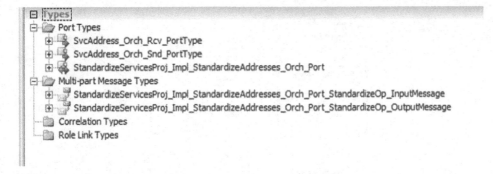

Figure 5-67. *Generated Port Types and Multi-part Message Types*

9. Open the orchestration, create the receive port, and map to the SOAP multi-part request type. To consume the two-way endpoint, you need to create an orchestration level SOAP request response port. When you are creating the two-way port, you need to select the WCF Wizard created port type. See Figure 5-68.

Port Configuration Wizard

Select a Port Type

A Port Type defines the set of operations that are permitted on the port.

Select the port type to be used for this port:

○ Create a new Port Type

◉ Use an existing Port Type

Available Port Types:

- Current Project
  - StdAddressClient.StandardizeServicesProj_Impl_StandardizeAddresses_Orch_Port

Communication Pattern: Request-Response.
Operations: StandardizeOp

[< Previous] [Next >]   [Cancel]

Figure 5-68. *Selecting Existing Port Types*

10. Finish the rest of the functionality in orchestration. Once finished, it looks like the sample orchestration shown in Figure 5-69.

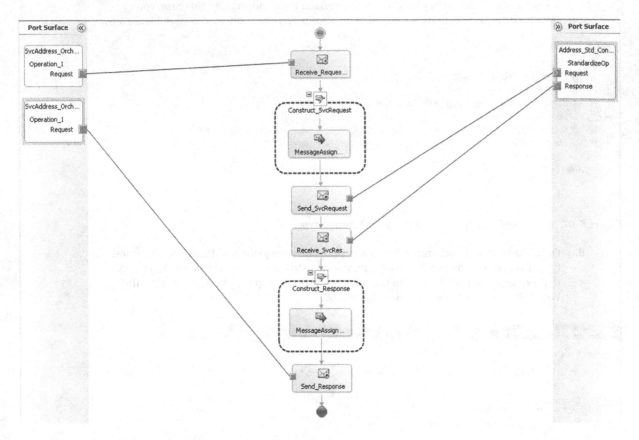

Figure 5-69. *Sample Orchestration consuming WCF Service*

How It Works

As outlined in this recipe, the WCF consuming Wizard generates the needed artifacts to simplify the service consumption steps for the developers. The Wizard generates the artifacts shown in Table 5-11. While this is valuable, and allows for services to be referenced and consumed directly in the orchestration, there are many cases where the best way to interact with a WCF service is within C# code in a referenced assembly. The assembly can be called from the orchestration, but the core interaction with the service is done within code in C#. Some examples of when this would be an appropriate approach include:

- When the WCF service is complex. Many services have complex interfaces that either have many methods, methods with many parameters, or structures that require the wizard to create complex hierarchical schemas. You will know your WCF service is complex when you run the wizard and it imports schemas and properties that you have no idea how to work with or call within your orchestration. When you see this, stop what you are doing and work with the service within .NET code.

- When the WCF service uses complex types as parameters. BizTalk does fine with simple strings and integers, but if the service expects objects to be passed in as parameters, this is most easily done in C#.

- When you don't want to weigh down your orchestration with a lot of auto-generated items. The wizard is great, but it produces a lot of weight and creates complexity that you may want to simply work around. The ODX file, the custom bindings, the numerous XSDs – all of these can be avoided by working directly in .NET code.

Table 5-11. *WCF Consuming Wizard generated artifacts*

Artifact	Description
XXX.BindingInfo.xml	Binding file for the normal (WCF-BasicHttp, TCP, WCF-WsHttp) send ports.
XXX_Custom.BindingInfo.xml	Binding file for the WCF-Custom adapter only send port. It gives a finer control on the adapter properties.
XXX.odx	A starter orchestration with the multi-part message types and port types is created.
XXX.xsd	Multiple schema files are created with request, response, and custom Fault schemas.

Many developers prefer to do all of the WCF service communication in C#, and leave all direct references to services completely out of the orchestrations.

CHAPTER 6

■ ■ ■

Adapters

The BizTalk engine uses adapters to communicate with outside systems, and adapters start and end any process within BizTalk. Adapters come in three basic flavors: protocol adapters, database adapters, cloud adapters and ERP adapters. In addition to these, BizTalk 2013 comes with several more protocol adapters and a new tier of adapters used to facilitate communication with the Microsoft Azure Service Bus (cloud adapters).

Hundreds of adapters are available from third-party vendors that enable the BizTalk engine to communicate with just about any system. In addition, if an adapter is not available, the BizTalk adapter framework facilitates custom adapter development in .NET. Commonly used adapters include the following:

- *Protocol adapters*: SFTP, REST, HTTP, File, and SOAP, WCF

- *Database adapters*: SQL, DB2, and Oracle

- *Cloud adapters*: SB-Messaging, WCF based Relay Adapters

- *ERP adapters*: SAP, PeopleSoft, and Siebel

An entire book would be necessary to cover all the adapters available and their proper use. ERP adapters in particular require an in-depth discussion of the ERP system in question before you are able to use the adapter for that system. This chapter will therefore focus on a few of the more basic protocol, database and cloud adapters that are included with BizTalk out of the box.

■ **Note**   Make sure to look at the BizTalk line of business (LOB) adapters (which include PeopleSoft, JD Edwards, TIBCO, and WebSphere) and the BizTalk Adapter Pack (which includes SAP, Siebel, and Oracle). All are available for download from Microsoft's site.

6-1. Configuring File Sends
Problem

You need to send a message from BizTalk with the File adapter.

Solution

The BizTalk platform offers numerous options to facilitate sending files. Within the BizTalk File adapter, various send options are natively available for the user to configure. The following steps demonstrate how to configure a send port:

1. Open the BizTalk Explorer, and create a send port that uses the File adapter.

■ **Note**   In alignment with standard BizTalk functionality, only static ports are defined to use a named File adapter.

---

2. In the send port properties, under the General options, click the ellipses for the Address (URI) property. The FILE Transport Properties dialog box appears.

3. Click the Destination Folder input box. Enter the value of the folder where you would like BizTalk Server to write the file.

4. ➤ Click the Copy Mode drop-down list, and ensure that the default value, Create New, is selected, as shown in Figure 6-1.

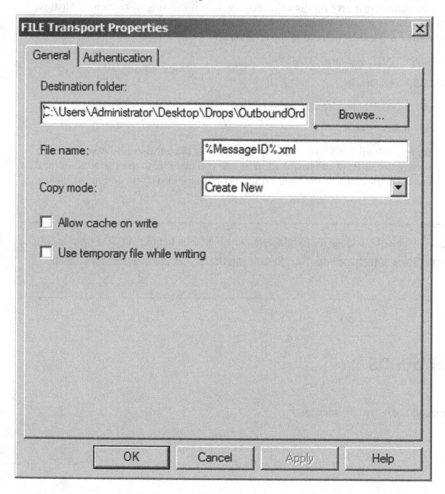

Figure 6-1.   *Configuring file sends in the FILE Transport Properties dialog box*

■ **Note**   The Copy Mode drop-down list offers the Create New, Append, and Overwrite options. In this recipe, we will use Create New.

5. Click the Authentication tab, ensure that the Use These Credentials When Host Does Not Have Access to Network Share check box is unchecked.

■ **Note**   BizTalk gives you the ability to specify a different user account if the security permissions are different from the running host user account.

6. Click OK.

How It Works

You can configure the File adapter either within the BizTalk Explorer (under a send port) or through code programmatically. The File adapter send configuration options encompass naming a file, using copy mode, implementing caching, and implementing security.

When naming files on the General tab of the FILE Transport Properties dialog box, you can configure a file send in conjunction with numerous macros to assist in making a file name more meaningful. For example, as shown in Figure 6-1, the File Name value is %MessageID%.xml. The macro, %MessageID%, will be substituted with the globally unique identifier (GUID) of the message in BizTalk Server at runtime when the file is named. This GUID comes directly from the message context property, BTS.MessageID. Please see Table 6-1 for a list of available macros. It is important to note you can use only these macros.

Table 6-1. *BizTalk Macros*

Type	Description
%datetime%	Sets the name of the file to the current UTC date in the format YYYY-MM-DD (example: 2010-07-01T103500).
%datetime_bts2000%	Sets the name of the file to the current UTC date in the format YYYYMMDDhhmmsss (example: 201007011035234).
%datetime.tz%	Sets the name of the file to the current local date plus the time zone difference from GMT in the format YYYY-MM-DDThhmmss-TZD (example: 2010-07-01T103500+700).
%DestinationParty%	The name of the file would be set to whatever value is in the message context property for BTS.DestinationParty. This field is only set in certain situations, therefore this macro is rarely used.
%DestinationPartyQualifier%	The name of the file would be set to whatever value is in the message context property for BTS.DestinationPartyQualifier. This field is only set in certain situations, therefore this macro is rarely used.

(*continued*)

Table 6-1. (*continued*)

Type	Description
%MessageID%	The most commonly used macro. This sets the name of the file equal to the unique identifier of the message. Using this macro guarantees that the name of the file will always be unique.
%SourceFileName%	The file will be named after the value in the FILE.ReceivedFileName context property. This property is only set if received by a File adapter. If the value is not available, the macro will name the file the actual string value of %SourceFileName%.
%SourceParty%	The name of the source party (if available) from the BTS.SourceParty context property. This macro is rarely used.
%SourcePartyQualifier%	The name of the source party (if available) from the BTS.SourcePartyQualifier context property. This macro is rarely used.
%time%	Sets the name of the file to the current UTC time in the format hhmmss (example: 103523).
%time.tz%	Sets the name of the file to the current local time plus the time zone difference from GMT in the format hhmmss-TZ (example: 103523+700).

Currently, the product does not support creating custom or user-defined macros, and it doesn't support using any other BizTalk context properties other than what is available via the macros. Using these file-naming macros has been described as somewhat problematic within the BizTalk user group community. It is worth noting that a macro will fail if the following is true:

- A corresponding system property is not set, for example, the exclusion of SourceParty or SourcePartyID.

- The file send macro is misspelled (including case-sensitive considerations).

  The value of the macro result causes an invalid file name, for example, the usage of the following characters: / \ ? < > . , * " |

A further consideration when using the File send adapter is to ensure the security/access permissions are set appropriately. This encompasses standard Active Directory security considerations for related share and folder permissions, as well as security considerations related to non-Windows environments. By default, the File adapter write activity uses the user account of the running BizTalk host. It is always a good idea to unit test a security scenario first to ensure a file can be written to the desired destination before introducing the File send adapter. This way, you can isolate permission issues, saving possible issue detection and resolution time.

6-2. Configuring File Receives
Problem

You need to receive a message in BizTalk using the File adapter.

Solution

Within the BizTalk File adapter, numerous options are available to facilitate receiving files. You can configure all these options natively within the adapter. The following steps outline configuring the File receive adapter:

1. Open the BizTalk Administration Console

2. In the desired BizTalk application, right-click the Receive Ports folder, and select New ➤ One-way Receive Port. Specify a name for the receive port. Leave the default settings on the remainder of the General tab, as shown in Figure 6-2.

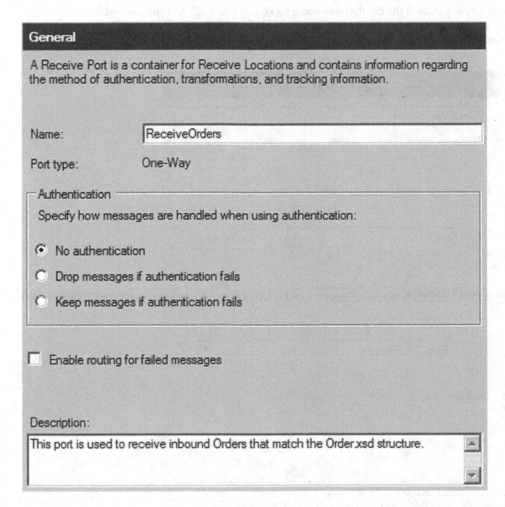

Figure 6-2. *General settings for a receive port*

■ **Note** You can add maps to a receive port; a map would be applied after a pipeline but before any subscribers (send ports or orchestrations) have processed the message. Some solutions can have maps but no orchestrations; the maps are added to the receive and/or send ports.

---

3. Click the Receive Locations tab, and click the New button. This will open a new window for configuring the receive location. A receive port can have one or more receive locations.

4. Give the receive location a name, and set the Type property to FILE.

5. The Receive handler property should be set the correct host application; this will depend on how you want to organize your environment. In many scenarios, only a single option is available here.

6. Set the Receive pipeline property to the correct pipeline. In this case, the `PassThruReceive` pipeline will be adequate; this means that any file will be picked up, and the contents will not be validated by any code. If the file that was being picked up was XML and you needed to ensure that it validated against a deployed schema, the correct receive pipeline would be `XMLReceive`. Figure 6-3 shows the configuration of the receive location so far.

General

Name: ReceiveOrderFile

Receive port: ReceiveOrders

Transport
Select a transport type and transport address below.

Type: FILE ▼ Configure...

URI:

Receive handler: BizTalkServerApplication ▼

Receive pipeline: PassThruReceive [Microsoft.BizTalk.Defau ▼ ..

☐ Make this the primary location

Description:
This will pick up the inbound Order.XML from a file drop. See other receive locations on this receive port for alternate options for inbound Order.XML files (such as FTP).

Figure 6-3. *General settings for the receive location*

7. Click the Configure button.

8. Enter the location of the file folder you want BizTalk Server to pull for files.

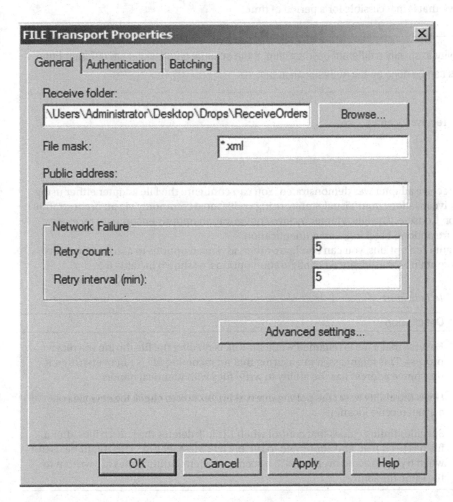

Figure 6-4. *Configuring file receives in the FILE Transport Properties dialog box*

9. Click the File Mask input area. Enter the value *.*.

■ **Note** The File Mask property allows the File adapter to consume files that match a specific file mask. In the instance of *.*, all files will be consumed by the wildcard mask. However, it is worth noting that you cannot set up two receive locations with the same mask, monitoring the same location.

---

10. Under the Network Failure options, set the retry values. The default options are 5 and 5 for Retry Count and Retry Interval but can be set at any value. If the retries are exceeded, the receive location will be automatically disabled. This would most commonly occur when polling a network drive that is inaccessible for a period of time.

■ **Note** BizTalk gives you the ability to specify a different user account, if the security permissions are different from the running host user account. This can be done on the Authentication tab.

---

11. Click OK to create the receive location.

How It Works

In this recipe, how to use the File receive adapter was demonstrated. You can configure the File adapter either using the BizTalk Explorer (within a receive location) from Visual Studio, using code (most commonly via an orchestration), or using the BizTalk Administration Console. The File adapter receive configuration options encompass receive location parameters, network failure options, batching, and authentication.

In addition to the basic configuration options, you can configure other advanced options to assist in the process of receiving files. The General tab contains some advanced configuration options, as shown in Table 6-2.

Table 6-2. *Advanced Settings for File Transport*

Option	Description
Rename Files While Reading	Ensures that a file is renamed while BizTalk is reading the file during the receive process. This might assist in ensuring that an incoming file is not overwritten if the source address has the ability to write files with identical names.
Receive Location Polling	Gives the ability to set the polling interval for BizTalk to check for new files on a given receive location.
Removing of Files	Specifies timing values that control when BizTalk deletes the source files after a file has been read and submitted to the BizTalk MessageBox. This might be useful when trying to avoid overwrites in a scenario where multiple files are written to the same file source.

The File receive adapter also allows for the configuration of file batching. Batching allows destination files to be submitted in a collective batch, allowing for the configuration of file consumption and file exception options on the entire batch. Within BizTalk's batch processing model, files that are processed successfully to the MessageBox are deleted from the source, files that are processed to the MessageBox with exception are suspended, and messages that fail to write to the MessageBox cause the entire batch to be rolled back. For example, a security permission issue might prevent the file from being open and consumed. This premise ensures that all files are preserved on the source file location. That is, the physical file deletion process does not occur until the entire batch has been processed.

6-3. Configuring SMTP Send Ports

Problem

You need to send a message from BizTalk with the Simple Mail Transport Protocol (SMTP).

Solution

This example configures a BizTalk send port using the SMTP adapter to send a message to a single email recipient. The following steps outline how to configure the SMTP adapter:

■ **Note** This recipe demonstrates how to create a static SMTP port. In many cases, you will need to specify dynamic values for an e-mail, including message content, recipients, subject line, and so on. All of this can be set dynamically using an orchestration and a dynamic send port.

If BizTalk needs to send each message to a different email address, use a dynamic port from an orchestration.

1. Open the BizTalk Administration Console.

2. Expand the BizTalk Server group, select the appropriate BizTalk application, and select the Send Ports folder.

3. Right-click the Send Ports folder, and select New ➤ Static One-Way Send Port to open the Send Port Properties dialog box. Give the Send Port a name.

4. Within the Transport section of the General tab, select SMTP from the Type drop-down list, as shown in Figure 6-5.

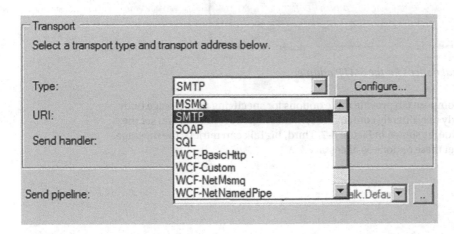

Figure 6-5. *Specifying the SMTP transport type*

5. Click the Configure button to open the SMTP Transport Properties dialog box.

6. On the General tab, enter the message recipient's e-mail address and the e-mail message subject, as shown in Figure 6-6. Additionally, request delivery and read receipts to get a notification e-mail when the message recipient receives or marks the message as read.

Figure 6-6. *Configuring the general options for the SMTP adapter*

7. The settings on the Compose tab provide three options for specifying the message body. First, the message body may directly contain the sent message. Second, you can set the message to a fixed value, as shown in Figure 6-7. Third, BizTalk can retrieve the message from a file location. Set these options as necessary.

Figure 6-7. *Configuring the Compose tab*

8. The Attachments tab allows you to configure the different ways BizTalk can include attachments. BizTalk can include the message being sent with the SMTP adapter as an attachment or include an external file as an attachment, as shown in Figure 6-8. Set these options as necessary.

Figure 6-8. *Setting the SMTP attachment*

9. The Handler Override tab contains SMTP configuration settings such as the SMTP server name, the From address used when sending email messages, and authentication settings. Instead of setting these configuration values for each send port using the SMTP transport, all SMTP send ports can share configuration values for the SMTP handler. Only change these values from the default settings if you need to override the default SMTP handler configuration.

■ **Note** This recipe demonstrates how to create a static SMTP port. In many cases, you will need to specify dynamic values for an e-mail, including message content, recipients, subject line, and so on. All of this can be set dynamically using an orchestration and a dynamic send port.

How It Works

BizTalk can only send email messages with the SMTP adapter. To receive a message via e-mail, you can use the POP3 adapter. Of course, in all cases, you can write a custom adapter or implement a third-party adapter if available.

The security settings of some SMTP servers disallow impersonation. Under these circumstances, the From address in an e-mail must match the account credentials provided to the SMTP server. The SMTP server must have an e-mail account created specifically for the credentials provided by BizTalk. For example, when specifying process account (NTLM) authentication, the identity of the BizTalk host instance must also have a valid e-mail address. If the From address does not match the e-mail address of the host instance identity, the e-mail will not be sent. You can configure settings on the adapter to be used by all send ports via the adapter. Configure the SMTP handler with properties that any SMTP send port can reuse with the following steps:

1. Connect to the BizTalk group in the BizTalk Administration Console, expand the Platform Settings folder, and expand the Adapters folder. Select the SMTP adapter.

2. Right-click the host appearing in the right pane of the BizTalk Administration Console, and select Properties.

3. Click the Properties button in the SMTP Transport Properties dialog box.

4. Set the default configuration values for the SMTP adapter. See Figure 6-9.

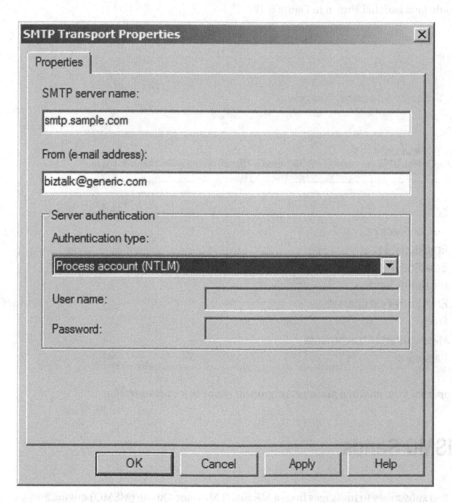

Figure 6-9. *SMTP handler configuration within Platform Settings*

You have three handler configuration options for authenticating with the SMTP server, as shown in Table 6-3. SMTP send ports have a fourth default authentication option, which specifies to use the handler configuration setting.

Table 6-3. *SMTP Handler Authentication Options*

Authentication Option	Description
Basic Authentication	Specifies specific credentials to authenticate with the SMTP server. BizTalk may pass these credentials over the network in clear text.
Do Not Authenticate	BizTalk provides no authentication credentials when sending an email message via SMTP.
Process Account (NTLM)	The adapter uses the host instance identity to authenticate with the SMTP server.

Finally, when setting SMTP values on a dynamic port from within an orchestration, use a message assignment shape to set the properties to the variable values. For example, if you want to set the e-mail body text to a dynamic value, the message assignment would look like that shown in Figure 6-10.

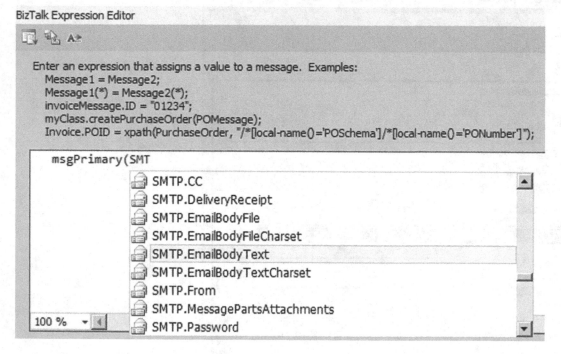

Figure 6-10. *Setting the SMTP Properties from within a Message Assignment shape in an orchestration*

6-4. Configuring MSMQ Sends
Problem

You are integrating with a system that subscribes to messages from a Microsoft Message Queue (MSMQ) queue, and you must configure BizTalk Server to send messages to MSMQ.

■ **Note** See Recipe 6–5 for further information about how to configure the MSMQ receive adapter.

Solution

You are building a solution that processes orders from an online commerce site and must deliver those messages to an ERP system via an MSMQ queue. To send messages to the destination queue, you must create a BizTalk Server send port that utilizes the MSMQ adapter. To configure the send port, follow these steps:

1. Open the BizTalk Administration Console.

2. Expand the BizTalk Server group, select an appropriate BizTalk application, and select the Send Ports folder.

3. Right-click the Send Ports folder, and select New ➤ Static One-way Send Port to open the Send Port Properties dialog box.

4. Give your send port a descriptive name, select the XMLTransmit pipeline, check that the subscriptions on the Filters tab are implemented, and select MSMQ as the transport type.

5. Click the Configure button to the right of the Transport Type field. This launches the MSMQ Transport Properties dialog box.

6. Set the Destination Queue property to the queue name that the ERP system accepts messages from, as shown in Figure 6-11. In this scenario, we are using a queue named ERPCommerceOrder.

Figure 6-11. Configuring an MSMQ send port

7. Leave all other properties with their default values, and click OK.

8. Click OK in the Send Port Properties dialog box to save the send port.

■ **Note** You can also create send ports in the BizTalk Editor view in Visual Studio.

---

9. Right-click the send port created in the previous step, and select Start.

How It Works

The BizTalk Server MSMQ adapter allows easy access to messages in MSMQ queues (MSMQ versions 2.0 and 3.0). The adapter relies on the local MSMQ service, which must be installed on the same computer hosting the adapter.

MSMQ Send Options

Although this example illustrates the simplest scenario for sending MSMQ messages to a specified queue, you can make a number of configurations against the MSMQ adapter:

- `Destination Queue`: Specifies the queue to which to send messages. See the following section for further information about how to format queue names.

- `Ordered Delivery`: Specifies whether the message order is persisted when delivering messages to the destination queue. This property enables a solution to implement ordered message delivery, although you must also ensure that all the previous processing (including the receipt of the message from the source queue) is handled serially if the order is to be maintained.

  You can additionally specify whether the send port should be stopped if errors are encountered when delivering a message to the destination queue. This setting helps enforce a strict ordered delivery requirement, although it has the side effect of completely disabling an interface if a single error occurs. This property is available only via the BizTalk Administration Console, under the Transport Advanced Options grouping of an MSMQ Send Port Properties dialog box. See Figure 6-12.

Figure 6-12. *The Ordered delivery setting for MSMQ ports*

■ **Note**   You can make this setting only via the BizTalk Administration Console, under the Transport Advanced Options grouping of an MSMQ Send Port Properties dialog box.

- `Encryption Algorithm`: Specifies the algorithm used to encrypt messages as they are written to the destination queue. The available values are RC2, RC4, and None. This property results in the `Message.UseEncryption` and `Message.EncryptionAlgorithm` properties being set.

- `Body Type`: Specifies the body type of MSMQ messages written to the destination queue.

- `Maximum Message Size (in kilobytes)`: Specifies the maximum size of the message batch to be delivered to the destination queue. The MSMQ adapter will fill the batch with messages from the MessageBox until this setting is reached.

- `Message Priority`: Specifies the priority for delivering messages. This setting is relative to the other send ports within your BizTalk environment. To nullify the functionality of this property, set the priority on all the send ports in your environment to the same value.

- `Recoverable`: Specifies whether messages will be recoverable if errors are encountered during the delivery to the destination queue. When this value is set to `True`, messages are persisted to disk in between being pulled from the MessageBox and delivered to the destination queue. If errors occur during delivery, messages can be recovered from the disk.

- `Support Segmentation`: Specifies whether the adapter allows large messages (larger than 4MB) to be segmented. This property should be set to `True` if you have implemented the large message extension—if the adapter attempts to deliver a message larger than 4MB and this property is set to `False`, an error is thrown and the message is not delivered.

- **Timeout**: Specifies the timeout value for which messages must be delivered (combined with the `Timeout Unit` property). This value applies only when the `Transaction` property is set to `True`. The MSMQ adapter treats messages not delivered within the specified timeout period as error scenarios.

- **Timeout Unit**: Specifies the timeout unit for which messages must be delivered (combined with the `Timeout` property). The available values for this property are `Days`, `Hours`, `Minutes`, and `Seconds`.

- **Use Journal Queue**: Specifies whether messages will be copied to the journal queue.

■ **Note** The journal queue is a system queue that is automatically created when MSMQ is installed and is meant to contain copies of messages that are sent or received.

- **Use Dead Letter Queue**: Specifies whether error messages will be sent to the dead letter queue.

■ **Note** The dead letter queue is a system queue that is automatically created when MSMQ is installed and is meant to contain undelivered messages.

- **User Name**: Specifies the user for accessing a remote queue. This property applies only when accessing remote queues. The MSMQ adapter's host account is used to access all local queues.

- **Password**: Specifies the password for accessing a remote queue. This property applies only when accessing remote queues.

- **Acknowledgement Type**: Specifies the type of acknowledgment to send upon the successful delivery of a message batch to the destination queue. The available acknowledgment types are defined in the `System.Messaging.AcknowledgeTypes` enumeration. You can select multiple acknowledgment types for this property.

- **Administration Queue**: Specifies the administration queue where acknowledgment messages are sent upon the successful delivery of messages to the destination queue.

- **Use Authentication**: Specifies that a certificate thumbprint will be used when delivering messages to the destination queue.

- **Certificate Thumbprint**: Specifies the certificate thumbprint used to attach to the message batch. You can use this certificate thumbprint to authenticate your BizTalk environment as the sender of the messages, helping increase the overall security of your integration solution. The certificate is stored in the `System.Messaging.Message.SenderCertificate` property.

■ **Note** You can find certificate thumbprints by viewing a certificate's details in the Certificate MMC snap-in.

- **Transactional**: Specifies whether the send port will deliver messages transactionally. This property must be set to `True` if the destination queue is transactional and `False` if the destination queue is not transactional.

If the Transactional property is set to True, the MSMQ adapter transactionally retrieves the appropriate amount of messages (as defined by the Maximum Message Size property) into a batch from the MessageBox and attempts to deliver the batch to the queue within the transaction. If any errors are encountered when delivering the batch (including a timeout, as defined by the Timeout and Timeout Unit properties), the MSMQ adapter attempts to redeliver the messages. If any errors are encountered when redelivering the batch, MSMQ suspends the messages, leaving them in a recoverable state in the MessageBox. Setting this property to True automatically implements the behavior defined by the Recoverable property. Messages within a batch are handled individually—those messages that do not encounter errors are delivered to the destination queue, even if other messages in the batch have errors.

If the Transactional property is set to False, the MSMQ adapter retrieves the appropriate number of messages (as defined by the Maximum Message Size property) into a batch from the MessageBox and attempts to deliver the batch to the queue. If any errors are encountered when delivering the batch (including a timeout, as defined by the Timeout and Timeout Unit properties), the MSMQ adapter attempts to suspend the messages. If any errors are encountered when suspending the batch, the messages are lost.

■ **Note** As a batch is delivered to the destination queue, errors can occur as messages. They pass through the send pipeline configured on the send port, pass through the map configured on the receive port, or are written to the destination queue.

MSMQ Queue Name Formats

To successfully send documents to an MSMQ queue, you must appropriately format the name of the queue via the Destination Queue property. The appropriate name depends on the type and location of the queue. The following list defines the way the Queue property should be entered for the commonly implemented queues:

- *Public queue*: ComputerName\QueueName

- *Private queue*: ComputerName\Private$\QueueName

- *Direct access to a queue via TCP*:
  DIRECT=TCP:IPAddressOfComputer\QueueName

- *Direct access to a queue via HTTP*:
  DIRECT=http://ComputerName/MSMQVirtualDirectory/QueueName, where MSMQVirtualDirectory is the Internet Information Services (IIS) virtual directory name of the MSMQ service

- *Direct access to a queue via HTTPS*:
  DIRECT=https://ComputerName/MSMQVirtualDirectory/QueueName, where MSMQVirtualDirectory is the IIS virtual directory name of the MSMQ service

- *Journal queue*: ComputerName\QueueName\Journal$

- *Dead letter queue*: ComputerName\Deadletter$

- *Transaction dead letter queue*: ComputerName\XactDeadletter$

By default, the MSMQ adapter prepends FORMATNAME:DIRECT=OS: to the Queue property, assuming the queue is referenced directly via the host computer's name.

6-5. Configuring MSMQ Receives

Problem

You are integrating with a system that publishes messages to an MSMQ queue, and you must configure BizTalk Server to receive messages from MSMQ.

Note See Recipe 6–4 for further information about how to configure the MSMQ send adapter.

Solution

You are building a solution that processes orders from an online commerce site that outputs order messages to an MSMQ queue. To receive messages from the queue, you must create a BizTalk Server receive location that utilizes the MSMQ adapter. To configure the receive location, follow these steps:

1. Open the BizTalk Administration Console.

2. Expand the BizTalk Server group, select an appropriate BizTalk application, and select the Receive Ports folder.

3. Right-click the Receive Ports folder, and select New ➤ One-way Receive Port to open the Receive Port Properties dialog box.

4. Give your new receive port a descriptive name, and click OK.

5. Right-click the receive port created in the previous step, and select New ➤ Receive Location. The Receive Location Properties dialog box appears.

6. Give your receive location a descriptive name, select the XMLReceive pipeline, and select MSMQ as the transport type.

7. Click the Configure button to the right of the Transport Type field. This launches the MSMQ Transport Properties dialog box.

8. Set the Queue property to the queue name that the online commerce site outputs messages to, as shown in Figure 6-13. In this scenario, we are using a queue named CommerceOrder.

Figure 6-13. *Configuring an MSMQ receive location*

9. Leave all the other properties with their default values, and click OK.

10. Click OK in the Receive Location Properties dialog box to save the receive location.

■ **Note**   You can also create receive ports and receive locations in the BizTalk Editor view in Visual Studio.

---

11. Select the Receive Locations folder in the BizTalk Administration Console, right-click the receive location created earlier, and select Enable.

How It Works

The BizTalk Server MSMQ adapter allows easy access to messages in MSMQ queues (MSMQ versions 2.0 and 3.0). The adapter relies on the local MSMQ service, which must be installed on the same computer hosting the adapter.

MSMQ Receive Options

Although this example illustrates the simplest scenario for receiving MSMQ messages from a specified queue, you can make a number of configurations against the MSMQ adapter:

- Queue: Specifies the queue from which to receive messages. Each queue must be polled by only one receive location per BizTalk environment. See the following section for further information about how to format queue names.

- Ordered Processing: Specifies whether the message order is persisted in the MessageBox. If this property is set to True, only one message is received in each batch (one message retrieved each time the receive location polls the queue). This property enables a solution to implement ordered message delivery, although you must also ensure that any subsequent processing (including the delivery of the message to a destination system) is handled serially if order is to be maintained. A True value for this property overrides the Batch property, essentially setting its value to 1.

- On Failure: Specifies the action the adapter should take on the receive location if an error occurs. These are the available values:

  - Stop: The receive location will be stopped.

  - Suspend (nonresumable): The receive location will remain enabled, with error messages being suspended in a nonresumable state.

  - Suspend (resumable): The receive location will remain enabled, with error messages being suspended in a resumable state.

- Batch Size: Specifies the number of MSMQ messages to be handled in a single batch. The default value of 0 indicates an unlimited number of messages in a batch. The MSMQ adapter retrieves messages from a queue and submits them to the MessageBox in batches of one to many messages.

- User Name: Specifies the user for accessing a remote queue. This property applies only when accessing remote queues. The MSMQ adapter's host account is used to access all local queues.

- Password: Specifies the password for accessing a remote queue. This property applies only when accessing remote queues.

- Transactional: Specifies whether the receive location will retrieve messages transactionally. This property must be set to True if the source queue is transactional and False if the source queue is not transactional.

  If the Transactional property is set to True, the MSMQ adapter transactionally retrieves the appropriate number of messages into a batch and attempts to submit the batch to the MessageBox within the transaction. If any errors are encountered when submitting the messages, the MSMQ adapter attempts to suspend the messages that have errors. If any errors are encountered when suspending the error messages, the MSMQ adapter rolls back the receive transaction (which leaves the messages in their original location—in the MSMQ queue). Messages within a batch are handled individually; those messages that do not encounter errors are submitted to the MessageBox, even if other messages in the batch have errors.

If the Transactional property is set to False, the MSMQ adapter retrieves the appropriate number of messages in a batch and attempts to submit the batch to the MessageBox. If any errors are encountered when submitting the batch, the MSMQ adapter attempts to suspend the messages. If any errors are encountered when suspending the batch, the messages are lost.

■ **Note**   The MSMQ adapter does not support transactionally receiving messages from a remote queue. If the queue is remote, message batches will be retrieved nontransactionally, regardless of the configuration of this property.

As a batch is submitted to the MessageBox, errors can occur in messages. They pass through the receive pipeline configured on the receive location, pass through the map configured on the receive port, or are written to the MessageBox database.

You should consider the performance impact when using the MSMQ adapter. It is important to understand the volume and size characteristics of the messages you expect to receive via MSMQ, because they can significantly impact your BizTalk Server resources. You should pay particular attention to the following:

Threading: BizTalk Server attempts to allocate threads to each MSMQ receive location as it polls its queue. Depending on how many messages are in the source queue, multiple threads may be allocated to each receive location. By default, the number of active threads allocated to the MSMQ adapter cannot exceed 25. If you have more than 25 messages being retrieved at any one time, it is possible to have latency.

Memory allocation: As message batches are retrieved by MSMQ receive locations, they are stored in memory until they are written to the MessageBox. The larger these batches are, the more memory is allocated. To throttle the amount of memory used by the MessageBox adapter, you can use the Batch and Serial Processing properties. You can limit the number of messages in any given batch by setting the Batch property to a low value. You can also set the Serial Processing property to True, which limits the MSMQ receive location to retrieving a single message in each batch. Memory allocation is particularly important if you have implemented the large message extension for message queuing, which allows messages larger than 4MB in size to be handled by the MSMQ adapter. See the SDK example devoted to this topic for further information.

It is important to understand the relationship of these configurations and the impact they have on system resources. The ideal configuration of threading, serial processing, and batch processing is specific to each BizTalk environment. Optimization should be part of the performance-testing phase for all solutions you deploy to your BizTalk Server environment.

MSMQ Queue Name Formats

To successfully read messages from an MSMQ queue, you must appropriately format the name of the queue via the Queue property. The appropriate name depends on the type and location of the queue. The following list defines the way the Queue property should be entered for the commonly implemented queues:

- *Public queue*: ComputerName\QueueName

- *Private queue*: ComputerName\Private$\QueueName

- *Direct access to a queue via TCP*: DIRECT=TCP:IPAddressOfComputer\QueueName

By default, the MSMQ adapter prepends FORMATNAME:DIRECT=OS: to the Queue property, assuming the queue is referenced directly via the host computer's name.

6-6. Sending Updategrams

Problem

You need to create an orchestration that inserts a record into a table in your SQL database. Specifically, you need to create an orchestration that inserts a new customer record in your ERP system based on an inbound customer creation message from your CRM system.

Solution

The solution reviewed as part of this recipe outlines how to use the SQL adapter within the context of an orchestration. The following instructions outline the tasks required to create and configure the physical SQL send port as well as the orchestration that implements the SQL adapter.

The solution has sample XML files to demonstrate how the SQL adapter inserts message content into a SQL table. The solution also includes a sample SQL table structure.

Task 1: Create Supporting Artifacts

Your first task is to create supporting artifacts. These include a database table and a BizTalk solution. Here are the steps to follow:

1. Create a new SQL database and table for which to insert the record. Compile the table definition listed in Listing 6-1.

    Listing 6-1. Listing Customer Table Definition

    ```
    CREATE TABLE [dbo].[Customer] (
        [CustomerID][int] IDENTITY (1,1) NOT NULL,
        [CustomerName][nvarchar](30) COLLATE SQL_Latin1_General_CP1_CI_AS NOT NULL,
        [Address][nvarchar](60) COLLATE SQL_Latin1_General_CP1_CI_AS NOT NULL,
        [City][nvarchar](30) COLLATE SQL_Latin1_General_CP1_CI_AS NOT NULL,
        [Region][nvarchar](30) COLLATE SQL_Latin1_General_CP1_CI_AS NOT NULL,
        [PostalCode][nvarchar](10) COLLATE SQL_Latin1_General_CP1_CI_AS NOT NULL,
    ) ON [PRIMARY]
    ```

2. Create a new BizTalk solution that will contain the objects that will insert customers into the Customer table in your SQL database. Next, create a sample message that matches the structure detailed in Listing 6-2. The schema for this message will be created as part of the solution as defined in the "Task 2: Create BizTalk Solution Artifacts" section of this recipe.

    Listing 6-2. Sample Customer Message

    ```
    <ns0:Customer_Request xmlns:ns0="http://SQLAdapterUpdategram">
      <ns0:sync>
        <ns0:after>
          <ns0:Customer CustomerName="Alice" Address="King" City="Seattle"
    Region="WA" PostalCode="98005" />
        </ns0:after>
      </ns0:sync>
    </ns0:Customer_Request>
    ```

Task 2: Create BizTalk Solution Artifacts

You will be using the Add Generated Items Wizard to generate the BizTalk artifacts for this recipe. The wizard will prompt you to specify your BizTalk environment (such as specifying the BizTalk MessageBox database, setting the connection string to the database you will be accessing, and identifying the type of SQL port you are creating, such as send or receive). The following steps describe this task in detail:

1. Choose Add Generated Items from the Solution Explorer tool menu. Verify that Add Adapter Metadata is selected. Figure 6-14 displays the Add Generated Items Wizard.

Figure 6-14. *Using the Add Generated Items Wizard*

2. On the Add Adapter Wizard screen that opens, select the SQL adapter, and verify the settings to your BizTalk MessageBox database.

■ **Note** You can leave the Port field empty unless you are specifying an already created SQL send or receive port. This sample will create a send port that you will specify later through the BizTalk Explorer.

---

3. Click Next, and set the connection string for the database to which you are connecting.

4. Next, in the SQL Transport Schema Generation Wizard, specify the target namespace as `http://SQLAdapterUpdategram`, the port type property as a Send port, the request document root element name as `Customer_Request`, and the response document root element name as `Customer_Response`. The wizard should look like Figure 6-15.

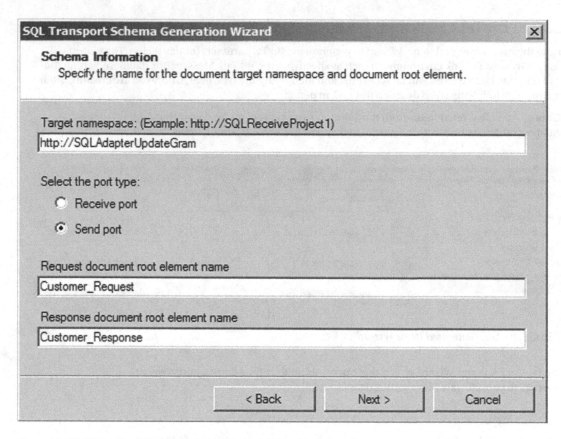

Figure 6-15. *Using the SQL Transport Schema Generation Wizard*

5. On the Statement type information page of the wizard, select Updategram as the type of statement.

6. On the Statement Information page of the wizard, select Insert as the type of the updategram to create. Additionally, on the same page, select the Customer table as the table name. In the Columns to Update list, multiselect the following columns: CustomerName, Address, City, Region and PostalCode. CustomerID is not required because SQL Server automatically generates the ID because of the column being an Identity column. The wizard should resemble Figure 6-16.

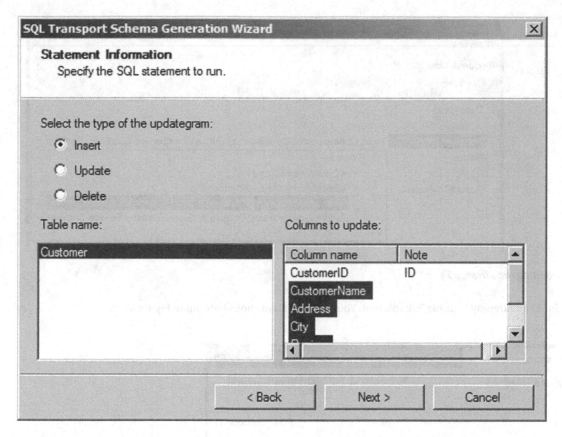

Figure 6-16. *Using the SQL Transport Generation Wizard's Statement Information dialog*

7. Click Finish, completing the wizard. When you complete the wizard, notice that BizTalk creates two artifacts for you: the BizTalk orchestration and `InsertCustomerService.xsd`.

■ **Note** The BizTalk orchestration allows you to perform additional processing of an inbound message before sending the message to the SQL database. The `InsertCustomerService` schema represents a multipart message within your orchestration. The first part of the message represents the request you will be sending to the SQL database, and the second part represents the response the database will return to you. In this recipe, we will use only the request portion of the multipart message.

---

8. Configure the BizTalk orchestration for an inbound receive and an outbound send. Set both the inbound and outbound ports to work with schemas of type `SQL_Adapter_ Updategram.InsertCustomerService.Customer_Request`. This property is set as shown in Figure 6-17. Make sure to set the Activate property on the receive shape of the orchestration to `True`.

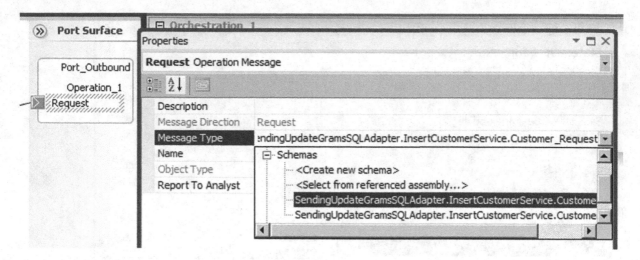

Figure 6-17. *Setting the Message Type*

9. Build and deploy your BizTalk solution. Your orchestration should resemble Figure 6-18.

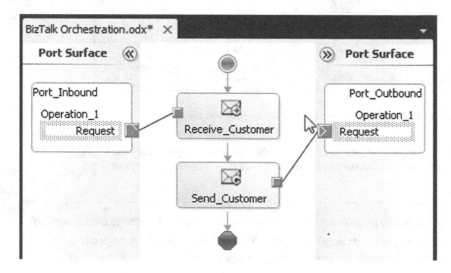

Figure 6-18. *Configuring the SQL updategram orchestration*

Task 3: Create Physical BizTalk Ports

To test this solution, you will need to create a physical file receive port to consume the inbound XML file and a SQL send port to send the message to the SQL database. A simple file receive port will consume the inbound XML document and activate the SQL updategram orchestration just created. Please see Recipe 6–2 for creating a file receive port. The following steps outline creating the SQL send port:

1. Open the BizTalk Administration Console.

2. From an appropriate BizTalk application, right-click the Send Ports folder, and select New ➤ Static One-way Send Port to open the Send Port Properties dialog box. Enter **Sample SQL Updategram Send Port** for the new send port's name. Within the Transport section of the General tab, select SQL from the Type drop-down list.

3. In the SQL Transport Properties dialog box, configure the connection string to the appropriate database by clicking the ellipses next to the Connection String field. Additionally, configure the document target namespace as http://SQLAdapterUpdategram. The Response Document Root Name can be set to any value; it is not used in this recipe. See Figure 6-19.

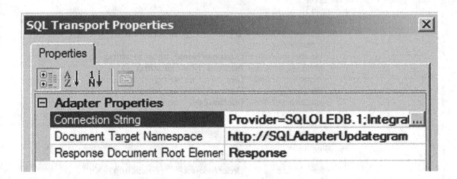

Figure 6-19. *Configuring the SQL updategram orchestration*

4. Set the Send Pipeline property to the Microsoft.BizTalk.DefaultPipelines.XMLTransmit pipeline.

5. Bind the deployed orchestration to the newly created send and receive ports.

Task 4: Test the Solution

Follow these steps to test the solution:

1. Place the customer test file in the file folder being monitored by BizTalk Server by the file receive port just created. BizTalk Server will consume the file, launch the orchestration, and send the updategram to SQL Server via the SQL send port configured.

2. Verify that the record inserted successfully into the Customer table.

How It Works

SQL updategrams are extremely useful when you need a lightweight implementation to insert, update, or delete data from a SQL table. This recipe demonstrates how to use the Add Generated Items Wizard as well as how to insert records into a SQL table. This recipe did not address the need to process exceptions that may occur when inserting records into a SQL table.

The focus of this recipe was to demonstrate how to insert a record into a single table; however, updategrams can also affect data in multiple tables. The Add Generated Items Wizard creates only a single schema for a single table. However, if you want to modify multiple tables in the same call, you can run the wizard multiple times and then copy the generated schemas into a single schema, or you can manually adjust the autogenerated schema and add the nodes. Assume you have a Customer table and an Order table. For each customer, you insert into the Customer table, you would also like to insert the corresponding orders to the Order table. If you knew the structure of the Order table, you could add the structure to the autogenerated schema, and BizTalk will know to insert the records into a table with the name of the node you specified. Figure 6-20 displays the structure of the modified schema to also insert records into the Order table. A better approach to modifying the autogenerate schema would be to consider using a SQL stored procedure to manage the insertion of data into multiple tables.

Figure 6-20. *Multiple table insert schema*

SQL updategrams allow you to update records at a table level, which is convenient. However, not all databases may allow access at a table level; they may require you to use other means to manipulate data in the specific table. Additionally, using an updategram locks you into using a deployed table structure, which presents a challenge from a maintenance perspective. When determining the best way to manipulate data in a SQL table, consider the following questions:

- Will the account with which you are accessing the SQL database have permissions at a table level?

- What is the likelihood of the table structure changing, and how does that affect the solution you are building?

- Is there logic at a database level that must be performed before the message from your orchestration can be processed?

- Do you need to affect data in many tables? Even though it is technically possible to insert data into multiple tables via an update datagram, inserting data into multiple tables can be better managed using a SQL stored procedure.

If any of the previous questions is true, you should consider an alternative to using an updategram. Recipe 6–7 discusses using SQL stored procedures as an alternative.

6-7. Calling Stored Procedures
Problem

You need to create an orchestration that inserts a record into a table in your SQL database via a stored procedure. Specifically, you need to create an orchestration that inserts a new customer record based on an inbound message.

Solution

The solution reviewed as part of this recipe outlines how to use the SQL adapter within the context of an orchestration. The following instructions outline the tasks required to create and configure the physical SQL send port as well as the orchestration that implements the SQL adapter.

The solution has sample XML files to demonstrate how the SQL adapter inserts message content into a SQL table via a stored procedure. The solution also includes a sample SQL table structure.

Task 1: Create Supporting Artifacts

The steps outlined for this task create the supporting solution artifacts. You will create the table, stored procedure, and inbound message structure for the message consumed by BizTalk. Here are the steps to follow:

1. Create a new SQL database and table for which to insert the record. Compile the table definition listed in Listing 6-3.

   Listing 6-3. Example Customer Table Definition

   ```
   CREATE TABLE [dbo].[Customer] (
       [CustomerID][int] IDENTITY (1,1) NOT NULL,
       [CustomerName][nvarchar](30) COLLATE SQL_Latin1_General_CP1_CI_AS NOT NULL,
       [Address][nvarchar](60) COLLATE SQL_Latin1_General_CP1_CI_AS NOT NULL,
       [City][nvarchar](30) COLLATE SQL_Latin1_General_CP1_CI_AS NOT NULL,
       [Region][nvarchar](30) COLLATE SQL_Latin1_General_CP1_CI_AS NOT NULL,
       [PostalCode][nvarchar](10) COLLATE SQL_Latin1_General_CP1_CI_AS NOT NULL,
   ) ON [PRIMARY]
   ```

2. If you do not have a stored procedure to insert individual customer records, compile the stored procedure listed in Listing 6-4.

   Listing 6-4. Example Insert Customer Stored Procedure

   ```
   if exists  (select * from sysobjects where name = 'BizTalkToCustomerInsert'
   and type = 'P')
       drop proc BizTalkToCustomerInsert
   go
   CREATE procedure BizTalkToCustomerInsert
                   @CustomerName nvarchar(60)
               , @Address nvarchar(120)
               , @City nvarchar(60)
               , @Region nvarchar(60)
               , @PostalCode nvarchar(60)
   ```

```
AS
/*
**
** Object: BizTalkToCustomerInsert
**
** Description: Inserts records into the Customer table for the SQL adapter
** stored procedure recipe
**
**
*/
BEGIN
    Declare @intReturnCode int
    select    @intReturnCode = 0

    /*Insert records that will be returned to caller*/
    Insert Customer (CustomerName, Address, City, Region, PostalCode)
    Values (@CustomerName, @Address, @City, @Region, @PostalCode)

    /* Set the outbound return code */
    select    @intReturnCode = @@error

    /* return the return code */
    return @intReturnCode
END

go
grant execute on dbo.BizTalkToCustomerInsert to public
go
```

3. Create a new BizTalk solution that will contain the components used to insert customers into the Customer table in your SQL database. Next, create a sample message that matches the structure detailed in Listing 6-5. The schema for this message will be created as part of the solution as defined in the "Task 2: Create BizTalk Solution Artifacts" section of this recipe.

Listing 6-5. Example Customer Input Message

```
<ns0:Customer_Request xmlns:ns0="http://SQLAdapterStoredProcedure">
  <ns0:BizTalkToCustomerInsert Address="1241 Little Overlook" City="Grand Jct"
CustomerName="Ciro
A" PostalCode="81502" Region="CO" />
</ns0:Customer_Request>
```

Task 2: Create BizTalk Solution Artifacts

Next, you will be using the Add Generated Items Wizard to generate the BizTalk artifacts for this recipe. The wizard will prompt you to specify your BizTalk environment (such as specifying the BizTalk MessageBox database, setting the connection string to the database that you will be accessing, and identifying the type of SQL port you are creating such as send or receive). Follow these steps:

1. Choose Add Generated Items from the Solution Explorer's tool menu. Verify that Add Adapter Metadata is selected.

2. On the Add Adapter Wizard page, select the SQL adapter, and verify the settings to your BizTalk MessageBox database. Figure 6-21 shows the initial connection screen.

Figure 6-21. *Using the Add Generated Items Wizard*

■ **Note** You can leave the Port field empty unless you are specifying an already created SQL send or receive port. This sample will create a send port that you will specify later.

---

3. Click Next, and set the connection string for the database to which you are connecting.

4. Click Next, and specify the target namespace as `http://SQLAdapterStoredProcedure`, the port type as Send, the request document root element name as `Customer_Request`, and the response document root element name as `Customer_Response`. The wizard should look like Figure 6-22.

Target namespace: (Example: http://SQLReceiveProject1)

http://SQLAdapterStoredProcedure

Select the port type:

○ Receive port

◉ Send port

Request document root element name

Customer_Request

Response document root element name

Customer_Response

Figure 6-22. *Using the SQL Transport Schema Generation Wizard*

5. On the Statement Type page of the wizard, select Stored Procedure as the type of statement, and click Next.

6. On the Statement Information page of the wizard, select the `BizTalkToCustomerInsert` stored procedure from the drop-down enumeration, and leave all the check boxes next to the input parameters empty.

7. Finally, click the Generate button, because it results in a generated execute script that is listed in the Generated Script field of the wizard. The wizard should resemble Figure 6-23.

Figure 6-23. *Using the SQL Transport Generation Wizard—the Statement Information page*

■ **Note** Because the stored procedure contains input parameters, they are displayed in the datagrid of the wizard. If there are default values that should be specified, you can enter those parameters next to the name of the input parameter. If the check box is selected, a null value will be submitted as the value for the input parameter.

---

8. Click Next and then Finish, completing the wizard. When you complete the wizard, notice that BizTalk creates two artifacts for you: the BizTalk orchestration and SQLService.xsd.

■ **Note** The BizTalk orchestration allows you to perform additional processing of the inbound message, and the SQLService schema contains the physical representation of the data returned from the stored procedure.

---

9. Configure the BizTalk orchestration for an inbound receive and an outbound send. The ports should be configured to receive and to send a message of type SQL_Adapter_Stored_ Procedure.SQLService.Customer_Request. Your orchestration should resemble Figure 6-24. Make sure to set the Activate property on the Receive shape to True.

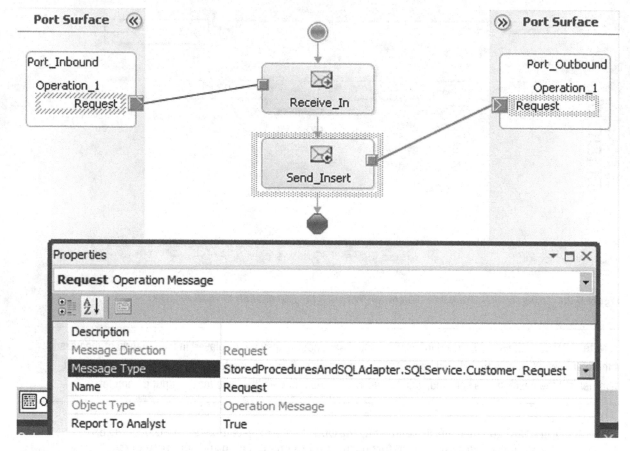

Figure 6-24. Configuring the SQL stored procedure orchestration

10. Build and deploy your BizTalk solution.

Task 3: Create Physical BizTalk Ports

Your next task is to create the physical BizTalk ports you will need to test the solution. Follow the process outlined in these steps:

1. To test this solution, you will need to create a physical file receive port to consume the inbound XML file and a SQL send port to send the message to the SQL database. Open the BizTalk Administration Console.

2. Find the appropriate BizTalk application, right-click the Send Ports folder, and select New ➤ Static One-way Send Port to open the Send Port Properties dialog box. Name the new send port **Sample SQL Stored Procedure Send Port**. Within the Transport section of the General tab, select SQL from the Type drop-down list.

3. In the SQL Transport properties, configure the connection string to the appropriate database by clicking the ellipses next to the Connection String field. Additionally, configure the document target namespace as http://SQLAdapterStoredProcedure.

4. Set Send Pipeline to the `Microsoft.BizTalk.DefaultPipelines.XMLTransmit` pipeline.

5. Bind the deployed orchestration to the newly created send and receive ports.

Task 4: Test the Solution

Your last task is to test your solution to be sure it works correctly. The procedure for testing is simple: place your sample customer test file in the folder being monitored by the file receive port, and verify that the record inserted successfully into the Customer table.

How It Works

Utilizing the SQL adapter to call stored procedures is a great way to insert data into a database or call a procedure to return data from a database. The benefits of using the SQL adapter over creating a component to make database calls include being able to use any BizTalk adapter (including guaranteed reliable message delivery, retry capabilities, and the ability to specify alternative mechanisms for message delivery). Additionally, a stored procedure is capable of taking an entire XML message or individual data elements as input parameters.

This recipe demonstrates how to use the SQL adapter and stored procedure to insert customer records in a SQL table. The stored procedure required input parameters but could have taken the entire contents of the XML message and parsed the contents of message.

6-8. Receiving Messages with the SQL Adapter
Problem

You need to create an orchestration that retrieves messages from a SQL table via a SQL stored procedure. Specifically, you need to create an orchestration that will receive individual customer records from your SQL database via a SQL stored procedure.

Solution

The solution reviewed as part of this recipe outlines how to use the SQL receive adapter within the context of an orchestration. The solution has a sample table and stored procedure to demonstrate how the SQL receive adapter routes messages based on message content. The following instructions outline the tasks required to create and configure the physical SQL receive port as well as the orchestration that implements the SQL receive adapter.

Task 1: Create Supporting Artifacts

Perform the following steps to create the SQL support artifacts that are used by this recipe:

1. Create a new SQL database and table for which to insert the record. Compile the following table definition, and insert the statements listed in Listing 6-6.

    Listing 6-6. Example Customer Table Definition

```
CREATE TABLE [dbo].[Customer] (
    [CustomerID][int] IDENTITY (1,1) NOT NULL,
    [CustomerName][nvarchar](30) COLLATE SQL_Latin1_General_CP1_CI_AS NOT NULL,
    [Address][nvarchar](60) COLLATE SQL_Latin1_General_CP1_CI_AS NOT NULL,
```

```
        [City][nvarchar](30) COLLATE SQL_Latin1_General_CP1_CI_AS NOT NULL,
        [Region][nvarchar](30) COLLATE SQL_Latin1_General_CP1_CI_AS NOT NULL,
        [PostalCode][nvarchar](10) COLLATE SQL_Latin1_General_CP1_CI_AS NOT NULL,
        [RecordStatus][tinyint] NOT NULL
    ) ON [PRIMARY]

    Insert Customer (CustomerName, Address, City, Region, PostalCode, RecordStatus)
    Values ('Shauna Marie', '9515 S Wally St', 'Bellevue', 'WA', '98004', 1)
    Insert Customer (CustomerName, Address, City, Region, PostalCode, RecordStatus)
    Values ('Pat Dean', '10034th 49th Ave NE', 'Redmond', 'WA', '95550', 1)
    Insert Customer (CustomerName, Address, City, Region, PostalCode, RecordStatus)
    Values ('Sherrie Long', '5015 48th Ave SW', 'Woodland Park', 'CO', '80863', 1)
```

■ **Note**   The table definition is different from the previous recipe. Make sure to use the table definition in Listing 6-6 or modify the previously created table definition.

---

2.   If you do not have a stored procedure to retrieve individual customer records, compile the stored procedure listed in Listing 6-7.

Listing 6-7. Example Retrieve Customer Record Stored Procedure

```
if exists(select * from sysobjects where name = 'CustomerToBizTalk' and type = 'P')
    drop proc CustomerToBizTalk
go
CREATE procedure CustomerToBizTalk
AS
/*
**
** Object: CustomerToBizTalk
**
** Description: Retrieves records from the Customer table for the SQL receive
**              adapter recipe
**
**
*/
BEGIN
    /*Populate temp table with records that will be returned to caller*/
    Select top 1 CustomerID
        , CustomerName
        , Address
        , City
        , Region
        , PostalCode
        , RecordStatus
    Into    #TempCustomer
    From    Customer
    Where     RecordStatus = 1
```

```
/*Update Status of retrieved record from the Customer table*/
Update      Customer
Set         RecordStatus = 0
Where       CustomerID = (select CustomerID from #TempCustomer)

/*Return records to caller*/
Select CustomerID
    , CustomerName
    , Address
    , City
    , Region
    , PostalCode
    , RecordStatus
from       #TempCustomer as Customer FOR XML AUTO, XMLData, Elements

/*Clean up temp table*/
drop table #TempCustomer
END

go
grant execute on dbo.CustomerToBizTalk to public
go
```

> ■ **Note**   Notice that the select statement in Listing 6-7 contains a FOR XML AUTO, XMLDATA, ELEMENTS clause.
> The SQL adapter requires select statements returning records to return them in XML format. Additionally, the XMLDATA
> clause is required only when running the wizard to generate the schema for the result set from the stored procedure.
> When you test the solution, make sure to remove the XMLDATA clause from your stored procedure.

Task 2: Create BizTalk Solution Artifacts

Next, use the Add Generated Items Wizard to generate the BizTalk artifacts for this recipe. The wizard will prompt you to specify your BizTalk environment (including specifying the BizTalk MessageBox database, setting the connection string to the database you will be accessing, and identifying the type of SQL port you are creating such as send or receive). This recipe assumes you have created an empty BizTalk solution. Here are the steps to follow:

1. Choose Add Generated Items from the Solution Explorer's tool menu. Select the Add Adapter Metadata template.

2. On the Add Adapter Wizard page, select the SQL adapter, and verify the settings to your BizTalk MessageBox database.

> ■ **Note**   You can leave the Port field empty unless you are specifying an already created SQL send or receive port.

3. Click Next, and set the connection string for the database to which you are connecting (this is where the table and stored procedure created in the previous task reside). Then, in the SQL Transport Schema Generation Wizard, specify the target namespace as `http://SQLReceiveAdapter` and the document root element name as `Customer_Response`. The wizard should resemble Figure 6-25.

Target namespace: (Example: http://SQLReceiveProject1)

`http://SQLReceiveAdapter`

Select the port type:

○ Receive port

○ Send port

Document root element name:

`Customer_Response`

Figure 6-25. Using the SQL Transport Schema Generation Wizard

4. Click Next, and on the Statement type information page of the wizard, select Stored Procedure as the type of statement. On the Statement Information page of the wizard, select the `CustomerToBizTalk` stored procedure from the drop-down enumeration, and click the Generate button. The Generate button results in a generated execute script that is listed in the Generated Script field of the wizard. Figure 6-26 displays the completed wizard.

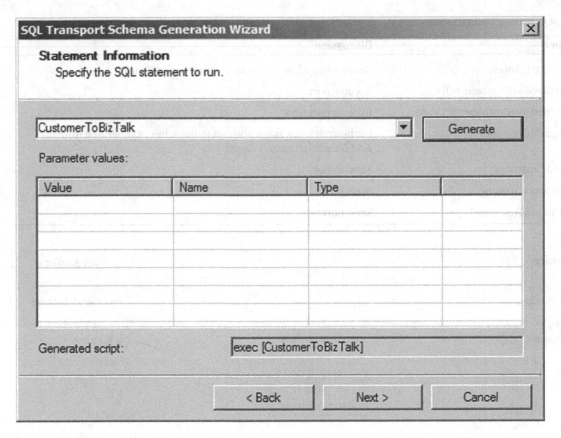

Figure 6-26. *Completed wizard*

■ **Note** If the stored procedure contained any input parameters, those parameters would display in the datagrid of the wizard. The wizard also depends on the select statement in the stored procedure to contain the XMLDATA clause in the FOR XML statement. The XMLDATA clause returns the schema layout for the structure returned by the select statement.

---

5. Click Finish, completing the wizard. When you complete the wizard, notice that BizTalk creates two artifacts for you: the BizTalk orchestration and SQLService.xsd.

■ **Note** The BizTalk orchestration allows you to perform additional processing of the inbound message, and the SQLService schema contains the physical representation of the data returned from the stored procedure.

---

6. Modify the BizTalk orchestration, configuring it based on the artifacts listed in Table 6-4. Configure the BizTalk orchestration for an inbound receive and an outbound send. See Figure 6-27.

Table 6-4. SQL Receive Orchestration

ID	Name	Discussion
1	Receive Customer	Receive shape. Set the Activate property to True.
2	oprtReceiveCustomerSQL	Receive port
3	oprtReceiveCustomerSQLType	Receive port type
4	msgSQLCustomer	Orchestration message pointed to the schema generated from the Add Generated Items Wizard
5	Send Customer	Send shape
6	oprtSendCustomer	Send port
7	oprtSendCustomerType	Send port type

Figure 6-27. Viewing the complete orchestration

7. Once your orchestration is complete, build and deploy your solution.

Task 3: Create Physical BizTalk Ports

Execute the following steps to create the SQL receive port that will call the stored procedure and route the message received to the deployed BizTalk solution:

1. To test this solution, you will need to create a physical SQL receive port to consume the inbound XML file and a physical file send port to send the message to a file share for examination.

2. From the BizTalk Administration Console, right-click the Receive Ports folder, and select add a one way Receive Port to open the One-Way Receive Port Properties dialog box. Name the new receive port **Sample SQL Receive Port**. Leave the rest of the settings with default values.

3. Right-click the Receive Locations folder, and select Add Receive Location. Select the receive port that was created in the previous step, and click OK. In the Receive Location Properties dialog box, configure the transport type, address, receive handler, and receive pipeline. Configure the dialog box settings specified in Table 6-5.

Table 6-5. *SQL Receive Location Configuration Settings*

Configuration Parameter	Value
Transport Type	SQL
Address (URI)	Location of your SQL server (See step 5 for more information.)
Receive Handler	BizTalk host instance (for example, BizTalkServerApplication)
Receive Pipeline	Microsoft.BizTalk.DefaultPipelines.XMLReceive

4. When configuring the Address (URI) property in the Receive Port dialog box, leave the Receive Configuration settings to the default values:

   a. Set Document Root Element Name to Customer_Response.

   b. Set Document Target Namespace to http://SQLReceiveAdapter.

   c. On the SQL Command page, navigate to the deployed BizTalk project and schema to set the SQL command properly (as shown in Figure 6-28). The completed SQL Transport Properties dialog box should resemble Figure 6-29.

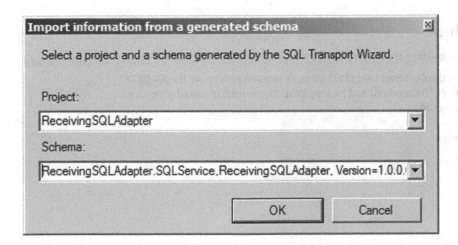

Figure 6-28. *Selecting the Schema from the Deployed Project*

Receive Configuration	
Poll While Data Found	**False**
Polling Interval	**30**
Polling Unit of Measure	**Seconds**
SQL Configuration	
Connection String	**Provider=SQLOLEDB.1;Integral ...**
Document Root Element Name	**Customer_Response**
Document Target Namespace	**http://SQLReceiveAdapter**
SQL Command	**exec [CustomerToBizTalk]**
URI	**SQL://WIN-LUNNMMJQUVE/Den**

Figure 6-29. *Viewing the completed SQL Transport Properties dialog box*

■ **Note** BizTalk uses the root element name and the namespace to route the inbound XML file. If the root element name and the namespace do not match the root element name and namespace of the SQLService.xsd file you created in the BizTalk solution, you will receive document routing errors and suspended messages when BizTalk tries to route the message from the SQL receive adapter.

---

5. Bind the deployed orchestration to the newly created send and receive ports.

Task 4: Test the Solution

Your final task is to test your solution. Here are the steps to follow:

1. Modify and recompile the CustomerToBizTalk stored procedure. Remove the XMLDATA clause in the FOR XML AUTO statement and recompile it. The resulting stored procedure should resemble Listing 6-8.

Listing 6-8. Revised Select Statement

```
/*Return records to caller*/
    Select CustomerID
        , CustomerName
        , Address
        , City
        , Region
        , PostalCode
        , RecordStatus
    from    #TempCustomer as Customer FOR XML AUTO, Elements
```

2. Start your orchestration and SQL receive port, and validate that a single XML file is created for each customer in your Customer table with the RecordStatus of 1. Also verify that the records in the Customer table have had their status set to 0 indicating that BizTalk has consumed the record. The resulting XML file should resemble Listing 6-9.

Listing 6-9. Customer Sample XML

```xml
<?xml version="1.0" encoding="utf-16" ?>
<Customer_Response xmlns="http://SQLReceiveAdapter">
  <Customer>
      <CustomerID>1</CustomerID>
      <CustomerName>Shauna Marie</CustomerName>
      <Address>9515 S Wally St</Address>
      <City>Bellevue</City>
      <Region>WA</Region>
      <PostalCode>98004</PostalCode>
      <RecordStatus>1</RecordStatus>
  </Customer>
</Customer_Response>
```

How It Works

Retrieving records via the SQL receive adapter is extremely useful and powerful when coupled with the use of stored procedures. Implementing the SQL receive adapter requires configuring and managing how records are retrieved from SQL. This recipe outlined how to use a stored procedure that selects records in a temporary table, updates the status of the individual record in the SQL table, and then returns the records to the SQL adapter. Additionally, this sample demonstrated how to use the FOR XML AUTO clause within a stored procedure.

Stored Procedure Configuration

The SQL receive adapter operates on the polling principle of retrieving records. The adapter will call the stored procedure on a configurable interval to retrieve records. However, the adapter does not maintain the state of which records it has consumed. Therefore, any stored procedure that the SQL receive adapter executes must maintain a level of state identifying the processed records. If you examine the stored procedure listed previously, you will notice that there is a RecordStatus column that is updated to 0 when the records are polled. You have many options for determining unprocessed records. For example, you can use the status flag, physically remove the record from the database, use the date range, and so on. If the stored procedure does not maintain state, BizTalk will continue consuming the same data.

In addition to maintaining state within the stored procedure, if you are returning a result via a select statement, then you must specify the FOR XML AUTO, XMLDATA clause for generating the SQLService.xsd schema. As explained, the XML AUTO clause instructs SQL Server to return the result set as XML, and the XMLDATA clause instructs SQL Server to return the schema layout for the returned result set. The SQL service adapter officially supports using the FOR XML AUTO clause.

You can also use the FOR XML Explicit clause, but it is not officially supported and should be used with care. Using FOR XML Explicit eliminates using the Add Generated Items Wizard to automatically generate the SQLService schema. However, you can create the SQLService schema manually. One benefit to using FOR XML Explicit over FOR XML AUTO is the greater level of control in the resulting XML structure that is returned to BizTalk. If you have a complicated XML message structure that is comprised of data from multiple tables, you can format the result set in the correct XML structure via the FOR XML Explicit clause. The select statement in Listing 6-10 demonstrates how to use the FOR XML Explicit clause.

Listing 6-10. Return Result Set Using the FOR XML Explicit Clause

```
select    1    as Tag, NULL    as Parent
  , NULL    as [Customer!1!element]
  , CustomerID as [Customer!1!CustomerID!element]
  , CustomerName    as [Customer!1!CustomerName!element]
  , Address as [Customer!1!Address!element]
  , City as [Customer!1!City!element]
  , Region as [Customer!1!Region!element]
  , PostalCode as [Customer!1!PostalCode!element]
  , RecordStatus as [Customer!1!RecordStatus!element]
from    Customer
FOR XML EXPLICIT
```

Adapter Configuration

The SQL receive adapter contains many items for configuration. Table 6-6 lists the items worth noting. The SQL adapter receive location differs from other BizTalk receive locations in that each SQL receive location identifies a specific message type that is received from a database. If you expect to receive multiple types of messages, you must construct a SQL receive port for each unique message type. The SQL adapter is configured for each unique message type through the Document Root Element Name node and the Document Target Namespace node. Additionally, each SQL receive location is configured to execute a specific SQL stored procedure or command.

Table 6-6. *SQL Receive Adapter Configuration*

ID	Configuration Parameter	Description
1	Poll While Data Found	Indicates whether to continue polling for new records in additional batches or whether to submit a single query result for the entire polling window.
2	Polling Interval	Identifies how often to poll for records.
3	Polling Unit of Measure	Identifies the unit of measure for polling.
4	Connection String	Identifies the connection string for the database containing data to be polled.
5	Document Root Element Name	Identifies the Root node that BizTalk will assign the inbound message.
6	Document Target Namespace	Identifies the namespace that BizTalk will assign the inbound message.
7	SQL Command	Identifies the SQL command the SQL adapter will execute.
8	URI	Identifies a unique identifier for the receive location. This value is autogenerated.

In addition to the configuration items identified previously, you must verify that MSDTC is configured correctly on the target system that is hosting the SQL database because BizTalk enrolls every call from the SQL adapter into an MSDTC-styled transaction.

6-9. Configuring HTTP Sends

Problem

You want to programmatically configure an HTTP send port from an orchestration using a Message Assignment shape.

Solution

This solution will describe how to post a document using a send port configured with authentication to post via a secure HTTPS site. The following solution assumes you have a BizTalk project open in Visual Studio with a BizTalk orchestration and a schema that can be used to create an orchestration message. Here are the steps to follow:

1. Create a new orchestration message by right-clicking the Messages folder in the Orchestration View window and selecting New Message. Enter **msgSend** for the message name, and give it a message type (this should be the schema of the document that will be sent via HTTP).

2. Setting HTTP properties requires constructing the message that will be sent. Drop a Message Assignment shape in the orchestration. This will create a Construct Message shape that should be configured such that the Message Constructed property is set to the message created in step 1.

3. Double-click the Message Assignment shape, and enter the property settings as shown in Listing 6-11. Figure 6-30 shows the properties available in the Message Assignment Editor. Click OK when complete.

Listing 6-11. Message Assignment Code

```
// Set HTTP send port properties; the username and password can be
// configurable by using the config file or BizTalk rules engine
// rather than hard-coded values
msgSend(HTTP.AuthenticationScheme) = "Basic";
msgSend(HTTP.Username) = "User"; // can be loaded from config file, also
msgSend(HTTP.Password) = "Password"; // can be loaded from config file
// configure additional parameters as appropriate
```

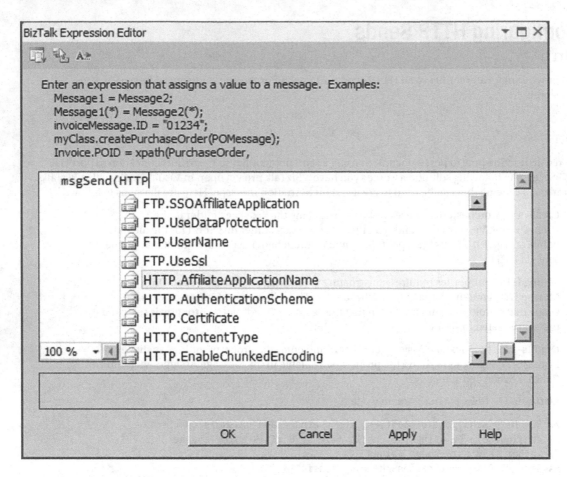

Figure 6-30. *Viewing the HTTP parameters in the Message Assignment Editor*

■ **Note** When selecting properties from the drop-down list in the Message Assignment shape, you'll see all the properties you can set. Specific to HTTP, both the Send and Receive properties are listed. A complete list of Send properties appears in Table 6-7.

Table 6-7. *HTTP Port Parameters*

Property	Type
AffiliateApplicationName	When using SSO, you can specify an affiliate application. You enter the name of the application as a string. When using this property, the UseSSO property must be set to True.
AuthenticationScheme	You can set four types of authentication: Anonymous, Basic, Digest, and Kerberos. When using Basic and Digest, you should set the Password and Username properties.
Certificate	If you are using a certificate (for HTTPS), you should enter the thumbprint of the certificate as a string here. Thumbprints are typically found in the properties of the certificate and are 40-digit hexadecimal values.
ContentType	The default value is Text/XML. This is a string.
EnableChunkedEncoding	Boolean value that indicates whether to send the document in chunked packets of information.
HttpCookie	Properties available if using cookies.
InboundHttpHeaders	The HTTP headers may be available on inbound HTTP messages.
MaxRedirects	The HTTP adapter can be set to allow for 0 to 10 redirects.
Password	Password used when posting to a secure site. AuthenticationScheme should be set to Basic or Digest.
ProxyName	If a proxy server is used, enter the name of the server as a string.
ProxyPassword	Password for proxy server. The UseProxy property should be set to True, and UseHandlerProxySettings should be set to False.
ProxyPort	Port for proxy server. An example would be 80.
ProxyUsername	Username for proxy server. The UseProxy property should be set to True, and UseHandlerProxySettings should be set to False.
RequestTimeout	By default, the timeout will be managed based on the size of the document. This can be overridden with a specific timeout value entered as a numeric entry (in seconds).
ResponseStatusCode	Properties available regarding the status code of the response.
SubmissionHandle	Submission handle, if available.
UseHandlerProxySettings	If set to True, other proxy properties that may be set are overridden, and the send port will use the proxy handler configuration.
UseProxy	Boolean value. Use other proxy properties in conjunction with this value.
UserHttpHeaders	HTTP headers, if available.
Username	Username used when posting to a secure site. AuthenticationScheme should be set to Basic or Digest.
UseSSO	A Boolean value indicating whether to use the SSO server. Use the AffiliateApplicationName property in conjunction with this.

4. Drop a Send shape on the orchestration surface. Set the `Message` property to the message created in step 1.

5. Right-click the port surface, and select New Configured Port. On the Port Binding page, set the parameters as indicated in the following substeps and shown in Figure 6-31:

    a. Set "Port direction of communication" to "I'll always be sending messages on this port."

    b. Set "Port binding" to "Specify now".

    c. Set Transport to HTTP.

    d. Set URI to the URL being posted to (`https://Sample`).

    e. Set the pipeline to the default `XMLTransmit` pipeline.

Figure 6-31. *Using the Port Configuration Wizard*

Table 6-7 describes the details of each of the port properties you can set for the HTTP port via code in an Expression shape of an orchestration. These are the same parameters you set when configuring an HTTP send port in the BizTalk Explorer.

How It Works

When sending documents via a send port, exceptions can occur—perhaps the HTTP server is unavailable or the URL is incorrect. In such cases, it is often useful to be able to catch the exception immediately in the orchestration, especially when specific error handling routines need to occur.

By default, send ports are set up to automatically retry in case of failure. This means an orchestration will call the send port and then continue processing asynchronously while the adapter manages the transmission of the document. If an exception is thrown, it is handled by the adapter and is never bubbled up to the orchestration. With the adapter operating asynchronously from the orchestration, exceptions that are thrown can result in lost messages and unexpected error messages.

To force the adapter to execute synchronously with the orchestration moving on to the next steps only when a message has been posted successfully by the adapter, you should set the `Delivery Notification` property on the send port to `Transmitted`, as shown in Figure 6-32.

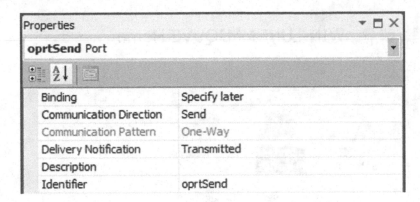

Figure 6-32. Setting the Delivery Notification *property*

6-10. Configuring HTTP Receives

Problem

You want to configure an HTTP receive location to allow posts from a client machine to BizTalk Server. Additionally, you want to understand how to configure IIS and create a virtual directory to allow the receive location to operate correctly.

Solution

This solution will describe how to configure an HTTP receive location to allow documents to be posted to BizTalk. The first task is to configure IIS to allow for the redirection of documents to BizTalk. The second task is to create a virtual directory to handle specific requests, and the third step is to configure the HTTP receive. The majority of servers will have IIS 7.0 installed, and this solution describes the steps necessary for 7.0 (IIS 5.0 and 6.0 have different configuration steps—refer to the BizTalk documentation for details). After IIS has been configured, you will work through the steps needed to create a virtual directory and configure an HTTP receive port.

To configure IIS 7.0, follow these steps:

1. Open Internet Information Services Manager by selecting Control Panel ➤ Administrative Tools.

2. Click the name of the server, and open the Handler Mappings in the IIS options (see Figure 6-33).

Figure 6-33. *Handler Mappings in IIS 7.0*

3. Under the Actions section, click Add Script Map, and set the properties as follows:

   a. Set the Request path property to BTSHTTPReceive.dll.

   b. Set the Executable property to the location of BTSHTTPReceive.dll (browse to BTSHTTPReceive.dll located in $\Program Files\Microsoft BizTalk Server 2010\HttpReceive).

   c. Set the Name property to BTSHTTPReceive.

■ **Note** If an error occurs indicating that the file is already required by another process, you don't need to continue, because the HTTP receive adapter has already been created and configured appropriately. Cancel out, and move to step 3.

---

   d. Click the Request Restrictions button. Set the value of POST on the Verbs tab, and the value of Script on the Access tab, as show in Figures 6-34 and 6-35.

Figure 6-34. *The Verbs tab in Request Restrictions of IIS 7.0*

Figure 6-35. *The Access tab in Request Restrictions of IIS 7.0*

      e.   Click OK, and save to exit Add Script Map settings.

      f.   On the Add Script Map dialogue box that opens, click Yes (shown in Figure 6-36).

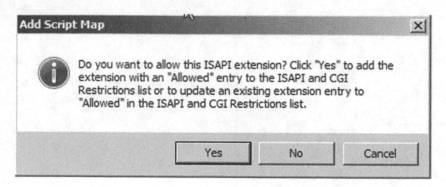

Figure 6-36. *Add Script Map dialogue box*

Once IIS is configured, the next order of business is to create a virtual directory. Each solution that requires an HTTP receive to be set up will require a separate virtual directory. BizTalk listens to this URL and, through the use of BTSHTTPReceive.dll and the HTTP receive adapter, passes the information to the BizTalk MessageBox.

The following steps demonstrate how to create a virtual directory. This directory is where clients will post HTTP requests to BizTalk.

1. In Internet Information Services Manager, expand the Sites folder, right-click the Default Web Site folder, and select Add Virtual Directory.

2. Set the following properties:

   a. The Alias of the virtual directory should be what you want exposed to clients. For example, SampleHTTPReceive would be exposed to the client as http://[server]/SampleHTTPReceive.

   b. Set the Physical path property to the location of the BTSHTTPReceive.dll file, generally located in $\Program Files\Microsoft BizTalk Server 2010\HttpReceive.

   c. For the Connect As properties, specify the appropriate credentials. The default is Application user.

   d. Validate the setting by clicking Test Connection, and click OK when the test is complete to save the settings.

At this point, IIS and the virtual directory are set up to route requests to BizTalk Server. The next steps are to create a receive port and configure a receive location for HTTP. These will be specific to each solution, so you will need to set up separate instances for different BizTalk solutions.

1. Using the BizTalk Administration Console, right-click the Receive Ports folder, and select New ➤ Request Response Receive Port. Give the receive port a name, and click OK to create the port.

2. Right-click the Receive Locations folder, and select New ➤ Request Response Receive Location. Select the port you created in the previous step as the container port.

3. In the Receive Location Properties dialog box that opens, use the following settings:

    a. Set Transport Type to HTTP. This will automatically set the receive handler to BizTalkServerIsolatedHost.

    b. Set Receive Pipeline to Microsoft.BizTalk.DefaultPipelines.XMLReceive.

    c. Set Send Pipeline to Microsoft.BizTalk.DefaultPipelines.XMLTransmit.

4. Click the Address (URI) ellipsis button, and use the following settings:

    a. Set the Virtual Directory plus ISAPI extension property to the virtual directory created during the IIS configuration earlier in this solution. The entry should follow this format: /SampleHTTPReceive/BTSHTTPReceive.dll.

    b. The Public address property is not used by BizTalk; instead, it is used for reference purposes only. The intention is for it to be configured such that it contains the full external address that clients would use to post to the receive location. The intended format for this reference field would be http://[servername]/SampleHTTPReceive.

    c. The Return Content-Type property is generally set to text/xml but can be modified depending on the format of the response expected.

    d. The Loopback flag is set when the request document is intended to be the response back. Generally, this flag is set for test purposes only. For this solution, it should be unchecked.

    e. The Return correlation handle on success property is for one-way ports only. It is intended to allow the creation of a unique identifier to be able to correlate the request to the document sent. Regardless of the setting, it will be ignored in this solution, because you are creating a request-response port.

    f. The Use Single Sign On property is to be used in conjunction with SSO. Leave this property unchecked.

    g. If checked, the Suspend Failed Requests property will, on error, suspend the document in the BizTalk MessageBox and will send an accepted notification to the client that posted the request (meaning the client will have successfully posted the document, but the document will be in a suspended state and will require administrative attention). If unchecked, any errors receiving the document will result in an immediate response back to the client indicating failure. For this solution, keep this property unchecked.

Figure 6-37 shows the final configuration.

Figure 6-37. *Viewing the final HTTP transport properties*

How It Works

You can set several configurations at the HTTP receive adapter level that will affect the way the adapter functions. You can set certain properties in the Registry that will provide for more control and optimization over large implementations that use the HTTP adapter. In many cases, however, the server and solution infrastructure may require that this default be reduced or increased. You can set this property using the following steps:

1. In the Registry Editor, locate the following path: HKEY_LOCAL_MACHINE\SYSTEM\ CurrentControlSet\Services\BTSSvc.3.0.

2. Right-click this path, and select New ➤ Key. Enter **HttpReceive** for the key's name.

3. Right-click the HTTPReceive key, and select New ➤ DWORD. Name the key **RequestQueueSize**. Give this a decimal value from 10 to 2048.

You can take the previous steps for the keys listed in Table 6-8.

Table 6-8. *HTTP Receive Adapter Registry Entries*

Property	Description
DisableChunkEncoding	DWORD whose default is 0. Any nonzero number turns off this setting. Indicates whether communications back to the client will be sent using chunked encoding.
HTTPReceiveThreadsPerCPU	DWORD whose default is 2. Can be set to any value from 1 to 10. Indicates the number of threads per CPU that are allocated to the HTTP receive adapter.
RequestQueueSize	DWORD whose default value is 256. Can be set anywhere from 10 to 2048. The value indicates the total number of concurrent requests that BizTalk will process simultaneously.

6-11. Configuring SOAP Sends and Receives
Problem

You want to understand how to configure a static request/response SOAP send port using BizTalk Explorer to allow client machines posting to orchestrations that have been deployed as web services.

Solution

SOAP ports are generally two-way (solicit-response) ports, because consuming web services generally result in a response to the calling party. The following steps guide you through the process of configuring a two-way SOAP port:

1. In BizTalk Administration Console, right-click the Send Ports folder, and select New ➤ Static Solicit-Response Send Port.

2. On the Property Pages dialog box that opens, select a transport type of SOAP.

3. Click the ellipsis for the Address (URI) property entry box. The Transport Properties dialog box will open with the General tab active.

4. Configure the General tab according to the requirements of the web service, with the following guidelines. See Figure 6-38.

   a. The value of the Web Service URL property should be entered in the format http://webservice.asmx.

   b. The four authentication types are Anonymous, Basic, Digest, and NTLM. The value selected for this property will depend on the requirements of the web service being consumed. Often, it will take some experimentation to determine the proper authentication settings, especially when additional security measures, such as certificates, are required.

   c. If a web service requires an SSL certificate, enter a reference to it in the Certificate Thumbprint property. You can access the thumbprint through the certificate properties and copy and paste it into this property.

Figure 6-38. *Configuring the General tab*

5. Configure the proxy settings on the Proxy tab according to any proxies that may be necessary to call the web service.

6. Configure the Web Service tab using the following guidelines:

   a. Generally, all calls to web services should be handled through the orchestration web port; this provides the robust capabilities for posting over the supported protocols inherent to SOAP.

   b. Occasionally, it may be necessary to specify a proxy class for a call to a web service. In such cases, a proxy class must be created. You can create a class using the command-line utility WSDL.exe. This tool will create an assembly that can be referenced using the Assembly Name property. Once referenced, the type and methods available on the original web service will be made available in the two remaining property fields.

7. Click OK to save the settings entered in the Transport Properties dialog box, and configure the remaining properties on the SOAP send adapter:

    a. Set the Send and Receive Pipelines settings according to the needs of the solution (generally XMLTransmit and XMLReceive).

    b. If a certificate is required for outbound encryption, set the Certificate Name property to the appropriate certificate. Only those certificates that have been installed on the machine will be available in the drop-down list.

    c. Set any inbound or outbound maps, and configure any filters that may be necessary.

8. Click OK to complete the configuration of the SOAP port.

How It Works

When calling a web service from an orchestration, it is often useful to be able to specify a dynamic URL. For instance, in a development environment, the URL being posted to will be a test URL, and the URL will need to change once the orchestration has been deployed to a production setting. You have several approaches to solving the need for supporting a dynamic URL, one of which is to set the address programmatically in an orchestration Expression shape.

One way to have a dynamic URL is to store the URL can be stored in a configuration file. Assuming that the BTSNTSvc.exe.config file is used to store a custom property, you can take the following steps:

1. In the BTSNTSvc.exe.config file, add a new key as follows (add this to the <appSettings> node):

    ```
    [<appSettings>]
            <add key="WSURL" value="http://sample.asmx"/>
    [</appSettings>]
    ```

2. Drop an Expression shape on the orchestration. You can enter the following code in the orchestration to read the configuration file and to set the address on the web port created in the previous steps:

    ```
    strURL = System.Configuration.ConfigurationSettings.AppSettings.Get("WSURL");
            Port_1(Microsoft.XLANGs.BaseTypes.Address) = strURL;
    ```

6-12. Creating Ports Through C# Applications

Problem

You want to create an external .NET application that can be used by administrators to create and modify ports on BizTalk Server.

Solution

You can create and modify a variety of components programmatically using the BizTalk Explorer object model. This solution will walk you through creating a basic C# Windows Form application that calls the object model.

■ **Note**   The `Microsoft.BizTalk.ExplorerOM.dll` assembly can only be used from 32-bit systems. You can reference it in Visual Studio on a 64-bit system, but it will not work once the code is compiled.

Here are the steps to follow:

1. In Visual Studio, create a new project of type Windows Forms Application (as shown in Figure 6-39).

Figure 6-39. *Creating a Windows Forms Application*

2. Add a reference to the assembly called `Microsoft.BizTalk.ExplorerOM.dll`. This assembly is located in `$\Program Files\Microsoft BizTalk Server 2010\Developer Tools`.

3. Create a new button on the form. The code will be implemented in the code behind this button for this demonstration solution.

4. Double-click the button to access the code behind, and enter the information listed in Listing 6-12.

Listing 6-12. *Creating Ports in C#*

```
private void button1_Click(object sender, EventArgs e)
{
 // instantiate new instance of Explorer OM
 BtsCatalogExplorer btsExp = new BtsCatalogExplorer();

 // connection string to the BizTalk management database where the ports will be created
 btsExp.ConnectionString = "Server='SR';Database='BizTalkMgmtDb';Integrated Security=true";

 // new BizTalk application
 Microsoft.BizTalk.ExplorerOM.Application app = btsExp.AddNewApplication();
 app.Name = "AppCreatedInCode";
 btsExp.SaveChanges();

 // new BizTalk File Send Port
 SendPort send = app.AddNewSendPort(false, false);
 send.Name = "SendCreatedInCode";
 send.PrimaryTransport.TransportType = btsExp.ProtocolTypes["File"];
 send.PrimaryTransport.Address = "C:\\Drops";
 send.SendPipeline = btsExp.Pipelines["Microsoft.BizTalk.DefaultPipelines.PassThruTransmit"];
```

```
// new BizTalk WCF-BasicHttp Receive Port
ReceivePort receive = app.AddNewReceivePort(false);
receive.Name = "ReceiveCreatedInCode";
receive.PrimaryReceiveLocation.TransportType = btsExp.ProtocolTypes["WCF-BasicHttp"];
receive.PrimaryReceiveLocation.Address = "http://demo/demofolder";
receive.PrimaryReceiveLocation.ReceivePipeline =
btsExp.Pipelines["Microsoft.BizTalk.DefaultPipelines.XmlReceive"];

// save all of the changes
btsExp.SaveChanges();
}
```

How It Works

You can access a wide variety of functionality through the BizTalk ExplorerOM assembly, including ports, applications, orchestrations, bindings, and party information. When using the BizTalk Administration Console is not the ideal option, the Explorer Object Model opens up a number of programmatic options.

6-13. Configuring SFTP Sends
Problem

You are building a solution that sends text files with batched financial transactions to a bank's secure FTP server using the SSH file transfer protocol. The bank has given you the server's SSH Host Key and also given a username and password that is required for client authentication.

Solution

Create a BizTalk Server send port to utilize the SFTP adapter. To configure the send port, follow these steps:

1. Open the BizTalk Administration Console.

2. Expand the BizTalk Server group, select an appropriate BizTalk application, and select the Send Ports folder.

3. Right-click the Send Ports folder, and select New ➤ Static One-way Send Port to open the Send Port Properties dialog box.

4. Give your send port a descriptive name, select the XMLTransmit pipeline, ensure any correct subscriptions are implemented (on the Filters tab), and select SFTP as the transport type.

5. Click the Configure button to the right of the Transport Type field. This launches the SFTP Transport Properties dialog box.

6. Set Security and SSH Server settings, and leave the rest as defaults, as shown in Figure 6-40.

Make the following security settings:

Set AcceptAnySSHServerHostKey to true.
Set the Password and Username properties

And make the following SSH Server settings:

Set AppendIfExists to false, if you don't want to append the existing file
Set FolderPath to the folder location where the file comes from
Set the correct Port (by default 22 is used)
Set Server Address to either the DNS name or the IP Address
Set TargetFileName with the BizTalk accepted Macros

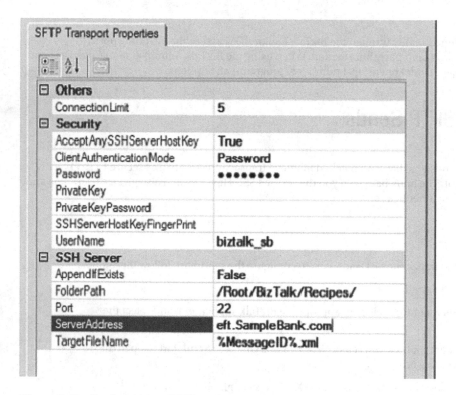

Figure 6-40. *Configuring an SFTP send port*

7. Leave all other properties with their default values, and click OK.

8. Click OK in the Send Port Properties dialog box to save the send port.

9. Right-click the send port created in the previous step, and select Start.

How It Works

The BizTalk Server SFTP adapter allows easy access to send files to secure FTP sites using SSH protocol and with various client authentication configurations. This new adapter introduced in BizTalk 2013 is significantly improved from the previous version of the FTP adapter.

SFTP Send Options

Although this example illustrates the simplest scenario for sending SFTP messages to a specified FTP location, you can make a number of configurations against the SFTP adapter. Following are some of the configuration options you can specify:

Connection Limit: The maximum number of concurrent connections that can be opened to the FTP server. Set it to zero if you don't want to limit the connections. It is defaulted to 5.

Access Any SSH Server HostKey: Specifies whether the send port accepts the SSH public host key from the server or not. If set to false, the port matches the host key with the key specified in the SSHServerHostKey property. If set to true, the port matches the key dynamically at the handshake. Otherwise, when set to false, the port matches the host key specified statically in SSHServerHostKey property. The default is false.

Client Authentication Mode: The authentication method that the send port uses for authenticating the client to the SSH Server. If set to Password, you must specify the value in the Password property. If set to PublicKeyAuthentication, you must specify the private key of the user in the PrivateKey property. Additionally, if the private key is protected by a password, specify the password as well for the PrivateKeyPassword property. It is defaulted to Password option.

Password: The SFTP user password, if you set the Client Authentication Mode to Password.

Private Key: The private key for the SFTP user, if you set the Client Authentication Mode to PublicKey Authentication.

PrivateKey Password: A private key password, if required for the key specified in the PrivateKey property.

SSH Server HostKey Fingerprint: The fingerprint of the server used by the adapter to authenticate the server if the Access Any SSH Server HostKey property is set to False. If the fingerprints do not match, the connection fails.

Username: Username for the secure FTP server.

Append If Exists: This property specifies whether the data from the file being transferred should be appended to the existing file. If set to True, the data is appended. If set to False, the file at the destination server is overwritten. It is defaulted to False.

Folder Path: The folder path on the secure FTP server where the file is copied.

Port: The port address for the secure FTP server.

Server Address: DNS server name or IP address of the secure FTP server.

Target File Name: The name with which the file is transferred to the secure FTP server.

■ **Note**   Macros can be used in forming the Target File Name. Refer to Table 6-1 for further details on the Macros that can be used for that purpose.

SFTP Security Setup

The improvement in the new SFTP adapter is in Security. Now the communication with the server is secured by SSH (Secure Shell) protocol. Also, authorized clients with proper credentials can send and receive files from the Secure FTP location. SSH protocol relies on public and private key based authentication, which is different from FTPS, a competing File transfer protocol standard which relies on SSL (Secure socket Layer).

SSH uses public-key cryptography to authenticate the remote computer and allow it to authenticate the user, if necessary. There are several ways to use SSH; one is to use automatically generated public-private key pairs to simply encrypt a network connection, and then use password authentication to log on.

Another is to use a manually generated public-private key pair to perform the authentication, allowing users or programs to log in without having to specify a password. In this scenario, anyone can produce a matching pair of different keys (public and private). The public key is placed on all computers that must allow access to the owner of the matching private key (the owner keeps the private key secret). While authentication is based on the private key, the key itself is never transferred through the network during authentication. SSH only verifies whether the same person offering the public key also owns the matching private key. In all versions of SSH it is important to verify unknown public keys, i.e., associate the public keys with identities, before accepting them as valid. Accepting an attacker's public key without validation will authorize an unauthorized attacker as a valid user.

The most probable security scenarios and dependent property set-ups are listed in Table 6-9.

Table 6-9. *Security property dependencies*

Security Scenario	Dependent properties
Statically setting SSH Host Key and setting client authentication modes	Set Access Any SSH Server HostKey to false. Set the SSH Server Host Key property with the key. If Client Authentication Mode is: Password: Set Password and Username properties. PrivateKey: Set Private Key property. PrivateKey Password: Set PrivateKey Password and Username properties.
Dynamically getting SSH Host Key and setting client authentication modes.	Set Access Any SSH Server HostKey to true. If Client Authentication Mode is: Password: Set Password and Username properties. PrivateKey: Set Private Key property. PrivateKey Password: Set PrivateKey Password and Username properties.

6-14. Configuring SFTP Receives
Problem

You are building a integration solution for a bank that receives and processes the files with batched financial transactions from a secure FTP server using SSH file transfer protocol. The bank uses the server's SSH Host Key and also a username and password for client authentication.

Solution

You are integrating with a system that publishes messages to a secure FTP site, and you must configure BizTalk Server to receive messages from FTP site. Create a BizTalk Server receive location to utilize the SFTP adapter. To configure the send port, follow these steps:

1. Open the BizTalk Administration Console.

2. Expand the BizTalk Server group, select an appropriate BizTalk application, and select the Receive Ports folder.

3. Right-click the Receive Ports folder, and select New ➤ One-way Receive Port to open the Receive Port Properties dialog box.

4. Give your new receive port a descriptive name, and click OK.

5. Right-click the receive port created in the previous step, and select New ➤ Receive Location. The Receive Location Properties dialog box appears.

6. Give your receive location a descriptive name, select the XMLReceive pipeline, and select SFTP as the transport type.

7. Click the Configure button to the right of the Transport Type field. This launches the SFTP Transport Properties dialog box.

8. Set Security and SSH Server settings, and leave the rest as defaults as shown in Figure 6-41.

Figure 6-41. *Configuring an SFTP receive location*

Make the following security settings:

> Set AcceptAnySSHServerHostKey to true
> Set the Password and Username properties

Make the following SSH Server settings:

> Set AppendIfExists to false, if you don't want to append the existing file
> Set FolderPath to the folder where the file comes from
> Set the correct Port (by default 22 is used)
> Set Server Address to either the DNS name or IP address
> Set TargetFileName with the BizTalk accepted Macros

9. Click OK in the Receive Location Properties dialog box to save the receive location.

10. Select the Receive Locations folder in the BizTalk Administration Console, right-click the receive location created earlier, and select Enable.

How It Works

The BizTalk Server SFTP adapter allows easy access to receive files from secure FTP sites using SSH protocol and with various client authentication configurations. This new adapter introduced in BizTalk 2013 is significantly improved from the previous version of the FTP adapter.

SFTP Receive Location Only Options

Although this example illustrates the simplest scenario for sending SFTP messages to a specified FTP location, you can make a number of configurations against the SFTP adapter:

> **Polling Interval**: The intervals at which the adapter will poll the server. To poll continuously, set this value to zero. It is defaulted to zero.

> **Unit**: The unit in which the polling interval is specified, for example, Seconds, Minutes, Hours, or Days. The default is Seconds.

■ **Note** Refer to Recipe 6–13 for further details on port level Security and SSH Server options.

6-15. Configuring WCF-WSHttp Request Response Ports
Problem

You are creating a WCF based web service to support an Internet facing order portal web application. The user logs into the order history page to view the order history. The order history page accesses the secure web service to retrieve the order details by client id. The WCF web service is required to securely transmit the order history over the wire to the portal web page.

Solution

You want to expose an orchestration as an interoperable WCF service that uses WS-* protocols, over HTTPS transport. To configure the two-way communication you need to create a request response port, and follow these steps:

1. Create an orchestration with a request response orchestration port to receive Orders Request and respond with Orders response. Figure 6-42 shows an example.

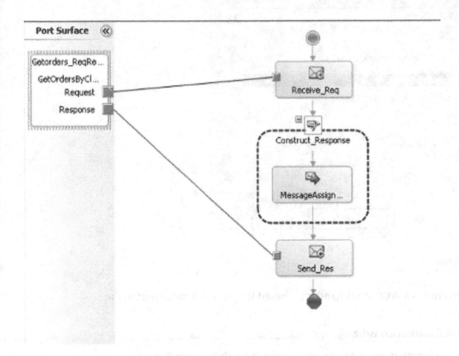

Figure 6-42. *Orchestration with Request Response Port*

2. Use WCF publishing Wizard shown in Figure 6-43 to expose the service using the adapter type WCF-WSHttp. Also, Enable on-premise metadata exchange, and Create BizTalk receive locations in the following application. Select the application in which you want the request response port to be created.

Figure 6-43. *WCF Publishing Wizard*

3. The publishing wizard creates a WCF-WSHttp adapter based Request Response port in the selected application.

4. Open the BizTalk Administration Console.

5. Double-click the Receive Location that is just created by the WCF Publishing Wizard (an example of this is shown in Figure 6-44).

Figure 6-44. *WCF-WSHttp Request Response Location*

6. Click on the Configure button to view the details on the adapter configuration. It will open a pop-up with options to modify the Address, Binding, and Contract (ABC of WCF service) information of the exposed WCF service.

7. To expose the service over https transport and use the Windows as client credential type, select the Security mode to Transport and select the Transport client credential type to Windows. See Figure 6-45 for the security settings.

Figure 6-45. *WCF-WSHttp Request Response Location – Security Tab*

8. To send the details of the failure to the client in SOAP Fault and suspend the message, go to Messages tab (see Figure 6-46) and enable Suspend request message on failure and Include exception details in faults in Exception Handling grouping.

Figure 6-46. WCF-WSHttp Request Response Location – Messages Tab

9. Leave the rest of the configuration as defaulted.

10. Click "OK" to save the configuration changes.

11. Finally, bind the WCF receive port with the orchestration, and the start the receive location and the orchestration.

How It Works

Windows Communication Foundation (WCF) has been a part of .NET framework since 3.0. It is a platform for developers to build service-oriented applications. BizTalk provides a group of WCF adapters to support service orientation. Through these adapters one can expose and consume a highly configurable, WS-* standards compliant interoperable web services. Through the WCF adapter configuration you can set the Address, Binding, and Contract of WCF services. These services can be hosted either in BizTalk runtime or in IIS (WCF-CustomIsolated adapter).

As a rule of thumb, use criteria given in Table 6-10 in selecting the appropriate adapter.

Table 6-10. *Adapter Selection*

Adapter	Selection criteria
WCF-BasicHttp	For providing backward compatiblity with HTTP and HTTPS protocols. Use this adapter for communicating through firewalls in the fastest possible way.
WCF-BasicHttpRelay	A WCF-BasicHttp adapter for cloud based service exposure and consumption.
WCF-Custom	For full control over adapter behavior and configuration. Service is hosted in BTSNTSvc.exe process.
WCF-CustomIsolated	For full control over adapter behavior and configuration. Service is hosted in IIS process.
WCF-NetMsmq	For services which need asynchronous, guaranteed, transactional message delivery.
WCF-NetNamedPipe	For an on-machine (service consumer and service processes are on the same machine) binary encoded message communication.
WCF-NetTcp	For intranet WCF-to-WCF communication (WCF issued both by service consumer and the service) using binary encoded messages.
WCF-NetTcpRelay	A WCF-NetTcp adapter for cloud based service exposure and consumption.
WCF-WebHttp	For REST based service exposure and consumption, over HTTP and HTTPS transports.
WCF-WSHttp	For building WS-* standards based interoperable services.

■ **Note** In case you want to expose the orchestration created in the recipe to cloud, all you need to create is a two-way WCF-BasicHttpRelay (or WCF-NetTcpRelay) receiving location and bind it to the orchestration. The port configurations are very similar to the current recipe. The cloud relay receive port has a few more options for configuring the security, and you will be setting Relay Client Authentication types, Service Discovery, and Access Control Service.

6-16. Configuring Azure Service Bus (SB-Messaging) Receives and Sends
Problem

You are working on a hypothetical hybrid integration scenario, where your framework subscribes to local weather events and proactively notifies the local fire department or an electricity grid for the upcoming impact. When the temparature reaches 120 degrees Fahrenheit in the valley, your framework alerts the local fire department for possible wild fires, or an electricity grid for the higher usage of power because of increased A/C unit usage.

Solution

You need to create an orchestration that subscribes to an Azure Service Bus Topic, apply a business logic, and send the outcome to an Azure Service Bus Queue. The solution reviewed as part of this recipe outlines how to use the SB-Messaging to receive an event from an Azure Service Bus Topic and send another event to a Service Queue.

It is implemented by a SB-Messaging adapter based receive location to subscribe to the event, an orchestration to process the event, and SB-Messaging adapter based send port to notify about the event. The following steps will guide you through the implementation:

1. Create a Service Bus Topic to subscribe the events from, and create a Queue to send the events to. Once created, the Namesapce page will appear as in Figure 6-47, the Queues page will appear as in Figure 6-48, the Topics page will appear as in Figure 6-49, and the Subscriptions page related to the Topic will appear as in Figure 6-50.

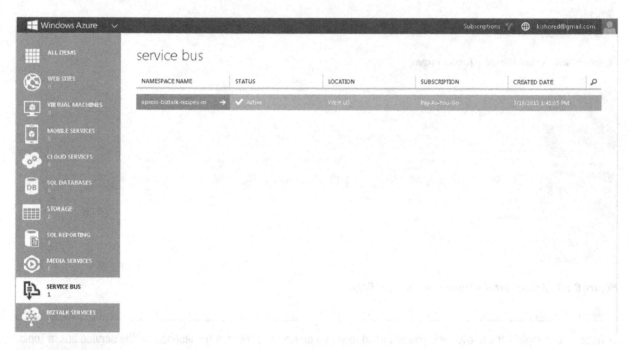

Figure 6-47. *Azure Portal – Namespace page*

Figure 6-48. *Azure Portal – Queues Page*

Figure 6-49. *Azure Portal – Topics Page*

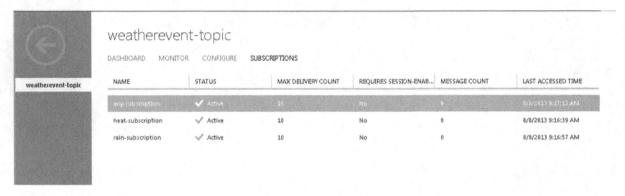

Figure 6-50. *Azure Portal – Topic Subscriptions Page*

■ **Note**   To complete the above task, you will need to set up an Azure Account, a namespace for the service bus, a Topic, and a Queue. For further details, refer to the Recipes in Chapter 12.

2.   Brokered messages and filter rules play an important role in creating subscriptions. For details on subscription filters refer to the Recipes from Chapter 12. To simplify the current Recipe, it is assumed that the Subscription Filter Rules are properly set up in the Azure Service Bus. In the current case, "heat-subscription" for the topic "weatherevent-topic" has a rule to subscribe to a heat event for a set of vulnerable areas (identified by zip codes). A Property Schema is created in a BizTalk project as shown in Figure 6-51.

```xml
<?xml version="1.0" encoding="utf-16" ?>
<xs:schema xmlns="http://EventConsumerProj.PropertySchema" xmlns:b="http://schemas.microsoft.com/BizTalk/2003"
    targetNamespace="https://EventConsumerProj.PropertySchema" xmlns:xs="http://www.w3.org/2001/XMLSchema">
  <xs:annotation>
    <xs:appinfo>
      <b:schemaInfo schema_type="property" xmlns:b="http://schemas.microsoft.com/BizTalk/2003" />
    </xs:appinfo>
  </xs:annotation>
  <xs:element name="EventType" type="xs:string">
    <xs:annotation>
      <xs:appinfo>
        <b:fieldInfo propertyGuid="b750788c-46f7-4351-b555-f8bb5d2dbfeb" />
      </xs:appinfo>
    </xs:annotation>
  </xs:element>
</xs:schema>
```

Figure 6-51. *BrokeredMessage Property schema and BizTalk message property schema*

3. Create an orchestration, as shown in Figure 6-52, to subscribe to the Heat event, and apply some business logic/rules to make a decision to rise as an alert to Fire department's Queue. Deploy it to a BizTalk application.

Figure 6-52. *Orchestration to receive subscribed events and to send events Queue*

4. Open the BizTalk Administration Console.

5. Expand the BizTalk Server group, select an appropriate BizTalk application, and select the Receive Ports folder.

6. Right-click the Receive Ports folder, and select New ➤ One-way Receive Port to open the Receive Port Properties dialog box.

7. Give your new receive port a descriptive name, and click OK.

8. Right-click the receive port created in the previous step, and select New ➤ Receive Location. The Receive Location Properties dialog box appears.

9. Give your receive location a descriptive name, select the XMLReceive pipeline, and select SB-Messaging as the transport type.

10. Click the Configure button to the right of the Transport Type field. This launches the SB-Messaging Transport Properties dialog box.

11. On the General tab, set the topic name as shown in Figure 6-53. Use the following format for the Queue or Subscription URL:sb://<**namespace**>.servicebus.windows.net/<**name of the topic**>/Subscriptions/<**name of the subscription**>/

Figure 6-53. *Receive Location's General Tab*

12. On the Authentication tab set the Access Control Service STS Uri, Issuer Name, and Issuer Key from the Azure portal, as shown in Figure 6-54.

Figure 6-54. *Receive Location's Authentication Tab*

13. On the Properties tab set the Namespace for Brokered Message Properties to the correct promoted properties schema namespace and enable Promote Brokered Message Properties, as shown in Figure 6-55.

Figure 6-55. *Receive Location's Properties Tab*

14. Right-click the Send Ports folder, and select New ➤ One-way Send Port to open the Receive Port Properties dialog box.

15. Give your send port a descriptive name, select the XMLReceive pipeline, and select SB-Messaging as the transport type.

16. Click the Configure button to the right of the Transport Type field. This launches the SB-Messaging Transport Properties dialog box.

17. On the General tab set the topic name, as shown in Figure 6-56. Use the following format for the Queue or Subscription URL:sb://**<namespace>**.servicebus.windows.net/**<name of the Queue>**/

General | Authentication | Properties |

Destination URL

sb://apress-biztalk-recipes-ns.servicebus.windows.net/firedepartment-que

Example:
sb://contoso.servicebus.windows.net/myservice/

Binding Properties

BatchFlushInterval (hh:mm:ss):   `00:00:00`

Open Timeout (hh:mm:ss) :   `00:01:00`

Send Timeout (hh:mm:ss):   `00:01:00`

Close Timeout (hh:mm:ss):   `00:01:00`

Figure 6-56. Send port's General Tab

18. On the Authentication tab set the Access Control Service STS Uri, Issuer Name, and Issuer Key from the Azure portal, as shown in Figure 6-57.

General | Authentication | Properties |

Specify the credentials to be used for authorization with Service Bus.

Access Control Service STS Uri:

https://apress-biztalk-recipes-ns-sb.accesscontrol.windows.net/

Issuer Name: `owner`

Issuer Key: `••••••••••••••••`

Figure 6-57. Send port's Authentication Tab

19. Click OK to save the settings.

20. Finally bind the orchestration with the Receive port and Send port.

How It Works

Windows Azure is Microsoft's cloud computing platform and infrastructure for building, deploying, and managing applications and services through a global network of Microsoft-managed datacenters. Azure provides a service bus that adds a set of cloud-based, message-oriented middleware technologies including reliable message queuing and durable publish/subscribe messaging. Service Bus is a messaging infrastructure that sits between applications, allowing them to exchange messages in a loosely coupled way, improving scalability and resiliency.

Queues offer First In, First Out (FIFO) message delivery to one or more competing consumers. That is, messages are typically expected to be received and processed by the receivers in the temporal order in which they were added to the queue, and each message is received and processed by only one message consumer. A key benefit of using queues is to achieve "temporal decoupling" of application components. In other words, the producers (senders) and consumers (receivers) do not have to be sending and receiving messages at the same time, because messages are stored durably in the queue. Furthermore, the producer does not have to wait for a reply from the consumer in order to continue to process and send messages.

In contrast to queues, in which each message is consumed by a single consumer, topics and subscriptions provide a one-to-many form of communication, in a "publish/subscribe" pattern. It is useful for scaling to very large numbers of recipients; each published message is made available to each subscription registered with the topic. Messages are sent to a topic and delivered to one or more associated subscriptions, depending on filter rules that can be set on a per-subscription basis. The subscriptions can use additional filters to restrict the messages that they want to receive. Messages are sent to a topic in the same way they are sent to a queue, but messages are not received from the topic directly. Instead, they are received from subscriptions.

The SB-Messaging handlers (receive and send) connect with Service Bus for receiving or sending messages. When receiving the messages from the queue or a Topic subscription, the "pre-fetching" configuration property will significantly improve the performance of processing the messages. When a receiver pre-fetches a group of messages, they are locked and cached locally. If these messages are not processed by the receiver before the time out period, then the lock will expire and the message will be available for another receiver processing it. Sessions can be enabled if a group of messages need to be processed in a session context. Sessions expire when there is inactivity after a specified session time out period. The Service Bus Access Control Service with proper Issuer Name and Key will authenticate the connection between BizTalk and Azure Service Bus.

6-17. Configuring SharePoint Receives and Sends

Problem

You are working on a human workflow scenario where a rules driven approval process needs to happen on certain financial decisions. These processes are long running and could take a few days to finish. For example, a marketing department employee needs to get approval for an initiative from his manager for budget of $20,000 or less, from the director for up to $50,000 and from the vice president for any thing above. He uses InfoPath to add an Approval Request document in the SharePoint Document Library, which is picked up by BizTalk's WSS receive location and which sends emails to appropriate level of management. Once the approval or rejection comes in an email in a few days, the Approval response is put in another document library.

Solution

The solution reviewed as part of this recipe outlines how to use the BizTalk's new WSS adapter for SharePoint 2013 to communicate with BizTalk 2013. You need to extend the SharePoint workflow to use BizTalk's long running process orchestrations, Business rules and adapters. This solution focuses on configuring WSS receive location and send port for the process. The following steps will guide you through the implementation:

1. Open the BizTalk Administration Console.

2. Expand the BizTalk Server group, select an appropriate BizTalk application, and select the `Receive Ports` folder.

3. Right-click the `Receive Ports` folder and select New ➤ One-way Receive Port to open the Receive Port Properties dialog box.

4. Give your new receive port a descriptive name, and click OK.

5. Right-click the receive port created in the previous step and select New ➤ Receive Location. The Receive Location Properties dialog box appears.

6. Give your receive location a descriptive name, select the `XMLReceive` pipeline, and select Windows SharePoint Service as the transport type.

7. Click the Configure button to the right of the Transport Type field. This launches the WSS Transport Properties dialog box. The following configuration picks up all the messages from Document View (ApprovalView) in a SharePoint site (`http://SomeSPServer.com`) using the provided SharePoint Online Username and Password, as shown in Figure 6-58. Update the properties listed in Table 6-11, and leave the rest of the configuration parameters as Defaults.

Figure 6-58. *WSS Receive Location Properties*

Table 6-11. WSS Receive Location Transport Properties

Grouping	Property	Notes
Advanced	Use Client OM	Yes (Default - because of SharePoint 2013)
General	Archive Filename	ApprovalMsg_%MessageID%.xml
General	Achive Location URL	ApprovalArchive_List
General	SharePoint Site URL	http://SomeSPSite.com/
General	Source Document Library URL	ApprovalRequestDocLib
General	View Name	ApprovalView, in case a subset of messages need to be processed from the Document Library
SharePoint Online	SharePoint Online Password	Set the password the SharePoint online account
SharePoint Online	SharePoint Online Username	Set the username for the online account, e.g., marketingUsr

8. Click OK to save the settings.

9. Right-click the Send Ports folder and select New ➤ One-way Send Port to open the Receive Port Properties dialog box.

10. Give your send port a descriptive name, select the XMLReceive pipeline, and select WSS as the transport type.

11. Click the Configure button to the right of the Transport Type field. This launches the WSS Transport Properties dialog box. The following configuration writes a message (formatted name) to Document Library (ApprovalResponseDocLib) in a SharePoint site (http://SomeSPSite.com) using the provided SharePoint Online Username and Password. Update the properties in Table 6-12, and leave the rest of the configuration parameters as Defaults, as shown in Figure 6-59.

Table 6-12. WSS Send Port Transport Properties

Grouping	Property	Notes
General	Destination Folder URL	ApprovalResponsesDocLib
General	Filename	Approval_%XPATH=//ar:RequestID%_%MessageID%.xml
General	Namespace Aliases	ar='http://schemas.apress.com/Approval'
General	Sharepoint Site URL	http://SomeSPSite.com/
SharePoint Online	SharePoint Online Password	Set the password the SharePoint online account
SharePoint Online	SharePoint Online Username	Set the username for the online account, e.g., marketingUsr

Figure 6-59. *WSS Send Port Properties*

12. Click OK to save the settings.

13. Finally bind the orchestration with the SharePoint Receive port and Send port. The orchestration receives the Approval Request through the receive port, applies Business rules based on the requested fund amount, and routes it to the appropriate executive's email address using SMTP. Once a response email is sent by the executive, POP3 receive port picks up the message and, based on the approval status, the orchestration constructs an Approval Response message and sends it to the destination SharePoint Document Library. Refer to Recipes from the Orchestration chapter for further details on creation and binding of orchestrations.

How It Works

WSS adapter facilitates communication between SharePoint's Human workflows and BizTalk's system integration capabilities. Through the WSS adapter framework, BizTalk receives documents from document libraries and sends them to SharePoint's document libraries. The adapter handles translation of different representations and also provides transformation services to handle InfoPath metadata.

The previous versions of BizTalk required the Server side Object model (SSOM) to be installed in SharePoint to enable communication between SharePoint and BizTalk. On some occasions, it was not possible to install SSOM on SharePoint, specifically when the SharePoint server was in a hosted environment. A special installation of SSOM (a web service called BTSharePointAdapterWS.asmx) is not required when integrating between BizTalk Server 2013 and SharePoint 2013; a SharePoint Client side object model (CSOM) is sufficient. When BizTalk 2013 adapter for SharePoint is communicating with older versions of SharePoint (2010, 2007, WSS 3.0, or SP2), an SSOM is required.

WSS Receive handlers connect to the SharePoint site and poll the Document Library for any outstanding documents at a specified polling interval in batches. Once the document is downloaded, the SharePoint web service deletes the document from the Document Library. In the event of any communication failures the document is left in the document library in a checked-out state. For further reliability, it is suggested to archive the documents instead of deleting them from the library. The documents can be archived with an overwrite option or use of a new name. The adapter handlers support good naming standards with various macros and also support XPATH expressions. The Receive handlers support InfoPath documents. Microsoft Office Integration property helps in handling the special processing instructions for the InfoPath documents. The property can be configured to either remove the InfoPath special processing instructions or preserve the instructions.

WSS send handlers connect with the SharePoint site and upload the documents to a specific document library. When uploading documents, one should give special care to their naming and prepare good names for the file and for the overwriting of the files as well. Use the File name property to control the name of the file. It allows the usage of Macros and XPATH for the file names. Send handlers support for uploading InfoPath documents to SharePoint document libraries. This behavior can be controlled by the Microsoft Office Integration property. To associate an XML message with the InfoPath, an XSN template is needed. A document library sometimes has multiple InfoPath templates. To select the correct template, note that each library will define a column that specifies an XML namespace. The column name and fallback column namespace are required for each of these templates.

6-18. Configuring REST (WCF-WebHttp) Receives and Sends

Problem

You are working for a company that specializes in shipping orders to customer addresses. The company loses a lot of money when it ships orders to wrong addresses. You are working on an Address Standardization web service that standardizes any North American address to your company's mobile Internet web application. The U.S. addresses are standardized internally by a packaged application, and the Canadian addresses are standardized by a 3ʳ-party REST web service.

Solution

You need to expose a REST based WCF service that also consumes another REST web service. The solution reviewed as part of this recipe outlines how to set up BizTalk's new REST (WCF-WebHttp) based adapter. The following steps will guide you through the implementation:

1. Create an orchestration to receive any address for standardization. U.S.-based addresses are standardized by applying business rules, and Canadian addresses are standardized by calling a third party provided REST service, as shown in Figure 6-60.

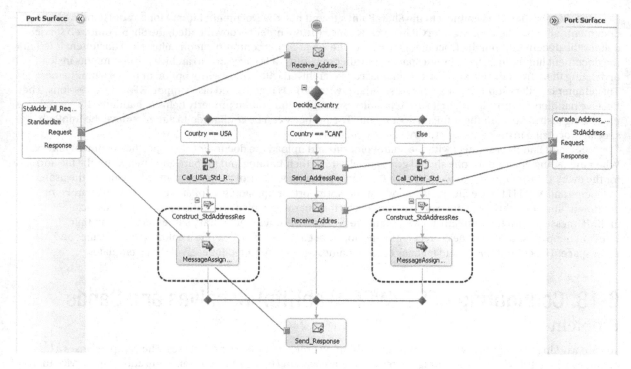

Figure 6-60. *Orchestration to be exposed as REST Web Service*

2. Create address standardization XML request and response. Promote "Country" element in the Request schema.

3. Deploy the orchestration and schemas project to the BizTalk Administration console.

4. Create a REST based web service by using the WCF Publishing Wizard, as shown in Figure 6-61.

Figure 6-61. *WCF Publishing Wizard with WCF-WebHttp Configuration*

5. Open the BizTalk Administration Console.

6. Expand the BizTalk Server group, select an appropriate BizTalk application, and select the Receive Locations folder.

7. Open the WCF-WebHttp receive location created by the WCF Publishing Wizard.

8. Click the Configure button to the right of the Transport Type field. This launches the WCF-WebHttp Properties dialog box. Update the properties listed in Table 6-13 and leave the rest of the configuration parameters as Defaults, as shown in Figure 6-62. The Same REST URL will be http://localhost/RESTService/StandardizeAddress.svc/Standardize.

Table 6-13. *WCF-WebHttp Receive Location Transport Properties*

Grouping	Property	Notes
General – Endpoint Address	Address(URL)	/RESTService/StandardizeAddress.svc
General – HTTP Address	HTTP Method and URL Mapping	<BtsHttpUrlMapping> <Operation Name='Standardize' Url='standardize'/> </BtsHttpUrlMapping>

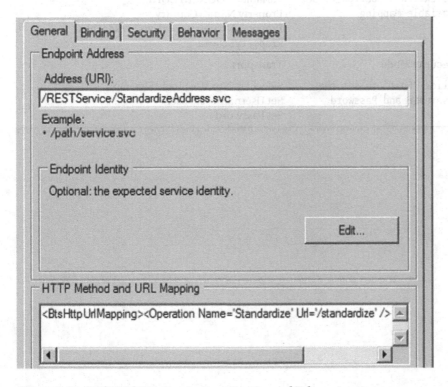

Figure 6-62. *WCF-WebHttp Receive Location General Tab*

The HTTP Request Body will have the Address Standardization request.

9. Click OK to save the settings.

10. Right-click the Send Ports folder and select New ➤ Solicit Response Send Port to open the Send Port Properties dialog box.

11. Give your send port a descriptive name, select the XMLReceive pipeline, and select WCF-WebHttp as the transport type.

    Click the Configure button to the right of the Transport Type field. This launches the WCF-WebHttp Properties dialog box. Update the properties in Table 6-14 and leave the rest of the configuration paramters as Defaults, as shown in Figure 6-63. The REST URL will be https://canadaservices.com/Standardize/CAN.

Table 6-14. *WCF-WebHttp Send Port Transport Properties*

Grouping	Property	Notes
General – Endpoint Address	Address(URL)	https://canadaservices.com/Standardize
General – HTTP Address	HTTP Method and URL Mapping	<BtsHttpUrlMapping> <Operation Name="StdAddress" Method="GET" Url="{countrycode}"/> </BtsHttpUrlMapping>
General – Value Mapping	Click "Edit" Button to Set Variable Mapping	Variable=COUNTRYCODE Property Name=Country Property Namespace=https://Recipes. PropertySchema
Security	Security Mode	Transport
Security – Username Credentials	Click "Edit" to set the Username and Password	Select Do Not Use Single Sign On Set Username: stdUser Set Password

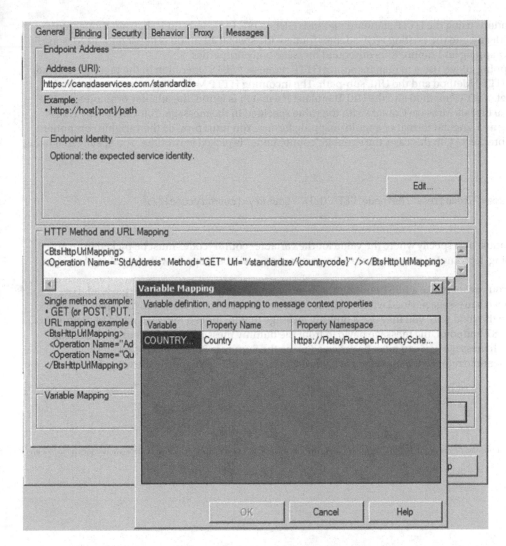

Figure 6-63. *WCF-WebHttp Send Port Value Mapping Configuration*

The HTTP Request Body will have the Address Standardization request.

12. Click OK to save the settings.

13. Finally bind the orchestration with the REST Request Response Receive port and Solicit Response Send port. Refer to Recipes from the Orchestration chapter for further details on creation and binding of orchestrations.

How It Works

Support for Representational State Transfer (REST) is finally fulfilled in BizTalk with the release of the WCF-WebHttp adapter. Now developers can participate in the most common cloud-based service integrations and in mobile application related services. Before BizTalk 2013, a limited set of REST functionality was possible through WCF behavior extensions by some third-party frameworks. The new adapter completely supports CRUD (Create, Update

Read, and Delete) operations using the HTTP standard methods GET, POST, PUT, and DELETE. Even though WCF-WebHttp adapter fits perfectly into the existing WCF adapter framework, special attention is needed for REST-specific configuration for value mapping and suppressing outbound message body properties.

BTS Operation Mapping allows users to map incoming HTTP requests to BTS Operation in the message context, based on the incoming HTTP Method and the URL sub-path. The incoming HTTP Method and the URL sub-path are matched against a set of HTTP method and the URI Template. If a match is found, the adapter promotes the BTS Operation property to the BizTalk Message Context with the value specified in the message. You can specify HTTP method to URL mapping as a singular format or a multi-mapping format. You must provide the variable component of the URL within curly brackets { }. In this case, the variable "countrycode" is picked at runtime. You specify that using Variable Mapping.

```
<BtsHttpUrlMapping>
        <Operation Name="StdAddress" Method="GET" Url="/Country={countrycode}"/>
</BtsHttpUrlMapping>
```

In such a case, you must also specify where the value for the variable "countrycode" must be picked from at runtime. In value mapping, a promoted property from a Property schema will be mapped with the value coming in the URL.

Based on the verb you use to invoke a REST endpoint, you may or may not require a message payload. For example, you may not need a message payload while using the GET or DELETE verbs. However, to trigger a call to the REST endpoint using the send port, you may use a dummy message that includes a message payload. Before the message is sent to the REST endpoint, the message payload from the dummy message must be removed. You can specify the verbs for which message payload must be removed using the Suppress Body for Verbs property.

For example, if you want to remove the message payload while using a GET verb, specify the value for this property as GET.

■ ■ ■

CHAPTER 7

Business Rules Framework

Business processes are changing at an unprecedented speed, and the IT systems that power business processes are being asked to keep up. In today's environment, to maintain a market advantage, organizations must react quickly to new markets, shifting consumer demand, shifting cost structures, and shifting business differentiators. The IT changes required to support dynamic business policies are taxing IT departments in terms of cycle time and hard costs.

At the root of this taxation are the complexities involved in designing and deploying traditional technical solutions. Current software development life cycle (SDLC) methodologies are time-consuming and expensive, and they often fail to deliver the set of features required by businesses within their time frames and budget targets. Although technologies such as .NET and BizTalk have shortened the cycle time to develop, test, and deploy solutions, often these technologies still don't meet the demanding cycle time requirements demanded by an agile business. For instance, consider a bank's business policy for granting credit to a customer. If you implement this logic within a BizTalk orchestration, the steps required to change the logic, compile the program, and redeploy are too numerous to enumerate here. In addition, this change requires that the system be taken offline while you enact the changes. Also, if the bank has a strong development methodology, it may require additional time to follow the process and obtain the necessary approvals. All this adds up to a sluggish, expensive process for changing the business policy.

The business rules framework is BizTalk's answer to reducing the business agility problem faced by traditional technologies. The business rules framework is a rules execution engine that allows you to create business policies that you can develop, deploy, and dynamically execute quickly without bringing your BizTalk process down. The framework comprises policies, facts, vocabularies, and rules. In conjunction, these artifacts combine to create a powerful tool for quickly changing business rules in near real time.

7-1. Creating a Business Policy

Problem

You want to understand the process for creating business rule policies. These policies are core components to all business rule development.

Solution

The business rules framework consists of policies, rules, vocabularies, and facts. A *business policy* is the container in which business rules are defined, versioned, tested, deployed, and executed. From within the business policy editing window, the first step before creating rules is to create a policy. The policy then may contain one or more rules for deployment. To create a policy, take the following steps:

1. Open the Business Rule Composer by selecting Start ➤ Programs ➤ Microsoft BizTalk Server 2010 ➤ Business Rule Composer.

2. If the Open Rule Store dialogue box opens, enter the correct connection information (see Figure 7-1).

Figure 7-1. *Initial Rule Store connection manager*

3. Within the Policy Explorer, right-click the Policies node, and click Add New Policy and give the policy a name.

4. By default, version 1.0 of the policy is created. You may change the version number if you want by selecting the version, navigating to the Properties window, and setting the Version property.

5. Right-click the version, and choose Save. See Figure 7-2.

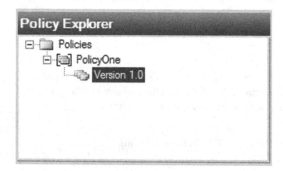

Figure 7-2. *The Policy Explorer frame within the Business Rules Composer*

How It Works

Creating a business rules policy is a relatively simplistic exercise but is the foundation to the business rules framework. Once you have created the policy, you can add rules and facts to the policy for testing and deployment. When calling the policy from BizTalk, the latest version will be selected for execution, unless you specify a specific version. The rules engine detects and deploys new versions of a policy, allowing changes to be made to the business policy in a live, deployed process. This creates a powerful environment to apply a dynamic business policy to deployed solutions with minimal work. The recipes in this chapter will guide you through adding rules, facts, and vocabularies to your business rules policy.

7-2. Creating and Testing Rules

Problem

You need to create and test a simple business rule that a business process can use. The business process needs to validate a document and receive the result.

Solution

You need to perform a number of basic steps to create a rule. These include the following:

1. Define the rule logic.

2. Define the input schema and XML instance.

3. Define the output schema and XML instance.

4. Define the facts that the rule uses, such as constants, functions, and predicates (vocabularies).

The first step to creating a rule is determining the logic of the rule. This example will use the logic in Listing 7-1 to construct the rule.

Listing 7-1. *Rule Logic*

```
If Age < Minimum Age Then Deny Application
If Age > or = Minimum Age Then Accept Application
```

We will show how to execute the rule in Listing 7-1 against an XML document containing the data that will be validated. For this example, we will use the NewHire schema (Figure 7-3) with the schema and XML instance (Listing 7-2).

Figure 7-3. *NewHire schema*

417

Listing 7-2. NewHire XML Instance

```xml
<ns0:NewHireList xmlns:ns0="http://CreatingAndTestingRules.NewHire">
  <DateTime>2010-08-04T18:00:00</DateTime>
  <Person>
    <ID>1</ID>
    <Name>Mary</Name>
    <Role>Office Manager</Role>
    <Age>31</Age>
  </Person>
  <Person>
    <ID>2</ID>
    <Name>Windy</Name>
    <Role>Organist</Role>
    <Age>38</Age>
  </Person>
</ns0:NewHireList>
```

■ **Note** The schema must define the `<Age>` element as an integer for the comparison to work in the business rule, which you will create in this solution. The rules engine will not implicitly convert a `String` to an `Int`.

The next step in this solution is to output a document. The document that is sent to the rules engine will be modified and returned to the calling entity. If the applicant's age is not a valid age, the document will be modified to display the text "INVALID APPLICANT" in the `<Role>` element (this element must exist in order for it to be set).

The following steps describe how to create the vocabulary using the Business Rule Composer:

1. Open the Business Rule Composer from the Start menu. If the Open Rule Store dialog box appears, select the appropriate SQL Server instance and authentication to log on (this should be the instance against which you want to develop).

2. Add a new vocabulary, which will contain the definition for the `Minimum Age` constant and the `Age` node in the input XML document. To do this using the Facts Explorer, right-click the `Vocabularies` folder, and create a new vocabulary named `AgeValidation`. See Figure 7-4.

Figure 7-4. *Creating a new vocabulary*

3. To add the Minimum Age constant, right-click the Version subfolder created in the previous step, and select Add New Definition. The Vocabulary Definition Wizard appears. Once the wizard is open, do the following:

   a. Add a new constant by selecting the Constant Value option. Enter **MinimumAge** for the Definition Name field. Give a description of the minimum age of the applicant. Click Next. See Figure 7-5.

Definition name:

MinimumAge

Definition description:

Minimum age of the applicant

Definition type

Which kind of definition do you want to create?

- Constant Value

- Range of Values

- Set of Values

Figure 7-5. Creating a new vocabulary

   b. On the final page of the wizard, set Type to System.Int32, and set Value to 18. Set Display Name to an appropriate value. Click Finish.

4. o add the reference to the Age node in the NewHire XML document, right-click the subfolder of the version that was created in step 2, and select Add New Definition. The wizard appears, and you should then perform the following steps:

   a. Select the XML Document Element or Attribute option, and click Next. See Figure 7-6.

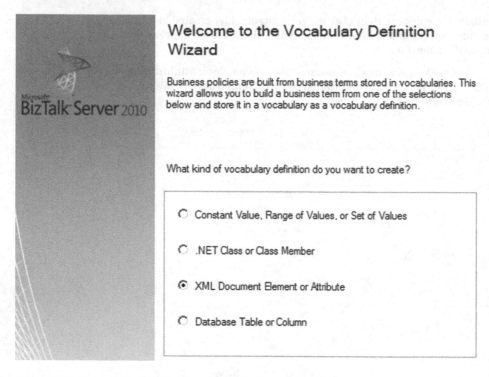

Figure 7-6. *New vocabulary based on an XML document element*

b. Enter **ApplicantAge** for the Definition Name field. Give a description of the actual age of the applicant.

c. Click the Browse button, and find the NewHire XSD schema. Once you have selected the schema, a new dialog box appears where you can select the Age node. Select this node, and click OK (See Figure 7-7).

Figure 7-7. *New vocabulary based on an XML Document Element Age*

    d.   In the Select Operation section, select the Perform "Get" Operation radio button.

  5.   Add a reference to the Role node in the NewHire XML document. Following the same procedure as defined in step 4, use these substeps:

    a.   Select the XML Document Element or Attribute option, and click Next.

    b.   Enter **ApplicantRole** for the Definition Name field. Give a description of the role of the applicant, which will be set to INVALID APPLICANT.

c.   Click the Browse button, and find the NewHire XSD schema. Once you have selected the schema, a new dialog box appears where you can select the Role node. Select this node, and click OK.

d.   In the Select Operation section, select the Perform "Set" Operation radio button. See Figure 7-8.

Definition name:

ApplicantRole

Definition description:

INVALID APPLICANT

XML document information

Document type: Instance ID:

NewHire   0

Schema:

C:\Users\Administrator\Documents\Visual Studio 2010\Projects\CreatingAnc   [Browse...]

XPath selector:

/*[local-name()='NewHireList' and namespace-uri()='http://CreatingAndTestingRules.NewHire']/*[loc

XPath field: Type:

*[local-name()='Role' and namespace-uri()=']   System.String   ▼

Select operation

⦿ Perform "Set" operation

○ Perform "Get" operation

Figure 7-8. New vocabulary based on an XML Document Element Role

e.   Click Next. On the final screen of the wizard, two steps are shown. For the first step, click the Edit button and set INVALID APPLICANT as the constant value. For the second step, keep the default values. Click Finish when this is complete. See Figure 7-9.

Definition name:

> ApplicantRole

Step 1 - Specify the display name/value for each parameter:

Parameters:

Position	Field/Attribute	Type	Value
{0}	*[local-name()='R...	System.String	INVALID APPLICANT

Edit...

Step 2 - Specify the display format string:

The display format string describes how the vocabulary definition is displayed in rule conditions and actions. For example, the display format string for the function "sum(x, y)" can be written as "the sum of {0} and {1}" where {0} and {1} are placeholders for the display names or values of the parameters x and y respectively.

Display format string:

> ApplicantRole {0}

Default

The definition for "ApplicantRole" will be displayed as follows when used in rule conditions and actions:

> ApplicantRole   INVALID APPLICANT

Figure 7-9. *Setting the values on the final page of the wizard*

6. Now, publish the vocabulary by right-clicking the newly created AgeValidation folder and selecting Publish. This allows the vocabulary to be used by a policy, which is where you define an actual business rule.

The steps up to this point have been putting into place the components needed to create a business rule. A *rule* (or set of rules) is defined within a policy and references preexisting functions, predicates, and any custom-defined constants (such as what you defined in the previous steps). The following steps show how to create the actual business rule and policy and use the vocabulary created previously:

1. In the Policy Explorer, right-click the Policies folder, and select Add New Policy. Enter **SamplePolicy** for the policy name.

2. A version appears. Right-click this version, and select Add New Rule. Enter **SampleRule** for the rule name.

3. Select the rule you created in the previous step. You will see an empty condition in the right pane. Take the following steps to create the rule (see Figure 7-10 for a full picture of the completed steps).

Figure 7-10. *Creating the rule*

a. In the Facts Explorer, expand the `Predicates` folder, and select the `Less Than` predicate. Drag and drop this on the rule condition.

b. On the `argument1` entry in the `IF` section of the rule composition window, drag and drop the custom vocabulary parameter `ApplicantAge` you created in an earlier step.

c. On the `argument2` entry in the `IF` section, drag and drop the custom vocabulary parameter `MinimumAge` you created earlier.

d. In the `THEN` section of the rule composition window, drop the `ApplicantRole` parameter (created earlier).

The rule is complete at this point. Save the rule (right-click Version, and select Save). You can now test the rule (and policy). Use these steps to validate and test the rule:

1. Right-click the `Version` folder of the rule you just created, and select Test Policy.

2. In the Select Facts dialog box that appears, click the schema name. The option to add an instance of the NewHireList XML will be available. You saw an example of this earlier in this recipe (refer to Listing 7-2). Click Add Instance, and browse to an instance of this XML document.

3. Once you have declared an instance, click the Test button. This causes the XML instance to be passed to the rule. A full trace appears in an Output window where you can verify whether the rule executed as expected (the value of the XML node should change).

4. Right-click the policy version, and select Publish.

5. Right-click the policy version, and select Deploy.

You can now call the rule and policy from an orchestration. To call the rule and policy from an orchestration, perform the following steps:

1. In an orchestration, create a message of the type that is to be passed into the rule and a message of the type that is expected back (in this case, the messages will both be the same `NewHireList` XSD type).

2. Drop a Call Rules shape in an Atomic Scope (or in an orchestration that has a transaction type of `Atomic`).

3. Right-click the Call Rules shape, and select the policy you created. There will be no input parameters.

■ **Note** The document type must match the namespace of the schema that will call it for the rule to be callable from an orchestration.

The XML instance shown in Figure 7-11 represents the generated output from testing the business rule created in this solution.

```
<?xml version="1.0" encoding="utf-8" ?>
- <ns0:NewHireList xmlns:ns0="http://CreatingAndTestingRules.NewHire">
    <DateTime>2010-08-04T18:00:00</DateTime>
  - <Person>
      <ID>1</ID>
      <Name>Mary</Name>
      <Role>INVALID APPLICANT</Role>
      <Age>31</Age>
    </Person>
  - <Person>
      <ID>2</ID>
      <Name>Windy</Name>
      <Role>Organist</Role>
      <Age>38</Age>
    </Person>
</ns0:NewHireList>
```

Figure 7-11. Final XML

How It Works

There are additional uses of the rules engine, including the ability to store parameters that can be accessed from orchestrations. Similar in nature to a configuration file that stores parameters that may need to change (such as connection strings) once a solution is in production, these constants allow for runtime modifications. Benefits to using the rules engine to store configurable parameters include ease of access, simple user interface, and enhanced read/write permissions (compared with a text file containing configurable parameters).

To add parameters that can be accessed from an orchestration, there are two basic steps: create the parameters, and access the constants through the rules engine API.

The first step is to create the parameters in a vocabulary in the rules engine and save them. You don't need to publish them unless versioning would be helpful. If they are not published, it is easier to modify them at runtime, because all that is required is to right-click the value that needs to be changed and select Modify. Once you have saved the vocabulary, running instances of orchestrations that reference these parameters will pick up the new values.

The second step is to add .NET code to a BizTalk Helper class to access the vocabulary through the rules engine API. The code shown in Listing 7-3 can be placed into a .NET assembly and should be referenced by a BizTalk project. The method can then be called from an Expression shape within an orchestration. This code also allows for a specific version to be called, if desired.

Listing 7-3. *Accessing Constants Through the Rules Engine API*

```
public bool blnGetVocabularyConstantValue(string strVocabularyName,
                              string strConstantName,
                              string strVersion,
                              ref string strConstantValue,
                              ref string strConstantType) {

    RuleStore rlsRuleStore;
    VocabularyInfoCollection vicVocabInfo;
    Vocabulary vocVocab;
    RuleSetDeploymentDriver rsdDriver = new RuleSetDeploymentDriver();
    Hashtable hshTable;
    LiteralDefinition litDef;
    Boolean blnConstantFound = false;

    rlsRuleStore = rsdDriver.GetRuleStore();

    if((strVersion == null) || (strVersion == "")) {
     vicVocabInfo = rlsRuleStore.GetVocabularies(strVocabularyName,
                             RuleStore.Filter.Latest);
    }
    else {
     vicVocabInfo = rlsRuleStore.GetVocabularies(strVocabularyName,
                             RuleStore.Filter.All);
    }

    // check to see that the vocabulary searched on has returned data
    if(vicVocabInfo.Count > 0) {
     for(int x=0;x<vicVocabInfo.Count;x++) {

     vocVocab = rlsRuleStore.GetVocabulary(vicVocabInfo[x]);

     // Check to see that the version equals the version being searched for
     // or that the version passed in was a wildcard (Null)
     if((strVersion == null) || (strVersion == "") ||
     ((vocVocab.CurrentVersion.MajorRevision + "." +
       vocVocab.CurrentVersion.MinorRevision) == strVersion)) {

      // Initialize the hashtable to the number of definitions on the vocabulary
      hshTable = new Hashtable(vocVocab.Definitions.Count);
      hshTable = (Hashtable)vocVocab.Definitions.SyncRoot;
```

```
        // check that the constant being searched for exists in the vocabulary
        if(hshTable.ContainsKey(strConstantName)) {
         litDef = (LiteralDefinition)hshTable[strConstantName];

         strConstantType = litDef.Value.GetType().ToString();
         strConstantValue = litDef.Value.ToString();

         blnConstantFound = true;

         // exit loop
         break;
        }
       }
      }
     }
  return blnConstantFound;
}
```

You can use the code in Listing 7-4 to invoke the previous class from an orchestration Expression shape. This allows for an alternate method of access to the rules engine without needing the standard call using the Call Rules shape and is useful when getting the value of a constant or other scalar value.

Listing 7-4. Calling the Object from the Orchestration Expression Shape

```
// the following string is the name of the vocabulary
strVocabularyName = "Project.BizTalk.Constants";
objVocab.GetVocabularyConstantValue(strVocabularyName, "ConstantName", "",
                                         "10", ref strValue,ref strType);
```

7-3. Creating Facts
Problem

You need to understand how to use the Facts Explorer to create a vocabulary that will be used within a business rule fact. You want to be able to store constants, predicates, and so on, that can be changed easily without redeploying code.

Solution

This solution will demonstrate how to create a vocabulary using a node in an imported XML schema. *Facts* are those items that are used to create rules. The Facts Explorer has four tabs, as follows:

- *Vocabularies*: These consist of all defined values that you can use when creating a rule, including constants, predicates, XML nodes, and so on.

- *XML Schemas*: You can use all schemas imported onto this tab when creating vocabularies or predicates (actions). You can drag and drop nodes on the XML Schemas tab in the Vocabulary window.

- *Databases*: You can add references to databases that will be used for creating facts on this tab. You can drag and drop tables onto the Vocabulary window.

- *NET Assemblies*: Assemblies, like databases and XML schemas, can be references in the Facts Explorer and used to create vocabularies.

Use the following steps to import an XML schema and create a new vocabulary:

1. In the BizTalk Business Rule Composer, click the XML Schemas tab in the Facts Explorer.

2. Right-click the Schemas folder, and select Browse. Locate a schema to import, and click Open. This imports the full schema into the window.

3. Create a new vocabulary by clicking the Vocabulary tab. Right-click the Vocabularies folder, and select Add New Vocabulary. Give the vocabulary a name.

4. Now, drag a node from the XML schema that was imported, and drop it on the vocabulary you created in the previous step. By holding down the mouse button as you drag the node, you can navigate between tabs.

5. The Vocabulary Definition Wizard immediately opens, with the XML Document or Attribute option automatically selected. Navigate through the wizard to finish creating the vocabulary. The fields will already be filled in for you.

How It Works

You can add the Database and .NET Assembly facts to the Vocabulary tab in a similar manner as described in this solution. Additionally, you can drop all facts in the condition or action (IF...THEN) of a rule. Once you have added a fact to a rule, right-clicking the condition or action allows you to browse to the original fact, as shown in Figure 7-12. Complex rules will have many facts referenced in them, and this allows you to keep track of all the disparate definitions.

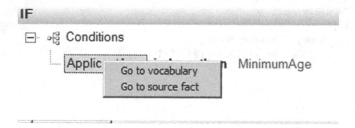

Figure 7-12. *Action with fact*

7-4. Setting Rule Priorities
Problem

You need to control the order in which the BizTalk rules engine executes rules. The order BizTalk executes rules in determines which rules take precedence, with the results of the last rule executing and potentially overwriting the results of the previous rules.

Solution

In many real-world scenarios, multiple business rules must execute in a predetermined order. In these situations, the second rule may overwrite the result of the first rule. Control the order in which the BizTalk rules engine executes rules by assigning a priority to each rule.

■ **Note**   This example assumes that the business rules already exist. For more information about creating business rules, please see the earlier recipes in this chapter.

The following steps demonstrate how to set the priority of a business rule:

1. Open the Business Rules Composer.

2. Navigate to the policy containing the rules.

3. Select the Use Preferred Shipper rule in the Policy Explorer, and change the Priority property to the value 1, as shown in Figure 7-13.

Figure 7-13. Setting the Priority property

■ **Note**   The BizTalk rules engine executes higher-priority rules first. Since the promotional shipping rate rule should override the preferred shipper rule, it must execute after the preferred shipper rule and must have a lower priority.

How It Works

The BizTalk rules engine executes high-priority rules first. Consequently, lower-priority rules execute after higher-priority ones and potentially can override the results of higher-priority rules. The BizTalk rules engine may execute rules with the same priority in any order. Remember that the priority of rules will affect the order BizTalk executes them in and has no direct effect on the importance of the rule's actions.

7-5. Creating Custom Fact Retrievers
Problem

You need to define business rules using facts that an orchestration cannot provide. The facts may not be available in the orchestration, or you may need to reuse a fact across many instances of the orchestration.

Solution

A business rule performs actions when conditions defined in the Business Rule Composer are true. For example, an action may modify a value in a message. The BizTalk developer creates a condition from facts, which are pieces of information the rules engine can examine. Most often, the rules engine will examine facts from the messages BizTalk directly processes. The orchestration invoking the rules engine directly provides these facts. However, sometimes a rule needs to be based on facts that are not available in the orchestration. The rules engine can retrieve these external facts with a custom fact retriever.

In this example, a business rule will schedule a customer's service request only if the customer's address is in the Northwind database. The customer's address may be different each time the orchestration invokes the rules engine. The customer's address is called a *short-term fact* because the orchestration provides the fact every time it invokes the rules engine. However, instead of opening a new connection to the database each time the orchestration invokes the rules engine, this example reuses the same connection to the Northwind database over and over again. Reusing the database connection makes it a *long-term fact*. The BizTalk developer must provide long-term facts to the rules engine with the IFactRetriever interface. The custom fact retriever created in this recipe provides the connection to the Northwind database to the rules engine.

■ **Note**   The Northwind database is a sample database that can be downloaded from Microsoft's site.

Use the following steps to create the custom fact retriever:

1. Open Visual Studio, and create a new class library project.

2. Add a reference to the Microsoft.RuleEngine.dll assembly. This assembly is located in the root of the BizTalk installation directory. This may be in either $\Program Files\Common Files\Microsoft BizTalk or $\Program Files\Microsoft BizTalk Server 2010\.

3. Implement the Microsoft.RuleEngine.IFactRetriever interface. This interface defines one method called UpdateFacts.

4. Within the UpdateFacts method, add code to check whether the factsHandleIn parameter is null. If the factsHandleIn parameter is null, create and return an instance of the Microsoft.RuleEngine.DataConnection class. If the factsHandleIn parameter is not null, simply return it from the method. When completed, the code should appear as in Listing 7-6.

Listing 7-6. Completed Custom Fact Retriever

```
using System.Data.SqlClient;
using Microsoft.RuleEngine;

namespace CustomFactRetriever
{
    public class AssertDBConnection : IFactRetriever
```

```
        {
    public object UpdateFacts(RuleSetInfo ruleSetInfo,
                             RuleEngine engine, object factsHandleIn)
    {
        object factsHandleOut;
        if (factsHandleIn == null)
        {
            SqlConnection SQLConn = new SqlConnection("
                                        Initial Catalog=Northwind;
                                        Data Source=(local);
                                        Integrated Security=SSPI;");
            DataConnection RulesConn = new DataConnection("Northwind",
                                            "Customers", SQLConn);

            engine.Assert(RulesConn);
            factsHandleOut = RulesConn;
        }
        else
            factsHandleOut = factsHandleIn;

        return factsHandleOut;
    }
  }
}
```

5. Compile the class library assembly, and deploy it to the Global Assembly Cache (GAC). This can be done via a command prompt using the `gacutil /if` command. After creating the custom fact retriever, define a vocabulary and business rules. This example will schedule a service appointment only if the customer's address is in the database.

6. Open the Business Rule Composer, and create a new policy with one rule. Define a vocabulary for accessing facts defined by an XML message. An orchestration must provide the message when the policy executes. This example gets the address a customer requested service at and decides whether to approve the service request.

7. Right-click the new vocabulary's version, and select Add New Definition. Select the option to create a new database table or column definition in the vocabulary, and click Next, as shown in Figure 7-14.

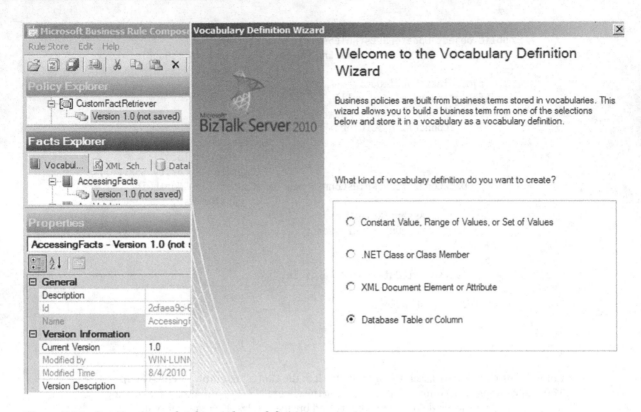

Figure 7-14. Creating a new database column definition

8. Give the definition an appropriate name, and leave the Binding Type set to Data Connection.

9. Within the Database Information section of the window, click the Browse button. After selecting a SQL Server instance with the Northwind database, browse to the Customers table. Select the Address column of the Customers table, as shown in Figure 7-15, and click OK.

Figure 7-15. *Setting the location of the customer's registered address*

10. Within the Select Operation section of the window, select the Perform "Get" Operation
radio button. Set an appropriate display name for display in the Business Rules Composer.
When complete, the Database Table or Database Table Column Definition window
appears, as shown in Figure 7-16.

Figure 7-16. Completing the definition

11. Click the Finish button to complete the vocabulary definition.

12. Select the policy version in the Policy Explorer section of the Business Rule Composer. The properties should appear in the lower-left region of the Business Rule Composer.

13. Select the Fact Retriever property of the policy version, and click the ellipsis that appears.

14. In the Select Configuration component, click the Browse button. In the list of assemblies that appears, select the custom fact retriever created previously in this example (shown in Figure 7-17).

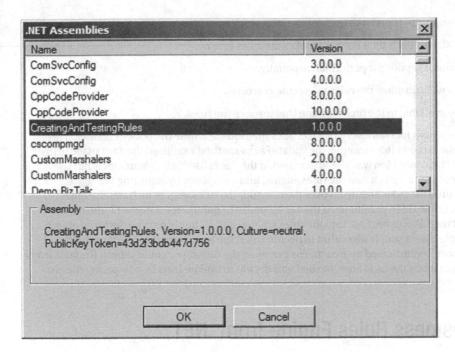

Figure 7-17. *Selecting the .NET assembly*

■ **Note** If you cannot locate the custom fact retriever assembly, verify that it is deployed to the GAC.

---

15. Select the class to complete configuring the custom fact retriever.

16. After creating the custom fact retriever to retrieve the DataConnection and configuring the policy to use the custom fact retriever, it is time to define the rules. So, define the business rule to compare the requested service address with the customer addresses already in the Northwind database. If there is a match, the service request will be scheduled.

17. Deploy the rules and invoke them from an orchestration, specifying the XML messages that the policy expects. The rules engine will invoke the UpdateFacts method of the custom fact retriever. The method will add a DataConnection fact to the Northwind database to the rules engine facts.

How It Works

The rules engine examines facts provided either directly from an orchestration or from a custom fact retriever. The facts provided directly from an orchestration are called short-term facts, and the orchestration supplies them each time BizTalk invokes the rules engine. The facts provided from a custom fact retriever are called long-term facts, and they can be reused each time BizTalk invokes the rules engine.

A BizTalk orchestration can also treat the DataConnection in this example as a short-term fact. Accomplish this by creating a DataConnection in an Expression shape and including it as a parameter to the Call Rules shape. However, each orchestration instance would create its own DataConnection. You can improve the scalability and performance of the application by treating the DataConnection as a long-term fact and sharing it each time BizTalk invokes the rules engine.

In general, treating a fact as long-term is preferable under the following conditions:

- The fact value can be shared each time BizTalk invokes the rules engine.

- Retrieving the fact incurs a significant performance penalty.

- Caching the fact value will still allow the rules to execute correctly.

- The fact is not directly available in the orchestration that invokes the rules.

The rules engine invokes the custom fact retriever's UpdateFacts method each time the policy executes. This method decides when to update the facts. In this example, the UpdateFacts method examines the factsHandleIn parameter to check whether the DataConnection was already created. If the factsHandleIn parameter is null, the method creates the DataConnection, inserts it into the rules engine, and completes by returning the DataConnection object. The next time the rules engine invokes the method, the rules engine includes the object returned by the method in the factsHandleIn parameter. If the factsHandleIn parameter is not null, the method knows that it has already inserted the DataConnection into the rules engine, and it simply returns the same object.

Although this solution example uses a simple algorithm to decide when the long-term fact needs updating, the developer can implement a more sophisticated approach. For example, the developer could refresh the facts every hour by returning a DateTime object when the facts are refreshed and decide to update facts by comparing the last refresh time to the current time.

7-6. Calling the Business Rules Engine from .NET
Problem

You are building a solution that must execute business rules based on dynamic information. These business rules are likely to change over time, and you want to minimize the impact on the solution when modifications are needed. To do this, you want to be able to call the rules engine from a .NET assembly.

■ **Note**   The problem within this recipe is the same as in Recipe 7-7. The solutions in the two recipes differ in how the business rules are executed.

Solution

This solution describes the steps necessary to call the business rules engine from a C# assembly. The steps detail how to build a .NET Windows application to process job applications and dynamically determine whether applicants meet a minimum age requirement. If the applicant is younger than a certain age, that person cannot be considered for employment. The minimum age is likely to change over time and needs to be easily configurable. The business rules engine that comes with BizTalk Server captures the business rule determining the minimum working age. Other recipes within this chapter detail the steps for creating rules.

■ **Note**   This recipe is based on the policy and vocabulary defined in Recipe 7-2.

This solution assumes that a rule exists in the business rules engine to determine whether an applicant meets the minimum age requirements. To call this rule from a .NET application, follow these steps:

1. Open the project containing the .NET application.

2. Add a project reference to the `Microsoft.RuleEngine.dll` assembly, which contains the classes required to call the business rules engine. This may be in either `$\Program Files\ Common Files\Microsoft BizTalk` or `$\Program Files\Microsoft BizTalk Server 2010\`.

3. Create the necessary policy and fact objects, and execute the business rule policy, as shown in Listing 7-7.

Listing 7-7. Calling a Business Rule from .NET

```
public void callSamplePolicy(ref System.Xml.XmlDocument newHireListDoc)
{
    // create the SamplePolicy policy object
    // specify policy name and version
    Microsoft.RuleEngine.Policy policy =
            new Microsoft.RuleEngine.Policy("SamplePolicy", 1, 0);

    // create the facts object array to hold the input parameters for the policy
    object[] facts = new object[1];

    // create the input parameter for the SamplePolicy policy
    // based on a typed BizTalk schema (fully qualified .NET type)
    Microsoft.RuleEngine.TypedXmlDocument typedXmlDoc =
      new Microsoft.RuleEngine.TypedXmlDocument("SampleSolution.NewHireList",
                                                              newHireListDoc);

    // add the input parameter to the facts object array
    facts[0] = typedXmlDoc;

    // execute the policy against the facts
    policy.Execute(facts);
    policy.Dispose();

    // set the parameter object
    newHireListDoc.LoadXml(typedXmlDoc.Document.OuterXml);
}
```

How It Works

Although the business rules engine comes as part of BizTalk Server, this solution shows that .NET assemblies outside the BizTalk environment can call into it. This allows external applications to use the same rule framework that the integration hub does, enabling companies to consolidate their business rules functionality onto one platform.

■ **Note**   You can extend this solution by using a web/WCF service method to access the business rules engine, allowing code on any platform to call into a common rule framework.

Executing a Policy

For a .NET project to call into the business rules engine, it must reference the `Microsoft.RuleEngine.dll` assembly. This assembly contains the classes used to access the rules framework, including those to execute policies. In this solution, you first create an instance of the policy object, with the appropriate name and version. The name must exactly match the name of the policy you want to execute. This solution specifies `SamplePolicy` as the policy name, which maps to the highlighted name in Figure 7-18.

Figure 7-18. *The name of the policy must match the .NET code exactly*

Following the policy name, you specify the major and minor versions of the policy you want to execute. You specify 1.0, which is the only version of the policy currently deployed. Alternatively, you could specify the name only when creating the policy object (no version parameters supplied to the policy's constructor method), which executes the most recently deployed version of the policy.

Next, you create a collection (array) of fact objects. This array holds all the objects necessary to execute the policy. These objects map to the different types of facts that the Business Rule Composer can create, including XML documents, .NET classes or class members, and database connections. The `SamplePolicy` policy uses only a single XML document fact, which you create next.

You use the `Microsoft.RuleEngine.TypedXmlDocument` class to create an XML document fact, specifying the document type (the fully qualified .NET type name) and XML document instance. Add this `TypedXmlDocument` to the fact collection.

Finally, you execute the policy against the facts collection. The facts collection is passed as a *reference* parameter, meaning any changes to the facts will be committed to the original instances. In this solution, the XML document fact will have the appropriate minimum age requirement logic applied.

It is also possible to execute a policy directly from an Expression shape within an orchestration. Listing 7-8 illustrates how you would execute the same policy as described in the "Solution" section of this recipe but from an Expression shape.

Listing 7-8. Calling Policy from Expression Shape

```
// create the SamplePolicy policy object
// policy variable has type of Microsoft.RuleEngine.Policy.  Create this in Orchestration View
Variables
policy = new Microsoft.RuleEngine.Policy("SamplePolicy", 1, 0);

// create the input parameter for the OrderShipping policy
// typedXmlDoc variable has type of Microsoft.RuleEngine.TypedXmlDocument
// NewHireListMessage has type of SampleSolution.NewHireList
```

```
typedXmlDoc =
  new Microsoft.RuleEngine.TypedXmlDocument("SampleSolution.NewHireList",
                                            NewHireListMessage);

// execute the policy against the facts
policy.Execute(typedXmlDoc);
policy.Dispose();
```

Although the policy executed in this recipe requires only a single XML document fact, facts can also be .NET classes or class members and data connections. By default, BizTalk Server requires you to provide an object instance for each fact used in a policy.

Passing Data Connection Facts

To pass a data connection fact to a policy, initialize a Microsoft.RuleEngine.DataConnection instance and pass it to the policy in the facts collection. If an update is being executed against the underlying database, you must also provide a transaction to the DataConnection object, as shown in Listing 7-9. If data is being retrieved only, no transaction is required.

Listing 7-9. Providing a Transaction

```
// create SQL connection object
sqlConnection = new System.Data.SqlClient.SqlConnection("ConnectionString");

// create SQL transaction object
sqlTransaction = sqlConnection.BeginTransaction();

// create Data Connection object
dataConnection = new Microsoft.RuleEngine.DataConnection(
        "SqlDataSetName",
        "SqlTableName",
        sqlConnection,
        sqlTransaction);
```

The .NET assembly can add this DataConnection object instance to a fact collection and pass it to the policy for execution.

7-7. Calling the Business Rules Engine from an Orchestration
Problem

You are building a workflow that must execute business rules based on dynamic information. These business rules are likely to change over time, and you want to minimize the impact on the solution when modifications are needed.

■ **Note**   The problem within this recipe is the same as in Recipe 7-6. The solutions in the two recipes differ in how the business rules are executed.

Solution

This solution will demonstrate how to call the business rules engine from an orchestration, without using a .NET assembly. The basic problem is similar to the previous recipe. The key points of the problem are as follows:

- Job applications must be processed, and it must be determined whether applicants meet the minimum age requirement.

- If the applicant is younger than a certain age, then that person cannot be considered for employment.

- The minimum age is likely to change over time and needs to be easily configurable.

■ **Note**   This recipe is based on the policy and vocabulary defined in Recipe 7-2.

This solution assumes that a rule exists in the business rules engine to determine whether an applicant meets the minimum age requirements. To call this rule from an orchestration, follow these steps:

1. Open the project containing the orchestration.

2. In the orchestration's Properties window, configure it to act as a long-running transaction by setting the Transaction Type property.

3. Create a new message, and specify the name and type. In this scenario, create a message named NewHireListMessage defined by the NewHireList schema.

4. From the toolbox, drag the following onto the design surface in top-down order:

   a. Receive shape to receive the initial order message—configure this shape to use the NewHireListMessage message to activate the orchestration instance and to use an orchestration receive port. Make sure to set the Activate property to True.

   b. Send the shape to deliver the NewHireListMessage message to an external port—configure this shape to use an orchestration send port.

5. From the toolbox, drag a Scope shape onto the design surface, in between the Receive and Send shapes configured in the previous step—configure this shape to act as an Atomic transaction.

6. From the toolbox, drag a Call Rules shape onto the design surface, inside the Scope shape configured in the previous step. Configure this shape by double-clicking it, which launches the Call Rules Policy Configuration dialog box. Select the appropriate business policy to call and the parameters to pass into the policy (SamplePolicy in this scenario).

■ **Note**   The Parameter Type list populates with all the data types expected as input parameters to the selected business policy. The Parameter Name list populates with all the orchestration variables and messages matching the parameter types.

How It Works

Calling the business rules engine from an orchestration is a straightforward task. It allows you to separate the business procedure and process flow from the business rules. This is particularly useful when the rules are used across many process flows, change frequently, or need audit logging and versioning capabilities.

This recipe's solution uses a message instance conforming to the NewHireList schema as an input parameter to the SamplePolicy business rule policy. This policy sets the <Role> element of the message to INVALID APPLICANT if the <Age> element is less than a certain age. You could then enhance the rule to apply different minimum age requirements for different roles or to retrieve real-time minimum age requirements from a government-run data source.

You could easily extend this solution to illustrate how the output from a business rule can facilitate business procedures and process flow within an orchestration. Business rule policies could define a complex set of rules to determine whether an applicant is valid for a role. As opposed to setting the <Role> element to INVALID APPLICANT, you could configure the policy to return a Boolean value indicating whether the applicant meets the minimum age requirements. The orchestration could then use this Boolean value in a Decide shape, allowing separate process flows to determine whether an applicant is valid for a role based on previous work experience, personal references, and salary requirements.

For an orchestration to successfully call a policy, you must make a few settings:

- The Call Rules shape must be within an Atomic Scope shape (this necessitates that the orchestration's Transaction property is set to Long Running).

- The policy must be published and deployed within the business rules engine.

■ **Note** The Call Rules shape will always access the most recently deployed version of a policy.

- An initialized instance of all variables referenced in the policy must be in the same scope as the Call Rules shape.

Although this solution uses only an XML message instance as input to the rules policy, policies can accept other types of input parameters as well. The Vocabulary Definition Wizard allows a .NET class or class member or a data table or column to be used as a business term. As previously stated, an initialized instance of all variables referenced in a policy must be in scope at the Call Rules shape in the orchestration. This means that if a .NET class and a data table or column are used in a policy, there must be an initialized instance of the .NET class and rules engine Microsoft.RuleEngine.DataConnection object available in the orchestration to pass into the policy as input parameters.

■ **Note** If there is no instance matching an input used in a policy's rules, that input parameter will not appear in the Call Rules Policy Configuration dialog box's Parameter list. This will prevent the policy from being successfully called from the orchestration.

The policy used in this scenario references vocabulary definitions based on two XML elements in the NewHireList schema: <Age> and <Role>. Take care when creating these vocabulary definitions, or the rule policy won't be able to appropriately handle the orchestration message. Specifically, set the Document Type property of the business term to be the fully qualified type name. If the fully qualified .NET type name is not used to define the BizTalk schema, BizTalk Server will not have enough information to uniquely identify the data field.

A finer point regarding the Call Rules shape is that it treats input parameters as reference parameters, which means rules may modify the objects passed and return them to the orchestration. Given that messages are immutable (once they are created, they cannot be modified) in BizTalk, how does this work? The answer is that, behind the scenes, the policy creates a modified copy of the original message. Although this saves the developer's time when creating their orchestration, it also has an important side effect: all promoted properties on the original message are removed from the message context. If properties on the message need to be maintained, make a copy of the message to allow the message context to be reset after the business rules engine is called.

7-8. Deploying and Undeploying Policies
Problem

You want to know the components that make up a rules engine policy and perform the steps necessary to deploy and undeploy a policy to make the rule sets available to business processes.

Solution

Deploying a policy requires that several components be in place prior to the deployment. The deployment is quite straightforward, and you can deploy in several ways. This solution describes the prerequisites to the policy deployment and walks through the deployment steps using the Business Rule Composer.

A policy consists of one or more rules. A rule comprises a set of facts. In this solution, we describe the process to deploy and undeploy all the components that make up a policy. Your first task is to define any facts that may need to be used in any rules that are part of the policy:

1. Define all the custom facts. Using the Business Rule Composer, open the Facts Explorer. Define any vocabulary, schemas, databases, or .NET assemblies that may be needed for any rule.

2. Once your custom facts are completed, save and publish any vocabularies that may have been defined. Right-click the vocabulary version, which will be used by a rule, and click Save. Right-click the version again, and select Publish. Once you have published a vocabulary version, you cannot modify it directly. Instead, it must be versioned—you can do this by copying the most recent version and then pasting a new version. The new version can be modified.

3. Your next task is to create a new policy and add all the rules that are part of the policy. In the Policy Explorer, create a new policy, and add one or more rules. As you create each rule, reference the appropriate version of the vocabularies, which have been published.

4. Save, publish, and test the policy by right-clicking the policy version and selecting the appropriate menu item.

5. The final task is to actually deploy the policy. Once the policy has been deployed, it cannot be deleted unless it is first undeployed. In the same manner as the vocabularies, it cannot be modified unless a new version is first created. Deploy the policy as follows: right-click the policy version that is to be deployed, and select Deploy. You can undeploy policies by selecting Undeploy, as shown in Figure 7-19.

Figure 7-19. *Undeploying via the Business Rule Composer*

How It Works

You have two basic approaches for deploying and undeploying policies. The first is to use the Business Rule Composer. Using the Business Rule Composer, you can define facts and policies that can be modified, published, and deployed. The second is to use the Rules Engine Deployment Wizard (see Figure 7-20). The wizard allows policy files to be exported and imported onto machines where they may not have been created.

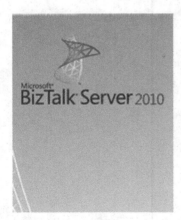

Welcome to the Rules Engine Deployment Wizard

This wizard guides you through the steps needed to perform the following tasks:

* Import or export a Policy/Vocabulary file.
* Deploy or undeploy a Policy in a Rules Engine database.

Figure 7-20. *The Rules Engine Deployment Wizard*

Use the following basic steps to deploy a policy in a distributed environment (See Figure 7-21 for all options):

1. Export the policy file. Open the BizTalk Rules Engine Deployment Wizard on the machine where the policy was created. Select Export Policy/Vocabulary file from database. Walk through the options, selecting the policy you want to deploy on a target machine. This process will create an XML file (or multiple files if exporting multiple vocabularies and policies) that can be copied to another machine.

2. Copy the XML file(s) created in the first step to the target machine. Open the wizard on the target machine, and select the Import and publish Policy/Vocabulary to database from file option. Walk through the options to publish the data to the target machine's rules engine (the vocabularies must first be deployed, and all referenced .NET assemblies must be placed in the GAC).

3. Run the wizard again on the target machine. This time, select the Deploy Policy option. All policies and vocabularies that have not been deployed will be available in the drop-down list. Select the object(s) you want to deploy, and walk through the rest of the wizard. The vocabularies and policies can now be referenced on the target machine by orchestrations or other components.

4. To undeploy, follow step 3, selecting Undeploy Policy rather than Deploy Policy from the first option list. Only those vocabularies and policies that have been deployed successfully will be available for undeployment.

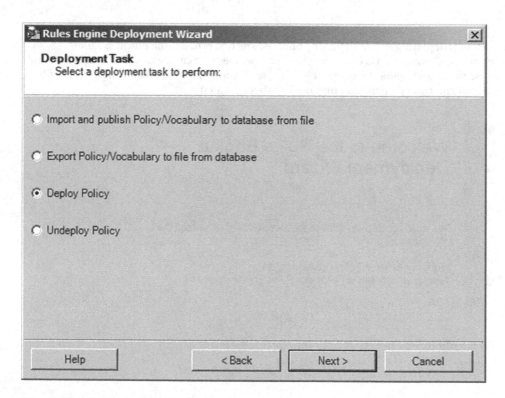

Figure 7-21. Using the Rules Engine Deployment Wizard

CHAPTER 8

■ ■ ■

EDI Solutions

BizTalk has been moving into the EDI (Electronic Document Interchange) space for a number of years. In early versions of BizTalk, EDI was accomplished with third-party adapters and a lot of development and configuration performed outside of the platform. With the release of BizTalk Server 2006 R2, EDI became a prominent part of the platform. With the advent of BizTalk Server 2010, all aspects of the EDI life cycle, including schemas, mapping, workflow processing, and trading partner management are fully developed and available.

The most compelling new functionality in the 2010 version of the product is how trading partners are managed. While managing partners was possible in previous editions, the new user interface and underlying data modeling allows users and administrators to easily create complex partner relationships and allows for multiple document types to be sent over numerous protocols to any combination of partner locations.

BizTalk 2013 doesn't make any changes to the functionality, but does ensure that all of the latest schemas are inline with the X12 and EDIFACTS standards. It also continues the support of HL7 and other accelerator standards.

This chapter will introduce the core components of implementing EDI solutions in BizTalk Server. Some of the most complex solutions to implement are EDI, due primarily to the intricate nature of some of the maps. The X12 837 healthcare claim, for example, is a massive schema with hundreds of nodes and elements, many of which are virtually identical. Versioning adds to the complexity, with some solution requiring both the 4010 and the new fully compliant HIPAA 5010 versions.

This chapter introduces all of the key features of working with EDI solutions. If you know BizTalk Server, jumping into EDI won't be too much of a stretch. However, don't underestimate the complexity of your first BizTalk EDI solution. There is a lot to work through (much of it outside of BizTalk), and you should approach it methodically and with a well-thought-out development approach. Maps, schemas, and orchestrations will all be familiar, but considerably more complex (as they would be on any platform, not just with BizTalk) and trading partner configuration and management will prove to be an area of BizTalk that you will not have used for other types of solutions.

8-1. Adding an EDI Schema to a Project
Problem

You are developing an EDI solution that will use the HIPAA–compliant X12 00401 837 Professional and Institutional schemas. You need to add these schemas to your project so that documents conforming to the 837 schema can be routed and mapped in BizTalk.

Solution

To add the BizTalk 837 schema to a Visual Studio project, take the following steps:

1. Right-click the project in Visual Studio, and select Add ➤ Existing Item.

2. Browse to the `$\Program Files\Microsoft BizTalk Server 2013\XSD_Schema\EDI\ HIPAA\00401A1` folder. You will see folders for the various health care claims. Select the `X12_00401_837_P.xsd` file, and click the Add button. Repeat this for the `X12_00401_837_I.xsd` file.

■ **Note**   You will need to extract the schemas using the `MicrosoftEdiXSDTemplates.exe` file, located in the root of the `XSD_Schema\EDI` folder.

Once added, the schemas can be referenced and used like any other schema. Figure 8-1 shows the 837 Professional schema in Visual Studio.

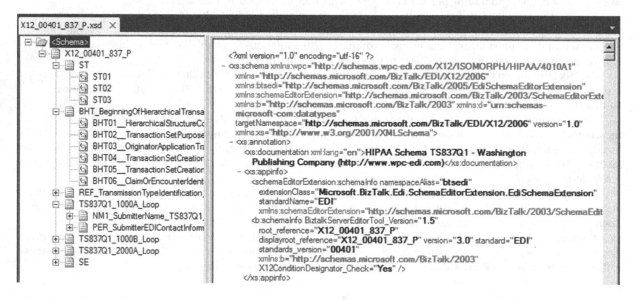

Figure 8-1. *The 837 Professional schema*

How It Works

There is no difference between an EDI schema and a standard BizTalk schema, except that the EDI schemas ship with BizTalk and are fully defined and ready to use. There are literally thousands of EDI related schemas available to choose from. EDI schemas generally are more complex than other types of schemas and come with a large amount of field restriction and validation on them.

For example, several of the elements in `BHT_BeginningOfHierarchicalTransaction_TS837Q1` have specific enumerations that are allowed. Figure 8-2 shows one of these enumerations. Data being processed through the EDI pipelines would fail validation if a value were in a field that didn't match one of the options in the enumeration.

Figure 8-2. *An enumeration*

■ **Note**   There is generally no need to modify the EDI schemas. On the off chance that one does need to be modified, it is sometimes easiest to modify in a text editor. The BizTalk schema editor can become slow with some of the larger EDI schemas (many are multiple megabytes in size).

8-2. Creating an EDI Map
Problem

You need to map an 837 EDI document to a document structure that matches an internal system.

Solution

You simply need to add a map to your Visual Studio project that contains the source and target schemas. Take the following steps to add a new map to your project:

1. Right-click the project in Visual Studio, and select Add ➤ New Item.

2. Select the Map template, give it a descriptive name, and click Add.

3. Set the source and target schemas.

4. Use functoids and other mapping techniques to implement the logic needed.

■ **Note**   There is a great book that covers EDI mapping in BizTalk Server, titled *Pro Mapping in BizTalk Server 2009* by Jim Dawson and John Wainwright (Apress 2009). All of the concepts related to EDI apply to the BizTalk Server 2013 platform.

How It Works

EDI maps are often notoriously complex. Some document types that are quite simple and don't require much in the way of mapping, but many EDI schemas are extremely complex and require careful planning, thoughtful development, many hours (or days or weeks!) of development, and a great deal of patience for administration and maintenance. An example of a complex EDI map is shown in Figure 8-3. Such a map is not an uncommon sight when you're walking into an existing EDI solution.

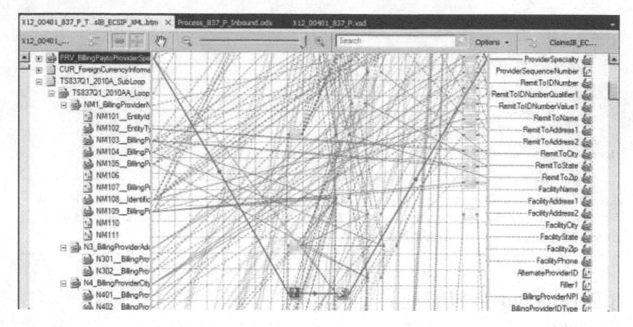

Figure 8-3. *A complex map*

■ **Note** When developing EDI maps, always think of the next person who is going to have to work with your map. If you can't remember where a functoid is or how a set of mappings works, you can't expect someone six months from now to understand what you have done. If a map becomes too complex, you can always work in a custom XSLT document, a .NET component, or other alternative mapping interface.

8-3. Defining Complex Mappings in External XSLT

Problem

Your map is getting out of control, and you want to move away from using the mapper.

Solution

In this solution, we will move all processing in the map to an external XSLT style sheet. Take these steps to accomplish this:

1. Create a new map, and specify the source and target schemas. This is the end of the traditional mapper; it is used simply to define the source and target schemas and house the external XSLT code

2. Create an XSLT document, and implement your mapping. An example of the header of an external XSLT document is shown in Figure 8-4.

```
File  Edit  Format  View  Help
<?xml version="1.0" encoding="UTF-16"?>
<xsl:stylesheet xmlns:xsl="http://www.w3.org/1999/XSL/Transform" xmlns:msxsl="urn:schemas-
microsoft-com:xslt" xmlns:var="http://schemas.microsoft.com/BizTalk/2003/var" exclude-result-
prefixes="msxsl var s0" version="1.0" xmlns:ns0="http://Institutional.Schemas.INTERNALOB_FF"
xmlns:s0="http://Professional.Schemas.ClaimsIB_INTERNAL_XML">
  <xsl:output omit-xml-declaration="yes" method="xml" version="1.0" />
  <xsl:template match="/">
    <xsl:apply-templates select="/s0:ECSIFIB_XML" />
  </xsl:template>

  <xsl:template match="/s0:ECSIFIB_XML">
   <ns0:ROOT>

   <!-- ALL MAPPING GOES HERE -->

   </ns0:ROOT>
  </xsl:template>
</xsl:stylesheet>
```

Figure 8-4. *An external XSLT*

3. To reference this file, click anywhere on the map surface, and look at the properties of the map. In the Custom XSLT Path property, set the path to your XSLT file (see Figure 8-5).

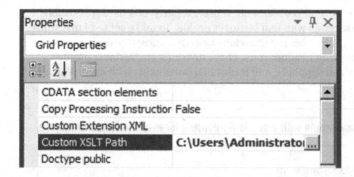

Figure 8-5. *Setting the Custom XSLT property of the map*

How It Works

When working with EDI maps, you will invariably encounter challenges that are difficult (or impossible) to solve with functoids. You will need to learn (or brush up on) your XSLT skills and approach mapping issues creatively. Using external XSLT is great for many activities, but for not all. Database lookups, callouts to .NET assemblies, and other similar processes are not possible. In many cases, more than a single map may be needed to successfully map a complex EDI document.

Testing maps with external XSLT documents is quite simple. Use the standard mapper functionality to test a map by defining the input document and other properties (see Figure 8-6). Note that it is very useful to *not* validate the inbound and outbound documents during development—make sure and set the Validate TestMap Input and Validate TestMap Output properties to False. Once you're ready, right-click the map file in Visual Studio, and select the Test Map option.

TestMap Input	Native
TestMap Input Instance	ɔps\pCNI10282009010021.837.txt ...
TestMap Output	XML
TestMap Output Instance	
Type Name	X12_00401_837_I_To_ClaimsIB_ECS
Validate TestMap Input	False
Validate TestMap Output	False

Figure 8-6. *Properties used for testing the map*

8-4. Creating and Configuring a Trading Partner

Problem

You are ready to begin trading EDI documents with an external trading partner. You need to configure this party's information in BizTalk in order to route documents properly.

Solution

Setting up and configuring a trading partner consists of several key elements: a BizTalk party, one or more business profiles on that party, and one or more agreements associated with that business profile. To make sense of this, think of the party as an organization, such as a supermarket chain. This supermarket chain may consist of one or more divisions, for example, North American and South American headquarters. These divisions are business profiles. Each division has individual agreements with vendors and suppliers, and trades EDI documents with each, which are configured as agreements on each business profile.

■ **Note** In many cases, you may have a single business profile with a single agreement for each party you configure.

To configure each of these components, take the following steps:

1. Create a new BizTalk party that represents the sender by clicking the Parties folder in the BizTalk Administration console. Right-click the white area in Parties and Business Profiles window, and select New ➤ Party (see Figure 8-7). Give the party a logical name.

Figure 8-7. *Creating a new party*

2. To create a Business Profile, right-click the party you just created, and select New ➤ Business Profile. Give the business profile a descriptive name, and then click the Identities tab. Configure the identities based on the information you have for this trading partner (see Figure 8-8).

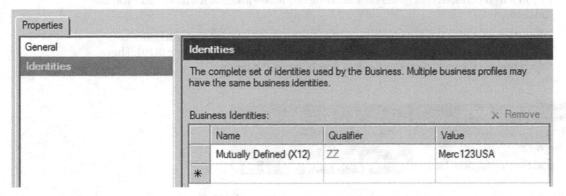

Figure 8-8. *Setting a business profile's identities*

3. Once the business profile has been created, you can set up an agreement, which is where the real heart of EDI configuration sits. Right-click the business profile you just created, and select Agreement. The Agreement Properties window will open (see Figure 8-9).

Figure 8-9. *The Agreement Properties window*

4. Give the agreement a descriptive name, and then set the key properties identifying what this agreement represents; also supply the Protocol and the Second Party settings. Protocol can be set to X12. The Second Party settings need to be set to a second BizTalk party (if you haven't created one, go ahead and create one now—just give it a name, and you are finished).

5. Once Party and Business have been set in the Second Party settings, you will notice two additional tabs appear within the Agreement Properties window (see Figure 8-10). These tabs represent the configurations for data flow between the parties.

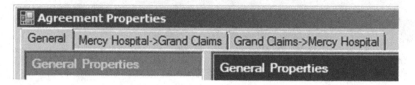

Figure 8-10. *Two new tabs appear once the Second Party properties are defined*

How It Works

The organization of parties, business profiles, and agreements allows for the configuration of any kind of document interchange between trading partners. Previous versions of BizTalk did not allow for the kind of flexibility and functionality that BizTalk 2010 and BizTalk 2013 provide. The entire trading partner management user interface is entirely new and is packed with features that ease setup, configuration, and maintenance.

■ **Note**   There is no direct migration path of EDI trading partners between BizTalk 2010/2013 and previous versions of BizTalk. The hierarchy and architecture is completely different, so a manual migration will be necessary.

8-5. Configuring an EDI Envelope
Problem

You need to configure BizTalk to populate the header and footer segments in outbound documents.

Solution

Sending an EDI document from BizTalk requires more configuration than a standard XML or flat file document. In addition to the standard adapter and port setup, and mapping, you also have to configure a BizTalk party and set up an agreement and related artifacts. Before we look at the steps involved in configuring an EDI envelope, let's look at what the envelope is. Listing 8-1 shows the document envelope of an 837 Professional file.

Listing 8-1. 837 Professional Envelope

```
ISA*00* *00* *ZZ*PROF123 *ZZ*Merc123USA *091028*1300*U*00401*000000701*0*P*<~

GS*HC* PROF123* Merc123USA *20091028*1300*701*X*004010X098A1~
ST*837*0001

[BODY CONTENT]

SE*32*0001~
GE*1*701~
IEA*1*000000701~
```

The envelope identifies a number of things about the document, most importantly, who the receiver and sender are. These values are stored in the sixth and eight positions of the ISA segment (ISA06 and ISA08). In the instance shown in Listing 8-1, these values are PROF123 (the sender identifier) and Merc123USA (the receiver identifier).

To set this up, take the following steps. This solution assumes that parties, a business profile, and an agreement have already been configured.

1. Open an agreement, and click one of the two tabs allowing for configuration of interchange information.

2. Click the Identifiers tab, and set the ISA properties as required (see Figure 8-11).

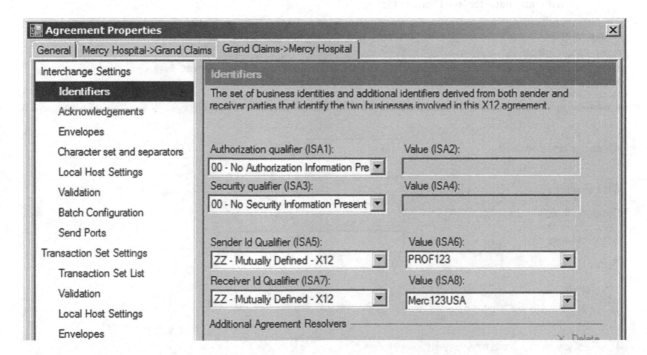

Figure 8-11. *Setting ISA properties on an Agreement*

3. Click the Envelopes tab, and set the identifiers, version, and usage ISA properties (ISA11, ISA12, and ISA15), as shown in Figure 8-12.

Envelopes

Interchange envelope settings derived from the sender party's profile .The derived settings can be customized within this agreement.These settings are not needed, if this BizTalk system is not used to send messages by the sender party.

ISA11 usage

○ Standard identifier: | U - U.S. EDI Community of ASC X12, TDCC an ▼ |

○ Repetition separator:

Control version number (ISA12): | 00401 - Standards Approved for Publication by ▼ |

Usage indicator (ISA15): | Test Data ▼ |

Figure 8-12. The ISA12, ISA13, and ISA15 properties

4. Click the Character set and separators tab. The character sets and separators define how an envelope (and the entire body of the document) is laid out. For example, setting the "Data element" field to an asterisk (*) ensures that each element of a segment is separated with this character (see Figure 8-13).

Character set and separators

Character Set and Separator settings derived from the sender party's profile. These derived settings can be customized within this agreement. The sender party's send pipeline uses these settings.

Character set to be used : | UTF8 ▼ |

Data element: | * | | Char ▼ |

Component element separator (ISA16): | : | | Char ▼ |

Segment terminator: | ~ | | Char ▼ |

Suffix:

● None   ○ CR

○ LF   ○ CR LF

☐ Replace separators in payload with: | $ | | Char ▼ |

Figure 8-13. Setting the properties that define the document structure

5. Once all of the properties have been configured as desired, click the OK button. Properties can be changed at any time and will immediately take effect.

How It Works

A large number of properties can be set on an agreement. Often, these properties will be common to all trading partners that you will do business with. Once you have worked through the configuration of a few agreements, you may decide that you don't want to set these up from scratch each time. If you have a configuration that is common, and you want to use as a starting point for other trading partners, simply export the settings as a template by clicking the Save As Template button at the bottom of the Agreement Properties window (see Figure 8-14). This template can be loaded and used when configuring future agreements.

Figure 8-14. *Saving settings as a reusable template*

8-6. Configuring Automatic Acknowledgements

Problem

You want to automatically send a 997 acknowledgement when an inbound EDI document has been received by BizTalk.

Solution

Configuring acknowledgements to trigger automatically is very straightforward. There are a number of options available on an agreement. Simply open an agreement, and click the Acknowledgements tab in the Interchange settings. Figure 8-15 shows a sample configuration.

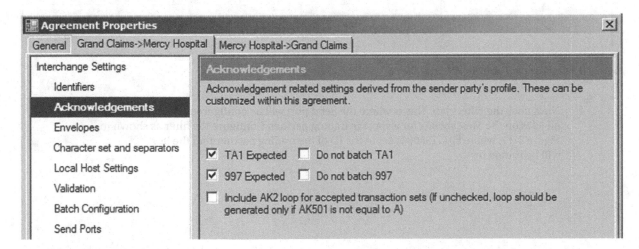

Figure 8-15. *Configuring acknowledgements*

How It Works

When BizTalk creates the acknowledgement, it drops it as a message on the MessageBox and treats it exactly like any other message. The only difference between an acknowledgement and other document types is that it is automatically generated by BizTalk. To configure the routing of a 997 to a file drop, take the following steps:

1. Create a new Send Port.

2. Set the Transport Type to FILE, and configure it to write to an appropriate folder.

3. Set the "Send pipelin"e field to EdiSend, as shown in Figure 8-16.

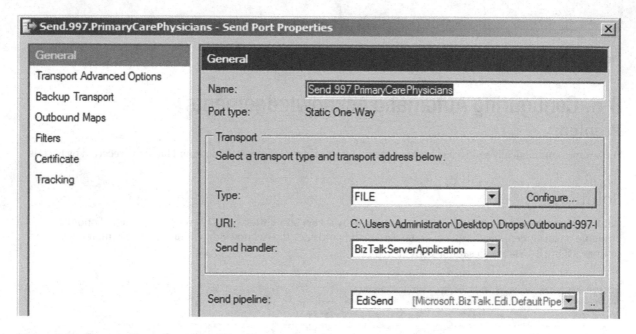

Figure 8-16. *Base configuration of Send Port*

4. Now, click the Filters tab. This is where the Send port will be configured to subscribe to all 997s on the MessageBox for a specific trading partner. Configure the filter as shown in Figure 8-17, where EDI.ISA06 is set to the ID of the trading partner that the 997 will be routed to.

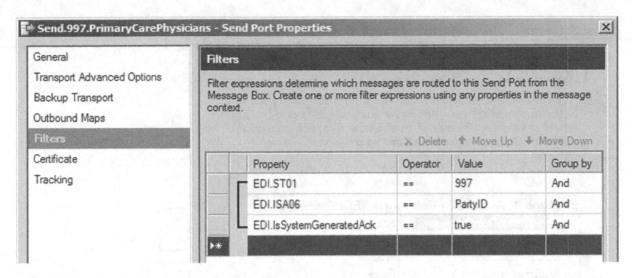

Figure 8-17. *Configuring the filter to subscribe to 997s for a specific party*

■ **Note**   You will need to configure one send port for each trading partner that will be receiving a 997 (for request/response ports, such as AS2 over HTTP, the 997 would be configured on the outbound response).

8-7. Configuring EDI Validation with Pipelines
Problem

You need to send and receive documents using the EDI pipelines to ensure that EDI validation takes place and that the envelopes of the documents are created correctly.

Solution

There are two primary steps in using the EDI pipelines. The first is to select the appropriate pipeline on the port that is being used. When you are sending documents, the port should be configured with the EdiSend pipeline. When you're receiving documents, it should have the EdiReceive pipeline. These pipelines have a number of configuration settings on them. Figure 8-18 shows the configurable properties of the EdiSend pipeline.

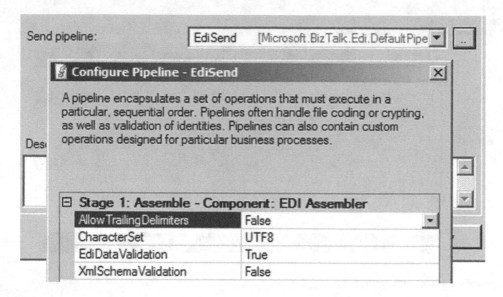

Figure 8-18. *Configuring the EdiSend pipeline*

■ **Note** There is a property on EDI pipelines named EdiDataValidation. While setting this to False would seem to cause EDI validation to be turned off, it doesn't always work that way. Make sure to test this functionality before you decide to use it. You schema and configuration may impact whether this setting has any effect or not.

How It Works

The pipelines perform validation, party resolution, envelope interpretation and creation and cause acknowledgements to be automatically created. The flow of the pipelines is as follows:

1. EDIReceive pipeline

   a. Examine the document type. This step interrogates the document to determine if X12 or EDIFACT and what the character set is. Properties are promoted on the document at this point (for routing purposes).

   b. Resolve parties. This step determines which party in BizTalk the document is intended for.

   c. Resolve and validate schemas. The document is validated against the schemas that have been deployed.

   d. Create an acknowledgement (if doing so is configured in the agreement).

2. EDISend pipeline

   a. Resolve parties, and match the context. When a document is sent, the envelope is attached in the pipeline. All of the settings for the envelope are determined at this stage.

   b. Resolve and validate schemas. The document is validated against the schema. If the document fails validation, it will be suspended.

8-8. Creating Custom EDI Pipelines

Problem

You want to add decryption as a stage in your processing of inbound EDI documents. The standard EdiReceive pipeline does not support this, and you need to create a custom pipeline.

Solution

This solution does not provide the code for the decryption custom pipeline component, but it does show how to reference a custom pipeline component and the EDI pipeline components to create a custom pipeline.

1. In your Visual Studio project, add a new pipeline by right-clicking the project, and selecting Add ➤ New Item. Select the Receive Pipeline template, and give it an appropriate name.

2. The Decode stage is where you will want to do the decryption. An inbound file must be decrypted before it can be run through the EDI components. Drag the decryption custom pipeline component from the Visual Studio toolbox to the Decode stage of the pipeline. Figure 8-19 shows the Decode stage with both a decryption and an archiving component.

Figure 8-19. *The Decode stage of a custom pipeline*

3. Next, drag and drop the EDI disassembler component onto the Disassemble stage of the pipeline, as shown in Figure 8-20.

Figure 8-20. *The Disassemble stage*

459

4. Set the EDI disassembler properties to the default values that you want. Note that these can all be overridden once the pipeline has been deployed, so these are just being set for the defaults. This can be done by right-clicking the EDI disassembler and selecting Properties. The properties are shown in Figure 8-21.

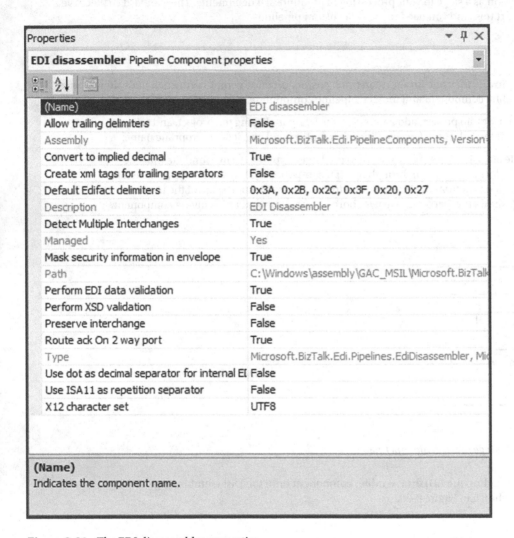

Figure 8-21. *The EDI disassembler properties*

How It Works

Creating custom pipelines is fairly easy; creating custom pipeline components is not. In this case, you want to create both a custom pipeline component (for decryption) and a custom pipeline (to house this custom component and to execute the standard EDI disassembly that occurs). Once the pipeline is fully configured and built, it can be deployed just like any other BizTalk artifact. The easiest thing to do is to right-click the BizTalk application where you want to deploy it and select Add ➤ BizTalk Assemblies (as shown in Figure 8-22).

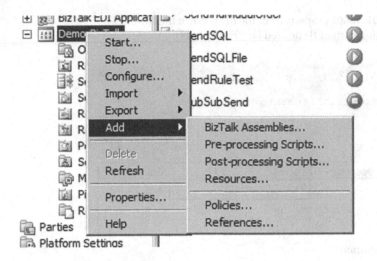

Figure 8-22. *Deploying the pipeline*

8-9. Subscribing to EDI Promoted Properties

Problem

You are receiving a large number of EDI documents from many different trading partners. You have an orchestration that you want to configure to subscribe to only EDI documents from a specific trading partner.

Solution

To filter what values are picked up by the orchestration, take these steps:

1. Right-click the initial Receive shape of the orchestration, and select Edit Filter Expression (shown in Figure 8-23). This receive shape should be subscribing to an EDI schema type. If it is not, no EDI properties will be promoted.

Figure 8-23. *Editing the filter on the Receive shape*

2. In the filter that opens, select the EDI.ISA06 property from the drop-down menu, and configure it to subscribe to the trading partner ID desired (see Figure 8-24).

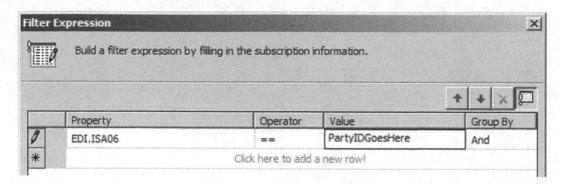

Figure 8-24. *Configuring the filter on the orchestration*

How it Works

A large number of EDI properties are promoted on a document. Among these are properties that pertain to the envelope. In this case, the orchestration needs to subscribe to the ISA06 property, which indicates the trading partner ID that is sending the document. There are many other fields available, some of which are shown in Figure 8-25.

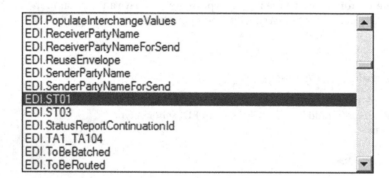

Figure 8-25. *Some additional EDI properties*

This solution showed how to configure an orchestration, but a send port can also be configured to subscribe to promoted EDI properties. To do this, open the send port, and click on the Filters tab, as shown in Figure 8-26.

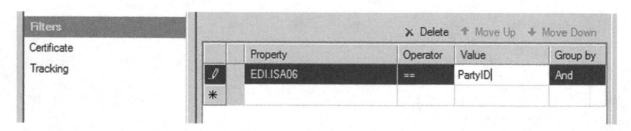

Figure 8-26. *Configuring the filter on a send port*

CHAPTER 9

Deployment

At the core of every BizTalk project is the necessity to deploy an integration project to the BizTalk execution environment. Given the complexity of the product, and the rich features it provides, this task has often been difficult and time-consuming. Every experienced BizTalk developer understands the time requirements to deploy, enlist, and start BizTalk artifacts, keeping in mind dependencies and ordering the steps accordingly. BizTalk has great functionality for this, so that a minimum of time is spent deploying solutions, and more time is available to develop new return-on-investment-producing solutions.

This chapter provides recipes for exporting and importing applications. It also covers how to start an application and begin processing within the BizTalk execution environment.

9-1. Exporting Applications
Problem

You have completed the build phase of a BizTalk project and need to migrate your work from the development environment to the test environment.

Solution

You must export the BizTalk application you have been building for use in the new environment. The BizTalk Administration Console provides the capability to export and import artifacts. Combined with the use of BizTalk applications, this allows for a simplified method of packaging your solutions and deploying them to new environments. The following steps outline the process for exporting a BizTalk application.

1. Open the BizTalk Administration Console.

2. In the left pane, navigate through BizTalk Server Administration to your BizTalk group, and expand the `Applications` folder.

3. Right-click the application you wish to export and select Export ➤ MSI File, as shown in Figure 9-1. This launches the Export MSI File Wizard.

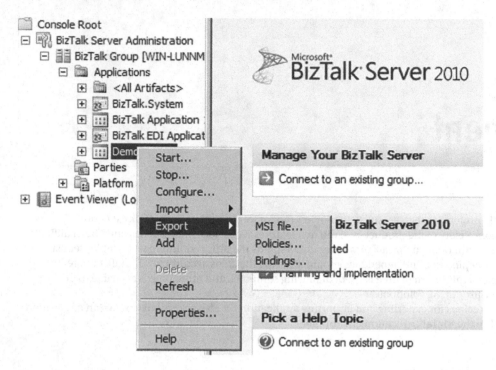

Figure 9-1. *Choosing to export an application*

4. Click Next on the Welcome page of the wizard.

5. On the Select Resources page, verify that the resources you need to include in the exported MSI package are selected. In the example shown in Figure 9-2, the resources consist of a number of BizTalk assemblies and their bindings and a referenced .NET assembly. Click Next to proceed.

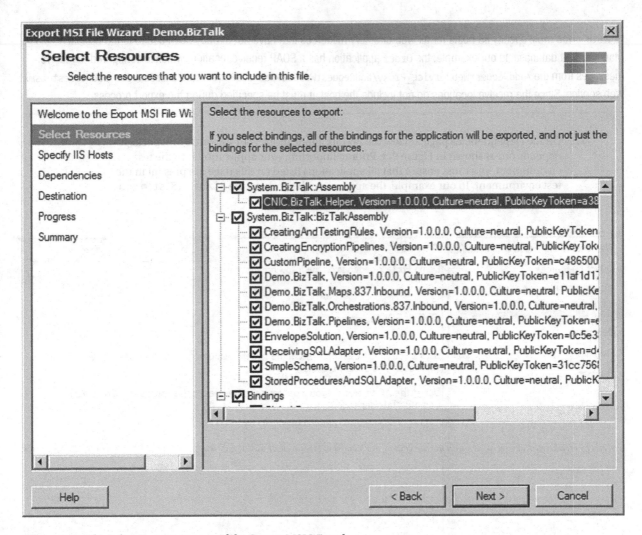

Figure 9-2. *The Select Resources page of the Export MSI Wizard*

■ **Note** Including bindings within your MSI package will automatically overwrite any existing bindings in the target application upon import. Exclude the bindings during the export process if you do not want to overwrite the bindings in your target application.

---

6. On the Specify IIS Hosts page, select the virtual directories you need to include in the exported MSI package. Click Next.

■ **Note** You must specify IIS hosts for all web directory resources that have not already been added to the BizTalk Management database. In our example, the `Order` application has a SOAP receive location, which is configured to receive messages from the `/addRequestWebService_Proxy/addRequestWebService_addRequestSPMLWebService_addRequest.asmx` web service. Since the receive locations do not include the host, it must be specified during the export process.

---

7. On the Dependencies page, review the BizTalk applications your exported MSI package depends on, as shown in Figure 9-3. Prior to importing your application into the test environment, you must ensure that all applications listed on this page are present in the test environment. In our example, the application depends on the `BizTalk.System` and `BizTalk EDI` applications. Click Next to proceed.

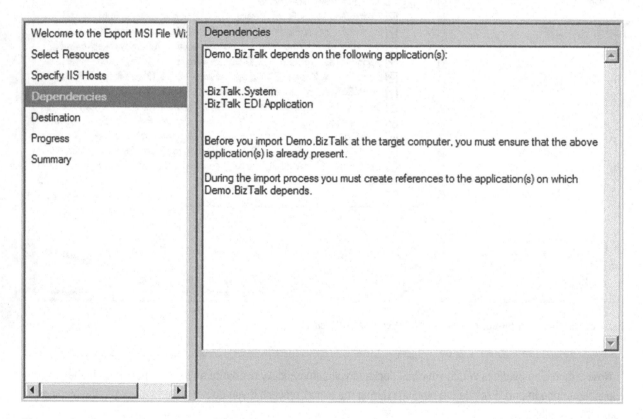

Figure 9-3. *The Dependencies page of the Export MSI Wizard*

8. On the Destination page, specify the destination application name (which indicates what the application will be named in the test environment after you have imported it) and the MSI package output location and file name, as shown in Figure 9-4. In our example, the application will be named the same as it was in the development environment (`Demo.BizTalk`) and the MSI package will be written out to a folder on the C drive.

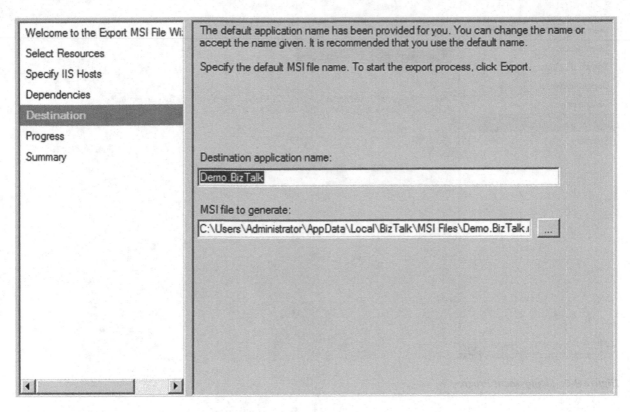

Figure 9-4. *The Destination page of the Export MSI Wizard*

9. Click Export to generate the MSI package.

10. The wizard displays the progress of the export operation and then shows a progress and summary screen when it has completed, as shown in Figures 9-5 and 9-6. The summary includes a list of steps necessary to import the application into a new environment, along with a link to the log file of the export operation. Click Finish to close the wizard.

Figure 9-5. *Deployment Progress*

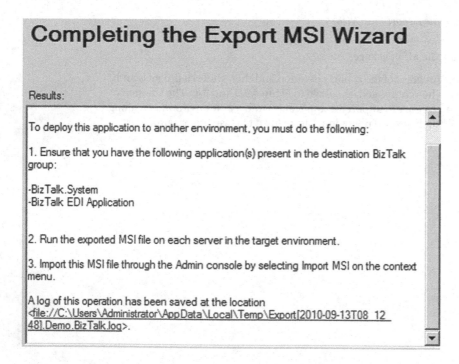

Figure 9-6. *The Summary page of the Export MSI Wizard*

How It Works

While exporting applications is an easy way to migrate solution artifacts between environments, it is important to note what is not included in exported MSI packages. Configuration values you have made in the BTSNTSvc.exe.config file are not exported. If one of your artifacts relies on a custom configuration value existing in this file, you must use another mechanism (manual or otherwise) to add that same configuration value to the target environment.

■ **Note** In general, only those artifacts that are specific to an application are exported. This means that BizTalk group configurations (performance values or adapter settings, for example) and Business Activity Monitor (BAM) artifacts are not included in the exported MSI package.

You should be careful with regard to security when exporting applications. Depending on your solution, your MSI package may contain sensitive information (such as passwords) and should be appropriately secured. One consideration is the use of passwords in port bindings. Passwords are removed from all bindings that you export directly from an application (as we did in our example). If you want to persist passwords in a binding file, you must create a binding file with the passwords in it and then add the binding file to the application as a file resource.

You should also pay attention to access rights on resources added to your application. All permissions on files and folders are removed during the export process. For web directory resources, the security settings in place at the time of export are written to the MSI package.

In addition to using the Export MSI File Wizard, you can access the same functionality via the BTSTask ExportApp command-line utility. This utility accepts the following parameters, which mimic the steps taken in the wizard:

- ApplicationName: The name of the BizTalk application to export

- Package: Path and file name of the MSI package to export

- ResourceSpec: Path and file name of the resource specification XML file

- Server: SQL Server hosting the BizTalk Management database housing the application to export

- Database: Name of the BizTalk Management database

In our recipe's example, the exported application includes relatively few artifacts—just several BizTalk assemblies, their bindings, and a required .NET assembly. Using the Export MSI File Wizard is simple and straightforward. It produces a single file that can be used to import the application into the test environment. On a larger project, it is likely that your application will have many more artifacts, including BizTalk assemblies, bindings, policies, and folder structures such as virtual directories and input/output folder hierarchies. Additionally, you might need to migrate only a subset of an application to a new environment. Using the BizTalk Administration Console, you can export application subsets, bindings, and policies.

Exporting Application Subsets

Exporting applications allows for all artifacts (or a subset of artifacts) associated with an application to be exported into an MSI package. All of the artifacts you select during the export process will be packaged into a single MSI file, which you can use to install your application to a different BizTalk environment.

In addition to exporting an entire application, you can use the Select Resources page to specify a subset of artifacts to export. Let's extend the solution one step further in the project life cycle to see how this functionality might be useful. Suppose that after testing the Order application in the test environment, you find and fix an error in the

Troubleshooting assembly. To apply your fix to the test environment, you need to export only the modified artifacts. Step through the Export MSI File Wizard a second time, and select only the Troubleshooting assembly on the Select Resources page. This produces an MSI package that includes only the selected assembly, which can be used to reimport the modified artifact in the test environment.

■ **Note**   Make sure that the assembly keeps the same strong name key and namespace on redeployment; otherwise, the .NET environment will consider the assembly a new component.

Exporting Bindings

Exporting bindings allows for bindings associated with an application to be exported into an XML file. Bindings are the links between your physical environment (for example, a specific MSMQ queue or web service URI) and your logical environment (for example, an orchestration receive port). You can export bindings for an entire BizTalk group or a specific BizTalk application or assembly.

You can use either the Export Bindings Wizard (right-click the appropriate application in the BizTalk Administration Console and select Export ➤ Bindings) or the BTSTask ExportBindings command-line utility to export bindings.

Exporting Policies

Exporting policies allows for Business Rule Engine policies associated with a BizTalk group (all policies in your BizTalk environment's Business Rule Engine database) or application to be exported into an XML file. Take the following steps to export policies for your BizTalk application:

1. Right-click the appropriate application in the BizTalk Administration Console and select Export ➤ Policies. This launches the Export Policies Wizard.

2. Select the policies and vocabularies you need to export, and specify a path and file name for the exported policy XML file, as shown in Figure 9-7.

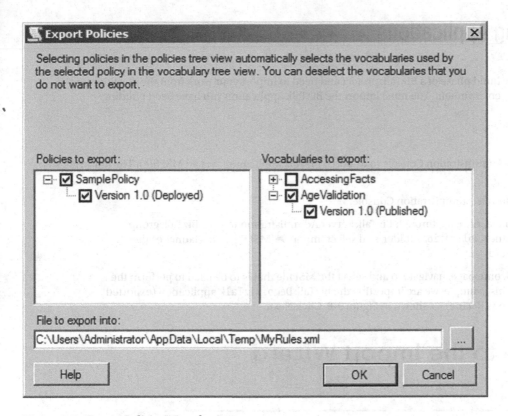

Figure 9-7. *Export Policies Wizard*

3. Click OK to export the policies.

It is recommended that you include all vocabularies contained in the policies you export. This prevents any missing vocabulary issues that can arise when one vocabulary references another.

In addition to using the Export Policies Wizard, you can export bindings using the BTSTask ListApp and ExportApp command-line utilities in combination, as follows:

1. Run the ListApp utility to create an XML file containing all artifacts for the BizTalk group or application for which you need to export policies. An example of using the List App utility is as follows:

```
BTSTask ListApp /ApplicationName:SampleApp /ResourceSpec:C:\SampleOutput.xml
```

2. Delete all artifacts from the XML file except the policies.

3. Run the ExportApp utility, specifying the updated XML file for the ResourceSpec parameter.

9-2. Importing Applications

Problem

You have completed the build phase of a BizTalk project and need to import your work from the development environment to another environment. You must import the BizTalk application you have been building.

Solution

You can use the BizTalk Administration Console to import a BizTalk application (via an MSI file). The following steps outline the procedure:

1. Open the BizTalk Administration Console.

2. In the left pane, navigate through BizTalk Server Administration to your BizTalk group. Right-click the Applications folder, and select Import ➤ MSI File. This launches the Import Wizard.

3. On the Welcome page, navigate to and select the MSI file that is to be used to perform the import. In this example, we are importing the BizTalk Demo.BizTalk application (exported in the previous Recipe), as shown in Figure 9-8. Click Next.

Figure 9-8. *Starting the Import Wizard*

4. On the Application Settings page, verify the settings for your application, references, and resources, as shown in Figure 9-9. In the list of applications available for reference, specify any references your target application has to existing BizTalk application assemblies and artifacts. You can also specify a new application (labeled during the export) or associate with an existing application within your BizTalk Management database. Click Next to continue.

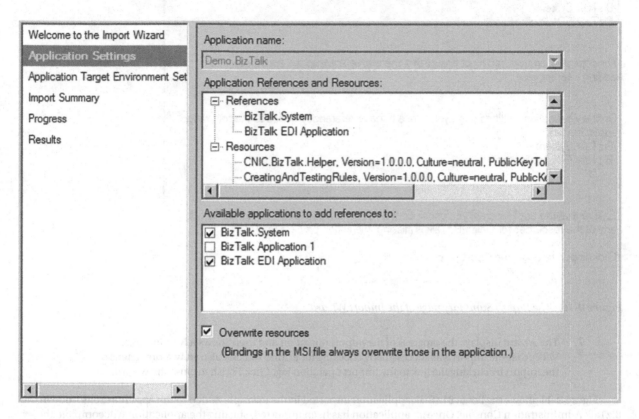

Figure 9-9. *The Application Settings page of the Import Wizard*

5. On the Application Target Environment Settings page, in the Target Staging Environment drop-down list, select the environment to which the application is to be deployed. This option allows for environment specific considerations. You can partition applications that have been imported with binding specific settings. By specifying an environment value at this stage, the Import Wizard will apply only to the environment specific configuration identified during the import process. If you leave the value set to <Default>, the configuration will be applied to all environments.

6. On the Import Summary page, verify the application import information presented, as shown in Figure 9-10. Click Import when you're ready to complete the import process.

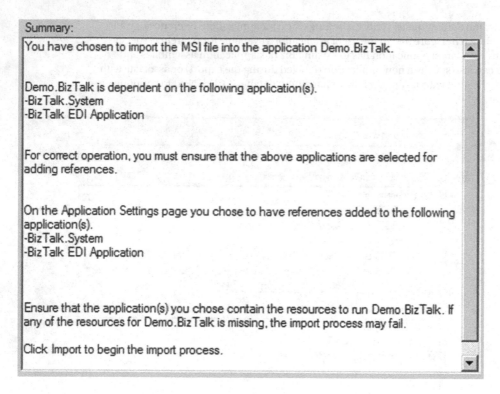

Summary:

You have chosen to import the MSI file into the application Demo.BizTalk.

Demo.BizTalk is dependent on the following application(s).
-BizTalk.System
-BizTalk EDI Application

For correct operation, you must ensure that the above applications are selected for adding references.

On the Application Settings page you chose to have references added to the following application(s).
-BizTalk.System
-BizTalk EDI Application

Ensure that the application(s) you chose contain the resources to run Demo.BizTalk. If any of the resources for Demo.BizTalk is missing, the import process may fail.

Click Import to begin the import process.

***Figure 9-10.** The Import Summary page of the Import Wizard*

7. The wizard displays the progress of the import operation and then shows a Results page. Verify that the import was successful by checking for errors. You can also view more details of the import by clicking the link to the import operation log. Click Finish to close the wizard.

Figure 9-11 shows the Demo.BizTalk application imported in the example added to the Applications node in the BizTalk Administration Console. Once an application has been imported, starting the application will complete the necessary deployment steps.

Applications

Name	Status	Description
<All Artifacts>		All artifacts within this BizTalk ...
BizTalk.System	Not Applicable	System Application
BizTalk Application 1	Stopped	BizTalk Application 1
BizTalk EDI Application	Started	
Demo.BizTalk	Stopped	

***Figure 9-11.** Demo.BizTalk application after import*

How It Works

The import process controls the sequence of shutting down services and provides the administrator with input to control and consider application references and dependencies. In addition, it controls the registering of BizTalk and .NET application artifacts into the Global Assembly Cache (GAC). This eliminates the need for IT users to know the sequence of specific BizTalk deployment steps and perform them manually, leading to faster and easier application deployment cycles.

In this recipe's example, we imported an MSI file, which contains application artifacts. You can also import policies (business rules artifacts) and bindings. Binding information examples could include an address (such as a file or queue location) port information, or specific properties that specify retries, security options, and so on. You could import bindings when the BizTalk solution artifacts already exist and the target requires only binding input/updates for deployment.

■ **Note** Importing an MSI file can include both bindings and policies. If these artifacts are specified in the application export process, they will be imported as part of the MSI file import process.

In addition to using the Import MSI File Wizard, you can access the same functionality via the BTSTask ImportApp command-line utility. This option could be useful when performing regular environment promotion activities, fully automated deployments, and so on.

■ **Note** BTSTask commands should not be used in a preprocessing or postprocessing script run during an application import. If this is done, any changes made during the import will not be visible to the scripts; therefore, the success of the deployment cannot be guaranteed.

The command has the following form:

```
BTSTask ImportApp /Package:value [/Environment:value]     [/ApplicationName:value]
[/Overwrite] [/Server:value] [/Database:value]
```

■ **Note** There are options on BTSTask that allow for the deployment of the assembly to the GAC.

When importing BizTalk applications, consider the following:

- *Overwrites*: Determine whether the import process should support overwrites. On the Application Settings page of the Import Wizard, you can set generic overwrites of BizTalk artifacts. If this check box is selected, existing artifacts will be overwritten on the target import. If this box isn't selected and a duplicate is found, the Import Wizard will raise an error.

- *Downstream components*: Keep in mind downstream components, such as URIs, files, queues, and HTTP URLs. For example, if your solution uses send port URIs, make sure that the URIs exist before running your BizTalk operation. If a location doesn't exist (for example, a receive location), BizTalk may detect this, raise an error to the Windows Event Viewer, and show the application status as partially started. Whenever an application is in the status of partially started, it's a good idea to check the application Windows Event Viewer for failures and information.

- *Runtime/operational considerations*: When deploying to an existing environment, keep in mind runtime considerations. Make sure that users have been notified and usages of running BizTalk processes are known.

- *Security*: By default, BizTalk does not store passwords for binding information unless they are explicitly referenced within the binding file build process. As a matter of caution, always verify your deployment, and update passwords and access rights appropriately within your BizTalk artifacts.

9-3. Manually Deploying Updates

Problem

You have a complex solution deployed with many orchestrations and other components. You want to deploy an update to one orchestration.

Solution

Deploying BizTalk solutions using an MSI file is great for the initial deployment but is of limited value once a solution is running in production and an update needs to be deployed. Manual deployment give the administrator 100% control over what is being deployed where, and chances for errors from incorrectly created MSIs are reduced to zero.

Manual deployment can best be summed up as follows:

1. Unenlist any orchestrations that will be redeployed. This can be done from the BizTalk Administration Console. If any orchestrations have running instances in memory, two options are available: 1) wait until these instances have completed before doing the update, or 2) terminate these instances (terminating instances can be done from the BizTalk Group Hub reports and administrative functionality).

2. Removed any maps and schemas that will be re-deployed. This can be done from the BizTalk Administration Console by right-clicking the maps/schemas (see Figure 9-12).

Figure 9-12. *Removing maps manually*

3. Once all objects that will be redeployed have been removed, right-click the BizTalk application you are applying the updates to, and select Add ➤ BizTalk Assemblies.

4. In the Add Resources dialogue box that opens, add the assemblies that you wish to redeploy, as shown in Figure 9-13.

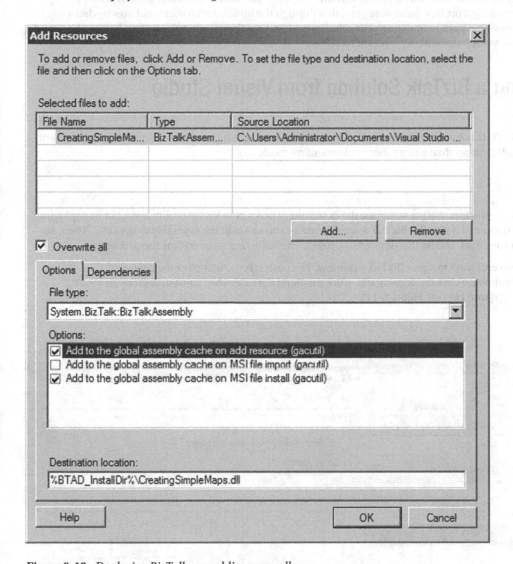

Figure 9-13. *Deploying BizTalk assemblies manually*

5. Click the "Overwrite all" check box to ensure that this overwrites the previous version of the assemblies. This will have to be done for every assembly in the list, so make sure to click each of them separately and click this "Overwrite all" option.

6. Make sure that the assemblies are added to the global assembly cache. This generally means clicking the first and third check boxes in the "Options" area of the dialogue box.

7. Click OK to deploy the BizTalk assemblies.

How It Works

Doing manual deployments will become one of the most common techniques you use once a solution has been successfully deployed to production. In fact, using the MSI deployment may not even be something you want to use at any point; manual deployments can be so much easier and less stressful, since you have complete control over everything.

When you are developing a project, make sure you think through the initial deployment and how updates will be deployed. Having an intelligent path to updating your solution prior to actual deployment is a great habit to have and one that will ease your development and deployment tasks.

9-4. Deploying a BizTalk Solution from Visual Studio
Problem

You have developed a BizTalk solution and wish to deploy the solution for testing in your development environment directly from Visual Studio, rather than using other deployment methods.

Solution

Since BizTalk projects compile into .NET assemblies, the deployment process in Visual Studio is similar to deploying other .NET projects. You must first sign the BizTalk assembly before you can add the assembly to the GAC. Then, set up the BizTalk project properties, and finally, deploy the project. The following steps outline the procedure.

1. There are several ways to sign a BizTalk assembly. The easiest is to right-click the project in Visual Studio and click the Signing tab. Click the "Sign the assembly" option, and create a new strong name key (see Figure 9-14).

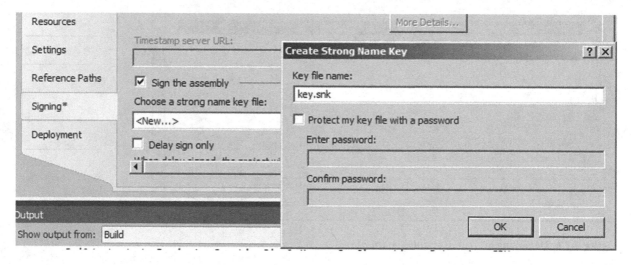

Figure 9-14. *Adding a strong name key to a project*

2. Next, click the Deployment tab.

3. Enter an application name for the project (this usually matches a BizTalk application that has already been created). Set other properties as desired (see Table 9-1). Figure 9-15 shows a project configured for deployment. Click OK to close the dialog box.

Table 9-1. *Visual Studio Deployment Properties*

Property	Description
Server	Defines the BizTalk deployment server. The local server name is the default setting for this property. If the project is shared across multiple development machines, set this value to localhost.
Configuration Database	Defines the name of the BizTalk configuration database. By default, and unless it was changed, the configuration database name will be BizTalkMgmtDb.
Application Name	Defines the application that will house this BizTalk project. Although leaving this property blank will cause the solution to deploy to the default application, it is a best practice to provide a value for this property.
Redeploy	Defines whether the deployment process will automatically delete the old deployed assembly before deploying the current assembly. This option is very useful, but should be used only within a development environment.
Install to Global Assembly Cache	Controls whether the assembly will be deployed to the GAC as part of the deployment process.
Restart Host Instances	Controls whether to restart the in-process host instance. By default, this property is False. Due to artifact caching during development, it is a best practice to change this setting to True to force the removal of artifacts from the cache. If this property is False, you may notice inconsistent behavior in your solutions, particularly during repeated deployments.

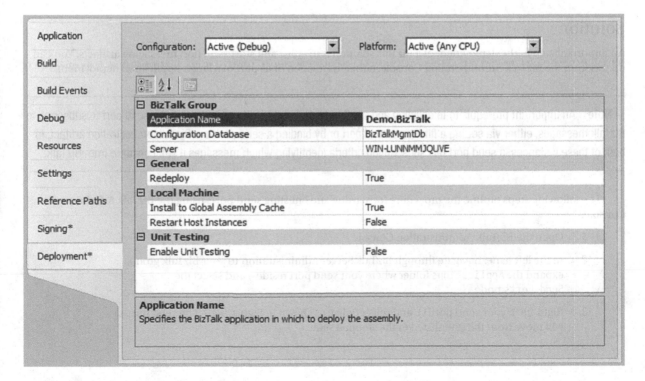

Figure 9-15. *Setting deployment properties*

■ **Note** The application name is not required, but it is a best practice to give all projects an application name to facilitate management of the project. If none is specified, the default BizTalk application will be deployed to.

---

4. Right-click the project or solution, and select Deploy.

5. Bind and start the artifacts.

Once you have bound an orchestration, the binding will be remembered the next time you deploy your project. In addition, if you have multiple projects within the solution, deploying from the solution will deploy all the projects within the solution.

How It Works

Deploying directly from Visual Studio is an alternative to exporting and importing BizTalk applications through the BizTalk Administration Console.

Within Visual Studio, several deployment properties are available, as described in Table 9-1.

9-5. Enlisting and Starting Send Ports
Problem

You have deployed a solution and need to validate that your send ports are enlisted and started.

Solution

An important step in the deployment of a BizTalk solution is to enlist and start send port messaging artifacts. You can do this from the BizTalk Administration Console, either in isolation or as part of a larger application deployment.

■ **Note** An important prerequisite to enlisting and starting a send port involves configuring the send port to subscribe to BizTalk messages, either via setting a filter on a send port or by binding a send port to a BizTalk orchestration artifact. In both of these instances, a send port has subscription criteria identifying which messages it will consume from BizTalk.

The following steps outline the procedure for starting and enlisting send ports using the BizTalk Administration Console.

1. Open the BizTalk Administration Console.

2. In the left pane, navigate through BizTalk Server Administration to your BizTalk group, expand the `Applications` folder where your send port resides, and select the `Send Ports` node.

3. Right-click your send port(s), and select Enlist, as shown in Figure 9-16. The send port(s) will move from the unenlisted to the stopped state.

Figure 9-16. *Enlisting send ports*

4. Right-click your send port(s) again, and select Start. Your send port(s) should now be started and enlisted.

How It Works

In this recipe's solution, we demonstrated how to enlist and start send ports via the BizTalk Administration Console. Enlisting and starting are two mutually exclusive states on a send port. Enlistment sets up the port and ensures that it is recognized and properly bound. Starting the port has it begin listening for the trigger that will cause it to execute. These are two logical mandatory steps to enable a BizTalk solution to be deployed.

■ **Note**   In this example, we demonstrated the explicit steps of enlisting and starting for demonstration purposes only. A send port can also be explicitly started from an unenlisted state.

Enlisting a port enables a subscription in the BizTalk MessageBox. If a send port is not enlisted, a message published to the MessageBox will not be subscribed to by the send port. If a subscriber is not found (the message had only the send port as the intended subscriber), a BizTalk error would be thrown, indicating that a matching subscription could not be found, and the message instance would be suspended but resumable in the MessageBox. (In previous versions of the product, this would have caused the message instance to be suspended but not resumable.)

If a message is published to the BizTalk MessageBox and a send port is not started, the message instance will sit in the MessageBox, waiting for the subscribing send port to be started. This situation is often hard to troubleshoot, as no error is thrown during the message submission process (an administrator would need to proactively look at what processes have been suspended using the Group Hub page).

In addition to administering send ports via the product tool set, BizTalk also has an object model available to allow programmatic administration via Windows Management Instrumentation (WMI). Send port administration is accessible via the base class `Microsoft.BizTalk.ExplorerOM.SendPort`. Within this class, a send port has a variety of methods available (for example, `ChangeSendPortStatus()`). Refer to the BizTalk product documentation for an inclusive list.

9-6. Enabling Receive Locations
Problem

You have deployed a solution and want to validate that your receive locations are enabled.

Solution

A receive location is the entry point into a receive port for pipeline processing and submission into the BizTalk MessageBox for subscribers and downstream processing. Receive ports can have multiple receive locations belonging to them. To allow messages to be received and consumed, you should enable a receive location.

■ **Note**   For a receive location to be enabled, make sure that the receive location has been associated with a receive handler and pipeline. The receive handler determines the security context (file access permissions) under which a receive location operates.

To enable a receive location, follow these steps:

1. Open the BizTalk Administration Console.

2. In the left pane, navigate through BizTalk Server Administration to your BizTalk group, expand the `Applications` folder where your receive location resides, and select the `Receive Locations` node.

3. Right-click your receive location, and select Enable, as shown in Figure 9-17.

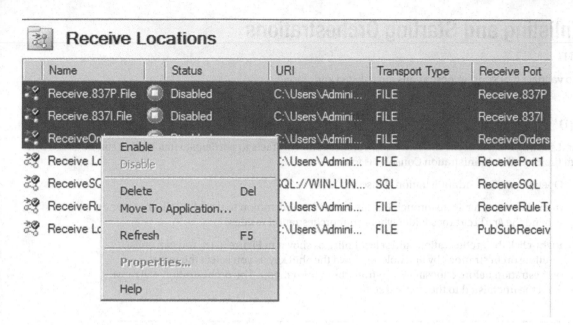

Figure 9-17. *Enabling a receive location*

■ **Note**   Multiple receive locations can be enabled by holding down the Shift key as you select the target receive locations. Then right-click and select Enable from the context menu.

How It Works

Enabling a receive location is an important deployment activity. If a receive location is not enabled, a message will reside in the physical adapter's transport receive location, and it will not be consumed by BizTalk. For example, the message could be a file in a folder for the file adapter or a message in an MSMQ queue for the MSMQ adapter.

A common problem when initially deploying and verifying receive locations is often security access and file permissions. When enabling a receive location, it is a good idea to check the Windows Event Viewer to ensure no errors are raised by BizTalk. Common errors with receive locations are often security related. Always check to ensure your receive location has been granted permission to the security credentials associated with the receive port's receive handler or the receive port itself.

■ **Note**   Once a receive location has been enabled, intermittent transport problems (for example, security or network access) will not disable the receive location. However, note that once a receive location is explicitly disabled, it must also be explicitly enabled to allow the receive location to function correctly.

9-7. Enlisting and Starting Orchestrations

Problem

You need to validate that your orchestrations are enlisted and started.

Solution

Enlisting and starting BizTalk orchestrations allows orchestration artifacts to participate in a BizTalk solution. You can do this from the BizTalk Administration Console, as follows:

1. Open the BizTalk Administration Console.

2. In the left pane, navigate through BizTalk Server Administration to your BizTalk group, and expand the Applications folder where your orchestration resides.

3. Right-click the orchestration, and select Enlist, as shown in Figure 9-18. You can enlist multiple orchestrations by first holding down the Shift key as you select the target orchestration before choosing Enlist from the context menu. The orchestration will move from the unenlisted to the stopped state.

Figure 9-18. *Enlisting an orchestration*

4. Right-click your orchestration again, and select Start. Your orchestration should now be enlisted, started, and ready for use.

How It Works

Enlisting and starting BizTalk orchestrations allows orchestrations to participate in BizTalk messaging and processing solutions. You can enlist and start orchestrations from either the BizTalk Administration Console or the Visual Studio environment. In this recipe's solution, we demonstrated using the BizTalk Administration Console.

Enlisting an orchestration is similar to enlisting a send port artifact. Enlisting an orchestration allows it to set up subscriptions with the MessageBox so it can receive messages published to it. In essence, enlisting holistically in the BizTalk product gives BizTalk artifacts (send ports and orchestrations) the ability to subscribe to the MessageBox for desired message contexts. Starting an orchestration allows an orchestration to physically consume and process a message.

Two important prerequisites to allow an orchestration to be started and enlisted are orchestration binding and host binding. Only orchestrations that have been bound can be enlisted; that is, an orchestration's port must be bound to a solution's physical send/receive port before enlisting. Unless an orchestration is a child orchestration or is directly bound to the message box, all ports must be bound to a physical host (see Figure 9-19 for a partially bound orchestration). If you attempt to enlist or start an orchestration when a host has not been bound, an error will occur, indicating that the enlisting has failed, as shown in Figure 9-20. In addition, an orchestration's configuration cannot be unbound when in an enlisted or started state.

Figure 9-19. *An unbound host*

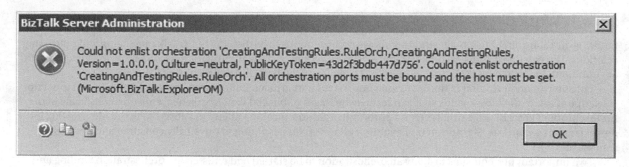

Figure 9-20. *Error trying to enlist an unbound orchestration*

It's also worth noting that entire BizTalk applications can be started and stopped. This activity ensures that all BizTalk artifacts under an application are enlisted, started, enabled, and ready (depending on the artifact), without any knowledge required by the user. Figure 9-21 shows starting a BizTalk application.

Figure 9-21. *Starting an entire BizTalk application*

CHAPTER 10

■ ■ ■

Administration and Operations

Integration solutions play a key role in many organizations' technology offerings. While much time and effort are typically spent on the actual implementation of these solutions, administration and maintenance tasks are often treated as second-class citizens. This reality can have costly consequences, as downtime of integration points can have large financial impacts on businesses.

Administration becomes an even bigger role with the introduction of hybrid integrations (on-premise and cloud) in BizTalk Server 2013. These workflows can now span multiple enterprise environment boundaries and can be shared by mobile devices. The Azure Service Bus Portal is used to administrate the service bus entities (service bus queues, topics, and relays), while the on-premise BizTalk Administration Console is used to manage the artifacts and components that communicate with the Service Bus entities. To allow for this expanded administrative need, a number of enhancements have been built into BizTalk Server 2013.

The BizTalk Administration Console includes two pieces of key functionality: the Group Hub page and application views. The Group Hub page exposes information for a single BizTalk Server, providing a view into the health of the server and allowing for troubleshooting and triage of issues. Specifically, the Group Hub page provides the following:

- Queries for work-in-progress and suspended items (service instances and messages)

- The ability to perform bulk operations (terminate, suspend, or resume) on service instances

- The ability to build and save custom queries to return information on service instances and messages

- Troubleshooting of service instances and messages

- Debugging of orchestrations

The application views expose information for a single BizTalk Server application. An application is a logical grouping of BizTalk artifacts. By grouping artifacts, applications allow them to be managed as a single unit, as opposed to individual items. Applications can be started and stopped, which starts and stops all the underlying artifacts, such as orchestrations, receive locations, and send ports. When an application is started or stopped, the individual artifacts are started or stopped in the correct order, accounting for all interdependencies. Applications also facilitate a number of deployment-related tasks, such as importing and exporting.

This chapter focuses on the use of the administration tools within the BizTalk Administration Console and the Azure portal and outlines how to ensure a well-managed BizTalk environment and a streamlined troubleshooting process.

10-1. Troubleshooting Suspended Services

Problem

Your integration solution has encountered an error, and you must determine what caused the fault.

Solution

A variety of tools can be used for troubleshooting suspended instances. The BizTalk Administrator Console is the first place to look in helping to identify why errors occur in an integration solution and to determine the best way to fix them. Other tools include the Windows event log, SQL Server, and other external applications.

Often, the event log gives the first indication an error has occurred in BizTalk, especially during the development stages of an integration project. BizTalk Server writes errors to the application event log each time it suspends a service instance. The error event contains helpful information on when, why, and where the fault happened. You can view errors posted to the event log by BizTalk Server through the BizTalk Administrator Console, which includes the Event Viewer MMC snap-in.

Frequently, the event log will have enough information to determine what action needs to be taken to fix the error (server name not specified on the SMTP adapter, for example), but often, further troubleshooting is necessary. To obtain more detailed information about the fault, you can use the BizTalk Administrator Console's Group Hub page, which provides a number of ways to search for suspended service instances.

The following steps outline a procedure for troubleshooting a suspended service.

1. Open the BizTalk Administration Console.

2. Expand the Event Viewer folder in the left pane, click Windows Logs, and select Application. You should see an error event relating to the service instance that was suspended. This event is flagged with a BizTalk related source, such as BizTalk Server or XLANG/s. See Figure 10-1.

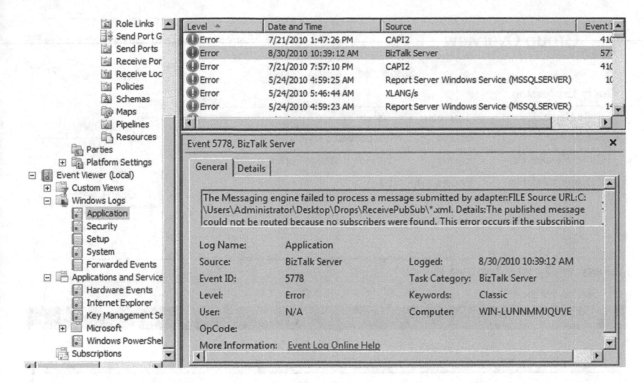

Figure 10-1. *The Application event log*

3. To obtain more detailed information about the event, expand the BizTalk Server Administration folder in the left pane, and select your BizTalk group. This opens the Group Hub page.

4. Click the Suspended service instances link in the Suspended Items section. Clicking this link launches a query window, as shown in Figure 10-2.

Figure 10-2. Suspended service instances query

■ **Note** The Group Hub page also provides filtered views of suspended service instances, including resumable service instances; nonresumable service instances; suspended MSMQT messages; and suspended service instances grouped by application, error code, service name, and URI. All queries are customizable.

---

5. Order the query results on the Creation Time column by clicking the column header. You can compare the creation date with the timestamp of the error event log entry to determine if they relate to one another.

6. Once you have found the appropriate suspended service instance in the query results list, double-click the row to launch the Service Details dialog box, as shown in Figure 10-3. The General tab of this dialog box includes high-level information regarding the suspended instance, including the BizTalk component that encountered the error, the service's status, and the instance ID. Knowing the particular component that encountered the error is a valuable and significant piece to the troubleshooting puzzle, as it assists in narrowing down where the fault occurred.

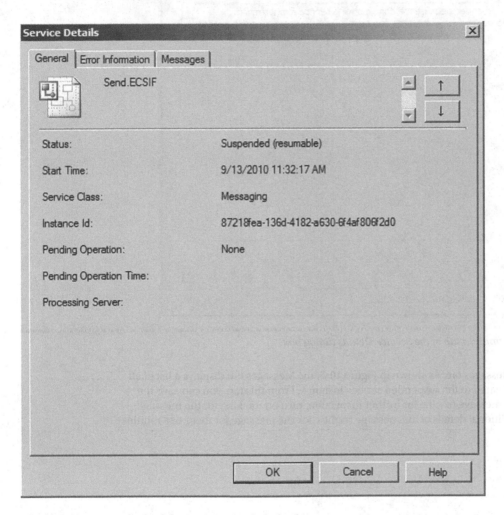

Figure 10-3. *General tab of the Service Details dialog box*

7. Click the Error Information tab. As shown in Figure 10-4, this tab displays the text of the exception that the suspended service instance encountered, which is the same as what is written to the application event log. The error text usually includes key stack information, indicating at what level the fault occurred and how it was bubbled up through BizTalk. In our example, the instance was suspended because the send port was stopped.

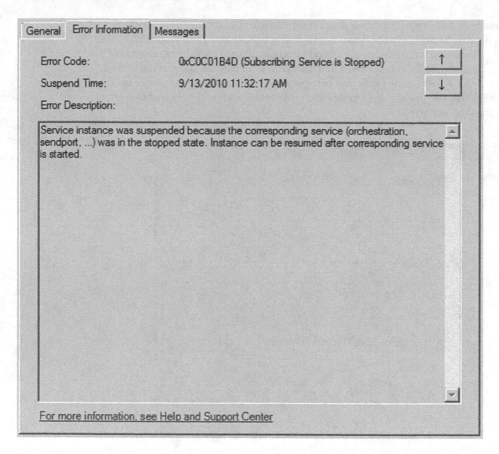

Figure 10-4. *Error Information tab of the Service Details dialog box*

8. Click the Messages tab. As shown in Figure 10-5, the Messages tab displays a list of all messages related to the suspended service instance. From this tab, you can save the suspended message to a file for further inspection, turn on tracking for the message, or view additional details of the message (right-click the message for these capabilities).

Figure 10-5. *Messages tab of the Service Details dialog box*

9. Double-click one of the messages, and select the Context section, as shown in Figure 10-6. This view displays the context of the suspended message, which can be especially helpful when troubleshooting. Particularly, it alerts you to what properties the message had when it was suspended and which were promoted.

General	Context			
Context	Name	Value	Type	Namespace
Message Parts	FileCreateDate	09132010	Promoted	http://CNIC.BizTalk.Sche...
part	FileDescription	412006324	Promoted	http://CNIC.BizTalk.Sche...
	RecordIdentifier	01	Promoted	http://CNIC.BizTalk.Sche...
	FileIdentifier	iCNI10212009060311.837...	Promoted	http://CNIC.BizTalk.Sche...
	FileSerialNumber		Promoted	http://CNIC.BizTalk.Sche...
	/*[local-name()='ECSIF_FF'...	iCNI10212009060311.837...	Not Promoted	http://schemas.microsoft.c...
	/*[local-name()='ECSIF_FF'...		Not Promoted	http://schemas.microsoft.c...
	/*[local-name()='ECSIF_FF'...	09132010	Not Promoted	http://schemas.microsoft.c...
	/*[local-name()='ECSIF_FF'...	412006324	Not Promoted	http://schemas.microsoft.c...
	/*[local-name()='ECSIF_FF'...	01	Not Promoted	http://schemas.microsoft.c...
	PartNames	System.String[]	Not Promoted	http://schemas.microsoft.c...
	PartyName		Not Promoted	http://schemas.microsoft.c...
	InterchangeID	{259E852C-CB83-4E08-92...	Not Promoted	http://schemas.microsoft.c...

Figure 10-6. *Context section of Message Details*

How It Works

When errors occur in your integration solutions, BizTalk typically suspends the service instance encountering the error. *Service* is a generic term used to describe an area of BizTalk processing, such as orchestration, messaging, or adapter. *Service instance* refers to a specific instance of the orchestration, messaging, or adapter component. The troubleshooting tools of BizTalk are primarily used by system/solution administrators and are not typically used (in a production environment) by developers or testers.

Finding the particular suspended service instance you are troubleshooting is the first step in solving the issue. In this recipe's solution, we compared the timing of event log errors and suspended services to find a specific instance.

This technique of timestamp comparison would not work well if you were troubleshooting a long-running service instance (in which case, the creation time of the instance and the time of the error may be significantly different). While our solution used a simple way of locating the suspended instance, more-advanced methods can be useful, especially in production, heavy-load, or long-running environments.

You can search for instances based on all sorts of information. To add additional filter criteria to the report, in the BizTalk Administration Console, take the following steps:

1. Click a new row in the Query Expression pane, under the Field Name column.

2. Add the desired column, as shown in Figure 10-7.

Figure 10-7. *Adding a column to the query results*

The BizTalk Administration Console also allows you to create your own queries to find suspended service instances. Click the New Query tab (shown in Figure 10-8) available in the BizTalk Group Hub Overview area. You can save and retrieve custom queries for future troubleshooting needs (a query can be saved by using the Save As button and storing the file for later retrieval).

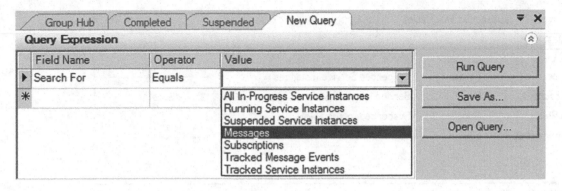

Figure 10-8. *BizTalk Administration Console Query Builder*

Once you have found your suspended service instance, the details that BizTalk Server tracks against the suspended instance provide a solid starting point for determining the best way to fix the issue. In general, you should use generic problem-solving skills when troubleshooting BizTalk errors: break down the problem into its component parts, and use the tools at your disposal to evaluate the fault using a bottom-up approach. Using the BizTalk Administrative Console allows you to break down complex solutions into manageable parts and troubleshoot the specific component encountering the error.

10-2. Resubmitting Messages
Problem

Your integration solution has encountered an error, and you need to resubmit the messages that have been affected by the fault.

Solution

The BizTalk Administrator Console allows you to resume service instances and resubmit their associated messages. You can locate the suspended service instance (which will contain the suspended message) that you need to resume and then choose to resume it, as follows:

1. Open the BizTalk Administration Console.

2. Expand the BizTalk Server Administration folder in the left pane, and select your BizTalk group. This opens the Group Hub page.

3. Click the Resumable link in the Suspended Items section. This launches a query window displaying all suspended service instances in your BizTalk environment that can be resumed.

4. If you are unsure if a particular suspended service instance contains the message you need to resubmit, right-click the instance record in the results pane, and select Show Messages. This displays a list of messages referenced by the service instance, allowing you to drill down further into the message details and interrogate the actual message, its context, and the flow the message took prior to suspension.

5. When you have located the service instance you need to resume, right-click the record in the results pane, and select Resume Instance, as shown in Figure 10-9. In addition to resuming single suspended service instances, you can also resume multiple instances by holding down the Ctrl key and selecting multiple rows in the results pane. To resume all instances, right-click the header record in the results pane, and select Resume Instances.

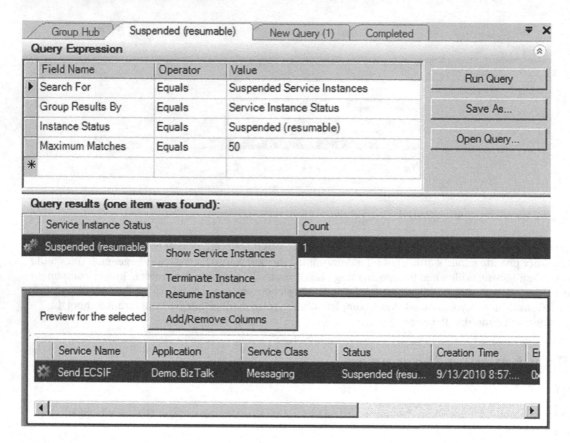

Figure 10-9. *Resuming a single suspended instance*

How It Works

BizTalk errors can be caused by a number of faults, including hardware or network failure or errors during pipeline or adapter processing. When errors occur in your integration solutions, BizTalk typically suspends the service instance that encountered the error. Services are areas of BizTalk processing—such as orchestration, messaging, or adapter—and service instances are specific instances of the orchestration, messaging, or adapter component. A service instance may contain one or more suspended messages. BizTalk differentiates between two basic types of suspension events: resumable (the service instance can be restarted) and nonresumable (the instance cannot be restarted).

Finding the service instance that contains the message you want to resubmit is critical. A number of methods for searching for suspended instances are provided by BizTalk. If you know that you must resubmit a message that was suspended in a specific orchestration, a quick way to search for service instances is to click on the Grouped by Service Name link on the Group Hub page, as shown in Figure 10-10.

Figure 10-10. *Viewing service instances*

In addition to resuming services instances normally, you can also resume service instances in debug mode. Resuming in debug mode will restart the service instance at the last successful persistence point prior to the error.

BizTalk also provides Windows Management Instrumentation (WMI) methods for resubmitting suspended service instances, such as `MSBTS_ServiceInstance.Resume` and `MSBTS_HostQueue.ResumeServiceInstancesByID`.

Finally, messages can be manually resubmitted. This process involves finding a particular service instance or message via the BizTalk Administrator Console, saving the message data, and using a resubmit mechanism (such as ports or administrative tools) to resend the message through BizTalk. To save a message, right-click the record (in the BizTalk Administrator Console), and select the option for saving the tracked message(s). While this method is generally more time consuming and task intensive, it can be particularly helpful when the error is such that it would be significantly difficult to successfully resume a suspended service instance. You should consider the following when manually resubmitting messages:

- Security, with regards to encryption and authentication

- Data privacy and protection for sensitive information

- User error if data is manipulated

10-3. Managing BizTalk Applications

Problem

You have BizTalk solution artifacts that should be grouped together for ease of management and maintenance. Specifically, you would like to group BizTalk Solution components so that you can easily deploy those components to another environment as well as start and stop the components together as a whole.

Solution

You can use a BizTalk application to group and manage BizTalk solution artifacts. As outlined in the following steps, the process involves creating the new application, configuring it, and then adding components. After creating the BizTalk application, you can import BizTalk MSI files and bindings and add previously created BizTalk assembly DLLs, scripts, and resources. The instructions in this solution describe the process for adding a BizTalk assembly DLL that contains multiple schemas.

1. Open the BizTalk Administration Console.

2. In the left pane, right-click the Applications folder, and choose New ➤ Application. This launches the Application Properties dialog box, as shown in Figure 10-11.

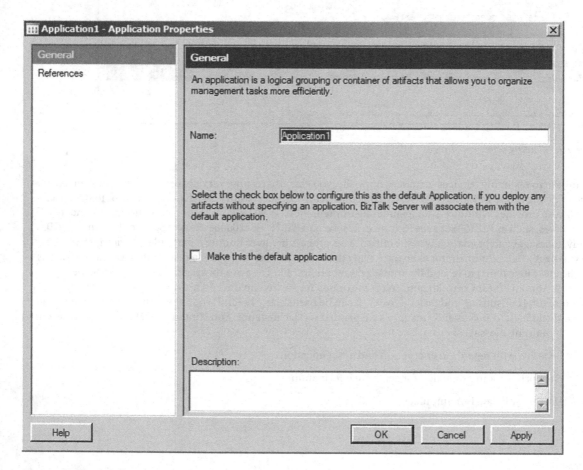

Figure 10-11. *Application Properties dialog box*

3. In the Application Properties dialog box, make the following settings, and then click the OK button to create the new BizTalk application.

- Enter the name of the application that you are creating.

- Specify if this application is the default application. Identifying your application as the default application is significant when deploying new BizTalk artifacts from Visual Studio. Unless you specify an application in Visual Studio, your BizTalk artifact deploys to the default BizTalk application. A BizTalk artifact that does not specify a deployment application name will be grouped in your newly created default application.

- Identify any application references. Identifying application references allows you to share resources across applications. For example, if you have a common set of shared schemas, maps, or pipelines, you can specify them as part of an application reference and not need to make multiple copies of those components for each BizTalk application.

4. After the application is created, verify that the artifacts have been bound appropriately. Right-click the application and choose Start.

■ **Note** When you start a BizTalk application, you have the choice of enlisting and starting all orchestrations, send ports, send port groups, receive locations, host instances, and resuming suspended instances.

---

5. To configure your application, from the BizTalk Administration Console, right-click it, and choose Configure. You will be presented with a Configure Application dialog box, shown in Figure 10-12. Here, you can configure binding, host, role links, and messaging/port settings for your application. Click OK after completing your configuration.

Figure 10-12. *Configure Application dialog box*

6. From the newly created application, right-click and choose Add ➤ BizTalk Assemblies. This launches the Add Resources dialog box, shown in Figure 10-13.

Figure 10-13. *Add Resources dialog box*

7. Click the Add button to identify the assemblies to add to the BizTalk application. You can add assemblies (BizTalk or custom), scripts, bindings, COM objects, and other objects to your BizTalk application. This dialog box includes the following settings:

- *Overwrite all*: This flag indicates whether to overwrite an existing resource in the Management database with the resource specified in the application. If you do not specify this flag and you have a resource that contains the same name, the process will fail when trying to add the object.

- *Options*: Depending on the type of resource being added, you have different options. For example, if you are adding an assembly to your project, you also have the option to add the assembly to the Global Assembly Cache (GAC), make the resource visible to COM, and register the component as a serviced component. Remember any assembly you wish to add to the GAC must be signed with a strong name key (this can most easily be done through the project properties in Visual Studio).

- *Dependencies*: You will receive a list of dependencies if you choose to add an assembly (BizTalk or custom) to your BizTalk application.

- *Destination location*: This is the location or path where the resource file will be copied when the application is installed. You may specify an absolute, relative, or UNC path. The default path copies the resource file to the application installation folder.

8. When you have selected the resources to add to you BizTalk application, click the OK button. Figure 10-14 shows an example of a BizTalk application with a schema resource added. Notice that BizTalk automatically manages the placement of the resource into the correct folder location within the BizTalk application.

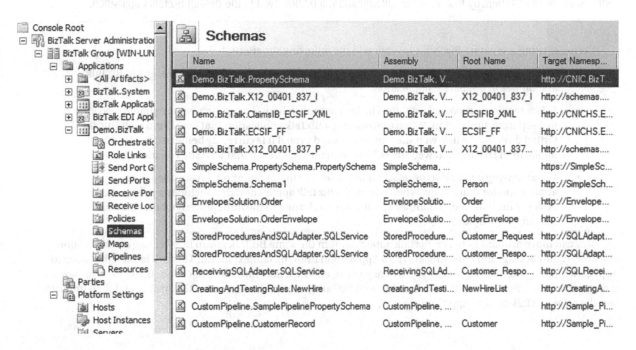

Figure 10-14. *Schema resource added to an application*

How It Works

BizTalk applications represent a powerful concept in organizing BizTalk artifacts into logical groupings. You can group like or related artifacts together in a BizTalk application. Once BizTalk artifacts are grouped logically, it is possible to export the application to another BizTalk environment. The concept of applications simplifies management, troubleshooting, and deployment of BizTalk artifacts.

The monitoring tools that are included in the BizTalk Administration Console take advantage of the BizTalk application concept. Multiple BizTalk solutions can be managed through logical application groupings.

BizTalk is set up with a default application container under which all BizTalk artifacts are deployed to by default. When you upgrade a previously created BizTalk solution, the artifacts will initially be placed in the default application. Additionally, in the following situations, BizTalk artifacts will be placed in the default application:

- When you deploy BizTalk artifacts from Visual Studio without specifying an application

- When you use BTSDeploy to deploy BizTalk artifacts (because this tool was created for a previous version of BizTalk)

- When you use BTSTask without specifying an application name

---

■ **Note** If you perform automated deployment, make sure to use the BTSTask tool instead of the deprecated BTSDeploy tool. With BTSTask, you can specify the application under which your BizTalk artifacts are deployed. If you continue to use the BTSDeploy tool, your BizTalk artifacts will be deployed to the default BizTalk application.

Consider using a separate BizTalk application in the following situations:

- *When sharing BizTalk assemblies across multiple applications*: In this situation, group BizTalk assemblies in a separate application.

- *When sharing a deployed web site*: The best approach here is to implement the shared web site in a separate application. When uninstalling a BizTalk application that contains a web site, the virtual directory of that web site will be removed even if it is currently being used. Any other application sharing that web site will encounter exceptions if that web site is removed.

- *When sharing a policy across multiple applications*: In this situation, create a separate application for that policy. When you stop a BizTalk application that includes a policy, the policy is undeployed. If another application is referring to the undeployed policy, you will encounter exceptions.

You can move artifacts between BizTalk applications in the same BizTalk group by selecting an application resource, right-clicking, and choosing Move To Application from the context menu. This will launch the Move to Application dialog box (see Figure 10-15), where you can choose a new BizTalk application. If you need to move artifacts to another BizTalk application in a different BizTalk group, you must export the artifact and then import it into the other BizTalk group's application.

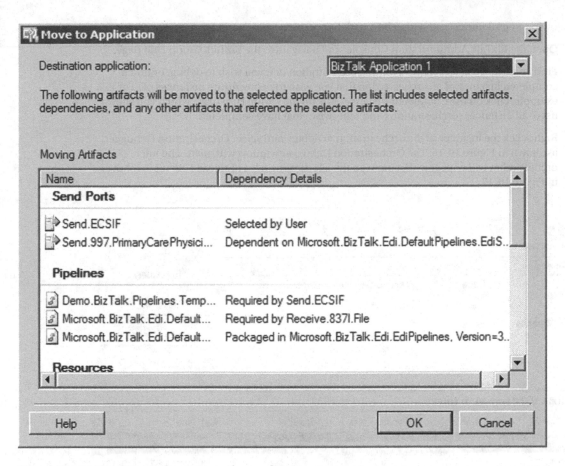

Figure 10-15. *Moving a send port to another application*

10-4. Debugging Orchestrations

Problem

You need to debug a BizTalk orchestration.

Solution

You can use BizTalk's Orchestration Debugger, which allows you to set breakpoints on any shape in an orchestration. Once an instance of an orchestration executes and encounters one of these breakpoints, it will go into a wait state in the BizTalk MessageBox, allowing a developer or administrator to manually step through the orchestration.

■ **Note** A *dehydrated orchestration* is an orchestration that has been removed from memory and persisted to SQL Server while it waits for its next action to occur, such as receiving a document. Upon this next action, the orchestration is returned to memory in the exact state prior to dehydration, and processing continues. This ability to dehydrate/rehydrate allows BizTalk Server to better utilize server resources.

The following steps demonstrate setting how to debug an orchestration.

1. Open the BizTalk Administration Console, and navigate to the BizTalk Group Hub page.

2. Find an instance of a currently running orchestration that you wish to debug, or find a completed instance of an orchestration that you wish to debug future instances of. For this example, click on the Completed Instances link on the Group Hub page, which will show a list of all instances (orchestrations and otherwise) that have completed.

3. Right-click the instance of the orchestration to debug, and select Orchestration Debugger, as shown in Figure 10-16. The Orchestration Debugger window will open. The full orchestration will appear with a pane on the left showing a list of tracked events, as shown in Figure 10-17.

Figure 10-16. Accessing the Orchestration Debugger

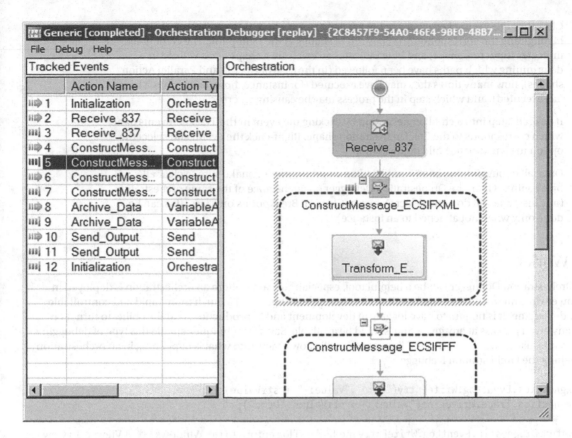

Figure 10-17. Orchestration Debugger window

■ **Note** Large orchestrations can take longer to load. Occasionally, with smaller development machines and larger orchestrations, you may need to wait for a while before the Orchestration Debugger window actually opens.

4. To set a breakpoint, right-click any shape, and select Set Breakpoint on Class.

5. Step through the orchestration by clicking tracked events in the left pane.

6. At any time, select Debug ➤ Attach. A new pane will open and display the values of all variables at the given stage of the orchestration. This allows for a full view into the state of the process. You'll notice a number of debugging actions are available on the Debug menu.

■ **Note** You can attach only to orchestrations that have not completed. If this is the first time that the orchestration has executed, it will likely have already completed. You may need to start a new instance before the orchestration will pause on a breakpoint that has been set.

7. Click through the tracked events in the left pane to see which steps have executed by highlighting the corresponding orchestration shapes in the right pane. The color green indicates input to a shape, and blue indicates an exit from a shape. This will aid in determining which paths have been followed (in the case of Decide and Parallel Action shapes), how many times they may have executed (for instance, how many times a loop has executed), and which step in the process may be causing an error.

8. If desired, step into a child orchestration by clicking the event in the Tracked Events pane, which corresponds to the Call Orchestration shape. Right-click the event, and select the option to step into the child orchestration.

9. Once all debugging has been completed on an orchestration, make sure to clear all breakpoints. Open the Orchestration Debugger on an instance of the same orchestration (any instance will do), and select Debug ➤ Clear All Breakpoints on Class (this can be done only when not attached to an instance).

How It Works

While the Orchestration Debugger can be a helpful tool, especially in cases where an orchestration is deployed in a production environment and is encountering errors, developers often need a much more rapid and controllable method for debugging. It is helpful to have logging in development and in production, and the ability to turn it on and off for any given process at any given time should be available. Several techniques enable this type of debugging.

For example, using two standard .NET lines of code will allow a view into what is happening in an orchestration without opening the Orchestration Debugger:

```
System.Diagnostics.EventLog.WriteEntry("Demo","Value: " + strValue);
System.Diagnostics.Trace.WriteLine("Value: " + strValue, "Demo");
```

The System.Diagnostic.EventLog.WriteEntry method will log entries to the Windows Event Viewer. To view this logged event, open the Control Panel, select Administrative Tools, and double-click Event Viewer. Events will be logged to the application log, and you'll need to refresh the display to see results as they are written.

■ **Note** The user that runs the orchestration (whatever the host user has been configured to be) must have rights to write to the Event Viewer to use the System.Diagnostic.EventLog.WriteEntry method.

The System.Diagnostics.Trace.WriteLine method will allow all of the trace outputs to be read by attaching to the main BizTalk executable and monitoring in Visual Studio. Use the following steps to do that monitoring:

1. In Visual Studio, select Debug ➤ Attach to Process.

2. In the window that opens, find BTNTSvc.exe, and highlight it. Click the Attach button.

3. Run an instance of the orchestration. Trace information will be made available in the Output window in Visual Studio.

One way to use the System.Diagnostic methods for debugging/tracing in orchestrations is to wrap the logging code in an If statement and create a TraceFlag that can be set in a configuration file, such as the BTSNTSvc.exe.config file in the root BizTalk Program Files folder. Here is an entry you could add to the BTNTSvc.exe.config file:

```
<add key=" TraceFlag" value="true"/>
```

Listing 10-1 demonstrates how to retrieve the TraceFlag and, based on its value, log information.

Listing 10-1. Configurable Trace Flag

```
// set the trace flag based on a value stored in the BizTalk Config File
// note that blnTraceFlag must be defined in the orchestration variables
blnTraceFlag = System.Convert.ToBoolean(System.Configuration.
ConfigurationSettings.AppSettings.Get("TraceFlag"));

// set the source to something unique for this orchestration
strSource = "DebugDemoOrchestration";

// Trace
if(blnTraceFlag == true){
strValue = System.Convert.ToString(intValue);
System.Diagnostics.EventLog.WriteEntry(strSource,"Value: " + strValue);
System.Diagnostics.Trace.WriteLine("Value: " + strValue, strSource);
}
```

When using this approach, keep tracing information separate in the orchestration from other functionality, and label it appropriately. You can do this by dedicating an Expression shape to a single trace event and naming it Trace (for example), as shown in Figure 10-18.

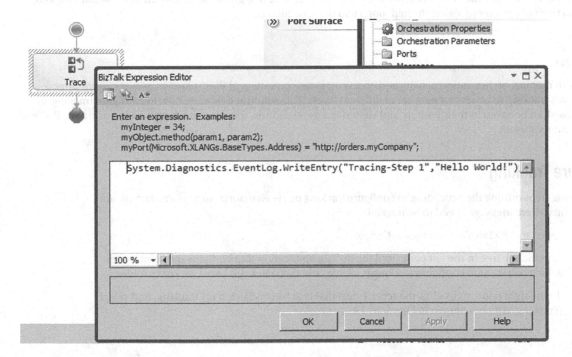

Figure 10-18. Expression shape for tracing

One of the most helpful ways to debug is to see the actual XML of a message, especially before and after mapping. This can be done by setting a variable of type System.Xml.XmlDocument equal to an orchestration message and then tracing the value of this variable, as shown in Listing 10-2.

Listing 10-2. Tracing XML

```
// set the xmlDoc variable equal to the message to be traced.
// msgOrch is an orchestration message
xmlDoc = new System.Xml.XmlDocument();
xmlDoc = msgOrch;
System.Diagnostics.EventLog.WriteEntry(strSource,"Value: " + xmlDoc.OuterXml);
System.Diagnostics.Trace.WriteLine("Value: " + xmlDoc.OuterXml, strSource);
```

■ **Note** The maximum size of a string that can be written to the Windows Event Viewer is 32KB. Often, XML messages will exceed this size. If a string longer than 32KB is written, an exception will be thrown, and the orchestration will terminate (unless appropriate exception handling is implemented). You can truncate the length using .NET code. There is no limitation to the size when using the `Trace.WriteLine` method.

10-5. Tracking Messages
Problem

You want to be able to view the contents of messages that have arrived in a given BizTalk solution to monitor messages and actions that have been processed through ports and orchestrations.

Solution

The ability to monitor orchestration activity and access message contents and flow is known as *tracking messages*. BizTalk allows tracking to be set at a number of different levels. This solution describes how to configure tracking so that messages can be saved in their entirety and viewed in any text editor. You can configure tracking using the BizTalk Administration Console.

Configure Tracking

The following steps outline the procedure to configure tracking on receive ports, send ports, and on any orchestrations where messages need to be tracked.

1. Open the BizTalk Administration Console.

2. Expand the tree in the left pane until the BizTalk application that contains the solution on which you want to configure tracking is visible, and then click the `Receive Ports` folder.

3. In the right pane, right-click the receive port that is to be configured for tracking, and select Tracking, which is shown in Figure 10-19.

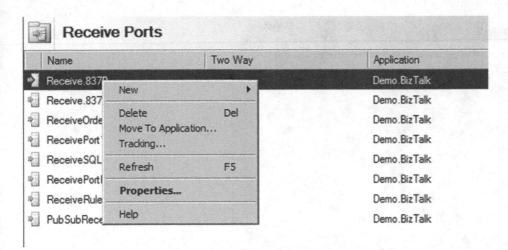

Figure 10-19. Configuring tracking within the BizTalk Administration Console

4. In the Tracking Options dialog box, set the desired options for tracking. The settings are generic across one-way and two-way ports.

- *Request Message Before Port Processing*: Request messages exist in one-way and two-way ports. Checking this value will track the message prior to being processed by the port (processing includes any pipelines or maps that may be on the port).

■ **Note** A message is a *request* if the message is initiated by the port/orchestration. A message is a *response* if the port/orchestration is receiving it from an external source.

- *Request Message After Port Processing*: Checking this value will track the message after it is processed by the port (processing includes any pipelines or maps that may be on the port).

- *Response Message Before Port Processing*: Response messages exist on two-way ports only. Checking this value will track the message prior to being processed by the port (processing includes any pipelines or maps that may be on the port).

- *Response Message After Port Processing*: Checking this value will track the message after being processed by the port (processing includes any pipelines or maps that may be on the port).

- If desired, configure tracking for send ports. Right-click the send port, select Tracking, and choose options in the Tracking Options dialog box.

- Configure tracking on the appropriate orchestrations. In the left pane of the BizTalk Administration Console, click the Orchestrations folder. In the right pane, right-click the orchestration, and select Tracking. In the Orchestration Tracking Options dialog box, you can configure tracking on events and on messages within the orchestration, as shown in Figure 10-20.

Figure 10-20. *Orchestration Tracking Options dialog box*

Access Tracked Messages

After you have configured tracking through the BizTalk Administration Console, access the tracked messages as follows:

1. Drop a message on the appropriate receive location to instantiate the orchestration.

2. Open the Group Hub page, and run a query that will return message instances.

3. Right click the message, and select Save to File to select a folder to save to, as shown in Figure 10-21.

Figure 10-21. *Saving tracked messages*

Depending on the complexity of the orchestration, the number of send and receive ports, and the level of tracking configured, there may be a few or a large number of messages written out to the directory specified. A combination of system messages and XML messages will have been tracked.

How It Works

There is a direct relation between the level of tracking configured for a given solution and the size of the underlying BizTalk databases. For solutions with high levels of tracking and a high volume of message transactions, databases can grow quickly. An intelligent approach to traditional SQL database management is required, especially as it pertains to table truncation and data backups.

10-6. Restarting the BizTalk Host Instance(s)
Problem

You have a number of new configurations in your BizTalk applications. You want to refresh everything and make sure all configurations are acknowledged by BizTalk Server.

Solution

Refreshing BizTalk Server is quite simple—restarting the BizTalk Host instance(s) essentially refreshes all of the configurations and running instances in the MessageBox. To perform the restart, take the following steps:

1. Open BizTalk Administration Console.

2. Expand the BizTalk Group, expand the Platform Settings folder, and click Host Instances.

3. Right-click the Host Instance that you want to restart, and select Restart (shown in Figure 10-22).

Figure 10-22. *Restarting the host instance*

How It Works

Occasionally, especially during development, you will need to restart the BizTalk host instances. When deploying new configurations, new referenced .NET assemblies, and new shared maps and schemas, it is important to restart the host to ensure all of the new artifacts are referenced properly (and that old references are forgotten). It is also helpful to stop the whole BizTalk host instance when you want to turn off all processing to ensure that nothing is received or sent, regardless of the status of the send and receive ports.

10-7. Throttle Orchestration Memory Usage

Problem

You need to optimize the memory use of orchestrations running on one of your BizTalk Server groups.

Solution

The new BizTalk Settings Dashboard allows for the configuration of a variety of core settings that control memory usage and performance. To access the tool, take these steps:

1. Open BizTalk Administration Console.

2. Right-click the BizTalk Server Group, and select Settings. The BizTalk Settings Dashboard will open.

3. Click the Host Instances tab.

4. Select the Orchestration Memory Throttling tab (see Figure 10-23).

5. Change the memory usage to the desired percentages.

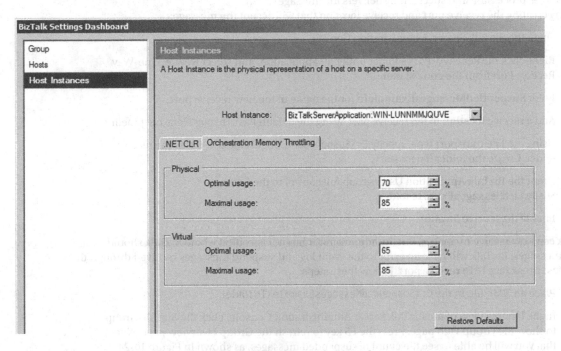

Figure 10-23. *Configuring memory in the BizTalk Settings Dashboard*

How It Works

The new BizTalk Settings Dashboard is hidden within BizTalk, but it is an extremely powerful tool. Orchestration performance is one of the features, but there are a wide variety of additional features that will prove to be useful. Take a look at the tool and see what properties will help improve the performance of your deployment. The default settings are usually fine to keep, but for advanced solutions, it may be necessary to make alterations.

10-8. Resuming Inbound Message Processing

Problem

BizTalk has encountered an error and suspended the processing of an inbound message. You need to fix the error and resume message processing to receive it successfully.

Solution

This example demonstrates the resumable inbound message-processing capabilities of BizTalk. BizTalk initially receives a message that has no recipients. In the publish/subscribe architecture of the MessageBox, the error message will indicate that BizTalk cannot find a subscriber to the message. After creating the appropriate subscription, this example resumes processing and successfully delivers the message.

Begin by creating the receive port and receive location that will accept the message:

1. Open the BizTalk Server Administration Console.

2. Right-click the Receive Ports folder under an application, and select New ➤ One-Way Receive Port from the context menu.

3. Enter **SuspendedMessagesExampleIn** for the name of the new receive port.

4. Add a receive location to the receive port, using the default PassThroughReceive pipeline.

5. Using the File transport type, specify C:\SuspendedMessagesExample\In as the receive folder. Create the folder if necessary.

6. Grant the BizTalk Application Users group full control to the C:\SuspendedMessagesExample folder.

7. Enable the receive location.

BizTalk can now receive messages, but the administrator has not specified where BizTalk should deliver the messages. BizTalk will raise an error to the event log and suspend messages received through the SuspendedMessagesExampleIn receive port. Follow these steps:

1. Place an XML file in the C:\SuspendedMessagesExample\In folder.

2. In the left tree view of the BizTalk Server Administration Console, click the BizTalk Group to show the Group Hub page. Press the F5 key to refresh the Group Overview page. Note that you will be able to see the count of suspended messages, as shown in Figure 10-24.

Work in Progress		Suspended Items	
Running service instances	0	Suspended service instances	5
- Dehydrated orchestrations	0	- Resumable	2
- Retrying and idle ports	0	- Non-resumable	3
- Ready service instances	0		
- Scheduled service instances	0		

Figure 10-24. Suspended message counts in the Group Hub page

3. Click the Suspended Service Instances link to open the Suspended tab. The Suspended tab will display all resumable suspended service instances, as shown in Figure 10-25.

Figure 10-25. Resumable service instance

Now that there is a suspended message in BizTalk, create a send port to deliver the message and resume message processing.

1. Create a new static one-way send port in the same BizTalk application as the receive port was created in.

2. Enter **SuspendedMessagesExampleOut** for the name of the send port, and configure the File adapter to deliver messages to the C:\SuspendedMessagesExample\Out folder. Create the folder if necessary. Use the default PassThruTransmit send pipeline.

3. In the left pane of the SuspendedMessagesExampleOut – Send Port Properties dialog box, select Filters.

4. Define a filter where BTS.ReceivePortName equals SuspendedMessagesExampleIn, as shown in Figure 10-26. This will create a subscription for all messages received through the SuspendedMessagesExampleIn receive port.

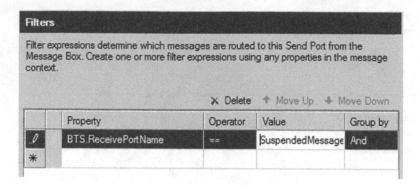

Figure 10-26. *Defining a message subscription*

5. Enlist and start the `SuspendedMessagesExampleOut` send port.

6. On the Group Hub page, return to the Suspended tab.

7. Select the Suspended (Resumable) query results to display the suspended `SuspendedMessagesExampleIn` service instance.

8. Right-click the suspended service instance, and select Resume Instance from the context menu. Click Yes when prompted to confirm. If the Resume Instance option is not available, verify that the selected service instance's status is Suspended (Resumable) under the query results.

9. Verify that BizTalk successfully delivered the XML message to the `C:\SuspendedMessagesExample\Out` folder.

How It Works

BizTalk supports resumable inbound interchange processing. It suspends the message while receiving it, and the administrator can resume the message after fixing the configuration error. The BizTalk administrator can perform extensive troubleshooting to identify the cause of a suspended message. Double-clicking the Suspended (resumable) service instance shown in Figure 10-25 opens a Service Details dialog box containing detailed information about the suspended message. The Error Information tab, shown in Figure 10-27, displays detailed error information indicating that the message was suspended because BizTalk could not identify a subscriber.

Service Details

| General | Error Information | Messages |

Error Code: 0xc0c01680 (Routing Failure)   ↑

Suspend Time: 10/22/2010 10:05:45 AM   ↓

Error Description:

The published message could not be routed because no subscribers were found. This error occurs if the subscribing orchestration or send port has not been enlisted, or if some of the message properties necessary for subscription evaluation have not been promoted. Please use the Biztalk Administration console to troubleshoot this failure.

Figure 10-27. *Viewing error information*

The Messages tab displays all the messages in the suspended service instance. Double-clicking a message opens the Message Details dialog box. Select Context in the left pane of the Message Details dialog box to display the message's context properties, as shown in Figure 10-28. BizTalk can use the Promoted context properties to identify the subscriber of a message.

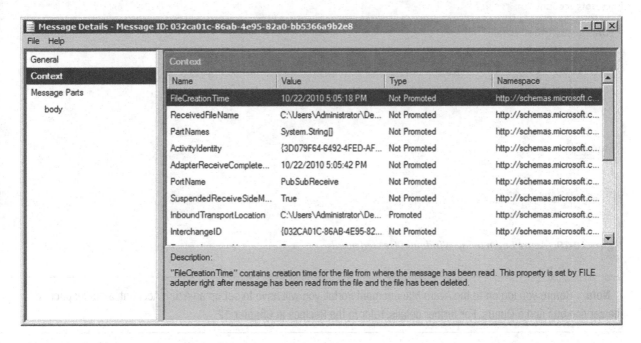

Figure 10-28. *Message context properties*

Back on the Suspended tab of the Group Hub page, the BizTalk administrator can right-click a suspended message and navigate the Troubleshoot Routing Failure submenu to identify the cause of a routing failure.

Although most suspended messages in BizTalk are resumable, in some situations, BizTalk cannot resume message processing. One example is when BizTalk uses order delivery messages in the same order BizTalk receives them. In this situation, resuming a message would also deliver it out of order, so BizTalk prevents resuming the message.

10-9. Monitor Message Flow Through the Azure Service Bus Queue
Problem

You are tasked to analyze the Azure Service Bus Queue to identify the patterns of usage. You also are to suggest potential quota changes based on the usage.

Solution

The Azure Management Portal manages subscriptions and provides dashboards for managed entities such as Azure Service Bus. Azure Service Bus entities are listed under a namespace. You can drill into the individual dashboards for each of these entities. To access the Dashboard for a Queue, take the following steps:

1. Log on to the Azure Management Portal using your Windows Live User credentials, as shown in Figure 10-29.

Sign in

Microsoft account What's this?

someacct@gmail.com

•••••••••

☐ Keep me signed in

Sign in

Can't access your account?

Sign in with a single-use code

Figure 10-29. *Azure Login using Windows Live credentials*

■ **Note**   Before you log on to the Azure Management Portal, you will have to set up an Azure Account, a namespace for the service bus and a Queue. For further details, refer to the Recipes in Chapter 12.

---

2.   You will now be on the Azure home page. Click the Portal link to view the Azure Management Portal's Central Administration and Dashboard page, as shown in Figure 10-30.

Figure 10-30. *User's Azure home page*

3.   Once you are in the Azure Portal, select the "Service Bus" option from the left side of the Portal Dashboard page. It will display the available namespaces under this subscription, as shown in Figure 10-31.

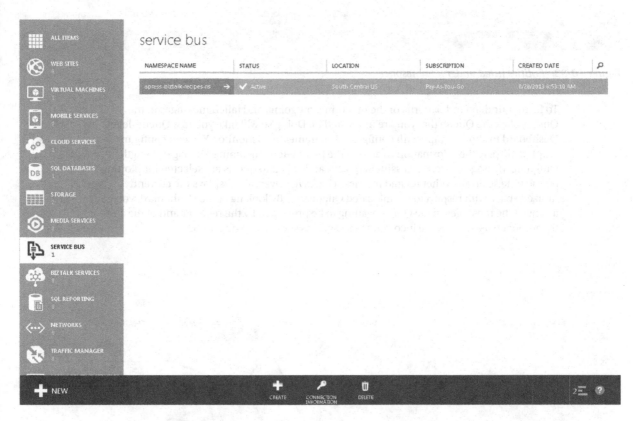

Figure 10-31. *User's Azure Management Portal*

4.   When you click the namespace (in this case, the only available namespace to click is apress-biztalk-recipes-ns), a list of entities (Queues, Topics, Relays, and Notification Hubs) that are under the namespace is displayed. This list page provides a summary of each of the entities (Status of the entity, Type of the entity, Size—Current & Maximum, and Last Access Type). Select the Queue you are interested in, as shown in Figure 10-32. In that figure, you see a queue named electricitygrid-queue that has a few messages waiting to be sent to the Queue message receiver.

apress-biztalk-recipes-ns

NAME	STATUS	CURRENT SIZE	MAX SIZE	QUEUE LENGTH	LAST ACCESSED ...
electricitygrid-queue →	✓ Active	595.63 KB	1 GB	775	10/4/2013 5:51:5...

Figure 10-32. *Entities listed under a namespace*

5. To further understand patterns of the incoming, outgoing, and failed messages in the Queue, click the Queue that you are interested in. Doing so will take you to a Queue-level Dashboard to show a graph with configurable parameters to monitor. You can configure graph to display the information related to the parameters; Incoming Messages, Length, Outgoing Messages, Size, Successful Requests, and Failed Requests are selected for plotting on the time scale and other related metrics. The Usage Overview displays the currently utilized space with respect to the allocated Queue size. By looking at the Dashboard, you get a view of the messages in the Queue waiting to be processed by the receiver and of the size of the Queue used up by the incoming messages, as shown in Figure 10-33.

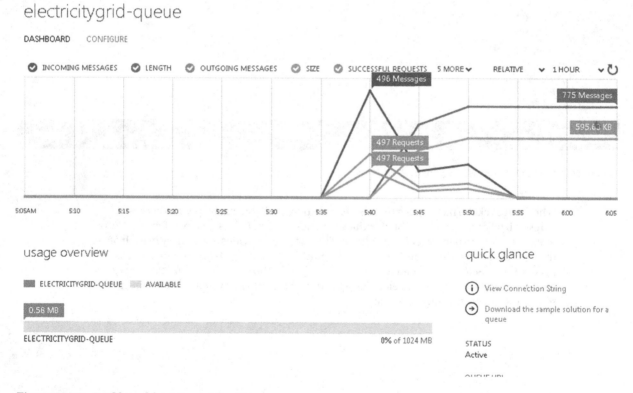

Figure 10-33. *Dashboard for a Service Bus Queue*

How It Works

A queue-level dashboard gives a high-level real-time view of the messages that are being processed by the queue and also shows the size of the queue (Queue Length) used by the current influx of messages. You can customize the Dashboard to view the specific parameters. Only six parameters can be chosen at a time.

Once you understand the queue length, and the time-based usage patterns of the queue, you can modify the configuration to suit current requirements. Figure 10-34 shows some of the parameters you can modify, and they are further described in Table 10-1.

electricitygrid-queue

DASHBOARD   CONFIGURE

general

DEFAULT MESSAGE TIME TO LIVE	30	seconds ▾
EXPIRED MESSAGE	☑ MOVE TO THE DEAD-LETTER SUBQUEUE	
DUPLICATE DETECTION HISTORY	20	seconds ▾
LOCK DURATION	30	seconds ▾
MAXIMUM DELIVERY COUNT	10	
QUEUE STATE	Enabled ▾	

shared access policies

NAME	PERMISSIONS
NEW POLICY NAME	▾

Figure 10-34. Service Bus Queue Configuration

Table 10-1. *Service Bus Queue Configuration Parameters*

Type	Description
Default Message Time to Live	Sets the message Expiration Duration. It is the duration after which the message is considered expired, if it is not picked up by the receiver. Possible time frames are seconds, minutes, hours, and days. The Default value is 14 days.
Expired Message—Move to the Dead Letter Sub-queue	Sets the move messages to Dead Letter Queue amount. The expired message can be moved to a secondary sub-queue called the Dead Letter Queue. Doing this will remove the bad messages from the real queue, and the receivers will not have to filter out the bad messages. Also, the bad messages can be processed by a separate workflow or audited for any bad configurations.
Duplicate Detection History	Sets the time span of the duplicate message history. A second message with the exact same parameters is considered a duplicate in a pre-specified time frame. Such duplicates will result in errors and show up in the Dashboard. The default is 10 minutes.
Lock Duration	Sets the time for which the message is peek locked from the other receivers. This means that receivers will not be able to access or "peek" into the message. The defaults are minimum 30 seconds and maximum 5 minutes.
Maximum Delivery Count	Sets the batch limit of number of messages to be delivered at a single time. The default is value is 10.
Queue State	Sets the current processing state of the queue. The possible configurations are: Enabled Disabled Send Disabled (Receive Only) Receive Disabled (Send Only) The default is Enabled.
Shared Access Policies	Shared Access Policies provide a control over the operations that can be performed by the users on this queue for a specific period of time. These policies are defined elsewhere and can be applied to this resource.

10-10. Monitor Message Flow Through Azure Service Bus Topic and Subscriptions

Problem

You are troubleshooting the message flow in a hybrid integration scenario, with Topic and Subscriptions. You are tasked to find the messages received by a specific subscriber for a Topic.

Solution

Azure Management Portal lists the Topics and rule-based subscribers for each Topic. To understand the usage patterns of a Topic and its related subscribers, the Dashboard should cover two levels of details: the summary at the Topic level, and another at the subscriber level. To access the Topic level Dashboards, take the following steps:

1. Log on to the Azure Management Portal using your Windows Live User credentials, as shown in Figure 10-35.

Sign in

Microsoft account What's this?

someacct@gmail.com

••••••••

☐ Keep me signed in

Sign in

Can't access your account?

Sign in with a single-use code

Figure 10-35. *Azure Login using Windows Live credentials*

2. You will now be on the Azure home page. Click the Portal link to view the Azure Management Portal's Central Administration and Dashboard page, as shown in Figure 10-36.

Figure 10-36. *User's Azure home page*

3. Once in the Azure Portal, select the "Service Bus" option from the left side of the Portal Dashboard page. Doing so will display the available namespaces under your subscription, as shown in Figure 10-37.

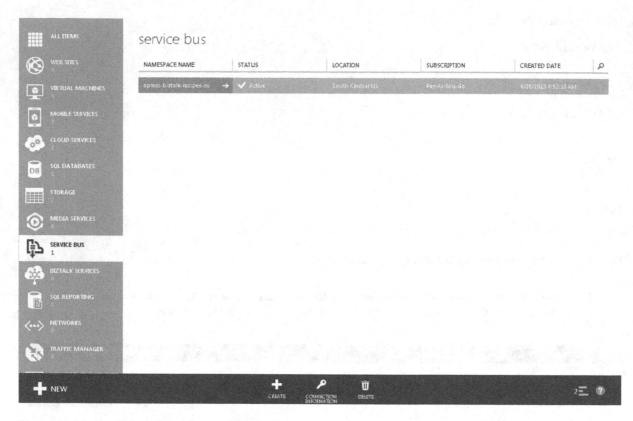

Figure 10-37. *User's Azure Management Portal*

4. Click a namespace to list the entities (Queues, Topics, Relays, and Notification Hubs) that are under the Namespace. You will find the summary of each of the entities (Status of the entity, Type of the entity, Size—Current & Maximum, and Last Access Type). Click the Topic (weatherevent-topic) to get the Topic Level Dashboard, as shown in Figure 10-38.

apress-biztalk-recipes-ns

ALL   QUEUES   TOPICS   RELAYS   NOTIFICATION HUBS   CONFIGURE

NAME	STATUS	TYPE	CURRENT SIZE	MAX SIZE	LAST ACCESSED TIME
electricitygrid-queue	✓ Active	Queue	595.63 KB	1 GB	10/4/2013 10:35:45 AM
weatherevent-topic →	✓ Active	Topic	0 B	1 GB	8/28/2013 9:09:15 AM

Figure 10-38. *Entities listed under a namespace*

5. The Dashboard for the topic will give the grand view of the real-time traffic flowing through the topic (the weatherevent-topic in Figure 10-38). The Dashboard for the selected topic shows a graph with configurable parameters to monitor. The usage overview displays the currently utilized space (Queue Length) with respect to the allocated queue storage size. By looking at the Dashboard, you can get a view of the messages in the topic waiting to be processed by the subscriber, as shown in Figure 10-39.

Figure 10-39. Dashboard for a Service Bus Topic

6. A topic can have multiple subscribers. The flow of messages through each of the subscriptions can be monitored by clicking the Monitor link located at the top of the topic dashboard. At this level, you have the option to select the parameters to monitor at a much more granular level. You can select the topic-level monitors or the subscriber-level monitors or mix them per your specific need, as shown in Figure 10-40.

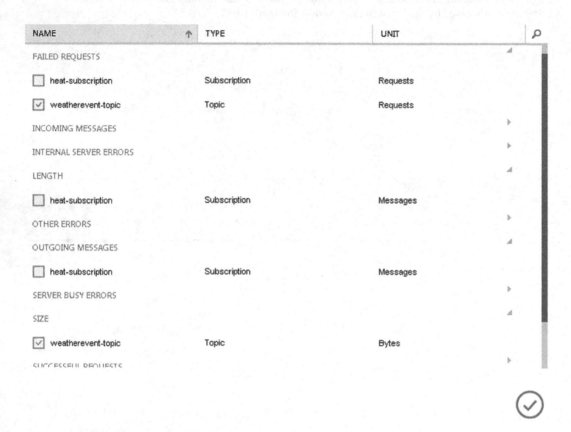

Figure 10-40. *Granular Subscription Level monitoring configuration*

7. You can now view both topic and subscription level message-flow details in the same graph, as shown in Figure 10-41.

weatherevent-topic

DASHBOARD **MONITOR** CONFIGURE SUBSCRIPTIONS

NAME	SOURCE	MIN	MAX	AVG	TOTAL
Internal Server Errors	Topic/weatherevent-topic	0 Requests	0 Requests	0 Requests	0 Requests
Failed requests	Topic/weatherevent-topic	0 Requests	0 Requests	0 Requests	0 Requests
Other Errors	Topic/weatherevent-topic	0 Requests	0 Requests	0 Requests	0 Requests
Server Busy Errors	Topic/weatherevent-topic	0 Requests	0 Requests	0 Requests	0 Requests
Incoming Messages	Topic/weatherevent-topic	0 Messages	0 Messages	0 Messages	0 Messages
Size	Topic/weatherevent-topic	0 B	0 B	0 B	---
Successful Requests	Topic/weatherevent-topic	0 Requests	59 Requests	45.43 Requests	318 Requests
Total Requests	Topic/weatherevent-topic	0 Requests	59 Requests	45.43 Requests	318 Requests
Failed requests	Subscription/heat-subsc...	0 Requests	0 Requests	0 Requests	0 Requests

Figure 10-41. *Granular Subscription Level Dashboard*

How It Works

Azure Management Portal manages the Topics/Subscribers and views the message flows. Dashboard at Topic level displays the high-level real-time view of the messages subscribed the Topic and its multiple subscribers. Unlike in Service Bus Queues, each message received by a topic is subscribed by multiple subscribers, based on some filter conditions. The Topic level dashboard can be drilled down to view the Subscriber level metrics.

Once the flow patterns for messages are set for the topic and the subscriber(s), the topic configurations can be altered, as required. Table 10-2 will help you understand the configuration details.

Table 10-2. Service Bus Topic Configuration

Type	Description
Default Message Time to Live	Sets the message expiration duration. It is the time period after which the message is considered expired, if it is not picked up by the receiver. Possible time frames are seconds, minutes, hours, and days. The default value is 14 days.
Duplicate Detection History	Sets the time span of the duplicate message history. A second message with the exact same parameters is considered a duplicate in a pre-specified time frame. Such duplicates will result as errors and show up in the Dashboard. The default is 10 minutes.
Publishing—Filter Message Before Publishing	If this parameter is checked, the messages are inspected, and filter rules are applied before the message is published to the topic.
Topic State	Sets the current processing state of the topic. The possible configurations are Enabled Disabled Send Disabled (Receive Only) Receive Disabled (Send Only) The default is Enabled.
Shared Access Policies	Shared Access Policies provide a control over the operations that can be performed by the users on this queue for a specific period of time. These policies are defined elsewhere and can be applied to this resource.

CHAPTER 11

■■■

Business Activity Monitoring

BizTalk implementations can be generally defined as business processes, and business processes generally create metrics and data, which are needed for reporting purposes. The ability to rapidly generate and access such metrics and reports about business processes is essential to many parties, including managers, developers, and integration partners. One of the core components of BizTalk Server 2010 is the Business Activity Monitor (BAM) framework, which allows you to create, deploy, and view information about running or previously run processes. BAM implementations publish the metrics and reports and make them available to users through custom interfaces, which are updated in near real time as data progresses through the system. This chapter will introduce the steps necessary to build, deploy, and access BAM implementations.

A business process within BizTalk consists of the combination of all the pipelines, ports, orchestrations, maps, and other components needed for the successful completion of a specific task or set of tasks. You can trace the full life cycle—from the moment a document arrives through all the steps of processing to the ultimate delivery of any documents—using the tools available through the BAM framework. Business analysts and developers must work together to define which steps in the business process are important to track and how these steps will be reported to users.

BAM is tied directly to the central BizTalk engine (that is, processes and databases) through OLAP *cubes*. These cubes are created automatically when a developer deploys a BAM report and profile, typically by using a combination of Microsoft Excel pivot tables and the BizTalk Tracking Profile Editor. Once all the BizTalk components are deployed and a running instance of an orchestration is executing, all defined steps of the flow will be subscribed to via the OLAP cubes and published via BAM components to the user. Users can access the published data via the Web, SharePoint, Excel spreadsheets, or applications that have been customized to display the information.

The recipes in this chapter include detailed information about working with standard BAM development and deployments, working with the BAM API, and viewing information available via the BAM engine.

■ **Note** There is a book focused solely on BAM, *Pro BAM in BizTalk Server 2009* by George Dunphy, Harold Campos, Stephen Kaufman, Peter Kelcey, Sergei Moukhnitski, and David Peterson (Apress, 2009). Make sure to refer to it for a great in-depth study of the technology and how to apply it to various business scenarios.

11-1. Creating BAM Activities and Views
Problem

You have business users requesting metrics, visibility, and business data from the execution of a deployed BizTalk solution and the associated artifacts. The business users are interested when any of the BizTalk processes execute the following steps: process begins, process ends, or process encounters exceptions. The business users are also interested in the following attributes of the messages consumed by the BizTalk processes: the transaction ID and transaction type.

Solution

This recipe outlines how to use Excel to create a BAM workbook that tracks milestones and business data for reporting. This recipe addresses the four categories of steps required in creating a BAM solution. Each category of steps plays an integral role in developing a useful, rich, and powerful BAM solution:

- Creating the BAM activity workbook
- Outlining the BAM view
- Identifying aggregations, dimensions, and measures
- Constructing the pivot table

■ **Note**   This recipe does not address how to use the Orchestration Designer for business analysts or the Tracking Profile Editor. These are covered in later recipes in this chapter.

Create the BAM Activity Workbook

BAM *activities* identify the milestones and tracking data an individual is interested in tracking. *Milestones* are the steps in an activity that are measured in time, and *tracking data* is the key data points in a process you are interested in tracking (such as a customer ID or name).

This category of steps outlines how to create a BAM activity in Excel. The activity defined in this recipe includes milestones that indicate when a process begins, ends, and encounters an exception. Additionally, the following steps outline how to create tracking data that captures the transaction ID and transaction type.

■ **Note**   All references in this recipe to Excel refer to Excel 2010. Previous versions of Excel will have slight variations to the steps outlined (the most obvious is that BAM is available on the main toolbar as opposed to showing under the Add-ins tab). Note that with the early version of BizTalk 2010, some errors could occur when using Excel 2010. If errors occur for you (such as the inability to save a workbook), roll back to using an earlier version of Excel. Later recipes in this chapter refer to Excel 2007.

---

1. Create a new Excel workbook, select the BAM menu item, and choose BAM Activity. Choosing the BAM activity will launch the Business Activity Monitoring Activity Definition Wizard.

■ **Note**   If the BAM menu item is an Excel add-in, the easiest way to get the BAM functionality is to start with a copy of the file named BAM.xla located in the ExcelDir of the root BizTalk Server 2010 directory.

---

2. In the Business Activity Monitoring Activity Definition Wizard, click the New Activity button to create a new activity. Name the new activity **Process Activity**.

3. Create the items listed in Table 11-1 for your activity, and click the OK button to complete the Business Activity Monitoring Activity Definition Wizard. The completed activity should resemble Figure 11-1.

Table 11-1. *Activity Milestones and Key Tracking Data Items*

ID	Item Name	Item Type	Data Type	Description
1	Begin	Business Milestones	Date Time	Identifies the date/time a process begins
2	EndSuccess	Business Milestones	Date Time	Identifies the date/time a process successfully ends
3	Exception	Business Milestones	Date Time	Identifies the date/time a process exception occurs
4	Transaction Id	Business Data – Text	Text (50)	Identifies the ID of the transaction being processed
5	Transaction Type	Business Data – Text	Text (50)	Identifies the type of the transaction being processed

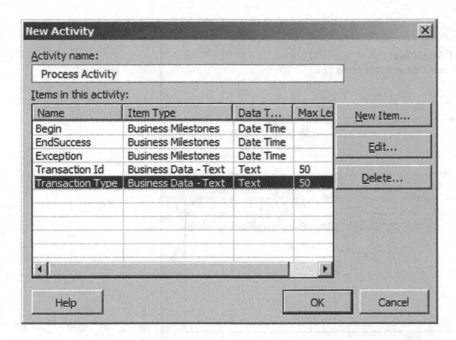

Figure 11-1. *New Activity dialog box*

4. Click the OK button twice to complete the wizard and create a BAM view.

Outline the BAM View

A BAM view is a representation of the milestones and business data tracked in one or more activities. A view may comprise multiple activities or multiple milestones from a single activity and can contain tracked data or milestones as well as provide aggregations or summaries of the tracked milestones and business data. Creating a BAM view is a necessary step because it defines which tracked milestones and business data to report. Typically, different views are created to show multiple audiences different aspects of the same tracked data.

This category of steps demonstrates how to outline your view and display tracked data items and milestones. The view created in this recipe summarizes how many processes execute successfully versus how many processes encounter an exception.

1. When the Business Activity Monitoring View Creation Wizard begins, click the Next button to advance the wizard and create a new view.

■ **Note**　If the wizard does not start, launch it by selecting BAM View from the BAM menu in the Add-ins section of Excel.

---

2. Name the view **Process View**, and select the Select All Activities box. The Business Activity Monitoring View Creation Wizard will resemble Figure 11-2. Click the Next button to advance the wizard.

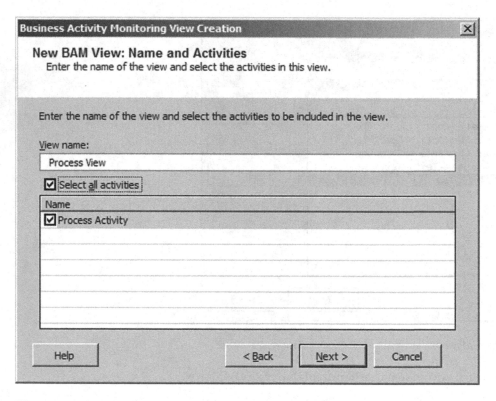

Figure 11-2. Business Activity Monitoring View Creation Wizard

3. On the New BAM View: View Items page of the Business Activity Monitoring View Creation Wizard, select the Select All Items box to add all the milestones and business data to the new view. Click the Next button to advance the wizard.

4. Click the New Group button to create a Group item, and select the box next to the milestones listed in Table 11-2. Figure 11-3 demonstrates the milestones to select.

Table 11-2. *Business Milestone Group*

Business Milestone Alias	Name	Activity
End	EndSuccess	ProcessActivity
	Exception	ProcessActivity

Figure 11-3. *New business milestone group*

■ **Note** The Group milestone allows related milestones to be treated as a single milestone. In this example, grouping the EndSuccess and Exception milestones is useful to indicate the completion of the process regardless of whether it completed successfully or failed.

5. Create a New Duration item with the parameters listed in Table 11-3 to record the total process execution time. Figure 11-4 demonstrates the New Duration creation dialog box.

Table 11-3. *Duration Properties*

Duration Name	Start Milestone	End Milestone	Time Resolution
ProcessDuration	Begin (Process Activity)	End (Process Activity)	Day

Figure 11-4. *New Duration dialog box*

■ **Note** A duration calculates the time between two business milestones and is useful when reporting the time elapsed between two milestones is important. In this sample, the duration will display the time elapsed for the process execution from the beginning of the process to the End milestone group created earlier.

---

6. The completed Business Activity Monitoring View Creation Wizard should resemble Figure 11-5. Click the Next button to advance the wizard and create aggregations, dimensions, and measures.

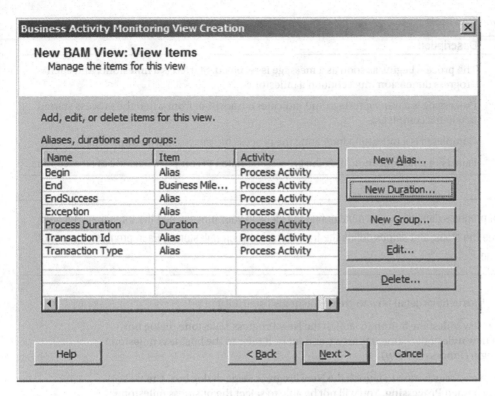

Figure 11-5. Completing the Business Activity Monitoring View Creation Wizard

---

■ **Note** All names used for aliases, durations, groups, dimensions, and measures must be unique for a single view.

Identify Aggregations, Dimensions, and Measures

Aggregations, dimensions, and measures in your BAM solution provide rich functionality for deriving computations and information based on the tracked data and milestones. This category of steps is not required; however, it adds richness to a BAM solution. After completing this category of steps, you must also complete the steps outlined in the "Construct the Pivot Table" section to organize the derived results.

1. Click the New Dimension button and create a new progress dimension. Name it **ActivityProgress**.

■ **Note** A *progress dimension* defines milestones and stages for a process. A progress dimension allows you to display how many processes are at an existing status at a given time. In this example, a progress dimension will display how many processes are in the middle of execution, how many encountered an exception, or how many processed without an exception. Table 11-4 lists the milestones and stages created in this example.

Table 11-4. Progress Dimension Items

Milestone/Stage Name	Description
Started	The process begins as soon as a message is received. Started is a milestone, and each progress dimension must contain a milestone.
Processing	Processing is a transient stage and indicates a transition from when the process started to when it completes.
Completed	Completed is a milestone indicating the process has successfully completed.
Failed	Failed is a milestone indicating the process has failed to complete because of an exception.

■ **Note**   When defining a progress dimension, you must define the steps in your process and the transitions between the steps. *Milestones* define the steps, and *stages* define the transitions between milestones. Each progress dimension must begin with a milestone.

2. The following instructions detail how to create the items listed Table 11-4:

    a. Click the New Milestone button to launch the New Progress Milestone dialog box. Create a new milestone, name it **Started**, and make it refer to the business milestone called Begin (Process Activity).

    b. Click the New Stage button to launch the New Progress Stage dialog box. Create a new stage named **Processing**. You will not be able to select the business milestone, because the wizard automatically selects the milestone.

    c. Click the New Milestone button to launch the New Progress Milestone dialog box. Create a new Milestone named **Completed**, and make it refer to the business milestone called EndSuccess (Process Activity).

    d. Click the New Milestone button to launch the New Progress Milestone dialog box. Create a new Milestone named **Failed**, and make it refer to the business milestone called Exception (Process Activity).

    e. Figure 11-6 demonstrates the completed progress dimension. Click the OK button to complete the New Dimension dialog box.

Figure 11-6. Finishing the progress dimension

3. Create a new measure with the properties listed in Table 11-5. A new measure will provide a count of processes currently executing. Click OK to complete the New Measure dialog box. Figure 11-7 demonstrates the New Measure dialog box.

Table 11-5. Measure Properties

Measure Name	Base Data Item	Aggregation Type
Count	Process Activity	Count

Figure 11-7. Creating a new measure

■ **Note** You must select Count as an aggregation type before you can select Process Activity as the base date item.

---

4. Click the Next button to complete the New BAM View: Aggregation Dimension and Measures page of the wizard.

5. Review the contents of the New BAM View: Summary page of the Business Activity Monitoring View Creation Wizard. Click the Next button, and finally, click the Finish button to complete the wizard.

■ **Note** At this point, you have successfully created a BAM activity and view (including aggregations, measures, and dimensions). The next step is to complete the pivot table layout for the BAM view.

Construct the Pivot Table

This final category of steps demonstrates how to lay out the computed items created in the earlier category of steps. If you did not complete the previous category of steps, you will not be presented with the option of creating a pivot table. The pivot table created in this recipe appears in the BAM portal and is the representation of the data for the user. An Excel pivot table allows you to lay out worksheet data in a grid to analyze trends over data as well as perform data aggregations. In this scenario, the progress dimension previously created is organized in the pivot table alongside the count measure also previously created.

After completing the Business Activity Monitoring View Creation Wizard, you will have a workbook with an empty pivot table that resembles Figure 11-8. The image displays the empty Pivot Table report and the Pivot Table Field List window. Data items from the Pivot Table Field List window are organized in the Pivot Table report.

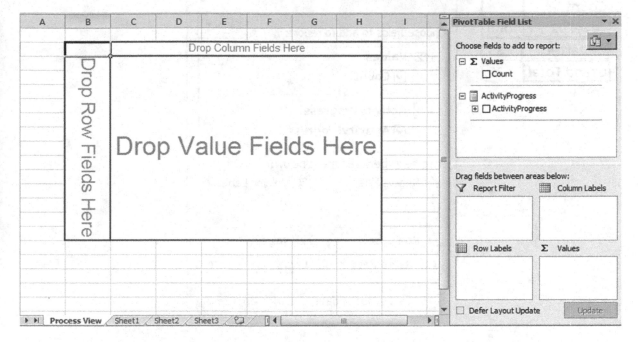

Figure 11-8. *Viewing the pivot table*

1. In Excel, drag the ActivityProgress dimension from the Pivot Table Field List window onto the Drop Row Fields Here section of the pivot table.

2. From the Pivot Table Field List window, drag the Count item to the Drop Value Fields Here section of the pivot table. The pivot table should resemble Figure 11-9.

Figure 11-9. *Viewing the pivot table's data items*

3. This step demonstrates how to expand the progress dimension to see all the defined stages and milestones. Double-click the Started milestone to expand and see the stages and milestones within the progress dimension. The completed pivot table will resemble Figure 11-10.

Figure 11-10. *Completed pivot table*

■ **Note**   If you receive an error message, verify that you clicked inside the Started milestone cell first before double-clicking the started milestone.

---

4.   Mark the pivot table as a real-time aggregation by clicking the Real-Time Aggregation button in BAM add-ins area of the Excel toolbar ribbon. Figure 11-11 shows where the Real-Time Aggregation button is located.

Figure 11-11. *The Real-Time Aggregation button is shown as the only button in the Toolbar Commands box*

5.   Save the workbook when you are finished.

How It Works

BAM is a flexible framework to expose key metrics about business processes modeled within BizTalk. Creating a BAM solution using the BizTalk tool set is a straightforward process requiring little custom development. As outlined earlier, creating and deploying a BAM solution requires four basic categories of steps.

Create the BAM Activity Workbook

The first category of steps in creating a BAM solution is defining the structure for recording data about a BizTalk process. The structure for recording process data is created in an Excel workbook via the BAM add-in tool. The workbook captures key performance indicators or milestones as defined by the user as well as defines how a user views the milestones. Keep in mind that the Excel workbook is independent from any of the BizTalk solution artifacts and serves only as a container for recording information and computing aggregations.

Using the BAM Excel workbook removes the need for the user to have familiarity with the physical BizTalk solution artifacts. In actuality, the user may be more interested in a logical process implemented through multiple BizTalk artifacts versus the specifics for a single artifact. Consider when you tell someone about a trip you have taken. Do you relay the highlights of the trip or all the travel details (such as flight number, gas station fill-ups, and so on)? The BAM workbook allows the user to specify the BizTalk process highlights to monitor.

■ **Note** As previously mentioned, the BAM workbook is an integrated add-in tool within Excel. If you have the BAM add-in tool enabled, you will be able to work on only a single Excel workbook at a time. If you try to open multiple workbooks, you will receive an Excel alert stating you cannot have multiple workbooks for the single Excel instance at the same time. However, you can open a new instance of Excel if you need multiple workbooks opened at the same time. Figure 11-12 shows the Excel exception alert.

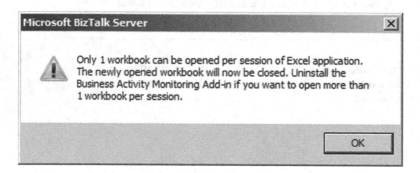

Figure 11-12. Workbook alert message

After creating the BAM workbook, the next step is to identify the key data items, milestones, or key performance indicators implemented through data aggregations. Again, keep in mind that the milestones are logical markers and are not tied directly to physical BizTalk artifacts. For example, a milestone could signify the start or completion of a process. After creating the milestone and deploying the workbook, you map the multiple BizTalk artifacts to that milestone or data item. A BAM activity is a reference to a group or collection of milestones or data items and can span multiple BizTalk artifacts. Table 11-6 describes the four types of items that can be created in a BAM activity. Please review the "Considerations" section of this recipe for additional information about relating multiple activities and grouping of activity items.

Table 11-6. *BAM Activity Items*

Milestone	Name	Description
1	Business Data – Milestone	Placeholder for a date/time marker. Use this type of milestone when interested when an event occurred.
2	Business Data – Text	Placeholder for a text type of data item. Use this type of milestone when reporting a specific textual value piece of data (such as a promoted property) that is a textual value.
3	Business Data – Integer	Placeholder for an integer type of data item. Use this type of milestone when reporting a specific number piece of data (such as a transaction ID).
4	Business Data – Decimal	Placeholder for a decimal type of data item. Use this type of milestone when reporting a specific piece of data requiring decimal precision (such as a dollar amount).

Outline the BAM View

After defining the BAM activity structure and necessary milestones, the next step is creating the view that will represent the tracked data items and milestones. The BAM view is a representation of the milestones and business data defined in a single activity or multiple activities. Views can contain both data and computed aggregations based on the data.

The BAM view also facilitates the creation of data aggregations. If you have distinct audiences interested in different data aggregations or representations of activity milestones, then using a BAM view to represent those views is advantageous. Additionally, you can restrict BAM views to specific audiences to limit the viewing of sensitive data or milestones. You can create a BAM view in one of two ways: using the Business Activity Monitoring View Creation Wizard or from the BAM add-in menu.

An optional task in creating a BAM view involves creating the necessary alias, duration, and group view items. These items are not required but offer extended desirable functionality to a BAM view. Consider view items as computed milestones that show the grouping of items or time durations between two milestones. Table 11-7 describes each view item.

Table 11-7. *BAM Computation Milestones*

ID	Name	Description
1	Alias	Allows the referencing of a previously created milestone.
2	Duration	Allows the monitoring of a span of time between two date/time milestones. For example, if you have a milestone for when a process begins and a milestone for when a process completes, you can create a duration milestone to report the time difference between the two milestones. The duration milestone will report on the following time scale (day, hour, minute, or second).
3	Group	Creates a new milestone for grouping of milestones into a single point in time. For example, if you have a milestone indicating when a process completes successfully or when a process fails, you could create a group milestone that indicates a process finished and group the process completes and process fails milestones. The composite or grouped milestone would identify when a process completed regardless of whether it completed or failed. Another common use is in the situation that you have a process that could fail at multiple points and you want to group all failures into a single process failed milestone.

Identify Aggregations, Dimensions, and Measures

Also optional when creating a BAM view is the inclusion of aggregations, dimensions, and measures based on the milestones and data items tracked. In this example, you created a measure to track the count of processes. Additionally, you created a progress dimension to show the progress of the process as it executes. These items are not required but offer additional flexibility to a BAM view.

Construct the Pivot Table

The final category of steps involves laying out the items of your view into a pivot table for reporting. In this recipe, you created a pivot table that displays the progress of your solution and aggregations of that process through a progress dimension, aggregations, and measures.

Activity Grouping and Multiple Processes

If you have an interest in categorizing multiple milestones into a single group, you should look at using activity grouping. Considering the milestones to be included in an activity and considering the scope of the activity can be challenging. A single activity can reference multiple activities; however, it may also make sense (depending on the level of detail) to create a single activity with the necessary milestones. Again, imagine a trip with multiple legs and side trips containing many details. If the user is interested in many details about the overall trip as well as the individual legs of the trip, it may make sense to create multiple activities to represent the trip as a whole as well as the individual trip legs. Alternatively, if the user is interested only in the trip highlights, it may make sense to create a single activity with those highlights for the entire trip (including trip legs).

In the recipe sample, milestones indicate when a process begins, ends, encounters an exception, and defines data characteristics about the processed transaction. Typically, these milestones include enough information for a user interested in a high-level view about the health of a business process.

Also think about the number of processes. In this example, you created a single activity to report on the behavior of a business process. If you create a solution that has multiple related processes, you may need to create and relate multiple activities. Creating related activities is also necessary in situations where you have a process that involves a looping structure (such as an orchestration with a loop). In the situation where you have a loop structure in an orchestration, you would create one activity for the orchestration and an additional activity for the events occurring within the loop. The physical act of relating activities occurs in the Tracking Profile Editor (or via code).

■ **Note**   When creating related activities, verify that the activities are included in the same BAM view. Additionally, verify that a shared attribute (for example, `MessageID`) relates the two activities.

Summary

BAM is a powerful extensible architecture that facilitates the sharing of key metrics and process milestones. This recipe outlined the basics of creating a BizTalk activity and view and demonstrated how to create relationships between activities and employ computed milestones via view items.

11-2. Deploying BAM Activities and Views

Problem

You have created a BAM activity and view within a BAM Excel workbook and must deploy the BAM artifacts within your environment.

■ **Note** This recipe uses the BAM workbook created in Recipe 11-1 as the basis for the scenario.

Solution

Successfully deploying a BAM activity and view involves a number of steps, typically performed by a few different users. After a business analyst creates the BAM activity and view within the BAM Excel workbook, an administrator deploys the artifacts to the BizTalk environment. The first set of steps to use the BAM Management Utility to deploy the activity and view defined in the BAM Excel workbook is as follows:

1. Open a command prompt by navigating to Start ➤ Run, typing **CMD**, and clicking OK.

2. Navigate to the folder containing the BAM Management Utility by typing the path similar to the following line at the command prompt, and pressing Enter:

    ```
    cd "C:\Program Files\Microsoft BizTalk Server 2010\Tracking\"
    ```

3. Use the deploy-all command to deploy the BAM activity and view defined in your BAM Excel workbook. For this solution, type the following line at the prompt, and press Enter:

    ```
    bm deploy-all -DefinitionFile:"C:\BAMWorkbook\BAMWorkbook.xls"
    ```

4. The status of the deploy operation appears in the console, as shown in Figure 11-13.

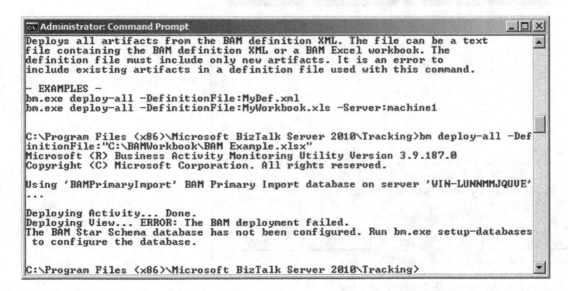

Figure 11-13. Deploying the BAM Excel workbook

> ■ **Note** If you get an error at this stage stating that the BAM Star Schema database has not been configured, this means that the Analysis Services has not been installed on SQL Server. To enable tracking and use of the BAM Portal, Analysis Services must be installed.

5. The next set of steps is for either a developer or an administrator to use the Tracking Profile Editor to define and deploy the mappings between the activities defined in the BAM Excel workbook and actual BizTalk artifacts, such as orchestrations and schemas. (BizTalk Server 2010 also allows pure messaging solutions to feed BAM.)

6. Open the Tracking Profile Editor by navigating to StartPrograms ➤ Microsoft BizTalk Server 2010 ➤ Tracking Profile Editor.

7. Import your BAM Excel workbook by clicking the Click Here to Import a BAM Activity Definition link. This link launches the Import BAM Activity Definition dialog box. Select the appropriate activity definition from the list. In this solution, select the activity definition named Process Activity, as shown in Figure 11-14.

Figure 11-14. *Import BAM Activity Definition dialog box*

8. Select the BizTalk artifacts you need to map the activity definitions to by clicking the Click Here to Select an Event Source link. This link launches the Select Event Source Parent Assembly dialog box. Select the appropriate BizTalk assembly containing the artifacts you will map to the activity definitions; in this solution, select the assembly named BAMProject, as shown in Figure 11-15. Click Next to proceed.

Figure 11-15. *Selecting the BizTalk assembly*

■ **Note** The list of assemblies contains all those BizTalk assemblies that have been deployed within your BizTalk environment.

9. In the Select Orchestration dialog box displayed next, select the orchestration containing the workflow and the links to the schemas that define the activity definitions. In this solution, select the orchestration named BAMProject.Process, as shown in Figure 11-16. Click OK.

Figure 11-16. *Selecting the BizTalk orchestration*

10. Now, map the orchestration steps in the right pane to the activity definition milestones in the left pane. Drag and drop the orchestration shapes to the activity definition milestones, as outlined in Table 11-8. Figure 11-17 shows how the Tracking Profile Editor looks after the orchestration steps have been mapped to the activity definition milestones.

Table 11-8. *Activity Definition Milestone Mapping*

Activity Definition Milestone	Orchestration Step (Shape)
Begin	Begin Process (Receive Shape)
EndSuccess	End Process (Send Shape)
Exception	Failure (Expression Shape)

Figure 11-17. Activity definition milestone mapping

11. Next, map the appropriate schema fields to the activity definition business data. Since the message containing the schema data fields you need to map is received by the Begin Process shape in the orchestration, right-click this shape, and select Message Payload Schema, as shown in Figure 11-18.

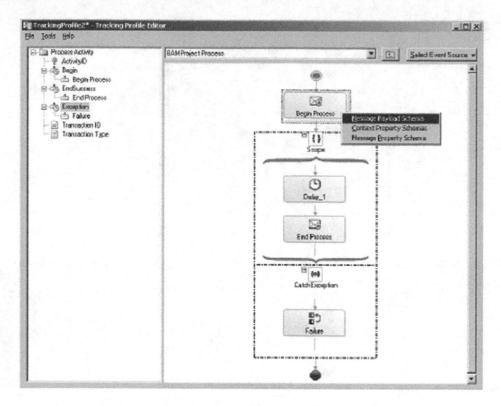

Figure 11-18. *Selecting the Message Payload Schema option*

12. Map the appropriate schema fields in the right pane to the activity definition business data fields in the left pane. Drag and drop the schema fields to the activity definition business data fields as outlined in Table 11-9. Figure 11-19 shows how the Tracking Profile Editor looks after the orchestration steps and business data have been mapped to the activity definition milestones.

Table 11-9. *Activity Definition Business Data Mapping*

Activity Definition Business Data	Schema Field
Transaction ID	ID
Transaction Type	Type

Figure 11-19. Activity definition business data mapping

13. Save the tracking profile by selecting File ➤ Save. Save the file as
    C:\BAMWorkbook\BAMTrackingProfile.btt.

14. Deploy the tracking profile by selecting Tools ➤ Apply Tracking Profile. Click OK
    to confirm the successful deployment of the tracking profile.

How It Works

Deploying BAM activities and views involves two BizTalk tools: the BAM Management Utility and the Tracking Profile Editor. The BAM Management Utility is a command-line tool used for managing your BAM environment. It includes a number of commands, but the one we'll focus on is deploy-all. The deploy-all command takes the following parameters:

- **DefinitionFile:** Path and file name of the BAM Excel workbook (or the exported XML file that can be generated from the BAM Excel workbook) containing the activities to deploy.

- **Server:** Name of the server to which to deploy the activities. If this parameter is not specified, the local server is used.

- **Database:** Name of the database to which to deploy the activities. If this parameter is not specified, the BAMPrimaryImport database is used.

This command reads the BAM Excel workbook specified in the `DefinitionFile` parameter and creates SQL Server database artifacts based on the activities and view defined in the spreadsheet. Specifically, this command creates the following:

- Tables within the BAM primary import database for capturing activity data in the live BizTalk environment.

- SQL Server Integration Services packages for transferring data between the live BizTalk databases and the SQL Server Analysis Services cubes.

- SQL Server Analysis Services OLAP cubes.

- A live data copy of the Excel workbook in the same folder as the original spreadsheet. Use the live data workbook to view up-to-date data within BizTalk Server after completing the deployment steps (including those involving the Tracking Profile Editor).

■ **Note** The BAM Management Utility has no update capabilities for BAM artifacts. You must first remove the old artifacts and then deploy the updated ones.

Use the Tracking Profile Editor to map the activities defined by the business analyst in the BAM Excel workbook to actual BizTalk artifacts, such as orchestration shapes and schema data fields. This task is absolutely critical in ensuring that the deployed BAM artifacts communicate the appropriate information. Although it is common to have a developer or administrator perform this task, this user should have a strong understanding of the business process. Applying the tracking profile places the hooks into the BizTalk Server environment used to record the necessary milestones and data fields, which map to the activities defined by the business analyst. The Tracking Profile Editor in BizTalk Server 2010 also provides functionality to feed BAM via pure-messaging scenarios (those that do not use orchestrations). To access schemas directly, click the Select Event Source drop-down list, and click Select Messaging Payload. This launches the Select Event Source Parent Assembly dialog box. Select the appropriate BizTalk assembly and then the appropriate schema.

Once the deployment steps have executed, you can see the activity data either through the live data copy of the BAM Excel workbook or through the BAM portal.

11-3. Using the BAM Portal
Problem

You need to create a solution that will track your company's business processes, compile the data into key performance indicators (KPIs), and develop a portal to display the information to executives. You have already created and deployed activities and views from a BAM worksheet to define and track the key performance indicators, and you would now like to consume that data from a portal.

Solution

Once you have developed and deployed BAM activities to track your KPIs, you may now consume the data from an ASP.NET portal without writing any code. You can accomplish this by utilizing out-of-the-box BizTalk reporting capabilities through the BAM portal. The BAM portal is a web-based portal built from ASP.NET that allows you to view and query cubed data created within the BAM framework. This recipe will cover three primary activities within the BAM portal:

- Accessing the BAM portal
- Performing an activity search
- Viewing aggregations

■ **Note**   Installing the BAM Portal on 64-bit machines requires that IIS allow for 32-bit applications. This can be easily accomplished by running the following command line script: `cscript %SYSTEMDRIVE%\inetpub\adminscripts\ adsutil.vbs SET W3SVC/AppPools/Enable32bitAppOnWin64 0`.

Accessing the BAM Portal

Take the following steps to access the BAM portal:

1. Deploy BAM activities and views.

■ **Note**   Please see the preceding BAM recipes in this chapter for further information about how to accomplish this task. If you do not have any activities and views deployed, you will not be able to view information in the portal.

---

2. Open the portal by navigating to Start ➤ All Programs ➤ Microsoft BizTalk Server 2010 ➤ BAM Portal Web Site.

3. Once you have opened the portal, you will notice three primary panes: the header frame at the top, the view frame to the left, and the content frame to the right. If you have deployed activities and views, they will be available under the MyViews tree.

Performing an Activity Search

BAM activities capture business processes milestones and business data at a specific point in time. An activity search allows you to define, save, open, and execute queries to retrieve that transactional business data. The activity search page has three main sections, as shown in Table 11-10.

Table 11-10. *Sections of Activity Search Page*

Page Section	Description
Query	This section of the page allows you to define, save, and open queries. Queries let you constrain which activities to return in the results window.
Column Chooser	This section of the page defines which columns to return in the result set.
Results	The section of the page displays the result set retuned by executing the query against the BAM activity data.

To perform an activity search, take the following actions:

1. Under the My Views tree, expand the view that correlates to the view name you have deployed.

2. Expand the Activity Search node, and click a deployed activity. This action will open a query window like the window displayed in Figure 11-20.

Figure 11-20. *Activity search query window*

3. Within the Query pane, build a query by configuring one or more constraints. To configure a constraint, follow these steps:

    a. Choose a field from the Business Data drop-down list.

    b. Choose an operator from the Operator drop-down list.

    c. Enter a value in the Value text box.

    d. Click the Add button to insert additional constraints.

■ **Note** You cannot create complex constraint logic, such as nested constraints. The portal will allow you to add constraints only with simple and/or relationships. By adding more than one constraint, an additional drop-down list will appear that will allow you to define the constraint relationship.

4. Within the Column Chooser pane, choose one or more columns to display in the Results pane.

5. Click Execute Query. The Results pane will display the query results.

Viewing Aggregations

Activity searches provide transactional business data from a specific point in time, and *aggregations* provide aggregated business data about a group of processes at a specific point in time. This aggregated data is processed and stored in OLAP cubes and accessed through pivot tables. The Aggregations page has two main sections, shown in Table 11-11.

Table 11-11. Sections of the Aggregations Page

Page Section	Description
Pivot Table View	Pivot tables provide for a way to summarize and work with data separate from the core spreadsheet. This section contains a standard pivot table. The table automatically points to the BAM framework and specifically the activities and views you have deployed.
Chart View	This section contains the chart view that displays, in chart form, the data filtering configured in the pivot table. It is also possible to change the chart view to any chart available through the office framework.

To view an aggregation, take the following actions in the BAM portal:

1. Under the My Views tree, expand the view that correlates to the deployed view name.

2. Expand the Aggregations node, and click a deployed pivot table. This action will open a window like the one displayed in Figure 11-21.

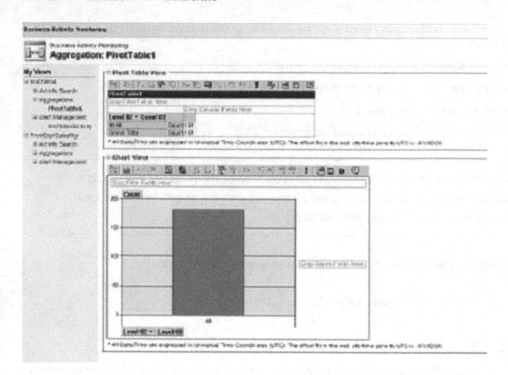

Figure 11-21. *Aggregations page*

> ■ **Note** If the BAM portal displays the "Safety settings on this machine prohibit accessing a data source on another domain" error in the pivot table, you need to change your security settings for Internet Explorer. Open the security settings by selecting the Tools ➤ Internet Options menu in Internet Explorer. Select the Security tab, and then click the Custom button. Once you are prompted with the Security Settings dialog box, locate the Miscellaneous heading, and select the Enable option for the Access Data Sources Across Domains choice. Finally, you will receive an error if no data exists in the cube.

3. From the pivot table View toolbar, click the Field Chooser icon. This will display a list of fields available with your BAM view.

4. Drag one or more total or detail fields to the center of the pivot table.

5. Next, drag one or more column fields to the column section of the pivot table.

6. Close the Pivot Table Field List control. Figure 11-22 shows what the pivot table with data should look like.

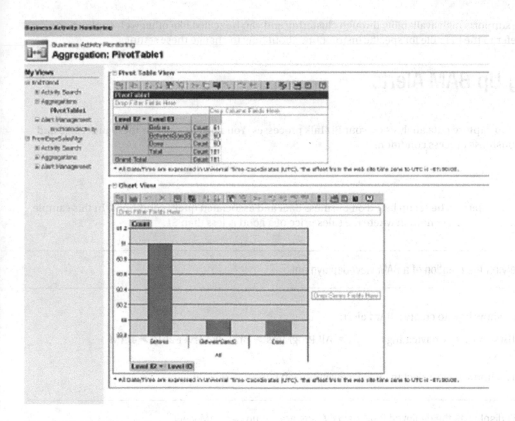

Figure 11-22. *Aggregations view*

■ **Note** The pivot table is a powerful tool, and this recipe does not go into the many features it provides. You should spend some time researching what this tool can provide and how to use it to its full potential.

How It Works

The BAM portal is a feature in BizTalk 2010 that facilitates the rapid consumption of business transactional and aggregated data, without writing any code. The portal is self-configuring, fairly easy to set up, and provides rich data retrieval capabilities. This recipe has provided a high-level understanding of what you can do with the portal, but it has an additional powerful feature, BAM alerts. BAM alerts allow you to configure and receive alerts related to specific changes in business data.

The BAM portal provides several areas of configuration: the look and feel of the main or dashboard page, the `web.config` file, a network load balancing (NLB) clustering. By default, the main dashboard, or Getting Started page, displays navigation instructions to the user. The content for the main dashboard page is located in the `MainPageContent.htm` file, which is located in the root of the BAM portal web site folder and can be altered.

Another area of configuration is `web.config`. This configuration file is similar to standard `web.config` files and allows you to configure security as well as environment settings for the BAM portal. The `web.config` setting highlights include referencing the BAM web services that may be hosted on different machines in a distributed environment, referencing a different main dashboard page file, culture support, and service timeout configuration. Additionally, the types of alert notifications are customizable in `web.config`.

Finally, BAM fully supports high availability through clustering and can be scaled like other web applications through NLB. Please refer to the help file for specific instructions about how to change these settings.

11-4. Setting Up BAM Alerts
Problem

You have to set up BAM to capture data analysis on your BizTalk processes. You need to monitor these processes and set up alerts based on business process conditions.

Solution

BizTalk's BAM tool enables alerts to be set up based on business data and associated query conditions. In this sample, you will be setting a BAM alert on a condition where the sales price of a good is less than $1.

■ **Note** BAM alerts rely on the creation of a BAM view deployment.

The following steps show how to create a BAM alert:

1. Open the BAM portal by navigating to Start ➤ All Programs ➤ BizTalk Server 2010 ➤ BAM Portal Website.

2. On the portal home page, select the BAM view in the left pane.

■ **Note** The portal will display all the deployed BAM views. Alerts are set up per BAM view.

---

3. Click the Activity Search link; Figure 11-23 shows the Activity Search page.

Figure 11-23. *Activity search*

4. Select your search criteria for the activity, and click Set Alert.

■ **Note** It might be a good idea to execute the query first to provide a sanity check on the query results. You can set up an alert before or after query execution.

---

5. The Alert Details screen will now display. At this screen, enter the details for your alert:

   - *Name*: Enter the name of the alert.

   - *Message*: Describe the message that should be displayed when the alert is fired.

   - *Priority*: Assign relative priority. This would be used as a priority identifier within your solution.

   - *Alert Security*: Allow this alert to be seen and used by other users.

6. Click Save Alert to save the alert details, as shown in Figure 11-24.

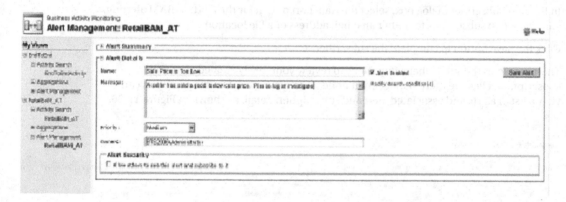

Figure 11-24. *Alert details*

7. Next, you must set up a subscriber to identify who should be notified and when the alert is fired, so click the Add Subscriber button. The Add Subscriber dialog box appears, as shown in Figure 11-25.

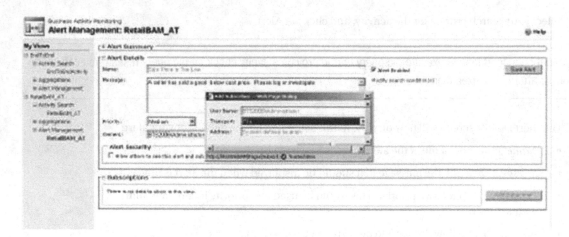

Figure 11-25. *Add Subscriber dialog box*

8. In the Add Subscriber dialog box, select the transport option for the alert. In BAM alerting, you can set up subscribers for either an email address or a file location.

9. Click the Save button to complete the subscriber setup.

10. This completes the subscriber setup. Now, to review your newly created alert and subscription, click the Alert Management node under your view. On this page, you can view a list of alerts and associated alert and subscription detail, as shown in Figure 11-26.

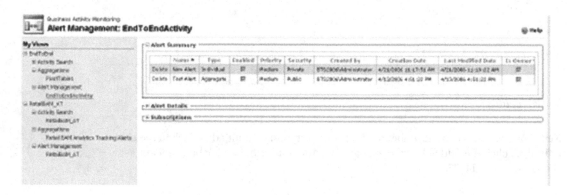

Figure 11-26. *Completed alert*

11. Finally, review that your subscription works. In this sample, you set up a subscription for a file location. Run your business process with data that will cause the alert to fire. When this occurs, an alert should be found in the alert location, as shown in Figure 11-27.

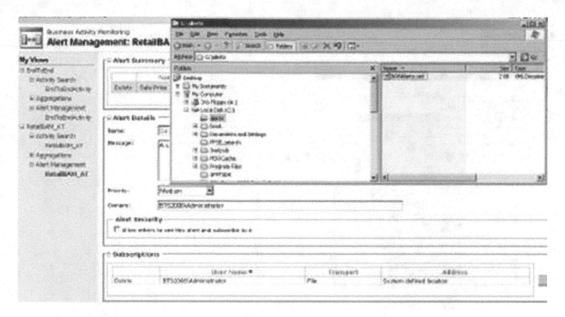

Figure 11-27. *BAM alert*

How It Works

BAM is a powerful tool in BizTalk that allows a solution that you can configure to monitor data passed through BizTalk without performing large amounts of custom development. BAM is based on SQL Server Reporting Services, and events are fundamentally triggered via SQL Server Notification Services. You must consider these prerequisites to successfully enable a BAM deployment:

- *Infrastructure*: Ensure your SQL Server environment and Windows server security configuration are all in working order. This can be problematic and a necessary step in ensuring a secure environment.

- *BAM workbook*: A BAM workbook with associated activities must be deployed in order to access BAM activity searches, aggregations, and associated alerts in the BAM portal.

- *Tracking Profile Editor*: You must deploy a Tracking Profile Editor to see queries and alerts within the BAM portal.

- *BAM alerts location*: You must specify a location to drop file alerts during installation/setup.

You can configure BAM alerts for aggregate or individual data conditions. You can create an alert initially or modify one after creation. An alert can be fired based on a condition of a row of data or as a condition of a summary of data (aggregate). To enable this, you have to set up individual data conditions by setting the alert in the activity search page (demonstrated in this sample) and set up aggregate alerts via acting on the pivot table on the Aggregations tab. Figure 11-28 shows this step.

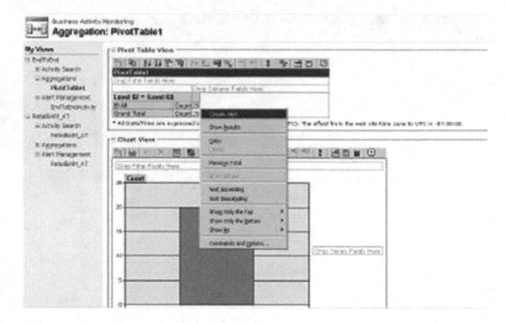

Figure 11-28. *BAM alert*

You can set subscribers for BAM alerts via two transport mechanisms:

- *Email*: Any valid email address or group alias, such as someone@apress.com. A link to the alert detail will be provided in the e-mail body.

- *File*: Alerts will be dropped to the file location specified during product install.

A receive location can be set up to allow consumption back into the BizTalk process for further examination and process action. In addition, aggregate alerts can have threshold limits set to ensure that subscribers are not saturated with repeated messages.

When deploying alerts, it is important to remember the testing aspects and notification success. If a file alert cannot be published as a result of incorrect setup, the alert can be lost. An error will be indicated in the application event log. However, the alert instance itself cannot be salvaged.

11-5. Using the BAM Interceptor
Problem

You want to send custom events to BAM and be able to track these events as if they were published by a core BizTalk component (such as an orchestration).

Solution

The BAM Interceptor is part of the API that is available to interact with BAM from a .NET code base (BizTalk or otherwise). The Interceptor is used primarily by the core BizTalk components, such as orchestrations and pipelines, but can be tied to custom code by a developer. By calling the Interceptor and the associated API methods, you have full control over when and what is sent to deployed and tracked BAM instances.

When orchestrations execute, they constantly send events to the BAM Interceptor. Events that are being subscribed to (tracked events, set in the BAM Tracking Profile Editor) will be saved, and all others will be ignored. When external components to the orchestration are called (such as referenced assemblies), however, they do not log to BAM, and events that occur can be inferred only by the surrounding events sent from the orchestration.

This solution will walk through the sample that is included in the BizTalk SDK. You can find the SDK project files at `Microsoft BizTalk Server 2010\SDK\ Samples\BAM\BamApiSample`.

You must go through several key steps to interface with the BAM Interceptor:

1. Create and deploy a BAM definition, and import it into the Tracking Profile Editor.

2. Create an Interceptor instance, which can be used to interface with the BAM Interceptor. This contains the configuration needed to associate the data in the custom event being fired with the event in the BAM definition.

3. Implement the code to call the BAM Interceptor.

The first thing to do is to import the BAM definition and understand how it corresponds to the rest of the files in the SDK:

1. Run the `Setup.bat` file. This will install the components.

2. Open the BizTalk Tracking Profile Editor. Click File, and then select Import BAM Activity Definition. Assuming the BAM definition has been deployed successfully, the option to select BAMApiPo will be available, as shown in Figure 11-29.

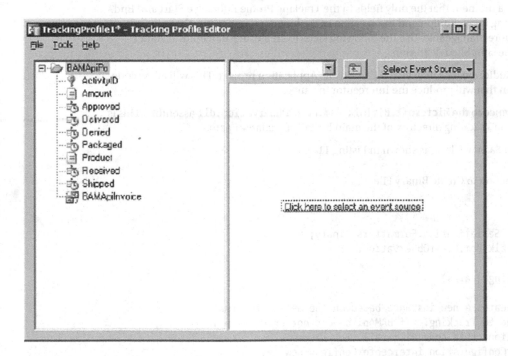

Figure 11-29. Tracking Profile Editor

During the setup process, two console applications are compiled. One of them is the InterceptorConfig.exe file, which takes a series of inputs to determine how to map data logged to the Interceptor to the BAM definition. The second is the BAMApiSample.exe file, which references the output of the InterceptorConfig.exe file to determine how to push data to the BAM Interceptor.

3. Open the BAMApiSample.sln file.

4. First, examine the InterceptorConfig.cs file to observe how it creates the binary file, which will be referenced by BAMApiSample. It creates an Interceptor instance, which is a binary file containing the information needed to map the values to the definition. The XPaths are in reference to the document, which is statically created within BAMApiSample.

An example of the mapping between the definition and BAMApiSample is as follows:

```
locNewInvoice [in BAMApiSample] = Received
  Event [in Tracking Editor]
@PoID [inBAMApiSample] = xpath in xml
  document to InvoiceID [in Tracking Editor]
```

5. Open the PurchaseOrder_config.xml document to see all the mappings as configured by InterceptorConfig.exe. You can change these values; however, you also have to change the document in BAMApiSample to match the new values.

6. Assume for a moment that the only fields in the Tracking Profile Editor are Start and End. By simplifying the definition and the creation of the binary reference file, the solution becomes more manageable. Use the following steps to create an Interceptor instance based on the simplified definition.

7. In Visual Studio, create a new Visual C# Console Application project. This will allow code to be written that will produce the Interceptor instance.

8. Add a reference to the Microsoft.BizTalk.Bam.EventObservation.dll assembly. This is located in the Tracking directory of the main BizTalk installation path.

9. The code in Main will look as shown in Listing 11-1.

Listing 11-1. Main Function to Create Binary File

```
using System;
using System.IO;
using System.Runtime.Serialization.Formatters.Binary;
using Microsoft.BizTalk.Bam.EventObservation;
// etc.
static void Main(string[] args)
{
 // the following creates a new instance based on the definition that
 // has been deployed to Tracking.  If BAMApiPo does not exist as a valid
 // deployed definition, this code will fail.
 ActivityInterceptorConfiguration interceptorConfig = new  ⮥
    ActivityInterceptorConfiguration("BAMApiPo");
 // registrations map the name of the tracked event to the
 // name that is in the binary file/Interceptor code.
 interceptorConfig.RegisterDataExtraction("Start","StartSample","");
 interceptorConfig.RegisterDataExtraction("End","EndSample","");
 // this is the indicator for when the Interceptor is to start and stop
```

```
// listening for events.  @ID is an XPath to where to locate the ID
// in the document passed in (see code for calling Interceptor, below)
interceptorConfig.RegisterStartNew("StartSample", "@ID");
interceptorConfig.RegisterEnd("EndSample");
// Create the Interceptor bin file
BAMInterceptor interceptor = new BAMInterceptor();
interceptorConfig.UpdateInterceptor(interceptor);
// write the file out
BinaryFormatter format = new BinaryFormatter();
Stream file = File.Create("BAMApiSample.bin");
format.Serialize(file, interceptor);
file.Close();
}
```

10. Build the solution. Run the executable. This will write out a binary file, which can now be referenced by the code to call the interceptor.

11. Additionally, an XML document could be generated, which would look like the following (this is not a required step):

```
<TraceInterceptorConfiguration xmlns:xsd="http://www.w3.org/2001/XMLSchema"↪
                xmlns:xsi="http://www.w3.org/2001/XMLSchema-instance">
                <TrackPoint Type="Start">
                <Location xsi:type="xsd:string">StartSample</Location>
                <ExtractionInfo xsi:type="xsd:string">@ID</ExtractionInfo>
                </TrackPoint>
                <TrackPoint Type="End">
                <Location xsi:type="xsd:string">EndSample</Location>
                </TrackPoint>
</TraceInterceptorConfiguration>
```

12. Now, open the BAMApiSample.cs file to observe how it is structured. The key items to look at follow:

   - *The class* MainApp: This class contains the main function that constructs the XML document and event stream that will be used to call the BAM Interceptor.

   - *The class* DataExtractor: This class contains the extractor that returns the data within a given node of the XML document based on the XPath passed as a parameter. The XPath comes directly from the binary configuration file created by the InterceptorConfig.exe file.

   - *The* #If *Interceptor statements*: All statements within these directives call the BAM Interceptor.

The following code is directly from one of the SDK's #If Interceptor directives. It shows how the binary file is loaded and how the OnStep method in the BAM Interceptor is called. In this case, the dataExtractor contains information about how to extract the data from a given node (with the XPath from the binary file), and locNewPo maps to the Received Activity in the Tracking Profile Editor.

```
BAMInterceptor interceptor=Global.LoadInterceptor("BAMApiPo_interceptor.bin");
interceptor.OnStep(Global.dataExtractor,"locNewPo",xePO,Global.es);
```

How It Works

The previous solution explored how to use the Interceptor API and introduced the concept of interaction with the BAM Interceptor. The functionality of this SDK sample is limited in use with true BizTalk implementations. The most likely use of calling the BAM Interceptor directly would be in the case of a custom assembly, which is called from an orchestration. Modifying the console application (BAMApiSample) to a .NET class is fairly straightforward.

Listing 11-2 shows a simplified approach to the application as a class that can be called directly from an Expression shape.

Listing 11-2. Interceptor in a .NET Class

```
class Sample
{
 // the EventStream and DataExtractor tie into Interceptor events
 public static EventStream es=null;
 public static DataExtractor dataExtractor=new DataExtractor();

 public void PassDocument(System.Xml.XmlDocument xmlDoc)
 {
  // instantiate the interceptor by referencing the binary file
  Stream file=File.Open("C:\BAMApiSample.bin", FileMode.Open, FileAccess.Read,
    FileShare.Read);
  BinaryFormatter format=new BinaryFormatter();
  BAMInterceptor interceptor=(BAMInterceptor)format.Deserialize(file);
  file.Close();

  // send an event that will start the tracking
  // xmlDoc is the instance of the document passed in
  interceptor.OnStep(Sample.dataExtractor,"StartSample",xmlDoc,Sample.es);

  // end the tracking
  interceptor.OnStep(Sample.dataExtractor,"EndSample",xmlDoc,Sample.es);
 }

 // add functions for constructing the EventStream and the DataExtractor
}
```

11-6. Creating a BAM Service Request
Problem

You have a deployed BizTalk solution and associated BAM artifacts. You have users viewing the BAM views and associated activities. The user would like additional information about one of the activity line items. Specifically, the user notices the process has terminated with an exception and would like the technical support team to investigate the exception. For this recipe, the sample BizTalk solution and BAM artifacts demonstrated are from the BAMEndToEnd sample project included in the SDK\BAM\Samples folder created with the BizTalk software installation.

Solution

This solution outlines how to use the BAM portal to view an activity line item and issue a technical assistance request for that activity line item. The following instructions assume you have deployed a BizTalk solution and the associated BAM artifacts and that the BizTalk solution has processed transactions. This solution outlines the steps required for creating a technical assistance service request from the BAM portal:

1. From the Start menu, select All Program Files ➤ Microsoft BizTalk Server 2010 ➤ BAM Portal Web Site.

2. Locate the view, and perform the activity search on the activity in which you would like to request technical assistance. Figure 11-30 displays a sample activity search.

Figure 11-30. *Activity search example*

3. Click the activity line item in which you would like to request technical assistance. The Activity Status screen will display and detail information about the chosen line item as well as the Assistance button. You should see a screen similar to Figure 11-31.

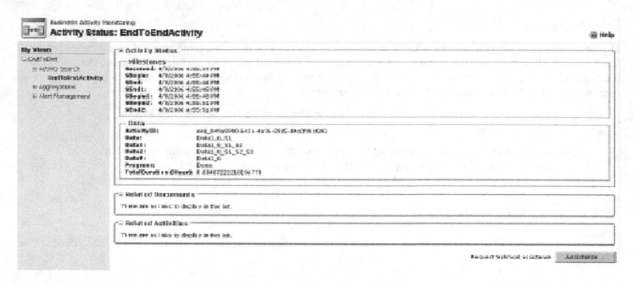

Figure 11-31. *Activity status example*

4. Click the Assistance button to open the Request Technical Assistance – Web Page Dialog dialog box, as shown in Figure 11-32. Enter the appropriate information for the technical request, and click the Send Report button.

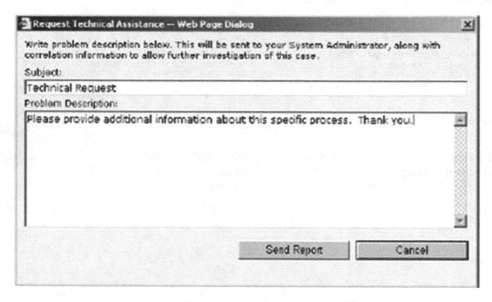

Figure 11-32. *Request Technical Assistance – Web Page Dialog dialog box*

5. Open the Event Viewer to verify that an event log entry has been created for the submitted request. Figure 11-33 demonstrates the generated event log entry for the submitted technical assistance request. The entry will be displayed in the Event Viewer as a success audit.

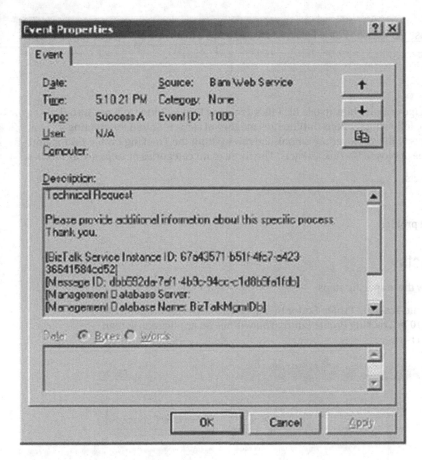

Figure 11-33. Event Viewer entry

How It Works

The Request Technical Assistance functionality included with the BAM portal allows the user to request additional information about a specific activity instance without having context to the business artifacts or the team supporting the solution. To take the greatest advantage of the Request Technical Assistance functionality, the support team should implement an automated solution to monitor Event Viewer entries or exceptions (such as the Microsoft Operations Manager). Via an automated tool, the support team could receive an e-mail or perform some automated action once receiving the technical assistance request.

By default, the Request Technical Assistance functionality creates an entry only in the Event Viewer of the BizTalk Server. For more advanced functionality, investigate how to use a tool that monitors the Event Viewer for new events and performs action based on those events.

11-7. Creating a Tracking Profile
Problem

You have deployed a BAM workbook and the associated BizTalk artifacts. You need to map the BizTalk artifacts to the deployed BAM workbook milestones, data items, and key performance indicators. Additionally, you need to save the mapped profile for deployment to other environments.

■ **Note**   Recipe 11-2 introduced how to use the Tracking Profile Editor; this recipe takes a more in-depth look at how to use it.

Solution

The example reviewed as part of this recipe outlines how to use BizTalk's Tracking Profile Editor to map BizTalk artifacts to an Excel BAM workbook. The following sections outline the category of steps required for creating a tracking profile, mapping BizTalk artifacts to the deployed workbook activities within the Tracking Profile Editor, and finally applying the tracking profile to the deployed BizTalk artifacts. The three main categories of steps are as follows:

- Select the activity and artifacts.
- Map events and data items.
- Save and apply the tracking profile.

Select the Activity and Artifacts

To select the activity and artifacts, follow these specific steps:

1. From the Start menu, open the Tracking Profile Editor by selecting Start ➤ All Programs ➤ Microsoft BizTalk Server 2010 ➤ Tracking Profile Editor. You will see an application screen that looks similar to Figure 11-34.

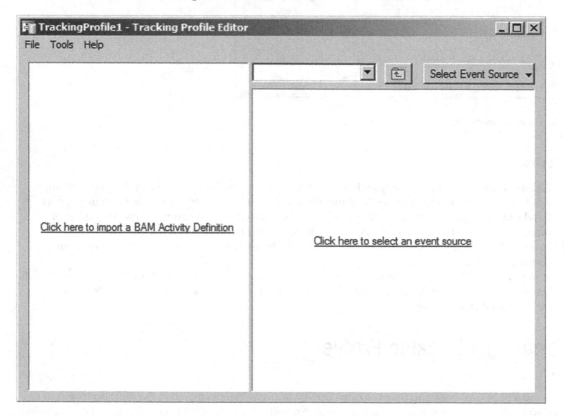

Figure 11-34. *Tracking Profile Editor*

■ **Note**   This solution assumes you have deployed a BAM workbook and BizTalk artifacts.

2. Click the Click Here to Import BAM Activity Definition link to load the deployed BAM workbook and associated activity:

    a. The BAM Import Activity dialog box will ask you to choose the activity to use in the Tracking Profile Editor. If you have deployed the BAM workbook created in Recipe 11-1, choose the Process Activity BAM activity.

    b. Leave the Retrieve the Current Tracking Settings for This Activity Definition box unchecked, and click the OK button to select the activity.

■ **Note**   If you have already applied a tracking profile to the selected activity, you can retrieve the results by selecting the Retrieve the Current Tracking Settings for This Activity Definition box.

3. Click the Click Here to Select an Event Source to load the BizTalk artifacts that will be used during the mapping activity. Identify the assembly that contains the orchestration to map, and identify the specific orchestration that contains data for mapping.

■ **Note**   In this example, a basic orchestration has been created that performs a message receive and send and that implements a catch block for any exceptions. In this example, the name of the assembly is BizTalk Server BAM Test, and the name of the orchestration is BizTalk_Orchestration_BAM.

    a. On the Select Event Source Parent Assembly page, locate the assembly that contains the orchestration you would like to map to the activity. Click the Next button to continue and to select the orchestration to map.

    b. On the Select Orchestration page, select the name of the orchestration you would like to map to the activity. Click the OK button to complete the Event Source Wizard. Figure 11-35 displays the example with a sample orchestration.

Figure 11-35. *Completed Event Source Wizard*

Map Events and Data Items

To map events and data items, follow these steps:

1. Drag the orchestration shapes to the Activity nodes listed in Table 11-12.

Table 11-12. *Sample Orchestration Step Mapping*

Activity Node	Orchestration Step	Description
Begin	Drag the Receive_Msg shape to the Begin activity node.	Captures the successful receipt of a message, which indicates that the process began successfully
EndSuccess	Drag the Send_Msg shape to the End activity node.	Captures the successful sending of a message, which indicates that the process completed successfully
EndException	Drag the LogException shape to the EndException activity node.	Logs an exception occurred in the process

2. Right-click the Receive_Msg shape, and choose Message Payload Schema.

   a. Expand the <Schema> folder icon, and navigate to the data items that are to be reported in BAM.

   b. Drag each reportable data item to the correct Activity node. Table 11-13 outlines the mapping of sample orchestrations to the deployed BAM activities.

Table 11-13. *Sample Orchestration Data Item Mapping*

Activity Node	Orchestration Step	Description
Transaction ID	Drag the `Customer.MessageID` node to the Transaction ID node.	`MessageID` is the unique identifier for the message received.
Transaction Type	Drag the `Customer.TransactionType` node to the `TransactionType` activity node.	`TransactionType` is the transaction identifier indicating the type of message received.

Figure 11-36 demonstrates the completed mapping between the sample orchestration and activity.

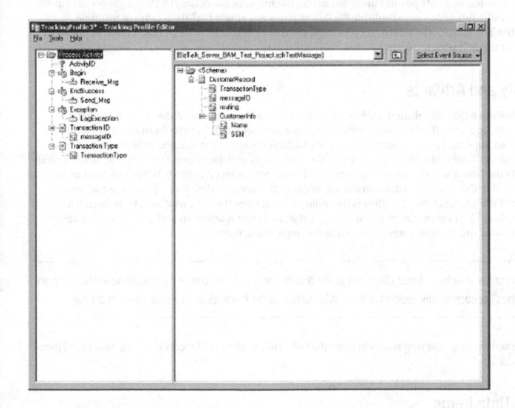

Figure 11-36. *Completed mapped activity*

Save and Apply the Tracking Profile

To save and apply the tracking profile, follow these steps:

1. From the Tools menu, select Apply Tracking Profile. Applying the tracking profile immediately sets the mapping to start recording data the next time the orchestration or process executes.

2. If you plan on deploying the tracking profile in other environments or would like to save a copy of the profile, then choose File ➤ Save As.

How It Works

As mentioned earlier in this chapter, BAM is a powerful tool and architecture for monitoring predetermined milestones and business data. Implementing BAM requires identifying the milestones and business data to report and then mapping those data points to the physical BizTalk solution artifacts. You can map milestones and business data to physical solution artifacts via the Tracking Profile Editor or via the BAM APIs and custom code.

This recipe outlined how to use the BizTalk Tracking Profile Editor to map between a deployed BAM workbook and physical BizTalk solution artifacts. This example outlined a simple scenario involving the mapping of a deployed activity to a single orchestration and data points contained within the message processed by the single orchestration. However, the Tracking Profile Editor can map multiple BizTalk artifacts to a single BizTalk activity or multiple activities. When using the Tracking Profile Editor, keep in mind the three categories of steps that were completed in this recipe, as outlined in the following sections.

Select the Activity and Artifacts

Before mapping an activity to a BizTalk solution artifact, you must choose the activity and the BizTalk artifact(s) that will be mapped. When you open the Tracking Profile Editor, you first select the activity from the list of deployed activities that will be receiving data. Once the activity loads, it will display each of the defined milestones and data items that were previously defined in the activity. The list of the milestones and data items is referred to as the *activity tree*. An activity tree lists the stages and business data items tracked in the deployed activity. When you load an activity in the Tracking Profile Editor, the stages identified in the activity and the business data items appear in the tree.

The basic premise of the Tracking Profile Editor is the ability to map from the deployed activity (which is a conceptual view of a business process) to the physical BizTalk solution. When loading an activity, in the Tracking Profile Editor the activity tree will list all the items created in the deployed activity.

■ **Note**　In addition to the list of activity items displayed in the activity tree, you can create four additional items. Please review the "Considerations" section of this recipe for more information about the additional items you can create.

After selecting the activity, the next step is to select the BizTalk artifacts that will be contributing data to the items listed in the activity tree.

Map Events and Data Items

The next category of steps involves the physical mapping between the BizTalk artifacts and the activity items listed in the activity tree. You map between a BizTalk artifact and an activity item by dragging the BizTalk artifact to the activity item. After dragging the BizTalk artifact to the activity item tree, the artifact will be listed in the activity tree.

Save and Apply the Tracking Profile

The final category of steps applies the tracking profile to the deployed BizTalk artifacts and allows you to save the tracking profile for deploying in other environments or making adjustments later.

Activity Tree Items

The activity tree typically lists the milestones and data items defined in an activity. However, you can also create four other types of items in the activity tree to further enrich your BAM solution. Table 11-14 outlines the items that are included as part of the deployed activity as well as the additional possible items available in the Tracking Profile Editor to help you map activity items to the solution artifacts.

Table 11-14. *Activity Tree Items*

Tracking Profile	Description	NotesEditor Item Icon
Stage	Automatically created in the activity tree when defining a milestone within an activity. The stages are listed when an activity is loaded.	Orchestration steps are mapped to this shape. Some orchestration steps cannot be mapped to this shape including Termination shapes and any steps included within a Loop shape.
Data Item	Automatically created in the activity tree when defining a data item within an activity. The data items are listed when an activity is loaded	You can specify data items from messages in orchestrations or pipelines. Additionally, you can specify context property information for those messages.
Activity ID	Uniquely identifies the instance of an activity that has executed and is automatically included within the activity tree.	This value can be user generated and identified from a message. However, the field must be unique, because it is a key in a SQL Server table. If no value is mapped in the Tracking Profile Editor, BAM will automatically generate this value.
Continuation	Inserts a new continuation folder within the activity tree.	Used in conjunction with ContinuationID to allow multiple components to populate the same activity. For example, if Orchestration A depends on Orchestration B and both contribute data to the same activity, then a continuation folder would be created and mapped to a data item in Orchestration A that is carried over to Orchestration B.
ContinuationID	Inserts a new continuation ID folder within the activity tree.	ContinuationID is mapped to the data item in Orchestration B that was passed from Orchestration A.
Relationship	Relationship folders are used to imply a relationship between one or more activities.	Relationships are especially useful in relating two activities for a single orchestration. For example, if you have an orchestration with a Loop shape, the orchestration and the Loop shape must be represented by separate activities. Via the relationship folder, you can create a relationship between the two activities.
Document Reference URL	Allows the linking of a document related to this instance of the activity.	The file name can be mapped from either a schema value or a context property on the message.

Activity Continuation

Activity continuation is the process of taking multiple BizTalk physical artifacts and combining data from those artifacts into a single activity. Combining data is a useful option when a business process spans multiple BizTalk solution artifacts. Think of the process of creating an activity as defining a database table structure with multiple columns representing the containers for the business data and milestones. When a process executes, it creates a new row in the activity database table recording the data as mapped in the Tracking Profile Editor. Multiple BizTalk artifacts reporting data to the same activity results in multiple rows created in the activity database table. For those artifacts to contribute to a single row in the activity, you need a continuation between the artifacts indicating their relationship.

A common business scenario where activity continuation is useful is the scenario of a life cycle of a purchase order. One company sends a purchase order to another company to purchase goods. The entity shipping the goods will typically send a shipment notice after receiving the purchase order. Additionally, the entity shipping the goods will usually send an invoice for payment of the shipped goods. Managing the sending a purchase order and the receipt of a shipment notice and invoice typically involves many BizTalk artifacts. However, it may be useful to have an end-to-end view of the purchase order life cycle (once issued to the receipt of an invoice) versus each artifact reporting independently. With activity continuation, all the artifacts involved in the life cycle of a purchase order can report information to a single activity, allowing for an end-to-end view of the purchase order life cycle.

Consider the following example: Orchestration A processes a message and transmits that message to Orchestration B for processing. When Orchestration B is finished, it sends a response message back to Orchestration A. When Orchestration A receives the response from Orchestration B, it completes processing. Figure 11-37 demonstrates the sample relationship between Orchestration A and B.

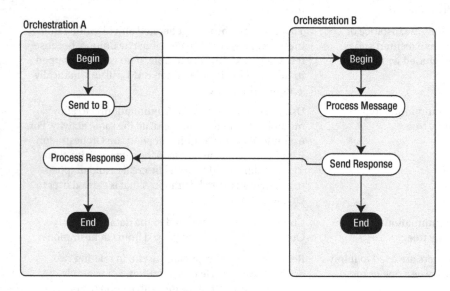

Figure 11-37. *Continuation sample*

Both Orchestration A and Orchestration B can be mapped to the sample activity. However, when the orchestrations execute, two data rows will be created in the activity table to record the information from the orchestrations (one for Orchestration A and one for Orchestration B). If both orchestrations need to contribute data to the same row in the activity, you must create a continuation in the activity tree to indicate the continuation of activity between Orchestration A and Orchestration B.

The following items are required to create an activity continuation between two orchestrations:

- A data item that relates the two orchestrations (or other BizTalk artifacts) and that can be an attribute in a message shared between the two orchestrations

- A continuation folder that specifies the data item in a parent orchestration that relates the two orchestrations

- A continuation ID folder identifies the data item in the child orchestration that relates the two orchestrations

---

■ **Note**   The name of continuation folder and the name of continuation ID folder must be identical in the activity tree. For example, if you create a continuation folder with the name of Continuation, you must create a continuation ID folder with the name of Continuation. You will receive an exception message if the continuation folder and continuation ID folder do not share the same name.

In the Orchestration A and Orchestration B example, the message ID in Orchestration A from the Send shape is mapped to the continuation folder. The same message ID in the Orchestration B Receive shape is mapped to the continuation ID folder. The message ID is the data item that links the two orchestrations and is also the data item in the continuation and continuation ID folders. The BAM end-to-end SDK sample included with the standard BizTalk installation provides a sample implementation of a continuation.

Activity Relationships

Activity relationships are different from activity continuations in that they allow implicit linking between multiple activities. Consider the Orchestration A and Orchestration B example. If both orchestrations represented different business processes, then it may not make sense to have them report to the same activity. If they report to different activities, it may be useful to represent that the activities have a relationship but are disparate. A real-world example of an activity relationship may be how a single purchase order represents multiple shipments. Each activity (purchase order and shipment) is a different activity but is related to the others.

Activity relationships are also necessary when needing to report on BizTalk orchestrations that contain the Loop shape. You can define the parent orchestration as one activity and the looping activity as a separate activity and still accurately report on the activity of the entire process.

When creating activity relationships, you must adhere to the following guidelines:

- Related activities should belong to the same BAM view.

- A relationship item must be created in each activity in the Tracking Profile Editor and must be given the appropriate name of the related activity.

Consider that Activity A reports on the activity in Orchestration A and Activity B reports on the activity in Orchestration B; you would create the relationships activity items listed in Table 11-15.

Table 11-15. *Example Relationship*

Orchestration Name	Activity Name	Relationship Item Name
Orchestration A	Activity A	Activity B
Orchestration B	Activity B	Activity A

After specifying the activity items in each activity, the data item that represents the relationship between the activities must be mapped to each activity item. After creating the relationship item in Activity A, a data item (for example, the message ID) that is shared between the activities would need to be mapped to Activity A. The same data item (that is, the message ID) is then mapped to the ActivityID item of Activity B. Mapping the data item to the ActivityID creates the relationship between the first and second activity.

CHAPTER 12

■■■

Cloud Solutions

In this new era of integration, enterprises must not only communicate with internal services effortlessly but also extend workflows beyond organizational boundaries. They are in need of cloud-enabled, managed services and an Internet service bus. Microsoft's Windows Azure Service Bus caters to such needs. Also, BizTalk Server, being central to Microsoft's hybrid integration strategy, is improved significantly on the cloud-readiness front.

BizTalk, until the current version, has provided a series of adapters to facilitate communication among various on-premise line-of-business systems. In BizTalk 2013, a group of new adapters was introduced to improve the communication between Windows Azure Service Bus entities in cloud and on-premise services. The new SB-Messaging adapters receive and send messages to service bus and WCF-based relay adapters for a two-way synchronous communication with cloud endpoints. In the previous version of BizTalk, the support for cloud integration was limited to relay adapters. Now, workflows can participate reliably and securely in one-way, two-way, and notification-based scenarios.

Apart from BizTalk Server enhancements, few others were introduced. Windows Azure BizTalk Services can significantly simplify the development of hybrid solutions where development is undertaken in Visual Studio and workflows are hosted in Windows Azure framework. It is a simple-yet-powerful service that provides Enterprise Application Integration (EAI) and business-to-business (B2B) capabilities for delivering cloud and hybrid integrations.

Considering the budgeting and resource-allocation complexities in setting up various on-premises BizTalk environments, Microsoft created a set of preconfigured virtual machines in Windows Azure. These virtual machines can be provisioned in a matter of minutes, compared to the days required previously. A virtual network can be created between on-premise servers and the Windows Azure–hosted virtual machines.

This chapter will introduce the core components of implementing hybrid solutions built and managed in BizTalk Server. It will shed some light on using the Azure Management Portal in configuring Service Bus entities, setting up one-way and two-way communications with Azure Service Bus, hosting BizTalk Server Virtual machine in cloud, and creating hybrid solutions with BizTalk Services.

12-1. Configuring Azure Service Bus Entities
Problem

Your enterprise is looking into a hosted, secure infrastructure for exposing the current on-premise workflows to cloud through Microsoft's Windows Azure Service Bus. You are tasked to set up an Azure subscription and configure Azure Service Bus entities before the development is started.

Solution

The financial decisions for such initiatives have to be approved by the key decision makers of your enterprise. Once they are approved, you, as an IT professional, will be tasked to create a Windows Azure subscription.

Execute the following steps to set up an Azure account, a Service Bus namespace, a queue, and a topic:

1. Create a Windows Azure subscription for your enterprise.

2. Go to https://account.windowsazure.com using your Internet browser. You will need a Microsoft Live Account to log on to the Azure Portal and create a Windows Azure subscription. If you don't have one, then create it, and use the username and password to set up an Azure subscription.

3. You will be selecting one of the many offers listed, entering the payment information, and agreeing to the Azure policies. In the current case, the "Pay-As-You-Go" payment offer is selected, as shown in Figure 12-1.

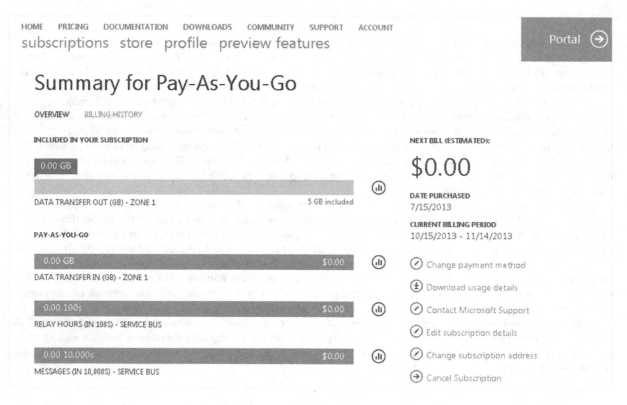

Figure 12-1. *Azure subscription summary*

4. Create an Azure Service Bus namespace to host the entities.

5. Click the Portal link to open the Management Portal page.

6. Select Service Bus from the left panel and click the Create a New Namespace link, as shown in Figure 12-2.

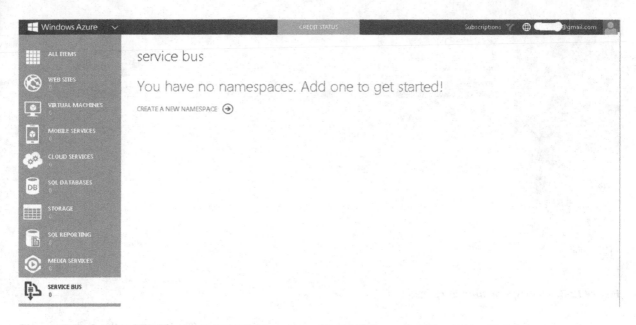

Figure 12-2. Create a New Namespace page

7. Give an appropriate name to the namespace. Select the region closest to your enterprise. Select the Azure subscription for payments. Click Check Icon to create the namespace. Table 12-1 offers some suggestions for specifying values that will help in namespace configuration.

Table 12-1. Namespace Configuration Parameters

Configuration Parameter	Value
Namespace Name	Give an appropriate name to the namespace, e.g., ApressRecipeNS.
Region	Select the region closest to your location, e.g., West US. The region will be useful in other areas of configuration.
Subscription	You might have multiple subscriptions. Choose the most appropriate one, e.g., Pay-As-You-Go.

8. The created namespace will be listed under the Azure subscription, as shown in Figure 12-3.

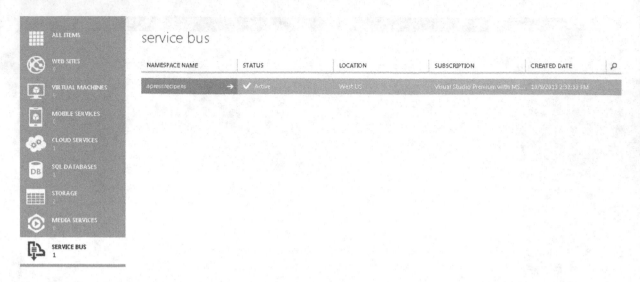

Figure 12-3. *Namespace summary page*

9. Click the namespace to view the connection details for the namespace. The issuer and the security key must be kept secret. Only authorized personnel should have access to that information.

10. Create an Azure Service Bus queue titled "ElectricityGridQueue" under the namespace.

11. Click the + New icon at the bottom left of the portal page to create a Service Bus queue, as shown in Figure 12-4.

Figure 12-4. *New icon on the portal*

12. To create a queue, you have to navigate to Quick Create, by clicking App Services ➤ Service Bus ➤ Queue ➤ Quick Create, as shown in Figure 12-5.

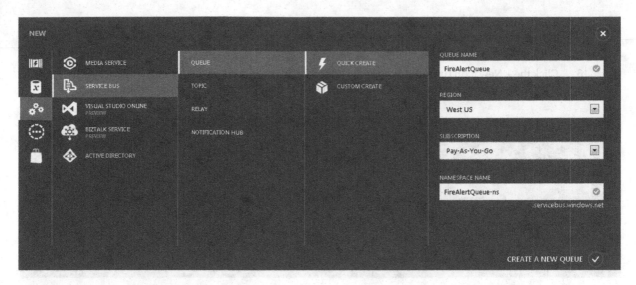

Figure 12-5. *Queue—Quick Create option*

13. Fill in the basic information for the queue and click Create a New Queue to complete the creation. Table 12-2 offers some hints for filling-in the required values.

Table 12-2. *New Queue Configuration Parameters*

Configuration Parameter	Value
Queue Name	Give an appropriate name for the queue, e.g., FireAlertQueue.
Region	Select the region that is closest to your location, e.g., West US. The region will be useful in other areas of configuration.
Subscription	You might have multiple subscriptions. Choose the most appropriate one, e.g., Pay-As-You-Go.
Namespace	All the namespaces under the subscription will be listed. Select the most appropriate one.

14. Once created, the queue will show up under the namespace. Refer to Figure 12-6.

Figure 12-6. *New queue under the namepsace*

15. Create an Azure Service Bus topic and a related subscription for the topic. In the current case, a Service Bus topic titled "WeatherAlertTopic" and a subscription named "FireAlertSubscription" are created.

16. Click the + New icon (usually found at the bottom left of the portal page) to create a Service Bus topic, as shown in Figure 12-7. Click Custom Create to set the extended properties.

Figure 12-7. *New topic create page*

17. This time, try the Custom Create option from the menu, which will provide more control over the topic configuration. This is a two-step process. First, give the topic a user-friendly name and select the region of the Azure data center. Second, select the subscription and the namespace and leave the rest as defaults.

18. The newly created topic will now appear under the namespace, as shown in Figure 12-8.

Figure 12-8. *Created topic under namespace*

19. Click the topic to see the dashboard for the topic, as shown in Figure 12-9.

weatheralerttopic

DASHBOARD   MONITOR   CONFIGURE   SUBSCRIPTIONS

usage overview

⬛ WEATHERALERTTOPIC   ⬜ AVAILABLE

0 MB

WEATHERALERTTOPIC   0% of 1024 MB

quick glance

ⓘ View Connection String

➲ Download the sample solution for a topic

STATUS
Active

TOPIC URL
https://apressrecipens.servicebus.windows.net/weatheralerttopic

Figure 12-9. *Topic details page*

> 20. Click the Create a New Subscription link to begin the creation of a subscription. Refer to Figure 12-10.

weatherevent-topic

DASHBOARD   MONITOR   CONFIGURE   **SUBSCRIPTIONS**

You have no subscriptions. Add one to get started!

CREATE A NEW SUBSCRIPTION ➲

Figure 12-10. *Create a New Subscription page*

> 21. Give a descriptive name to the subscription and leave the rest of the configuration information defaulted, then click Check Icon to save it.
>
> 22. The subscription will show up under "weatheralerttopic," as shown in Figure 12-11.

weatheralerttopic

DASHBOARD   MONITOR   CONFIGURE   **SUBSCRIPTIONS**

NAME	STATUS	MAX DELIVERY COUNT	REQUIRES SESSION-ENAB...	MESSAGE COUNT	LAST ACCESSED TIME
FireAlertSubscription	✔ Active	10	No	0	10/18/2013 10:16:27 AM

Figure 12-11. *Created subscription for the topic*

How It Works

The Azure Management Portal provides a web-based interface for managing the Windows Azure platform as well as dashboards to determine the health of various deployed services. The Azure Management Portal manages the following Windows Azure capabilities:

Compute: Cloud Services, Web Sites, Virtual Machines, Mobile Services

Data Service: Tables, Blobs, SQL Databases, HDinsight (Hadoop), SQL Reporting

Networking: Virtual Network, Traffic Manager

App Services: Identity, Performance, Messaging (Queues, Service Bus, Workflow Manager, Media Services)

Commerce: Store, Marketplace

Of the various capabilities provided, the one of interest in the current recipe is the Service Bus management capability of the Azure Management Portal. Azure Service Bus provides a messaging channel for connecting cloud applications with on-premise services and systems. Through Service Bus, messages can be exchanged in a loosely coupled manner for improved scale and resiliency. Service Bus queues, topics, and relays are central to hybrid integrations.

Service Bus queues provide FIFO (first-in-first-out) message delivery over a range of messaging protocols (REST, WS-*, AMQP). Messages can be put in or pulled off the queue through the queue API. A Service Bus queue typically participates in one-sender-to-one-consumer (one-to-one) -based messaging scenarios. Through the Azure Management Portal, one can visually manage (create, update, and delete) queues.

Unlike Service Bus queues, topics deliver messages to multiple subscriptions and fan out message delivery at scale to downstream systems. Using topics, each incoming message can be subscribed to by multiple subscribers to create a one-to-many messaging scenario. The subscribers select to receive the messages, based on a particular message criteria. At the current state of the Azure Management Portal, it is possible to create topics and subscriptions but not the subscription rules.

The Azure Management Portal provides dashboards for the entities (queues, topics, and relays) from which the user will be able to determine the usage patterns of the entity and also view the grand status of the messages flowing through the entities. A configurable dashboard can show information such as the following:

- Incoming Messages
- Internal Server Errors
- Length
- Server Busy Errors
- Outgoing Messages
- Failed Requests
- Size

- Successful Requests
- Other Errors
- Total Requests

An Azure Service Bus namespace creates a logical grouping for the entities. Each namespace is attached to Access Control Service (ACS), to authenticate the access to the messaging entities within the namespace. The Access settings can be changed in the ACS Management Portal.

12-2. Configuring Queues and Topics from Visual Studio
Problem

You are working on an integration scenario that requires a Service Bus queue and a topic with some advanced subscription rules. You want to set up these Azure entities directly from Visual Studio, without logging in to the Azure Service Bus Portal.

Solution

Azure Service Bus queues and topics can be configured from Visual Studio's Server Explorer add-on by the Azure Integration Developer or by the Azure Administrator, through the Azure Management Portal. The advantage of using Visual Studio is the advanced control on the queue and topic creation. Also, the rules for the subscriptions can only be created in either Visual Studio's Server Explorer or through the Service Bus Management API. The Azure Management Portal currently does not have the ability to set the subscription rules. The following steps will guide you through the configuration of queues and topics:

1. Open Visual Studio and expand Server Explorer. Right-click Windows Azure Service Bus and select the Add New Connection... option from the menu, as shown in Figure 12-12.

Figure 12-12. *Server Explorer—Add New Connection*

2. You will have the option either to select the configuration file or manually set up the connection string by providing the connection and security details. In this case, the Windows Azure Service Bus is manually configured by providing the namespace and the issuer details, as shown in Figure 12-13. You can preview the connection string in the Read-Only text box in the Configuration window. Click OK to connect to the Service Bus namespace.

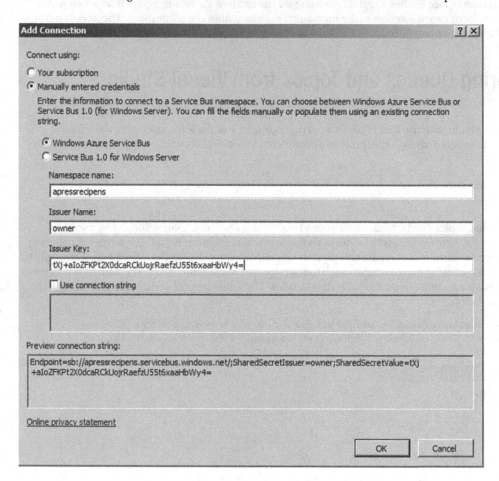

Figure 12-13. *Server Explorer—Add Connection*

3. Once connected to the Service Bus, you will have the option to create new queues and topics. Expand the Azure Service Bus tree to view queues and topics. A queue can be created by right-clicking the Queues node and selecting the Create New Queue option from the Context menu. In this case, only Name and User Description are populated, and the rest is left defaulted, as shown in Figure 12-14. Click the Save button to create the queue under the selected Azure Service Bus namespace.

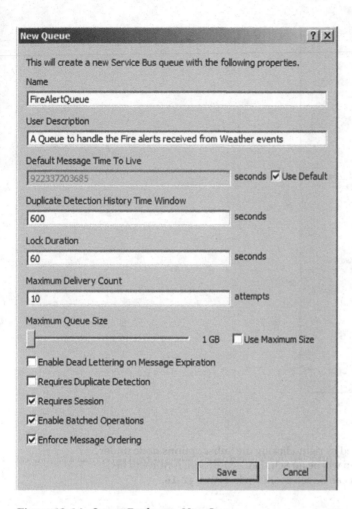

Figure 12-14. *Server Explorer—New Queue*

4. Similarly, a topic can be created by clicking the Create New Topic option in the Context menu and setting topic properties, as shown in Figure 12-15.

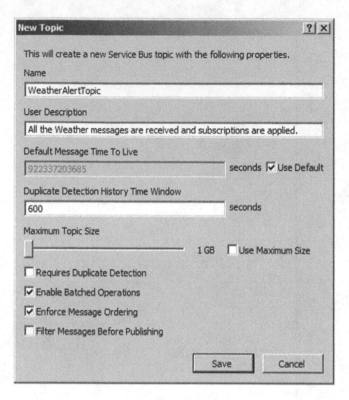

Figure 12-15. *Server Explorer—New Topic*

5. Subscriptions for the topics can be created by right-clicking the Subscriptions node under the Topics tree. A rule for the subscription will be an SQL-like expression. A rule will be used in filtering and routing messages. It can be set, as shown in Figure 12-16.

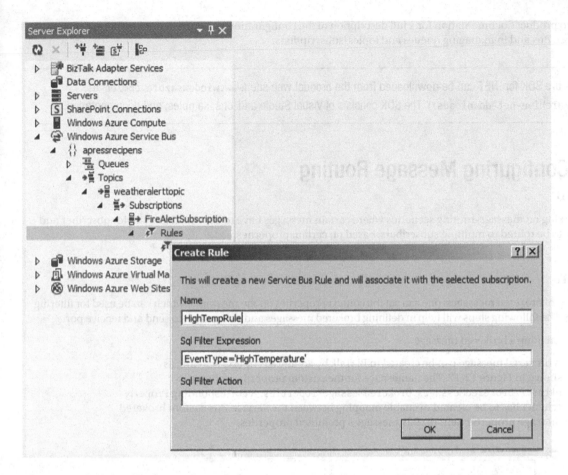

Figure 12-16. Server Explorer—Create Rule

How It Works

Visual Studio's Server Explorer is the Server Management console for Visual Studio. The Windows Azure Tools for Microsoft Visual Studio include Server Explorer support for managing Service Bus messaging entities, such as queues and topics. Once connected to the Service Bus namespace, one can create, delete, and modify the properties of messaging entities in a given service namespace. The following list details connection details and management of entities in Visual Studio.

> *Add connection to Azure Subscription*: The subscription details for the connection can be set either by manually typing or by downloading the subscription file. In Server Explorer, it is possible for developers to connect to Azure Service Bus using issuer and namespace details or to connect locally to Service Bus for Windows Server. The Service Bus for Windows Server is a set of installable components providing messaging capabilities of Windows Azure Service Bus on Windows. With the help of Service Bus for Windows Server, one can build and test message-driven applications in self-managed environments.

> *Manage queue, topic/subscriptions with advanced configuration control*: Just like the Azure Management Portal, the Server Explorer is capable of managing the queues and topics. Unlike the Portal, it is possible to define subscription rules in Server Explorer.

Refer to product documentation for a full description of the configuration parameters used in connecting to Azure Service Bus and in managing queues and topics/subscriptions.

■ **Note**   Azure SDK for .NET can be downloaded from the product web site (`www.windowsazure.com/en-us/ downloads/archive-net-downloads/`). The SDK consists of Visual Studio add-ons, samples, and documentation.

12-3. Configuring Message Routing
Problem

You are working on message-routing scenarios where certain messages have to be routed to a single subscriber and others have to be routed to multiple subscribers, based on certain properties.

Solution

With the help of brokered messages, one can set the context properties on the messages, which can be used for filtering and routing. The following steps will help in defining brokered messages and using them to send and receive ports.

1.   Creating a brokered message

A brokered message can be created in BizTalk by adding a property schema, as shown in Figure 12-17. The namespace for the custom properties schema is `https://BrokeredMessages.BrokeredMessageProperties`. A corresponding Property schema has to be created to enable mapping between the Service Bus custom brokered message properties and BizTalk message's promoted properties.

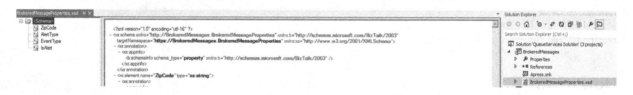

Figure 12-17. *BrokeredMessageProperties schema setup*

2.   Using the BrokeredMessage in an SB-Messaging adapter-based Receive location

BrokeredMessage can be associated with an SB-Messaging adapter (Service Bus queue or topic) –based Receive location by setting the Properties, as shown in Figure 12-18. The namespace for Brokered Message Properties is set to the custom namespace specified in the previous step. When the Promote Brokered Message Properties check box is enabled, the custom brokered message properties will be promoted into the BizTalk message with the standard brokered message properties. If not checked, only a subset of standard Service Bus message properties is promoted to the BizTalk message context. Refer to Recipe 6-16, "Configuring Azure Service Bus Sends and Receives," for further details on port configurations.

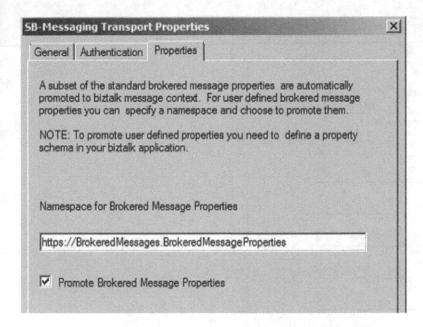

Figure 12-18. *Properties setup screen for Receive Location*

3. Using the brokered message in an SB-messaging adapter-based Send port

Brokered messages can be associated with an SB-messaging adapter (queue or topic) -based Send port by setting the Properties, as shown in Figure 12-19. If the outgoing BizTalk message has any of the standard brokered message in its context, then the adapter will automatically set them as Brokered Message Properties. In addition, you could also specify defaults as part of the Send port properties.

Figure 12-19. Properties setup screen for Send Port

4. Using brokered messages in content-based routing and processing logic

When BizTalk receives a message from Service Bus, the context properties of a brokered message are mapped into BizTalk's promoted properties. These promoted properties of the BizTalk message can be used in business logic of an orchestration, as shown in Figure 12-20.

Figure 12-20. Orchestration-based routing with Brokered Message Properties

The Brokered Message Properties can be used in Azure BizTalk Services in routing the messages to various destinations.

5. Associating Brokered Message Properties to the message:

Finally, a brokered message with custom context properties can be created and sent to a queue, as shown in Listing 12-1. In the following code, a brokered message is created with few custom properties added to the context of the message, and a Fire Alert–type message is added to the body of the brokered message.

Listing 12-1. Setting Brokered Message Properties in .NET

```
class QSender
    {
        const string QueueName = "firealertqueue";
        static string ServiceNamespace = "apressrecipens";
        static string IssuerName = "owner";
        static string IssuerKey = "Some Valid Issuer Key";

         public static void SendQ(FireEvent fireEvent)
        {
            TokenProvider credentials =
               TokenProvider.CreateSharedSecretTokenProvider(
                   QSender.IssuerName, QSender.IssuerKey);
            Uri serviceUri = ServiceBusEnvironment.CreateServiceUri("sb",
                                                QSender.ServiceNamespace, string.Empty);

            MessagingFactory factory = null;
```

```
        factory = MessagingFactory.Create(serviceUri, credentials);

        QueueClient qClient = factory.CreateQueueClient(QSender.QueueName);

        BrokeredMessage brokeredMessage = new BrokeredMessage(fireEvent,
                                    new DataContractSerializer(typeof(FireEvent)));
        brokeredMessage.Properties.Add("ZipCode", fireEvent.ZipCode);
        brokeredMessage.Properties.Add("AlertType", fireEvent.AlertType);
        brokeredMessage.Properties.Add("EventType", "Weather");
        brokeredMessage.Properties.Add("IsAlert", true);

        qClient.Send(brokeredMessage);

        Console.WriteLine("press enter to exit....");
        Console.Read();
    }
}
```

How It Works

Using Azure Service Bus, one can develop two types of hybrid messaging solutions. A relay service provides synchronous communication with the service endpoint hosted in cloud. The second is a messaging solution that uses brokered messaging capabilities for asynchronous and loosely coupled solutions. Loosely coupled messaging solutions support publish-subscribe, temporal decoupling, and load-balancing scenarios.

A brokered message is a Service Bus message envelope with a message header and payload. The header of a brokered message can hold a set of standard Service Bus–specific metadata and also a set of custom properties that can be used in filtering and routing of messages. These custom properties can be set, based on a business scenario. The queues and topics use Brokered Message Properties in filtering and routing. The business processes handling these messages will have the ability to apply business logic, based on these properties.

A brokered message in a BizTalk context is a BizTalk message with promoted properties. While handling the brokered messages, the properties are transferred as promoted properties from Service Bus entity clients to BizTalk. These promoted properties can be used for filtering and content-based routing.

In the current scenario, the QSender class sends a brokered message with custom properties (ZipCode, AlertType, EventType, IsAlert) to the Azure Service Bus queue. A Receive location in BizTalk picks up the message and passes it on to an orchestration. The received orchestration can apply some business logic using the promoted property of the BizTalk message.

12-4. Exposing a Relay Endpoint Through Azure Service Bus
Problem

You are tasked to securely expose an existing on-premise WCF web service to cloud through Azure Service Bus.

Solution

BizTalk Server 2013 introduced a new set of relay adapters to help this process. Before BizTalk 2013, exposing a relay endpoint was accomplished through the WCF Service Publishing Wizard. Now it can be done with the WCF Service Publishing Wizard and through port bindings.

In the current recipe, an orchestration is exposed as a service. This lookup orchestration takes a client ID and returns the orders for the client. This orchestration is deployed to BizTalk Server. Now, it has to be exposed as a relay service. For the sake of simplicity, an on-premise WCF service is already created, and a MEX endpoint is deployed to IIS.

■ **Note** Refer to Recipe 5-24 for creating an on-premise WCF service using the BizTalk WCF Service Publishing Wizard. The wizard can create a WCF service endpoint and add the port to the BizTalk Application or create a MEX endpoint in IIS for an existing WCF port.

The following steps will let you expose the existing on-premise WCF service to the cloud as a relay service.

A WCF MEX endpoint is deployed to the BizTalk Administration Console with the configuration shown in Figure 12-21.

Figure 12-21. *Receive location for on-premise WCF service*

1. In the desired BizTalk application, select the receive port under which you want to add an Azure Service Bus relay receive location. Right-click Receive Port and select New ➤ Receive Location. It opens the Receive Location Properties Window.

2. Give the receive location a name, and set the Type property to WCF-BasicHttpRelay.

3. The Receive handler property should set the correct host application, depending on how you want to organize your environment. In many scenarios, only a single option is available here.

4. Set the Receive pipeline property to the correct pipeline. If the message that was being picked up was XML, and you needed to ensure that it validated against a deployed schema, the correct receive pipeline would be XMLReceive. Figure 12-22 shows the configuration of the receive location so far.

Figure 12-22. *General settings for the receive location*

5. Click the Configure button.

6. Enter the value of the Azure Service Bus endpoint URI from where the relay endpoint is accessed, as shown in Figure 12-23.

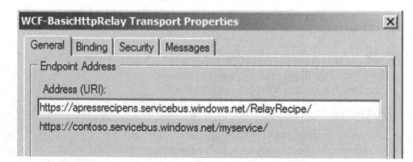

Figure 12-23. *Configuring WCF-BasicHttpRelay Transport Properties—General tab*

7. Click the Security tab to set the Service Bus Security. Here you will set the Security Mode, Client Security, and Access Control Service details. In this case, the Security Mode is set to Transport, because https is used for communication, and Client Security is set to None. Click the Edit button in the Access Control Service section to fill in the Security Token Service (STS) URI, Issuer Name, and Issuer Key, as shown in Figure 12-24.

Figure 12-24. *Configuring WCF-BasicHttpRelay Transport Properties—Security tab)*

8. Click OK to create the receive location.

Now the relay endpoint will be listed in the Azure Service Bus Portal, as shown in Figure 12-25.

apressrecipens

⚡ ALL   QUEUES   TOPICS   RELAYS   NOTIFICATION HUBS   CONFIGURE

NAME	RELAY TYPE	LISTENERS
RelayRecipe	HTTP	1

Figure 12-25. *Azure Service Bus relay listed under namespace*

How It Works

BizTalk Server 2013 introduces two new adapters for the Service Bus relays. The configuration of WCF-BasicHttpRelay and WCF-NetTcpRelay adapters are very similar to the existing WCF-BasicHttp and WCF-NetTcp adapters, except in the way security is configured. Refer to Recipe 6-15 to understand the details of two-way WCF receive-location configuration.

The Azure Service Bus relay securely exposes the on-premise WCF service to the public cloud. Before Service Bus functionality was released, such relay functionality was possible only through opening ports in the firewall, to permit external clients to access the corporate networks. This was not a preferred choice for the network administrators, because of security vulnerabilities that these non-policy driven activities were creating. There is no need to create special accommodations for the service communication.

Secure communication between the cloud consumer and the on-premise WCF service occurs in three stages. First, on-premise WCF service registers the relay endpoint with Azure Service Bus, by providing proper Access Control Service (ACS) credentials. Second, the Azure Service Bus framework validates the ACS credentials. If they are valid, it registers and exposes the endpoint for the public cloud to consume. Finally, the consumer connects to the relay endpoint using the proper ACS credentials. Azure Service Bus validates the credentials and issues a token. After validation, the client is now able to send a request message to the on-premise WCF service. The WCF service performs the business logic and sends the response to the consumer.

While configuring the security of the relay adapters (WCF-BasicHttpRelay, WCF-NetTcpRelay), the following have to be considered:

- The Security mode specifies the type of security to be used. The possible security modes are no security (None), transport-level security only (HTTPS, TLS over TCP, or SPNego), message-level security only (SOAP message security), or transport with message credentials (SOAP message security with HTTPS/TCP transport security). The message client credential type (Username or Certificate) and the appropriate encryption algorithm have to be selected for security modes Message and TransportWithMessageCredential. When using the message-type security mode, the service certificate for the receive location has to be provided through the Service certificate—Thumbprint property.

- The relay client-authentication type specifies the option to authenticate with the Service Bus relay endpoint from where the message is received. The possible options for this configuration are no authentication required or use the RelayAccessToken. RelayAccessToken specifies that the security token has to be used to authorize the Service Bus relay endpoint. To successfully set the RelayAccessToken, you must have the Access Control Service STS URI, Issuer Name, and Issuer Key.

The rest of the configuration, apart from Security, is very close to the traditional WCF on-premise adapters.

12-5. Setting Up a Virtual Machine with BizTalk 2013 in Cloud

Problem

You are tasked to provision a virtual machine with the BizTalk 2013 server installed in it for a short-term development initiative.

Solution

Provisioning a virtual machine means acquiring licenses, setting up operating systems, installing all the prerequisite software, and, finally, configuring BizTalk Server. Because of the current licensing models, the cost and effort to set up an internal BizTalk environment could be expensive, particularly when the initiative is only for a short term. To help resolve the problem, Microsoft offers pre-built images for such needs. These pre-built images can be brought up and down in only a few minutes, as you need them. The following steps will help you in provisioning a BizTalk 2013 virtual machine in Azure:

1. Log into Azure Management Portal, and click the + New icon of the page to open the options. Navigate to Compute ➤ Virtual Machine ➤ From Gallery, as shown in Figure 12-26.

Figure 12-26. Navigating to From Gallery

2. Select the virtual machine image from the gallery. In this case, you can select a virtual machine with BizTalk 2013 Enterprise, Evaluation, or Standard Version. Select the Virtual machine image to suit your needs. The information in Figure 12-27 shows the virtual images that are available for you to select from.

Figure 12-27. Selecting VM with BizTalk 2013

3. Select Virtual Machine Configuration information. Set the Machine Name, Size, and User details, as shown in Figure 12-28.

CREATE A VIRTUAL MACHINE

Virtual machine configuration

VIRTUAL MACHINE NAME

APressRecipeVM

SIZE

Medium (2 cores, 3.5 GB memory)

NEW USER NAME

adminusr

NEW PASSWORD CONFIRM

•••••••• ••••••••

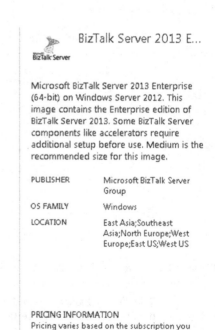

BizTalk Server 2013 E...

Microsoft BizTalk Server 2013 Enterprise (64-bit) on Windows Server 2012. This image contains the Enterprise edition of BizTalk Server 2013. Some BizTalk Server components like accelerators require additional setup before use. Medium is the recommended size for this image.

PUBLISHER Microsoft BizTalk Server Group

OS FAMILY Windows

Figure 12-28. *Virtual machine configuration—1*

  4. Set up the Cloud Service, Storage Account, and Availability Sets, as shown in Figure 12-29.

CREATE A VIRTUAL MACHINE

Virtual machine configuration

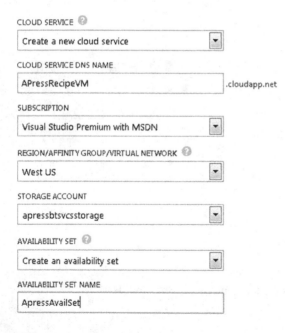

CLOUD SERVICE

Create a new cloud service

CLOUD SERVICE DNS NAME

APressRecipeVM .cloudapp.net

SUBSCRIPTION

Visual Studio Premium with MSDN

REGION/AFFINITY GROUP/VIRTUAL NETWORK

West US

STORAGE ACCOUNT

apressbtsvcsstorage

AVAILABILITY SET

Create an availability set

AVAILABILITY SET NAME

ApressAvailSet

BizTalk Server 2013 E...

Microsoft BizTalk Server 2013 Enterprise (64-bit) on Windows Server 2012. This image contains the Enterprise edition of BizTalk Server 2013. Some BizTalk Server components like accelerators require additional setup before use. Medium is the recommended size for this image.

PUBLISHER Microsoft BizTalk Server Group

OS FAMILY Windows

LOCATION East Asia;Southeast Asia;North Europe;West Europe;East US;West US

PRICING INFORMATION
Pricing varies based on the subscription you

Figure 12-29. *Virtual machine configuration—2*

5. Finally, pick the virtual machine endpoints and agree to the licensing and privacy statements, as shown in the Figure 12-30.

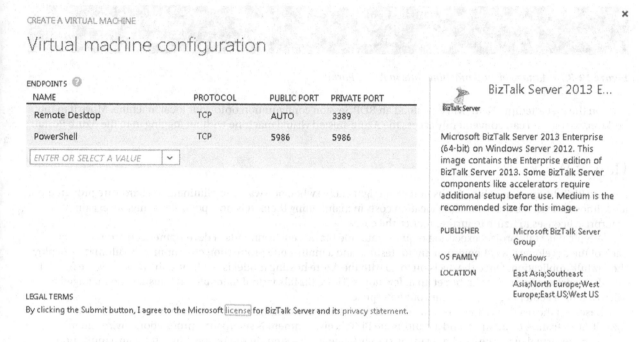

Figure 12-30. *Virtual machine configuration—3*

6. In a few minutes, the virtual machine will be set up and start running, as shown in Figure 12-31.

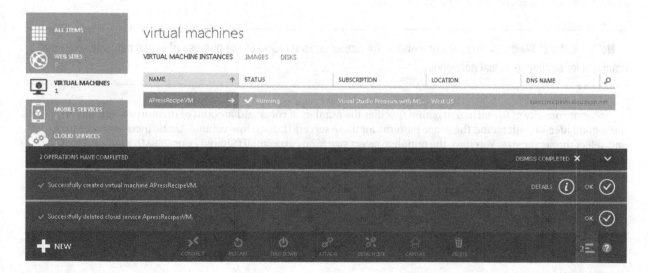

Figure 12-31. *Created virtual machine Azure Portal*

7. Now you will be able to manage the state of the virtual machine. You can Connect, Restart, Shut Down, Attach, or Delete the virtual machine, as shown in Figure 12-32.

Figure 12-32. Manage virtual machine state in Azure Portal

On the first attempt, Azure will download an RDP Session configuration onto your local machine. Move it to the desktop, so that you can conveniently access the Azure-hosted virtual machine without logging in to the Azure Portal.

How It Works

Hosting BizTalk virtual machine is absolutely the right choice when one wants to eliminate the hardware procurement lead times and reduce the resource-allocation costs in maintaining them. It is now possible to migrate existing enterprise licenses to Azure to further reduce the costs.

A typical BizTalk project execution requires multiple BizTalk environments, a development environment for each of the developers, a QA environment for testing, and a multi-node production environment to ultimately deploy the BizTalk application. Once the decision to go with the Azure hosting model is made and the financials are figured out, the entire environment can be set up in few hours. These BizTalk virtual machines are hosted and managed in Microsoft data centers in a region near your enterprise.

Based on the need, a virtual machine image is selected. For example, a single virtual machine is selected for a BizTalk 2013 feature evaluation, and a multi-node BizTalk environment is set up for a production environment.

A single virtual machine can be set up by simply following the steps in the recipe, but setting up a multi-node BizTalk server environment requires some up-front planning. Understanding the following setup properties will help you in creating and configuring Windows Azure–hosted virtual machines.

Virtual network provides the capability to extend the corporate network into Windows Azure and treat the deployments in Windows as a natural extension of the on-premise network. It has to be set up before configuring a multi-node BizTalk Server environment.

■ **Note** Refer to Windows Azure documentation for further understanding of the purpose of virtual networks and best practices for setting up virtual networks.

Size or capacity of the virtual machine specifies the number of cores and amount of memory for the servers. It is a good idea to understand the usage patterns for these servers (bursts, low volume, traffic increases over time) and select the server size. You have the option to select size from extra small (Shared core, 768MB memory) to A7 (8 cores, 58GB memory). It is a good idea to size the server correctly initially, rather than change the configuration on an ad-hoc basis, even though it is possible to do so.

Selection of Region or Affinity Group is very helpful in improving the performance. When a virtual machine or network is hosted in a region closest to your enterprise, all your server traffic will go through fewer network hoops. Affinity Group lets you group your Windows Azure services to optimize the performance. All the services within an affinity group will be located in the same data center. An affinity group is required when a virtual network is created. Choose Affinity Group over Region, if you already have one created.

A Cloud Service can be created to host one or more virtual machines. You can load-balance multiple virtual machines by hosting them in a single cloud service. Windows Azure provides round-robin load-balancing of network traffic to publicly defined ports of a cloud service. A load-balanced endpoint is a specific TCP or UDP endpoint used by all members of a cloud service.

An Availability Set helps you avoid the risk of single-point failures for the applications. The virtual machines in an availability set will be deployed across multiple fault domains.

A Storage Account gives the applications access to Windows Azure Blob, Table, and Queue services located in a geographic region. A storage account can use up to 200TB of storage space. The storage account gives your virtual machines access to Windows Azure Blob services located in a geographic storage.

12-6. Creating Content-Based Routing

Problem

You are tasked to create a content-based routing scenario, using Windows Azure BizTalk Services (WABS). Your workflow is supposed to receive, enrich, and route the incoming messages to multiple destinations.

Solution

Consider a scenario where a weather event is raised to indicate a high temperature or high wind in a valley area prone to wildfires. When such an event is raised, a local fire department is alerted to the possibility of a wildfire. For areas other than a valley, the critical non-fire event is subscribed to by multiple subscribers. All other non-critical events are logged for future analysis.

Such content-based routing can be achieved by configuring a rich endpoint in Windows Azure BizTalk Services. The endpoint will receive the weather event, introspect the event, enrich the event with certain meta properties, and route the event to the appropriate destination(s). In this scenario, an XML one-way bridge receives the weather event and enriches the message with certain routing properties (IsAlert, EventType, Temperature). The enriched message is routed to various destinations, based on the properties. The following pseudo-logic best captures the routing logic:

```
If (EventType = 'HighTemperature' OR EventType= 'Wind') AND Temperature > 110
Then Send a Fire Alert event to Fire Department Queue
Else If (EventType = 'Cold'  OR EventType = 'Flooding')
     Then Send the Weather Event to a Weather Alert Topic
Else IF (IsAlert = False)
     Then Send the Non-Critical Events Queue
```

■ **Note** This recipe assumes that BizTalk Services are already configured. Refer to Microsoft's documentation for details on setting up BizTalk Services for your subscription and installing the related SDKs. Once the prerequisites are set up on the local development environment, you will observe a new set of templates added to Visual Studio for BizTalk Services–based solution development.

The following steps will guide you through the implementation:

1. Open Visual Studio and create a new BizTalk Service project, as shown in Figure 12-33.

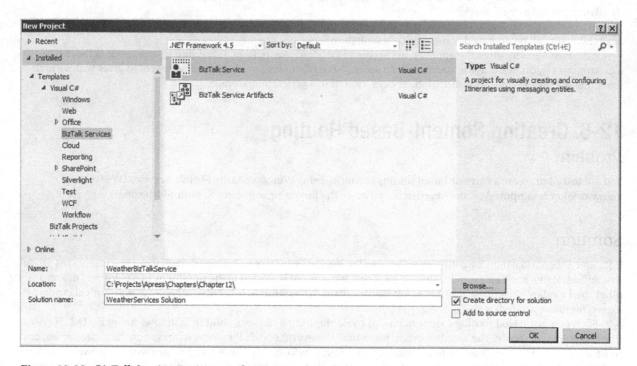

Figure 12-33. BizTalk Services Project template in Visual Studio

2. Create the two required schemas (WeatherEvent.xsd and FireEvent.xsd), as shown in Figure 12-34 and Figure 12-35. Also, create a map between Weather Event and Fire Event (WeatherEvent_To_FireEvent.trfm), as shown in Figure 12-36. Observe that the redesigned Map surface looks very close to on-premise BizTalk maps, and it is saved with a file extension .trfm.

Figure 12-34. *Weather Event schema*

```xml
<?xml version="1.0" encoding="utf-16" ?>
- <xs:schema xmlns="http://WeatherBizTalkService.WeatherEvent" xmlns:b="http://schemas.microsoft.com/BizTalk/2003"
    targetNamespace="http://WeatherBizTalkService.WeatherEvent" xmlns:xs="http://www.w3.org/2001/XMLSchema">
  - <xs:element name="WeatherEvent">
    - <xs:complexType>
      - <xs:sequence>
          <xs:element minOccurs="1" maxOccurs="1" name="EventType" type="xs:string" />
          <xs:element minOccurs="1" maxOccurs="1" name="Temperature" type="xs:int" />
        - <xs:element minOccurs="1" maxOccurs="1" name="PrimaryAffected">
          - <xs:complexType>
            - <xs:sequence>
                <xs:element minOccurs="1" maxOccurs="1" name="AffectedArea" type="xs:string" />
                <xs:element minOccurs="1" maxOccurs="1" name="ZipCode" type="xs:string" />
              </xs:sequence>
            </xs:complexType>
          </xs:element>
        - <xs:element minOccurs="0" maxOccurs="1" name="SecondaryAffected">
          - <xs:complexType>
            - <xs:sequence>
              - <xs:element minOccurs="1" maxOccurs="unbounded" name="Areas">
                - <xs:complexType>
                  - <xs:sequence>
                      <xs:element minOccurs="1" maxOccurs="1" name="AffectedArea" type="xs:string" />
                      <xs:element minOccurs="1" maxOccurs="1" name="ZipCode" type="xs:string" />
                    </xs:sequence>
                  </xs:complexType>
                </xs:element>
              </xs:sequence>
            </xs:complexType>
          </xs:element>
          <xs:element name="IsAlert" type="xs:boolean" />
        </xs:sequence>
      </xs:complexType>
    </xs:element>
  </xs:schema>
```

Figure 12-35. *Fire Event Schema*

```xml
<?xml version="1.0" encoding="utf-16" ?>
- <xs:schema xmlns="http://EventConsumerProj.FireEvent" xmlns:b="http://schemas.microsoft.com/BizTalk/2003"
    targetNamespace="http://EventConsumerProj.FireEvent" xmlns:xs="http://www.w3.org/2001/XMLSchema">
  - <xs:element name="FireEvent">
    - <xs:complexType>
      - <xs:sequence>
          <xs:element minOccurs="1" maxOccurs="1" name="AlertType" type="xs:string" />
          <xs:element minOccurs="1" maxOccurs="1" name="AlertColor" type="xs:string" />
          <xs:element minOccurs="1" maxOccurs="1" name="Temperature" type="xs:int" />
          <xs:element minOccurs="0" maxOccurs="1" name="AlertMessage" type="xs:string" />
        </xs:sequence>
      </xs:complexType>
    </xs:element>
  </xs:schema>
```

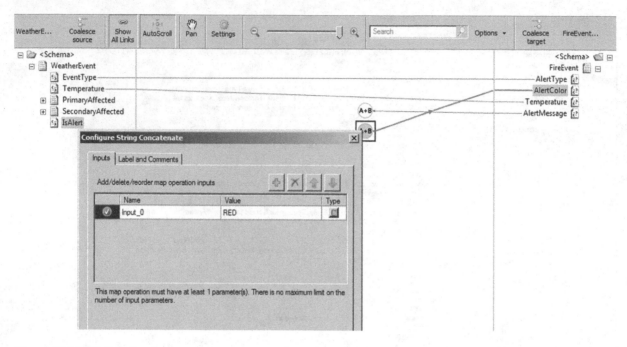

Figure 12-36. *BizTalk Services mapper*

3. Open the file MessageFlowItinerary.bsc to configure the rich endpoint. Observe that the toolbox has the necessary shapes for Bridges, Destinations, and Sources, as shown in Figure 12-37.

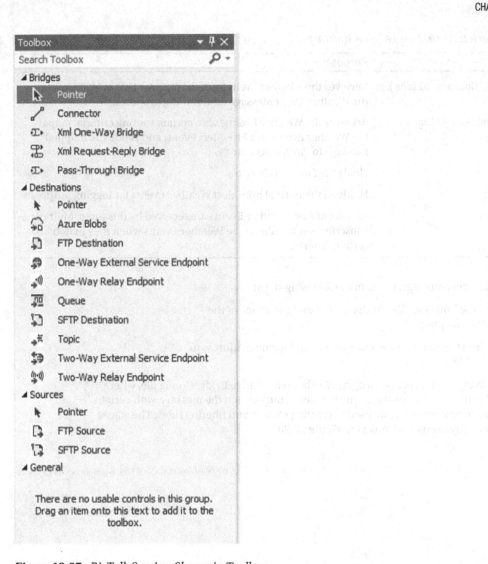

Figure 12-37. *BizTalk Services Shapes in Toolbox*

4. To fulfill the current need, you will require two Xml One-Way Bridges, two Service Bus Queues, and one Service Bus Topic. The following table (Table 12-3) summarizes the purpose of the bridges, queues, and topic/subscription.

Table 12-3. *Purpose of Each Entity in Message Flow Itinerary*

Entity	Purpose
WeatherEventBridge(XML One-Way Bridge)	Receives the Weather Event from the Source. This bridge enriches the Weather Event Message with routing properties
FireAlertBridge(XML One-Way Bridge)	Receives the Weather Events, with certain routing criteria, maps the Weather Events to a Fire Alert Event; and sends the mapped message to FireAlertQueue
FireAlertQueue(Queue)	Holds the Fire Alert Events
NormalEventQueue(Queue)	Holds all the normal non-alert Weather Events for logging purposes
WeatherAlertTopic(Topic)	All critical alert Weather Events are received by this topic. Multiple subscribers subscribe to the Weather Events when they match certain criteria.

To configure the WeatherEventBridge, perform the following steps:

5. Drag and drop the Xml One-Way Bridge on the design surface of the MessageFlowItinerary.bsc.

6. Select the bridge shape and set the Entity Name and Relative Address to WeatherEventBridge.

7. Double-click WeatherEventBridge to open WeatherEventBridge.BridgeConfig file, where you will be able to select the message type to receive, then enrich the message with certain properties. These properties will be used in creating routing and filtering rules. The stages of the Xml One-Way Bridge will look as in Figure 12-38.

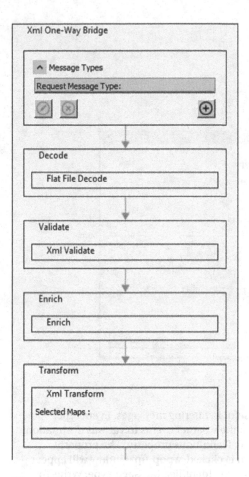

Figure 12-38. Xml One-Way Bridge

8. The message type to receive is configured by clicking the "+" button at the Message Types selection stage. This opens a pop-up to pick a message type from the available schemas in the project. Once the schema is picked and the Arrow button is clicked, the Request Message Type is selected. Click OK to add the message type to the Message Types selection stage, as shown in Figure 12-39.

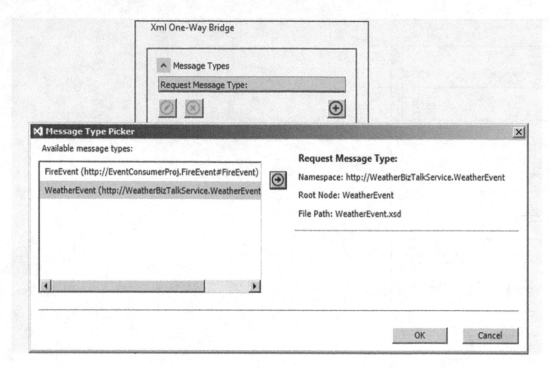

Figure 12-39. Xml One-Way Bridge—Message Type selection

The Message Properties defined as part of the Enrich stage will be useful in filtering messages. EventType, Temperature, and IsAlert properties are useful in content-based routing of the weather events to various destinations. They can be defined by selecting the Enrich stage and clicking the Property Definitions property. The property definitions can be added by clicking the Add button. When the Add button is clicked, a pop-up window will appear to receive the details. You will be able to select the Source Type of the property, Identifier, Message Type, Write To Property Name, and Data Type. In the following figure (Figure 12-40), the property named IsAlert of Data Type Boolean is set from the WeatherEvent schema by selecting the value of IsAlert Xml node. Similarly, you can set EventType and Temperature properties. Once completed, these three properties are added to the context of the incoming message of type WeatherEvent.

Figure 12-40. Xml One-Way Bridge—Property Definitions

9. Drag and drop another Xml One-Way Bridge onto the design surface of MessageFlowItinerary.bsc. Change the name of the bridge to FireAlertBridge.

10. Double-click FireAlertBridge to select the incoming message type to WeatherEvent.

11. Now go to the Transform stage of the bridge and select the map to transform the WeatherEvent to the FireAlert schema, as shown in Figure 12-41.

Figure 12-41. Xml One-Way Bridge—Maps Selection

12. Configure two queues and one topic. Perform the following steps to configure them:

13. Drag and drop the queue shape to the design surface of MessageFlowItinerary.bsc.

14. Select the queue and change the Entity Name to FireAlertQueue. Now the name of the Configuration file is changed to FireAlertQueue.Config, as shown in Figure 12-42.

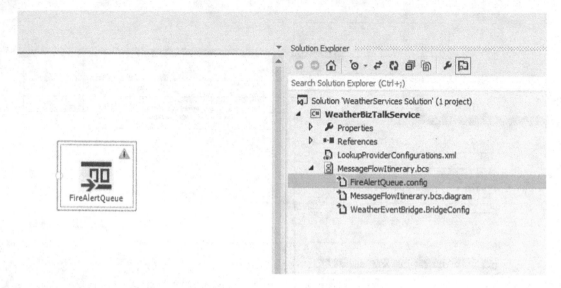

Figure 12-42. Fire Alert Queue selection

15. Double-click to open the FireAlertQueue.Config and put the correct values for Shared Secret and for the queue address, as shown in Listing 12-2.

Listing 12-2. FireAlertQueue.Config file

```
....
<behaviors>
    <endpointBehaviors>
      <behavior name="serviceBusCredentialBehavior">
        <transportClientEndpointBehavior>
          <tokenProvider>
            <sharedSecret issuerName="owner" issuerSecret="Some Issuer Secret" />
          </tokenProvider>
        </transportClientEndpointBehavior>
      </behavior>
    </endpointBehaviors>
  </behaviors>
  <bindings>
    <netMessagingBinding>
      <binding name="binaryEncodedSoapEnvelopeBinding" />
    </netMessagingBinding>
    <customBinding>
      <binding name="textEncodedMessageBodyBinding">
        <webMessageEncoding>
          <readerQuotas maxDepth="2147483647"
                              maxStringContentLength="2147483647"
                              maxArrayLength="2147483647"
                              maxBytesPerRead="67108864"
                              maxNameTableCharCount="2147483647" />
        </webMessageEncoding>
```

```
        <netMessagingTransport />
      </binding>
    </customBinding>
  </bindings>
  <client>
    <clear />
    <!-- Use this endpoint if the receiver is Thick client or REST based -->
    <endpoint
      name="TextEncodedMessageBody"
      address="sb://apressrecipens.servicebus.windows.net/firealertqueue"
      binding="customBinding"
      bindingConfiguration="textEncodedMessageBodyBinding"
      contract="System.ServiceModel.Routing.ISimplexDatagramRouter"
      behaviorConfiguration="serviceBusCredentialBehavior" />
    <!-- Use this endpoint if the receiver is a WCF service -->
    <endpoint
      name="BinaryEncodedSoapEnvelope"
      address="sb://apressrecipens.servicebus.windows.net/firealertqueue"
      binding="netMessagingBinding"
      bindingConfiguration="binaryEncodedSoapEnvelopeBinding"
      contract="System.ServiceModel.Routing.ISimplexDatagramRouter"
      behaviorConfiguration="serviceBusCredentialBehavior" />
  </client>
...
```

Follow the same steps for configuring WeatherAlertTopic and NormalEventQueue. Then continue as follows:

16. Connect the shapes as in Figure 12-43 and put the filter Conditions for the connections. This can be done by connecting the shapes with a Connector shape from Toolbox.

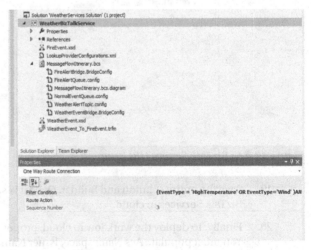

Figure 12-43. *Route Filter Configuration*

17. To update the filter condition for the connection between WeatherAlertBridge and FireAlertBridge, you have to highlight the connection. In the properties for the connection, select the Filter Condition Property. It opens up a Route Filter Configuration pop-up window. In the filter, put the appropriate filter condition, as shown in Figure 12-43. You can see further details on filter configurations in Table 12-4.

Table 12-4. *Filter Configuration*

Connections	Filter Configuration
WeatherEventBridge to FireEventBridge	(EventType = 'HighTemperature' OR EventType= 'Wind') AND Temperature > 110
WeatherEventBridge to WeatherAlertTopic	EventType = 'Cold' OR EventType = 'Flooding'
WeatherEventBridge to NormalEventQueue	IsAlert = False
FireEventBridge to FireAlertQueue	1= 1 (Match All)

18. Set the BizTalk Service URL by clicking anywhere on the design surface of MessageFlowItinerary.bsc, as shown in Figure 12-44.

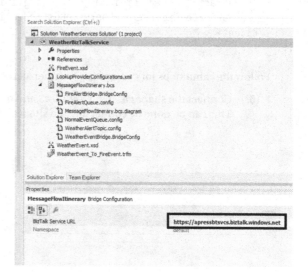

Figure 12-44. *BizTalk Service URL setup*

19. Save the entire solution and Build it. Once it is successfully built, it has to be deployed to BizTalk Services in cloud.

20. Finally, to deploy the workflow to cloud, proper deployment credentials have to be given. You must populate Acs Namespace, Issuer Name, and Shared Secret and click Deploy, as shown in Figure 12-45.

```
┌─────────────────────────────────────────────────────────────┐
│ ⋈  WeatherBizTalkService Deployment                      [×] │
├─────────────────────────────────────────────────────────────┤
│                                                               │
│  Deployment Endpoint:    https://apressbtsvcs.biztalk.windows.net/def │
│                                                               │
│  Acs Namespace:          apressrecipebtacs                    │
│                                                               │
│  Issuer Name:            owner                                │
│                                                               │
│  Shared Secret:          ●●●●●●●●●●●●●●●●●●●●●●●●●●●●●●●       │
│                                                               │
│  ☐ Refresh service after deploy (the service will be unavailable for a few │
│     minutes)                                                  │
│                                                               │
│                              [  Deploy  ]   [  Close  ]       │
│                                                               │
└─────────────────────────────────────────────────────────────┘
```

Figure 12-45. *WeatherBizTalkService Deployment*

How It Works

Azure BizTalk Services is a scalable and extendable cloud integration platform that provides simplified EAI and B2B capabilities for delivering cloud and hybrid integration solutions. The BizTalk service integration runs on a secure, dedicated per-tenant environment that can provision on demand, while it is being managed and operated by Microsoft. Before the release of Azure BizTalk Services, such hybrid integrations had to be developed and deployed to the on-premise production BizTalk server farm. Microsoft identified the need to simplify the development and deployment of such common usage patterns (EAI and B2B) and created managed, robust, and extendable and dedicated hosting services in Windows Azure.

With the advent of BizTalk Services, the workflows are now built into Visual Studio and deployed straight to the Azure BizTalk Services platform, and there is no need for any on-premise BizTalk servers to host these hybrid integration workflows. Also, by dedicating the processing capabilities, the BizTalk Services platform can create isolation for computation and storage. This way, these managed services perform predictably.

■ **Note**   Azure BizTalk Services SDK can be downloaded from Microsoft's Download center (www.microsoft.com/ en-us/download/details.aspx?id=39087). BizTalk Services SDK installs the Visual Studio project templates for creating a BizTalk Service project for EAI and BizTalk Service Artifacts for Electronic Data Interchange (EDI). It provides the tools to develop and deploy EAI Bridges and Artifacts.

BizTalk Services Bridges

A bridge in the context of BizTalk Services is a single processing unit for managing sources, pipelines, and destinations. Typically, bridges receive messages from multiple sources, enrich the messages in a pipeline, and route the messages, based on content, to various destinations. Bridges involve the following elements:

Sources receive messages and pass them to pipelines. A bridge endpoint receives a message from at least one source, HTTP. Apart from the HTTP source, multiple other sources can be configured as bridge endpoints. Some of the accepted sources are HTTP, FTP, and SFTP.

Pipelines look very similar to BizTalk pipelines. The pre-defined stages of the BizTalk Services pipeline can be configured based on the need. A property is nothing but an interesting piece of data associated to the message. The properties in a message will be useful at various stages of the pipeline. A property can be derived from transport headers, from the node of a message, from an external data lookup, or from system properties. These properties will be useful in creating filter expressions. In addition, pipelines can include multiple transformations.

Destinations are the locations to which messages are routed. The messages are routed to various destinations, based on content. Some of the configurable destinations are Service Bus, Web Service, SFTP, FTP/S, HTTP, and Blob storage.

Enterprise Application Integration Patterns

BizTalk Services provide rich processing and messaging capabilities to enable communication between disparate applications. The applications can be cloud-hosted or on-premise. With the help of bridges, the following enterprise application integration needs can be fulfilled:

> *Protocol Bridging*: The messages coming on various transports can be received and processed uniformly by the bridges.

> *Schema Validation*: The messages flowing through the bridges can be validated against the deployed schemas

> *Message Transformation*: The messages arriving at the bridge may not conform to the requirements of the destination endpoint. Message format and message type mismatches can be cleared per destination endpoint requirements.

Message enrichment via a group of custom properties can be added to the message context. These context properties can be used for routing and filtering messages.

Content-Based Routing with BizTalk Services

The incoming messages to the EAI Bridge can be routed, based on content, to the destination. The required information for the routing can be added to the message context properties, and these properties can be derived from various sources, such as the following:

- From transport level metadata (SOAP, HTTP, FTP, SFTP)

- By applying XPath on the XML Body

- By performing a custom lookup

Based on the content of the messages and the context properties, the messages can be routed to destinations, by applying routing filters and routing actions. These act as follows:

> *Routing Filters*: Enable messages to be routed to the designated endpoints based on filter expressions. The filter expressions use the same syntax as SQL92 standards.

> *Route Actions*: Bridge the protocol mismatch. They are used for writing specific headers to the message sent to a destination. For example, a bridge takes a message from an HTTP source and adds some SOAP headers to the message, before sending it to the WCF service destination.

12-7. Setting Up LOB Communication with Adapter Services
Problem

You are working on a cloud-based integration scenario where Windows Azure BizTalk Services (WABS) must make a two-way communication with a line-of-business (LOB) solution to get sales orders for your company.

Solution

WABS relies on adapter services to facilitate the two-way communication with on-premise LOB solutions. Under the current scenario, when a request is sent to the two-way EAI bridge, it is transformed into an LOB request, and the response from the LOB system is mapped to the expected response before it is sent out over the bridge. To simplify the scenario, an SQL Server is chosen as an LOB system. A stored procedure is accessed to get the sales orders for a company.

■ **Note** This recipe assumes that BizTalk Services are already configured for this cloud-based EAI workflow. Refer to Microsoft's documentation for details on setting up BizTalk Services for your subscription. Also, you have to install Windows Azure BizTalk Services SDK and Adapter Services. After the installations, a project template for BizTalk Services will be added to Visual Studio. Refer to Recipe 12-6 for further details on creating a BizTalk Services project based on the Visual Studio template and for adding schemas and maps to the project.

The following steps will guide you through the implementation of LOB adapter configuration and in building the two-way bridge:

1. Create a BizTalk Server Project in Visual Studio and add the request and response schemas to it.

2. Now you have to set up an LOB Target to communicate with the SQL Server and get the target schemas and construct maps. To set up an SQL Type of LOB Target, you must go to the Server Explorer ➤ Expand BizTalk Adapter Services ➤ Expand the WCF Management Endpoint ➤ Expand LOB Types ➤ Right-click SQL to Add SQL Target, as shown in Figure 12-46.

Figure 12-46. *Add SQL Target selection*

3. When Add SQL Target is clicked, an Add Target Configuration Properties window will appear. In the Properties Window, you will be able to configure Connection parameters, Operations, Runtime Security, and Deployment.

4. Click Next> on the Welcome screen to configure Connection parameters, as shown in Figure 12-47. You must type the name of the server on which SQL databases are hosted, type the name of the SQL Instance, supply the name of the SQL database (Catalog), and specify the credentials to use for this target.

Figure 12-47. *Add a Target—Connection parameters*

5. Click Next> on the Connection parameters screen to configure Operations. In the current case, a strongly-typed procedure named [dbo]. GetSalesOrdersByCompanyCode is selected. Click the Properties button to view the generated WSDL, Target namespace, and SOAP Action for the selected operations, as shown in Figure 12-48.

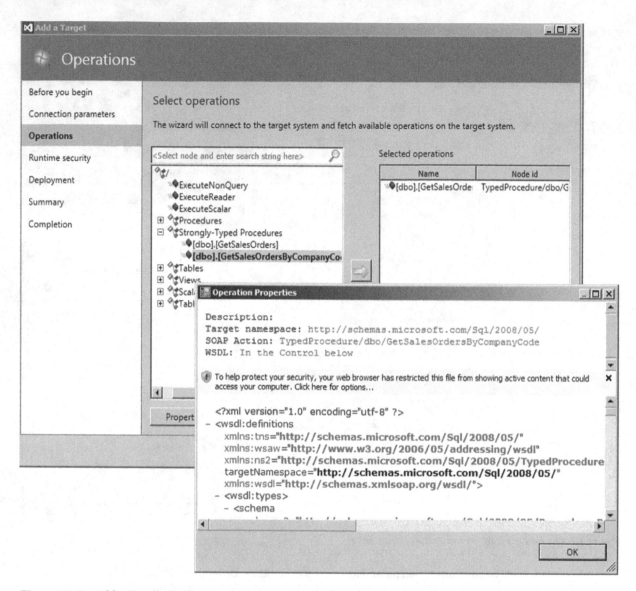

Figure 12-48. *Add a Target—Operations*

6. Click Next> to specify the security. On the Security setup screen, you will be given the option to select the type of security and to provide the needed attributes for it. In the current case, Fixed Windows credentials are selected for runtime security. The Username, Domain, and Password are provided, as shown in Figure 12-49.

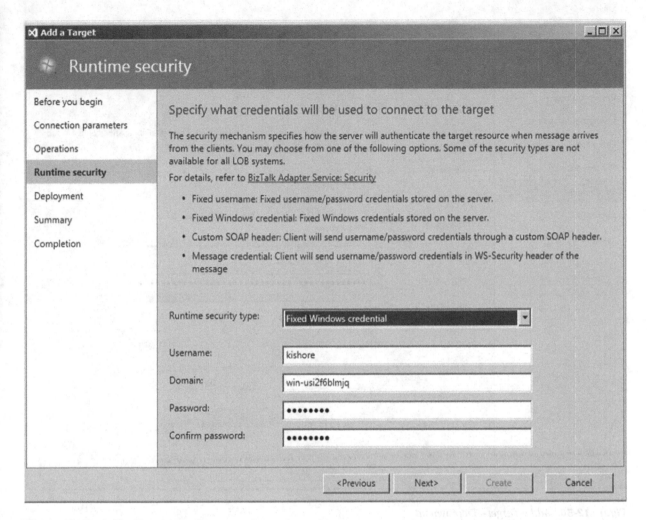

Figure 12-49. *Add a Target—Runtime security*

7. Click Next> to configure the Deployment Properties for the LOB target. In this window, you will specify the LOB relay and subpath. A combination of relay path and subpath will uniquely provide a URL for the LOB Target. The consuming applications will connect with the Service Bus relay endpoint to make one-way or two-way communications. If you have existing relay paths, you can select the existing relay paths and the subpath for the Target. Otherwise, you can create a new relay path and link the Target subpath to it. In the example, a new relay path is created, as shown in Figure 12-50.

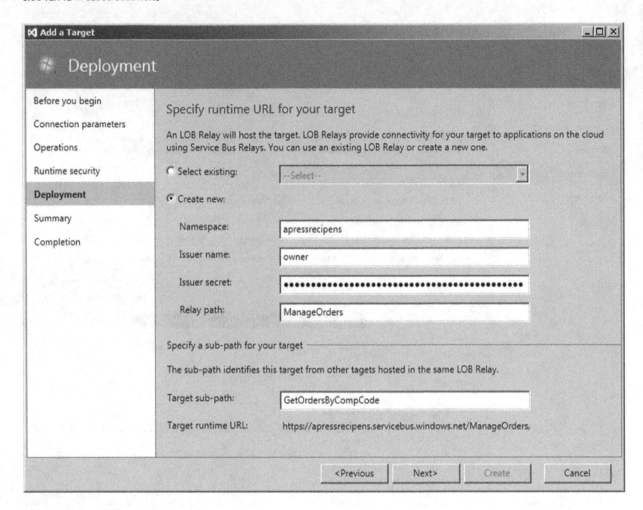

Figure 12-50. Add a Target—Deployment

8. Click Next> to view the summary and, finally, click the Create button to create an LOB Target under the SQL node of Server Explorer, as shown in Figure 12-51.

Figure 12-51. Server Explorer—SQL LOB Target

9. From the newly created LOB Target, you can get the LOB schemas. These schemas will be used in inbound and outbound maps. They can be imported into the project by right-clicking the LOB Target and selecting Add Schemas to the LOB two-way project. A pop-up window will appear, from which you will be able to configure the names for schema prefixes and use LOB Credentials to import the schemas in the project, as shown in Figure 12-52.

Figure 12-52. *LOB Schema Generation*

10. Create the maps to transform the incoming request message to the bridge into an LOB Request message and the response from LOB into the bridge's response message.

11. Double-click the file MessageFlowItinerary.bcs in Visual Studio project LOB Two-Way. Once it is opened, drag and drop the Xml Two-Way Bridge onto the design surface. Double-click the bridge to configure the request and response schemas and the related maps, as shown in Figure 12-53.

Figure 12-53. Xml Two-Way Bridge configuration

12. Drag and drop the SQL LOB Target that was just created onto the design surface and connect the bridge and the LOB Target, as shown in Figure 12-54. Set the filter expression to pass all the request messages coming into the two-way bridge to pass to the SQL LOB Target. Also, make sure that the WABS connection is set up and the configuration file for the LOB Target is given the proper secret key.

Figure 12-54. Finished workflow

13. Save the entire Project and Build it. Once it is successfully built, it needs to be deployed to Windows Azure BizTalk Services.

14. Finally, to deploy the workflow to cloud, the proper deployment credentials have to be set up. You have to populate Acs Namespace, Issuer Name, and Shared Secret and click Deploy, as shown in Figure 12-55.

Figure 12-55. LOBTwoWay Deployment

How It Works

BizTalk Adapter Services facilitate communication between cloud applications and on-premise LOB applications that are behind the corporate firewall. With the help of BizTalk's adapter pack (BAP), BizTalk Adapter web services executes operations on the LOB system and relays back the response to the cloud endpoint consumer.

Adapter Service Features

The Adapter services are set up when BizTalk Services SDK is installed. As a part of installation, a web site is created in IIS for BizTalk Adapter services, as well as a database to store the configuration information.

Development will be on-premise through Visual Studio, and any items added as LOB Targets will be saved in SQL Server. As part of development, the developer sets up an LOB Target and imports generated schemas into the project. These schemas will be used in maps between incoming requests and responses with LOB-generated schemas. The developer will be able to deploy the BizTalk Service project to cloud by providing proper credentials.

The runtime of BizTalk Adapter Services manages the connectivity and message relays between cloud consumers and various LOB systems. When a message is sent to the Service Bus endpoint in cloud, it is relayed to the on-premise LOB Target. The BizTalk Adapter Service runtime confirms the target details from the SQL data store, executes the operation on the target, and sends the response to the Service Bus endpoint.

Configuring an LOB Target

Connection parameters vary, based on the type of LOB system being configured. In the case of the SQL Server, database servers with instance names, database names, and the credentials are specified for the connection.

Multiple Operations can be selected from the list. The interface lets you search for the operations of interest to you. In the case of SAP, a list of BAPI, RFC, tRFC, and IDOC are listed.

Runtime Security specifies the security type. It can be a fixed username and password, a custom SOAP header where username and password are included, or in the Message Credential in the WS-Security header.

Deployment specifies the LOB Relay information. An LOB Relay is a URL that provides a connection to the cloud using Service Bus Relays. An LOB Relay acts as a container for the LOB Targets and can be used with multiple LOB Targets. An LOB Relay is configured by selecting the namespace for the Service Bus, Issuer Name, Issuer Secret, and target relay path and subpaths.

12-8. Setting Up EDI Trading-Partner Communication

Problem

You have to set up agreements with your trading partners to receive and send EDI documents using BizTalk Services.

Solution

Consider a scenario where your enterprise (ABC Devices, Inc.) has a trading-partner agreement with a supplier that we will refer to as Supplier X. You, being the medical device maker, work with a partner to supply components for your products. You participate in a sequence of EDI document transmissions in the workflow, as shown in Figure 12-56. To simplify implementation of the recipe, only the invoice transmission (X12 EDI 810) and the corresponding acknowledgments (X12 EDI 997) are considered.

Figure 12-56. *EDI document transmission sequence between partners*

The following steps will guide you through the deployment of a BizTalk Services–based EDI itinerary and in setting up trading partners in the Azure BizTalk Services Portal:

1. Before a trading partner is configured, the required EDI schemas and the maps to the canonical schemas have to be deployed to the BizTalk Services framework. An EDI BizTalk Services project must be created in Visual Studio, as follows:

2. Import the EDI schema X12_00401_810.xsd into the BizTalk Services project. The latest version of EDI schemas (MicrosoftEdiXSDTemplates.zip) can be downloaded from the product web site. Refer to product documentation for further details on download instructions.

3. Create a canonical XML schema (Invoice.xsd) for mapping the EDI schema.

4. Create a BizTalk Service Map to map the EDI schema (X12_00401_810.xsd) into canonical schema (Invoice.xsd).

5. Open the BizTalk Services itinerary file (MessageFlowItinerary.bcs).

6. Drag and drop an Xml One-Way Bridge and configure the bridge to receive the EDI message and transform it to Invoice.xsd.

7. Drag and drop a Service Bus Queue onto the itinerary and configure the queue to use the proper Service Bus credentials.

8. Finally, build the BizTalk Services project and deploy it to the Windows Azure BizTalk Services framework.

■ **Note** Refer to Recipe 12-6 for further details on developing a content-based routing scenario with BizTalk Services. The EDI schemas have to be downloaded from the product web site and unzipped onto the local development environment. When unzipped, you will find all the X12 EDI schemas. The required EDI schemas should to be copied into the BizTalk Services Project.

---

9. Log in to the Azure Management Portal and navigate to the BizTalk Services summary screen. Click on the Manage image link at the bottom of the screen, as shown in Figure 12-57.

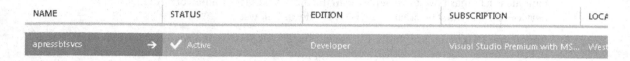

Figure 12-57. BizTalk Services summary page

10. When clicked, a BizTalk Services Management portal will be displayed. On the first attempt, you will be required to put the BizTalk Service Name, Issuer Name, and Issuer Secret of ACS for the namespace, as shown in Figure 12-58.

Figure 12-58. BizTalk Services Register Account

11. After the registration, the summary page for the current BizTalk Service will appear. Here, you will have the option to manage Partners and Agreements.

12. The Bridges and Resources pages will show the deployed bridge endpoints and schemas, as shown in Figure 12-59 and Figure 12-60.

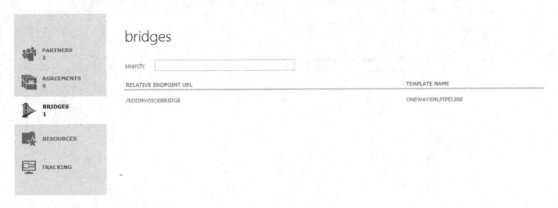

Figure 12-59. *BizTalk Services Management Portal—Bridges*

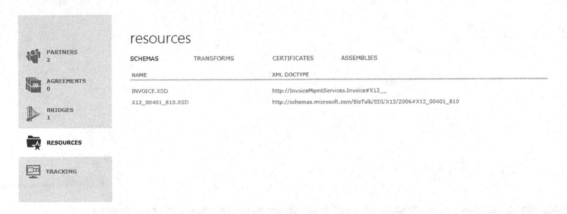

Figure 12-60. *BizTalk Services Management Portal—Resources*

13. Now you must create a host partner for ABC Devices, Inc., as shown in Figure 12-61. Similarly, you have to create a trading partner for Supplier X.

new partner

*Partner name:	ABC Devices
Description:	Medical Device makers, partnering with suppliers.
First name:	John
Last name:	Doe
Email ID:	jdoe@abcdevices.com
Phone:	111-222-3333
Website URL:	abcdevices.com
Country:	USA
Address (Line1):	123 Main St
Address (Line2):	
City:	Foothill Ranch
State:	CA
Postal Code:	92610

SAVE   CANCEL

Figure 12-61. New Partner creation page

14. After creating the trading partners, an agreement has to be created between ABC Devices, Inc., and Supplier X. This agreement will define the contract between these two business partners and specify the transacting messages over the communication protocols. An agreement configuration in the portal is very detailed and spans multiple pages before it can deployed. Once the general settings for the agreement are configured, you will have the option to create Receive and Send sides of the agreement. Table 12-5 will guide you through the settings. Note that an agreement requires both Receive Settings and Send Settings. In certain scenarios, you might have to default the send side with certain values before the agreement can be deployed.

Table 12-5. *Setting Up EDI Agreement Between Partners*

Grouping	Property	Notes
General Agreement	Name	Provide a descriptive name for the agreement.
	Host Partner–Partner Name & Partner Profile	Select the managed partner for the agreement. A managed partner is a partner managed by the service provider and to whom the pipelines are deployed during agreement deployment. Typically, partners managed by the service provider are configured as a managed partner, while the enterprise partners are not designated as managed partners. In the current case, ABC Devices, Inc., is the Host Partner, and the default Partner profile is selected for this configuration.
	Guest Partner–Partner Name & Partner Profile	Select the other Supplier X as the Guest Partner.
	Host Identifies–Qualifier & Values	Select an authenticating qualifier that provides unique business identities to the trading partners. Set the name and the value of the Host Identifier. Name: ZZ-Mutually Defined. Value: Host.
	Guest Identifies–Qualifier & Values	Name: ZZ-Mutually Defined. Value: Guest.
	Tracking	The received and sent message can be tracked for detailed analysis. You can either track the message properties or the entire message.
Receive Settings	Transport	The receive-side Transport settings let you select the transport on which the EDI document is received. In this case, leave it defaulted. The endpoint specifies the URL to which Supplier X sends the Invoice message.
	Protocol	The Protocol details are set up in this screen. Here, you will specify the Identifiers, Acknowledgments, and expected X12 schemas. In this case, leave the Defaults for Identifiers. Enable TA1 expected Enable 997 expected Under schemas, click + to set the expected schema to receive (/X12_00401_801.xsd) and set the Sender Application to Guest.
	Transform	Select the map to be used by the bridge when it receives an X12 Invoice message. Select the appropriate map from the deployed list of maps.
	Route	It specifies the destination to route to, after the EDI message is mapped. You will have the option to specify routes for good messages and suspended messages. Click the Add button to configure multiple routing filters and destinations. A special destination can also be set up for the suspended messages. In this case, all the good messages are routed to InvoiceQueue, and the suspended messages to BadInvoiceQueue.

(*continued*)

Table 12-5. (*continued*)

Grouping	Property	Notes
Sender Settings	Inbound URL	Specifies the input endpoint URL address to send messages to the Send pipeline. In the BizTalk Services Portal, this address is fixed and defined by the EDI pipeline. You can also use this page to promote properties from the incoming SOAP or HTTP message headers. These properties can be used later for batching configuration. In the current case, leave it as defaulted.
	Transform	Specifies the outbound maps. Leave it defaulted.
	Batching	Specifies the batching criteria for the outgoing EDI messages. In the current case, leave it defaulted.
	Protocol	As with the Inbound Protocol setting, you can set up an outbound Protocol. In this case, set the Version to 00401, Transaction Type to 810, and Schema to X12_00401_810.xsd.
	Transport	As with the Inbound Transport setting, you can specify the outbound Transport. You can specify the Transport Settings both for good EDI messages and suspended ones.

15. Finally, click the Deploy button to deploy the agreement.

The deployed BizTalk Services EDI Bridge can be tested using the MessageSender tool. To help test the deployed Service Bus endpoints, Microsoft released two command line tools (`MessageSender.exe` and `MessageReceiver.exe`) as part of the SDK samples. `MessageSender.exe` is used to send a message to a one-way or a request-reply bridge deployed in Service Bus. `MessageSender.exe` takes the following parameters:

```
MessageSender.exe <ACSNamespace> <IssuerName> <Issuerkey> <RuntimeAddress> <MessageFilepath>
<ContentType>
```

`MessageReceiver.exe` is used to receive messages from a Service bus queue, one way-relay, and two-way relay. While receiving messages, if the entity doesn't exist, then the tool creates it. The `MessageReceiver.exe` utility takes the following parameters:

```
MessageReceiver.exe <ServiceBusNamespace> <IssuerName> <Issuerkey> <EntityPath> <Mode>
```

How It Works

Through the BizTalk Services Management Portal, one can create and manage trading partners and agreements among the partners on the Web. After configuring the trading partners, the EDI documents can be communicated among the partners on various transport protocols (HTTP/S, AS2, FTP/S) to the endpoints where the agreements are deployed. Because the BizTalk Service itineraries for EDI processing are hosted in a managed single-tenet environment, they can be scaled appropriately, per the client's needs. Because of the simplified configuration, the time to on-board new partners has significantly decreased.

■ **Note** Refer to Recipes in Chapter 8 for detailed information about EDI schemas, maps, and trading-partner management. For extended discussion on the individual properties in trading partner agreement setup, refer to Microsoft product documentation.

Index

■ T

Get the eBook for only $10!

> Now you can take the weightless companion with you anywhere, anytime. Your purchase of this book entitles you to 3 electronic versions for only $10.

This Apress title will prove so indispensible that you'll want to carry it with you everywhere, which is why we are offering the eBook in 3 formats for only $10 if you have already purchased the print book.

Convenient and fully searchable, the PDF version enables you to easily find and copy code—or perform examples by quickly toggling between instructions and applications. The MOBI format is ideal for your Kindle, while the ePUB can be utilized on a variety of mobile devices.

Go to www.apress.com/promo/tendollars to purchase your companion eBook.

Apress®
THE EXPERT'S VOICE™